# TELUGU VERBAL BASES

*A Comparative and Descriptive Study*

# TELUGU VERBAL BASES

*A Comparative and Descriptive Study*

*by*

BHADRIRAJU KRISHNAMURTI

MOTILAL BANARSIDASS
PUBLISHING HOUSE • DELHI
*Email: mlbd@mlbd.in • Website: www.mlbd.in*

*2nd Reprint : Delhi,* ***2021***
*First Edition : 1961 (University of California Press, Berkeley & Los Angeles)*



ISBN: 978-81-208-2324-2

*Printed & Published by*
Rajendra P Jain *for*
Motilal Banarsidass Publishing House
A-44, Naraina Industrial Area, Phase I,
New Delhi–110 028 (INDIA)
*Email: mlbd@mlbd.in*
*Website: www.mlbd.in*

IN

FOND MEMORY OF

MY FATHER

# PREFACE

It is now over a century since Dravidian philology came into existence with the publication of Robert Caldwell's Comparative Grammar of the Dravidian Languages in 1856. Linguistic science, both historical and descriptive, has since made tremendous advances throughout the world; but the progress made in the Dravidian field has not been commensurate with what could be expected in a full century. However, with the employment of better methods, and the help of the contributions of many Western philologists as well as some Indian scholars, we have now at least a better understanding of the many problems of Dravidian phonology, although no progress worthy of mention has been made in solving the problems of comparative morphology of Dravidian.

The present work, which may be regarded as a pioneering attempt in the field of Dravidian philology, was undertaken nearly five years ago with little knowledge of its magnitude. It was believed at that time that a thorough study of the derivation of the Telugu verb on a comparative level would provide a basic sample for phonological observations and form a basis for investigation of noun-formation in Telugu, eventually facilitating the preparation of an etymological dictionary of Telugu. Four years were spent at Andhra University, India, mainly devoted to the gathering and studying of comparative material—a period of trial and error. This monograph has been cast into final form during 1955-1956 at the University of California, Berkeley, under the direction of Professor M. B. Emeneau.

Difficulties soon appeared as I started my study in India in 1950, primarily on account of the absence of any reference book for Dravidian etymologies and of the lack of established phonological equations for etyma in the various languages. An etymological dictionary for Dravidian has remained a desideratum throughout the century of life of Dravidian philology, and this fact has been in the main responsible for the absence of much incentive for intensive research in Comparative Dravidian. Thanks to the labors of Professors Burrow and Emeneau, this long-felt need will be filled soon. With a patient study of comparative vocabularies over the years and with the help of the latest scholarship in the field, I finally succeeded in reconstructing Proto-Dravidian phonology, at least as a working hypothesis, and in setting up a comparative phonology for Telugu.

Though the treatment in this work is confined to the verbal bases, most of the observations in phonology and derivation are equally valid of application to the other parts of the vocabulary. An attempt has been made to show, if not to decide, the place of Telugu in the whole family of the Dravidian languages by setting up isoglosses for the distribution of phonological, derivational, and also partly morphological features. A number of problems have been originally worked out with encouraging results. To name a few: the conditions for the occurrence of the so-called "aphaeresis" in Telugu have been laid down more precisely than heretofore (§§1.121 ff.); a satisfactory interpretation has been offered for the problem of alternations i/e and u/o in South Dravidian (§§1.267 ff.). It has been shown, in various places, how certain phonological developments are closely associated with the changing patterns of syllable structure in the individual languages, e.g., loss of medial vowel leading to metathesis or assimilation, etc. Besides, a few observations of phonemic alternations of a deeper nature (i.e., belonging to the PDr. stages) have been shown, e.g., *n/*ṯ alternation, *c/*ḻ alternation, lack of contrast in length for all root-vowels except *a before y, and so on.

An exhaustive index of the Telugu verbal bases is given as Part II of this work. Homonyms, which are usually put together under a single item in the traditional dictionaries, have been meticulously separated on the basis of comparative evidence. Reconstructions for the root element (and also for the suffixes, where possible) have been set up in conformity with the developments described in the phonology.

The sources for the preparation of the Index are in the main the published Telugu Dictionaries, including the latest Sūryarāy-āndhra-nighaṇṭuvu (SAN), of which four volumes, i.e., A to N have so far appeared. The remaining volumes of this Dictionary have been in the press for a long time. I had the opportunity to refer to these also during the summer of 1952 with the kind help of Dr. G. V. Sitapati, the present editor of the Dictionary. Some items under P and all those under M and V have thus been secured. The next source is Śabdaratnākaramu (Śab.R.), which is still considered to be an authentic (if not complete) dictionary for literary Telugu. The remaining sources include Brown's Telugu-English Dictionary, which quotes a number of dialect forms besides the literary forms, and Āndhra-vācaspatyamu (ĀVāc.), which is also useful, though not consistent in giving authority from literature for a given gloss. The Telugu Academy of Kākināḍa published, in 1930, a book entitled Āndhra-dhātumāla (Dh.M.), whose authorship was disputed. This book consists of verbal stems, colloquial as well as classical, simple as well as compound; glosses are given first in Sanskrit, followed by a Telugu translation. In spite of a number of errors in confusing r/r̲, etc., and giving sometimes inaccurate glosses, it is a very useful collection, though not exhaustive. A number of the items reported as "colloquial" occur in this book.

In addition to these, a number of forms from my own knowledge of the modern usage have also been included. Some of my friends and students at Waltair provided me with certain items from their own areas; especially, the Rāyalasīma dialect forms were furnished by Mr. T. Donappa. A note on the transcription is given below (p. xxvii).

Since this work was spread over a period of nearly five years, grateful acknowledgement is due to many persons and institutions for their help and coöperation.

I am grateful to Professor G. J. Somayaji for having suggested this topic to me and for his constant material help and encouragement during the early stages of this work. I am also indebted to Sri A. Ramakrishnarao, Librarian, Andhra University, for his invaluable aid in securing for me a number of rare books from various libraries in India.

I owe a special debt of gratitude to Professor M. B. Emeneau for his capable direction and many acts of kindness. Not only has he made a number of very valuable comments and suggestions to improve the quality of this monograph, but he also patiently read every word of it with especial care and interest and corrected a number of flaws in usage and style which would have disfigured this work otherwise. He further placed at my disposal his whole personal library on Dravidian and created every facility for rapid and organized work. I am also deeply indebted to him for supplying me with his unpublished indices of Kota and Toda verbs. I am deeply grateful to Professor T. Burrow for his suggestions for my work from time to time through correspondence.

I am also indebted to Professors Z. S. Harris, H. M. Hoenigswald, and Leigh Lisker of the University of Pennsylvania, to whom I owe my knowledge of structural linguistics and its application to historical problems.

Grateful acknowledgement is due to the Rockefeller Foundation under whose fellowship aid this work has been accomplished at Berkeley during 1955-1956. I am also thankful to the United States Educational Foundation in India and the related bodies, for having selected me for an award under the Fulbright and Smith-Mundt program for advanced training in linguistics at the University of Pennsylvania during 1954-1955, following which the Ph.D. degree was awarded in 1957 after submission of part of this monograph as a dissertation.

Last, but not least, I am thankful to Miss Barbara Dantzler for undertaking and accomplishing the major part of typing the manuscript of this work, in spite of its exacting nature.

Berkeley
August 14, 1956 Bh. K.

[Additions and corrections made since 1956 include especially references to some more recent works by various authors, including myself, and the completion of chapters III and IV. I owe several corrections and improvements in chapter III to Professor Gordon Fairbanks, who read through the draft thoroughly, and offered valuable comments during his stay at Deccan College, Poona (India), during 1958-1959.]

Waltair
September, 1959 Bh. K.

# CONTENTS



## PART I

## A COMPARATIVE AND DESCRIPTIVE ANALYSIS

# BIBLIOGRAPHY


Aiyar, L. V. Ramaswami, "Aphaeresis and Sound-Displacement in Dravidian," QJMS, XXII, 448-480.

_______, The Evolution of Malayam Morphology. Ernakulam: Cochin Government Press, 1936.

_______, "Initial Labials in Dravidian," ER, XXXVII (1931), 98-105.

_______, "Morphology of the Old Tamil Verb," Anthropos, XXIII (1938), 747-781.

_______, "Materials for a Sketch of Tulu Phonology," IL, VI, 385-439 (Calcutta: Linguistic Society of India).

_______, "Notes on Dravidian" ('Nasals and Nasal Articulation in Dravidian'), ER (1928), 447-460.

_______, "The Old Tamil Verb," QJMS, XXX (1939), 1-12 (reprint).

_______, "A Primer of Malayāḷam Phonology," Bull., Ramavarma Research Institute, vols. V, VI, and VII.

_______, "A Problem of Dravidic Phonology: Tamil Medial -y-, -ś- and Kannada -s-," JOR, VI (1932), 11-21.

_______, "Tamil L̲," JOR, IX, 140-147 and 195-210.

_______, "The Tamil-Malayalam Alveolar Plosive," JOR, VIII, 1-51 (reprint).

Anavaratavinayakam Pillai, S., Dravidic Studies III: The Sanskritic Element in the Vocabularies of the Dravidian Languages. Madras: Superintendent, Government Press, 1923.

Āndhra Dhātumāla. Kākināḍa: The Telugu Academy, 1930 (authorship disputed).

Arden, A. H., A Progressive Grammar of Common Tamil. 4th ed. Revised by A. C. Clayton with an appendix on Tamil phonetics by J. R. Firth. Madras: Christian Literature Society for India, 1934.

Bagchi, Prabodh Chandra (Trans.), Pre-Aryan and Pre-Dravidian in India. Calcutta: University of Calcutta, 1929.

Bhaduri, Manindra Bhusan, A Mundari-English Dictionary. Calcutta: Calcutta University Press, 1931.

Biligiri, H. S., "The Nasal Phonemes of Kannada," IL, XVI (1955), 306-308.

Bloch, Jules, "The Intervocalic Consonants in Tamil," IA (1919), 191-195. (Extracted with additions from MSL, XIX (1914), 85 ff.; trans. by J. D. Anderson.)

_______, "Some Problems of Indo-Aryan Philology," BSOS, V, 720-756.

_______, Structure grammaticale des langues dravidiennes. (Publications du Musée Guimet, Bibliothèque d'études, 56.) Adrien-Maisonneuve: Librairie d'Amérique et d'Orient, 1946.

Bray, Denys, The Brahui Language. Part I. Calcutta: Superintendent, Government Printing, 1909.

Bray, Sir Denys, The Brahui Language. Part II. The Brahui Problem; Part III. Etymological Vocabulary. Delhi: Manager of Publications, 1934.

Brigel, J., A Grammar of the Tuḷu Language. Basel Mission Book and Tract Depository, 1872.

Brown, Charles Philip, A Telugu-English Dictionary. 2nd ed., revised by M. Venkata Ratnam, W. H. Campbell, and K. Veeresalingam Pantulu Garu. Society for Promoting Christian Knowledge, 1903.

Bucher, J., A Kannaḍa-English School-Dictionary. 2nd ed., revised by Prof. Christanuja Watsa. Mangalore: Kanarese Mission Press and Book Depot, 1923.

Burrow, T., "Dravidian Studies I," BSOS, IX, 711-722.

_______, "Dravidian Studies II," BSOS, X, 289-297.

_______, "Dravidian Studies III," BSOAS, XI, 122-139.

_______, "Dravidian Studies IV," BSOAS, XI, 328-356.

_______, "Dravidian Studies V," BSOAS, XI, 595-616.

_______, "Dravidian Studies VI," BSOAS, XII, 132-147.

_______, "Dravidian Studies VII," BSOAS, XII, 365-396.

_______, "Some Dravidian Words in Sanskrit," TPS 1945, 79-120.

_______, "Some Loanwords in Sanskrit," TPS 1946, 1-30.

_______, and Bhattacharya, S., "Field Notes on Kolami (Kinwaṭ Dialect)" (included in Emeneau, Kolami, A Dravidian Language, 277-286).

_______, The Parji Language: A Dravidian Language of Bastar. Hertford: Stephen Austin and Sons, Ltd., 1953.

Caldwell, Rt. Rev. Robert, A Comparative Grammar of the Dravidian or South-Indian Family of Languages. 3rd ed. London: Kegan Paul, Trench, Trübner and Co., Ltd., 1913.

Chatterji, S. K., "Old Tamil, Ancient Tamil and Primitive Dravidian," IL, XIV (1954), 1-19.

Chettiar, A. C., "Aphaeresis, Syncope and Apocope in Tamil," Journal of the Annamalai University, IX, 50-53.

Chinnayasūri, Paravastu, Bālavyākaraṇamu [in Telugu]. Rajamundry: Satyanārāyaṇa Book Depot, n. d.

Dawson, James, "Gondi Words and Phrases," JASB (1870), 109-117 and 172-198.

Droese, Ernest, Introduction to the Malto Language. Agra: Secundra Orphanage Press, 1884.

Emeneau, M. B., "An Alphabetical Index of Toda Verbal Roots" (unpublished).

_______, "An Alphabetical Index of Kota Verbal Roots" (unpublished).

_______, "The Dravidian Verbs 'come' and 'give,'" Lg., XXI (1945), 184-213.

_______, Kolami, A Dravidian Language. University of California Publications in Linguistics, Vol. 12. Berkeley: University of California Press, 1955.

_______, Kota Texts, Part I. University of California Publications in Linguistics, Vol. 2. Berkeley and Los Angeles: University of California Press, 1944.

_______, "The Nasal Phonemes of Sanskrit," Lg., XXII (1946), 86-93.

_______, "Phonetic Observations on the Brāhūī Language," BSOS, VIII (1937), 981-983.

_______, "Toda, a Dravidian Language," TPS 1958, 15-66.

_______, "Proto-Dravidian *c-: Toda t-," BSOAS, XV, 98-112.

_______, "The Vowels of the Badaga Language," Lg., XV (1939), 43-47.

Fitzgerald, A. G., Kuviṅga Bassa [The Language of the Western Khonds]. Calcutta: Catholic Orphan Press, 1913.

Friend-Pereira, J. E., A Grammar of the Kūi Language. Bengal Secretariat Book Depot, 1909.

Gai, G. S., Historical Grammar of Old Kannada (based entirely on the Kannada Inscriptions of the 8th, 9th, and 10th Centuries A. D.). Poona: Deccan College Post-Graduate and Research Institute, 1946.

Godavarma, K., "The Change of a to e in the Indo-Aryan Loan Words of Malayāḷam," BSOS, VIII, 559-562.

_______, Indo-Aryan Loan-Words in Malayāḷam. Vavelikara: Ramavarma Bros., 1946.

Grierson, G. A., Linguistic Survey of India, Vol. IV. Calcutta, 1906.

Grignard, A., A Grammar of the Oraon Language and Study in Oraon Idiom. Calcutta; Catholic Orphan Press, 1924.

_______, An Oraon-English Dictionary. Calcutta: Catholic Orphan Press, 1924.

Gundert, H., A Malayalam-English Dictionary. Mangalore: Basel Mission Book and Tract Depository, 1872; London: Trübner and Co.

Hislop, Stephen, Papers Relating to the Aboriginal Tribes of the Central Provinces. Nagpur, 1866.

Kanapati Pillai, K., "The Enunciative Vowel in Dravidian," University of Ceylon Review, I (1943), 35-41.

_______, "The Palatal ñ in Tamil," University of Ceylon Review, I (1943), 66-73.

Katre, S. M., "A Comparative Etymological Index to Formation of Konkaṇi," BDCRI, III, 291-348.

Kittel, F., A Grammar of the Kannada Language in English Comprising the Three Dialects of the Language (Ancient, Mediaeval and Modern). Mangalore: Basel Mission Book and Tract Depository, 1903.

_______, A Kannaḍa-English Dictionary. Mangalore: Basel Mission Book and Tract Depository, 1894.

Krishnamurti, Bh., "Evolution of Proto-Dravidian ḻ in Telugu," Saṃskṛti (Telugu journal), Rajamundry, I, II (1953-1954).

_______, "Field Notes on Koṇḍēkōr Gadaba" (unpublished).

_______, "The History of Vowel-Length in Telugu Verbal Bases," JAOS, LXXV (1955), 237-252.

_______, "Proto-Dravidian *ẓ," IL—Turner Jubilee Volume I (1958), 259-293.

_______, "Alternations i/e and u/o in South-Dravidian," Lg., XXXIV (1958), 458-468.

Kuiper, F. B. J., "Zur Chronologie des Stimmtonverlusts im dravidischen Anlaut," BSOAS, XI, 987-1001.

Mãnner, A., Tuḷu-English Dictionary. Basel Mission Press, 1886.

Master, Alfred, "Indo-Aryan and Dravidian III," BSOAS, XII, 340-364.

_______, "Intervocalic Plosives in Early Tamil," BSOAS, IX, 1003-1018.

Meile, Pierre, "Sur la sifflante en dravidien," Journal Asiatique, CCCCXLVII, 73-89.

Mitchell, A. N., A Grammar of Maria Gondi, as spoken by the Bison Horn or Dandami Marias of Bastar State. Jagdalpur: Bastar State Press, 1942.

Narasimhia, A. N., A Grammar of the Oldest Kanarese Inscriptions. Mysore: University of Mysore, 1941.

Pope, G. U., Outlines of the Grammar of the Tuda Language (published as App. to W. E. Marshall, A Phrenologist Amongst the Todas, London, 1873).

Ramachandra Dikshitar, M. A., Studies in Tamil Literature and History. London: Luzack and Co., 1930.

Ramakrishnaiya, K., Dravidian Cognates. Madras: University of Madras, 1944.

Sankaranarayana, P., A Telugu-English Dictionary. Madras: V. Ramaswami Sastrulu and Sons, 1927.

Schulze, F. V. P., A Grammar of the Kuvi Language. Madras: Graves, Cookson and Co., 1911.

_______, Vocabulary of the Kuvi-Kond Language. Madras: Graves, Cookson and Co., 1913.

Sekhar, A. C., "Evolution of Malayalam," Bulletin of the Deccan College Research Institute (1951), 1-216.

Sethu Pillai, R. P., "Tamil—Literary and Colloquial," JOR, II (1937-1938), 1-60.

Setumadhava Rao, P., A Grammar of the Kolami Language. Hyderabad, 1950.

Siddheswara Varma, Critical Studies in the Phonetic Observations of Indian Grammarians, London (1929).

Sitaramacaryulu, Bahujanapalli, Śabda Ratnākaramu (Telugu-Telugu Dictionary). Madras: The Madras School Book and Vernacular Literature Society, 1937.

_______, Triliṅgalakṣaṇaśēṣamu (Prauḍhavyākaraṇamu) in Telugu. Madras: Vāviḷḷa Rāmaswāmiśāstrulu and Sons, 1929.

Sitaramaswami Sastri, Vajjhala Cina, Āndhra-vyākaraṇa-saṃhitā-sarvasvamu (AVSS). Waltair: Andhra University, 1951-1952.

Sreekantaiya, T. N., "Affricates in Kannada Speech," IL, XIV (1954), 83-90.

_______, "The Mutation of i, u, e and o in Kannaḍa," Transaction and Proceedings of the All India Oriental Conference, VIII (Mysore, 1935), 769-800.

Subbayya, K. V., "A Primer of Dravidian Phonology," IA, XXXVIII (1909), 159-170 and 188-221.

_______, Dravidic Studies II: The Pronouns and Pronominal Terminations of the First Person in Dravidian. Madras: Superintendent, Government Press, 1923.

Subrahmanya Sastri, P. S., Comparative Grammar of the Tamil Language. Tiruvadi, Tanjore Dt., 1947.

_______, History of Grammatical Theories in Tamil and Their Relation to the Grammatical Literature in Sanskrit. Madras: Journal of Oriental Research, 1934.

_______, Tolkāppiyam. Vol. I. Eḻuttatikāram. Madras Oriental Series, No. 3. Madras: Journal of Oriental Research, 1930.

Sūryarāyāndhranighaṇṭuvu [in Telugu], Vols. I-IV. Kākināḍa: Āndhrasāhitya Pariṣattu, 1936-1944.

Švarný, Oldřich, and Zvelebil, Kamil, "Some Remarks on the Articulation of the 'Cerebral' Consonants in Indian Languages, Especially Tamil," Archiv Orientální, XXIII (1955), 374-434.

Syāmala Kāmasāstri, Koṭra, Āndhra Vācaspatyamu (Telugu-Telugu Dictionary), Vols. 1-4. Kākināḍa: Author, 1934-1940.

Tamil Lexicon, 6 vols. Madras: University of Madras, 1924-1939.

Thyagaraju, A. F., "The Development of Dravidian ḻ," Vyāsasaṅgrahamu (1933), 75-88.

Trench, C. G. Chenevix, Grammar of Gondi, as spoken in the Betul District, Central Provinces, India. Vol. II. Vocabulary, etc. Madras: Superintendent, Government Press, 1921.

Turner, Ralph Lilley, A Comparative and Etymological Dictionary of the Nepali Language. London: Kegan Paul, Trench, Trübner and Co., Ltd., 1931.

Tuttle, Edwin H., Dravidian Developments. Language Monographs, No. 5. Linguistic Society of America, 1930.

_______, "Dravidian Researches," AJP, L (1929), 138-155.

_______, "Some Dravidian Prefixes," BSOS, VIII (1936), 13-15.

Weinreich, Uriel, Languages in Contact: Findings and Problems. New York: Linguistic Circle of New York, 1953.

Whitney, William Dwight, Sanskrit Grammar. 7th issue of the 2nd ed. Cambridge, Mass.: Harvard University Press, 1950.

Williamson, H. D., Gondi Grammar and Vocabulary. London: Society for Promoting Christian Knowledge, 1890.

Winfield, W. W., A Grammar of the Kui Language. Bibliotheca Indica, No. 245. Calcutta: Asiatic Society of Bengal, 1928.

_______, A Vocabulary of the Kui Language [Kui-English]. Bibliotheca Indica, No. 252. Calcutta: Asiatic Society of Bengal, 1929.

# ABBREVIATIONS

## JOURNALS, ETC.

| | |
|---|---|
| AJP | American Journal of Philology |
| BDCRI | Bulletin of the Deccan College Research Institute |
| BSO(A)S | Bulletin of the School of Oriental (and African) Studies |
| EI | Epigraphia Indica |
| ER | Educational Review |
| IA | Indian Antiquary |
| IL | Indian Linguistics |
| JA | Journal Asiatique |
| JAOS | Journal of the American Oriental Society |
| JASB | Journal of the Asiatic Society of Bengal |
| JOR | Journal of Oriental Research |
| Lg. | Language |
| LSI | Linguistic Survey of India |
| NDI | Nellore District Inscriptions |
| QJAHRS | Quarterly Journal of Andhra Historical Research Society |
| QJMS | Quarterly Journal of Mythic Society |
| SII | South Indian Inscriptions |
| TPS | Transactions of the Philological Society |

## LANGUAGES

| | |
|---|---|
| A. | Assamese |
| B. | Bengali |
| Brah. | Brahui |
| CDr. | Central Dravidian |
| Dr. | Dravidian |
| G. | Gujarati |
| Go. | Gondi (as recorded by Trench)<br>(Dawson: see Bibliography)<br>(Williamson: see Bibliography) |
| GoA. | Gondi, Adilabad dialect (Field-notes of Burrow and Bhattacharya, included in Emeneau, Kolami, see Bibliography) |

| | |
|---|---|
| GoM. | Gondi, Maṛia dialect (Mitchell: see Bibliography) |
| H. | Hindi |
| IA | Indo-Aryan |
| Ka. | Kannaḍa |
| KGad. | Koṇḍēkōr Gadaba |
| Klm.(SR) | Kolami: Setumādhava Rao (see Bibliography) |
| (E) | Emeneau (includes Kinwaṭ dialect (Kin.); see Bibliography) |
| Ko. | Kota |
| Koḍ. | Koḍagu |
| Ku. | Kumaonī |
| Kui | |
| Kur. | Kurukh |
| Kuvi (S) | Schulze (see Bibliography) |
| (F) | Fitzgerald (see Bibliography) |
| M. | Marathi |
| Ma. | Malayāḷam |
| MIA | Middle Indo-Aryan |
| Mlt. | Malto |
| NDr. | North Dravidian |
| Nep. | Nepalese |
| NIA | New Indo-Aryan |
| Nk. | Naiki |
| O. | Oṛiya |
| OIA | Old Indo-Aryan |
| Oll. | Ollari |
| Pa. | Pāli |
| PDr. | Proto-Dravidian |
| Pj.(Sth.) | Parji: Southern dialect |
| (N) | Northern dialect |
| (NE) | North-eastern dialect |
| Pkt. | Prakrit |
| PSDr. | Proto-South-Dravidian |
| S. | Sindhi |
| SDr. | South Dravidian |
| Sgh. | Singhalese |
| Skt. | Sanskrit |
| Ta. | Tamil |
| Te.(ĀVāc.) | Telugu: Āndhra-vācaspatyamu (Koṭra Syāmalakāmaśāstri: see Bibliography) |

| | | |
|---|---|---|
| Te.(Brown) | Telugu: | see Bibliography |
| (Dh.M.) | | Āndhra-dhātumāla (see Bibliography) |
| (Śab.R.) | | Śabda-ratnākaramu (Sitaramacaryulu: see Bibliography) |
| (SAN) | | Sūryarāy-āndhra-nighaṇṭuvu (see Bibliography) |
| To. | Toda | |
| Tu. | Tuḷu | |

## CITATIONS

| Name of the literary work | Telugu | Date in centuries |
|---|---|---|
| Acalā. | Acalātmajāpariṇayamu | 18 |
| Appak. | Appakavīyamu | 17 |
| Āmu. | Āmuktamālyada | 16 |
| UR | Uttararāmāyaṇamu | 18 |
| UH | Uttaraharivaṃśamu | 14 |
| Kavij. | Kavijanāśrayamu | ? 12 |
| Kaḷā. | Kaḷāpūrṇōdayamu | 16 |
| Kāś. | Kāśīkhaṇḍamu | 14-15 |
| Kāḷ. | Kāḷahastimāhātmyamu | 16 |
| Krīḍ. | Krīḍābhirāmamu | 14-15 |
| KS | Kumārasambhavamu | 11 |
| Ghaṭikā. | Ghaṭikācalamāhātmyamu | 16 |
| JBh. | Jāiminībhāratamu | 15 |
| Daś. | Daśakumāracaritramu | 13 |
| Daśā. | Daśāvatāracaritramu | 18 |
| Dvā. | (Siṃhāsana)dvātriṃśika | 15 |
| Dvi.Nal. | Dvipadanalacaritramu | 16 |
| Dvi.Bhr. | Dvipadabhāratamu | 16 |
| Dvi.H. | Dvipadahariścandrōpākhyānamu | 14-15 |
| Nava.N. | Navanāthacaritramu | 15 |
| Naiṣ. | (Śṛṅgāra)nāiṣadhamu | 14-15 |
| Nirv. | Nirvacanōttararāmāyaṇamu | 13 |
| Nṛs. | Nṛsiṃhapurāṇamu | 14 |
| Paṇḍ. | Paṇḍitārādhyacaritramu | 13-14 |
| Pāṇḍ. | Pāṇḍuraṅgamāhātmyamu | 16 |
| Pārij. | Pārijātāpaharaṇamu | 16 |
| Prabhā. | Prabhāvatīpradyumnamu | 16 |
| BP | Basavapurāṇamu | 13-14 |
| Bhg. | Bhāgavatamu | 15-16 |

| | | |
|---|---|---|
| Bhīm. | Bhīmakhaṇḍamu | 14-15 |
| Bhōj. | Bhōjarājīyamu | 15 |
| Bhr. I | Bhāratamu (by Nannaya) | 11 |
| II | (by Ṭikkana) | 13 |
| III | (by Er̲r̲āpreggaḍa) | 14 |
| BhR | Bhāskararāmāyaṇamu | 12-13 ff. |
| Manu. | Manucaritramu | 16 |
| Mārk. | Mārkaṇḍēyapurāṇamu | 13-14 |
| RR | Raṅganātharāmayaṇamu | 13-14 |
| Rasika. | Rasikajanamanōbhirāmamu | 17-18 |
| Vasu. | Vasucaritramu | 16 |
| Vikram. | Vikramārkacaritramu | 15 |
| Vijñ. | Vijñānēśvarīyamu | 13 |
| Vi.Pu. | Viṣṇupurāṇamu | ? 16 |
| Vēm. | Vēmanaśatakamu | 16 |
| SivaR. | Sivarātrimāhātmyamu | 14-15 |
| Sakunt. | Sakuntalāpariṇayamu | 15 |
| Hara. | Haravilāsamu | 14-15 |
| HariV. | Harivaṃśamu | 14 |

| Name of the literary work | Tamil | Date in centuries |
|---|---|---|
| Akan. | Akanān̲ūr̲u | Sa. |
| Aiṅk. | Aiṅkur̲un̲ūr̲u | Sa. |
| Ilak. | Ilakkaṇaviḷakkam | 17 |
| Kamp. | Kamparāmāyaṇam | 12 |
| Kallā. | Kallāṭam | Sa. |
| Kalit. | Kalittokai | Sa. |
| Kur̲r̲. | (Tiruk)kur̲r̲āla ūṭal | |
| Kr̲ḷ. | (Tiruk)kur̲aḷ | Sa. |
| Kur̲un. | Kur̲untokai | Sa. |
| Cilap. | Cilappatikāram | Sa. |
| Cir̲up. | Cir̲upāṇār̲r̲uppaṭai | Sa. |
| Cīv. | Cīvakacintāmaṇi | 10 |
| Cūṭā. | Cūṭāmaṇinikaṇṭu | 16 |
| Taṇikai. | Taṇikaippurāṇam | 16 |
| Tan̲ip. | Tan̲ippāṭaltiraṭṭu | |
| Tirikaṭu. | Tirikaṭukam | 18/19 |
| Tirumuru. | Tirumurukār̲r̲uppaṭai | Sa. |
| Tiruvāc. | Tiruvācakam | 7 |

| | | |
|---|---|---|
| Tiv. | Tivyappirapantam | 9 |
| Tivā. | Tivākaram | 8 |
| Tēv. | Tēvāram | 7 |
| Tolk. | Tolkāppiyam | c. 2 B.C. |
| Nar̲r̲. | Nar̲r̲iṇai | Sa. |
| Nan̲. | Nan̲n̲ūl | 12 |
| Nāl. | Nālaṭiyār | 7 |
| Neṭu. | Neṭunalvāṭai | Sa. |
| Patir̲. | Patir̲r̲uppattu | Sa. |
| Parip. | Paripāṭal | Sa. |
| Pārata. | Pāratam | 14 |
| Piṅ. | Piṅkalanikaṇṭu | 8 |
| Pu.Ve. | Pur̲apporuḷveṇpāmālai | 12 |
| PN | Pur̲anān̲ūr̲u | Sa. |
| Periyapu. | Periyapurāṇam | 12 |
| Perump. | Perumpāṇār̲r̲uppaṭai | Sa. |
| Porun. | Porunarār̲r̲uppaṭai | Sa. |
| Maṇi. | Maṇimēkalai | Sa. |
| Maturai. | Maturaikkāñci | Sa. |
| Malaip. | Malaipaṭukaṭām | Sa. |
| Mullaip. | Mullaippāṭṭu | Sa. |

Sa. stands for Sangam literature. The Texts have not been definitely dated but can be placed roughly between the 3rd century B.C. and the 4th century A.D. The dates indicated above are taken from P. S. S. Sastri, Historical Tamil Reader (Annamalainagar, 1945), pp. x-xi and Ramachandra Dikshitar (see Bibliography).

## GENERAL

| | | | |
|---|---|---|---|
| acc. | accusative | class. | classical |
| adj. | adjective | colloq. | colloquial |
| allom. | allomorph(s) | cpd. | compound |
| alt. | alternant(s) | dat. | dative |
| altern. | alternatively | denom. | denominative |
| aux. | auxiliary | der. n. | derivative noun(s) |
| caus. | causative | dial. | dialectal |
| cent. | century | ety. dub. | etymology dubious |
| cf. | confer | hab. | habitual |

| | | | |
|---|---|---|---|
| id. | idem (the same as before) | prob. | probably |
| imper. | imperative | q. v. | quod vide (which see) |
| inf. | infinitive | refl. | reflexive |
| inscr. | inscriptional | s. v. | sub voce (under the word) |
| intr. | intransitive | sg. | singular |
| lex. | lexical | st. | stem |
| loc. | local (dialectal) | tr. | transitive |
| l. w. | loan word | v./vb. | verb |
| M. | Middle | var. | variant(s) |
| Mdn. | Modern | v. i. | verb intransitive |
| n. | noun | v. s. v. | vide sub voce (see under the word or words) |
| neg. | negative | v. tr. | verb transitive |
| pp. | past participle | | |
| ppl. | participle | | |

# TRANSLITERATION

As far as Telugu, Old and Modern, is concerned, the transcription is phonemic (see §§1.1-9).[1] For Kota, Toda, Kolami, and Parji also, the transcription is phonemic. For the rest, what we have here is a sort of 'broad transcription. In the Tamil writing system [n] and [n̲] are distinguished, but on distributional grounds they seem to belong to one phoneme /n/; [n], dental nasal, occurs word-initially and before dental stops; [n̲] alveolar nasal intervocalically, in gemination and before /r̲/ (see chapter I, note 53). /l̲/ is a voiced retroflex fricative, occurring in Ta., Ma., OKa., and OTe. [-r̲-], a voiced alveolar trill, is an allophone of *t̲ (probably a voiceless alveolar stop) in SDr. in the intervocalic position. In the Toda material ü = high front rounded vowel, ï = high back unrounded vowel, ö = central mid rounded vowel; c = ts, ʒ = dz, č = tš, ǰ = dž, θ = voiceless dental fricative, x = voiceless velar fricative; ł and ł̣ are voiceless laterals of the alveolar and retroflex series respectively. Among the sibilants, s̲ z̲ are alveolar, š ž alveolopalatal, and ṣ ẓ retroflex (for further details, see Emeneau, "Toda, a Dravidian Language," TPS 1958, p. 19). In both Toda and Kota /t̲ d̲/ are alveolar stops, voiceless and voiced respectively. Tulu u̥ = ï (high back unrounded vowel); è = æ (higher low front unrounded vowel).

In the material of Central Dravidian there is reason to believe that [ṛ] represents a retroflex flap. rr written in Gondi records is of uncertain phonetic value; could it be an alveolar trill contrasting with the flap r? Kuvi (S) ẓ = ts, ch = č; we do not know how Fitzgerald's vw- is to be pronounced.

Kur. and Brah. k̲h̲ and Malto q may represent varieties of voiceless uvular (or post-velar) fricative; the corresponding voiced ones are transliterated as g̲h̲ and g̵ respectively. Droese says that th in Malto is "a lightly sounded English sharp 'th'" (p. 1). We do not know whether it sounds like 'th-' as in 't̲h̲in' or in 't̲h̲en.' There is no indication of the phonetic value of [n̲] in Malto.

No attempt is made in this work to change the transcriptions found in the different source-books, except in the case of vowel-length for which /¯/ is used uniformly in the place of symbols occurring variously as [´] [·] [¯]. [ṅ] is used to represent the velar nasal in SDr., since

[1] Subject to the interpretation of [˜] and the dipthong ai̯ in phonemic terms (§§1.3, .4).

its use is uniformly prevalent in all the lexicons of the literary languages; however, [ŋ] is employed for this sound for Klm., Nk., Pj., Oll., and KGad. as in their source-books.

In the vocabularies of many languages, the verbal bases are entered along with the infinitive morphemes as follows: Ma. -ka/-kka, Tu. -uni/-pini, -puni/-vuni, Go. -ānā, Kui -pa/-ba/-va, Kuvi (F) -ali, Kuvi (S) -nai/-inai, Kur. -ānā, Mlt. -e. While studying the comparative etyma, these elements have to be eliminated. The form in parentheses following the entry of a verb-root of any language is the past stem of the root, unless otherwise stated, e.g., Ta. cel (ceṉ-ṟ-) to go, etc.

An asterisk preceding a Telugu entry in Part II means that the verbal base in question has very restricted distribution in paradigm. An asterisk following an entry of Telugu shows that the form is archaic and does not continue in Modern Telugu as known to the author. Elsewhere, an asterisk indicates reconstruction. A Roman figure (II to V) following each entry in Part II refers to its inflectional class keyed to the description in chapter III (§§3.26-.33). Entries unaccompanied by a Roman figure belong to Inflectional Class I.

# PART I
# A COMPARATIVE AND DESCRIPTIVE ANALYSIS

CHAPTER I

# A COMPARATIVE AND HISTORICAL PHONOLOGY

## PHONEMES

### Old Telugu

§1.1. On the basis of early inscriptions and literary works, the following phonemes can be set up for the native element of Old Telugu:[1]

Consonants

| | Lab. | Dent. | Alv. | Retro. | Pal. | Vel. | Glot. |
|---|---|---|---|---|---|---|---|
| Stop | p<br>b | t<br>d | | ṭ<br>ḍ | | k<br>g | |
| Affricate | | | | | c<br>j | | |
| Spirant | | s | | *l̲ | | | h |
| Nasal | m | | n | ṇ | | ṅ | |
| Lateral | | | l | ḷ | | | |
| Flap | | | r | | | | |
| Trill | | | r̲ | | | | |
| Semi-vowel | v | | | | y | | |

Vowels

| | Front | Non-Front |
|---|---|---|
| Close | i | u |
| Half-close | e | o |
| Half-open | | |
| Open | | a |

All vowels contrast in length, e.g., paḍu to fall : pāḍu to sing.

[1]See p. 126.

§1.2. A large amount of borrowing from Old Indo-Aryan introduced the following aspirated stops and sibilants in Old Telugu:

| | | | | |
|---|---|---|---|---|
| ph | th | ṭh | ch | kh |
| bh | dh | ḍh | jh | gh |
| | | ṣ | ś | |

The traditional Telugu grammars have also included the nasal [ñ] in this list but it can be interpreted as an allophone of /n/ in Te. (§1.4) as well as in Sanskrit.[2] The Sanskrit visarga [:], transcribed ḥ, which is also classed with these in traditional grammars, occurs only within words and compounds, but not utterance finally as in Sanskrit, e.g., duḥkhamu distress, tapaḥphalamu the fruit of penance. It can therefore be assigned in Telugu to the phoneme /h/ as its voiceless variant occurring before voiceless labial and velar stops.

§1.3. In poetry ai̯ and au̯ are treated, on the one hand, as monosyllables rhyming with long vowels, and on the other, as disyllables (viz., ayi, avu) rhyming with VCV sequences. This is applicable only to the diphthongs belonging to the native element.[3] Skt. diphthongs occurring in loanwords are always treated as monosyllabic, equivalent to long vowels; therefore, their distribution is only partially similar to the native ai and au. The phonemic status of Skt. ṛ ṝ and ḷ ḹ is doubtful even in the borrowed element in OTe.; word-initially, at least, they are treated as consonantal r and l.[4]

As far as the structure of the OTe. verbal bases is concerned, the phonemic system given in §1.1 is adequate.

Allophones:

§1.4. Very little is known about the phonetics of Old Telugu beyond what is broadly obvious. /c j/ have two allophones each as gathered from the descriptions of traditional grammars and also supported by modern usage; viz., [t͡s d͡z] dental affricates before the back vowels, and [č ǰ] palatal affricates before the front vowels.[5] [ñ], which occurs only before palatal affricates, can be assigned to /n/. Across morpheme boundaries [ñ] is in free variation with [n].[6] /m/ and /n/ contrast initially, and /m/, /n/, and /ṇ/ contrast intervocalically. Contrast between /n/ and /ṅ/ occurs in such cases as: kinka anger; kānka gift, offering (alternatively, kinuka, kānuka), as opposed to /koṅku/ to hesitate.[7] /ḻ/, which is considered to be a retroflex fricative in Ancient Tamil, is a Proto-Dravidian phoneme which occurs only in the early Telugu inscriptions as a separate phoneme. By the beginning of the literary period (i.e., early 11th century), it had already fallen together with /ḍ/ and /r/ in complementary environments. /r/ and /r̲/ are separate phonemes in OTe. as can be attested by numerous minimal pairs, e.g., arugu to go : ar̲ugu to decay, to be digested. However, there is evidence that this contrast was occasionally blurred even during the period of the early classics (§1.107, note 60).

Following the Skt. system of writing, an anusvāra [O] was used in the orthography of early Telugu inscriptions primarily in the place of the nasals [m ñ ṅ] before stops and affricates, but it gradually replaced the whole series of nasal phonemes before stops and affricates and came to serve as a cover symbol for all of them. Since [O] occurs only before stops and affricates, its phonemic status is automatically determined, i.e., /m/ before labial stops, /n/ before dental stops and affricates, /ṇ/ before retroflex stops, and /ṅ/ before velar stops. But historically, these pre-consonantal nasals were all lost regularly after long vowels, but optionally after short vowels. So, a form like /ēṅgu/ of inscriptional Te. or even Pre-Te. is always /ĕgu/ in literary Te.; but an older form /kalaṅgu/ to be disturbed, is either /kalagu/ or /kalaṅgu/. Old Telugu grammarians devised a name for this alternating value of [O] (Romanization ṃ) and called it ardhānusvāra or arasunna (literally, half-nasal or half-circle).[8] In all the environments of homorganic nasals they wrote the symbol of pūrṇānusvāra or full circle [O], since its phonetic value (i.e., presence or absence of articulation) is determined by the length of the preceding vowel; therefore forms written [ēṃgu] and [kalaṃgu] were phonetically and phonemically ēgu, kalagu/kalaṅgu, respectively. It was only from prosody that one could know whether [O] was meant to be articulated as a full nasal or not in a given stanza after short vowels. In conformity with the meaning of arasunna (half-circle) the Te. printing system of classical texts introduced [C] as opposed to [O]. [C] means that it is a free alternant of a full nasal after short vowels and has a zero alternant after long vowels. Throughout this work I have followed the printing system by using a tilde [˜] in the place of [C], because this has, at the same time, a morphophonemic advantage as well as a historical suggestivity in description. Therefore, a form like ē̃gu, in this work, is phonemically /ēgu/ but historically from an older /ēṅgu/; a form like /kalā̃gu/ is phonemically /kalaṅgu/ freely alternating with /kalagu/, of which /kalaṅgu/ is older. In present day spoken Telugu, the alternating value of [C] no longer exists; it is lost everywhere.

This description is adequate to identify the phonemic value of [˜] occurring within the verbal bases where it is always a part of the derivative suffixes. This is also used in the place of the morphophonemic variants of an inflexional -n (see §3.7 and note 7 of Chapter III).

§1.5. /ṇ ṅ ḷ y/ do not occur initially in a word. /v/ never occurs before /u o/. All the remaining consonants occur initially before all the five vowel phonemes. The frequency of occurrence of the various classes of consonants in the root-initial position is as follows in a descending order: voiceless stops; nasals; semivowel /v/; voiced stops; trills; laterals, and spirants. The only consonant groups admitted in the initial position consist of one of /p t k b d g m v s/ + /r/, e.g., pr-, tr-, kr-, etc. These never occur medially in native words. A root may begin with any of the five vowel phonemes or any of the consonants or consonant groups as described above.

§1.6. Each syllable has a vowel as nucleus (peak). Any consonant or consonant group not preceded by a vowel belongs to the following one. Single consonants occurring between vowels always belong to the following vowels; but consonant groups in this position are divided between the preceding and the following vowel nuclei, the first member of the consonant group belonging to the preceding nucleus and the second member to the following nucleus, e.g., /ka|da|lu/, /kruc|cu/, /īḍ|cu/. The alternative analysis as /kru|ccu/ and /ī|ḍcu/ is not admissible, since sequences of the type cc- and ḍc- are not possible onsets in Telugu. A long syllable is one which has a long vowel as its nucleus, or a short vowel plus a consonant, e.g., /nā|ku/ : /nak|ku/; a short syllable is one which has a short vowel as its nucleus and also as syllable final, as in the above example /ka|da|lu/. This description of the syllable structure conforms to the metrical system of Old Telugu prosody.

## Modern Telugu

§1.7. The phonemic picture of Modern Telugu is considerably different. Among consonants, a labio-dental voiceless fricative /f/ is introduced through English loanwords like coffee /kāfī/, office /āfīsu/, etc. Contrast between /r/ and /r̲/ is completely lost. The contrast between /th/ and /dh/ is also eliminated; only /dh/ occurs for both. The Modern Telugu phonemes can be charted as follows:

Consonants:

| | | | | | | | | | | | | |
|---|---|---|---|---|---|---|---|---|---|---|---|---|
| p | ph | | t | | | ṭ | ṭh | c | ch | k | kh | |
| b | bh | | d | dh | | ḍ | ḍh | j | jh | g | gh | |
| | | f | | | s | ṣ | | ś | | | | h |
| m | | | | | n | ṇ | | | | | | |
| | | | | | l | ḷ | | | | | | |
| | | | | | r | | | | | | | |
| w | | | | | | | | y | | | | |

Vowels:

| | |
|---|---|
| i | u |
| e | o |
| æ | a |

**§1.8.** In the sub-standard speech aspirated stops are replaced by the corresponding unaspirated ones; even among standard dialect speakers, aspirates and unaspirates freely vary in the retroflex, palatal, and velar series. Single voiceless stops are tense and slightly aspirated (in the case of unaspirated stops) in the initial position after an open juncture and are lax medially between vowels. Voiced stops of the dental and velar series are slightly spirantized intervocalically. /ḍ/ has a flap [ṛ] allophone in the same position. /n/ has four allophones: a dental nasal [n] before dental stops, a palatal nasal [ñ] before the palatal allophones [č ǰ], a velar nasal [ṅ] before velar stops, and an alveolar allophone [n̲] elsewhere. /c j/ have two allophones each as in Old Telugu (see §1.2). Single /m/ has a nasalized bilabial frictionless spirant allophone [w̃] utterance finally, intervocalically, and before /s w h/ in consonant clusters; elsewhere, it is a bilabial nasal continuant. /w/ is a bilabial frictionless continuant everywhere, except in gemination, where it a labio-dental fricative [v]. /r/ is an alveolar trill [r̲] in gemination; elsewhere, an alveolar single flap [r].

**§1.9.** Vowel length is phonemic, indicated in this work by a superscript bar /ˉ/. /æ/, which does not occur in Old Telugu, is a phoneme in Modern Telugu; however, it always occurs with length, e.g., /koṭṭāka/

don't beat! (imper., 2 sg.): /koṭṭǣka/ after beating; /koṭṭǣw/ you beat (past) : /koṭṭĕw/ you might beat, don't (admonitive, with high-falling pitch).

## CONSONANTS: INITIAL

§1.10. Etymologically, most of the Telugu verbal bases can be divided into two elements each, viz., a root of type (C)V̄̆- or (C)V̄̆C-, and a derivative suffix of type -(C)C or -V̄̆(C)C.[9]

Family likeness or traces of cognation in Dravidian occur mainly in the root syllables; the choice of derivative suffixes is generally not uniform among the members of all the sub-groups (§§2.8 ff.). In the following sections, a brief comparative and historical account of each Telugu phoneme involved in the radical syllables is given.

### k-

§1.11. Te. k- < PDr. *k- before all vowels except the front series ī̆ ē̆. Te. k- occurring before the front vowels is exceptional and all such forms with k- before ī̆ and ē̆ may be considered loanwords from Kannada or some other neighboring language in which k- remains before the front vowels;[10] for instance:

1. kiniyu to be angry; Ka. kinisu; Ta. ciṉa; Ma. cinikka.
2. kiṭṭu to approach; Ka. kiṭṭu, giṭṭu; kiḍu n. approach; Tu. kiṭṭa, giṭṭa proximity; Ta. kiṭai, kiṭṭu; Ma. kiṭayuka, kiṭṭuka; Mlt. kiṭa near.
3. keḍayu to fall down, crash; Ka. keḍe; Tu. keḍaguni; Ta. kiṭa; Ma. kiṭakuka.
4. keralu to increase, spread; Ka. keraḷu, keḷar; Ta. kiḷar to be abundant; Ma. kiḷaruka.
5. kelayu to cry, etc.; Ka. kele; Tu. kelevuni; Ta. cilai; Ma. cilekka.

The above Telugu forms are obviously taken from Kannada at a pre-literary period, by which time c- < *k- before front vowels was no longer in operation.

§1.12. There are, however, a few more forms in Telugu with kī̆-/kē̆-, for which correspondents in Ka. or Tu. are missing and hence their immediate sources are obscure:

1. kiduku to fret, to groan (as a child on waking from sleep); the closest related form occurs in Brah. kijj- to fret, groan; Ka. giji a sound denoting confusion.

2. kēru[1] to chuckle with joy; to cry out; Ka. keraḷ to cry; Tu. kērle sound, noise; Ta. cirarru to shout, call.

3. kēru[2] to laugh; kēr-inta laughter, mockery; kēr-aḍamu, krēṇi id.; Kui grēspa to mock, ridicule; Klm.(SR) kaiŋ-, (E) kayŋg-[11] to laugh; Go.(W) kīrī derision; *kay-r-/*key-r- > kēr- is the etymology which best explains all forms, including Go. i- < *ey-.

Further forms of this category are kiṭṭu to kill (Bhr. II), kiniyu to approach, and kivvu to perish (Brown), for which no reliable etymologies could be discovered.

§1.13. Before all other vowels (i.e., ă̄, ŏ̄, ŭ̄), Te. k- corresponds to South and Central Drav. k- (or g-), Kur. Brah. kh- and Mlt. q-;[12] Burrow has given most of the forms in his article and the few Telugu verbs not included in his lists are as follows:

1. kaḍugu to wash, clean, cleanse; Ka. karcu; Ta. kaluvu; Ma. kaluku; Kui kahpa to wash the face; Kur. khajj- to cleanse the head with clay; Mlt. kaje to wash (as clothes).

2. kaniyu to ripen; Ta. kani id.; Ma. kaniyuka; Kuvi kamb- to become ripe; Kur. khañj- to bear fruit; Mlt. qanjpe a fruit.

3. kappu to cover; Ta. Ma. Ka. Tu. kappu; Kuvi kaph- to outflank; Kur. khap- id.

4. kūḍu to assemble; Ka. Tu. kūḍu; Ta. Ma. kūṭu; Kur. khōṇḍ- to bring together, gather; khōṇḍr- to assemble.

5. koṅku, koncu to hesitate, fear (< *to shrink, bend); Ka. koṅku to be bent; koñca inferiority; Kui kōga to shrink; Klm. gogg- id.; Kur. khŏngh- to bend; Mlt. qonk- to bend (knees).

The others (occurring also in Burrow's list) are: kanu, kāncu to see; karacu (1) to bite; (2) to learn; kalāgu to be stirred; kāyu to heat; kāgu id.; kācu to protect; wait; kuluku to shake; koṭṭu to beat; kōyu to pluck, cut.

§1.14. In all the above forms the phonetic correspondence as formulated by Burrow holds regular. There are, however, a considerable number of forms in which Kur. Mlt. and Brah. have k- instead of kh-/q- before non-front vowels:

1. kaṭṭu to tie, bind; build; Ka. Tu. Ta. kaṭṭu id.; Klm. kaṭṭ-; Go. kaṭṭ- to shut (door); Kui kaṭru twisted : Kur. kaṛ- to twist together; Mlt. kaṛke to tighten: kaṭe a bank: Te. kaṭṭa id.

2. kaḍacu to cross; to exceed; Ka. kaḍe; Tu. kaḍapuni; Ta. kaṭa; Ma. kaṭakka; Kui gṛāsa, gṛāpa to cross over; Kuvi grāñc- id. : Kur. kaṭṭ- id.; Mlt. kaṭe id., kaṭtre to help cross; Brah. kharr- to proceed.

3. kappu to overspread; SDr. and Kui and Kuvi kapp-, kap- : Kur. kapp- to overspread with limbs; cf. also khap- to cover exactly.

4. kasaru to be angry, to scold, chide; n. anger; kasi vengeance; cf. Tu. kastu violent; Ta. katavu to be angry with; katal̲ id.; Ma. kayarka to start in anger : Kur. kackacr- to be annoyed; cf. kael broken in spirit.

5. kuṭṭu to stitch, sew; Go. kōṭṭ- id. : Kur. kuḍ-/kuṛ- to string, pierce; Mlt. kuḍe to pierce; kuṭye to nail.

6. kūyu to cry out, call; Ka. kū, kūku, kūgu; Tu. kūguni; Ta. kūvu; Ma. kūka; kūkkuka; Go. (kōr)-kūs- (cock) to crow; Klm. kūg-; Kui kūpka id. : Mlt. kūkre to call out; Brah. kūk- shout, cry.

7. kūrku to doze; kūru- adj. sleepy; Tu. kūruni id.; Kui kōra to lull to sleep; Go. kūrk- to nod in sleepiness : Kur. kūg- to doze; Mlt. kūge id.

These correspondences are too obvious to allow any question regarding their correctness. This does not, of course, challenge Burrow's formula but only makes out a case for a number of residuary forms, whose development is to be sought in other factors,[13] e.g., dialect mixture, borrowing and diachronic developments (for which no material is available). These examples also do not show any evidence for the existence of a different velar phoneme here in Proto-Dravidian, since many of the languages agree in pointing to an original *k-. The existence of doublets in k- or kh- beside k̲h̲- forms in Kur. Mlt. is also to be taken into account; see especially Kur. k̲h̲onchā/koccā, khap-/kap-, etc.

c-[14]

§1.15. Te. c- < PDr. *c-, before all vowels. This phoneme is represented in some Dr. languages by c- and in others by s-; Tamil, Malayalam, Telugu, Koḍagu, Parji, Kuruk̲h̲, and Malto belong to the first group, while Kannada, Gondi, Kui, Kuvi, Kolami, and Naiki belong to the second; in some languages there is free variation like Kota and K. Gadaba.[15] Toda represents it always by t-.[16] Some dialects of Gondi, Kuvi, and sometimes Brahui change it to h-, which tends to disappear in the Gondi dialects.[17]

1. canu to go; Ka. sal; Tu. sanduni; Ta. Ma. cel; Kui salba; Kuvi han-; Go. hand-; Brah. hin-.

2. cācu to extend, stretch out as limbs; trans. of cā̃gu/sā̃gu; Ka. cācu; Tu. cācuni; Kui sāspa; Kuvi hāh-; Go. sāha-t-.

3. cikku to be caught, be stuck; Ka. sikku/silku; Tu. sikkuni; Ta. Ma. cikku; Klm. sik-; Pj. cirŋg-; Go. hilk-; Kui sinḍu a snare.

4. cī̃du to sneeze, blow the nose; Ka. sīnu; Ta. cīntu; Ma. cīntuka; Kui jīnja; srīnda; Kuvi (F) sind-.

5. cuṭṭu to revolve, to wind; Ta. Ma. cur̲r̲u; Ka. Tu. suttu; Pj. cuttu.

6. cūcu to see, also cūḍ- in certain forms; Ka. suṭṭu to show; Tu. tū-, sū-; Ta. Ma. cuṭṭu to point out; Ma. cuṇṭu to show; Kui sūṛa to see; sūṭ- to show; Go. sūr- to expect; GoM. huḍ- to see; Brah. hur-, hun- id.

7. cēru to reach, approach; Ka. sēr; Ta. cēr; Ma. cēruka; Klm. Nk. sēr-.

8. cokku to be stupefied, intoxicated; Ka. sokku/sorku; Tu. sorkuni; Ta. cokku; Ma. corukkuka; cf. Ta. Ma. sōr to languish; Kui sōsa to be intoxicated.

9. cōpu to drive off (as flies, etc.); send; insert; Ka. sō, sōvu id.; Nk. sōrtān sent (LSI iv, p. 572); Kui dōpa to insert; Kur. job- to thrust.

§1.16. Telugu has preserved the PDr. *c- in a number of forms, while some of the South Dravidian languages have either changed it to t- or altogether lost it (see §1.23).[18] t- < *c- has wider distribution than zero < *c-, which latter change is confined only to the Southern group. It should, however, be noted that these developments are scattered and not regular in any particular language. Following are some typical examples of Te. c- < *c- paralleled by t-/zero in some of the Southern languages:

1. cadiyu to be crushed; cadupu to smash; Ka. sade, v.t. id.; tade id.; sadaku/tadaku id.; Tu. sadi beating; Ta. tatai to be shattered; catai to crush; tatar to be crushed; Ma. catayuka to be squashed; catekka id.

2. car̲acu to slap; tar̲aṭu to beat with a rope; Kui jaṛsa a whip : Ta. tar̲ai to beat down; ar̲ai to slap, hammer; Ma. ar̲ayuka id.; Tu. tarapuni to rivet; Kur. taṛ- to flog, lash; Mlt. taṛce id.

3. callu to sprinkle; Ka. caḷe sprinkling; Tu. call-/cell- id. : Ta. Ma. Ka. taḷi to sprinkle, scatter; Tu. talipuni id.

4. cinuku to drizzle; to rain; Ka. jinugu; Ma. cinar̲uka to be spilt : Ta. ir̲ai to sprinkle; Ma. ir̲uka; Ka. er̲acu; (r̲/n̲ alternation common in Drav., see §1.96).

5. cō̃ku to touch; sōku, soṅku, sokku id.; Tu. soṅkuni, sōṅguni, sōkuni : Ta. tōy- come in contact with; touch; Ma. tōyuka to be united; Tu. tōku collision; toy- to strike.

Other forms of this type are: caduvu to read; cā̃du to rub into paste, chafe; cālu to be sufficient; ciluku to spill; cī̃du to blow the nose; cē̃du to bale out water; cēru to reach; colayu to faint; cōpu to chase, send; for which see Part II.

§1.17. Te. c- < *k- before front vowels, i.e., ī̆ and ē̆; Ta. Ma. c-, all others k-; even Tamil and Malayalam do not palatalize if the front vowels precede a retroflex consonant, ṭ, ṇ, ḷ, or ḻ.[19]

1. cikku to be reduced (as persons); Ta. ciṟuku to be stunted in growth : Kota kilgaṭ-/-gac to be small for one's age; Go. kiṟkwāl very thin (of a man).

2. cidumu to nip, pluck; Ta. citai to pluck : Ka. kittu id.; Kui kisa to pinch; Kuvi GoM. kic-; Go. kidīt- to shred chillies; Klm. kism-; Kur. kicc-; Brah. kishk- (*kic- > *kit- > *cit-).

3. cekku to insert; Ka. sekku/serku, prob. l.w. < Te.; Ta. ceruku, cerumu; Ma. cerukkuka : Kur. k̲h̲err- to insert; Mlt. qere to thrust in, tuck in.

4. ceḍu to perish; be spoiled; Ka. kiḍu/keḍu; Tu. keṭṭa bad; Ta. Ma. keṭu; Go. kaṟi-t-; Mlt. qerme to destroy.

Others are: cirūgu to be torn; cidiyu, ciduku to be crushed; cimuḍu to be spoiled by overboiling; civuku to be rotten; ceṇḍu to cut, chop; cedaru to be scattered; cenaku to touch, provoke; ceppu to tell; ceralu to be jubilant; to grow enraged; cerugu to sift, winnow; ceruvu to tuck in; celayu, celāgu to cry, etc.; cēyu to do.

§1.18. As Burrow has noted, Telugu is the South Dravidian language most affected by palatalization, and in this respect it is independent of similar developments in Tamil and Malayalam.[20] Inscriptions record this development from the 5th century onwards[21] but we do not know how long it existed before. However, the forms krinda-, krī- below, krēva side, krēṇi ridicule, indicate that palatalization of kī̆- and kē̆- commenced after the completion of the metathesis of radical phonemes, which affected a large number of forms (see §1.139 ff.). In any case, it appears that this is to be attributed to the early period of the separation of Telugu from the main body of South Dravidian.

§1.19. In a few forms, there seems to be an irregular palatalization, i.e., *k- > c-, before non-front vowels:

1. cuṭṭu to roll up, wrap, wind; Ta. Ma. cuṟṟu; Ka. Tu. suttu; Kui sursuri curly; cf. Ma. cuṟayuka to turn around : Kui grūpa to encircle; Kur. guruñjta'ānā to twirl, whirl; Mlt. guryare to whirl, revolve; Brah. kūr- to roll up; kurr- to shrink; see also Ta. kuruḷ to curl, etc.

2. cūḍu to burn (v.t.); Ka. suḍu; Tu. suḍpuni; Ta. Ma. cuṭu; Klm. suḍ-; Go. surr- : Kur. kuṟ- to become hot; cook on embers (past st. kuṭṭ-).

3. coccu to enter; also cor-; Kui sōlba to enter; sōṟpa cause to enter; put in; Go. sōṟī-t-; Klm. sōng- : Kur. kōr- to enter; Mlt. kor- id., kortr- to let enter, thrust in.

Similarly we have also in South Dravidian:

1. koṅku to be bent, curved : Ma. coṅga, coṅgu crookedness; coñcu id.

2. kunuku to doze (< *to bend); Ma. kuniyuka to bend; Ta. kūṉ-, Ka. kūn- : Ma. cunikka to make a curve in writing; cunippu arch; if this cuṉ- is taken to be a variant of cuṟ- (cf. Te. cuṭṭu) we seem to have a close connection of this set with kuṉ-/kuṟ- with similar meaning (see §1.96 for ṉ/ṟ alternation).

3. kuriyu v.i. and v.t. to drizzle, rain : ?Ta. Ma. cori id.; Ka. suri.

It may be that these are cases of mere accidental resemblance, or else that they indicate some principle of vocalism so far not discovered.

§1.20. In one form Te. c- develops out of an Indo-Aryan t-, palatalized before i, with the blend of a Dravidian suffix:

cemaru to melt down (HariV.), cemar-cu to sweat; cemmaṭa, cemaṭa sweat; cemma moisture; also tēma id.; Tu. semma, temma cold; cf. Skt. tim- (stim-) to become wet; tema-, m. wetness; [Nep. sim- bog; P. simmṇā to ooze; L. simmaṇ; S. simaṇu, sima, f. ooze (see s.v. sim, Turner, Nep. Dict.); M. tevaṇẽ to liquefy; Pali temto wet.]

The suffix -ar is probably formed on the analogy of a similar set in Dravidian; compare Te. cemaru with Ka. bemaru, bevaru to sweat, perspire; Tu. bege, begar; Ta. viyar id. The base cem- has no obvious cognates in Dravidian.

§1.21. There is one more c- form for which proper etymologies are lacking in Dravidian. Te. caduvu to read, recite : ?Ta. Ma. ōtu; Ka. Tu. ōdu; this correspondence is difficult. Burrow is inclined to connect this form with Ta. catur ability, etc. deriving the Skt. catura- skillful as a loan word from Dravidian.[22]

## t-

§1.22. Te. t- < PDr. *t-, before all vowels:

1. tappu to miss, fail; to violate; Ta. Ma. Ka. Tu. tappu id.; Kuvi (S) tapp- to misdo.

2. tā̃ku to touch; Ka. tāku, tāṅku; Tu. tākuni; Ta. tākku; Ma. tākkuka; Kur. tak- to give a slight knock; Mlt. tak- to touch.

3. tinu to eat; Ka. tin, tinnu; Tu. tinpini; Ta. tiṉ, tiṉṉu; Ma. tinnuka; Kui tinba; Kuvi tinn-, tinj-; Go. tind-; Kur. Mlt. tind- to feed.

4. tuḍucu to wipe, erase; Ka. tode; Tu. tuḍepuni, toḍepuni; Ta. tuṭai; Ma. tuṭekka; Kui tuhpa to cast away.

5. ter̲acu to open; Ka. ter̲e; Tu. terapu space; Ta. tir̲a; Go. tarī-t-; Kui dari adj. opened out; trēppa to lay out; ?cf. Ma. tur̲akkuka to open.

6. toḍuku to touch; Ka. tuḍu, toḍu to join, etc.; Ta. Ma. toṭu to touch; Tu. toṭṭuni to hold fast; Go. tunḍ- to be stuck; Brah. tor- to hold fast.

7. tō̃cu to appear; Ka. tōr̲-/tōr̲u; Tu. tōjuni; Ta. tōn̲r̲u; Ma. tōn̲n̲uka; Kui tōmba, tōnja; Kuvi(F) tonja aiyali id., tōss- to show; Pj. tōnd- id.

§1.23. In a considerable number of forms Te. t- develops out of a PDr. affricate *c- as attested by the preservation of this phoneme (i.e., *c) in some of the languages. This assumption is based on the presence of t-/zero alternation in many languages which can be explained only by positing an original *c due to the absence of *t > zero in any position.[23] Again there is also evidence from loan words that an IA s- develops to t- in a few cases in OTa. where we expect a zero, e.g., Skt. sēnā- > Ta. tān̲ai army; this could happen by substituting Dravidian c- for Skt. s-, viz., Skt. sēnā- > *cēn̲ai > tān̲ai (for ā/ē after c-, see §1.240). The change of t > c also occurs in Dravidian but to a restricted extent, mostly in association with the front vowels or the semivowel /y/. Examples for t- < *c- are as follows:

1. taḍiyu to be soaked, wet; taḍupu to make wet; taḍi dampness; Ka. taḍi wet, damp; taṇ cold : Ka. caḷi cold, coolness; Ta. caḷi cold; Ma. caḷi mud, mire; caḷḷu bog, caḷumpu id.

2. taniyu to be satisfied; to grow cool; tanu cool; Ka. taṇi to be satisfied; grow cool; Ta. taṇi id. : Tu. saṇipuni, saniyuni, taṇiyuni to grow calm, cool; Ta. Ma. Ka. Tu. caḷi coldness; Te. cali id.; this is etymologically connected with the previous item.

3. tar̲umu to chase away, drive; Kui tāja to wipe : Kur. caṛ- to expel.

4. talāku to shake, fear, etc.; Ka. taḷḷal̲a fear; Tu. taḷḷaṇa wavering; Mlt. talqro weak, delicate; cf. Te. talaru to fear, tremble; Ka. taḷar; Ta. taḷar droop; grow weary; Ma. taḷaruka id. : Ma. caḷuṅṅuka to shake, to be frightened; cāḷuka to stagger; Tu. caḷḷu, callu timid, weak (see §§1.211, 2, .213).

5. tiṭṭu to scold, abuse; Ka. tiṭṭu; Ta. tiṭṭu : Ka. siḍuku to scold, chide; n. wrath; siṭṭu anger, wrath; Brah. jirk- to rebuke.

6. tirugu to revolve, turn, etc.; Ta. Ma. Ka. tiri id.; Ka. tirigu; Tu. tiṙg-; Go. tirīt-; Klm. Nk. tirg-; Pj. tirk- to writhe; Kuvi trig-, tiṛv- : Brah. sīrr- to recoil; cf. tar- to spin.

7. tīḍu to rub, whet; Ka. tīḍu; Ta. Ma. tīṭṭu id.; Tu. tīṇṭu : Tu. sīṇṭuni to rub.

8. tur̲ugu, tur̲umu to stuff in, cram; Ka. tur̲uku; Ta. Ma. tur̲u : Ka. curcu/cuccu to insert.

9. tū̃gu to swing, rock : ū̃gu id. (< *cūṅku, see §1.213, 2).

10. tūlu to reel, stagger, etc.; Tu. tūluni to totter, reel : Te. sōlu id.; Ka. cōl to become slack; Ta. uyal/tuyal id.; Tu. oyaluni id.; ultimately from *cuyil/*coyal (see §1.295).

Similarly, in torā̃gu to ooze, tor̲ā̃gu to give up, shed, tolā̃gu to step aside, tō̃gu to bathe, t- has developed out of an original c-. However, in items 5, 6, and 7 above, one cannot be certain whether *c- or *t- is the original initial phoneme because even *t with a following front vowel can yield *c (see Te. cemaru §1.20).

n-

§1.24. Te. n- < PDr. *n- before all vowels:

1. nagu to laugh; navvu id.; Ka. nagu; Tu. nakali ridicule; Ta. naku; Ma. nakekka; Brah. makh- id.

2. niṇḍu to be full; Ka. ner̲e; Tu. neriyuni; Ta. nir̲ai; Ma. nir̲ayuka; Kui Kuvi nenj-; Kur. nīnd-, Mlt. nind-.

3. nūr̲u to crush, nur̲ucu id.; Ta. Ma. Ka. nūr̲u id.; nur̲i id.; Tu. nuriyuni; Go. nōr- to grind; Kuvi nūi- to mill; Brah. nus- id.

4. neṭṭu to push out; Ta. ner̲i, ner̲r̲u; Tu. nesipini; Kui nasa to press, push; Go. natt- to dash down; Kur. nepp- to brush up (while sweeping); Mlt. nerme id.

5. noccu to suffer, grieve; Common Dravidian noy- (see Part II).

§1.25. An initial n- with a following vowel alternation of ā/ē or a/e is supposed to have derived from a PDr. *ñ- with either ā̆ or ē̆ following. The few Telugu verbs with na- corresponding to na-/ne- of Ka. are as follows.[24]

1. narayu hair to grow grey; nara greyness; neriyu (Mdn. Te., dialectally, besides nariyu); Ta. narai, Ma. narekka; Tu. narevuni : Ka. nare/nere; < *ñār- (see §1.233).

2. naccu to be agreeable; to trust; Ta. naccu to desire, love : Ka. naccu/neccu to desire; trust; n. love, etc.; Ta. nacai to love; naya to be pleasing, agreeable.

3. nattu to stammer; Tu. nattiṅgĕ a man partially dumb : Ka. nattu/nettu to stammer.

Of these, there is reason to attribute the a/e variation in naccu/neccu to the fact that it was originally ay/ey as in naycc- (or *naytt-) and neycc- (*neytt-), which is treated under the phonology of vowels (§1.283); in the case of nattu, lack of literary usage and etymologies makes its derivation from an original ñ form highly dubious. Corresponding to Te. nāku lick, nāṭu to fix, and nānu to be soaked, Ka. has na-/ne-forms with short vowel, while the long vowel forms show ā in agreement with the forms of the other languages, which do not show any alternation between ā/ē. *ñā- > nē- is the usual development in Ka. by which we expect nē- forms instead of nān-, nāṭ- in Ka., if *ñā- were original.

§1.26. In the following forms an original ñ- is preserved in Tamil and/or Malayalam:

1. naggu to be crushed; nakku a notch, a chip; Ka. naggu to become bruised; neggu to crush; Tu. narguni to be bruised; Ta. neruṅku, naruṅku; Ma. ñeruṅṅuka to be pressed.

2. namalu to chew; nemarcu id.; nemaru rumination; Ka. namalu, nevaru id.; Tu. naunt-, naump- to chew; nauntu squeezing, chewing, crushing, etc.; Ta. ñemuṅku to squeeze, crush; Ma. ñamuṅṅuka id.; Koḍ. ñavṇḍ- to squeeze.

3. naḍūku to shake, tremble (out of cold, fear, eto.); Ma. ñaḻuṅṅuka id.; Ta. naḻukku, naḻir id.

4. navayu to languish, sink, droop; Ka. name, nave to wear away; Tu. name id.; Ma. ñamuṅṅuka to yield under pressure; Ta. ñemuṅku id.; Ta. namuku id.

§1.27. The conclusions of Burrow on this phenomenon are the following. A PDr. *ñā- develops to nā- in later Ta. and nē- in all other languages. *ñā- remains in Old Tamil and Old and Modern Malayalam. There were two sets of forms in PDr. beginning with *ña- and *ñe- which were confused in Old Tamil, but faithfully preserved in Malayalam. Modern Tamil na- and ne-, wherever they are secondary,[25] correspond to original *ña- and *ñe- respectively.

§1.28. On a closer study of the material presented by Burrow, it appears that some of his assumptions have to be modified. The situation in PDr. seems to be that there was no contrast between ā̆ and ē̆ after *ñ-. Lack of contrast between two phonemes in a certain environment would mean two things. Phonemically, either ā̆ fell together with ē̆ or vice versa, and there was only one phoneme here, either ē̆ or ā̆, which was a pool of both *ē̆ and *ā̆. Later, there could be a drift again in some area or other, i.e., either from *ā̆ > ē̆ or *ē̆ > ā̆, according as the resultant phoneme of merger was ā̆ or ē̆ in this position. In short, there was probably a period when ā and ē were distinct after *ñ-, secondly a period of merger, and again a period of secondary shift. This is similar to the problem of the merger of PDr. *i and *e before a into *e and again the drift of this *e to i in pre-Tamil (see §1.278). Phonetically, this means that the border line of distinction between the articulatory ranges of ā̆ and ē̆ was blurred. This is very similar to the lack of contrast between ā and ǣ in Modern Telugu after a palatal affricate /c/; after any other consonant, e.g., ḍ, the two vowels are clearly distinguished in their phone ic ranges, whereas after /c/ ā tends to be much more fronted and even raised and is to be placed nearly halfway between ā and ǣ, slightly tending toward ǣ; this could therefore be interpreted as a member of the ǣ phoneme. But the fact of lack of phonetic demarcation or the occurrence of overlapping in the articulatory ranges of two phonemes in a certain environment has an important relation to the problem of writing. It seems purely impressionistic and arbitrary whether a scribe prefers to write this "neutralized phone" as ā̆ or ē̆. To take the Modern Telugu example again, since there is no symbol for ǣ in Telugu orthography, it is usually represented either by ē or ā. Wherever a minimal contrast between ē and ǣ is suggested (e.g., koṭṭēw you might beat! [admonitive] : koṭṭǣw you beat [past]), one is usually inclined to use the ā symbol for ǣ; on the contrary where a minimal contrast is suggested between ǣ and ā (e.g., koṭṭǣka after beating: koṭṭāka don't beat!), one usually employs ē in the place of ǣ; but after c where we get only ǣ, but not ā, this is represented graphemically either by ā or by ē, for instance, vaccāka/vaccēka after coming, for /vaccǣka/. Similarly in Ka. both a and e occur in free variation after c in written records very frequently, e.g., caccu/ceccu to crush, grind; caccara/ceccara haste, speed; caṭṭi/ceṭṭi earthen pot; cannu/cennu beauty; cambu/cembu copper; callu/cellu to scatter.

§1.29. Studying the problem of ā̆/ē̆ after *ñ- in view of the above remarks, it appears that there was a similar neutralization between the phonetic ranges of these two vowels in that particular environment. Ancient Tamil grammarians fixed the phonemic value of this by the statement that only an ā or an e can occur here (but not an ē or a, Tolk. Eḻut. 64). This indicates that ñā- < *ñā- or *ñē-, and *ñe- < *ña- or *ñe-, which means that the neutralized phoneme *ā̆/*ē̆ was more a-like when long, but e-like when short. Since there is no phonetic (and therefore phonemic) contrast between ā̆ and ē̆ here, how these vowels are represented in writing does not necessarily prove or indicate the original (pre-merger) vowel qualities any more than Ka. a/e in the above examples represents the historically original quality after *c-. Malayalam, which separated as an independent language from Middle Tamil during the 10th century or thereabouts, has to be treated as only a dialect of Old Tamil while discussing this development, since it goes back to the common Tamil-Malayalam period. Then, Burrow's material can be shown as follows (op. cit., pp. 603-606):

| Tamil | | Malayalam | |
|---|---|---|---|
| ñāñcil | a plough | ñĕṅṅōl, nĕññil | |
| ñāl | to hang down | ñāl/ñēl | |
| . . . | | ñāṟal/ñēṟal | Eugenia jambolana |
| . . . | | ñeṅṅuka/ñaṅṅuka | to become soft |
| ñaṇṭu/ñeṇṭu | crab | ñaṇṭu | |
| ñemuṅku | to yield to pressure | ñamuṅṅuka | |
| ñemiṭu | to squeeze | ñamuṇṭu | |
| ñaral/ñeral | to sound | ñaraṅṅuka | |

These sets show that within the Old Tamil area there was a considerable amount of vacillation in the representation of *ā and *e, each of which is a result of merger of two phonemes. The employment of different vowels in different dialects and later a dialect mixture in literary texts could also be a source for this divergent representation of pre-Tamil *ā and *e.

The real difficulty in the problem is to know whether *ñ- shifted to n- in all other languages after or before the merger of vowels, or whether merger of the vowels took place only in pre-Tamil or PSDr. At least the double developments in vowels in Central and North Dravidian corresponding to *ñā- or *ñe- of Tamil should lead us to suspect that the merger was only confined to pre-Tamil.

1. Ta. ñāṇ a cord : Kui nōṇe; Go. nōne id.

2. Ta. ñālam earth : Kui nēḍe ground; Go. nēli.

3. Ma. ñerippu fire : Go. nirw- to burn; Te. nippu fire; Mlt. nare flame.

4. Ma. ñarampu tendon, nerve : Kur. narī pulse, nerve; Mlt. nāru veins.

Cases 1 and 3 above seem to indicate that even more than two vowels (ā and ē) were probably involved in the merger.

§1.30. Since, corresponding to Ta. ñā-, most other languages of South and Central Dravidian show nē-, the phonetic probability is that an original *ă merged with *ĕ through the palatalizing influence of the preceding *ñ-.

Of these earlier sequences, i e ; *ñĕ and ñe, *ñē shifted to ñā in pre-Tamil.

§1.31. It is again doubtful whether ñ-, wherever it occurs, is PDr. Even in Ancient Tamil there were cases with ñ-/y- alternation: yān- : ñān- I; yāl̲ : ñāl̲ lute; ñāṅkar there : (later) āṅku (< *yāṅku);[26] similarly there are cases where we notice a ñ-/zero alternation as in Ta. ñemuṅku : Ka. avugu, avuku; Ta. ñaṇṭu : Te. eṇḍri, etc. In these and similar instances, it is just to consider y- original and ñ- secondary. Tolkāppiyam has stated that yā- becomes ñā- when it immediately follows a final ṇ or n̲ of the preceding word (see El̲uttu. 147); according to Tolkāppiyam this was only seen in verbs, e.g., maṇ yāttu > maṇ ñāttu.[27] On the basis of this the following Te. verb had, presumably, an original y- in the initial position, since n- and zero alternate, followed by vowel alternation:

nĕmu to sift, winnow; Ta. nèmpu, nòmpu; Ma. nĕmpuka, nāvuka (see Burrow, DS V, p. 604), to which may be added Go. yĕm- to sift out husks of rice, pulses, etc.; Kui ĕmba to separate rice grains from straw by shaking.

According to Burrow an original ñā- produces nĕ- in Go. and Kui; on the contrary we have a vowel in these languages in the initial position instead of n-. We can posit a PDr. *yāmp- to explain this discrepancy.

§1.32. There is another set of forms, in which, corresponding to Te. n- (< *n-), some members of the Dravidian family attest forms without it. This is a very common case of the instability of initial n- in Dravidian observed in every one of the descendants to a greater or less degree (see also §1.218).

1. nilucu to stand; Ta. Ma. Ka. Tu. Koḍ. nil-; Go. nill-/nitt-; Kui nīlba, nisa : Klm. ill-; Kur. il-, Mlt. il-; Kur. ild- to set up.

2. nevulu to grieve; nevva trouble; pestilence : Ta. evvam affliction, distress; pestilence; ĕval poverty, want (< *nev-ul-).

3. nĕyu to weave; Ka. Tu. Ta. Ma. ney-; Kuvi nĕh- : Kur. ess- to weave, plait; Mlt. es-; cf. Kui ĕspa to spin.

Cases showing the instability of n- within Telugu will be treated elsewhere (§1.219). The reason for this development is presumably a wrong division of word junctures where an /n/ is involved.[28]

## p-

§1.33. Te. p- < PDr. *p-, before all vowels:

1. paṇḍu to ripen; Ka. paṇ fruit; Tu. parnduni; pandaḍe fructification; Ta. pal̲un̲u to grow ripe; Ma. pal̲am fruit; Go. paṇḍ- v. id.; Klm. paṇḍ-; Kur. pā̃n-, Mlt. pā̃n- id.

2. pāḍu to sing; Ka. pāḍu; Ta. Ma. pāṭu; Klm. pāṛ-; GoM. pār-; Kur. Mlt. pāṛ-; Kuvi (F) pacū a song.

3. piṇḍu to squeeze, to milk; Ka. piṇḍu, pili id.; Tu. puṇṭuni to wring (a wet garment), purñc- to squeeze a lemon; Ta. pili; Ma. piliyuka; Klm. pīnḍ-; Go. pīr- id.; Kuvi pīc- to milk; Mlt. pilq- to squeeze; Brah. pilh- id.

4. puḍūku to handle, grasp; Ka. puḍuku, puḍuṅku; Tu. puḍu grasping; Kuvi brūc- to snatch; Klm. puṛk- to touch.

5. perugu to grow, flourish; Ka. percu id.; Tu. percuni; Ta. Ma. peruku; Klm. perg-; Go. pirr-; GoM. pērs- to extend; Kui beri beri inba to swell; Kur. pard-; Brah. pir- to swell.

6. poṅgu to swell up, boil; Ka. poṅgu; Tu. poṅguni; Ta. poṅku; Ma. poṅṅuka; Kui poṅga to be spilt (by overflowing); Kuvi (S) poṅg-; Go. pōng- to overflow (as a river); pōṛ- to swell; Kur. por$^{o}$kh- to swell (river, etc.); Mlt. pōngje to be increased; porg- to become fat.

§1.34. In one or two cases v- of some CDr. forms corresponds to Te. and SDr. p-, for instance, Te. piṇḍu to milk : Kui vṛīsa id.; Te. pāḍu to sing : Go. wāṛ- id.[29]

m-

§1.35. Te. m- < PDr. *m-, before all vowels:

1. manu to live, stay; Ta. mannu to live, remain; Kui Kuvi man to be; Kuvi (F) manj- id.; Go. mand-; Pj. men-, mend-; KGad. men-; Kur. man- to occur, become; Brah. manning to be, become.

2. minuku to shine, twinkle; Ka. minuku; Tu. minukuni, miṇkuni; Ta. minnu, minuṅku id.; Ma. minnuka; Pj. minnal spark.

3. mugiyu to end; Ka. Tu. mugi; Ta. muki; Kui mūga to be finished; mūpka to complete; Kur. munj- to finish off.

4. mēyu to graze; Ka. mēy, mē-; Tu. mēpuni; Ta. mēy; Ma. mēyka; Kuvi (F) mē-; mey-; Go. mēī-; Pj. mēy-; Nk. mīy-; cf. Kur. men- id.; Mlt. min- id.

5. morugu to bark; Ka. more to cry aloud; Tu. morè a cry; Ta. morumoru to grumble; Kui muska to bark; Kuvi mōkh- id.; Go. mohch- to bark; cf. Brah. marrām shout, call.

§1.36. Te. m- irregularly alternates with v- of Ma. and Go.[30]

1. malayu[1] to roam, wander; Klm. malay- id. : Ma. valayuka to wander about; Go. walī-t- id.

2. malayu[2] to be distressed; valiyu id.; Ta. malai to afflict; to distress : Ma. valayuka to be distressed; valekka to vex; valaccal, vallāyma distress.

The m-/v- variation is widespread in one set of forms: Te. maḍāgu, maṇāgu to bend, with stems in mā̆ḷ-, mā̆ṇ- on the one hand and vā̆ḷ- and vā̆ṇ- on the other, occurs in all SDr. languages (see §1.42).

§1.37. Corresponding to Te. m- (< *m-), Brah. has b- in a few forms:

1. Te. muriyu to crumble; Ka. Ta. Ma. muṟi id.; Kur. mur$^{u}$k- to cut; Mlt. murk- id. : Brah. bur- to crumble.

2. Te. meṭṭu a step; v. to step; Ka. meṭṭu id., v. and n. : Brah. biṭ a mound, hillock; cf. Te. meṭṭa, miṭṭa id.

3. Te. mēyu to graze (see §1.35 above) : Brah. bei grass fit for grazing; bei kanning (v. t.) to graze.

## v-[31]

§1.38. Te. v- < *v- before all front vowels and ā̆; similarly, *v- remains in Ta. Ma. Kui Kuvi Go. Klm. and Pj., but it develops to b- in Ka. Tu. Koḍagu Baḍaga Kur. Mlt. and Brah. In Ka., the beginning of this shift has been traced to the 9th century A.D.[32] We have no knowledge as to when it took place in the northern group.

1. vaccu to come; Ta. vā-, var-; Ma. varuka; Kui vāva; Kuvi wa-; Go. wai- : Ka. bar-, bā-; Tu. bā-; Koḍ. bā-; Kur. bar-; Mlt. bar-; Brah. ba-, bar, ban-.

2. viccu to blossom; viriyu id.; Ta. viri to expand; Ma. viriyuka; Kui vrīva to break out; Go. viṛsut- to enlarge; extend : Ka. biccu, bircu to expand; biri to burst; Tu. biriyuni; bicc- id.; Kur. bird- to pierce; Brah. birr- to separate out.

3. velūgu to shine; velayu id.; Ta. veḷ white, shining; Ma. veḷi light; Go.(W) weṛchī light; Kuvi (F) vella white; Klm. velang light, Naiki walang id. (Hislop, p. 22) : Ka. beḷagu to shine; Tu. beḷaguni id.; Kur. bilc- to shine; billī light; Mlt. bil-bilr- to shine.

§1.39. In Mdn. Te. an on-glide [w-] develops on all initial back vowels. This is also true of Ta. and Ma.; in Tu., PDr. *vi-, *vī-, *ve-, and *vē- change to bu-, bū-, bo-, and bō- respectively in most cases,[33] obviously through *vu-, *vū-, *vo- and *vō-. This development is more common when retroflex consonants accompany these vowels. Ka. also has a similar tendency which came into effect after *v- > b-; as va- > ba- > bo-; baggu to bend (< *vaggu) : boggu id. Comparable developments in Te. are rarely found, and nowhere in the verbs.

In SDr. va-/o- alternation is found to be a common occurrence and also vā-/ō- to a limited extent; this problem is treated elsewhere (see §§1.234, .242).

§1.40. In the following cases Te. and SDr. v- is paralleled by p- in Kui:

1. vaṅgu to bend (< *vaṇ-ku); Ka. Tu. baggu; Ta. vaṇaṅku, vaḷai; Ma. vaṇaṅṅuka, vaḷekka : Kui palga to bend, stoop.

2. vīgu to get swollen, to be proud; Ka. bīgu to become bulky, large; be proud; Ta. vīṅku to swell, increase in size; Ma. vīṅṅuka id. : Kui pīga to be heavy; pigu adj. heavy.

§1.41. Some of the Dravidian languages have a sporadic m- corresponding to Te. v-. v/m alternation is common in Telugu in the medial position but not so initially; initially v-/m- is very common in Ma. and to some extent in Ta. The following examples illustrate Te. v- : Ma. Ta. m-.

1. vānu to fashion (as pots); Ka. bān id.; Pj. vāñ- to make pots; Mlt. bānde the way of doing : Ta. vaṉai, maṉai to make, fashion; Ma. manayuka id.

2. vekku to sob, hiccough; Ka. Tu. bikku; Ta. vikku; Kur. bekkh- to be choked; Mlt. beq- : Ma. vikku, mikku id.

A sporadic alternation of Te. and SDr. v- : Kui Kur. Mlt. Go. m- occurs in the following few cases:

1. vaṇḍu to cook; Kui vaja to cook; Go. wanji rice : Kur. maṇḍī rice (cooked); Mlt. manḍi rice water; Kuvi (F) manji rice (raw).

2. vinu to hear; Ta. viṉ- to hear, question; Ma. vinayuka to ask; Kui venba hear, ask; Kuvi wen-; Klm. vin-; Brah. binning : Kur. men- to hear, ask; Mlt. men- id.; Mundarí men- to tell, say (Bhaduri).

3. vēcu to look for, expect; Kuvi bēc- to look, see : Kui mehpa look attentively; Kuvi meh'- to view.

4. vīcu to blow (wind, etc.), to fling; Ta. Ma. vīcu; Ka. Tu. bīsu; Kui vīka to blow with the mouth : Go. mihi-t- to throw down violently.

5. vēyu to throw, cast, also vaḻcu id. : Kui mespa to let fall, drop into.

§1.42. In one form v-/m- alternation is so widely represented in SDr. that it probably goes back to PSDr.:

1. maḍāgu, maṇāgu to bend, besides vaṅgu (< *vaḷ-aṅku); vālu to bend down, hang down; Ka. vālu, mālu id.; Tu. māluni, māḷuni id.; all forms derive from PDr. vă̄ḷ-/vă̄ṇ-, mă̄ḷ-/mă̄ṇ-.

## s-

§1.43. Comparative evidence does not warrant the postulation of an *s phoneme besides *c either for PDr. or for PSDr., since there are no Dravidian etyma where *c and *s contrast. There is only one phoneme here in PDr., and it is more likely to be an affricate (*c) originally than a sibilant (§1.90). The daughter languages provide an isogloss in their phonetic representation of the PDr. *c- : some show it as an affricate [č] and some as a sibilant [s]; in a few others there is free variation between [č] and [s] (§1.15). Te. primarily belongs to the c-group, but because of a large amount of borrowed vocabulary from Skt. and Pkt. and from the neighboring Kannada (which is an s-language), c- and s- have developed contrast in the initial position even in the OTe. period. There are however relatively few s-forms of Dravidian origin in OTe. which cannot be attributed to borrowing. In modern spoken Telugu s- occurs in the sub-standard dialect corresponding to c- of upper class speech, e.g., caduvu/saduvu to read, cilaka/śilaka a parrot.

§1.44. Among verbs, eliminating the unattested lexical items, for which etymologies are also not available, there are fifteen forms with an initial s-. Some seven of these occur in OTe. classics, of which six appear to be early loanwords from Kannada. Of the rest, four are assimilated loans from OIA or MIA, and four occur as free alternants of c-forms in literature.

§1.45. The following are considered to be the early loanwords from Kannada:

1. samayu to perish, be destroyed; Ka. same, save, samasu id.; Ta. camai, cavu.

2. sā̃ku to foster, rear; Ka. sāku; Tu. sāṅkuni, tāṅkuni; Ta. tāṅku; Ma. tāṅṅuka (t- < *c-, see §1.23).

3. suḍiyu to whirl, to turn round; Ka. suḻi; Tu. suḷipuni, tuḷipuni; Ta. cuḻi; Ma. cuḻiyuka.

4. sorā̃gu to droop, sink away; Ka. soragu; sōr-; Ta. cōr id.

5. sōlu to swoon, fail, stagger; Ka. sōlu be defeated, fail; fall off; Ta. Ma. tōl.

6. salupu to ache; salupu, saḷupu (colloq. Te.) a shooting pain; Ka. saḷe/seḷe to pull, draw; suffer spasms (as the muscles of limbs); Kui jelba to pull, draw (a/e alternation due to the preceding *c-, see §1.232).

§1.46. In one form Te. and Ka. nave different meanings: surugu to run, disappear, flee; Ka. surugu n. withered dry portion of a plantain leaf (no class. usages); this may better be compared with Ka. surku to contract, shrink; fade, but this latter form occurs in Te. as srukku id. with metathesis. Tu. surugu n. sinking, sliding is the nearest.

§1.47. The following three verbal bases are assimilated loanwords from IA.

1. saṇugu to mutter (Brown, not in Dh. M. or Śab. R.); also saṇa-saṇa-l-āḍu to mutter in dissatisfaction (colloq. Te.); because of ṇ, this form must be a post-classical introduction probably from M. saṇkā whizz; cf. Guj. saṇko whizz; B. sana id.; H. san (Pali sanati, saṇati, Pk. saṇa- m., saṇia) possibly from Skt. svanáh m. noise, etc., svánati sounds (see s. v. sankanu go mad, get very angry, Nep. Dict.).

2. sarudu/sardu (also sarusu, Śab. R.) to distribute equally; to economize (colloq.); sari equal, equality; well; Ka. sari put in a proper order; sari, saru equality; Tu. sari adj. equal, right; Ta. cari id.; Kui sarna adj., adv. straight, outstretched; Go. sarko straight (Hislop, p. 34); Kur. sarya- put in its proper place; Mlt. saryare to be cured; < Pkt. sari-, saria- equal; Pali sari-, sarisa- < Skt. sadṛśa- equal, comparable.

3. saĩcu to bear, tolerate (< *sayincu < *sah-incu; classical; sah-incu also occurs as a tatsama verb); saĩpu toleration; Ka. sahisu/sōsu to bear (§1.284, 1).

Obviously the above three verbs have an IA origin but are assimilated into the Telugu syllable pattern of simple bases through the addition of native derivative suffixes. Only Telugu has the -gu, -du suffix forms in items 1 and 2 above.

§1.48. There is one more form which is also a borrowing from MIA occurring without any additions since it neatly fits into the native al-ending bases; the medial consonant is deaspirated to suit the native phonemic system:

saḍalu to become loose, slack, etc. (classical; colloq. saḷḷu); Ka. saḍil, saḍal id.; Tu. saḍilu̥ (adj.) loose, slack, loosened; < Pkt. saḍhila-, Skt. śithilá-; (for ḍīlu with the loss of s- cf. A. ḍhilā, Beng. ḍhilā̃, M. ḍhilā (also saḍhal), Guj. ḍhīlum [see L. Gray, Indo-Iranian Phonology, p. 17; Nep. Dict., v. s. v. ḍhilo]).

Kittel gives this form in his dictionary under native items and it is also not included in the traditional Ka. list of IA loanwords (see Kittel's Kannada Gram., p. 437), but the evidence for taking this form as a loanword from IA is too obvious to dispute.

§1.49. The following forms have s- as a free variant of c- in literature:[34]

salupu/calupu to pass (time), to do, make, trans. of canu to go, proceed; sāgu/cāgu to go, to extend, prolong; solayu/colayu to swoon, faint (< *cōl-ay-), cf. sōlu id.; sõku/cõku to touch; to be contaminated, touched. All these forms have good etymologies and are traceable to PDr. *c-forms.

§1.50. There is one difficult case with s-, which is not explainable on any of the above grounds and which is also attested in early classics:

sogayu (past st. sogas-) to be intoxicated, swoon, faint; Kui sōsa to be intoxicated; Ta. toy to languish; cf. Te. sōlu to droop, Ka. jōl, etc.

One possible explanation is that it is a loanword from pre-Kui before vowel contraction took place in that language. Comparing Ta., Te., and Kui forms, *coy-a- can be reconstructed (§1.295). The contracted base *cō- underlies Te. sōlu, Ka. Ta. cōr to droop, etc.; Ta. toy- < *coy-. Therefore, the Te. form is from *coy-a with the common development of -g- < *-y- (see §1.79).

§1.51. s-forms for which reliable etymologies are not available:

1. saḍapu to steal, misappropriate; cf. Tu. saḍita a bet, wager.
2. sarugu to increase, grow (? < sari-).
3. selāgu, selayu to cut, chop; cf. Kui silpa to shave (of beard, etc.); Tu. selè a crack, chink.
4. selayu to swell, rise, riot; cf. Ta. cilai to sound, etc.

§1.52. The presence of certain forms in s-, even in OTe., without parallels in Ka. and the occurrence of native suffixes on a few s- loans only in Telugu may be taken as good evidence for positing an s- dialect in pre-Telugu (probably in an area contiguous to Kannada), from which the s-forms spread to the other dialects.

### h-

§1.53. There is no *h in PDr. It is possible, however, to set up an *h for pre-South-Dravidian which could have occurred as an intermediary stage between PDr. *c- and the SDr. zero-. Such a suggestion was made by Meile ("Sur la sifflante," p. 82) and Burrow (DS VI, p. 146). Following the development of *c- to h- in Kuvi and certain Gondi dialects (as well as Brah.), it is likely that PDr. *c- shifted to *s- and then to *h- in PSDr. before it was lost in the individual languages. Some IA languages as well as many other languages of the world have shown, during the historical period, a shift of s > h (> zero), e.g., Greek and Avestan.

§1.54. In Kannada PDr. *p- developed to h- probably through an intermediary *ph- (§1.217). Te. has two verbs with h- which are borrowed from Kannada.

1. hattu to hold fast, hold, adhere; Ka. hattu, pattu to stick, to join; Tu. hattuni, pattuni; Ta. parru; Ma. parruka. The regular Te. form is paṭṭu < PDr. *pattu.

2. heccu to increase; Ka. heccu, peccu, percu; Tu. heccuni, percuni id.; PDr. pĕr-.

The isogloss of h- < *p- also includes Badaga, an off-shoot of Ka. (Emeneau, "The Vowels of the Badaga Language," Lg., 15, p. 43). It is not certain whether Tulu and Koḍagu are also covered by the isogloss or the h-forms in these languages are merely loanwords from Ka. h- < p- began to disappear from the 13th century onwards and is completely lost in the uneducated dialects of Modern Kannada.

## Voiced Stops

§1.55. Caldwell's assumption[35] that there were no initial voiced plosives in PDr. as reflected in Ta. and Ma. was contradicted by Jules Bloch on the basis of the history of a few words like ghōṭaka horse and drāviḍa name of a people, which, according to him, were originally native to Dravidian.[36] This view received support from some quarters[37] and contradiction from others. Burrow argued for Caldwell and analytically put forth evidence to show that voicing of initial stops appearing in some of the Dravidian languages, was only secondary and did not represent PDr.[38] He contended that if PDr. had initial voiced plosives we should at least expect to find some common words and verbal roots shared by most of the Dravidian languages, if not all, commencing with voiced plosives (op. cit., p. 721).

§1.56. Among the Telugu verbal bases, there are a number of forms with initial g-, j-, ḍ-, d-, and b-, of which g-, j-, and d- can be traced to original k-, c-, and t-. d- also develops regularly from an older ḍ- (§§1.64, .129). In a few forms d- < *t- < *c- or < *j- < *c-. Initial ḍ- and b- do not regularly result from ṭ- and p-, though a few cases may be shown for p- > b- under certain conditions. ḍ- usually develops from radical ḻ or ṭ (also sometimes ḷ), occurring in non-initial position, through metathesis with, sometimes, vowel contraction. b- forms in Telugu are mostly loanwords from Kannada, where the shift of b- < *v- was in operation from classical times. In a few words b- develops out of an original m-, especially in clusters with r as the second member, as br- < *mr-. The following examples suffice to show these developments.

g-

§1.57. g- < k-:

1. gaṇṭu to wound; an opening (of wound); Ka. kaṇḍi, kaṇame a hole, opening; Te. gaṇḍi, kanuma id.; Tu. kaṇḍi, gaṇḍi a gap, opening; kaṇi a trench; Ma. kaṇṭi n. id.; Klm. gaṇḍ- to prick; Brah. kanḍ n. gap; PDr. *kaṇ-.

2. gillu to pinch, nip off; Ka. giṇḍu id.; Tu. kiṇkuni, kinkuni; Ta. Ma. kiḷḷu id.; all other languages have forms with k- as initial (see s.v. giccu, Part II).

§1.58. There is one form in which g- has developed out of an original v- as shown by Ta. and Ma.

gelucu to win, defeat; Ka. gel, geli, gelu, gellu; Klm. gell-; Kuvi (S) gelh-; Kuvi (F) gelp- to save; Tu. gelpuni, genduni id. : Ta. vel(lu) to conquer, subdue; v.i. to excel, prosper; Ma. velluka id. Ta. keli id. is probably a loanword from Kannada. g/v alternation is common in South Dravidian and more so in Telugu, when they are in the medial position. Initially g- < v- is an aberrant change in Telugu, though there are a few instances of this change in bound forms which occur always in the company of free forms in the preceding position: -gāru (< *vāru, honorific suffix) occurs after the names of persons; -guru < *-vuru the masc.-fem. plural suffix in numerals, for instance, Te. āṟuguru, āṟuvuru six people; iruvuru two people, Ka. ibbar < irbar < *ir-var.

§1.59. The palatalization of g- is much less common than that of k-, when followed by the front vowels.[39] We, therefore, have a number of unpalatalized g-forms before ĭ and ĕ: giccu to pinch; ginju to flutter the limbs; giṭṭu to accrue to; giṟuku, giṟupu to wink the eye suggestively; to scribble; gīyu, gīcu, gĭku, gīṟu to scratch, rub; geṇṭu to push out; genayu to prosper; gentu to hop; gelucu to win; for most of these forms k- could be attested as the original from comparative sources. It may quite probably be assumed here that voicing took place in these forms before the onset of palatalization in this language, which obviously left the forms unaffected.

j-

§1.60. j- < *c-.

1. jaḍiyu to shake, fear; jaḷupu, jaḍupu fear, dread; daḍa palpitation, throbbing; Ka. jaḍi, jaḍe to threaten; daḍa quivering; Tu. jaḍu fright : Ka. caḷi to succumb; jaḷḷuga a weak man; Ma. caḷuṅṅuka to be frightened; Tu. caḷḷu imbecile, weak.

2. jaṅku to fear, shiver, hesitate, < *caṇ-ku, of which *caṇ- is

the alternant of *caḷ- underlying the above series and many others (see §1.161); Ka. jaṅkisu to scold.

3. jarugu to slide, elapse as time; Ka. jarugu; jari to slip; Tu. jariyuni id. : Ta. cari to slip away; carukku id.; cār- id.; Ma. carikka to move, walk; cariyuka to slide; Ka. sari move, go, slide; ? Klm. (SR) sarkīl- to get away.

Similarly jimmu/cimmu, jilugu, and jīru are traceable to forms with c- initials.

d-

§1.61. d- < *t-.

diddu to set right, rectify; Ka. tiddu, tirdu; Tu. tidduni; Ta. Ma. tiruttu id.; from tir- to change, turn, etc.

§1.62. d- < *t- < *c-.

1. dā̃ṭu to cross, leap; Ka. dāṇṭu, dāṭu id.; tāṇṭu to jump; Klm. dāṭ-; Ta. Ma. tāṇṭu to jump : Ma. cāṭuka to leap; cāṭṭam a leap; PDr. *cāṇṭ-.

2. dēvu to lade out, bale out; Tu. tēpuni to irrigate; Ma. tēkuka, tēvuka to bale out : Te. cē̃du to bale out, Ka. sēdu id.

§1.63. d- < *j- < *c-.

daḍiyu to be afraid; also jaḍiyu id.; daḍa throbbing of heart (see s.v. jaḍiyu, §1.31); < *caḷ-.

§1.64. d- < *ḍ- < *-ṭ- or *-ḻ-.

There is a large class of forms where an initial d- has regularly developed out of an older ḍ-, which itself is the result of metathesis from an original *-ṭ-/-ḍ- or *-ḻ-. (For a detailed account of this change see §§1.124 ff.).

1. daggu to cough (< ḍaggu).

2. dayyu to be tired (< ḍayyu).

3. dā̃gu to be hidden (< ḍā̃gu); Kui ḍāpa lie in wait; Klm. ḍāp- to hide.

4. dāyu to near (< ḍāyu); dāpu nearness.

5. digu to descend (< ḍigu < *iḻg-); Ta. Ma. Ka. iḻi; Tu. iḷi; GoM. ḍig-; ḍīkt- fell (Nandgaon Go. dial., LSI IV, p. 522); Kui dīva to descend; Kur. elkhr-, Mlt. elq- to descend.

6. dūyu to draw out a sword; strip off leaves, etc. (< *ḍūyu/*ḍuy-yu); cf. Te. duvvu to comb; Kui ḍupka to scrape together; sweep up; ṛūsa to scrape; Kuvi rūch- to comb.

7. dollu to roll down (< ḍollu); cf. Ta. uḻal to roll down.

The shift of ḍ- > d- seems as old as Telugu literature, but d- forms preponderate as time goes on. In Modern Telugu d- has almost invariably replaced ḍ- and survivals are few. In this connection it is interesting to note that Maṛia Gondi and Klm., etc. preserve the archaic forms of Telugu with initial ḍ-, which these languages might have borrowed from the neighboring Te. before d- < ḍ- commenced in it, i.e., sometime before the 8th or 9th century A.D.

b-

§1.65. b- < *v-.

Initial b- forms in Telugu are to be ranked amongst the earliest borrowings from Kannada, where b- < PDr. *v- appears as early as the 7th century A.D.[40] E.g.:

1. baḍalu to be tired; Ka. ba<u>l</u>al; Tu. baḷalike tiresomeness; Ta. va<u>l</u>alikkai weariness; Kui vaha; Kuvi wah- to be tired (h- < *s- < *<u>l</u>-).

2. bigiyu to be tightened; Ka. bigi; Tu. bigiyuni; Ta. vici to bind (< *viki), viku to be tight; Ma. viṅṅuka id.

3. bedaru to be alarmed; Ka. beda<u>r</u>-, beda<u>r</u>u; Tu. beduru fear; Ta. vita<u>r</u>u to tremble; Ma. vita<u>r</u>uka.

§1.66. There are, however, a few forms for which parallels in Kannada are not discoverable. Therefore, the sources for these are not clear unless we say that the b- < *v- isogloss included some part of the Telugu area besides that of Ka. Tu. and Badaga.

1. balayu to surround; Tu. balepuni to enclose; Ta. vala id.; a loanword from Tu.

2. beḍiyu to break; to be spoiled (a work due to obstacles); Ta. veṭi to crack, explode; Ma. veṭiyuka to open; to explode.

The sources of b- in the following forms are also obscure: bijugu to lie; buliyu to be in great glee; beṇaku to be sprained; beḷaku, besuku to shake, move.

§1.67. Sometimes there seem to be a few independent formations in Telugu with b- < v- (through contamination with the Kannada forms) without direct borrowing:

1. bādu to flog, beat; cf. Ka. bay to put; Ta. vai id.; Mlt. baje to strike.

2. beṇãku to move, n. motion; Ka. beḷpaḷe trembling; Ta. viṇviṇai to throb as the eye (Tolk.); < *veṇ-/*veḷ-.

3. beḷũku to shine; cf. Te. velũgu id. from PDr. *veḷ-; Ka. beḷ-.

§1.68. b- < *p-.

1. baraṭu to scratch, scrape; Ka. paraḍu; Ta. paṟǎṇṭu; Kui paṛja to be burred over.

2. boṅku to lie (< *poyṅk-); Ka. pusi; Ta. Ma. poy- id.; GoM. bus-.

3. bollu to lie, etc.; Ka. poḷḷu hollowness; Ta. poḷḷal fault; poḷḷaṉ a liar.

§1.69. b- < *m-. These forms are relatively few:

1. bokku to gobble up; Ka. mukku; Tu. mukkuni; Ta. mukku; Kui muka; mukal mouthful; Kur. mŏkh-, Mlt. mŏq- to eat.

2. bruṅgu to sink, be hidden; Ka. muḻuṅgu to sink; Tu. murkuni; Ta. Ma. muḻuku; Kui bṛuḍga sink completely; Kuvi mrūkh-; Go. murung-.

3. bruyyu to perish; bruncu to kill; Tu. murk- to be ruined; Ta. muruṅku to be ruined; Kui mrūva to die; brunga to be plucked out.

Conclusion:

§1.70. A few general remarks on the causes of voicing of initial stops in Telugu will not be out of place here. Though a precise formulation is not possible, it can be found that certain environments are in some way responsible for the production of voicing in the initial plosives as against others; for instance, we notice this:

1. When the root-syllable possesses a liquid, nasal, or trill (or flap), as in gillu, ganṭu, jaṅku, guṟucu, jarugu, etc. There are relatively fewer cases with voicing when the base has finally a plosive or fricative, e.g., kappu, tappu, cekku, paṭṭu; kōyu, cēyu, etc.

2. When Telugu forms consonant clusters with r initially through metathesis, gruccu, groccu, gruddu, groyyu, drobbu, etc. When the suffix syllable has a voiced plosive geminate, initial voicing is almost regular; when it is a voiceless stop geminate, it is optional in many cases: cf. gruddu, drobbu, as against kruccu/gruccu; kroccu/groccu; kruṅku sun to set, Mdn. Te. guṅku (< gruṅku).

3. When the radical final liquid is assimilated to the suffix-sonant, the initial consonant is also brought under the influence of the suffix in the matter of voicing: diddu to rectify (< *tirdu).

4. When the base-final y, r, l, or ḻ is lost before a nasal-plosive suffix: boṅku to lie < *poyṅk-; gõku to scratch (< *kŏrṅk-). The effect is similar even when the base has a final nasal followed by a plosive suffix not preceded by a nasal: ganṭu < *kaṇ-ṭu, jaṅku < *caṇ-ku, danḍu < *taṇ-tu, etc.

§1.71. All the above environments put together do not still sufficiently cover the whole of the data over which this phenomenon operates. While the general principle seems to be the extension to the initial voiceless stop of voicing occurring in the succeeding syllables, there are also innumerable cases where initial voicing is not produced under the same circumstances. However, voicing is more widespread in constructions which are capable of being analysed (in PDr.) into a base plus a derivative suffix than in unsuffixed stems as kappu, tappu, tannu, etc. Again the relative susceptibility of the various voiceless stops to the assimilative influence of the succeeding sonorants is also to be taken into account. Thus, k- is more easily influenced to alternate with g-, than c- with j- and t- with d-; p- > b- is extremely rare, while ṭ- > ḍ- never occurs on account of the lack of forms with ṭ- in Dravidian.

§1.72. The distribution of the initial voicing is also a matter on which it is hardly possible to systematize. It is often found that for some voiced forms, there are doublets with voiceless stop initials: giṭṭu$^2$/kiṭṭu$^2$; gatuku/katuku; guppu/kuppu; gur̲ucu/kūrcu; daṇḍu/taṇḍu; jimmu/cimmu; gruccu/kruccu; groccu/kroccu; sometimes either Ka. or Te. shows the voiced variety, while the other has the unvoiced one or lacks it altogether: Te. gīṭu, gīcu, gīyu : Ka. gīcu, kīsu; gīr̲u, kīr̲u; Te. gir̲uku scribble : Ka. kir̲uku; Te. diddu : Ka. tirdu, tiddu; Te. gaṇṭu to wound : Ka. Tu. kaṇḍi an opening; Tu. gaṇḍi id.

§1.73. Lack of etymologies for a number of forms with voiced initial plosives is another striking feature. There are as many as twenty verbs from Telugu itself for which there are no parallels in the cognate languages: giṭṭu, gilubu, gunuku, geṇṭu, gadumu, genayu, gremmu, jeḷuku, jīru, jō̃ku, danıyu, danuku, dō̃cu, dōru, baḍiyu, bijugu, buliyu, etc. are without etymologies. Even when unequivocal etymologies are available, it is the voiceless plosive that is more widely distributed than the voiced one (see, especially, giccu, gī̃cu, gillu, guppu, jaḍiyu, jarugu, dā̃ṭu, diddu, doralu, etc.); not even a single proto-stem could be discovered from the mass of Dravidian vocabulary with a widespread distribution of initial voicing to merit the assumption of a PDr. voiced initial even to a small extent. All these circumstances uphold the views of Caldwell, Subbayya,[41] and Burrow that PDr. had only surds in the initial position; voicing in some of the descendants in this position is only secondary.

## CONSONANTS: MEDIAL

### Intervocalic Stops

§1.74. Caldwell assumed that the "law of convertibility of surds and sonants," as operating to the fullest extent in Ta. represented "the Dravidian phonetic system."[42] This meant that, originally, there were only sonants in the medial (intervocalic and post-nasal) position, and surds always in the initial position and in gemination. As far as the initial position is concerned this problem has been dealt with in earlier sections. Jules Bloch on the basis of the supposed history of three Sanskrit words, ghōṭaka- horse, gǎrdabha- ass, and drāviḍa n. pr. of a people, and a passage from Kumārila Bhaṭṭa's Tantravārtika, arrived at the following conclusions: (1) that voiced plosives (and even aspirated stops) existed in Common Dravidian in a remote past; (2) that, in Tamil, loss of sonority occurred sometime between the beginning of the Christian era and the time of Kumārila (c. 700 A.D.); (3) and that again, about the time of Na<u>nn</u>ūl, i.e., 1200 A.D., intervocalic surds became sonants.[43] He also brought in the striking similarity between Indo-Aryan and Dravidian in the weakening of intervocalic consonants. Therefore, he thinks, by implication, that Te. and Ka. preserve the PDr. system of initial and medial stops as against OTa.

P. S. Subrahmanya Sastri, contesting Caldwell's theory of the sonantization of medial stops in Ancient Tamil, states that these are very recent developments in Tamil and do not belong to the literary dialect. He brings in Te. iṅku to dry up, vaṅki a hook, kǡka heat, and ance stair, and Ka. vaṅki, kāke, and añce to show that the presence of voiceless plosives in these languages even after nasals is a proof that voicing is not an ancient characteristic attributable to the parent speech.[44] Alfred Master, on the other hand, agrees with Bloch and even goes further to say that "there is no ground for supposing that there was any period in which Tamil lacked voiced plosives."[45] His main evidence is the spirantization of PDr. *-p- and *-c- to -v- and -y- even in Ancient Tamil, which is a clear indication of its weakened articulation of the medial stops (op. cit., p. 1006).

§1.75. Chatterji in a recent article in Indian Linguistics (Vol. 14, 1954, pp. 1-19), entitled "Old and Ancient Tamil and Primitive Dravidian," partly upholds the view of Jules Bloch, and makes the following assumptions: In Primitive Dravidian both unvoiced and voiced stops were phonemic. It was so even in Ancient Tamil of the pre-Sangam or pre-Tolkāppiyam period. The unvoicing of initial stops in Tamil started "in the early centuries of the Christian era or even still earlier but it must have become established in Ta. by 600 A.D." In the non-initial (i.e., intervocalic and post-nasal) position voicing started as late as 1350 A.D., the period when Old Tamil ends and Middle Tamil begins (pp. 12-15).

The approaches of both Bloch and Chatterji suffer from the shortcomings of ignoring the internal evidence of Dravidian (i.e., comparative vocabulary, etc.) as a means of reconstruction, and of relying too much on the still doubtful evidence of loanwords and a string of ethno-paleographic theories. Still no etymology can be found in Dravidian for the alleged native Damila or Dramiḍa (Chatterji conveniently attributes it to the Cretans of the Mediterranean). Again the arguments of Burrow and Master have not been disproved with Dravidian evidence; especially the evidence of Alfred Master about the shift of *-p-, *-c- to -v-, -y- (< *-s-) is conclusive. He has also shown proof for the occurrence of *-t- as -d- in Ancient Tamil (op. cit., p. 1007). To this should be added the evidence of a weakened articulation of intervocalic -k- in all South Dravidian languages, which is often dropped with the contraction of vowels flanking it on either side. In this respect, -k- behaves in the same way that fricative -y-, -v- behave, e.g., Ta. mikai, mikal greatness, abundance : mē-, mēl id. (< *meka-, *mek-al); Ta. Ma. tuk-al skin, Ka. tog-alu; Tu. tug-alu̥; Ta. Ma. Ka. Te. Klm. Pj. Nk. Oll. Go. Kuvi tō-l skin (see §§1.277, .295). Again, the weakening of PDr. alveolar stop *-ṯ- to a trill -ṟ- in all SDr. languages is an additional proof of this. The foregoing evidence shows clearly that some intervocalic stops were voiced and some spirantized, certainly in PSDr. if not in PDr. Tamil is no exception to this.

However, there is reason to set up a period for PDr. when the stops still remained voiceless in the intervocalic position; especially note the alternation of *-c-/*-t- in SDr. (§§1.88-.90), and the palatalization of k before front vowels in Tamil, which must have taken place before these stops became voiced; e.g., Ta. potukku to wrap, conceal : Kui poja; Kur. pojj- to wrap, etc.;[46] Ta. viku, vici to bind (< *viki) : Ka. bigiyu id.

§1.76. While dealing with the problem of intervocalic plosives in Dravidian, we have to make a distinction between the plosives contained in the root-syllables and those in the suffixes. In the succeeding chapter, it will be shown that, in trisyllabic forms, the consonant of the second syllable invariably belongs to the root, while the following vowel is a part of the suffix. In disyllabic forms with final -ku, -ṅku, -kku, etc. the radical element exists in the first syllable itself (see §§1.160 ff.). The radical plosive occurring in the intervocalic position is always voiced in the trisyllabic bases. This is also true of Kannada. It is only the suffix-consonants that lack uniformity in the matter of voicing in Telugu and Kannada.

As far as Old and Middle Tamil and Old Malayalam are concerned, one could set up only one set of stop phonemes, viz., /k c ṭ ṯ t p/ with allophones as follows: root initially always voiceless stops [k c t p] (/ṭ t̲/ do not occur in this position). Intervocalically, when single, [g ḍ d] voiced or even probably spirantized. In this position /c p/ have spirantized allophones [s v]. In gemination, there occur always voiceless [k c t t̲ p]; but after nasals, voiced [g j ḍ d̲ d b]. Probably in Old Tamil the last of these could be voiceless, following the system of Telugu and Kannada in this respect.

As a rule voiceless consonants do not occur in literary Telugu as part of radical syllables between vowels except as simplification of geminates or secondarily through assimilative influence of the following voiceless plosives; the second part of the statement applies only to verbs with -d-. For instance, Ancient Telugu aduku, kaduku, uduku, koduku, ciduku, piduku have developed doublets in the post-classical period with -t- for -d- under the influence of the following -ku, which proceeds from *-kku; Modern Telugu uses forms with -t-. This development does not take place when the following suffix-consonant is not a voiceless stop, e.g., Te. adumu to press down (there is no corresponding *atumu). Among forms with -g-, -j-, -ḍ-, and -b- there is no such alternation even under the same circumstances, e.g., puḍuku to grasp; ubuku to swell over; there are, of course, a few forms with -k- and -ṭ- of a different type; they are either onomatopoetic, or dialectal, or only lexical forms of late origin; e.g., pekalu to come out, a Modern Telugu variant of pegalu in certain dialect areas; cikilu to weep winking the eyes (as children) occurs in a 16th century work of little literary standing; ciṭulu, peṭulu to make a cracking sound, to crack, explode are onomatopoetic words. Barring these forms, which are by no means exceptions, only voiced stops occur intervocalically in trisyllabic forms, when they form part of the radical syllable. (Since the suffix consonant does not occur in this position, -g-, -j-, -ḍ-, -d-, and -b- of the second syllable always belong to the root). This statement also holds good in the case of Kannada. Here, we have to exclude later formations and borrowings, both in Telugu and Kannada. Early loanwords conform to the usual rule of no weakening of surds between vowels.

§1.77. In the matter of suffixes, there is no uniformity between Te. and Ka. in voicing: e.g., Te. iṅku to evaporate; Ka. iṅgu id.; Te. naḍũku to tremble, Ka. naḍugu; Te. cinuku to rain, Ka. jinugu; sometimes Ka. has both the varieties: Te. toḍãgu to commence, Ka. toḍaku, toḍaṅku, toḍagu; Te. muḍugu to shrink in, Ka. muḍuku, muḍugu; Te. podugu to hide, encase; Ka. poduṅku, pudugu id.; Te. tur̲ugu to stuff in, Ka. tur̲uku, tur̲ugu id.; etc. In view of this, P. S. S. Sastri's examples from Te. and

Ka. do not show anything to prove the preservation of Proto-Dravidian voiceless plosives in medial position, since all such plosives are suffix-consonants.

§1.78. The occurrence of voicing in the intervocalic root-consonant, which is thoroughly regular in Te. and Ka., along with the spirantization of -c- and -p- to -y- and -v- in Ancient Tamil almost proves that the weakened articulation of these consonants was already present in Proto-South-Dravidian, though it was not universal at the time of the separation of the descendants. The village and personal names recorded in the early Telugu and Kannada inscriptions also attest this view.[47] The voicing of suffix-plosives has become regularized in Middle and Modern Tamil and Malayalam. Ancient and Modern Malayalam suffixes -ṅṅ- and -ññ- can more reasonably be derived from -ṅg- and -ñj- than from -ṅk- and -ñc-; this indicates that in Middle Tamil itself voicing of suffix-stops was already complete. We, therefore, approve of Caldwell's statement in a modified form that voicing of the radical voiceless stops in intervocalic position was ancient in all the literary South Dravidian languages and also probably represents a Proto-Dravidian dialect condition, while voicing of the suffix-stops is attributable to a period after the separation of the various cognate languages and hence independent in each of them. Tamil and Malayalam have levelled this development by voicing all stops that occur in the non-initial position except in gemination.

## -g-

§1.79. Te. -g- < PDr. *-y-; sometimes -y- itself is a weakening of an older *-c-; this development is also shared by Ta. Ma. Ka. and Tulu.[48] Though its occurrence in Central and North Dravidian is not borne out by clear evidence, a few stray cases can be shown:

1. egudu to obtain (Paṇḍ.) : Te. eydu id., also eyidu; Ka. aydu; Ta. Ma. eytu.

2. tagulu to be joined; to join, touch; to strike; Ka. tagu! id.; tagu to be joined, to fit; Ta. takai to seize : Ta. tai (i.e., tay-) to join, tie, put on; tai-vā to touch (Tolk.); Ma. taikka to hit.

3. pagulu v. i. to break; Ta. paku be split, to separate; Ma. pakayuka to divide; pakuka to be separated: Te. pāyu v. i. to separate; Go. pai(y)- to be split; Kui paṅga to be split, papka (< pak-p-) to split; Klm. Nk. payk-, Pj. payp-, payt-; cf. Ka. pasu to divide, distribute; paccu (pp.); Ta. paṅku portion (< *pay-ṅk-); Te. Ka. pañcu to distribute.

4. bigiyu to be tightened; Ka. bigi to bind; Tu. bigiyuni id.: Ta. vici

to bind tightly (< *viki); to be swollen, to be stiff : Ma. viṅṅuka (< *viyṅgu-) to be tight; cf. Ta. vīṅku to be stiff, tight; Ka. bisu to be stiff; Kui bija to be enormously swollen; Kur. bithra-, Mlt. bithg- to expand; PDr. *viy- < *vic-.

5. mugiyu to end; Ka. mugi; Tu. mugiyuni; Ta. muki; from the common Dravidian muy- < muc- : Kui mūga to be completed; Kuvi muth- (< *muc-) id.; Kur. muñj- to finish off; SDr. muy-, mūy- to close (s. v. mūyu, Part II).

6. vagacu to consider, contemplate; Ta. vakai to consider; Ka. bage, Tu. bageyuni to think, consider : Ta. vai to consider (Kṟḷ.), to meditate (Cilap.); vaittu-koḷ to suppose.

Similarly in pogayu to be smoked; migulu to remain; mogucu to contract, close; nogulu to pain, ache; etc., -g- proceeds from an older *-y-; that -y- passed through the stage of -k- is evident from Ta. vici (< *viki) corresponding to Te. Ka. bigi < *viki < *viyi; another striking proof of this can be found in the following etymology: Te. vākili doorway; Tu. bākil; Ka. bāgil; Ta. vāyil, vācal; Ma. vātil (Ma. -t- < *-c-). The past-stem forms of the verb agu 'to become' have a -y- in the place of -g- as ay-i-, ay-ina-, etc. which indicate the original base to be *ay- or *āy- (see Ta. Ka. ā- id. with the loss of y, before inflexional suffixes).

§1.80. Te. -g- < PSDr. *-v-; sometimes the -v- itself is a weakening of an older -m-:

1. iguru, ivuru, iṅku to evaporate; Ka. igaru, imaru, imiru, imuru id.; Ka. Tu. iṅgu to dry up. The PDr. base is *im- with suffixes -ku, -uru, etc.; intervocalically, -m- > -v- > -g-.

2. tegaḍu to rebuke, slight; Ka. tegaḻ id.; Tu. teguni to rebuke; tegelè reviling : Ta. tevvu enmity, hostility.

3. tigiyu to pull, draw : Te. tiviyu, tivvu id.; Ka. tivi to take off, remove; Klm. tivv- to pull.

4. niguḍu to spread, to rise, be extended; Ka. nigur, niguḷ; also nīḷ id.; nimir id.; Tu. nigacuni to stretch : Ta. nivar, niva to rise high; nimir to be outstretched; Ma. nikakka, nikaḷuka to rise; niviruka, nivirka, nīrka to rise, etc.; the m/g alternation can be explained through an original *-v-.

§1.81. The alternation of -v-/-g- is not on the same level as that of -y-/-g-, since -v- and -g- are in free variation in many forms in the literary period. In the whole list of forms with an intervocalic -g-, the following forms occur with v/g alternation in literature: pogayu, povayu to smoke; egucu, evucu to chase; tagulu, tavulu to hit; migulu, mivulu to remain; negulu, nevulu to grieve; tigiyu, tiviyu; iguru, ivuru; tegaḍu, tevaḍu; negaḍu, nevaḍu. No such free variation occurs in the following forms: vagacu to consider; egayu to rise, fly; bigiyu to be tightened; mugiyu to end; mogiyu to undertake; pegalu to come out. It is, obviously, not the environment that causes this variation, since in either series there are both front and back vowels, following as well as preceding the phoneme in question; or does this indicate different sources historically, viz., wherever there is free variation between -v- and -g-, -v- is original, while in cases where there is no such variation -g- < *-y-? This does not turn out to be true in all the forms, though it seems to hold good in some; for instance, in egucu, tagulu, migulu, negulu, and pogayu, where there is -g-/-v- alternation, the -g- is traceable to an earlier -y-. One could still hold the above assumption, if analogy is evoked to explain the irregularities and overlapping.

-ḍ-

§1.82. Te. -ḍ- < PDr. *-ṭ-, corresponding to Ka. Tu. -ḍ-; Ta. Ma. -ṭ-; Pj. Klm. -ḍ-; Nk. -ṛ-; Kui -ṭ-/-ṛ-, sometimes -r-; Kuvi -r-; Go. -ṛ-, -r-, or -rr-; Kur. Mlt. -ṭ-/-ṛ-, sometimes -s-:

1. aḍãgu to be suppressed, concealed; to diminish; Ka. aḍagu, aḍaṅgu; aḍe to shut up; Tu. aḍeṅguni, aḍepuni id.; Ta. aṭai to conceal; aṭaṅku to yield; Ma. aṭaṅṅuka; Kui āṭpa/āṛpa to conceal; Kur. aṛk- to knead; Mlt. aṛk- to thrust or wedge in.

2. iḍiyu to break, crumble; Ka. iḍi; Tu. iḍè a chasm; Ta. iṭi to break; to pound; Ma. iṭika id.; n. stroke; cf. Kui reṅga to be broken; Kur. eṭ- to tear to pieces; Mlt. eṭ- to destroy; eṭro broken; cf. Kur. es- id.

3. iḍu to put, place; Ka. iḍu; Tu. iḍpini; Ta. Ma. iṭu; Pj. iḍ-, itṭ-; Klm. iḍ-; Nk. iṛ-; Go. irr- id.; Kui iṭa.

4. kaḍacu to pass (time); to cross; Ka. kaḍe id.; Tu. kaḍapuni to cross; Ta. kaṭa; Ma. kaṭakka; Kui gṛāpa (gṛā-t-) (< *kaṭ-a-) to cross over; gṛāsa to step over; Kuvi grānc- to cross over; Kur. katṭ-; Mlt. kaṭ-; Brah. <u>kh</u>arr- to proceed.

5. pāḍu to sing; Ka. pāḍu; Ta. Ma. pāṭu; Go. wāṛ-; GoM. pār-; Kur. Mlt. pāṛ-; Pj. pāḍ-.

6. puḍuku to grasp, snap; Ka. puḍuku, -ṅku; Tu. puḍu grasping; Ta. puṭai a snap (as a carpenter's string); Kui pṛunga to be snapped; plucked; Kuvi·brūch- to snatch; Klm.(E) puḍk-, Klm.(SR) purk- to touch; Nk. puṛk- id.

Similarly in āḍu to play; uḍugu to be shrunk; kuḍucu to eat, drink;

kūḍu to gather; cūḍu to burn, v.t.; ceḍu to be spoiled; toḍayu to smear; toḍaru, toḍāgu to attempt, commence; tuḍucu to wipe; naḍacu to walk; nāḍu to pierce; nuḍuvu to speak; paḍu to fall; vāḍu to wither, etc., Te. -ḍ- < *-ṭ- of PDr.

§1.83. In a considerable number of cases, we notice an alternation of -ṭ- and -ḷ- in South Dravidian, of which -ḷ- may be considered the original, since similar variation does not occur in forms where ḍ can be traced to an original ṭ. Again, it should be remembered that only in the medial position do we have -ḷ- > -ḍ-, while the unsuffixed bases show final -ḷ or -ḷḷ(u). There is also -ḍ-/-ṇ- alternation in certain forms, indicating an original -ḷ-/-ṇ-:

Te. -ḍ- < *-ḷ-:

1. aḍugu to ask; Pj. aḍ- id. : Ta. aḷavu to enquire after one's health; aḷi to speak, express.

2. taḍayu to delay (< *stop, tarry); Ka. taḍe id.; Tu. taḍeyuni to halt, stop; taḍavu delay; Ta. taṭu to detain, taṭai to hinder, stop; Ma. taṭayuka to be obstructed : Ka. taḷvu, taḷuvu delay; to delay; taḷu to hinder; Tu. talepuni id.; Ta. taḷ to stop, hinder; taḷai id.; taṭṭu, v.t. to stop (< *taḷtu); cf. Te. talāgu to be interrupted; to remove; Kur. taṇḍ- to hinder, prevent; PDr. *taḷ-/taṇ-.

3. taḍiyu to become wet, soaked; taḍi moisture; Ka. taḍi, n. id. : Ka. taṇ- coolness, cold; Tu. sani-yuni, -puni to grow cool; Ta. taṇ- coolness; taḷi coolness; Ma. taṇiyu grow cool; taṇ- cold; the root that can be abstracted from this group as *taḷ-/*taṇ- can further be resolved into *caḷ-/*caṇ- (see §1.23, 1).

4. miḍiyu to frisk, jump; be proud; miṭṭu id.; Ka. miḍuku arrogance; miḍi to hop; mīṭu jumping; Ta. miṭukku pride; Ma. miṭi a tap, fillip; miṭṭuka to fillip : Te. mīṭu to fling; Ka. mīṇṭu to jump; Tu. mīṇṭuni/mīṭuni to raise with a lever; Ta. Ka. miḷir to jump; Ma. miṭantuka to jerk with a lever; cf. Kui mīnja to pounce upon. The PDr. base is *mīḷ-/*mīṇ-; or ultimately *mi-/*mī- is the base with -ḷ/-ṇ as suffixes; other forms derived from this base, migulu, mincu, for which see Part II.

So also poḍucu to pierce, bore; vaḍāku/vaṇāku to shake.

We notice within Telugu itself -ḍ- (< *-ḷ-) alternating with -ṇ-; the -ḍ-/-ṇ- alternation takes place in Telugu where -ḍ- is followed by a nasal as part of the suffix: aḍāgu/aṇāgu to be suppressed; vaḍāku/vaṇāku to tremble; kaḍāgu/kaṇāgu to undertake, begin; toḍāgu/toṇāgu to commence; maḍāgu/maṇāgu to be bent; in all these forms it is to be assumed that an original stem-final -ḷ or -ṇ has become ḍ in the intervocalic position.

§1.84. Te. -ḍ- < PDr. *-l̲-;[49] Ta. Ma. -l̲-; OKa. -l̲-; Middle and Modern Ka. -ḷ-, -ṇ-; in closed syllables -r-; Tu. -r- or -ḷ-; Kui -ṛ- mostly, but -r- in some consonant groups; in a few cases ḍ-/d- (initially through metathesis); Go. -ṛ-, sometimes -r-/-rr-; in a few cases -s-; Klm. Nk. -r-; Pj. -ṛ-; KGad. -ḍ-; Kur. Mlt. -c-/-s-, in a few cases -r- or -l-; Brah. -r-.

1. goḍāgu, goṇāgu to grumble, mutter; Ka. goṇagu id.; Ta. kul̲aku to wheedle.

2. aḍalu to be distressed; Ka. al̲al to grieve; Tu. arluni to burn; Ta. al̲al to burn; Ma. al̲aluka id.

3. kaḍugu to wash; Ka. karcu id.; Ta. kal̲uvu id.; Ma. kal̲ukuka; Kui kahpa to wash (< *kaspa); Kur. khajj- cleanse the head with clay; Mlt. kay- wash (clothes).

4. kōḍu to sift (rice from husks); Ka. koccu (< *korcu); Ta. kol̲i; Ma. kol̲iyuka; Kui kṛohpa; Kuvi(S) kloh-, Kuvi(F) korss-; Go. kōss-.

5. pūḍu to be filled up (as a pit); Ka. pūl̲, hūl̲, hūṇ; Ma. pūl̲uka; Ta. pul̲ai a hole; pūl̲i dust; Kur. putt- to set (of sun).

The remaining forms under this category: vāḍu to make use of; oḍuku to spin; īḍu to milk; ūḍu to leave, fall off; ōḍu to ooze; piḍucu to squeeze; suḍiyu to revolve; baḍalu to be tired.

§1.85. In South Dravidian, in a few cases, alternative forms occur in -r̲- (< *-t̲-) for those with -ḍ- (< *-ṭ-). This probably reflects the PDr. alternation between t̲ (alveolar) and ṭ (retroflex), of which the former had a subphonemic variant (i.e., allophone) r̲ in the intervocalic position; in other positions contrast was lost between *t̲ and *ṭ in many of the Dravidian languages including Telugu (§§1.163b, .195). This situation is evident not only in the etymologies of many forms but also in certain morphological contexts of certain forms in the individual languages; for instance, Old Telugu transitives of āḍu to play, ōḍu to be defeated, kūḍu to gather, ceḍu to rot, and paḍu to fall, suffer, are ār-cu, ōr-cu, kūr-cu, cer̲-u-cu, and par̲-u-cu respectively. This indicates that -ḍ- in these forms is originally from *-t̲- instead of *-ṭ-; the -r̲-/-r- allophone preserved in the transitives is a clear testimony to this. So also in the following forms PDr. *-t̲- fell together with -ṭ-, presumably before *-t̲- > -r̲-:

1. vaḍalu, vāḍu to wither, dry up; Ka. vaḍi, oḍi heat; Ma. vaṭiyuka to dry up; Ta. Ma. vāṭu; Ka. Tu. bāḍu id. : Ta. var̲ai, Ta. Ma. var̲u to dry; Ka. bar̲e, Kui vasa to dry (s < *r̲); GoM. vārt- to wither; Kur. bār- to fry in oil; Brah. bārr- to wither; PDr. root *vāt̲- alternating with *vāṭ-.

2. iḍiyu to break, crumble; Ta. iṟu to break, crack; Kui iska to collide; Kur. isig- to crack; es- to break by force; eṭ- to destroy.

The foregoing examples show that the PDr. phoneme has fallen together with ṛ or r in most of the Central and North Dravidian languages, and with ṭ or ḍ in South Dravidian. In most cases *ṯ has remained still a separate phoneme [ṟ] in all the South Dravidian languages (Old Ta. Ma. Te. Ka., and Toda). Tamil and Malayalam preserve the alveolar phoneme *ṯ in geminates as distinct from the geminate ṭṭ (retroflex). This problem will be dealt with in detail under the history of the ṟ phoneme.

§1.86. Telugu and South Dravidian have lost a radical nasal in the following forms: toḍāgu to commence : Kui ṭōṇḍa to begin; Te. kūḍu v.i. to gather : Kur. k͟hōṇḍ- id.

-d-

§1.87. Te. -d- < *-t-, corresponding to -t- or -d- of the other languages:

1. cadiyu to be crushed; cadupu to crush; Ka. sade id.; sadaku/tadaku to beat; tade id.; Tu. sadi striking; Ta. catai to be bruised; to crush; tatai to be shattered; tatar to be crushed; Ma. cata crush; catekka to squash; (t- < c-).

2. cidiyu to be squeezed; Ta. citai; Ka. kittu to pluck out; Mlt. kithwr- to burst open.

3. cedaru to be scattered; Ta. citar, citaṟu; Ma. citaṟuka; Ta. citai to be scattered; Ka. kedaṟu; Tu. kedaruni; Kur. khetr- be thrown off; k͟hett- to shake off (through jerks).

4. bedaru to be startled; Ka. bedaṟu; Tu. bedaru a start, fright; Ta. vitaṟu, vitir to tremble; Ma. vitaṟuka; Kuvi pedṛ- to be startled.

5. medugu be pounded or ground into powder, paste, etc.; meducu, v.t.; Ka. midi (< *medi); Tu. medupuni; Ta. meti; Ma. metiyuka; to be bruised; metikka to thrash; Kui meda a blotch on the skin; Kuvi med- to push; Mlt. medgr- to discolor by bruise; medgo discolored by bruise.

§1.88. The development of a dental plosive from an affricate is common in Dravidian, especially in the Southern group. This has been discovered by Burrow, who demonstrated its application in the initial position.[50] The reverse change of t >.c also occurs in South Dravidian, but only in a few cases, where t is associated with a front vowel or the semivowel. We find c > t also in the medial position, which the following examples suffice to show:

-d- < *-t- < *-c-

1. aduru to tremble; shake; v.t. adur-cu, adru-cu; Ka. adir, adaru; Tu. adaruni, aduruni; Ta. atir; Ma. atiruka : Te. asi(y-āḍu) to tremble; asadu slenderness; Ka. asi to tremble; slenderness; asumbu id.; Ta. acai to move, stir; to be slender; ayakku v.tr. to shake; aî slenderness; Kur. asr- to tremble; cf. Mlt. adyare to be agitated.

2. aduku to join, unite; to suit, etc.; Ka. adaku, aduku; Ta. Ma. atuṅku to be compressed; atukku to press; Kuvi ath- to inclose; att- to inhere; cf. Kur. att- to put on; Mlt. at- id. : Ka. asa fitness, propriety; Ta. acai to join with, tie, bind, etc.; Kuvi ass- to fit, catch; Kur. assg- to adhere, stick; Mlt. asg- id.; cf. Kota ac- to seize.

3. piduku to milk; squeeze; Ta. pitukku press out, squeeze out; Ma. pitukkuka; Ka. hiduka id.; Kur. ped$^{e}$k̲h̲- id. : Te. pisuku to squeeze, mash; Ka. pisuku, hisuku, -uṅku; Tu. piskuni, pīsuni id.; Ta. picakku to press between fingers; picai to knead; Ma. piccuka to pinch; Kuvi (F) pīc- to milk, wring; Go. pisk- to knead flour; with c > y > zero : Pj. pīk- to crush, Kur. pīk̲h̲- press for oil, squeeze; Mlt. pīq- wring, etc. (> l.w. Skt. picc- to press, see T. Burrow, TPS, 1945, pp. 109-110); it is clear here that c-forms are more widely represented than the t-forms which are later formations.

4. uduku to wash, drub, as clothes; Klm. sutk- id.; Go. suhk- wash clothes (< *susk-); Kui jōga id. (< *ocag- or < *sohg-) : ? Go. usūm- wipe, clean (with a cloth); Klm. usm- to wipe, apply; Kuvi ūss- to anoint; Te. usumu to clean clothes; cleanse.

5. podugu to cover; to embed; set in; Ka. pudugu to insert; poduṅku to hide; pode to wrap round; Tu. pudepuni to put in clothes, inwrap; Ta. potukku to conceal; putai to be buried; pote to cover, hide; pottu id.; Ma. potiyuka, pudayuka id.; pottuka to cover : Kur. pojj- to wrap round; Kui poja to pack; Mlt. poj- id.; Brah. puch clothing; cf. Ta. Ka. Te. potti a cloth, garment.

These examples attest Te. -d- < *-c-, through *-t- This development also throws light on the phonetic nature of the Dravidian affricate at the time of the shift.

§1.89. In loan words Tamil drops an Indo-Aryan s, initial as well as medial.[51] E.g., Ta. āyiram, Ka. sāsira, sāvira, Tu. sāvira, sāra thousand, < IA sahasra-; Ta. īyam lead, Skt. sīsa- id.; Ta. (*tēyam >) tēm a country, Skt. dēśa-; an intervocalic affricate of IA remains in Tamil, Skt. sūci a needle, Ta. ūci id. The development of a Skt. sibilant to a dental stop in the intervocalic position is a Middle Tamil characteristic, operating to the fullest extent in Malayalam, which branched off from Middle Tamil as a separate language.[52] Therefore, Ta. ātaṉam < Skt. āsana- a seat; tātaṉ < Skt. dāsa- a servant; mātam < Skt. māsa- month, etc. are all later developments which are in clear contrast to the early Tamil loss of the intervocalic sibilants.

§1.90. An intervocalic -d- can develop from two sources here, when a -c- is the ultimate original: -c- > -j- > -d-; or -c- > -t- > -d-. Of these the first development runs against the PDr. sound system, since the early Dravidian development is to spirantize a medial -c- to -s- (see §§1.112, .114). However, -c- > -j- occurs as a later feature in Ka. and Te. in loanwords, e.g., sūdi (< *sūji); these forms are not many. From these data, we can assume that when PDr. -c- developed to -t-, it was still an occlusive and had not developed into a sibilant, since, otherwise, [-s-] cannot alternate with -t- in early South Dravidian. So the shift of *-c- > -s- is probably later than that of *-c- > -t-; also the loss of occlusion of -c- (> [-s-]) was coeval with or later than the borrowing of the first IA words with sibilants, lost in all positions. The forms with -t- alternating with -s- are not to be matched with the Middle Tamil forms of -s-/-t- alternation in loanwords, since the former are attested in works of early Tamil (i.e., Sangam Tamil works). Collins wrongly thinks that Skt. s, ś > Ta. y or zero was later than their development to -c- (see Remarks to "Dravidic Studies" III, p. 59).

-n-

§1.91. Te. -n- < PDr. *-n-, corresponding to Ta. -ṉ- and -n- of all other languages; the PDr. -n- seems to have more alveolar allophones than dental; a dental allophone probably occurred in consonant groups with a following dental plosive:[53]

1. tinu to eat; Ka. tin, tinnu; Tu. tinpuni; Ta. tiṉ, tiṉṉu; Ma. tinnuka; Kui ṭinba; Kuvi tinj-; Go. tind-; Pj. Klm. Nk. tin-, tind-; Kur. tind- to feed; Mlt. tind- id.

2. vinu to hear; Ta. viṉ to ask, hear; Ma. vinavuka to ask; Kui venba; Kuvi wen-; Klm. Nk. vin-; Pj. ven-, vend-, vett-; Kur. Mlt. men- to hear, ask; Brah. bin-.

3. manu to live, stay; Ka. Tu. mane house; Ta. maṉṉu to live long; Ma. mane house; Kui manba to exist; Kuvi manj-; Go. mand-; Pj. men-, mend-; Kur. man-; Brah. man-.

§1.92. Telugu shares with North Dravidian and Pj. Klm. Nk. Go. of Central Dravidian the change of PDr. -ṇ- to -n-. This shift was in progress in the pre-literary period itself as shown by the inscriptional evidence and was completed by the 11th century.[54] This falling together of *ṇ with n has led to confusion and inverse spellings in the writings of later inscriptions. The following examples demonstrate Telugu -n- < PDr. *-ṇ-:

1. kanu to see; kannu eye; also *kān- and kāñcu to see; Ta. Ma. Ka. kāṇ- to see, past stem kaṇḍ-.

2. tinuku to strain (as at stool); Ka. tiṇuku; tiṇi to be full or packed; Ta. tiṇuṅku to become close; Ma. tikku straining; Mlt. tinq- to strain.

3. penãgu to be entwined, twisted; to fight; Ka. peṇagu; peṇe to intertwine; Ta. piṇaṅku, piṇai id.; Ma. piṇayuka, v. i.; cf. GoM. piṛang- to entwine.

So also in enayu, ponaru, pūnu, etc.

§1.93. There was in PDr. an alternation between -ṇ- and -ḷ-. So, whenever we have an alternation of -n-/-l- in Telugu, we can normally trace it to the PDr. alternation *-ṇ-/*-ḷ-, which was also widely represented in the other South Dravidian languages.

1. konu to buy, take; also auxiliary verb in reflexive stems; causative is kolupu; early Te. inscriptions koṇ-; Ka. koḷ, Tu. koṇuni; Ta. Ma. koḷ, koḷḷu; Klm. koṛ- to buy; Kui Kuvi koḍ- to buy, take up; PDr. *koḷ-/*koṇ-.

2. taniyu to be satisfied, contented; cf. tanu, adj. cool, cold; Ta. taṇi id.; taṇ coldness; Ma. taṇiyuka id.; Ka. taṇ coldness, cool; Tu. taniyuni to be allayed; these forms arise from the PDr. stem *caḷ-, *caṇ- cold, etc. (see §1.23), cf. Tu. saṇipuni to cool; (t- < c-).

Similarly in uṇḍu to be, ceṇḍu to cut, uṇ- and ceṇ- have alternative bases *uḷ- and *keḷ- in the other languages.

§1.94. There is one form in which -n- derives from an original -l̲-. This is unexpected, since in Telugu an intervocalic *-l̲- invariably becomes -ḍ-. This form is obviously a loanword from Kannada, where *-l̲- > -ṇ- is one of the normal developments (§1.84).

munũgu, v.i. to sink; Ka. muṇugu, muṇigu; mul̲uṅgu, mul̲ugu; Tu. muṇuguni, murkuni; Ta. mul̲uku, mūl̲ku; Ma. mul̲ukuka; Kui bṛuḍga; Kuvi mrūkh-; Kur. mul$^{u}$kh-, Mlt. mulg̣-; certain dialects of Mdn. Te. still preserve the ṇ in muṇugu, which is proof of its later introduction into the language since it does not conform to the usual shift of -ṇ > -n of early Telugu.

§1.95. The alternation of -l-/-n- operates dialectally to a great extent in Modern Telugu,[55] but in the early speech it was very much restricted. However, there is evidence to show that there was -n-/-l-alternation in PDr., which is seen in many cases in Ta. The following Te. form with -n- has an alternant in -l- in the transitive, reflecting a similar alternation in the parent speech:

canu to go, to elapse; calupu tr. to pass (time); Ka. sal, sallu; Tu. sanduni; Ta. cel-; Ma. celka; Kui salba; Kuvi han-; Go. hand-; Brah. hin-.

§1.96. Te. -n- < PDr. -n- [*-ṉ-], alternating with *-ṯ- [*-ṟ-]:

1. mānu to be healed; to subside; v.t. to give up : Ta. māṟu : to be cured; to cease; māṟṟu to cure; Ma. māṟuka id.; māṟṟuka to remove; Kui māṛa to be healed; Kuvi mānp- to heal.

2. kanu to bring forth (human beings); cf. kandu a child; Ka. kandu the foetus of beasts; kanda a young child : Ka. kaṟu a calf; Ta. kaṉṟu id.; Ma. kaṉṉu the young of cattle; kaṟṟu a boy, calf; Brah. khan- to bring forth. The n form of the verb is preserved in Te. and Brah. only.

3. cinuku to sprinkle; to rain; a drop of rain; Ma. cinaṅkuka; Ka. cinuku a drop; jinugu id.; Ta. ciṇuṅku id. (l. w. < Te.) : Ma. Ta. iṟu to drip; (loss of c-, see §1.210). The base *cin- occurs in Te. cindu to be spilt, etc.

In items 1 and 3, the n/[ṟ] alternation is attested by the occurrence of -ṟ- intervocalically in Ta. and Ma. In item 2, Ka. kaṟu could be from PDr. *kaṉṯu following the usual Ka. development of losing a pre-consonantal nasal, but we do not normally expect this in forms of short-vowelled bases of two syllables; it is, of course, common in disyllabic forms where the radical vowel is long: Te. nānu to be soaked, Go. nānd- : Ka. nāṟu (< *nāṯ- < *nānṯ-); Te. ūnu, ū̃du to hold; Ta. ūṉṟu to be fixed : Ka. ūṟu to lean, stay, fix (< *ūṯ- < *ūnṯ-). Other items pointing to an original n/ṯ [i.e., ṉ/ṟ] alternation are: Te. minuku/meṟayu to shine (< *min-/ *miṯ-); kunuku to doze, kruṅgu to sink, bend; nanucu to blossom (< *nān-/ *nāṯ-), etc. (see Part II).

-m-

§1.97. Te. -m- < PDr. *-m-:

1. kumulu to smoulder, grieve; cf. kummu embers; Ka. kome to burn; Tu. gumulu n. fire burning in embers; gumuluni to be hot as in fever; Ta. kumai to be overboiled; be hot; distressed; Ma. kumuṟuka to be hot; with a consonantal derivative suffix, cf. Ta. kumpi heat of fire; kumpu become overburnt; Ma. kumpal n. id.; Ka. kumpaṭe, Te. kumpaṭi a furnace; PDr. base *kum-.

2. cimuṭu to wink; Ka. cimuṭu; Ta. Ma. cimiṭṭu id.

§1.98. Many of the SDr. languages show a frequent variation between intervocalic v and m from the earliest times; sometimes it becomes difficult to ascertain which of the two is historically the original. In the following two cases Te. -m- develops out of an original -v-, judging on a statistical basis:

-m- < *-v-

1. nemaku to search, seek; cf. Ka. nīvu, nivaru to pass the hand gently over; Ta. nīvu id.

2. nimuru to rub gently (< *nivur- < *nīv-ur-); Ta. Ka. nīvu id.

§1.99. In the following cases, where -v-/-m- alternation is more widespread than in the above two examples, it seems justifiable to consider -m- as being the original, for two reasons: (1) -m- occurs or can occur in closed syllables as well as in the intervocalic position, whereas -v- occurs only intervocalically. -v- may be considered a positional free variant of -m-, since the later has a wider distribution. (2) Bases with a final -v- are, in fact, very few.

1. amaru to be ready, be accomplished; to be fit; Ta. amar v. i. to fit; amai id.; Ma. ameyuka id.; Ka. amar to be agreeable; Tu. amāruni to suit; Ta. camai to be suitable; Ka. same, save id.; samaṟu, savaṟu id.; Te. savarincu to set right.

2. kamaru, kamalu to be singed, burnt; Tu. gameluni to be hot; gameyuni id.; Ta. kamaṟu to be excessively heated; Ka. kamuru id.; all from *kam-ar, cf. Ka. kāvu heat, cauterization; kāviri heat (< *kav-al- < *kāval).

3. namalu to chew; nemarcu to ruminate; Ka. namalu, nevaru; Mdn. Ka. nemaru; Tu. naẙnt-, naẙmp- (< *navunt-, *navump-) to chew; *ñam- (§1.233).

§1.100. Sometimes -v- developing to -m- in Te. is a reflex of *-p- in the intervocalic position:

-m- < *-v- < *-p-

1. kamucu to seize, catch hold of, gulp; also kaviyu, kavucu, kavvu; Ka. kavi, kavaru; Ta. kavi; Ma. kaviyuka id.; Ta. Kur. kapp- to swallow; Te. kappa frog (which pounces to seize); Kui kappa id.

2. camaru to slap with palm; crush to death under feet; kill; (< *cav-ar- < *cap-ar- < *cap(p)-ar-); the original meaning is "to slap, flatten." Cf. Te. appaḷincu to slap (c- lost, §1.210); Ka. cappaḷisu id.; appaḷisu; Tu. appaḷipuni; (see Part II s. v. samayu; also Burrow, TPS 1945, pp. 99, 100).

Similarly in umiyu to spit, tamaku to falter, fail, hesitate, samayu to perish, -m- is from an original *-p- through *-v-.

-r-

§1.101. Telugu -r- < *-r- in common with all the Dravidian languages:

1. torāgu to flow, gush out; Ka. sōr to drop, drip; suri id.; Tu. sōr-, tōr-; Ta. cori; Ma. coriyuka; Kota corv-, cord-; To. twar- (Emeneau, BSOAS, XV, 102); Kui tōṛa to flow, trickle; sṛohpa to issue from; Kuvi (F) torg- to fall; tōranga a teat; Kur. curuk̲h̲- to leak; Mlt. curg̣- id.; Brah. curr- to flow, to gush; trump drop of water.

2. perugu v.i. to grow; Ka. piri largeness; percu to increase; Tu. perc- id.; Ta. peruku; Ma. perukuka id.; Kuvi perh- to raise; GoM. pērs- to extend; pirr- to grow; Klm. perg- id.; Kur. pard- to grow in number; to prosper; Brah. pir- to swell (of body).

3. paracu to be spread; to spread (as mat); Ka. pari, pare; Tu. paraturuni; Ta. para; Ma. parakka; Kui prahpa to spread out as grain; Kuvi (F) press- id.; GoM. parh- to spread.

Other forms of this type are: baraku to scratch; karāgu to be melted; marāgu to be addicted; jarugu to slide; move; cirūgu to be torn; tirugu to turn; berayu to be joined, mixed; morayu to sound (as an instrument); uriyu to burn; eriyu to burn; kuriyu to rain; virugu to be broken, etc.

§1.102. In a few cases, Go. Kui Kur. Mlt. show -ṛ- instead of -r- corresponding to SDr. -r-, see s.v. marāgu to be attached to; to be tamed; orayu to be rubbed; assayed; murugu to rot; in most cases Brah. has -rr-.

-r̲-

§1.103. It has been established that the PDr. *t̲, which occurs only in the non-initial position, is an alveolar plosive.[56] The daughter languages have preserved this value in the post-nasal position and in gemination. In most languages *t̲ of *-nt̲- and *-t̲t̲- has developed either to a dental stop or a retroflex stop;[57] in Ta. and Ma. in the older stages, the phonemic value of the alveolar stop is preserved in these positions as distinct from a dental or retroflex stop.[58] Intervocalically, all SDr. languages developed it to a trill which has fallen together with the alveolar (or pre-alveolar) flap r in the modern dialects except in Toda, where r̲ and r are still phonemically distinct.

§1.104. Te. -r̲- < PDr. *-t̲-, corresponding to Ta. Ma. Ka. -r̲-, Tu. -r- (less frequently -j- or -d-), Kui -ṛ-/-r-, Kuvi Klm. Go. Kur. Mlt. -r-, occasionally -ṛ-:

1. car̲acu to whip, slap; tar̲aṭu to flog; Ka. ar̲e; Ta. ar̲ai, tar̲ai; Ma. ar̲ayuka; tar̲ekka; Tu. tarepuni to rivet; Kui jaṛsa whip; Kur. taṛ- to flog; Mlt. taṛc- to slap.

2. ter̲acu to open; Ka. ter̲e; Tu. terapu space, room; Ta. tir̲a; Ma. tur̲akka; Go. tarī-t- id.; Kui trēppa to lay out; dari, adj. opened out; Kur. tāṛ- to put out of the way; clear of obstruction.

3. nar̲aku to cut, fell; Ta. nar̲ukku; Ma. nar̲ukkuka; Go. nark- to cut; GoM. naṛk-; Mlt. nark- to claw, scratch.

4. mur̲iyu to be broken; cut into pieces; cf. mukka a slice (< *mur̲ka); Ka. mur̲i to break; sever; Tu. murku fragment; Ta. mur̲i id.; Ma. mur̲ikka; cf. mūr̲uka to cut; Kui muṛpa to split wood; mrunga to be torn; Go. muṛī-t- to be dislocated; Kur. mur$^{u}$k- to amputate; murch- to twist and break; Mlt. murk- to cut and break; Brah. bur- to crumble.

§1.105. Corresponding to the SDr. (literary) -r̲-, Kui also shows in some cases -s-/-j-, Tu. -d-/-j-, Kur. Mlt. -j-.[59] It should however be noted that this is not a regular correspondence, since sometimes only one language has -s-/-j- while the others show the regular -r-/-ṛ-. A few such forms are given below:

1. tar̲ugu to chop; to cut, slice; Ka. tar̲i, tar̲e id.; Tu. tarapuni, tajapuni; Ta. tar̲i; Ma. tar̲ikka : Kui tahpa to chip off (< *taspa); Klm. targ-; cf. Kur. Mlt. tār- to fell; Brah. taṛ- to cut, slaughter.

2. tūr̲u to enter, pierce through; tur̲ugu to stuff; Ka. tūr̲u to enter, pierce; tur̲uku to stuff; Ta. tur̲u to enter; insert; Ma. tur̲uka id.; Go. durs- to fit in or on another : Kui tuspa to pierce, make a breach; Kur. turd- to pass through; tūr- to pierce through soft matter; Mlt. turg- to bury, etc.; Brah. trujj- to choke.

3. pār̲u to run; flee; Ta. Ma. Ka. pār̲u id.; Tu. pāruni to run; parapuni to flow; Go. parī-t- id.; Mlt. parc- id. : Kui pānja fly, leap.

In these cases, even where Kui shows a -j- or -s- for a SDr. -r̲-, it is the trill that is more widely distributed than the affricate or sibilant. Kur. and Mlt. have a preponderant representation of -ṛ- or -r- for a SDr. -r̲-. Out of twenty-one correspondences that Mlt. has for SDr. -r̲- forms in verbs, it has -r- in fourteen and -ṛ- in six and -s- alternating with -r- in one. Kuruk̲h̲ has eight forms with -ṛ- and seven with -r- out of a total of twenty cognates. Even allowing a margin for doubtful etymologies, there still remains a considerable proportion to justify the equation of SDr. -r̲-: Kur. Mlt. -ṛ-/-r-, all of which are traceable to a single PDr. phoneme *t̲.

§1.106. There is one clear case of -r̲-/-s- alternation in Dravidian which has a wide range of distribution:

kar̲acu to bite; kāṭu n. a bite; Ka. kaḍi, karcu; Tu. kajepuni to chew; Ta. kaṭi, kar̲i; Ma. kaṭikka; Kui kasa; Kuvi kach-; Go. kacc-, kask-; Klm. Pj. kacc-; Kur. k̲h̲acc-; Mlt. qasw-.

This is a very interesting case since we find in SDr. an alternation between -r̲- and -ṭ-, which also throws light on the phonetic value of -r̲ as originally a voiceless alveolar plosive. Therefore, -ṭ- must have developed out of *-t̲- before *-t̲- lost its occlusive articulation in the intervocalic position and developed into an alveolar trill. It will not be unreasonable to consider the affricates of Kui, Kur., and Mlt. as having developed from the PDr. phoneme *-t̲- in its occlusive state before the final break-up of the parent speech. The paucity of such forms points to their relative antiquity, whereas the preponderance of the trill-type allophone shows that this was almost accomplished in the proto-stage itself. Kur. and Mlt. also show forms of the latter stage for the above etymology: Kur. k̲h̲ār- to gnaw, Mlt. qār- to bite off. So, these two developments in NDr. and Kui represent different chronological layers rather than two different sources of origin. In this connection we have to recall the instances where a SDr. -ḍ- (< *-ṭ-) is paralleled by Kui, Kur., and Mlt. -s- (§1.82, .85).

§1.107. -r̲- and -r- are different phonemes in PDr., but they have fallen together and lost contrast in Ta., Ma. (certain dialects), Ka., and Telugu.[60] This development seems to have taken place even in some ancient Telugu forms; as a result we have doublets with -r- for an original -r̲- and vice versa; e.g., er̲āgu, erāgu to bow; Ka. er̲agu; Tu. eraguni; Ta. ir̲aṅku; Ma. ir̲aṅṅuka.

Similarly for an original -r̲- in the following forms, Te. has both -r̲- and -r- forms side by side in the literature: or̲āgu, orāgu to bend; mur̲ugu, murugu to rot; pār̲u, pāru to run; pēr̲u, pēru to curdle; mīr̲u, mīru to exceed; tēr̲u, tēru to be appeased; ur̲u, uru to behoove, to be suitable, etc. Some have an -r̲- corresponding to an -r- of Ta. Ma. Ka.: Te. mar̲alu, maralu to return : Ka. malar; Te. varalu, var̲alu to shine, flourish: Ta. vaḷar id. (metathesis in the two above instances); Te. ūru to ooze, spring up as water; cerugu to winnow (for *ūr̲u and *cer̲ugu respectively). This sort of alternation between -r̲- and -r- also appears in some ancient Tamil and Kannada words.[61]

-l-

§1.108. Te. -l- < PDr. *-l- corresponding to -l- of all the Dravidian languages; sometimes *-l- develops to -r- in Tulu:

1. kalãgu to be in agitation (as water), to be disturbed; Ka. kalaku, kalaṅku v.i., v.t.; Tu. kalaṅkuni; Ta. kalaṅku; kalai to be scattered; Ma. kalaññu; Kur. k͟halk͟h- to disturb, make water muddy; Mlt. qalg-; Kui glahpa to stir, to confuse.

2. olucu to flay, peel (skin, rind, etc.); Ka. suli; Tu. sulipuni; Ta. Ma. coli; Kur. chol-, Mlt. cōlye; Brah. sil n. skin, hide.

§1.109. Te. -l- < *-ḷ-; this development Te. shares with all the languages of Central and North Dravidian, while Ta. Ma. Ka. Tu. Kota Toda and Koḍagu of SDr. preserve the PDr. *-ḷ-; Naiki has -ḷ- after all vowels except i and sometimes ē; in other positions it has only -l- (see Emeneau, Kolami, p. 149); Gondi sometimes has -ṛ- corresponding to *-ḷ-.[62]

1. velũgu to shine, n. shining; Pj. vili- to be white; Oll. viled white; Kuvi vella white; Klm. veleŋ n. light; Kur. bilc- to shine; Mlt. bilpu the moon: Ta. viḷaṅku; Ma. viḷaññu; Ka. beḷagu; Tu. beḷaguni; Kota veḷg-; To. pö̃ɫx-; Go.(W) weṛcī light.

2. teliyu to be known, become clear; Kuvi (F) tellali to awaken; telk- to know; telp- to interpret; cf. Brah. tipp-, titt-, neg. of chā- to know (Bray I, §261); Klm.(E) telmi adj. white: Ta. teḷi to become clear, teḷ id., teḷḷu id.; Ma. teḷiyuka; Ka. tiḷi; Tu. tiḷi adj. clear; Koḍ. teḷi; Kota teyḷ- (teḷc-).

§1.110. In a few cases, Central and North Dravidian members have -ṛ- (or -ḍ-) corresponding to PDr. -ḷ-, for instance, Te. polucu to shine : Kuvi pṛoth- to light; Te. molucu to sprout : GoM. mōḍiy- to sprout; etc.

-v-

§1.111. (a) Te. -v- < *-p-:

1. javuku to grow weak; to be shaky; Ka. javagu, jōgu swampy ground; Ka. tavu to dwindle; save id.; Ta. cavu become weak; tavu to be reduced; cf. Ta. tapu to perish.

2. kaviyu to pounce; overspread; Te. Ka. Ta. Ma. kappu id.; cf. Te. kamucu.

3. javaru to flog; cf. camaru to crush; < *capp- (§1.197).

(b) Te. -v- < *-m-:

1. civuku to rot < *cim-uku < *kim-uku; cf. Te. cimuḍu to be overboiled; Ka. kimul̠ to be spoiled.

2. navayu to be reduced, emaciated; Ka. name, nave; Tu. name to wear away; Ta. namukku to yield to pressure; Ma. ñamuṅṅuka to sink.

(c) Te. -v- < *-k- [-g-]:

tiviyu to pull, attract; also tigiyu id.; Ka. tivi id.; teg- to draw, pull, diminish; Tu. teguni to take; Ta. tikai to be taken aback; subside; tekku to take, receive.

-s-

§1.112. Of all reconstructed phonemes of PDr., *c seems to be the most complicated, with numerous divergent developments in the descendant languages. Since many of these developments occur in almost every language and are not clearly marked out by any language boundaries, they have to be ascribed to the parent language itself with dialect mixture in the pre-separation period. The correspondences of PDr. non-initial *c in Telugu and the other languages may be analyzed into two main sets:

I. *-c-
  1. -c- [-č-] > -t- [-d-]
  2. -c- [-s-] > -y- > -k- [-g-] (> -v-)/-zero-

II. *-c-/-l̲-

§1.113. The course of development in the correspondences of Set I is clear since it is always in one direction, and the usual reconstructional procedure yields only a single phoneme *c. Set II is difficult in that two divergent series of correspondences occur in a number of etymologically related forms leading to the reconstruction of two phonemes for PDr., viz., *c and *l̲; now the evidence is preponderant for *c and now for *l̲.[63] We may infer from this that the *c/*l̲ alternation occurred in PDr. itself and was the result of the split of a pre-Dravidian phoneme other than *c or *l̲. Though there is no definite evidence to set up either *c or *l̲ as being primary in PDr., the chances are that *l̲ has secondarily developed either as a dialectal or as a positional variant of *c. In OTa., for instance, Skt. śēṣa- > Ta. cēl̲am (Dravidic Studies III (1919), pp. 32-34). This may suggest that a dialectal (less probably positional) variant of *c-, having a phonetic value similar to Skt. ṣ, was replaced by l̲ with a later dialect mixture which produced two series of correspondences in the same languages.

§1.114. It has been discussed earlier (§1.90) that -c- > -t- is earlier than -c- > -s- because of the improbability of the latter developing to -t- instead of to -y-/zero. In the following forms, corresponding to Te. -s- (< *-c-) certain languages show -t- or zero.

1. osāgu to give; a present; Ka. osage a gift; Ta. utavu to give, etc.; utavi gift (Kalit.); oy/uy to give; oyyal giving, present; PDr. *oc-.

2. kasaru to scold, rebuke; n. anger, dislike; kasi vengeance; kasu adj. bitter, unripe (of fruit); Ka. kasa ill-humor; kay bitterness; gajaṟu/gadaṟu to scold; Ta. kaippu bitterness, aversion; katavu to be angry with; n. anger (Kalit.); kataḻ id.; Ma. kayarka to start in anger; cf. Kur. kackacr- to be vexed; kackac vexation : Ta. kacaṅku to be displeased with; kaca to be disgusted with; kāy to be wearied, displeased (Tolk.); PDr. *kāc- : *kac-V-.

3. masāgu to break forth as a passion, increase, swell, etc.; Ka. masagu id.; masaka vehement emotion; mā id.; Ta. maintu (= mayntu) strength (Tolk.), infatuation of love (Parip.); connected with this set are: Te. masaru to be proud, arrogant; impassioned; n. pride; Ta. matar to increase; be affected by frenzy; be arrogant; n. pride; matam/mataṉ strength, arrogance (PN); maiyal pride. All these forms point to a PDr. *mac- to increase, swell, be proud, etc. It is interesting to compare these with NIA: Pkt. maccai is excited; K. macar m. madness; H. macnā to be excited; Nep. macāunu/maccāunu to make rise, flourish; G. macvũ to swell; M. macṇē to swell (R. L. Turner, Nep. Dict.). Turner connects these forms with Skt. mac- (Dhātupāṭha), macate to be arrogant. He rejects Bloch's derivation of these from Pkt. majjai, Skt. mádyati because of the difficulty of the consonant, i.e., c instead of j in NIA. Therefore the Skt. verb is likely to be a borrowing from PDr. when the form had still the occlusive *c in the non-initial position.

§1.115. Following are a few examples for PDr. -c- > [-s-] > -y-. Here the -t- forms do not occur.

1. esāgu to shine; appear, increase; esakumu excellence; Ka. ese to shine, be distinguished; esaka splendor; Ta. iyakkam excellence; icai to fit, harmonize; iyal/ēl fitness (loss of y from PSDr. *eyal); PDr. *ec-.

2. musuru to overspread, pounce upon; swarm as bees, etc.; mũgu id. (< *muy-ṅg-); Ka. musuṟu id.; Ta. moci, moy to crowd as flies; mūcu to swarm about; Go. moi-, moitt- to rush at, close with. This is obviously connected with the base *muc- to close, shut.

Other forms: nusulu to move; nusũgu to hide.

§1.116. In a few cases Te. and SDr. -c- [-s-] may be a part of the derivative suffix rather than being the PDr. base final, e.g., visaru to blow (wind), hurl, fling; Ka. bisur; Ta. viciṟu to fan, fling; Ma. visaruka id. : Te. Ta. vīcu id.; Ma. vīsu, vīyu; Tu. bījuni; Kui vīka, vīnja. On the basis of the Kui form the ultimate PDr. root is *vī- with the c suffix in SDr.; the long vowel is shortened later before the vowel derivatives, i.e., PDr. *vī-c- : *vic-V-.[64]

§1.117. There are numerous sets to establish *c/*ḻ in PDr. The following Te. verbs in -s- provide a few typical examples: pisuku squeeze, press; Ka. pisuku, pisuṅku; Tu. piskuni, pīsuni; Ta. picai, picakku; Go. pisk-; Kuvi (S) pic-; Nk. pustum drawing (LSI, IV, p. 574); Pj. pīk- to crush; pīc- to grind (> Skt. piccayati squeezes; pich- to press flat, wring)[65] : piḍucu to squeeze, wring, press out; Ka. piḻi; Tu. pureñcuni, purecuni; Ta. piḻi; Ma. piḻiyuka; Go. pīr-; Mlt. pilq-; Brah. pil̲h̲- id. These two series of forms are clearly related and yield two PDr. forms *pic- and *piḻ-. Burrow derives Skt. picc- < *pirc- (ibid.), but, since the assimilation of a liquid + stop to stop + stop is a very late characteristic in divided Dravidian, it is more likely that Skt. pich-, picc- are based on the c alternant of PDr. *pic-/*piḻ-.

Another such set is the words meaning 'to delay,' 'to procrastinate,' 'be dull,' 'dim,' etc.: masalu to delay; Ka. masal delaying; masuḷ to hide oneself; madaḍu dullness; Tu. madaḍu slothful; n. a lazy man; Ta. macaku to linger, hesitate; macaṅku become confused, dull; macakkam dullness; macaṇai a dullard (< PDr. *mac-) : Ta. maḻuṅku become dull in mind; maḻuppu to delay; Ma. maḻukkuka to delay (< PSDr. *maḻ-). A majority of forms occur with c, meaning to be dim, dull, etc.; see s.v. māyu in Part II.

For similar cases pointing to PDr. *c/*ḻ, see s. v. usugu, usumu to scour; osulu to be loose.

§1.118. The following is an interesting case for reconstruction since Kuruk̲h̲ itself shows forms which reflect the original dichotomy of developments, viz., PDr. *c/*ḻ: nusulu to shrink, hide oneself; Ka. nusuḷ, nuguḷ (< *nuyuḷ) to hide oneself, retreat, n. subterfuge; Kur. nūk̲h̲r- to hide oneself, be kept secret (< *nuy-k-); all from PDr. *nuc-/*nuy- : Kur. nuṛ- to conceal, hide; stow away (out of sight), Mlt. nuḍgre, v.i. to hide oneself, disappear; nuḍe v.t. to conceal (< *nuḻ-).

§1.119. In the following case, corresponding to -c- > -y- > -k- of SDr., Kur. and Mlt. show -k- obviously derived from PDr. *-y- and preserved in its original unvoiced condition (§1.79) : nusulu v.i. to shake, stir; Ka. nugicu to slip; Tu. nugupuni, nuguruni to loosen, slacken; Ta. nukai become loose : Kur. nuk$^{u}$r- to be shaken; nuk- to shake (up and down, wind shakes tree); Mlt. nukre to swing, rock; nuk- to shake. Kur. nuk$^{u}$r- is suggestive of the original intervocalic position of -k- which is not shown by the transitive stem and by the Mlt. forms.

§1.120. No reliable etymologies are available for the following forms in -s-: kasugu to mutter; kusulu to be discontented; tasuku to coquet; nusumu to pull, draw; masulu to boil, simmer.

## INITIAL ḍ-, r-, ṟ-, l-
## (Metathesis and Vowel Contraction—I)[66]

§1.121. From a comparative study of Dravidian vocabularies, one observes that the retroflex consonants (ṭ ṇ ḷ ḻ) and the liquids of the alveolar series (r ṟ l) do not occur initially in Common Dravidian etyma. But, in pre-Kui-Telugu certain phonetic changes took place (in the pre-historic period), resulting in a shift of these consonants to the initial position in forms in which they were originally medial. Soon after the start of this development in Common Kui-Telugu, there seems to have been a historical separation between Kui and Telugu leading to different methods of carrying out the shift with the same result, viz., the change in the position of certain consonants from non-initial to initial. Tulu and Gondi also show evidence for the operation of a similar phonetic development in certain words, which are not borrowings from Telugu or Kui.[67]

§1.122. As far as Telugu is concerned the etyma that underwent this shift originally consisted of an initial vowel (one of a i e u o) followed by one of the consonants: ṭ[-ḍ-] ḻ ḷ l r ṟ, which in turn is followed by a derivative suffix beginning with a vowel or consonant. When a consonantal derivative follows, metathesis has occurred in the phonemes of the root-syllable with the doubling of the suffix consonant if it is single; when a vowel derivative follows, metathesis has occurred in the phonemes of the root syllable attended by a contraction of the vowels of root and (derivative) suffix syllables. These statements and the resulting sequences of vowel contraction may be presented as formulas as follows:[68]

$V^1$ root-vowel; $V^2$ suffix-vowel;

$C^1$ root-consonant; $C^2$ suffix-consonant;

'-' marked within a form denotes the etymological boundary which separates the root from the derivative suffix.

Type 1. $V^1C^1$-$C^2$- > $C^1V^1$-$C^2C^2$-

Type 2. $V^1C^1$-$V^2$- > $C^1\bar{V}^1$-

$C^1$ standing for any one of the medial consonants: ṭ ḻ ḷ l r ṟ, the following will be the vowel sequences in the contracted forms of Type 2.

(a) $aC^1$-a- > $C^1$ā-
(b) $eC^1$-a- > $C^1$ē-
(c) $oC^1$-a- > $C^1$ō-
(d) $iC^1$-i/u- > $C^1$ī-
(e) $eC^1$-i/u- > $C^1$ẹ̄-
(f) $uC^1$-i/u- > $C^1$ū-
(g) $oC^1$-i/u- > $C^1$ō-

(It should be noted that in PSDr., in the environment [-a, PDr. *i *u merged with *e *o respectively; consequently in contractions of the above type, we always get an ē for PDr. *i-a, *e-a, and ō for PDr. *u-a, *o-a, see §§1.277, .138.)

§1.123. After the completion of this shift in Telugu, -l̲- fell together with ḍ-, and -ḷ- fell together with l-; this refers to the period of early Telugu inscriptions when l̲ was still phonemic in Telugu. In Classical Telugu, the distinction between r and r̲ was still preserved in some of these metathesized forms. During the early literary period itself (11th century), ḍ- (which was a pool of three PDr. phonemes *ṭ, *l̲, and ḷ) started to fall together with d- and was gradually replaced by it as time passed. In Modern Telugu r- and r̲ merged into one phoneme /r/. Dealing with the forms of verbal bases obtained from the literary compositions, one finds in Telugu only four consonants, ḍ-, r-, r̲-, and l- occurring initially as a result of this shift.

ḍ-

§1.124. Type 1: $V^1C^1\text{-}C^2\text{-} > C^1V^1\text{-}C^2C^2\text{-}$

1. l̲acc(ina-) (that) destroyed, effaced (< *al̲-c-) (inscriptional; 625 A.D., EI 27, p. 230); Ta. Ma. Ka. al̲i to be destroyed, effaced; to ruin, etc.; also Inscr. Te. al̲is(ina-) (that) destroyed. Later inscriptions have the form ḍacc(-i, -ina) with the orthographic replacement of l̲ by ḍ following the sound shift. In Classical Telugu this form occurs with the stem ḍayy- (ḍass-) to diminish (as strength), to decay, > to be tired; see ḍappi destruction (Bhr. II, Śāṃti., 1.52); cf. Klm. (E) day-, ḍayt- to become thin.

2. ḍiggu/ḍigu to descend, dismount (< *l̲i-gg- < *il̲-g-); Klm. (SR) ḍig-, Klm. (E) dıg-, Kinwaṭ dial., ḍigg-; Ka. il̲i to descend; Ta. il̲i id.; Ma. il̲ika; Pj. iṛv-; Oll. iṛg-; KGad. iḍg-; Kui dīva (past st. dī-t-); Kur. elkhr- to set (of sun), Mlt. elqr- id.

3. ḍindu to decrease, diminish (strength), become low, subside; to perish (< *l̲i-nd- < *il̲-nd-); from the same etymon as the last, cf. Ta. il̲i fall, be reduced, v. t. to lower (past stem ıl̲int-); Ma. il̲ikka to lower; Ka. il̲i to become less, be humbled.

Similarly, dunnu (< *ḍu-nn- < *l̲u-nn < *ul̲-n-) to plough; ḍullu (< *l̲u-ll- < *ul̲-l-) to fall off (§1.127); ḍulcu/ḍulucu to loosen; cause to fall; duvvu (< *ḍu-vv- < *l̲u-vv- < *ul̲-v-) to comb; the earliest noted usage of this last form is in a 14th century text with d- < *ḍ- : Ta. ul̲u; Pj. uṛv-; KGad. uḍuv-; Kuvi rūss- to dress another's hair; rūca comb; cf. Kui ṛūsa to rub, scrape.

§1.125. Type 2: $V^1C^1\text{-}V^2\text{-} > C^1\bar{V}^1\text{-}$

$aC^1\text{-}a\text{-} > C^1\bar{a}\text{-}$

1. ḍãgu [ḍāṅgu] to be hidden; to disappear (< *aṭ-ank); Kui ḍāpa (ḍā-t-) to lie in wait for; Klm.(E) ḍāŋg-; Te. aḍãgu/aḍaṅgu to be hidden; to be suppressed; lie hidden; Ka. aḍaṅgu id.; Ta. aṭaṅku be subdued; disappear; aṭakku to hide; Ma. aṭaṅṅuka be enclosed; Tu. aḍāvuni to hide, be concealed; deṅguni be hidden (loss of a- through aphaeresis); Kui āṭpa to conceal, hide.

2. ḍāyu (ḍās-) to approach; ḍāpu proximity (< *aṭ-a-); Ka. aḍasu to join, to be near; enter closely; aṭṭu closeness; Ta. aṭaicu to be joined; aṭai joining (/aṭay/); Ta. aṭu, Ma. aṭukka to approach; Kui aṭpa to join together (pp. aṭṭ-); aṛse together, with; Mlt. aṭge near, close.

$uC^1\text{-}u\text{-} > C^1\bar{u}$

3. ḍūyu/ḍuyyu to pass through, as an arrow; to draw (sword from scabbard); to strip off leaves (passing the hand through) < *ḻū < *uḻ-u-; Kui ṛūsa to rub, scrape; cf. Te. ūḍcu (< *ūḻ-) id.; Go. ūch- to pluck, to strip (feathers of a bird); Ta. uḻu to scratch, incise; pass fingers through the hair.

§1.126. In two cases ḍ- seems to have arisen from *t- before a preconsonantal nasal of the retroflex series.[69] A similar consonantal assimilation also characterizes Parji, Kui, Kuruḵẖ, and Malto.[70]

1. ḍakku to be obtained; to come within one's control (< *taṇ-k-); Ka. dakku to accrue to; remain, be preserved (l. w. < Te.); Tu. daksuni, dakkuni to be retained; Ta. taṅku to remain (Kṟḷ.); be under control; takku to come to stay; become permanent as possession; be profitable; Ma. taṅṅuka come into possession; takkuka to be obtained; Te. dakku id.; Klm.(E), Nk. tak- stay, remain. No language shows evidence for a final ṇ in the radical syllable. Still, it has to be assumed on account of initial ḍ- in OTe.; or else the Te. form could be a hyperstandardization of dakku since, probably, ḍ- forms were considered more archaic than d- forms due to the prevalence of the shift ḍ- > d- already by the time of early literary texts.

2. ḍaṅgu to be pounded (grain), ḍancu/dancu to pound; these forms occur with ḍ- in the 11th century inscriptions. Kui ḍāmba to pound; Ka. taḷḷu to thrash, pound; Tu. taḷḷuni/talluni to thrash, as paddy; Go. dals- to pound; Mlt. dalye to grind; Ka. taḷisu to pound; (> l. w. Skt. taṇḍula- husked rice);[71] through the common Dravidian alternation of ḷ/ṇ, *taṇ-k can be set up as the earlier stage of Te. ḍaṅgu. But, Kui ḍā- seems to indicate an earlier *aḍ-a-. Alternatively, one could connect the Te. and Kui forms with the derivatives of *aṭ- to beat, strike,

etc.: Ta. aṭu to strike, beat; Ka. aḍacu to cuff; aḍi beating; Te. aḍucu to strike, etc.; Pj. aṭṭ- id.; Te. ḍaṅg- < *aṭ-aṅg-, with secondary shortening of the radical vowel after contraction, i.e., ḍaṅg- < *ḍāṅg- < *aṭ-ank-.

In pre-Telugu, sequences of a long vowel followed by nasal-consonant groups had two later developments, viz., either the nasal was lost or the long vowel was shortened. See loṅgu/lõgu to be subdued (< *ḷōṅg- < *oḷ-ang-). According to this, an original *ḍāṅg- developed to ḍaṅg- rather than to ḍā̃g- possibly to avoid homonymy with ḍā̃gu to be hidden (< *ḍāṅg- < *aṭ-ank-). It is to be noted that Kui shows the long vowel ḍāmba (*aḍ-amp-). These secondary developments in Telugu were based on a pattern of syllable grouping into which long vowels followed by two consonants (double consonants or consonant groups) no longer fitted. A long vowel plus a single consonant or a short vowel plus two consonants became the two acceptable types in disyllabic forms. Essentially these two represent a single type since, by definition, a long syllable has either a long vowel, or a short vowel plus a consonant (§1.6).

There is another such set: Te. ḍoṅku to perish, subside, sink; Ta. oṭuṅku to be restrained; be hidden; to sink. Te. ḍoṅku is therefore from < *ḍōnku < *oḍ-ank-; the alternative development appears in dõku to sink, used in a 14th century literary work.

§1.127. An understanding of this principle will also explain such forms as ḍullu/ḍollu to fall off: Te. ūḍu, v.i. to leave off, be loosened; fall off, etc.; Ka. uḻal to swing, be unsteady, be loosened; Ta. uḻal to oscillate; Mlt. uṭr- to fall (or urgr- to fall off); all these indicate a PDr. *ūḻ- : *uḻ-V; the derivative suffix could be -al/-il/-ul, though Ta. Ka. show only -al. The vowel variation in ḍullu/ḍollu can be explained in one of the two following ways:

*ḍūl-/ḍull- < *uḻ-ul

*ḍōl-/ḍoll- < *uḻ-al (see §§1.138, .27);

or, ḍull- by simple metathesis from *uḻ-ᵘl with a loss of a weakened u or i of the suffix *-ul or *-il; derivative a (of suffix -al) is not usually lost, hence vowel contraction in $uC^1$-a- > $C^1$ō : *uḻ-al > *ḻōl-/*ḻoll- > ḍōl-/ḍoll-.

§1.128. Etymologies are not available for the following verbal bases with ḍ-: ḍeppu/deppu to abuse, taunt (not attested in early works; deppu common in Mdn. Te.); ḍēku/dēku to creep or slide along the ground on posteriors (also not found in classical texts; common in Mdn. Te. both with d- and ḍ-); ḍokku to grow old; adj. old (no classical usages; lexical); ḍõku/dõku pare or shave the ground cutting up the turf ( ? < *tōṇ-k-, see Te. tō̃ḍu, Ta. tōṇṭu to dig, excavate, etc.; occurs only in Mdn. Te., listed by lexicons); ḍō̃gu/dō̃gu to crawl on the hands and knees (in a text of 14th century A.D. with d-). This last form is the alternative development of ḍoṅgu to crawl, which occurs in a 12th century work of a Śaiva poet (see Part II). Both these may be connected with the series derived from *oṭ-ank/-ang > *ḍōṅk-/*ḍōṅg- > Te. ḍoṅku to be hidden; to sink; ḍō̃ku to sink; ḍoṅgu to hide oneself, to steal; doṅga a thief; GoM. dong- to steal; Klm.(E) ḍoŋga a thief.

§1.129. ḍ- forms preponderate in Bhr. I of the 11th century; both ḍ- and d- forms occur frequently in works of the 12th and 13th centuries. From the 14th century onwards d- forms occur more often, though the ḍ- forms have always remained in literature as archaic literary survivals. The occurrence of duvvu to comb, without any ḍ- alternant is a clear proof that d- had already replaced ḍ- and it could not be revived by poets in their works, since, presumably, it was not recoverable either from the oral tradition or from the earlier literary works. Before the shift of ḍ- > d- took place in Telugu a few neighboring languages like Kolami, Maṛia Go., and Pj. borrowed a number of words which occur with initial ḍ- in those languages to the present day.

r-

§1.130. Of the eighteen forms with initial r-, etymologies are available only for ten; a few others have doubtful cognates in some of the other Dravidian languages. Following are the examples:

Type 1: $V^1C^1$-$C^2$- > $C^1V^1$-$C^2C^2$-

1. rajju to prate, talk empty words; n. prattle, empty talk (<*ar-j-); Klm.(E) raz-, ras-t- talk nonsense; cf. Kui ṛaspa to ring, make a reverberating sound; Ka. arcu to emit indistinct sounds; cry aloud; racce crying aloud.

2. ruddu to scrub, rub, scour, etc. (< *ur-d-); Kui rūsa crush, grind : Ka. urdu/uddu to rub, etc.; ujju id.; Tu. urduni to rub, file; Ta. urai rub into paste (past stem, uraitt-); Ma. uruṅṅuka id. (< *uruṅk-); PDr. base *ur-, see s.v. orayu in Part II.

3. rubbu to grind, crush into paste (< *ur-b-), the same base as above with a different derivative, i.e., < *ur-upp-.

§1.131.

Type 2: $V^1C^1$-$V^2$- > $C^1\bar{V}^1$-

1. rāyu to be rubbed; rācu v. t. to rub (< *ar-a-); Kui rāga be worn away; rāpka (< rākpa) cause to rub together; Kuvi (F) rāc- to

clean : Ka. are/ari to grind, crush; ari to grind on a slab; Tu. areyuni to pulverize by pounding; Ta. ari destroy by rubbing; grind, pulverize; Ma. arayuka.

2. rālu to fall, drop off (fruits, leaves, being detached); Klm. rāl- to fall, rāp- to fell; Nk. rāl- to fall out, rāl-p- to fell : Ta. ar̲-al becoming detached by cutting; ar̲u to be severed; to break asunder, cut off, sever.

3. rēyu to increase, rise, rage, cf. r͂ēgu id. (< *er̲-a-): Ta. ir̲a to excel, go beyond; n. height; Ta. Ma. Ka. ēr̲u to rise, ascend, increase; Tu. ēruni id.

4. rōyu[1] to seek, look for (< *or-ay-) : Ta. ōr to examine, consider; ōrppu, ōrcci investigation; Ma. ōr to consider, etc.; Ka. ōru to consider, inquire.

5. rōyu[2] to hate, dislike, renounce (< *or̲-a-); Ka. rōsu to dislike, feel disgusted; rōte dirt, filth : Ta. or̲u to punish, rebuke; dislike, be disgusted; ur̲ai to rebuke, disgrace; alternatively, cf. oruvu to abandon, renounce.

In items 2, 3 and 5, Telugu has r instead of r̲. This is additional evidence for the assumption made earlier (§1.105) that contrast between r and r̲ began to be lost even during the earliest period of Telugu literature.

§1.132. The r-forms without reliable etymologies are the following:

1. rakku (Dh. M.) to rend with nails; Śab. R. gives as r̲akku; may be compared with Ta. Ma. ar̲u to cut off.

2. ragulu/ravulu to be kindled; to take fire; may be connected with forms meaning "friction"; cf. ~avva a spark.

3. rā̃ju to take fire, be kindled (classical); seems to be connected with the above; are both these from *ar-a-, to be rubbed, etc.? This probably reflects the way in which fire used to be made in ancient days.

4. runju (Dh. M.) "nāsayākarṣaṇe" to draw in through the nose.

5. ruttu (Śab. R.) to flog.

6. remmu to pull out; pluck out; to snatch by force; cf. Tu. rumbuni to pluck off.

7. rollu to prattle; n. prattle.

8. rō̃ju to pant; gasp.

r̲-

§1.133. There are only four verbal bases with r̲-, of which only one has a clear etymology fitting it into the formula of vowel contraction:

Type 2: $V^1C^1\text{-}V^2 > C^1\bar{V}^1\text{-}$

r̲ōlu to lament, cry (< *or̲-al) : Te. or̲alu, Ka. or̲al id.; Kuvi oṛhali to groan; cf. Ta. or̲u to afflict.

§1.134. The etymologies of the following forms seem plausible:

Type 1: $V^1C^1\text{-}C^2 > C^1V^1\text{-}C^2C^2\text{-}$

1. r̲uppu/r̲uvvu to fling with force; pelt, etc. (< *ur̲-p-) : Ka. ur̲ubu/ur̲uvu violence of wind; speed, force, rapidity.

2. r̲oppu (Śab. R. roppu) to roar, shout (< *or̲-appu); Ka. r̲oppu to roar; grunt like a hog; Ta. urappu to shout, vociferate; bluster, roar, sound loudly.

§1.135. The one without etymology is: r̲immu to throw, cast, fling; Ta. Ma. er̲i to throw, etc. may be compared, but the difficulty is the disagreement in radical vowels.

## l-

§1.136. Most of the forms with l- belong to the second type of development, i.e., metathesis with vowel contraction.

Type 2: $V^1C^1\text{-}V^2\text{-} > C^1\bar{V}^1\text{-}$

1. lācu to long for, desire, hanker after (< *aḷ-a-) : Ka. aḷipu to hanker after, long for.

2. lāyu to approach (< *aḷ-a); cf. Ka. aḷa to approach; proximity.

3. lē- to be not (< *il-a-; irreg. verb, governs the infinitive of a verb): Ta. il, illai not; Ma. illa; Ka. il, illa; Kui siḍa; Pj. cila (indecl.) not; GoA. sile; Mlt. cile (prohibitive). This item is very important in that it shows that metathesis and vowel contraction took place in Telugu after the loss of *c- in the initial position.

4. loṅgu/lō̃gu to be subdued, become humble; low, etc.; lō̃-baḍu to fall within one's control (lit. to fall within); this form is apparently connected with the words meaning 'inside, within, etc.' arising out of *uḷ-/*oḷ- (§1.223); cf. Ka. oḷavu power, authority.

5. lēcu to wake up, rise (< *el-a-); Klm.(SR) lēs- id. : Ta. ēl to rise, wake up, etc. Many of the earlier writers have connected the Te. form with Ta. Ma. Ka. el̲u to rise, etc.,[72] but this etymology has to be rejected, since PDr. *l̲ does not develop to l in Telugu except in loanwords from Ka. where *l̲ > ḷ; the form in question is clearly not a loanword from Ka. since there is absence of metathesis and vowel contraction in Ka.

§1.137. The rest of the forms, for which etymologies are not available: lā̃gu to pull, drag; lā̃cu to be excited; be roused; loḍupu (Dh. M.)

to stir up; loḷḷu (Dh. M.) to bark (of dogs); lǒḍu to stir with the fingers.

§1.138. From a comparison of this development with the results of our study about i/e and u/o alternation in SDr., we note the following points of relative chronology:

As far as Telugu is concerned, metathesis and vowel-contraction took place after the merger of PDr. *i *u with *e *o respectively in SDr.; consequently, we get the following sequences among contracted forms: *i/*eC-a- > Cē-; *u/*oC-a- > Cō-. Where the derivative vowel is i or u, as in iC-i/u-, we get Cī-; e.g., Te. ḍī(konu) to butt, oppose, attack, hit against (< *iṭ-i/u-); Ta. iṭi to butt; iṭu to hit against; Mlt. iṛmbe to collide. Again, this should have taken place after the loss of *c- in SDr. Since Kui has comparable developments with different vowel sequences in contraction and also without the loss of *c-, these developments presumably started in pre-Kui-Telugu followed by a sudden historical separation of the two languages.

Since this development does not operate in all forms that have the necessary conditions for its operation, we infer that it took place in pre-Telugu in a dialect area probably somewhere in the north where it was contiguous to Kui; forms affected through this process later spread to the other dialects through literature and other means of language-spread.

## CONSONANT GROUPS: INITIAL
### (Metathesis and Vowel Contraction—II)

§1.139. The occurrence of consonant groups in the initial position is not a Common Dravidian characteristic; but, during the prehistoric period Telugu and Kui formed initial consonant-clusters through metathesis attended by vowel contraction in some cases. The only consonant groups admitted in the initial position in Old Telugu through this process are those with r as the second member of the cluster; the first member can be one of the phonemes: k t p g d b s m v, combining with r as kr-, tr-, pr-, and so on. This development is comparable to the one involved in the formation of initial ḍ- r- r̲- l-, except for two differences: viz., while all these consonants can occur initially (through metathesis and vowel contraction), only r occurs as part of initial consonant groups; secondly, in the initial position r- develops out of PDr. *r and *r̲, whereas in consonant clusters *r derives from three PDr. phonemes, *r *ṯ[-r̲-] and *l̲. It has already been stated that *l̲ develops to ḍ- initially (§1.123).

§1.140. Though Telugu and Kui agree in the basic principle of this development, viz., forming initial consonant clusters, they differ greatly both in the scope and in the results of this shift. Kui, for instance, has a wider range of consonants involved in initial-clustering. As the first member of the clusters, Kui has also j and ḍ in addition to k t p g d b s m v (which it has in common with Telugu); as the second member, Kui has also ṛ and l in addition to r, which it shares with Telugu. There is also evidence for an *nṛ- in Proto-Kui which developed to ḍṛ-, ḍr-, or dr- in the language recorded during this century, in the following examples: Ta. Ma. naṭa- to walk; Ka. naḍe, Te. naḍacu : Kui ḍṛāmba a step, threshold; Ta. Ma. narampu a nerve, tendon; Tu. narambu; Te. naramu : Kui ḍrāmbu id. (Burrow, DS V, p. 605); Ta. neruppu fire : Kui drē- n. ignition, a flare; Ta. Ma. nīṭu to grow long; Te. niḍu- adj. long: Kui ḍrīnja to be elongated; adj. lengthened.

§1.141. Many Dravidian scholars have discussed these developments and attempted to define the conditions under which they took place in these two languages. Of these, mention should be made of L. V. Ramaswami Aiyar and Alfred Master, whose articles provide etymologies for a number of forms with initial consonant clusters and analyze the developments involved with some success.[73] L. V. Ramaswami Aiyar and his predecessors observed that accent shifted in these forms from the first syllable (radical syllable) to the second, resulting in the loss of the radical vowel; before this development took place the vowel of the derivative syllable was assimilated in quality to the first.[74] Master rightly rejects the explanation of accent-shift, though he does not clearly set forth the conditions governing vowel length in radical syllables. He calls the process involved in these developments proenthesis.[75] Again, none of the earlier writers has realized that this change took place in Telugu after the merger of PDr. *i and *u with SDr. *e and *o, before a (§§1.268 ff., .277).

Eliminating the doubtful etymologies, one could explain these forms as resulting from metathesis of the last two phonemes of radical syllables, accompanied by contraction of vowels of root and suffix syllables under certain conditions (§1.144). As far as Telugu is concerned we can separate four stages in the whole course of this development from prehistoric times.

§1.142. The first of the pre-metathesis stages (which is pre-SDr. or PDr.). In this stage all forms that later underwent certain changes leading to metathesis had the following sequences: a radical syllable of a CVC-type followed by a derivative syllable of a -V, -VC or -VCC type.

Of the radical CVC-, the initial C could be one of the phonemes k t p c m v;[76] the vowel following the initial C may be any one of the five short vowel phonemes; the final C is either r or r̲ or l̲. We can tabulate this as follows:

| C | V | C |
|---|---|---|
| p | a | r |
| t | i | r̲ |
| k | u | l̲ |
| c | e | |
| m | o | |
| v | | |

With each initial consonant (except v which occurs only before a i e) there are five vowel possibilities and with each vowel there are three final consonant possibilities. This gives us fifteen possible combinations of root syllables with each of the five initial consonants p t k c m, and nine with v, i.e., 75 + 9 = 84 different radical syllables. But the frequency is much less with c-. A few radical syllables are given below for illustration:

| | |
|---|---|
| *par- | Te. par-acu to spread |
| *tir- | Te. tir-ugu to turn, wander |
| *kol̲- | Ta. kol̲-al a tube |
| *cur- | Ta. cur-ukku to shrivel up |
| *ver̲- | Te. ver̲-acu to be afraid; Ta. ver̲-i n. fear |

The derivative suffix syllables following these roots are of three main types with the following sequences:

[V = vowel admissible in that position; L = a sonorant (a non-occlusive including r̲ < *ṯ); N = pre-consonantal nasal; P = voiceless stop]

| | | | | |
|---|---|---|---|---|
| (1) V | = | a, i, u | | |
| (2) V + L | = | a, i, u | + | l, r, r̲, ḷ, l̲, m, n, y, v, (rarely ṇ) |
| (3) V + P | = | a, u | + | k, c, ṭ, t, p |
| + NP | = | a, u | + | nk, nc, ṇṭ, nt, mp |
| + PP | = | a, u | + | kk, cc, ṭṭ, tt, pp |

e.g., V: Ta. (par-)a to spread

VL: Ta. (kal̲-)al to shake, be loose

| | | |
|---|---|---|
| VP: | Ta. (meḻ-)uku | to plaster |
| VNP: | Ta. (miḻ-)uṅku | to swallow |
| VPP: | Ta. (tir-)uppu v.t. | to turn v.t. |

The above statements can be charted as follows:

| | | | |
|---|---|---|---|
| 1 | a i u | | |
| 2 | a i u | L | (u) |
| 3 | a u | P NP PP | u |

A final non-morphemic u occurs optionally after VC (where C is an L) but regularly after all other sequences with a final P.

§1.143. The second stage is the one that immediately preceded the shift. During this period, the vowel u occurring initially in derivative suffixes is lost but the vowel a is maintained. This loss of u is more common when the vowel is followed by nasal-stop or stop-stop sequences (see chart NP or PP).

| E.g., | Stage I | | Stage II |
|---|---|---|---|
| | *miḻ-uṅku | > | *miḻ-ṅgu |
| | *kaḻ-al | > | *kaḻ-al |

Irregular voicing in the suffix stops may be attributed to this stage, i.e., the change of PDr. NP to NB (where B is a corresponding voiced stop); e.g., PDr. *kar-aṅku to be melted > kar-aṅgu id. (Te. Ka.); similarly *-unt > -und, *-ump > -umb, etc.[77]

§1.144. The third stage is the one when the shift actually took place. During this stage, metathesis occurred in both the above types in the last two phonemes of the radical syllables. The result of this is a simple metathesis in the first type and metathesis with vowel contraction in the second type:

| Stage II | | Stage III |
|---|---|---|
| *miḻ-ṅgu | > | *mḻi-ṅgu |
| *kaḻ-al | > | *kḻa-al > *kḻā-l |

We do not know whether there was a stage in pre-Telugu without vowel contraction, as *kḻa-al, or whether both metathesis and vowel-contraction occurred simultaneously. In Kui, at least, there is evidence for the co-occurrence of vowels without hiatus-prevention or contraction.[78] Similarly, it is possible that there was a stage in pre-Telugu also when both the vowels that came together through metathesis remained without contraction; but as there is no useful purpose served descriptively by separating this stage, we can as well put together metathesis and vowel contraction as constituting a single development. In these vowel contractions, the following sequences of long vowels occur:

| Stage II (Vowels uncontracted) | | Stage III (Vowels contracted) |
|---|---|---|
| CaC-a- | > | CCā- |
| i.-i/u- | > | ī- |
| u.-u/i- | > | ū- |
| e.-a- | > | ē- |
| o.-a- | > | ō- |

(Before -a- derivative, e (< *i and *e), and o (<*u and *o), see §§1.268 ff.)

To the third stage itself, we can assign the phonemic changes in the consonants after the shift, viz., the falling together of *-ṯ-[-ṟ-] and *-ḻ- with *-r-.

§1.145. The fourth stage is historical and post-classical in Telugu, during which the second member of all the initial consonant clusters is progressively lost.[79] This cannot be precisely dated, but there is evidence that it started during the Middle Telugu period which begins approximately in the 12th century A.D.[80] In modern spoken Telugu none of the OTe. consonant clusters belonging to this development remains. Of course, consonant clusters in loanwords (i.e., tatsamas) from Skt. and other languages occur in modern usage without simplification.

§1.146. There are seventy-five verbal bases in Telugu which are quoted with initial consonant clusters in dictionaries; at least two-thirds of these have reliable etymologies and can be traced through the different stages of development described above. Following the above analysis the whole corpus of material is divided into two major groups, viz., forms involving simple metathesis and those involving both metathesis and vowel contraction. Both these groups are again subdivided into three classes each, according as the composition of the derivative suffix is VL, VNP, or VP/VPP respectively. The forms, in which P, PP, or NP is replaced by a single voiced stop before metathesis, are treated as Class 4 in Group I and are considered as a separate set for reasons detailed in §1.153.

This classification may be charted as follows:

| Group I (Forms with simple metathesis) | | Group II (Forms with metathesis and vowel contraction) | |
|---|---|---|---|
| Class 1 | with L-suffixes | Class 1 | with L-suffixes |
| Class 2 | with NP-suffixes | Class 2 | with NP-suffixes |
| Class 3 | with P- or PP-suffixes | Class 3 | with P- or PP-suffixes |
| Class 4 | with B-suffixes (i.e., voiced P) | | |

§1.147. In Group II, after long vowels (resulting from contraction), geminates or consonant groups cannot occur since the OTe. pattern of syllabification requires either a short vowel + CC or a long vowel + C. To suit this pattern an early (inscriptional and earlier) Telugu sequence of a long vowel + two consonants has either shortened the long vowel or replaced the two consonants with one, i.e., the final stop, voiced or voiceless. (Cf. loṅgu/lō̃gu both in literature, see §§1.126, .127).[81] Sometimes even the two admissible patterns alternate between themselves, e.g., ḍūyu/ḍuyyu.

Following are a few typical examples of Group I (i.e., forms with simple metathesis in radical syllables):[82]

§1.148. Class 1. With L (sonorant) suffixes:

1. krammu to overspread, extend; overflow (< *kl̲a-m- < *kal̲-m-); Ta. kal̲-umu to grow, be full; overflow; n. denseness (as tuft of hair; Tolk.); Kui garja to spread out, increase; multiply, grow thick and outspreading.

2. krovvu to grow fat; n. fat (< *kl̲o-v- < *kol̲-v-); Kui krōga n. fat; Ka. korvu, korbu, kobbu id.; Ta. Ma. kol̲u n. id.; Klm. Nk. koru; Pj. koṛv- be fat; GoA. koṛvinj n.; Kur. k̲h̲ōr- to flourish, thrive; Ta. kol̲u to flourish, be fat.

3. travvu to dig, root up, etc. (< *tar̲-v-); Kui tāṛa to burrow, dig out; Go. tarr- to root up; taṛ- dig, scratch up (of pigs); Kur. caṛ- (caḍḍ-) to root, root up; pull out, etc.

Other forms of this class include krayyu to join, get in; kriyyu to be reduced; krummu butt with horns; kruyyu to withhold oneself; kruḷḷu to rot; gremmu to lengthen a metal on anvil; treḷḷu to fall, perish; trevvu to be cut off; treyyu id.; bruyyu to perish, be destroyed; some of these have doubtful etymologies.

§1.149. Class 2. With NP (nasal-stop) suffixes:

1. kruṅgu to sink, fall down (< *kur̲-ṅg- < *kur̲-uṅk-); Ka. kurgu/kuggu to be bent, depressed; to decrease; kuggu be humbled; Ta.

kur̲uku to grow short, shrink; be reduced (Tolk.); kur̲u become short; diminish; Kui kṛumba sink beneath; die out; kṛūva id.; Kuvi krūiyali to sink (past krūt-).

2. bruṅgu to sink, be immersed; be hidden (< *ml̲u-ṅg- < *mul̲-ṅg- < *mūl̲-unk-); Ka. mul̲uṅgu, mul̲gu; Tu. murkuni; Ta. mul̲uku to be immersed; mūl̲, mūl̲ku id.; Ma. mul̲uku; Go. murung-; Kui bṛuḍga to sink completely in.

3. mriṅgu to swallow, devour (< *ml̲i-ṅg- < *mil̲-ṅg-); Ta. vil̲uṅku to swallow, gulp down (Kr̲l.); mil̲uṅku/mul̲uṅku id. (colloq.); Ma. mil̲uṅṅuka id.; Klm.(SR) ming- id. (l. w. < Te.).

Following are the remaining forms belonging to this class: krandu to lament, to sound; kruṅku to set (of sun, etc.); truṅgu be crushed, to break, fall; trencu to cut to pieces; snap, tear; mraṅgu fall down, perish; be abated; mrandu[1] die, perish; mrandu[2] to burn; mroṅgu to jump up.

§1.150. Class 3. With P or PP (voiceless stop) suffixes:

1. gruccu/kruccu to pierce, prick, thrust, drive in a pointed instrument (< *kl̲u-c- < *kul̲-c, ultimately from *kul̲-icc-); Kui kuta to prick (thorn); Ka. kul̲i make a hole, dig, etc.; Tu. kurepini bore, drill, etc.; Ta. kul̲i to be hollowed, to form pits; Ma. kul̲ikka to dig a hole.

2. traccu to churn (< *tar-c-); Pj. terip-/terit- to churn (Pj. e < *a, see Burrow and Bhattacharya, The Parji Lg. §2).

3. trokku to tread, trample upon; crush under feet (< *tl̲o-k- < *tol̲-k-); Ka. tul̲i (< *tol̲i) to tread on, crush; Tu. torpuni to kick; tread; Ma. tol̲ikka to kick, etc.

The other forms belonging to this class are: krakku to vomit; kraccu to surround, (with refl. -konu) to spread, overspread; krukku to stuff, cram; grukku to swallow (of liquids), gulp down; groccu to dig; trikku to remain, be left over; trippu v.t. to turn, revolve; pruccu to rot; mrakku to become dim, lustreless; mrokku to bow in respect; vraccu to tear to pieces; srukku to faint, languish; fade, etc.

§1.151. Class 4. With voiced stop suffixes:

1. gruddu to cuff, give a blow (< *gur-d-); Ka. gurdu/guddu; Tu. gudduni; Ta. kur̲r̲u to pound, to butt; kur̲u to pound (in mortar); Ka. gurdu < *kur̲-t- < *kur̲-utt- (-tt- might be originally the causative or preterite morpheme).

2. mraggu to perish; to be obliterated (< *mar-g- < *mal̲-g-); Ka. maggu/mal̲gu grow pale; be destroyed, perish; Tu. margu̥ adj. dead; Ta. mal̲uṅku to be lost (Kalit.); be deprived of glory; Kui mrāṅga to be lost; mrāpka (< *mrākp-) to lose, obliterate; Kuvi(F) mṛakh- to obliterate.

Other forms of this class are as follows: drobbu to push, shove; prabbu to spread; braduku to flourish, live; mruggu to ripen (off the tree); mroggu to bend; sraggu to rot.

§1.152. In all the above classes of forms belonging to Group I, one notices the loss of the vowel beginning the derivative suffixes before metathesis has taken place. This could be seen clearly in forms of Class 4 where Ka. shows the immediately earlier pre-metathesis stage. The comparative evidence shows that the vowel lost is u. In contrast to these forms those in Group II show lengthening of the radical vowel, and the derivative vowel in the unmetathesized stage is a in most of the instances. The only difference between forms of Group I and those of Group II is therefore the occurrence of different vowels in derivative syllables in the Proto-Dravidian stage; obviously this difference in the derivative vowels is the basis for the difference in their respective developments in the metathesized condition.

Class 3 forms differ from the others in that they possess nasal-occlusive suffixes in the pre-metathesis condition which have remained even after the shift, e.g., mri-ṅgu < *miḻ-ṅg-. In Classes 1 and 4, the suffix is more often a single consonant than a geminate, see especially Class 1, items 1 and 2, and Class 4; in Class 2, the original suffix is more likely to be originally a geminate than a single consonant, as in *maḻ-ukku, *moḻ-ukku, etc., whence mrakku, mrokku; cf. Te. trippu v.t. to turn : Ta. tiruppu id.

§1.153. In this Group the basis for separating forms with voiced stop suffixes (Class 4) from the class of forms with voiceless ones is partly structural and partly chronological. Forms like mraggu, mroggu, etc., arise from *maḻ-ugu/*maḻ-gu, moḻugu/moḻgu (< *maḻ-uṅk-, *moḻ-uṅk-), etc. respectively. In Ka. a nasal-stop group of the derivative syllable frequently alternates with a single corresponding voiced stop, e.g., *nk > g; *nt > d; *mp > *b > v; *ṇṭ > ḍ; this has taken place obviously before the loss of the preceding vowel u, which begins the derivative suffixes. Consequently, corresponding to Ta. maḻuṅku, Ka. has maḻugu/maḻgu. The normal pre-Telugu development is the loss of u, but the preservation of the nasal-consonant group as in *maḻ-ṅg-, *muḻ-ṅg-. This sequence can have two possible developments in early Te.: either the pre-nasal ḻ (or r) is lost, or metathesis takes place in the radical syllable; either *maṅgu, *muṅgu or *mraṅgu, *mruṅgu, but not *mar-gu as in Ka. (see §§1.167, .144).

In view of this one can notice that the forms given under Class 4 in Group I fit well into the Ka. development rather than into the Te. one.

So, all forms under this Class may probably be considered as early borrowings into Te. from Ka., and metathesis has taken place in Te. after the borrowing. This assumption is supported by the inscriptional evidence of the 9th and 10th centuries; during this period there are still forms like perggaḍa chief, minister, besides preggada in the inscriptions.[83] Therefore, there is reason to believe that metathesis in forms of this Class is the latest to take place.

§1.154. Whether the suffix consonant is single or double in the unmetathesized stage, it is always double in the metathesized forms. The fact seems to be that in derivative words nowhere do the single and double consonants contrast after r (or r̲ or l̲). Orthographically all consonants (except l) are often written double after r in inscriptions and early manuscripts. This is also true of the Ka. orthographic tradition.[84] It is possible that all these consonants were originally pronounced long in this position; of course, this orthographic tradition continued even till recent years in palm leaf manuscripts. Another plausible explanation for doubling of the suffix consonants in metathesized forms is the pressure o syllable pattern. Among disyllabic forms Te. has two predominant types, CV̄C or CVCC, but not CVC. Following this pattern, since an original *kal̲-m- cannot become *kl̲a-m· /*kra-m-u, the final consonant had to be doubled. This falls in line with the tendency on the part of all the South Dravidian languages to double a Proto-Dravidian base-final consonant, e.g., *kap- to cover, Ta. Ma. Ka. Te. kappu; *kiḷ- to nip off, Ta. kiḷ, kiḷḷu; Te. gillu.

Following are a few typical examples of Group II (i.e., forms with vowel-contraction):

§1.155. Class 1. With L (sonorant) suffixes:

1. krāyu to vomit, to hawk, spit (< *kar̲-ay); Ka. kār̲u id.; Tu. kāruni; Ta. kār̲u to hawk; Ma. kār̲uka to retch, spit; kāruka to hawk, vomit; cf. Te. krakku to vomit (< *kar̲-ukku).

2. krōlcu to sing (of birds), produce noise (of birds); Ka. koral, koraḷ sound, voice; koralcu to call or cry out; Tu. korenjuni to make noise; Ta. kural voice, word; kurai to shout, jubilate; n. noise; Ma. kural n. sound, voice.

Other forms belonging to this category are the following: krālu to move, shake; krēṭu to clear the throat; krōyu to stretch out the tongue, as a serpent; krōlu to drink; trōlu to drive away (cattle, etc.); prēlu to prate; mrālu to faint, languish; mrōyu to sound (musical instruments, etc.); vrāyu to write; vrālu to incline, bend; to perch; vrēyu to strike with a weapon; vrēlu to hang down.

§1.156. There is one case of long ī from *iC-i/u, vrīlu to be disunited (vir-il). Since PDr. *i and *u fell together with *e and *o in SDr. before [-a in most of these contractions, we get only ē and ō in metathesized contracted forms in pre-Telugu. In this particular case long ī can be explained by positing a vowel other than a in the derivative syllable, even though no language shows the form with the derivative -il/-ul.

vrīlu v.i. to be separated, to break off; viriyu to break, fall apart; Ka. biri id.; Tu. biriyuni; Ta. viri id.; Ma. viriyuka to expand; Kui vringa, vrīva to fall to pieces; Pj. viriŋg- to be loosened; Kur. bird- to break through; Brah. birr- to separate out.

In the whole class of forms that underwent metathesis there is hardly one per cent of items with long ī and ū; this proves our theory that the vowel contraction took place mostly in forms with a derivative -a-, and that only three vowels existed in the root syllables, viz., a e o in this environment, due to the above mentioned merger in Proto-South-Dravidian.

§1.157. Class 2. With NP (nasal-stop) suffixes:

1. krā̃gu (= krāṅgu) to be burnt (< *kar-ank-); Ta. karuku to be scorched; Tu. karṅka the state of being burnt; Ta. Ma. Ka. kari to be scorched; cf. Kui kāṛa to be hot.

2. mrō̃gu (= mrōṅgu) v.i. to sound (as a drum, bells, etc.) (< *moḻ-aṅg-); Ka. moḻ-agu; Ta. muḻaṅku; Ma. mulaṅṅuka; Kur. murr- to thunder.

The remaining forms include prā̃ku to spread, creep; prāmu to smear over (< *prāmp- < *par-amp-).

§1.158. Class 3. With P or PP (voiced or voiceless stop) suffixes (see note 77):

1. trāgu to drink (< *tar-agu); Pj. tār- to swallow; KGad. sark- to drink (of oxen, etc.).

2. trōcu to push out; brush aside, etc. (< *tor-ac-); cf. also trōyu id.; Kui trōpa to press forward with fingers (past trōt-); Ta. tura tô drive away, expel; Ma. turattuka id.; Pj. turkip-/turkit- to push; KGad. turus key- to push out.

The other forms of this class are: prōcu to sustain, protect; mrēgu to smear, plaster.

§1.159. It is possible to work out a relative chronology for this development as far as Telugu is concerned. Except Class 4 in Group I, all other classes may be considered to have arisen in the pre-inscriptional period, which we call pre-Telugu. The first undoubted case of metathesis with vowel contraction occurs in a 5th century A.D. inscription, in a village name prālūru, lit. rice-town.[85] Other early inscriptional forms include the following: Group I: kl̲occe, vl̲accina (739 A.D.);[86] pl̲aki (632 A.D.);[87] Group II:[88] pl̲ōlanānḍu (732 A.D.); cēṃbrōlan (930 A.D.); trōva (10th century A.D.); ml̲ēka (7th century A.D.); vrāse (7th century A.D.).

As there are a few forms like krī- below, krēva side (*kil̲-i-, *ker̲-av- respectively), in which we expect the palatalization of *k- before front vowels, it can be concluded that metathesis (and contraction) have taken place before the start of palatalization in pre-Telugu. The development described in the foregoing sections is similar to the one involved in the forms where a medial *r, *r̲, and *l̲ shifted to the initial position. It was already stated that this development took place after the loss of *c- in Proto-South-Dravidian. From these facts it appears that metathesis (and contraction) in Telugu took place after its separation from Proto-South-Dravidian when it was still bound to Kui with the isogloss of this development. The merger of PDr. *i *u with *e *o before a and the loss of PDr. *c- are features common to all SDr. languages and therefore belong to the PSDr. period.

## CONSONANT GROUPS: NON-INITIAL

§1.160. In disyllabic bases of (C)VCCV-type, the consonant group following the radical vowel is frequently either a nasal plus an occlusive, or a geminate stop. The formation of geminates will be treated under a separate head. Among the nasal-stop groups, historically sometimes the nasal is part of the root and sometimes of the suffix. In any case the final stop is always a part of the suffix. In the following forms the preconsonantal nasal is etymologically a part of the ultimate root:

§1.161. -ṅku < *-ṇ-k- and *-m-k-; -ṅgu < *-ṇ-g-

1. jaṅku to be frightened; shake, tremble (< *caṇ-k-); the PDr. base is probably *caṇ-, an alternant of *caḷ- with the usual ḷ/ṇ alternation (§1.83). Ma. caḷuṅṅuka shake, to be frightened; Ka. caḷi to fear; Tu. caḷḷu imbecile, weak; with -ḍ- < *-ḷ-, Te. jaḍiyu id.; Ka. jaḍi to threaten; Tu. jaḍu fright; cf. Ta. caṅku to be dispirited (l. w. < Te.).

2. iṅku to sink, evaporate (< *im-k-), im-uru, iv-uru, ig-uru id.: Ka. iṅgu, imaru, imiru, imuru id.; Tu. iṅguni.

3. vaṅgu to be bent (< *vaṇ-g-); Ta. vaṇaṅku to bend; Kuvi (S) wang- id.; with the ḷ alternant of the root, Ka. baḷku, baḷaṅku, baḷuṅku; Ta. vaḷai to bend; Ma. vaḷayuka id.; Kui palga to bend down, stoop; PDr. *vaḷ-/*vaṇ-.

§1.162. -ncu < *-ṇ-c- and *-n-c-

1. pancu to send (on an errand), to command (< *paṇ-c-); Kui paṇḍa to send; Kuvi (S) panḍ-, pant- id.; Klm. pank- (panak-t-) to send; Nk. pank- id.; Ta. paṇi to order, command; n. a command, etc.; cf. Te. panupu, pampu a commission.

2. incu to be sweet, agreeable; n. sugar cane (< *in-c-); Ka. in sweetness; Tu. impu agreeable; Ta. i<u>n</u>i to be sweet; i<u>n</u>imai sweetness; Ma. iniya sweet.

§1.163. (a) -ṇṭu < *-ṇ-t-

1. aṇṭu v.i. to stick; v.t. to touch (< *aṇ-t-); Ta. Ka. Tu. aṇṭu id.; Klm. anṭ-; Pj. anḍ- attach string to bow; PDr. *aṇ-/*aḷ- : Ka. aṇe to touch; Tu. aṇepuni to come in contact, to paste; Ka. aḷa, aḷ contact, light touch, etc.

2. gaṇṭu to cut, wound; n. a notch, wound (made through an arrow or knife) (< *kaṇ-t-); Ka. kaṇḍi/gaṇḍi, kaṇame a hole, opening; Ta. Ma. kaṇṭi a chop, slash; Klm.(SR) gaṇḍ- to prick. Cf. Te. kanuma a mountain pass; gaṇḍi a hole, opening, aperture; Brah. kanḍ gap, breach, hill pass.

3. kuṇṭu to limp (< *kuṇ-t-); Ka. Tu. kuṇṭu id.; kuṇṭa a cripple; Ka. kuṇi move in a hopping or jumping manner; kuṇmu to bend; Ta. kuṇaku to become bent or crooked; Tu. kōṇṭ- to limp; Klm. kuṇṭ- to limp; Go. kūṭ- id. PDr. base is *kŭṇ-/*kŭḷ-; cf. Ka. kuḷḷu, kuḷir to bend, stoop.

(b) -ṇḍu < *-ṇ-d- and *-n-ṯ- < *-n-t-

1. daṇḍu to collect (taxes, subscriptions), also taṇḍu id. (< *taṇ-d-); PSDr. *taṇ-/*taḷ- : Ta. taṇṭu to collect, taxes, etc.; Ka. taḷe to receive, take; Tu. daṇḍiyuni to put forth; stretch hand to receive anything; cf. Ka. taṇḍa a mass; taṇḍakāṟa one who amasses.

2. eṇḍu to dry up, evaporate (< *en-ṯ- < *el-nt-); Ta. e<u>nr</u>u sun; el sun, sunshine; ellai sunshine; Mlt. eṛye to parch grain; Pj. nendi (NE. nenḍi) sunshine, heat; Go. addi id.

Other forms of this class are: uṇḍu to be (< *uṇ-d-); cuṇḍu to dry up due to heat (< *cuṇ-d-); ceṇḍu to chop off (< *keṇ-d-); niṇḍu to be filled (< *nin-ṯ-); maṇḍu to burn (< *man-ṯ-); meṇḍu to lever up (< *men-ṯ-); vaṇḍu to cook (< *van-ṯ-).

§1.164. The PDr. consonant-group *-nt̲- normally develops to -ṇḍ- in Telugu, but there are several cases of its occurrence as -nd-: -ndu < *-n-t̲- < *n-t-.

1. kandu to be scorched (through heat); to grieve (< *kan-t̲-); here the root is *kan- alternating with *kar̲- (see §1.96); Ta. kan̲r̲u become scorched; Ka. Tu. kandu id.; Te. kanalu to burn; the -r̲- forms: Ka. kar̲e blackness; Ta. kar̲u grow dark, get angry; Ma. kar̲ukka id.; Kui kāṛa to be hot; be distressed.

2. indu to be palatable, sweet (< *in-t-); Ta. in̲i to be sweet, etc.; see s.v. incu (§1.162, 2).

3. cindu to spill; also ciluku id. (< *cin-t-); cinuku to pour, spill; n. a drop; Ta. cintu id.; Ma. cinnuka id.; Ma. cinar̲uka to be spilt, scattered. If the PDr. combination is *-n-t- we do not expect -nt- in Ta. Ma. ? Loans from Te.

Similarly kundu to decrease (< *kun-t-); ondu to get at; reach (< *on-t-).

§1.165. The PDr. sequence *-n-t̲- arises from *-n-t- through the assimilation of t (suffixal) to the preceding alveolar *n [n̲]. The correspondences of this consonant group in the various languages can be divided into four sets:[89]

Set 1. OTa. n̲r̲, Mdn. Ta. nn/ṇṭ (see note 58)
Ma. n̲n̲
Kota, Toda d̲

Set 2. Te. ṇḍ, less often nd
KGad., Oll. nḍ (material insufficient)
Pj. nd/nḍ (dialectally)

Set 3. Ka., Koḍagu, Go., Klm., Nk., Kur., Mlt. nd

Set 4. Kui (Kuvi) nj/s
Tulu nj

For Set 1, *nt̲ can be reconstructed even from the evidence available during the historical period. Since Kui, Tu. j represents a phoneme other than PDr. *t or *ṭ (which remain in these languages), we have to reconstruct *nt̲ as the earlier stage of nj, with the equation PDr. *t̲ in the environment *n] = Kui, Tu. j. PDr. *t̲ appears also as j in these languages even intervocalically (see §1.103).

In Set 2, Telugu preserved *nt̲ as nr̲ in the early inscriptions as opposed to ṇḍ. The shift *nt̲ > ṇḍ was well on the way by the 9th century and orthographic replacement of nr̲ by ṇḍ appears from the 10th century onwards. From the discussion of the forms in §1.164 it has been suggested that there might be a dialect in OTe. in which d instead of ḍ replaced ṯ. Pj. shows a dialectal variation in the representation of PDr. *nṯ, i.e., nḍ and nd. The material for Ollari and KGad. is too scanty to set forth the correspondence clearly; but the available material shows nḍ < *nṯ. On the whole, this set also, as Emeneau rightly supposed, lends to a reconstruction *nṯ as its immediately earlier stage.

In Set 3, though the usual development is the substitution of a dental stop for *ṯ, there is evidence for different developments within Go. and Kur., e.g., Go. uṇḍī one (Mandla dial. LSI IV, p. 480), undī one (Betul, Trench, p. 48);[90] Kur. oṇṭā; cf. Ta. oṉṟu, Te. oṇḍu, PDr. *onṯ-. Following the developments in the other groups, it is justifiable enough to suppose that, even in these languages, there has been a two-fold treatment of PDr. *ṯ on a dialectal basis.

All these facts indicate that PDr. *nṯ remained in all Dr. languages for a long time after the separation of the individual groups and it was only a few centuries ago that the merger of *ṯ either with a dental or a retroflex stop started to operate independently in each sub-group. This period may be different in each group, but in any case it cannot be earlier than the 7th or 8th century A.D.

§1.166. Telugu has four nasal phonemes: /m n ṇ ṅ/ (see §§1.1, .4). Before velar stops PDr. *m and *ṇ fell together with /ṅ/. Before the palatal stop *ṇ fell together with /n/. Before the alveolar stop *n [n̲] fell together with /ṇ/ in some cases and remained in others.

§1.167. In the forms so far quoted the pre-consonantal nasal is shown to be a part of the bases. In the following forms the nasal-occlusive groups occurring after the radical vowels proceed from similar groups of PDr. belonging only to the suffix morphemes; in many of these cases the PDr. roots had a final y, r, or ḻ which was either lost before the following nasal-occlusive suffix or assimilated to the nasal element. Following are a few typical examples:

1. boṅku to lie; n. a lie (< *poy-ṅk-); Ka. Tu. boṅku id.; Ta. Ma. pokkam falsehood (-kk- by assimilation from *-ṅk-) : Ta. poy to lie; Ma. poykka id.; Ka. pusi (< *poci) id.; GoM. bus- to lie.

2. pancu to divide, separate (< *pay-nc-); Ka. pañcu, Tu. hañcuni id.; Ka. pasu to divide, cut, etc.; Kui pahpa to apportion; papka to split (< *pak-p-); Ta. Ma. paṅku a portion; Go. pai-; Pj. payp-/payt-; Klm. Nk. payk- id.

3. poncu to waylay (< *por$^{u}$nc-); Ka. poñcu id.; Kui pōrpa to lie in wait; Kuvi (F) pōrh- id.

4. paṇḍu to ripen; a fruit (< *paḻ-nd-; -ṇ < *-ḻn-); Tu. parndu fruit; parnduni be ripe, mature; Pj. Klm. panḍ- to ripen; Pj. paṟñ-

id.; Oll. paṛŋ(g)- to become ripe; Go. paṇḍ-; Kur. paṇḍuār- to take a yellow-red appearance; the PDr. root *pal̲- occurs in Ta. pal̲u to ripen, etc.

5. pondu to obtain (< *por$^{u}$nd- < *porunt-); Ka. pordu, poddu id.; Tu. porduni; Ta. poruntu; Ma. porunnuka; cf. Te. porayu to obtain, etc.; Ka. pore id.

6. pambu to spread, increase (< *parmp-); Ka. parbu, pabbu id.; Tu. pabbuni id.; Ta. pampu to spread like water; parampu to extend, spread; see Te. paracu to spread; Ka. pare, etc.

Other forms of this class include the following: kaṅgu to grow dark, be scorched (< *kar-ṅg-); mincu to exceed (< *miy-nc-); muncu to immerse, plunge (< *mul̲$^{u}$nc-); anju to fear (? < *ay-nc-); piṇḍu to squeeze, express; milk (< *pil̲-nd-); vandu to be dejected, grieve (< *var-nd-); cendu to reach, to be obtained (< *cer$^{u}$nd-).

§1.168. It is probable that some of the bases contain simply PDr. roots in final vowels, of (C)V- type; for instance: koṅku to fear; koncu to hesitate, shrink, fear (original meaning *to bend, to shrink); Ka. koṅku to be bent (< *ko-ṅk-/-nc-); Kui kōga become small, decrease; kōpka (< *kōk-p-) tr.; Mlt. qonq- to bend, indent; cf. Ma. kō-ccuka to be contracted; Ma. koṅki a hook.

Similarly poṅgu to swell, overflow; many languages show *po- as the radical syllable and *-ṅk- as the suffix. On the whole, forms of this type are few.

§1.169. In a considerable number of forms the boundary between the root and the suffix cannot be marked due to lack of reliable etymologies, i.e., whether the boundary is after the nasal (as in Group I) or before the nasal (as in Group II); such are: naṅgu to speak with nasalization, twang; ceṅgu to lose a game; deṅgu to cohabit; toṅgu to bend, stoop; ginju to writhe, struggle to escape; gunju to draw, pull; gentu to jump.

§1.170. The foregoing discussion about the formation of nasal-stop groups in disyllabic verbal bases in Telugu may be summed up in the following chart:

| Te. | PSDr. | PDr. |
|---|---|---|
| -ṅk- | -ṅk- | -nk-<br>-ṇ-k-<br>-m-k- |
| -ṅg- | -ṅk- / -ṅg- | -nk-<br>-ṇ-k-<br>-m-k- |

| Te. | PSDr. | PDr. |
|---|---|---|
| -nc- | -nc- | -nc-<br>-n-c-<br>-ṇ-c-<br>(-m-c-) |
| -ṇṭ- | -ṇṭ- | -ṇ-t- |
| -ṇḍ- | -ṇṭ-/-ṇḍ-<br>-nṯ-/-nḏ- | -ṇ-t-<br>-n-t-/-n-ṯ- |
| -nd- | -nt-/-nd-<br>-nṯ-/-nḏ- | -nt-<br>-n-t-/-n-ṯ- |
| -m-/-mm-<br>-mp-<br>-mb- | -mp-/-mb- | -mp-<br>-n-p-<br>(-m-p-) |

No examples are available in verbs for the sequences in brackets, though they are theoretically possible.

§1.171. In the verbal bases of the (C/CC)V̄̆C-type where the radical syllable consists of a long vowel followed by a nasal-plosive group, the nasal is, as a rule, lost in Telugu, whether it is a part of the base or of the suffix. Such finals are no longer consonant-groups as far as Te. is concerned. This loss was marked in ancient Te. by the symbol called ardhānusvāramu or arasunna which was only an orthographic remnant of a lost nasal phoneme; it is phonetically a zero after long vowels and a free alternant of the respective nasal phoneme after short vowels in the second syllable (see §1.4); a few examples of this are quoted:

(V̄̃)ku < *-ṅk-: tā̃ku to touch (< *tāṅk-); sā̃ku to nourish; gī̃ku to claw, scratch; pī̃ku to pull out; gō̃ku to scratch; sō̃ku to touch; be infected.

(V̄̃)gu < *-ṅg-: ā̃gu to be stopped; kā̃gu to be boiled; sā̃gu v. i. to lengthen; mā̃gu to ripen (off the tree); vā̃gu to prattle; nī̃gu/ī̃gu to be rid of; to discard; vī̃gu[1] to swell, be proud; vī̃gu[2] to disappear; ū̃gu to swing; tū̃gu id.; mū̃gu to swarm (flies, etc.); ē̃gu to go; vē̃gu to grow hot; be roasted; tō̃gu to bathe.

(V̄̃)cu (< *-nc-): ē̃cu to inflict; vē̃cu to trouble; to make suffer, burn; saī̃cu to tolerate.

(< *-n-c-): nō̃cu to observe a religious ceremony (< *nōn-c-).

(V̄̃)ḍu (< *-n-d-): ū̃ḍu to be planted, fixed

(< *-ṇ-d-): vē̃ḍu to request; tō̃ḍu to bale out

(V̄̃)tu (< *-nt-): pā̃tu to plant

(V̄̃)du (< *-nd-): ī̃du to swim; cī̃du to sneeze;

(< *-n-d̲-): ū̃du to plant, fix.

§1.172. PDr. *-mp- becomes -m- in Te. after long vowels in disyllabic bases and after short vowels in trisyllabic bases; in disyllabic bases it develops to -mm- after a short vowel (-mm- will be treated under the history of geminates). Examples for:

(a). *-mp- > Te. -m- in disyllabic bases with radical long vowel:

ōmu to preserve, cherish (< *ō-mp-); Ta. ōmpu to protect, guard; cherish, nourish; Ma. ōmpuka id.; Ka. ōvu id. (-v- < *-mp-); ō to be fond of; to love; be pleased with.

(b). In the following case Te. -mu (< *-mp- < *-n-p-):

nōmu to observe religious ceremony, see nō̃cu id. (< *nōn-p-); Ka. nōn to perform any austerity, etc.; nōmpi any religious obligation; Tu. nōmbuni to fast; nōmbu fast; penance; Ta. nōn̲pu ceremonial fasting; Ma. nōnpu penance, fasting.

The formation of nasal-occlusive groups in this class of forms is similar to the one described under short-vowelled bases (§§1.161-.170).

## DOUBLE CONSONANTS

§1.173. Excluding the forms with gemination resulting from metathesis of the radical phonemes, there are 135 verbal bases with double consonants following the radical vowel. All these forms are disyllabic and of type (C)VCCV where the final vowel is always u and has no morphological value. Etymologically, this type can be traced to two main PDr. types, viz., a root + derivative suffix type with the etymological boundary occurring as (C)VC-C- or as (C)V-CC-; or a root type or primary type without any derivative suffix following, i.e., CVC-. In the first case gemination is due to the assimilation of a root-final sonorant with the following stop; or the assimilation of the preconsonantal nasal with the following stop. In the case of the second type, i.e., CVC-, the final consonant occurs doubled in the daughter languages regularly if it is a stop and optionally if it is a sonorant; in OTe. this consonant is always doubled whether a stop or a sonorant. In certain forms CV-CC- is from an older *CV(C)-CC-, in which the root-final consonant is either lost or assimilated to the following consonant sequence (see also §1.167).

The consonants that are geminated are voiceless stops k c ṭ t p; voiced stops g j ḍ d b; nasals n m; trill ṟ; lateral l ḷ; semivowel v. It is useful to deal with each set separately; however, ṭṭ and ḍḍ are separated from the stop series since they involve certain special developments.

Type CVC-C- where the root-final consonant is r, ṟ, ḻ, or rarely l or ḷ:

Voiceless stop geminates: kk, cc, tt, pp.

§1.174. kk:

(a). kk < *r-k

cekku to pare, shave (wood); n. rind (< *cer-k- < *ker-k-); Ta. cirai shave, cut with sickle; Ma. cirekka; Ka. kere, kiri; Klm. kerk- to shave; Mlt. qĕr- shave; qĕrtr- be shaved; (it is probably better to separate the meaning to scrape, which many of these forms have, from to shave, because To. Tu. Pj. and Kur. forms have only the meaning to scrape, while Mlt. has two separate words qerc- to scrape; qĕr- to shave [see Kolami 379]). Burrow derives Te. cekku from *ketku, comparing it with Ka. kettu, and Ta. cetukku (DS III, p. 124), but the assimilation of two such stops is nowhere else met with in Dravidian. The form, if it remained in Te., would be *ceduku; cf. Te. piduku to squeeze : Ta. pitukku id.

(b). kk < *l-k

cikku to be caught, to be stuck; be obtained (< *cil-k-); Ka. sikku, silku, siluku id.; Tu. sikkuni, silkuni; Ta. Ma. cikku; Go. hilk- to be entangled; Kui sinḍu (pl. siṭka) trap for small birds.

(c). kk < *ḷ-k

nikku to become erect; to strut; n. erectness, pride (< *niḷ-k- < *niḷ-uku/-ukku); Ka. niḷku stretch oneself full, rise up; nilku, niluku to stretch one's self; to stand on tip-toes; Ka. Ta. nīḷ intr. to extend, stretch out; Ma. nīḷuka grow long.

(d). kk < *ṟ-k

mukku to strain (at stool), grunt in pain, labor, etc. (< *muṟ-k-); Ta. muṟku inarticulate sound; mukku to strain as a woman in travail; Ma. mukkuka/mikkuka to strain, grunt; murukku n. writhing agony; muṟukkuka to be constipated; Ka. mukkare, mukkiṟi to strain, etc.; Tu. mukkuruni to growl.

§1.175. cc:

cc < *r-c

viccu to blossom; to open, burst; v.t. to open, loosen; adj. open; cf. viriyu to blossom, viri flower; virugu to be broken; vrīlu to crack, open up; Ka. biccu, bircu to loosen, open a bundle; biri to burst open; Tu. biccuni id.; biriyuni burst open; birkè a crack; Ta. viri intr. to expand, open; v.t. expand, untie (past viritt-); Ma. viriyuka v.i. id.; also the Central and North Dravidian languages have forms with radical final r.

§1.176. tt:

tt < *l̲-t

There is only one form of this type: mettu to apply, plaster with mud, cement, etc. n. plastering (< *mel̲-t-); cf. Ta. mel̲uku; Te. mrēgu to smear, anoint; Ta. Ka. Tu. Pj. Klm. Nk. mett- to plaster; Kui mrāṇḍa smear; plastering; Go. maṟhutt- to paint cattle for Pola or Diwali festival; Brah. mir- to plaster.

§1.177. pp:

(a). pp < *r-p

mappu to train, familiarize; marupu to accustom, habituate (Classical); macc-ika (< *mar-c-) tameness; marāgu/marugu to be accustomed to; to long for (governs accusative); Ta. maruvu be accustomed to (Kr̲ḷ.); Ma. maruvuka to become familiar; maruṅṅuka be tamed, accustomed; marukkuka to tame; Ka. maccu/marcu attachment; maccika approbation; Tu. marcuni to be tamed; Kui mrāspa to train; Kuvi (S) mrih- to teach, tame; Brah. marrī tame.

(b). pp < *r̲-p

neppu to push out (< *ner̲-p-); see neṭṭu id. Ta. ner̲i to press firmly with hand (Kalit.); Tu. nesipuni to press down; Kui nasa to push; Go. natt- to dash down; Kur. nepp- seize with a sweeping movement; Mlt. nerm- to clear away anything which adheres.

§1.178. Other forms that come under this development are as follows:

kk < *r-k: ukku to be stuffy (of warm weather); cekku to insert; cokku to be intoxicated; vikku to be loosened.

kk < *r̲-k: cikku to become thin (of persons); nokku to indent, pinch.

kk < *l-k: mekku to gobble up.

kk < *l̲-k: ekku to climb, rise up.

cc < *r-c: accu to be in debt; to pay (tax, etc.); uccu to pass through; penetrate; coccu to enter; maccu to attract.

pp < *r-p: vippu to untie, open a bundle.

§1.179. From the above lists one notes that more consonants are involved in assimilation with k than with the other stops. Before assimilation r̲ fell together with r in consonant clusters, where it is the first member; this change was recognized even in the earliest classical dialect, e.g., mār̲u to be changed: mār-cu to change (trans.) (< *mār̲-c-).

Burrow worked out a relative chronology for the formation of double consonants in Telugu through assimilation. GoA. serpum, Go. sarpum shoe, sandal corresponds to Ta. ceruppu, Te. ceppu, and Ka. kerpu. Since Go. preserves *k- before front vowels also, we expect *kerpum instead of serpum. So this form must have been borrowed by Go. from the neighboring Telugu "before the r was assimilated to the following p, that is, before the beginning of the literary period in Telugu" (DS III, p. 129). As far as Telugu is concerned the assimilation of root-final r, etc. with a following voiceless stop is much earlier than that with a voiced stop; of these the latter change can be assigned to the historical period, whereas the former change belongs even to pre-inscriptional Te., which is pre-Telugu.

Voiced stop geminates: gg, jj, dd, bb.

§1.180. The formation of the voiced stop geminates is on the same line as that of voiceless ones except for the fact that the former belongs to the historical period in Telugu. In the early Telugu inscriptions of the 7th and 8th centuries, one still finds forms where the root final r, ṟ, or ḻ has not yet been assimilated to the following voiced stop, e.g., mardavalli (name of a village; 660 A.D.; IA X, p. 244, line 17), now known as maddāli (< *madda-valli); perdaḷ the grown-up ones (6th century A.D.; IA XIII, p. 187, line 27; Classical: peddalu); irbbali name of village (663 A.D.; EI XVIII, p. 3, lines 20-21). By the 9th century assimilation has already taken place as attested by the following forms: pedda trōva lit. a big way (name of a village; EI V, No. 27; pedda < *perda- big); iggalūru (9th century) lit. a town of two stones (ir + kal + ūru; EI I, p. 350).

§1.181. gg:

(a). gg < *r-g

kaggu to turn black (through heat, smoking) (< *kar-g-); cf. krãgu to be charred (< *kar-aṅgu); Ka. kargu id.; n. blackness; kari to be charred; Tu. kar̤ṅka state of being burnt; Ta. karuku to be scorched; grow dim; kari id.; Ma. kariyuka id.; Kui kāṟa sun's heat; Klm.(SR) kārī black; Go. karw- to burn; Kur. kharai derangement characterized by great heat in the bowels (happens during the hot season); Brah. khar adj. angry.

(b). gg < *ḻ-g

taggu to be diminished, reduced; become low, shrink, abate (< *taḻ-g-); Ka. taggu, targu, taḻgu id.; tāḻ being low; Tu. tagguni to be humble; Ta. tāḻ to be lowered, sink, decrease; tr. to degrade, lower; Ma. tāḻuka intr. id.; ? Kui jãmba to subside; Kuvi (S) tah- to tranquilize;

Kur. tār- to fell; tarkā quiet, calm; Brah. tamm- (? < *tarm-) to get down, to fall.

(c). gg < *r̲-g

nuggu be powdered; to powder; n. powder; see nūr̲u to crush; nur̲ucu id.; Ka. nuggu, nurgu, nur̲ugu to reduce to small bits or powder; Ta. nur̲uṅku be powdered; n. grit (Tolk.); nur̲ukku to powder; Ma. nur̲uṅṅuka to be broken; Go. nōr- id.; Ta. Ma. Ka. Te. nūr̲u to powder.

§1.182. jj:

jj < *r-j

There is only one case with -jj among verbs, which is quoted from a single text, viz., a work of the 13th century which is regarded as representative of Classical Telugu: vijju intr. to spread (UH.), probably from *vir-j-, see Part II viriyu to spread; cf. Ka. bijje greatness.

§1.183. dd:

(a). dd < *r-d

diddu to correct, to rectify (< *tir-d-); Ka. tiddu/tirdu id.; Tu. tidduni id.; Ta. tiruttu to rectify (PN); tiruntu to be corrected; Ma. tiruttuka tr. to correct, etc.

(b). dd < *l̲-d

addu to dye, dip in a liquid; to press (< *al̲-d-); Ka. addu, ardu, al̲du (also ajju) to immerse, dye; Tu. arduni to wash (of clothes); Ta. al̲untu be pressed, immersed; al̲uttu to press down; al̲uṅku be pressed; Go. āhch- to massage.

§1.184. bb:

bb < *r̲-b

ubbu to swell, be bloated; grow proud; n. swelling (< *ur̲-b- < *ur̲$^{u}$b-); Ka. ubbu, urbu id., ur̲ubu to rise; Tu. ubbuni id.; Ta. ur̲uttu to increase; ur̲ai to swell; Ma. ur̲uppu a large bag; Te. Ta. ūr̲u to swell; Brah. hūring- id.

§1.185. The rest of the forms of this type are:

gg < *r-g-: naggu to be dimpled, be reduced to powder;

gg < *l̲-g: iggu to pull down; to bend back;

dd < *l̲-d: biddu to die;

bb < *r-b: ? abbu to be obtained, to accrue.

From a study of the foregoing forms of the *CVC-C(V) type, one notes that assimilation between the root-final C (r, r̲, l̲, etc.) and the following stop is brought about in most cases by the weakening of an u-vowel originally occurring between these two elements. Strong support for this development comes from Ta. and Ma. forms where a similar reduction of the 'union-vowel' does not take place as in Te. Ka. and Tu.; the other languages for which we have no earlier records show a complete reduction of this vowel whatever its quality. This is in contrast with the Middle Ka. and Te. development of the loss of only an u (or sometimes an i) vowel but not usually of the vowel a. This has partly been discussed in earlier sections (§1.143). An alternation of light (short-vowelled) and heavy bases in closed syllables points to an intermediate stage with vowel derivatives, e.g., Te. addu to immerse; Ka. al̲-du id.; Ta. Ma. Ka. āl̲- to sink; the intermediate stage is obviously preserved in Ta. al̲-untu to be immersed; al̲-uttu to immerse. This form with the weakening of u yields *al̲-tt- > Ka. al̲-d- with voicing of t after a sonorant. This development will be treated in detail under the history of vowel-length in the Telugu verbs (see §§1.289 ff.).

Type CV-CC(V):

§1.186. Final CC in forms of this type proceeds from PDr. sequences of nasal + stop in which the nasal has been assimilated to the following stop in PDr. itself, viz., kk < ṅk, cc < nc, ṭṭ < ṇṭ, tt < nt, mm < mp.[91] The root syllable is originally a CV or a (C)VC-sequence in which the final consonant is either lost or assimilated to the following suffix groups (§§1.167, .168). Examples are not available for all of these sequences in Te. verbs but the following will suffice to establish the developments.

§1.187. kk:

kk < *ṅk or *(y)-ṅk

pokku to blister, n. a blister; Tu. pokke a blister; Ta. pokku to be blistered; Ma. pokkuḷ a blister : Tu. poṅku n. a kind of boil or sore; cf. Te. poṅgu to boil over; Ka. poṅgu id.; Ta. poṅku to boil up, bubble up; Ma. poṅṅuka id. Similarly, pikku to draw back, colloq. to withhold money, be miserly (< *pi-ṅk-); vikku to swell with pride, to stretch out (< *viy-kk- < *viy-ṅk-).

§1.188. cc:

There are actually no examples for cc < *nc in Telugu verbs though it is theoretically possible as seen from the assimilation of other similar groups, kk < ṅk, etc. As far as Telugu is concerned, cc in disyllabic bases is traceable to two sources in PSDr., i.e., cc or ytt; in the latter case tt is probably an original past tense or causative morpheme, which is palatalized following the root-final y.

cc < *cc or *y-cc

naccu to be agreeable; to trust, like; see nammu to trust (< *namb- < *nay-mb-); Ka. naccu/neccu to desire, trust; Ta. nac̆cu to desire, love; n. desire, liking; nacai to love (Kr̲l̲.); naya to long for, rejoice (PN); nay-am joy, excellence; Te. nayamu better, excellent; Ka. Tu. naya tenderness; nase/nasi adj. soft, gentle. It is obvious that the PDr. base here is *nac-/*nay-. It is also possible that the Te. form is directly from PDr. *nac- rather than *nay-cc-, but since Ka. shows an alternation of a/e in naccu/neccu, this can be explained only by positing an earlier nay-/ney- (see §§1.25, .283).

The other forms of this category are iccu to give (< *iy-tt-); caccu to die (< *cay-tt-); teccu to bring (< *tey-tt-); meccu to praise (< *mey-cc- or *mey-tt-); noccu to suffer (< *noy-tt-); veccu to be heated (< *vey-cc- or *vey-tt-);[92] of these -cc is more widely distributed in SDr. in the cases of meccu to praise and veccu to be heated. Both possibilities can be assumed here, i.e., a PSDr. cc-suffix or y-tt, since Ancient Ta. and Ka. also show the development of palatalization of t in the company of y (§2.45).

§1.189. There are two difficult forms, puccu to send and vaccu to come, for which the sources of cc in Telugu cannot be definitely reconstructed:

1. puccu to send (allomorph pu- in pu-ttencu/-ttēru to send away); cf. Ta. puku to reach, enter, go; pukku to put in (Tolk.), cause to enter; Ma. puku to enter; pukkuka put in; Ka. pogu, pugu to enter (past pokk-); Tu. pogguni to enter; Ta. Ma. Te. pō- to go; Ka. pōgu; Tu. pōpini id. SDr. pō- arises from PSDr. *pok-a- with the loss of -k- and vowel contraction. However, the remaining forms show two original vowels, both u and o. Ka. Tu. might have re-formed the root-vowel in pogu on the analogy of pō-. Ta. Ma. and Te. point to an original *pu- as the PDr. base with different stop derivatives (§1.247, 2).

2. vaccu to come (rā- in certain forms). With the help of the exhaustive study of this verb by Emeneau in all Dravidian languages, one can set up two PDr. stems *va-/*vā- with r as a detachable suffix (see Lg. 21, pp. 187, 199, 200). The Te. form can arise either from *var-c- with assimilation of r-c > cc or from vā-cc- where cc is a derivative suffix (op. cit., p. 208).

§1.190. mm:

mm < *mb < *mp or *y-mp

1. nammu to believe, trust (< *na-mb- < *nay-mp-); Ta. Ma. nampu to believe, etc.; to like, long for; Ka. nambu id.; Tu. nambuni,

nammuni id.; Kuvi (S) namm-, Kuvi (F) nām- id. (see s. v. naccu §1.188).

2. vemmu to be heated, scorched (< *ve-mb- < *vey-mp-); Ta. vempu to be very hot (Kalit.); veppu, veppam heat; Ma. vempuka vb. id.; Ka. bem heat; Tu. boppu moderate heat; PDr. base vey-/vē- < *vec-. Similarly ommu to be suited (to one's constitution) < *o-mb-; pammu/ pambu to spread < pa-mb- < *par-mb-.

<u>Type (C)VCC-:</u>

§1.191. The reconstructed PDr. light bases of the (C)V̆C- type have for their final any one of the stop (P) or sonorant (L) consonants except ñ (i.e., stops: p t ṯ ṭ c k; sonorants: ḻ m n ṇ r l ḷ v y).[93] In unbound root morphemes, if the final consonant is a stop, all SDr. languages generally show it as a double consonant, e.g., *kap- : Ta. Ma. Ka. Te. kappu to overspread. If it is a sonorant, it optionally turns up as a geminate in SDr.; in this respect not all the literary languages are uniform, e.g., PDr. *cel- to go: Ta. Ma. cel-; Ka. sal, sallu; Tu. salluni; Te. cellu. As stated already, a final C of PDr. roots always occurs as a geminate in Te. whether it is a stop or sonorant.[94] One can with equal justification reconstruct for PDr. either a single consonant or geminate in this position. Since there is no contrast between single and double consonants in the root-final position, whichever solution we choose is only a matter of descriptive facility and pattern uniformity. When the stops become medial by the addition of vowel derivative suffixes, they are always single and are probably voiced in PSDr., for instance, Te. Ta. vittu, Ka. bittu to sow : Ta. vitai seed; Ma. vitekka to sow; Te. veda sowing; Ka. bede id.; here it makes no difference whether one reconstructs *vitt- or *vit- for PDr., if one makes a statement that a final C is CC finally and C medially.

In the following the final geminate in Telugu proceeds from a PDr. root-final stop, i.e., Te. (C)VPPu < PDr. *(C)VP-:

§1.192. kk:

kk < *k

vekku to hiccough, sob; be choked in sobbing; n. vekkili hiccough; Ta. vikku to hiccough (Kalit.); vekkuḷ n. id. (Kṟḷ.); Ma. vikku/mikku to stammer; Ka. bikku sob, pant, hiccough; Tu. bikkuni id.; bikku n.; Kui veka to cough; Kur. bekkh- be choked; to cough; weep; Mlt. beq- id.; the i/e alternation seems to arise from the fact that the base is primarily onomatopoetic. Similarly bokku to gobble up (< *mok-), see Part II.

§1.193. cc:

cc < *c

giccu to pinch; Kui kisa id.; Kuvi (S) kich- to nip; Kuvi (F) kic- to pinch; Go. kisk- id.; kicc- pick green leaves for salads; Pj. kicc- pluck (with finger); kīk- pinch (< *kiyk-); Oll. kisk- pinch; Klm. kism- id.; KGad. kicc- to pluck; Kur. kicc- break into very small pieces with fingers; Brah. kishk- to pluck. All these forms undoubtedly indicate a radical final *-c in PDr., but a comparison with SDr. forms like Te. gillu to shread, pinch, Ta. kiḷḷu, Tu. kiṇk-, etc. indicates that *ki- is probably the ultimate root with ḷ and c as different suffixes. Even in that case it should be admitted that c has been incorporated into the root morpheme in PDr. itself and does not behave any differently from an original base final stop (see §2.149).

There are actually very few survivals of PDr. root-final c as cc in the daughter languages due to its shift to y or l̲ in this position (§§1.112 ff.). Of all languages, Ka. shows evidence for many of these base final c forms, cf. Te. ēyu to throw : Ka. esu/isu (past ecc-); so also Ka. pasu to divide (past pacc-); most languages show the weakened form here, viz., pay- (s.v. pagulu, Part II; also see Kittel, Kannada Grammar, §164, 9, 10).

1.194. tt:

tt < *t

1. pittu to fart; Kui Kur. Mlt. pīt- id.; Go. pitt-. If this is to be connected with the Common Dravidian *pī- excrement, or *pi- behind, we have again another case of incorporated suffix in PDr. itself.

2. vittu to sow seed; n. seed; veda sowing; Ta. bittu to sow; n. seed; bede n. id.; Tu. bittuni/buttuni v.; Kui vīti adj. scattered; Kuvi vīcanga semen; Go. wīt- to sow; GoM. witt-; Kur. biṛā seedling; Mlt. bīcī seed (> Skt. l. w. bīja-, see Burrow, TPS 1946, p. 10).

Another case of tt < *t is Te. mottu to strike, blow.

§1.195. ṭṭ:

PDr. *t̲ fell together with *ṭ in pre-Telugu. PDr. *t̲ has a trill type allophone in the intervocalic position which is represented by r̲ in SDr. and by r or ṛ in Central and North Dravidian. Radical finally and in consonant clusters *t̲ preserves its occlusive character in most of the languages and has fallen together with either a dental stop /t/ or a retroflex stop /ṭ/. In Te. it fell together with ṭ in geminates, but seems to have two developments in the consonant group PDr. *nt̲, viz., nd, ṇḍ (that is to say that *t̲ fell together with dentals in some forms and with retroflexes in others, probably in different dialects originally; a parallel development occurs in Pj. also, see §§1.165 ff.).

(a). ṭṭ < *ṭ

kiṭṭu to approach; Ta. Ma. Ka. kiṭṭu id.; Ta. kiṭai to meet; Ma. kiṭayuka to knock against; Mlt. kiṭe near, nigh.

(b). ṭṭ < *ṯ

vaṭṭu to dry up; vaṟugu n. that which is dried (dry pickle); Ta. Ma. vaṟṟu id.; Ka. battu; Tu. baccuni; Go. vatt-; Klm.(E) vat- to parch; Pj. vett-; Oll. vaṭ- wither, dry; Kur. batt-; Mlt. bat-; Brah. bārr- to become dry; cf. Ta. vaṟu dry up, grow lean; Ma. vaṟuka; Ka. baṟe; Kui vasa to wither.

Out of twenty-four verbal bases ending in ṭṭ in Telugu, sixteen belong to ṭṭ < *ṭ, and six to ṭṭ < *ṯ; two forms have doubtful etymologies.

§1.196. There is a small class of verbs with tt < *ṯ, which is obviously borrowed (even during the classical period) from Ka., where this is the normal development:

ettu to raise, lift; Ka. ettu; Tu. ettuni; Ta. ēṟṟu (tr. of ēṟu to rise) to lift up; Ma. ēṟṟuka to raise, etc.; Go. att- to take into one's lap; since a long vowel does not occur before a geminate in Te. and Ka. it is shortened. Other forms of this type are: attu, hattu to be attached; united : Ka. hattu, pattu; ottu to press, squeeze.

§1.197. pp:

pp < *p

1. tappu to miss, fail; err; to violate; break; n. error; Ka. Tu. Ta. Ma. tappu to err, fail, miss; Kuvi tappu to misdo; cf. Ta. tavaṟu to slip; n. failure; taval id.

2. ceppu to say, speak (< *kep-); Ta. Ma. ceppu id.; Ma. ceppi ear; Tu. keppu deafness; Kur. keb- (kepp-) to lecture; to scold; cf. Ta. Ma. Te. cevi ear; Ka. kivi (< *kevi); Tu. kebi; Klm. kev; Go. kawī; GoM. kev; Brah. khaf. Ma. ceppi ear and the weakening of *-p- to -v- in most of the languages is the evidence in this case to set up a PDr. *p. Burrow derives the Ma. form from *kerpi (DS IV, p. 335), but we do not expect the weakening of a secondary pp in the intervocalic position in Dravidian; on the other hand Ma. does not belong to the group of languages that assimilate *rp to pp. The meaning connection is natural enough in Dravidian when one compares sets like *kay hand and *key to do, which originally derive from the same base.

Other forms of this type are kappu to overspread; cappu to chew, masticate; uppu to boil; guppu to shoot (of arrows, etc.); oppu to consent; suit.

Type *(C)VC- with final sonorants.

I.e., Te. (C)VLLu < PDr. *(C)VL-:

§1.198. nn:

nn < *ṇ

pannu to plan; make ready; cf. pani work; Ta. Ma. Ka. paṇṇu to make, accomplish, scheme; paṇi a work; Tu. paṇipuni to give a shape.

So also ennu to count; *minnu to speak (minnaka silently); tannu to beat.

§1.199. mm:

mm < *m

ammu to sell (Classical) : Go. mamm- to sell (? m- intrusive. Cf. Go. āmōṭ we : māmēṭ id., Seoni Dial.; LSI, IV, p. 514). The verb form does not occur in any other language, but one can suspect its occurrence in the following complex forms: Te. Ka. Tu. aṅgaḍi a shop; Ta. aṅkāṭi bazaar (Cilap.); Ma. aṅṅāṭi; these forms may be analyzed as *am-kăṭi meaning a selling place; see Te. kaḍa a place; Ka. kaḍe, gaḍi id. Ta. amai to effect, accomplish, may be compared with the verb.

So also tummu to sneeze (< *tum-).

§1.200. ll:

(a). ll < *ḷ; *ḷ fell together with l in Telugu during the preliterary period.

allu to plait, weave; Ka. aḷḷu id.; aḷa joining; Tu. aḷḷ-āvuni to mix; Ta. aḷḷu to be dense; thickly interwoven; to knit; Kui alpa to weave together; Pj. alṭ- to be twined around; Klm.(SR) all-; Kuvi (S) all- id.

Similarly gillu to nip off, pinch; callu to sprinkle; nollu to suck fingers (of a child); bollu to lie.

(b). ll < *l:

cellu to suit, fit; to be valid as coin; to pass as time; cf. canu to suit, to go; Ta. Ma. cel to pass as time; to occur, suit, etc.; Ka. cellu; Tu. salluni be proper; Kota. cal- be acceptable to; be suitable; To. sal- to belong to (Emeneau, BSOAS XV, p. 109).

§1.201. There are no genuine cases of PDr. root-final *v which occurs as vv in SDr.

The two main types of the formation of geminates in Telugu so far described are not peculiar to Telugu; especially type CV-CC(V) and type (C)VCC- (§§1.183 ff., .191 ff.) occur in all the SDr. languages. There are a few more forms with double consonants in which none of the above types seems to have been involved. These forms are peculiar to Telugu and are not shared by the other literary languages. They have therefore to be explained from the internal evidence of Telugu itself. They are forms with vv and r̲r̲:

(a). vv:

1. navvu to laugh; n. laughing; nagu to laugh; Ta. naku, nakai to laugh (past of naku is nakk-); Ma. nakekka id.; Ka. nagu, nage id.; Tu. nakali ridicule; nakeruni to titter; cf. Brah. mak̲h̲- id.

2. tivvu to pull, etc.; tiviyu id.; Ka. tivi to take off or remove staff with which dogs are led to chase; tege (pp. tekku) to pull out; Tu. teguni to take; deppuni to pull out; Ta. tikai to be taken aback; tekku to take; Ma. tikayuka to be finished; Klm. tivv- to take off, remove.

Since the past stem shows kk in Ta. etc. for naku, one can take *k as original with v developed from it intervocalically (see §1.111c). In Telugu vv seems to have resulted from the contraction of final -iyu leading to the gemination of the preceding consonant to conform to the canonical pattern of syllables: So we have tiv-iyu : tivvu, probably through *tivyu; on the analogy of this, navvu < *nav-iyu.[95]

(b). r̲r̲:[96] Te. r̲r̲ < *r̲-y < *r̲-iy

There are only three forms: bir̲r̲u to become stiff; kur̲r̲u to cry, yell (Brown); jur̲r̲u to sip with noise. These forms do not occur in the early classics and the standard works of later times. In Mdn. Te. jur̲r̲u occurs with a long trilled [r̲] which is the allophone of /r/ in gemination.

1. jur̲r̲u to sip with noise; Ta. ur̲i id.; Ka. sur̲i; Ka. juru juru n.; Kur. sur$^{u}$p- drink with a noisy sucking of the lips.

2. kur̲r̲u to cry, groan; cf. Te. gur̲aka snoring; Ma. kur̲ummuka to snore, onom.

3. bir̲r̲u to become stiff; n. hardness; Ka. bir̲uvu, bir̲ubu n. id.; Tu. biru strong; Ta. ver̲i stand stiff; vir̲ai grow stiff; Ma. vir̲akka id.

§1.202. There are two forms with ḍḍ whose origin is difficult. Following the general trend of phonological developments in SDr., ḍḍ can arise from the assimilation of a base-final ṭ with a following voiced dental suffix d, i.e., *ṭ + d > *ḍ-d > *ḍ-ḍ, because assimilation across morpheme-boundaries shows both regressive and progressive operation. See Ta. *ḷ-t > *ṭ-t > ṭṭ, nīḷ to be long, past stem nīṭṭ- < *nīḷ-t-.

1. aḍḍu to obstruct (< *aṭ-d-), aḍḍamu obstruction; Ta. aṭai to block; be obstructed; Ma. aṭekka to obstruct; Ka. aḍe to be shut up; aḍḍi an obstacle; Tu. aḍḍa n. id.; aḍepuni to shut up; Brah. aḍ kann- to stop.

2. oḍḍu to place, put; to lay (< *oṭ-d-); Ka. oḍḍu to place; to oppose; Tu. oḍḍuni to hold, stretch out as the hand; Ta. oṭṭu to stake; advance, challenge; Ta. Ma. oṭṭam wager.

## CONSONANTS: FINAL

§1.203. As far as OTe. is concerned, the traditional grammarians have taken the vowel-ending allomorphs of the verbal bases as the basic alternants. They formulated a rule that all verbs have -u before consonants, and correspondingly zero before vowels. The only exception to this is a small class of verbs in -nu which has the consonant-final allomorphs before the past tense suffix -t-, e.g., aṇ-ṭ- from anu to say, kaṇ-ṭ- from kanu to see, etc.; before the present tense -c-, both the vowel- and consonantal-ending allomorphs occur in free variation, e.g., anu-c-/an-c- saying. For Mdn. Te. it is more convenient to take the forms with final consonants as the basic alternants. This topic will be dealt with in detail in Chapter III.

§1.204. All PDr. final consonants become medial in Te. because of the occurrence of a final -u in all cases. In phonological developments $C^1$ in PDr. $\check{V}\underline{C}^1$ does not behave any differently from that in $V\underline{C}^1VC(V)$. The only exception to this is the treatment of PDr. *y.

§1.205. PDr. *y develops to Te. g in the intervocalic position in trisyllabic bases, e.g., nog-ulu < PDr. *noy-ul-, pagulu < *pay-ul- (see §1.79). In disyllabic or trisyllabic forms with final -u, PDr. y remains in Telugu. Again, PDr. *c remains in most cases in Te. and Ka. intervocalically in trisyllabic bases (e.g., osagu, masagu, kasaru, etc. See §§1.112 ff.), but in the final position *c fell together with y in most of the languages including Telugu; this latter development is therefore attributed to PDr. itself.

§1.206. In the following case PDr. root-final *y (from earlier *c or *y) remains in Telugu.

(a). Te. y < PDr. *y

kāyu to shine (of sun); Ka. kāy/kāyu to grow hot; Tu. kāyuni; Ta. Ma. kāy; Kui kāg- to warm oneself (by fire); kāspa to make hot; Klm.(E) kāŋg-; Pj. kā-p- to heat; Oll. kay-p- id.; Kur. khāy- become dry; khaid- make dry; Mlt. qāy- become dry; qeyr- be hot, boiled.

Similarly, īyu to give, kūyu to cry, cēyu to do, tēyu to be worn, mēyu to eat, graze, vēyu to throw, kōyu to cut, nōyu to suffer.

(b). Te. y < PDr. *y (< **c)

māyu to become dimmed, dirty; to vanish; perish, be destroyed; Ka. māyu id.; Tu. māyuni be extinguished; be put out; Ta. māy v.i. to hide, vanish (Maturai.); become lustreless (Kalit.); to perish (Kr̲ḷ.); tr. to hide (Maturai.); destroy, kill; Ma. māyuka wear away, grow dim; vanish; etc. : Ka. māsu, māju, masuḷ grow dim, fade; decrease; Tu. māsuni/mājuni id.; Ta. mācu spot, stain; defect (Kr̲ḷ.), dust, darkness (Kr̲ḷ.); macaṅku become dim, dull; Ma. mācu n. filth; māccu dirt; Kui māsi n. filth, dirt, stain; Kuvi (F) maci dirt (of body); Mlt. masge to vanish or disappear (as person); Brah. mashā<u>kh</u> scarred; in addition to these, there are also forms pointing to PDr. *l̲ which is also evidence for an original *c/*l̲ in PDr. from which *y developed secondarily. It is likely that only *mā- is the ultimate root here, with *c/*l̲ (> y) as derivative suffixes. In any case these elements were incorporated into the root in the PDr. stage itself.

Other items of this type are ēyu to throw; pūyu to smear; pōyu to pour, etc.

§1.207. In Telugu all bases in final -y(u) have alternate stems in final -s(u) before front vowel suffixes, e.g., kāyu to shine, kās-i having shone; kalayu to meet; kalas-i having met. s in these cases is not to be mistaken as representing the PDr. *c from which y developed. It will be shown in the following chapter that it was originally a part of the past tense morpheme (preserved in Gondi), which was wrongly divided and assigned to the base rather than the inflexional suffix; for instance the course of changes is somewhat as follows: *kāy-ci > *kāci/kāsi > Te. kās-i. The original y stem occurs in non-past forms; similarly *kalay-ci > *kala-ci/si > Te. kalas-i. Loss of y before stops is a Common Dravidian development. These developments are treated in detail in the following chapter under the history of suffixes -y, -ay, and -iy (§§2.43 ff.).

## VOWELS: INITIAL

§1.208. Generally most of the Dravidian languages agree in showing the same vowel-qualities in radical syllables. The percentage of agreement is highest if the vowel in question is traceable to a PDr. long vowel and occurs long in all the languages compared. Many of the qualitative variations in vowels among the Dravidian languages are explainable through the influence of the neighboring consonants. In some languages at least, certain of the consonants which are responsible for a vowel-alternation were later lost and are discoverable only through comparative evidence, for instance, the loss of *c- in SDr. after producing an ă/ĕ alternation (§§1.232, .240) and the loss of *y- in Ta. Ma., etc., with an original ā/ē merger in the following vowel (§1.216).

§1.209. Initial vowels in some of the Telugu verbal bases go back to PDr. *CV- sequences, of which the consonants are lost in Telugu. One such consonant is *c- which has suffered a sporadic loss in all the SDr. languages; other consonants of this type include *y- and *ñ-. A few cases of movable *n- have also been attested for many of the Dravidian languages, of which it is not certain whether it is a case of loss or of intrusive growth. During the historic period, Telugu has lost an h- in words borrowed from Ka. with h- < *p-. Each of these developments will be treated in detail in the following sections.

§1.210. It is now established that PSDr. has a tendency to lose a PDr. *c-, which is maintained in Central and North Dravidian with the exception of Brahui.[97] This phoneme indifferently appears as an affricate [č-] in some and as a sibilant [s-] in others; sometimes the same language has both the phonetic variants in different dialects. In certain Gondi dialects and in Kuvi and Brahui, it develops to h-; in Brahui, this h- alternates with zero without any apparent connection with the change that took place in SDr. in the prehistoric period. In the following Te. verbal bases with initial vowels a PDr. *c- preceding the vowels is lost as shown by comparative evidence:

> aḍalu to grieve; amayu, amaru to be suitable, etc.; arugu to approach; aluku to be afraid; iccu to give; imuḍu to be contained; iluku to be sprained; uduku to wash; umiyu to spit; ū̃gu to swing; ūṟu[1] to well up, as water; ūṟu[2] to grow fat; ēdu to be reduced; ēṟu to sift; oliyu, olucu to flay.

§1.211. Many of these items appear in the lists of Meile and Burrow and the rest that belong here are the following:

1. arugu to approach; Ka. arugu vicinity; Tu. aru brim, edge; Ta. aruku to approach; n. nearness, edge; arukal n. id.; Ma. aruvu n. id. Ka. sār to approach; sāraṇ nearness; sāre id.; Ta. cār to approach; Ma. cāruka id.; cf. Ka. sari to go, etc.

2. aluku to fear, tremble; Ka. aḷuku; aḷku id.; Tu. aḷkuni id.; Ta. aḷukku, Ma. aḷukkuka id. : Ma. caḷuṅṅuka to shake, to be frightened; Ka. caḷi to be deprived of one's power; Tu. caḷḷụ weak, timid.

3. imuḍu to be contained, to remain within; imuḍ-cu to thrust in a given space; Ta. imiḻ to restrain; imai to shrink, diminish : cimiḻ to tie, bind.

4. uduku to wash, to drub (as a garment) : Klm. Nk. sutk- to wash (clothes); Go. suhk- id.; cf. Kui jōga wash clothes, n. washing.

5. umiyu to spit (< *uv-iyu < *cuv-iyu < *cup-iyu); Ka. ugi (< *uv-i); ugu̲l (< *uv-u̲l) id.; Tu. ubbiyuni; Ta. umi, umiḻ (< *uv-i, *uv-iḻ); Ma. umiyuka id. : Kui sūpa to spit; Kuvi hūpali id. (see Burrow, DS IV, BSOAS, XI, p. 339).

6. ūṟu[1] to well up, as water; to ooze; uṟiyu id.; Ka. ūṟu, oṟe; Tu. ūjuni, ūsuni; Ta. ūṟu, uṟu, uṟai; Ma. ūṟu, uṟakka; Brah. hūring-/ūring- to swell up : Kui sūga a spring; Go. sū-sū a little wet (Meile, op. cit., p. 86).

7. ūṟu[2] to grow fat, etc.; uṟuvu bigness; excess; Ka. uṟuvu n. id.; uṟe abundantly; urvu to rise, swell; Tu. urubu n. increase; Ta. ūṟu, uṟuttu to increase; uṟai greatness : Kui sūja to be fat, thick.

§1.212. ā and ē alternate after an initial *c in a number of cases. The following two forms with ē- in Telugu, corresponding to ā- of the other languages, have lost an original initial *c, as attested by comparison:

1. ēdu v.i. to diminish, to cease, fail, etc. (*ēy-du < *cēy-tu); Ta. āy to be diminished, reduced; āyvu diminution : Ta. cāy to be emaciated; cāyvu deficiency; cf. Klm. sāy to leave; Pj. cāy to leave, abandon.

2. ēṟu to select, pick up; sift, etc.; Ka. ēṟ id. : Tu. sāruni to sift; Kur. cāj- to choose, pick out the best; Kuruk͟h -j- is the reflex of a SDr. [*-ṟ-] (see DS IV, p. 346), and hence the early SDr. form would be *cāṟ-; cf. Ta. tāṟṟu to winnow, sift (loc.), perhaps a transitive of an obsolete [*tāṟu] < [*cāṟu].

§1.213. Burrow has further discovered that the PDr. *c- also develops to t- in many of the Dravidian languages, including the SDr., where it alternatively tends to be lost. On this basis he assumes an original *c-, wherever there is an alternation between t- and zero even though no language preserves the phoneme in question.[98] This principle can be tested with forms for which a c-/s- is still preserved in some language or other, e.g., Te. aluku to fear : talāku, talaru id. : Ma. caḷuṅṅu, Tu. caḷḷu̥ weak, etc.; Te. umiyu to spit (< *uviyu < *cuviyu) : Ta. Kur. Mlt. tup- id. : Kui sūpa id. There are only two verbs, for which an original c- has to be assumed on the basis of t-/zero-alternation in the initial position:

1. aḍalu to grieve; aḍaru to burn; Ta. aḻal to burn; n. heat; Ma. aḻaluka to burn from grief; Ka. aḻal id.; Tu. arluni to burn : Ta. taḻal to glow; Pj. taṛi to be hot; PDr. base *caḻ-, suffix -al; (Te. -ḍ- develops out of an older ḻ in the intervocalic position).

2. ū̃gu to swing, rock; ū̃cu, ū̃pu, v.t.; Ta. ūṅku; Klm. ūng-, ūp-; Go. ūng-; Kuvi ūmp- to swing : Te. tū̃gu to swing, to doze; Ka. tūgu id.; tuṅku to dangle, wave; Tu. tūṅkuni; Ta. tūṅku to swing, sleep; tuñcu to doze, droop; Ma. tuṅṅuka; Kuvi tūṅg- to sway; Kuvi (F) tūkh- to swing; Kuvi (S) tūnai to throb. Item 2 has certain complications, in that Central Dravidian shows forms without c-/s-. It is likely that they borrowed these forms from the neighboring Telugu at a very early period, since they all preserve the preconsonantal nasal, which Telugu had lost sometime before the commencement of literature. This assumption is justified by the Central Dravidian forms meaning 'sleep,' where an ancient s- is preserved: Kui sunja to sleep; Kuvi hunjali id.; Go. (Seoni dial.) suñcī sleeping; GoM. hunj-, v.; cf. Ta. tuñcu to sleep; therefore, ū̃gu/tū̃gu < *cuy-nk-. The base *cuy- underlies Ta. uyal, tuyal to swing, wave, shake; Te. Tu. tūlu to reel, etc. (see DS VI, p. 142).

§1.214. Meile and Burrow are agreed on the point that this change has affected the SDr. alone; but it is curious that Kuru<u>kh</u> and Malto too seem to attest the occurrence of this development to a limited extent. The evidence includes a part of the material under discussion:[99]

1. aluku to fear : Kur. Mlt. elc- (§1.211, 2).

2. ūṟu[2] to be bloated : Kur. uskār- to swell up slightly (§1.211, 7).

§1.215. Similar to the loss of *c- in SDr. is the loss of *y- in all the Dravidian languages except Ancient Tamil.[100] Previous to this loss there was a merger of ā and ē after *y- in PDr. itself in one direction or another. This vowel is always ā in Ta. both before and after the loss of *y-; in Ma. and Ka. it is ā; in Te. and the languages of the Central Dravidian group it is frequently ē.

§1.216. The loss of PDr. *y- is postulated for the following forms on the basis of Te. ē : Ta. Ma. Ka. ā:

1. ēḍcu to weep, lament; Ta. Ma. Ka. aḻu; Tu. arpini; To. oṛ- (oṛy-); āḍ- (Pope); Pj. aṛ-; KGad. āḍ-; cf. Kui ṛīva id.

2. ēlu to rule, govern : Ta. Ma. Ka. Tu. āḷ id.

In many similar sets with ā/ē alternation Ancient Tamil generally preserves the PDr. *y-. In the above two cases, since Ta. does not show *yā- forms, the loss of *y- should have started before the period of early literary works in Ta. and was carried through the Middle Tamil period, i.e., 10th century or so.

§1.217. A third set consists of three verbs with the loss of an h-; these forms are obviously early borrowings from Ka., where h- < *p- was already widely prevalent in the prose writings of the 10th century A.D.[101]

1. attu to hold, to be held; to stick to (< *hattu < *pattu); Ka. hattu, pattu id.; Tu. hattuni, pattuni; Ta. pa<u>rr</u>u; Ma. pa<u>rr</u>uka; the regular Te. form is paṭṭu.

2. uṭṭu to be born; to occur (< *huṭṭu < *puṭṭu); cf. Te. puṭṭu id.; Ka. uṭṭu, huṭṭu, puṭṭu; Tu. puṭṭuni; n. uṭṭu, huṭṭu, puṭṭu birth; Go. puṭṭ- vb.

3. eccu to increase; n. increase (< heccu < peccu < *percu); Te. peccu increase; Ka. eccu, heccu, peccu, percu to grow, etc.; Tu. heccuni, percuni id.; PSDr. pĕr- big.

Of these attu appears in Bhr. II of the 13th century, while the other forms appear in later works. However, the loss of h- in early Ka. loanwords in Te. may have been independent of a parallel development in Ka., which began in the 13th century to a restricted degree but became established in the speech of lower classes later. Forms like hattu and heccu appear again in relatively later writings in Te., which are probably reintroductions from Ka.

§1.218. Burrow has mentioned an n-movable in the initial position occurring in many Dravidian languages without definite features of distribution.[102] On the contrary, there are many cases in which a PDr. *n- is preserved in all the languages, e.g., the word *ney oil. The only explanation that could be given at this stage of our knowledge for the presence or absence of this movable *n- is that it is due to wrong division of words at syntactic junctures, as Eng. an apron < a napron.

§1.219. In the following forms Telugu alone shows the forms without n- side by side with those with n-; therefore *n- may be considered original here, with loss in Telugu due to wrong division of words at junctures:

1. āḍu/nāḍu v.i. to pierce into, to be fixed, as an arrow, etc. (Bhr.); Te. nāṭu to fix, be fixed; Ka. nāṭu; Ta. Ma. nāṭṭu to fix, plant.

2. ī̃gu/nī̃gu to be rid of (sins, etc.); tr. remove, discharge a debt; Ka. nīgu to quit, abandon; Ta. nīṅku; Ma. nīṅṅuka id.

3. īlugu/nīlugu to be fully stretched out, as the body; (metaphorically) to die (Bhr.); Ta. Ma. Ka. nīḷ- to be extended; Ka. niḷuku, niluku, nilku id.; Tu. nīcuni to extend.

4. ulumu/nulumu to rub over the eyelids after sleep (Bhg.), to twist; Te. nulumu to twist, rub together; Ka. nuli to wring, twist; Kui nōlba id.; Kur. nō̃ẽnā id.

5. egayu/negayu to fly, rise up; Ka. nege; Tu. negiyuni, negipuni; Ta. niva- id.; Ma. nikakka; Klm. negay- to jump.

6. ovvu/novvu to be spoiled, to grieve (Bhg.); cf. novvu pain; PDr. stem noy-/no- (v.s.v. noccu, nogulu, Part II).

§1.220. There are two more forms with vowel-initials, for which doublets in n- do not occur in the usage of Telugu, whether classical or modern:

1. ī̃du to swim; Ka. īju, īsu; Tu. ījuni, besides nīduni; Ta. nīntu, nīncu; nīccu, n.; Ma. nīntuka; Klm. īnd-.

2. usumu to rub, scour; cleanse, anoint; also usugu id.; Go. usūm- to wipe, clean with a cloth; Kuvi ūss- to anoint; ūsp- to plaster; Klm. usm- to wipe, apply : Mlt. nusg- to rub, clean.

Of these, the first word ī̃du to swim seems to connect itself with a large group of Dravidian forms with a similar movable n- meaning water, arising from the stems nīr/īr, of which nī-/ī- are the ultimate roots. In the case of the second word it is uncertain as to which, viz., us- or nus-, is original, but the absence of n- in the majority of languages is a point in favor of considering it intrusive in Malto.

§1.221. As stated earlier, many cases of divergence in radical vowels among the various Dravidian languages can be explained in terms of the immediate phonemic environments, i.e., certain neighboring consonants which are responsible for alternations in radical vowels. There still remain a few cases of disagreement in radical vowels among the languages which are difficult to explain in the present state of our knowledge of Dravidian. We have to consider such cases of disagreement on two levels: those occurring among the literary languages, and those occurring between the literary and the non-literary languages. The later are numerous and difficult to explain due to the lack of their earlier records.

Generally the degree of agreement in radical vowels among the literary languages is high. Many cases of divergence among these languages can be resolved through internal reconstruction carried out with the help of their earliest literatures; those which cannot be resolved indicate a disagreement of a deeper and more archaic character which should be attributed to the PDr. stage.

In the following cases Telugu and the other literary languages disagree in initial radical vowels.

## a-

§1.222. a-/e-/i-

Te. anu to say, speak, also an- (past aṇṭ-); Ka. anu, annu; Tu. anpini; Nk. yantēr said (boy) (LSI, IV, p. 574); Kur. Mlt. ān- : Ta. eṉ; Ma. ennu; Ka. en, ennu; Pj. en- (end-); Nk. en- (LSI, op. cit.) : Tu. inpini; Kui inba; Go. ind-; Klm. in-; KGad. in- (only as a connective in indirect speech).

u-

§1.223. u-/o-

uḍugu to shrink, to subside; to sink (in water, etc.); v.t. to give up, stop (as a function, etc.); caus. uḍucu; uḍupu id.; Ka. uḍugu to shrink; stop; v.t. to bend, to remove; Kui ḍūmba to be shrunken; ḍūppa to shorten, draw in; cf. ṛumba to sink down, dive; Kur. uṭ- to close, stop, gag; uṭ$^{u}$rnā to be intercepted behind, to set, be hidden; Mlt. uṭe to close, fill up : Te. ḍoṅku to subside, shrink, perish; ḍoṅgu to be hidden; Ka. ḍoṅku to be bent; adj. bent; Tu. ḍoṅku crookedness; oḍiyuni to stoop, bend, etc.; Ta. oṭuṅku to be restrained, to shrink, to be hidden; (Kṟḷ.), to sink, cease, stop, etc.; oṭukku to subjugate, reduce; n. contraction; Ma. oṭuṅṅuka to come to an end, die; oṭukkuka to finish; oṭuvu n. end. Both u and o are widely represented here, almost in one-to-one proportion. A solution to this variation is likely to be found in the Ta. forms oṭuṅku to be hidden (Kṟḷ., 838), oṭukkam a place of concealment. The other connected meanings as recorded by the Ta. lexicon are from the later texts and some of them are actually recent. If this meaning is considered the nucleus, we can trace this series to a base which appears both as uḷ- and oḷ- in Dravidian meaning 'inside' with the following derivatives: Ta. oḷi to be hidden; to hide, conceal; Ma. oḷikka to hide oneself; to conceal, suppress; Ka. uḷi to be hidden; oḷ that is hidden; Te. lō̃gu, loṅgu to be subjugated, restrained (< *ḷōngu, by metathesis from *oḷang-); -lō inside; Kur. ulā inner room (also a post-pos.); Mlt. ule inside, within.

e-

§1.224. e-/a-

1. Te. eydu, eyidu, ēdu to go, reach, obtain; Ta. eytu; Ma. eytuka : Ka. aydu to go, reach, approach; to obtain. Burrow sought to explain the vowel variation in these forms through an original *yayt- which he reconstructed by comparing the Dravidian forms with the Uralian (see DS V, BSOAS XI, p. 602). An alternative explaination is also possible. Here, the common stem is ey-, which along with its variant ē- has a wide range of representation in Dravidian : Te. ē̃gu to go (*ey-ng-); Ta. ēku id.; Tu. eipuni to tread; Kui epa to arrive (past et-); Kuvi (F) ej- to reach, arrive; GoM. ēvd- to arrive; Klm. edg- to drive away; Pj. ēd- to arrive; Kur.-Mlt. ēk- to walk. All these forms point to an original *ey-. The development of Ka. with a-

instead of e- seems to arise from the common interchange of *ay and *ey in Dravidian in prominent syllables (see §§1.283 ff.). The alternative form of this base *ay- underlies many words in SDr.: Ma. ayekka to send away, to let go; to leave; Tu. agapini to depart, agapāvuni to cause to go, send away (< *aya-); Ka. agal to go away from; agalcu to remove; Ta. akal v. i. to leave; akarru to expel; akai (< *a-yay) to send forth; Ma. akaluka to part, etc.; cf. Kur. amb- to send away; set free; give up.

2. Te. erūgu to know; Ka. Ta. ari; Ma. ariyuka; Koḍ. ari; Ko. ar-; To. ary-; cf. Brah. *harr- in harr-if- to ask (-if- is the causal suffix).

First of all the idea of 'knowing' is something abstract, and probably has arisen from some concrete concept as in the case of other similar combinations in Dravidian; for instance, Ta. āy- to search, examine; to sift, separate; select, choose; Ma. äyka to select; Ka. āy to select, cull; Tu. āyuni to select; Kui āska; Go. āc-; Mlt. āde to select, discriminate, judge. In this group 'examining' is obviously a semantic extension of a concrete 'selecting or picking up,' which is the widest represented meaning. Similarly it is possible to derive Te. erūgu : Ta. ari-, etc. from an original *căr-, which has been reconstructed to explain Te. ēru to pick up, choose; Tu. sāruni; Ta. tārru; Kur. cāj- to select, to be fastidious. There are a number of instances where an original initial c- has caused an alternation (actually a merger) of ā/ē irrespective of whether the original vowel was ā or ē (§1.212). Therefore, the formula is PDr. *căr : *cēr (with the loss of *c-) > *ār- : *ēr. *ēr- underlies Te. ēru to choose, pick up; besides erūgu to know, to find out. *ār, the alternate root, underlies Ta. Ma. Ka. ari < *ār-i-; cf. Ka. arasu to inquire after, seek, search; n. inquiry, research; arake, arike searching. The absence of cognates in Central Dravidian and the occurrence of h- in Brahui also lend support to positing a form for PDr. with an initial *c-

§1.225. With these few exceptions Telugu has a fair agreement with the other SDr. languages in the matter of initial vowels; but divergences between Te. (and SDr.) and the non-literary languages of Central and North India are manifold. The reasons for a variety of correspondences in these languages for a given phoneme in SDr. are shrouded in the bygone history of these languages, which can only in part be reconstructed for want of any of their ancient records. All that can be done at present is to list all such correspondences, and present them in sets as far as possible.

§1.226. Te. a- : Kur. Mlt. e-

1. aḍugu to ask; Pj. aḍ, aḍi id. : Kur. eṛ- to call, summon (past eḍḍ-, eṛ-); Mlt. eṛye to speak with fluency.

2. aṇṭu to stick to, to adhere; v.t., to touch, etc.; Ka. aṇṭu; Tu. aṇṭu; Klm. anṭ-; Pj. anḍ- : Kur. eṭṭ- to remain stuck at one place.

3. aluku to sprinkle (as seeds, etc.); Pj. Klm. alk- to sprinkle; Kui lănja, Kuvi (S) lanz- id. : Kur. elkh- to pour liquids out by tilting.

§1.227. Te. ā- : Kui ē-

1. ānu to lean, recline; Ka. ān, ānu; Tu. ānipuni; Kur. ān- to cause pain by being pressed against (gravel, etc.); Mlt. āṉṛeṭe to lean or rest on pillows : Kui (tlau) ĕṇba v.t., to recline (the head upon).

§1.228. Te. i- : Kur. Mlt. e-

1. iḍiyu to be broken, to burst, crack; Ka. iḍi; Tu. iḍe n. a split, chasm; Ta. iṭi id.; Ma. iṭika; Kui iska to butt, collide : Kur. es- to break, crush; esr- to be broken; Mlt. eṭgre to be broken; eṭe to destroy.

2. iṟiyu to be squeezed; iṟuku to be thrust; to thrust into; n. tightness; narrowness; Ka. iṟuku, iṟuṅku to make tight; Tu. iriyuni to squeeze between; Ta. iṟuku to become tight; tr. iṟukku; Ma. iṟukuka, tr. iṟukkuka : Mlt. eṛge to shut, imprison; cf. Kur. eṭṭ- to be too tight; hiṭ$^{i}$ṅg- to remain stuck.

§1.229. Te. u- : Kur. Mlt. ō-; PDr. *ūr- : *ur-V-

1. uriyu v.i. to burn; uralu id.; Ka. uri; Tu. uriyuni; Ta. uru to burn, smart : Kur. ōr- to be heated; impers. to be warm weather; Mlt. ōrtre to make red-hot; ōthre become red-hot (< ōrth-).

2. Te. ŭ̄ṭu to drink completely (as oxen, the water, etc.) (colloq.); Ka. ūḍu to eat; Ka. Tu. ūṭă food; Ta. Ka. Ma. uṇ- to eat or drink; Central Dravidian uṇ-/ūṇ- : Kur. ōn- to eat or drink; Mlt. ōn- to drink.

§1.230. Te. ō- (< *oy-) : Kur. uĩ-

1. Te. ōmu to look after, cherish, love, etc. (< *ōmbu); Ka. ō to be fond of; love; ose to be delighted; ōvu to guard, take care of; Tu. ōmana darling; fondness; Ta. ōmpu; ōmpuka; cf. Mlt. oje to bring forth young, to keep : Kur. uĩ- to let grow; to watch over.

## VOWELS: MEDIAL

§1.231. Stability of the root vowel is the rule in Dravidian, without regard to its position in a word (i.e., initial or medial), but certain consonants, especially c-, *ñ-, y-, and bilabials (p, b, m, and v), preceding these vowels influence their quality in some of the Dravidian languages. At least, the differences in vocalism subsisting among the various South Dravidian languages are to a large extent explainable on this basis.

### -a-

§1.232. a/e alternation following an initial c- in SDr.:

1. Te. canu to go, to pass; to be fit, proper; Ka. sal, sallu to pass; to be proper; be current as money (pp. sandu); Tu. salluni to be fit; sanduni to pass (as time); to be paid; Kui salba to go; Kuvi han- id.; Go. hand- to go; Kur. calr- to go on; be current as coin : Te. cellu to be suitable, proper; to pass as time; to be valid as coin; to be paid, etc.; Ta. cel to go, pass; to be suitable; pass as coin, etc. (past ce<u>nr</u>-); Ma. celka to pass on; to be current; to cost.

2. callu to sprinkle water, etc.; to scatter seeds; Ka. caḷe scattering; caḷeya sprinkling; callu, calaku, calaṅku, calaṅgu id.; Tu. calluni; Ta. callu id. (perh. l. w. from Te.); replacing c- by t-, Ka. taḷi to strew, sprinkle; Tu. talipuni id.; Ta. taḷi to drip; v.t. to sprinkle; Ma. taḷikka id. : Ta. teḷi to strew, scatter, sprinkle as water (Akan.); to sow seeds, etc. (< *ceḷi); Ka. cellu, celaṅku, celaṅgu id.; Tu. celluni.

3. caccu to die (cā- in certain stems); Ka. sā id. (pp. sattu); Tu. saipini; Kui sāva; Kuvi hānai; Go. sai; Pj. cay- (cañ-): Ta. cā id. (past cett-); Ma. cā- id. (pp. cettu).

It is clear from a study of the above that the e forms are less widely represented than the a forms, and that this variation prevails in SDr. only.

Kannada normally represents the PDr. palatal stop or affricate phoneme by s-. Among the c- forms, a few are probably survivals of an ancient stratum like caḷe, caḷeya, etc., but most of the others in c- are clearly loanwords from Telugu. A variation between a and e is found in Kannada mostly after c- but not after s-,[103] which indicates that the alternation is caused by the preceding affricate. Kannada has this variation irrespective of whether the original vowel following c- is a or e, e.g., callu/cellu < *cal-; keda<u>r</u>u/cada<u>r</u>u to be scattered, a loanword from

Te. cedaru (r̲ under the influence of the normal Ka. form kedar̲u). It appears that this development in Ka. is not an ancient one, since it does not affect words belonging to a linguistically earlier stratum like caḷe, caḷeya, caḷi, etc.

According to Tolkāppiyam, the vowel a never occurs after an initial c- (Eḻut. 62). Hence, a PDr. *ca- sequence has three possible developments in OTa., viz., either c- is lost, or c- is replaced by t- (with which either a- or e- can occur), or ca- is changed to ce-. The use of forms with ca- in the initial position has gradually increased in the post-Sangam and Middle Tamil periods. There is no evidence for the confusion of a/e after c- in Mdn. Ta. In Ma. sometimes a alternates with e after c-, as cali/celi, cari/ceri; but this tendency does not characterize the ancient language.

Telugu rarely confuses a and e after c- in the historic period, since the pronunciation of c- before each of these vowels is so different that it keeps their qualities thoroughly distinct. It is [t͜s-] before a and [č-] before e. It is likely that a similar confusion existed in pre-historic Telugu, perhaps before this allophonic distinction between [č-] and [t͜s-] had appeared in the language.

In view of these remarks we can now explain the variation in the above forms. Corresponding to Te. canu, only Ta. and Ma. show an e form in cel-, which is obviously the Ancient Tamil approximation of the PDr. *cal-. Te. cellu might be either an early borrowing from Tamil or a pre-Telugu variant of *cal (later canu), which, however, seems to be less probable. The original form of the second word in the above list is *caḷ-, preserved in OKa. caḷe, caḷeya, etc. Since ca- does not occur in OTa., t- is substituted for c- as in taḷi to sprinkle, etc., but the variant teḷi id. testifies to the existence of an alternative form for *caḷi, viz., *ceḷi, which must have gone out of use long before the Sangam period; otherwise, a/e alternation after t- is abnormal and unexpected. The original quality of the vowel in item 3 is difficult to decide. To judge from Go. sai-, which faithfully preserves the PDr. diphthongs, it might be originally *-ay-. Ka. sāy- and Tu. sai- strengthen this view. With the usual loss of the base final -y before an occlusive in Dravidian, the past stem emerges as *catt- < *cay-tt-, as attested by Ka. pp. sattu, Te. cacc- (where -cc- < *-ytt-); in Te. the past stem is extended to other forms of the verb later on. Ta. past cett- is, therefore, its approximation to an older (i.e., pre-Tamil) *catt-. Attempts have been made to connect this form with Kur. khe- to die; Mlt. keye id., and Brah. kahing id.,[104] but this etymology does not seem to me to carry much conviction.

§1.233. a/e alternation following an original ñ-.

This phenomenon is dealt with at length by T. Burrow in his Dravidian Studies V (BSOAS XI, pp. 603-616). He observed that a and e tend to alternate after an initial ñ- in Kannada and to some extent in Telugu. The following forms among Telugu verbs come under this development.

1. narayu to become grey (of hair); nara greyness; grey; Ka. nara, n. id.; Tu. narevuni, vb.; Ta. narai; Ma. narekka : Te. nerayu id. (dial.); Ka. nere.

2. namalu to chew; Ka. namalu; Tu. nauntuni, naumpuni to chew; nauntu squeezing, pinching, crushing; chewing (Tu. nau- < *navu-); Ta. Ma. namukku to yield to pressure; namai v.i. to wear : Te. nemaru rumination; nemarcu to ruminate; Ka. nemaru, nevaru to chew; Ta. nemir to be crushed; ñemuṅku to be squeezed, pressed; Ma. ñamuṅṅuka to yield to pressure.

In item 1, no language preserves the form with ñ-, but Burrow assumes it to have originally existed, on account of the a/e alternation in Ka. after n-. The following forms, however, seem to possess the same root as those under this item: Ta. nārai white stork; Ma. ñāra heron, also nāra; Tu. nōrè, naraye id. The PDr. base is, therefore, *ñār-/*ñēr- with the suffix *-ay > *ñeray > naray/neray. In item 2, Tulu nauntu provides the semantic link between Te. and Ka. on the one hand and Ta. and Ma. on the other. The original form in this case will be *ñam- or *ñem-, with -ar, -al, -uṅku, etc. as suffixes (§1.26).

§1.234. a with a preceding v- alternates with o- in SDr.; this development is also shared in some degree by Central and North Dravidian.

1. vaḍiyu to ooze; fall in drops; Ta. vaṭi to drip, trickle; Go. waṛ- to leak (of houses) : Te. ōḍu id.; Ka. oḍi to flow gently; Tu. oḍḍuni to flow; cf. Kui ōṛa a channel.

2. vaḍuku to spin : Te. oḍuku id.; Ta. oḻukku to draw out as gold thread; Kui osa to weave, sew; Kur. ōj- to spin; Mlt. ōj- to twist.

3. vaṇḍu to cook; cf. Kui vaja id.; Kuvi (S) wajinai : Kuvi onda rice (cooked); SDr. does not possess reliable correspondents for this, but Ta. vaṟu to be fried, etc. may be compared (note SDr. [-ṟ-] = Kui -j-).

4. vadaru to prate, cry out; Ta. vataṟu id. : Te. odaru id.; Ka. odaru to shout, howl; Ta. utampu to scold, rebuke; utappu id.; cf. Ta. ōtai/ōcai sound, noise, clamor.

5. vadalu (v.i. and tr.) to leave, release, loosen; to become loose; to leave off; adj. loose : Te. udalu v.i. to leave off; udalcu to loosen, release; Ka. odaru to shake off; udir to shake off; udir to fall off, down, etc.; Tu. udaruni, uduruni, udruni to fall, hand down; Ta. utir

to drop off; to be shaken; Ma. utiruka id.; Kur. od°kh- to render less tight, to detach.

6. vanaru to grieve; vanaṭa grief; exact etymologies are wanting but different forms with the same radical element seem to be found in the other sister languages as follows: Ka. baṇagu a wretch (< *vaṇagu) : Ka. oṇagu to dry, emaciate; Tu. voṇugelụ dry, lean; Ta. uṇaṅku to dry, to be emaciated; to be dejected in mind; Ma. uṇaṅṅuka id.; all from *vaṇ-/*oṇ-

7. vasulu to become loose as joints, etc. : Te. osulu id.

8. valacu to agree, like, love; Ka. val id.; Ma. val id. : Te. *ol-, an allomorph of val- in negative stems (§3.31:12); Ka. ol to like, etc.; oli, ole id.; Tu. oliyuni to favor; olapuni to love; Ta. ollu to agree, etc.; Ma. olluka to consent, love; neg. ollā/vallā.

9. valiyu to be reduced; distressed; to pine; Tu. baliyuni id.; Ta. vali to be painful; n. trouble, etc.; Ma. valayuka to be distressed; Kui valga to be thin, emaciated : Te. *oll- in ollābŏvu to be distressed; Ta. olku to grow weak; to pine; olli thinness; Kui oṛpa to pine for; Kur. ol°kh- to lament; Mlt. olg- to cry, weep.

From a study of these forms, it seems difficult, at least in some cases, to decide whether va- or o- represents the original. Many of the modern South Dravidian languages give a bilabial value to the consonant v, which, combined with a low back vowel a, sounds nearly like o, e.g., Te. vaccu to come, colloq. occu. Tolkāppiyam and Nannūl describe v as a labio-dental.[105] We find in the Dravidian languages a number of instances showing an alternation of v/m and v/p initially and medially. PDr. v- regularly becomes b- in Ka. Koḍ. Tu. Kur. Mlt. and Brah. All these factors seem to give a bilabial character to the PDr. v, and the change in the degree of lip contact might have led to the various local differences. Ramaswami Aiyar thinks that the descriptions of the Tamil grammarians might have been prompted by an imitation of the Sanskrit system.[106]

On statistical considerations, an o- is more widely distributed than va-, which latter appears preponderant in one or two items: vaṇḍu, vaḍiyu. In the last case, i.e., valiyu, both va- and o- are equally distributed and it is uncertain as to which is the original. On the whole it appears that, in some forms at least, a free variation between va- and o- was prevalent in the parent speech itself.

§1.235. A variation between a and o following an m- is found in the following case:

magucu to turn, to cause to return; Tu. magapuni to turn over : Ka. magucu, mogucu to turn round; to return; v.t. to turn.

§1.236. Barring the few above exceptions Telugu -a- agrees with the -a- of the other SDr. languages; but Malayalam has one divergent form in -e- corresponding to -a- of the others : Te. paḍu to fall (others have forms in pa-) : Ma. paṭu, peṭu; the latter is not found in early inscriptions. It appears only from the 13th century onwards, and no reason has been shown for this development (see A. C. Sekhar, Evolution of Malayalam, p. 19).

§1.237. There are a few isolated cases of variation between Telugu (and SDr.) and the other languages of the family.

vaṅgu to bend; to be curved; Ka. Tu. Ta. Ma. Kui Kuvi have etymologies with -a- : Kur. beṅk- v. t. to bend, to curve; beṅkō curved, crooked; besides baṅkā curved.

§1.238. Te. -a- : Kui -e-

baruku to scratch with nails; to claw, tear; to scribble; Tu. parṅkuni to scratch with nails : Kui verka to scratch (a part that itches); scratching.

§1.239. There is one difficult case of a/e/i variation after m-, for which a solution is not possible in the present state of our knowledge of Dravidian:

maragu to be addicted; to become familiar; v.t. marapu to familiarize; to train; tame; Ka. marcu, maccu to be very much devoted; Tu. marcuni, Ta. maruvu to be accustomed to; Ma. maraṅṅuka id.; Kui mrāspa to train; Brah. marrī tame, domesticated : Ka. meccu (= marcu); Ma. meraṅṅuka to be tamed, etc. : Kuvi (F) mrīss- to accustom; mrīh- to be accustomed; Mlt. mínje to become familiar.

-ā-

§1.240. Fluctuation between ā and ē is common following c- in South Dravidian:

1. c$\bar{\breve{a}}$du to rub into paste; to triturate; rub on floor, etc.; n. paste; Ta. Ma. cāntu sandal paste; Ta. cāttu to daub, smear; Tu. sādike smearing; cf. Ka. caccu to grind, crush : Te. tēyu to be rubbed; Ka. ceccu to grind; tē, tēy-, tēyu to triturate; Tu. tēpuni; Ta. Ma. tēy-. The Telugu form, stripped of its suffix -ndu, is perhaps nearer the PDr. base, which would be *cāy-, alternatively *cēy-. It is clear that this alternative form is the source of the group tē-/tēy- with the substitution of t- for c-.

2. tāru to move; to approach; tār-konu to meet; tār-asamu proximity; tār-cu to take to; cause to reach; Ka. tār to lead or conduct near; alternatively we have in Telugu, -tēru in (kaḍa)-tēru to be finished; lit. to reach (the end); tr. -tērcu to conduct, as a bound form with identical meaning. Both these forms are traceable to older cār-/cēr- to go, reach, found in Ta. Ma. Ka. and Tu. Telugu has cēru to go, reach; -ē- is more widely represented here than -ā-, since the Central Dravidian forms also show only -ē-.

Telugu does not attest any case of cā-/cē- alternation during the historic period probably on account of the allophonic variation of /c-/ before these vowels. It seems on the whole that a confusion between ā and ē after c- had been at work in certain forms in South Dravidian at a very early stage, certainly before the loss of *c-. The examples of ēdu and ēṟu justify this conclusion (§1.212).

§1.241. Corresponding to Telugu nā- of the following, Kannada shows a variation between na- and ne-, which, according to Burrow, points to an original ñ- in the place of n-:

1. nāku to lick, Ta. Ma. Tu. nakku; Kui Kuvi Klm. Go. nāk- : Ka. nakku/nekku.

2. nāṭu to be planted; to plant; Ta. Ma. naṭu to fix : Ka. naḍu/neḍu to fix firmly; Tu. naḍpini, neḍpini; forms with a long vowel are also found in Ta. etc., viz., Ta. Ma. nāṭṭu; Tu. nāḍuni; Ka. nāṭu to enter into (as a thorn), v.t. to fix.

3. nānu to be soaked; to become wet; Ka. nāndu, nādu to make damp; nān to get wet; Tu. nānuni to be moist; Ta. nāntu id.; Ma. nāntuka; Go. nānd- id.; Mlt. nāṉye cold season; forms with short vowel occur in Ta. naṉai; Ma. nanayuka; Tu. naneyuni : Ka. nane, nene to become moist; Kui nenja to water plants.

In the above cases a peculiarity that attracts one's attention immediately is the existence of forms both in long and short radical vowels, and also the fact that the variation in Ka. occurs only in short vowels. If we consider *ñā- as original in all these forms Ka. should have an alternation in long vowels, viz., nā-/nē-. On the other hand, if we take *ña- as original, vowel-length in the other forms cannot be satisfactorily explained. On that score we cannot separate these two series as etymologically unconnected, since the close phonetic-semantic resemblance does not warrant that. Therefore, there might be more than one reason for this sort of variation between a and e after n-. Vowel harmony and analogy too might have had a role to play, besides others.

§1.242. Te. ā with preceding v- alternates with ō- of other languages; this is similar to the alternation of va-/o- described in an earlier section (§1.234).

1. vāgu to chatter, babble; talk senselessly cf. Ta. vāṅku to abuse : Kui ōga to boast.

2. vārcu to wait, look for; expect : Ta. ōr to examine; Ma. ōrka to expect; to consider; Ka. ōru id.

3. vālu to bend, incline; Ka. vālu, mālu to bend; Tu. māluni to lean; cf. Ta. vaḷai to bend; Ma. vaḷayuka : Ka. ole to bend; ōl- swinging about; Tu. ōleguni to sit, recline; olaṅguni to incline, lean.

§1.243. Following are a few cases of isolated interchange between Te. ā on the one hand, and ē and ō of some of the non-literary languages, on the other.

(a). Te. -ā- : Go. -ē-, Kui Pj. -ō-

kācu to guard, protect; to tend cattle, etc.; Ka. kā- to guard; Tu. kāpuni; Ta. kā; Ma. kākkuka; Klm.(SR) kaipeng to watch; Kur. k͟hāp- id.; Brah. k͟hwāf- to make to graze : Go. kēp to guard, watch, esp. crops; Kui kōpa to tend cattle, to herd; Pj. kōp-/kōt- id.

(b). Te. -ā- : Kui -ō-, -ē-

1. sā̃ku to rear, bring up; Ka. sāku id.; Tu. sāṅkuni; Ta. tāṅku; Ma. tāṅṅuka : Kui jōṅga to hatch; take under the wings; to serve out food.

2. rācu to rub, grind; smear; Ka. are to grind; ari id.; Ta. arai; Klm. rāka to rub teeth; Kui rāga to be rubbed; rāpka to wear out (by friction); Kuvi (F) rāc- to clean; cf. Go. arī-t- to drag along the ground : Kui rēsa to rub, chafe; n. rubbing.

## -i- and -ī-

§1.244. Whether initially or medially, i and ī seem to be the most stable of Dravidian vowels in radical syllables. In South Dravidian there is only one difficult case of i/e alternation, for which an explanation is not found: Te. tiviyu, tigiyu to pull, draw, attract; take; to be withdrawn, as an army; to subside, as a tide; also tivvu, tīyu id; Klm. tivv- to pull, drag : Ka. tege to draw towards oneself; take off; pull; to be taken away, diminish; Tu. deppuni to take, receive; pull out, remove; Ta. tekku to take, receive; tikai to subside; Ma. tikayuka to be finished.

§1.245. Corresponding to -i- of Telugu, some languages have -u- after a bilabial consonant. This development is more common in Tu. than in others.[107]

1. piḍucu to squeeze, wring out; Ka. piḻi; Ta. piḻi; Ma. piḻiyuka : Tu. purecuni, pureñcuni; purñcuni to squeeze as a lemon.

2. piṇḍu to wring, to milk; Ka. piṇḍu; Tu. piṇḍi what is squeezed : Tu. punṭuni to wring, press; Naiki pustum drawing (LSI, IV, p. 574).

3. pittu to fart; Kui Kur. Mlt. pīt-; Go. pitt- : Ka. hūsu id. (< *pū-su); Tu. pūpuni (< *pī-); pūki a fart.

4. pilucu to call; Ta. viḷi to call; v.i. to roar; n. sound; piḷippu sound, calling : Tu. buḷpuni to cry aloud; buḷpu a cry, clamor.

5. miḍuku to grieve; Ka. miḍuku : Ma. muṭukuka.

6. viḍucu to leave, quit, give up; viḍu id.; Ta. Ma. viṭu; Ka. biḍu; GoM. biḍs- to abandon : Tu. buḍupini to leave, forsake.

7. vittu to sow seeds; Ka. bittu; Tu. bittuni; Ta. vittu; vitai; Ma. vitekka : Tu. buttuni.

8. mriṅgu to swallow (< *mḻiṅg-); Ta. viḻuṅku; Ma. miḻuṅṅuka : Ta. colloq. muḻuṅgu.

§1.246. In a few cases certain Central and North Dravidian languages show an -e- corresponding to -i- of Te. and SDr.; this development is especially found in Kui, Kur. and Mlt., but the conditions of such variation are not clear:

1. tirugu to roam, wander, move; revolve; SDr. *tir-; Go.(W) tirhat- v.tr. to turn; Kuvi trig- to shiver; ṭric- to twist; tiṛv- to twist; Brah. sīrring to recoil : Kui terpa to twist; trēba to wander; trehpa to cause to wander; Kur. ter$^{e}$m- to roll up.

2. ninḍu to be full; Go. ninḍ- id.; Kur. nīnd-; Mlt. nind-; Klm. ninḍ- : Kui Kuvi nenj- to be full; Kui nespa to fill.

3. piduku to express, squeeze, milk; Ka. hiduku; Ta. pidukku; Ma. pitukkuka id. : Kur. ped$^{e}$k̲h̲- v.t. to press hard, squeeze, strain.

4. vinu to hear; SDr. *vin-, except Kota, where it is vent- (veynt-) to ask; Klm. vin-; Brah. bin- : Kui venba; Kuvi venjali; Pj. and KGad. ven-; cf. Kur. Mlt. men-.

5. viriyu, virugu to be broken, to crumble; Ka. viri; Tu. biriyuni; Ta. viri; Ma. viriyuka; Kui vriṅga; vrīva id.; Kuvi(F) bri- : Kur. berr- to get out of shape by expanding sideways or falling under weight, as a mud wall, etc.

On account of the absence of -i- < *-e- under these circumstances in South Dravidian, it is to be assumed that -i- represents the original phoneme here, while the -e- forms are later developments in the languages in which they occur. A really complicated case is vinu for which one South Dravidian language, viz., Kota, shows an -e- in agreement with Central and North Dravidian, while all others have only -i-

-u-

§1.247. The following cases evidence an alternation of -u-/-o- in South Dravidian:

1. kuṭṭu to stitch, sew; prick; sting; Ka. kuṭṭu to prick; kuṭuku to sting (as an ant); kuḍuku to peck; Ta. kuḻi to pierce (of an arrow, etc.); Tu. kuḷipuni to sting (as an ant); Klm. Nk. kuṭṭ- to sew; Pj. kuṭṭ-, Oll. kuṭ- : Ta. koṭṭu to sting as a scorpion or wasp; koṭukku n. sting of a wasp, etc.; Ma. koṭukka id.; Te. Ka. koṇḍi id.; Go. kōṭṭ- to sew leaves, bore ears; to peck at; cf. Brah. k͟hull- to pierce, stab.

2. puccu to send, send away, pu-t-tencu, pu-t-tēru id.; Ta. puku to reach, enter (pp. pukk-), pukutu to enter; pukku to cause to enter, put in; Ma. pukuka to enter, pukkuka to put in : Ka. pogu, pugu to enter (pp. pokku); Tu. pogguni to enter, interfere.

3. musuru to swarm as flies, cf. mũgu id. (< *muyṅg-); Ka. musuṟu; Ta. mūcu swarm about; n. swarming : Ta. moy to swarm, crowd as flies; moci swarm; Go. moi-, moitt- to rush at, close with.

Of these, the alternation in item 1 could be due to two reasons: (1) i/e and u/o alternate in Dravidian in a number of cases when they precede a retroflex consonant, or an affricate c, or y (this also explains item 3); or (2) there might be an amalgam of two series of meanings here introducing contamination in forms; Ta. koṭṭu to sting, for instance, seems to be the result of contamination between *kuṭṭu to sting and koṭukku a sting. We can separate the ku- series with the meaning 'to sting,' from the ko- series with the meaning 'a sting.'

Structurally the ḷ forms are basic rather than the ṭ forms. Therefore kuṭṭ- < *kuḷ-t- (see Tu. kuḷipuni); Ta. koṭukku a sting < *koḷ-u-, Te. Ka. koṇḍi < *koṇ-t (< *koḷ-nt-).

In item 2, the PDr. vowel is definitely *-u-. Ka. and Tu. might have re-formed the stem on the basis of pō- to go, which is a contraction of PSDr. *pok-a- < *puk-a- (see §1.277, IIa).

-ū-

§1.248. In the following forms Te. and SDr. ū alternates with ō of certain languages of the Central and North Dravidian groups:

1. kūḍu v.i., v.tr. to meet, join; add together; to agree; Ka. kūḍu; Ta. Ma. kūṭu; Kuvi (S) kūḍ-; Tu. kūṭuni, kūṇṭuni to mix, mingle : Kur. k͟hōṇḍ- v.t. to bring together, assemble; cf. Mlt. gōnje a crowd, multitude.

2. kūrku to sleep, be drowsy; Tu. kūruni be sleepy; Kui kūra to lie down, prostrate; Go. kūrk- to nod in sleepiness : Kui kōra to lull to sleep.

3. nūṟu to powder, crush; Ta. Ma. Ka. nūṟu id.; Tu. nūruni; Kuvi (F) nui- : Go. nōr- to grind.

4. nulucu to twist; nūlu thread; Ka. nūl to spin; Tu. nūpini, nuppuni id.; Ta. nūr to spin; Kui nūḍu, Kuvi lūlu n. : Kui nōlba to twist; Kur. nō̃ẽ- id.

5. pūcu to blossom, flower; Ta. Ka. pū- id.; Ma. pūkka id.; Tu. pū a flower; Kui pūju, Kuvi (F) pūyū flower; Kur. puỹd-, puyd- to flower, blossom; Mlt. pūthe id. : Go. poi- to flower; Klm.(Kin.), Nk. pokke a flower.

6. pūnu to put on; Ta. pūṇ id.; Ma. pūṇuka; Kur. pūn a necklace; Mlt. pūn- to put on one's neck : Go. pōnḍ- to put on a dhoti, etc.

7. pūyu to besmear, daub; Ka. pūsu; Tu. pūjuni; Ta. Ma. pūcu : Kur. pot- to whitewash, plaster.

It has already been stated that higher and lower vowels alternate in Dravidian before an affricate c or a semivowel y, i.e., i/e, u/o, a/e. Of the above cases, comparative evidence shows that ū in items 2, 3, 4, 5, and 7 has resulted from *uy which would alternate with *oy, following the above formulation. The languages with long ō should have formed it on the *oy alternant. Since more languages show the *uy alternant, we can set this up for PDr. with *oy as a dialectal variant. In items 1 and 6 the vowel alternation may be attributed to the influence of the following retroflex eonsonants, though this development is not common with long vowels. In item 6, the preceding bilabial stop could have partly contributed towards obscuring the distinction between ū and ō.

-e-

§1.249. Among verbs there is one case of disagreement between Te. and the other literary Dravidian languages in the radical vowel in medial position:

teccu to bring, tē-, tēr- (other stems); Ta. Ma. Ka. Koḍ. Ko. Go. Kui Kuvi—all these show stems with the radical syllable in tā- (see Emeneau, Lg. 21 (1945), p. 188). Kur. tai-/tey- to send; Mlt. tēy- id. may be compared. A PDr. *tay- alternating with *tey- will solve the problem of Te. with ē < *ay/*ey. This is also supported by the Kur. Mlt. evidence if those forms are taken to belong here in spite of the meaning discrepancy. We actually have to set up three variants for PDr.: *ta-, *tā-, and *tay-, of which *ta- and *tā- are distributed complementarily (see Emeneau, op. cit., table 2, p. 188). The isogloss of *tay- encloses Te. and Kur.-Mlt. We can presume that *tā- and *tay- were dialect variants in PDr.

§1.250. Telugu e (radical e whether initial or medial) is frequently paralleled by Go. a; sometimes Kui, Kur. and Mlt. also show -a- corresponding to Telugu -e-:

1. ter̲acu to open (of a door, box, etc.); Ka. ter̲e; Tu. terapu space, room; Ta. tir̲a id. : Go. tarī-t- id.; Kui dari adj. opened out, cf. trēppa to lay out.

2. telucu to adore, praise : Go. talehk- to beg, ask for anything; cf. Go. temb- to beg for alms (? < *ten-b-).

3. neṭṭu to push (in, down or off); Ta. ner̲i to press firmly with hands (Kalit.); ner̲r̲u to thrust, dash; cf. Kur. nepp- to brush out sweepings, etc.; Mlt. nerm- id. : Go. natt- to dash or throw down; Kui nasa to press, push, crush.

4. perugu to grow, increase, etc. pĕr- adj. big; Ka. Tu. Ta. Ma. peru/pēr adj. big : Kur. parda'- to raise, increase; par$^{i}$cha'- to rear, breed up.

§1.251. The following cases record an alternation between e of Telugu (and the other South Dravidian languages) and i of some members of the Central and North Dravidian groups:

1. teliyu to be known; become clear; v.t. to know; Ka. tiḷi become clear, bright; Tu. tiḷi transparent; clear; Ta teḷ become clear; teḷi id.; Ma. teḷiyuka id. : Kui tiri adj. clear, shining, bright, pure, holy; tirna clearly; Kur. tiltil adj. of a fresh appearance; tiltil$^{i}$r- be fresh and healthy; Brah. tir- neg. stem of cā- to know (see Brahui Grammar, §261).

2. perugu to increase, grow (see above); GoM. pērs- to extend : Brah. pir- to swell (of body); this *e > i appears in the Go. form also, pirr- to grow, germinate.

3. per̲uku to pull up, pluck out, weed out : Go. piṛang- to pull.

4. mettu, mrēgu (< *mel̲aku) to daub, plaster; Ta. Ma. mel̲uku to anoint, paste; Ta. mel̲uku n. cow dung, wax; Ma. mel̲uku wax : Brah. mir- to plaster; cf. Go. maṛhutt- to paint, etc.

5. velugu to shine, become bright; SDr. *veḷ- bright : Kur. bilc- to shine, glitter; bilte light, flame; Mlt. bil-bilr- to shine brilliantly; bilpu the moon.

Of these, in items 1, 4 and 5, the alternation of e/i is explainable through the following retroflex consonant.

§1.252. In one case, which appears primarily onomatopoetic, Telugu e corresponds to i of Ta. Ma. Ka. and Tu.:

vekku to hiccup, sob; vekkili n. hiccup; vegacu vb. id.; Ka. Tu. bikku take a deep breath; Ta vikku to hiccup; vikkuḷ n. (Kṟḷ.); Ma. vikku/mikku to rise in the throat; (with loss of v-, Te. ekkili hiccup; Ma. ekkil, ekkiṭṭu hiccup); Kui veka to cough; Kur. bekkh- to be choked (of animals); to cough; Mlt. beq- to be choked.

-ē-

§1.253. The following etymologies with Telugu -ē- preceded by *c indicate an alternation of ā and ē in this position in PSDr. (see also §§1.212, .240).

1. cē̃du to draw up, bale out water; Ka. sēdu, sēndu; Ta. cēntu; Ma. tēkuka, tēvuka (with t- < *c- and with a different derivative suffix); cf. Te. dēvu to bale out with the hand : Ta. cāmpu to pull by jerks; pump, draw in.

2. cēru to reach, approach; also -tēru occurs in compound verb-forms, e.g., kaḍa-tēru to reach the end; to end; to be over, tr. kaḍatērcu; Ka. sēr; Ta. cēr; Ma. cēruka; Klm. sēr-; Kuvi hēr-; Go. sēṛ- enter a house : Te. tāru (< *cār-) to approach; tārcu to conduct, take near; Ka. sār to approach, tr. sārcu; Ta. cār id., cārttu to join; Ma. cāruka be attached; cāra near, close; cārttu to join : Te. arugu to approach; Ta. ār to combine with (with loss of *c-, see §§1.210 ff.).

3. tēyu to be worn out (by rubbing) ( ? l. w. < Ka. as no early literary usages are quoted in dictionaries); Ka. tē-, tēy- to grind, triturate; Tu. tēpuni; Ta. Ma. tēy- to waste by rubbing : Te. cā̃du to rub, polish (< *cāynd-); Ta. cāttu to smear; Ka. caccu/ceccu to grind, crush; PSDr. *cāy/*cēy.

There is no way of deciding whether originally ā fell together with ē or vice versa. The area of this merger seems to have extended to Central Dravidian also. Notice Go. sārung six; Pj. sējēn (< *sēṟ-) (LSI, IV, p. 554) : Ta. Ma. Ka. Te. āṟu id.; Ta. āmai : Kui sēmbi tortoise; Te. tā̃bēlu (-ēlu derivative suffix); Ka. ēve, āme, āve; Tu. ēme (DS VI, p. 138). The ē forms are more widely distributed than those with ā, and hence it could be taken to be the quality of the phoneme after the merger of ā and ē after *c- in certain of the forms.

§1.254. In the following etymology Te. nē- : Ma. nā- is explained by Burrow through an original *ñ- in the place of n- (see DS V, p. 604; also §§1.25 ff.).

nēmu to winnow, sift; Ta. nēmpu/nōmpu id.; nĕmpuka; Kui ĕmba to separate rice from straw by shaking; Go. yĕm- to sift out husks of rice, pulses, etc. : Ma. nāvuka id.

The evidence is not enough to set up a PDr. *ñ- in the initial position. Burrow does not quote the Go. and Kui forms which clearly belong here. These two languages indicate an original *ĕ- or *yĕ- (or *yă-), in which case, a secondary *ñ- could be set up for SDr. In this case it may be recalled that secondary *ñ- out of *y- is attested for Ta. in certain morphophonemic situations (viz., when *y- follows n or ṇ across morpheme boundaries, see §1.31).

-o-

§1.255. Telugu has o in the following case corresponding to o/u of the other languages. As shown earlier, the alternation could be due to the following retroflex consonant:

koṭṭu to beat, strike, etc. Tu. korpini beat, flog; koṭṭu a spade; Ta. koṭṭu to beat, as a drum, hammer, clap; pound as paddy, etc.; n. stroke, beat (Aiṅk.); Ma. koṭṭuka beat as a drum; Kui kospa to beat; kōḍu a pestle; Go. kohk- to pound (as chutney), butt with horns; goṭṭ- to poke, thrust at; Kur. khoṭṭ-; Mlt. qoṭ- break, knock at : Ka. kuṭṭu to beat, strike, pound; Tu. kuṭṭuni to give a blow; pound, crush, bruise; Ta. kuṭṭu to cuff; Ma. kuṭṭuka to pound; Klm.(SR) kuṛk-/kuḍk- to beat; Klm.(E) to pound (grain); Nk. kuṛk- to pound; Pj. kuṭip-/kuṭit- to punch, knock (door); (South) kuṭṭ- to strike foot against stone (> l. w. Skt. kuṭṭ-, see Burrow, DS III, BSOAS XI, p. 139; for IA, see Nep. Dict. kuṭnu).

The vowel alternation may also be due to a confusion between two series of etyma originally distinct, one with *koṭ- meaning to beat (drum), to hammer, strike, etc. and another with *kuṭ- meaning to pound in a mortar, to cuff, butt, etc. This assumption derives from the fact that more of the ku- forms have 'pounding' and related meanings; the Skt. l. ww. with ku- also mean 'to pound,' kuṭṭayati crush, bruise, pound; kuṭṭima a pounded floor (see Burrow, op. cit., p. 134), while Pāli koṭṭeti beat, smash, pound, akoṭeti beats, pounds, stamps, indicate that these were borrowed from some Dravidian language having an o variant. There was reborrowing from IA into North Dravidian with ku-/ko- (see Burrow, op. cit., p. 139).

§1.256. There is another form which shows an alternation of o/u before the retroflex lateral ḷ:

nollu(konu) to suck the finger (as a child); Mdn. Te. to grab, to be avaricious; Ka. noṇe to swallow; to clean with tongue the substance lodged between the teeth (Mdn.); Ta. noḷḷu to swallow, devour; Kur. nun$^{u}$<u>kh</u>- to swallow, gulp; the Kur. form provides a solution for Ta. nuṅku/noṅku id. (< *nuṇ-k/*noṇ-k-), Ma. noṅṅu, Ka. nuṅgu, in which the alternation o/u is because of the pre-consonantal nasal being originally a retroflex consonant.

§1.257. After bilabial consonants there occur alternations between o and u, o and a, i and u, and e and o among the various Dravidian languages. The following examples illustrate some of these variations:

1. pogulu to grieve, lament, weep; Ka. puyalcu to cry out, lament; puyyal n. lamentation; Tu. buguḷuni to be grieved; Ta. pukai to burn, grieve; n. distress; pūcal lamentation, distress; cf. Tu. pojakoṇuni to be distressed, grieved.

2. mogiyu to overspread; spread (as darkness); moguḍu to close, contract (as flower); mogucu, moguḍcu to close, shut up (v.t.), to fold (hands), etc. : mūyu to close (Common Dravidian *muy-, *muc-, see Part II).

3. moṭṭu to rap with knuckles; Mdn. Te. moṭṭi-kāya a rap with knuckles ( ? < Skt. muṣṭighāta-); Ka. moṭṭu id.; Ta. Ma. muṭṭu id.; Kur. muṭga'-/muṭka'- id.; Mlt. muṭi fist; Brah. muṭ fist, muṭrī shampooing with the fist (l.ww. < IA; cf. Pa. Pkt. muṭṭhi-, Skt. muṣṭi- m.f. fist, see s.v. muṭh Nep. Dict.). In this last case the original vowel is obviously u since it is a loanword from IA muṭh-. Alternatively, o in Te. and Ka. could be due to contamination between Dravidian mottu to beat and *muṭṭ- from IA muṭh-

§1.258. In the following cases some Central or North Dravidian languages show a u-variant corresponding to o of Te. and SDr.:

1. porayu to join, get, obtain; v.i. to occur; Ka. pore to join (v.i., tr.); Ta. poru to join, unite; Ma. poruka to meet : Kur. pur$^{u}$m- to mix, unite; Mlt. purm- to mix, etc.

2. podugu, poduvu to cover, envelope; Ta. potuṅku to conceal; pottu to inlay; clothe; Kui poja to pack; Kur. Mlt. poj- to wrap around, bundle, pack : Brah. putunk bundle; puch clothing, clothes.

3. polucu to shine, polupu brilliance; Ta. poli to shine, brightness; Ma. pularuka to dawn : Mlt. pulpulr- to shine through whiteness.

4. mo<u>r</u>ugu to bark (as a dog); Go. mohc- id.; Kuvi mōkh- : Kui muska to bark.

In all the above cases o should be taken as the PDr. quality by virtue of its wide distribution and u as a local development in the languages of the non-literary group.

§1.259. Variation between o and a/e is seen in a few etymologies when preceded by a bilabial consonant:

1. poncu to waylay, watch for, lurk (< *pornc- < *por$^{u}$nc-); Ka. poñcu, hoñcu id.; Kui pōrpa to watch for, lie in wait; spy; Kuvi pōrh- to lie in wait : Ta. Ma. Ka. pār to watch, wait for, look for.

2. poṭlu to burst, break, explode; Ma. poṭṭuka to burst, explode; Tu. puḍāvuni to burst, break : Te. peṭlu, peḍulu to break, become brittle; Ka. peṭlu a cracking sound; peṭal, peṭalu id.

3. *mor̲āgu to hide (in the cpd. kanu-mor̲āgu to cheat, lit. to hide the eye); Ka. mor̲e the state of being hidden : Te. mar̲ūgu be hidden, concealed; Ka. mar̲e being hidden; Tu. madeyuni be out of sight; Ta. mar̲ai to hide; Ma. mar̲ayuka id.

In the above cases o is clearly secondary in item 3; even in item 1, ō in Kui Kuvi Ka. and Te. is likely to be secondary since the bilabial stop p might have imparted lip-rounding to the unrounded back vowel ā.

§1.260. This shift of a > o in the vicinity of bilabial consonants is frequent in Modern Telugu, and is obviously not a recent tendency, e.g., moguḍu husband < OTe. magāḍu; poḍucu a young woman < paḍucu (cf. āḍa-boḍucu sister-in-law); pogulu daytime (in lower class dialect) < pagalu. On the contrary in compound constructions long ō becomes ā; moga-mōṭamu (shyness, lit. hiding the face), moga-māṭamu; tiraga-māta seasoning (< tiruga-mōta < *tirugā-bōta, lit. pouring again); rā-vāku don't come (< rā-bōku, Guntur dial., in another dialect rā-mōku).

The forms treated elsewhere for an o-/va- alternation may be recalled here (§1.234).

### -ō-

§1.261. *-ō- remains in Telugu:

kōḍu to sift, winnow; Ta. kol̲i; Ma. kol̲ikka; Go. kōss- to sift in a 'sūpa' with a sidelong swing; Kui kṛōhpa to winnow; Kuvi(S) kloh- id., Kuvi(F) kṛōh- id.

§1.262. So far we have discussed only those cases in which the correspondences are not regular between Telugu and some of the other Dravidian languages in the matter of radical vowels, initial and medial. It is therefore to be assumed that there is a fair amount of regularity in radical vowels in the rest of the cases among the various Dravidian languages.

§1.263. This is probably the right place to include two types of somewhat regular series of correspondences between Te. on the one hand and Go. and Pj. on the other: Te. radical e (< PDr. *e) : Go. a, GoA. e.

1. eṇḍu to dry up (< *en̲ṯu < *el-nt-); eṇḍa sunshine; Ta. el, en̲ṟu sun; Pj. nend, (NE.) neṇḍi sunshine : Go. (Trench) addi the heat of the sun; GoA. eddi; GoM. yēd sunshine, summer.

2. teṟacu to open (of a door, box, etc.); Ka. teṟe; Ta. tiṟa : Go. tarī-t- to open (of a door).

§1.264. There are a few cases where Go. shows i for Te. (and PDr.) radical e (see §1.251).

1. perugu to grow : Go. pirr- id.

2. peṟuku to pull out : Go. piṛang- id.

This probably indicates a dialect mixture in our records of Gondi.

§1.265. Corresponding to Telugu ă̄ (< PDr. *ă̄), Parji shows ĕ̄ in radical syllables in a considerable number of cases (see The Parji Language, pp. 1, 2, §2).

1. vaccu to come (Common Dravidian var-, vā-) : Pj. ver id.

2. āṟu to become cool : Pj. ēd id.

§1.266. On the contrary there are also some forms in Pj. which do not show this alternation, and others which show the reverse development, i.e., PDr. *e : Pj. a, similar to the one in the Go. dialect recorded by Trench (see The Pj. Lg., ibid.). This situation again seems to point to the development of differences originally on a dialectal basis and a subsequent admixture of different dialects.

## ALTERNATIONS i/e AND u/o[108]

§1.267. In PDr. disyllabic and trisyllabic forms of $(C^1)V^1C^2\text{-}V^2$ or its extended types the etymological boundary occurs between $C^2$ and $V^2$; whatever precedes this is the root element and whatever follows is a part of the derivative suffix. $V^1$ stands for any one of the five short vowel phonemes, viz., i e a o u, and $V^2$ stands for any one of the phonemes i a u. $C^2$ can be any PDr. consonant except *ñ- which does not occur in this position.

§1.268. In contrast to this PDr. situation the situation in the older stages of the literary languages of SDr. is as follows:

When $V^2$ (i.e., the derivative vowel) is *i or *u or zero all the four languages preserve the PDr. *i *e *u and *o in the position $V^1$ (radical vowel); but when $V^2$ is an *a Ta. and Ma. always show i or u (but not e or o), and Te. and Ka. e or o (but not i or u) for $V^1$. This situation is briefly charted in the following:

| PDr. | | Ta. Ma. [*-i [*-u [*-zero | [*-a | Te. Ka. [*-i [*-u [*-zero | [*-a |
|---|---|---|---|---|---|
| *i | > | i | > i (*i, *e) | > i | > e (*i, *e) |
| *e | > | e | | > e | |
| *u | > | u | > u (*u, *o) | > u | > o (*u, *o) |
| *o | > | o | | > o | |
| (*a | > | a | > a | > a | > a)[109] |

Examples of the foregoing:

1. PDr. *iṭ-i

Ta. iṭ-i to break, crumble; Ma. iṭ-i(ka); Ka. iḍ-i; Te. iḍ-iyu.

2. PDr. *iṭ-u

Ta. iṭ-u to put, give; Ma. iṭ-u(ka); Ka. iḍ-u; Te. iḍ-u.

3. PDr. *teḷ-i

Ta. teḷ-i to become clear; to know; Ma. teḷ-iyu(ka); Ka. tiḷ-i (< *te-ḷ-i, §1.279); Te. tel-iyu to be known, become clear

4. PDr. *keṭ-u

Ta. keṭ-u to perish, decay; Ma. keṭ-uka; Ka. keḍ-u/kiḍ-u; Te. ceḍ-u.

As opposed to:

5. PDr. *eṇ-a- > PSDr. ? eṇ-a/iṇ-a

Ta. iṇ-ai v.i. to agree, to unite; Ma. iṇ-ayu(ka); Ka. eṇ-e equality; eṇ-asu to add together; Te. en-ayu to agree; suit.

6. PDr. *piṇ-a- > PSDr. ? piṇ-a-/peṇ-a-

Ta. piṇ-ai v.i. to entwine; v.t. to join, link; Ma. piṇ-ayu(ka); Ka. peṇ-e to intertwine, etc. (-e < *-ay); Te. pen-ayu id.

Similarly with the *u *o vowels.

§1.269. It is clear from the foregoing chart that before a derivative *-a, both the PDr. *i and *e turn up as i in Ta.-Ma. and as e in Te. and Ka.; similarly PDr. *u, *o > Ta.-Ma. u, and > Te. Ka. o. Therefore, given for these languages only a set of forms in which an a-vowel begins the derivative suffix, one cannot be certain whether the original vowel is *i or *e, or *u or *o. There are only two possible interpretations for this situation. (1) Of the four PDr. vowel phonemes *i *u and *e *o, *i *u fell together with e o in Te. Ka., and *e *o fell together with i u in Ta. Ma. in this environment. Since these mergers move in opposite directions, one has to assume that they took place independently in each set of languages:

In the environment [Ca

| Ta. Ma. | Te. Ka. |
|---|---|
| *e → i | *i → e |
| *o → u | *u → o |

It is, however, an extreme accident that two simultaneous shifts, yielding the same result (i.e., loss of contrast between each set of two vowels), should have taken place in neighboring languages independently of each other. Again, if we mean this as a development immediately following the PDr. stage, we thereby imply a strong language boundary which ties up Te. Ka. as against Ta. Ma.; there is no other isogloss to support this assumption. On the contrary, Telugu is nearer to its northern neighbors in the matter of phonology than to its southern or southwestern ones.

§1.270. (2) An alternative and more plausible explanation is as follows: Since all the four languages have one feature in common, namely, lack of contrast between i, e on the one hand, and u, o on the other, this should have taken place at a period common to all these languages, say, in PSDr. In other words, in PSDr. itself the convergence of the four PDr. vowel-qualities into two has taken place. Let us assume for the time being that we do not know the qualities of these two vowels, whether they were i u-like or e o-like. Then we symbolize the resultant qualities of this merger as X and Y; PDr. *i, *e-[a > PSDr. *X-[a; PDr. *u, *o-[a > PSDr. *Y-[a. In our records of Ta. Ma. X = i and Y = u; on the other hand, in Te. Ka. X = e and Y = o. If we have some means of knowing whether X and Y were i u-like or e o-like after the merger in PSDr., we can easily attribute a later shift to one group or another within SDr. This interpretation differs from the earlier one in that we are assuming three stages here, instead of two, viz., PDr., PSDr., and SDr., and again the shift is stated to have taken place in one direction only at a time. Instead of setting up two simultaneous and independent mergers in Ta. Ma. and Te. Ka. respectively, we are actually setting up only one shift in PSDr. with a later change in the divided SDr. which brought about the juxtaposition in developments.

Here there are two problems to solve:

(1) how can one discover the PDr. vowel qualities, and

(2) in what direction did the merger take place in PSDr. (i.e., *i *u > *e *o; or vice versa) ?

§1.271. Most of the earlier writers on this problem took it for granted that the Ta. Ma. vowels represented PDr. and attributed the later shift in all cases to Te. and Ka.[110] For the first time Burrow proposed a useful procedure of internal reconstruction within SDr. itself.[111] Since all the languages in question preserve the PDr. vowel qualities when the derivative suffix begins with a consonant, i, u, or zero, he proposed a comparison of forms having a derivational a-vowel "with kindred words in which the radical i (e) and u (o) are not followed by a or ai" (op. cit., p. 291). Obviously the radical vowel occurring in closed syllables or in forms with a following derivative i or u represents the PDr. quality, e.g., Ta. oṭ-i to break: uṭ-ai id. (< *oṭ-ai).

§1.272. The general principle is to discover reliable etymologies where an a vowel does not occur at the beginning of the derivative suffix (i.e., $V^2$). Therefore, two broad environments can be set up for this purpose: (1) where the radical vowel occurs in closed syllables, i.e., when the radical syllable is (C)V̆C or (C)V̄C; the heavy base (long-vowelled base) alternates regularly with the light base (short-vowelled base) when vowel-derivatives follow (see §§1.289-.294); (2) where the radical vowel occurs in open syllables with i or u beginning the derivative suffix.

Sometimes the evidence of the non-literary languages of Central Dravidian and North Dravidian may be found useful in tracing the quality of the PDr. radical vowel, though it does not help in tracing the derivative vowels due to their almost complete loss in all these languages. Many divergences from the PDr. vowel system appear in these languages even in radical vowels, so that one cannot set up regular sound-correspondences to explain all the material. But if two or more geographically distant or historically unconnected languages show the same vowel quality, it could be taken to represent PDr.

In a few cases the evidence of Go. is useful since the PDr. radical *e always occurs as a in the dialect that Trench treated. The Adilabad dialect as reported by Burrow and Bhattacharya preserves the PDr. *e. PDr. *i remains in these two dialects.

The solution to the second question, i.e., the identification of the PSDr. vowel qualities which have resulted from the merger of PDr. vowel sets will be postponed to the end of this topic.

§1.273. Among Telugu verbs there are sixty-nine e-[a forms and forty-nine o-[a forms of which the PDr. vowels can be reconstructed for over sixty per cent, following the above principles. Only a few typical examples are given below.

§1.274. In the following forms the PDr. vowel quality is identified through its occurrence (either long or short) in closed syllables:

*i

nel-ayu to stay, remain; live; nelavu abode; Ka. nelasu become established, settle, stay; Tu. nelasu̥ bottom, soil; Ta. nilai to remain, stay; Ma. nilekka come to a stand : Common Dravidian *nil to stand (see Part II s.v. nilucu to stand).

*e

teg-aḍu to slight, blame, neglect; Ka. tegal̲ id.; Tu. teguni to abuse, revile; tegelè n. reviling : Ta. tevvu enmity, hostility; teviḷ to loathe, dislike.

*u

mon-ayu to begin, commence, undertake (a battle); to occur, happen; mona a battle-front; Ka. mone an affray; Ta. mun̲ai be deeply engaged in; Ma. munayuka to go before : Ta. mun̲n̲u to get to, join, adhere to; mun̲ adv. in front.

*o

os-ãgu to give; a present; Ka. osage a present, gift; Ta. utavu to give (-t- < *-c-); Ma. utakuka to serve out : Ta. oy send forth, give; oyyal giving, forwarding.

§1.275. In the following the quality of the PDr. vowel is reconstructed on the basis of its occurrence in open radical syllables with i or u beginning the derivative suffixes:

*i

pen-ãgu to be twisted, to struggle, fight; pen-ayu to be entwined; Ka. peṇagu/peṇagu id., peṇasu to wrangle; peṇe to intertwine; Ta. piṇai to entwine; piṇaṅku to be intertwined, linked; Ma. piṇayuka be entangled : Ta. piṇi to fasten with ropes; Ka. piṇil a braid of hair; Go. piṛang- to entwine.

*e

ced-aru v.i. to be scattered; to disperse; Ka. kedar̲u; Tu. kedaruni; Ta. citai, citar to be scattered; citar̲u to disperse; Ma. cıtar̲uka id.; citar dust : Ta. cet-iḷ dust (Cīv.); Kur. k̲h̲ettr- be thrown off; k̲h̲ett- shake off or out by a jerk.

*u

tol-ãku, ton-ãku v.i. to spill (of water); Pj. tolk- to spill; Ta. tuḷaṅku to move, shake; tuḷakku v.t. to shake; Ma. tuḷaṅṅuka to be shaken : Ta. tuḷ-i to sprinkle; Ta. Ma. tuḷ-umpu v.i. to shake, to be agitated; Ka. tuḷuku, tuṇuku, tuṅku id.; Tu. tuḷi to churn; tuliyuni id.; cf. Kur. Mlt. tund- to spill.

*o

por-ayu to get, obtain, to reach; v. i. to occur; Ka. pore to be joined; to join, come near : Ta. poru tr. to reach, join; extend; unite; Ma. poruka to meet; also see Ta. poruntu come in contact, reach, Ma. porunnuka, Ka. pordu, poddu, Te. pondu.

§1.276. In the following the evidence of the non-literary languages is utilized to reconstruct the PDr. vowel quality (no examples are available for PDr. *i).

(a) *e: Kur. Mlt. e; Go. a, GoA. e

1. er̲-āgu bend, bow down; Ka. er̲agu bend, bow, alight, come down; Tu. eraguni; Ta. ir̲aṅku to descend, bend, alight; ir̲aiñcu id.; Ma. ir̲aṅṅuka to descend; ir̲akkuka to put down : Kur. ett- to descend; Mlt. et- to go down (tt < *t̲t̲; see §1.195, b); Go. ragg- to descend; reht- to cause to descend; Kuvi (F) rech- to descend; reph- to lift down.

2. ter̲acu to open (of doors, etc.); Ka. ter̲e; Tu. terapu space; Ta. tir̲a to open : Go. tarī-t- to open (of a door); Kui trēppa to lay out.

3. ved-aku to seek, search; Ka. bed-aku v. and n.; Kur. bedd- to seek, search; Mlt. bed- id.

(b) *u

1. mrōgu (< *mol̲-aṅku) to sound, thunder; Ka. mol̲agu; Tu. muresuni; Ta. mul̲aṅku to roar, thunder; Ma. mul̲aṅṅuka id. : Klm.(SR) muray to utter threats; Pj. mur- to growl (as a tiger); Kur. murr- to thunder.

2. tor̲āgu to leave, give up; Ka. tor̲e; Tu. torepuni; Ta. tur̲a id. : Kui tuhpa to leave, cast away; give; sṛūva/jṛūva to shed; juṛpa cause to shed.

(c) *o

pogayu be fumigated; be smoked; seasoned; poga smoke; Ka. poge; Tu. puge; Ta. pukai; Ma. pukekka : Pj. Klm. Nk. pog smoke; GoA. poya id.; cf. Ta. pō- to be stretched out, extended.

Similarly in pogaḍu to praise, trōcu/trōyu to push forth, the PDr. vowel is *o on the basis of the evidence of the non-literary languages.

§1.277. The second problem is to determine the phonemic status of *X and *Y of PSDr., i.e., the vowel qualities that resulted from the merger of PDr. *i, *e and *u, o respectively. Evidence is now available which seems to solve this problem.

In all the SDr. languages it is a common development that the root and suffix vowels have contracted with the loss of the medial consonant when it is one of the following: *-k- [-g-], *-y- (< *-y- or *-c-), or

-v- (< *-v- or *-k-). A series of long vowels have resulted from such contractions as follows:

I (a). *iC-[i, u > ī
(b). *iC-[a > ē
(c). *eC-[i, u, a > ē

II (a). *uC-[i, u > ū
(b). *uC-[a > ō
(c). *oC-[i, u, a > ō

From the above we notice that in contracted forms PDr. *e and *o do not change their qualities but are simply lengthened when any one of the three admissible vowels occurs in the derivative suffix. On the contrary, PDr. *i and *u in the sequences *iC-[a and *uC-[a behave in the same manner as original *e and *o in producing ē and ō in contractions. In contrast to this *i and *u preserve their quality even in contractions when they are not originally followed by a. In other words, in the environment [C-a all the SDr. languages show ē and ō in contracted forms irrespective of whether the PDr. quality is *i *e or *u *o respectively. The following examples, though they are not from Te. verbs, illustrate the above formulas:

I (a). *iC-u > ī : *niv-u > nī-

Te. niv-ur̲u ashes; also nīr̲u; Ta. Ma. Ka. nīr̲u; Go. nīr

I (b). *iC-a > ē : *tiy-a- > tē-

Ta. tīy-am sweetness; Te. tīy-amu/tiyy-amu id.; Ka. siyy-ane sweetly : Ta. tē-m sweetness, honey, honey-bee; tē-n̲ honey (-n̲ < *-m); Ma. tēn; Ka. jēn, tēnu; Kota tēn; Koḍ. tēn; Te. tēne; tēṇ-ṭ-i bee; Klm. Nk. tēn- : Pj. tīni honey bee; Oll. tīn honey; KGad. tīnu id.; Kur. tinī bee; tīnn- to have a sweet taste.

I (c). *eC-a > ē : *key-a- > kē-

Ka. kes-avu, kes-u a sort of yam (Arum colocasia): Ta. cē-mpu, cē-mpai id.; Ma. cēmpu; Tu. tēvu, cēvu; Te. cēma.

II (a). *uC-a- > ō : *puk-a- > pō

Ta. puku to go, proceed; puk-avu entering (Aiṅk.); Ma. pukuka to enter, etc. : Ta. pō to go; Ma. pōga; Ka. pōgu; Tu. pōpini; Te. pō-, pōvu.

II (b). *oC-a > *ō : *tok-a- > tō-

Ta. Ma. tuk-al skin, etc. Ka. togalu; Te. tovalu; Tu. tug-alụ, Kur. cokkā the skin or shell of fruits, peelings; Te. tokku id. : Ta. Ma. Ka. Te. Klm. Nk. Pj. Oll. Go. Kuvi tōl skin, etc.

§1.278. The foregoing examples are sufficient to enable us to deduce the following conclusions:

(1). Before contraction took place PDr. *i and *u fell together with *e and *o respectively before the derivative *-a.

(2). Since these contractions are common to all the South Dravidian languages their occurrence should be attributed to a period common to all these languages, the period before their separation, viz., PSDr. From these it follows that in PSDr. before a derivative *-a there were only *e and *o for PDr. *i *e and *u *o respectively. The phonemic identification for *X and *Y is *e and *o.

(3). After the break-up of PSDr. Ta. shifted these occurrences of *e and *o to i and u in most cases. There are, however, a considerable number of survivals of this merger stage in OTa. literature (i.e., e-a and o-a sequences) which probably point to a dialect in which this later shift did not come about. Among these survivals there is a form with e, viz., peyar name, from PDr. *piyar, which is a clear indication that these survivals reflect the presence of the original merger stage in Ancient Tamil before the later shift.

(4). This provides an additional isogloss for the languages with *c- > zero as opposed to the languages with *c- > c-.

(5). Metathesis and vowel contraction in Telugu has to be ascribed to the post-merger period and the period after the loss of *c- in SDr.

§1.279. In classical Ka. there occurred another phonetic shift independently, by which radical e and o fell together with i and u respectively when followed by closed vowels, i or u.[112] This shift is dated to about the 8th century A.D. A few examples to illustrate this shift: idir opposite < *edir, Te. eduru; Ta. etir; suri to pour down < *cori, Ta. cori, Te. torāgu; puri to fry < *pori, Te. porāṭu, Ta. pori.

§1.280. The developments described in the foregoing sections belong only to the ancient stages of the SDr. languages made available to us through their literary records. The situation in modern speeches is altogether different. In Ta. and Ma. i, u in the situation before a have tended to be pronounced as e, o as in the case of Te. and Ka., e.g., Ta. ilai > elai; iṭam > eḍam; ciṟai > cerai; uṭal > oḍal; kuraṅku > koraṅgu, etc.[113] In Mdn. Te. and Ka. sequences of i-a and u-a are very common in present day speech, for instance, Te. cilaka parrot, miḍata a grasshopper, uḍata a squirrel, etc.; Ka. tigaṭu rind, nilavu standing, huḷa a worm. In most of the cases it is the derivative vowels that have undergone alternation through vowel harmony rather than the radical vowels.

## DIPHTHONGS

§1.281. Although ai and au are traditionally treated as diphthongs in the literary languages, they can be structurally interpreted as *ay and *av for PDr. *y and *v pattern with the other sonorants like n l ḷ etc., in that they occur in the final position of radical syllables and derivative suffixes, e.g., *cal to go; *vin to hear; *koḷ to take; *kāṇ eye : *kay hand; *ur-ay to be rubbed. That i in ai is *y is also supported by historical evidence, which shows that in most cases -i [y] is from an original *-c. It should also be noted that it is only after a short a that i and u are written as non-syllabic vowels; elsewhere, i.e., after ā and ĭ, ĕ, ŏ, ŭ, they are always written as consonants y and v in the literary languages.

§1.282. In both Classical and Modern Telugu ai and au freely alternate with ayi and avu respectively (§1.3). In Kannada "the radical forms of ai are ay, ayi, and those of au are avu, ava" (Kittel, Kannaḍa Grammar, §§21, 217; §150 remarks). For Tamil Tolkāppiyam says that "a and y when pronounced together sound like ai" (Eḻut. 56) and that "the symbol i is sometimes used for y at the end of words," e.g., nāi for nāy dog (Eḻut. 58). As in the other literary languages, in Ta. au may be replaced by av.[114] Mdn. Ta. radical ai is changed to a in closed syllables, aindu five > aiñju > añju.[115] On the other hand, an original au is pronounced as two syllables: savukkiyam joy < Sanskrit sāu̯khya-.[116] In earlier tadbhavas Skt. āu > ō in SDr.,[117] e.g., Sanskrit kāupīna- > Ta. Ka. kōvaṇam; Skt. drāupadi- (n.pr.) > Te. drōvadi. In Malayalam also ai = ay, and is preserved in radical syllables.[118]

All the above facts support the PDr. reconstructions *ay and *av as sequences of V + C rather than V + V. However, it is clear that in SDr., at least, these sequences have alternative values, monosyllabic as well as disyllabic. Due to the rarity of bases ending in v, we do not usually meet with etyma for which a PDr. *av has to be reconstructed.

### *ay

§1.283. PDr. *ay has different developments in radical and derivative syllables. In radical syllables comparative evidence points to an alternation of *ay/*ey in PDr. Among the SDr. languages Te. shows in many cases reflexes for both the alternants, i.e., *ay = ay and *ey = ē. Go. preserves the PDr. *ay alternant in most cases. The remaining Central and North Dravidian languages seem to have the *ey base more often than *ay, e.g.:

1. Ta. Ma. kai, kaya- to be bitter; Ma. kaikka; Ka. kay, kayi; Tu. kaipe bitterness; Te. cē̃du (< *key-nd-) adj. and n.; Koḍ. kay- vb. id.; Pj. kēp-, kēt-; Go. kehkē bitter. The SDr. languages and Kuvi Kur.-Mlt. have -c/-s forms (*-y < *-c); PDr. *kac-/*kay-.

2. Ta. kai hand; Ma. kai, kayyi; Ka. kay, kayi, keyyi; Koḍ. kay; Tu. kei; Te. cēyi, also kai-, and kē(lu); Go. kai; Kui kaju (-j- < -y-); Kuvi kēyu; Klm. Nk. kī; Pj. key; Oll. ki; KGad. kiyyu; Kur. k̲h̲ekkhā; Mlt. qeqe; PDr. *ey = CDr. ī̌.

In contrast to this development, if the PDr. sequence is *ey, all the languages show a single series of correspondences: PDr. *ney oil, fat: Ta. ney oil, fat, ghee, grease; Ma. ney; To. nīy; Ka. ney, nēy; Koḍ. ney; Tu. neyi, nēyi; Te. neyyi, nēyi, nē- (before consonants) ghee; Klm. Nk. ney id.; Pj. Oll. ney oil; Go. nī id.; Kui nīju id.; Kuvi (F) nīyū id.; Kur. nē̃ta fat, grease; Mlt. ne̱nya id. (see Emeneau, Kolami Vocab. No. 590).

From the foregoing it is clear that wherever the comparative evidence points to a wide-spread alternation of *ay/*ey, it is always *ay that is original in PDr. with *ey as a secondary development. On the other hand, if all languages point to an *ey only, in that case it is the original sequence in PDr. as opposed to *ey < *ay. The *ay/*ey alternation is in keeping with the general alternation of higher and lower vowels before y in many Dravidian languages (§1.248).

§1.284. In Telugu there are only two verbs with the ai diphthong: vaicu to put, place; saĩcu to tolerate. Of these the latter is not native, though it is assimilated to the native pattern by the addition of an -ncu suffix:

1. sa̭ĩcu to bear, tolerate; sair-incu id., to forgive; sairaṇa toleration, forgiveness; Ka. sahisu, sōsu to bear; sairisu/sayrisu to endure; cf. Ta. caki- to bear; Kur. sah- id. (< IA sah- id.). Since this is probably a later loanword, it does not show the usual ay/ey alternation common in the native forms.

2. PDr. *vay-/*vey-:

va̭icu to put, place, altern. vēyu to throw, put down, strike, etc.

*ay alternant forms: Te. vaicu : Ka. bay; Ta. vai; Ma. vaikkam what is deposited; Kur. baĩ to thatch.

*ey-alternant forms: Tu. vēy cover as a building, thatch; put on as a garland; Ma. vekka to put, lay, build; Tu. bēpuni to thatch a roof; ? Kui vēnga to be spread out; vēpka to stretch out; vega to thatch; Kuvi (S) wē- to beat, smite, strike; wēng- to outspread; Kuvi (F) vīka thatch.

§1.285. In the following form Telugu in common with Central and North Dravidian shows the *ey alternant of PDr. *ay/*ey:

vēgu/vēvu to dawn; Ta. vaiku id.; Kui vēga; Pj. vēv-, vēy-; Nk. KGad. vēg-; Kur. bijj-; Mlt. bij- id.

§1.286. In the derivative position *ay has altogether a different series of developments:

PDr. *-ay : Ta. -ai, Ma. -a, -ay(u); Ka. -e, -a; Te. -a, -ay(u).

Caldwell, in his treatment of this diphthong, speaks only of the derivative -ay (see p. 136). K. V. Subbayya, while correctly rejecting the existence of diphthongs in PDr., derives the Ta. derivative -ai from PDr. -a.[119] But there is no basis for taking the diphthong as peculiar to Tamil. Te. Ma. -ay and Ka. -e all point to an original *-ay preserved everywhere in Ta. An example of the foregoing correspondences: orayu (< *uray-) to rub, test, graze; be slightly bruised; orapu friction (< *uray-ppu); Ka. ore to rub on; orasu id.; ore, ora, orasu friction, etc.; Tu. oresuni to wear off, to rub; urepuni to array, rub; Ta. uracu, urai wear away by friction; uraicu/uraiñcu to rub (Kalit.); Ma. urasuka, urekka to rub; Kui rūsa to grind, crush.

§1.287. In a considerable number of cases the PSDr. *-ay has to be reconstructed only on the evidence of Te. Ka. developments, e.g.:

1. mer̲ayu to shine, glitter (< *mer̲-ay); Ka. mer̲e id.; mir̲u shining (< *mer̲u); Tu. mereyuni, merevuni to shine; Ta. Ma. do not have forms like *mir̲ai as we should expect.

2. morayu to sound, resound (a flute, etc.); Ka: more to hum, buzz, to sound (of instruments); Tu. moresuni, muresuni to rumble; Ta. mural to make sound; Ma. muraḷuka to hum, buzz (note different suffixes in Ta. and Ma.); Klm. muray- to sound.

The OTe. -ay ending of verbs has lost the final -y in Mdn. Te.; e.g., Old Te. orayu is in Mdn. Te. orus-/oruv-. It is interesting to note that Kolami preserves the -ay forms still, which it must have borrowed from the neighboring Telugu in the pre-literary period (see Emeneau, Kolami, pp. 68, 69, §5.17; there are as many as five such verbs shown).

## VOWEL-LENGTH[120]

§1.288. There are only two grades of phonemic length in Dravidian, viz., short and long. Earlier, the historical changes in the quantity of vowels in Dravidian have been attributed to the play of accent.[121] Since there is no evidence for phonemic stress in Dravidian this theory has been rejected. In Te. and the other SDr. languages certain changes in vowel quantity have occurred even in the undivided stage, which can be explained through certain canons of syllable patterning.

§1.289. For PDr. we have to set up two types of consonant-ending root syllables, viz., light bases (C)VC-, and heavy bases (C)V̄C-. Of these (C)VC- can occur free or bound, whereas (C)V̄C- mainly occurs free; when a derivative vowel is added to (C)V̄C-, the radical vowel is shortened and this type falls together with (C)VC-. Consequently, when vowel derivatives follow, only the (C)VC- type occurs in the preceding position. A few examples of this alternation:

(C)VC-V- < (C)V̄C-

1. cer-ugu to winnow (< *cēr̲-ugu); Ka. kēr̲u; Ma. cēr̲u; Ko. kēr̲-; Pj. Klm. Nk. kēd-, KGad. Oll. kēy-; Kur. kẽs-; Mlt. kēs-.

2. par̲acu to run, fly, flee; Ta. par̲-a fly; par-i to escape, flow; Ma. par̲akka to fly, flee; Go. parī-t-, to fly; par- adj. flying; Mlt. paṛc- to run away : Ta. Ma. Ka. Te. pār̲u id. : Tu. pāruni; Kui pānja to fly; n. flying.

§1.290. There is no general rule to show which languages preserve the original grade and which the shortened grade. Since this alternation can be discerned in all the languages to some extent, it should have been present in PDr. itself. There are a number of cases where Te. preserves the long grade while Ta. etc. show the shortened one:

1. *vāl̲ : *val̲-V-; vāḍu to use (an object, word, etc.); vāḍuka usage : Ta. val̲-aṅku to be in use; val̲-akku usage; Ma. val̲i usage; Ta. Ma. val̲i, Ka. bal̲i a way, path.

2. *vān- : *van-V-; vānu to make, fashion (as pots); Ka. bān id.; Pj. vāñ-; Mlt. bānde the way of doing : Ta. van̲ai to form, shape; man̲ai to make, create; form, fashion; Ma. manayuka id.

§1.291. In certain cases Telugu itself possesses both the grades, long and shortened, e.g., pār̲u to run : par̲acu id.; nūr̲u to crush, grind; nur̲ucu to thrash; kōru to wish : kor̲alu id.; tūr̲u to pierce through, pass through : tur̲ugu, tur̲umu to insert, stuff in; nūlu thread : nulucu to twist.

§1.292. In numerous cases the derivative vowel which is originally responsible for the reduction of the radical long vowel is later weakened and dropped leading to three developments in Telugu.

1. Assimilation of the root-final consonant (usually r, r̲, or l̲) with the suffix stop:

cokku to be intoxicated; Ka. sokku, sorku; Tu. corkuni : Ma. corukkuka to feel dizzy; corukuka to be stupefied : Ta. cōr to languish, faint; Ka. sōr id.; Kui sōsa to be intoxicated; (*corku < *corukku < *cōr-ukku).

2. Loss of the root-final consonant:

kaṅgu to be singed (< *kar-ṅg- < *karuṅg- < *kār-uṅk-); Tu. karṅka the state of being singed; Ka. kariṅku blackness; kargu to turn black : Ta. Ma. Ka. kār blackness; Te. kār- adj. black; Klm.(SR) kārī black.

3. Metathesis in the radical phonemes:

bruṅgu to be immersed, to be hidden (< *mḻuṅgu < *muḻ-ṅg- < *muḻ-uṅg- < *mūḻ-uṅk-); Ka. muḻuṅgu; Tu. murkuni; Ta. muḻuku; Ma. muḻuku : Ta. mūḻ, mūḻku id.; Kuvi (F) mṛukh-; Pj. būṛ- to sink; cf. Kur. bōr to immerse.

We notice from the above that when the suffix contains a nasal-stop combination following the lost derivative vowel, either the root final liquid is dropped, or the radical phonemes are metathesized.

§1.293. Since the reduction of the radical long vowel is caused only when a vowel derivative occurs in the following syllable, we have to reconstruct this syllable in many cases, even if no language preserves it; e.g., cendu to reach; to belong; centa proximity, adv. near; South and Central Dravidian cēr/sēr to reach (see Emeneau, BSOAS XV, pp. 110, 111). Here the Telugu form should be traced to *cer-nd-, following (2) above, which proceeds from earlier *cer-und-/-unt- < *cēr-unt-.

§1.294. In many cases the heavy base (the long-vowelled base) itself can be etymologically resolved into $(C)^{1}\bar{V}\text{-}C^{2}$- where $C^{2}$ is a part of the derivative; but this development should be attributed to the period preceding the Common Dravidian stage to which all the languages are traced back. Since (C)V̄-C- does not behave any differently from (C)V̄C-, there is no reason to distinguish these two types for the PDr. stage. The following example is a useful case in question: Te. Ka. tūṟu to enter, penetrate; Kur. tūr- to pierce through soft matter : Te. tuṟugu to insert, cram; Ka. tuṟuku id.; Ta. tuṟu to be thick; to cram; Ma. tuṟuka to be stuffed; tuṟuttuka to force in; Pj. tutt- to be blocked up; Kur. turd- to pass through any narrow aperture; Mlt. turg- to bury the ashes of the dead. For all the above forms we reconstruct *tūṟ- : *tuṟ-V- for PDr. This may be compared with the following: Ta. Ma. tū-mpu tube, sluice, outlet; Te. tū-mu; Ka. Tu. tū-mbu; besides, cf. Te. tū-pu an arrow (that which pierces through). This latter set yields a PDr. *tū- base with *-mpu as the suffix; comparing *tū- with *tū-ṟ- we can separate -ṟ- as a derivative suffix since it is structurally substitutable for *-mp-.

Again, the above etymology shows, on account of Kur. tūr- : turd-, that the reduction of heavy bases to light in the company of vowel derivatives is a Common Dravidian feature, though these vowels have all been generally lost in the non-literary languages.

## Lengthening of short vowels

§1.295. One type of lengthening common to many of the languages including South Dravidian arises from the contraction of the root and suffix syllabics when a spirant type of consonant intervenes between them, viz., *-y-, *-v-, or *-k- [-g-]:-

1. ūrcu to breathe, respire, sigh (< *uy-$^{i}$rc-); Ta. Ma. uyir to breath; Ta. uy to live; uyirppu respiration; Te. ūrpu id.; Ka. usir to breathe; Tu. usuru n.; Kur. Mlt. uj- to breathe.

2. kōru to wish (< *koy-ar < *kos-ar); Ta. Ma. kōr̲u; Ka. kōr̲u; Tu. kōruni; Te. kosaru to desire, n. a desire; Ka. kosaru to hanker; desire; n. eagerness.

Similarly kūlu to fall (< *kuy-il); tūlu to reel, totter (< *tuy-il); sōlu to swoon, faint (< *coy-al); pīlu to burst out (as seams) (< *piv-ul).

As far as Telugu verbs are concerned the forms with the loss of an intervocalic -v- leading to vowel contraction are later than those where -y- is involved, because the former appear during the historic period in Telugu and also lack parallels in the other South-Dravidian languages.

§1.296. The second type of lengthening in vowels which is peculiar to Telugu, with certain parallels in Kui, is also a result of contraction of root and suffix vowels without the loss of the intervening consonants. This consonant, which etymologically belongs to the radical syllable, is metathesized with the radical vowel; e.g., rācu/rāyu to rub (< *ar-a-). It is possible that there intervened a stage without vowel-contraction, as ra-a- < *ar-a-, between the *ar-a- stage and the rā- stage, especially judging from the Kui evidence where two vowels can occur together with hiatus and without coalescence. Since this development has been treated elsewhere (§§1.122 ff., .144 ff.) we refer to those sections for fuller information and examples.

§1.297. One more case of the occurrence of long vowels, rather than lengthening, in Telugu, is when the radical vowel is followed by y. A comparison of vocabulary where radical vowel (other than a) is followed by y, shows that long and short vowels do not contrast in this position in most of the Dravidian languages. Sometimes in the same language both grades occur freely; e.g., nēyu to weave, plait (< *nē̆y- < *nec-); Ka. ney, neyi, neyyu; nē, nēy, nēyi, nēyu, pp. nēdu/neyidu; Tu. neyyuni; nēyipini, nēpini, nēyuni; Ta. ney; Ma. neyka; Kuvi neh-/nēh-; Kur. ess- to weave, plait; Mlt. es- id.

§1.298. In Classical Telugu, in all forms with the sequence vowel (other than ă) + y, the vowel is always long; e.g., ēyu to throw; kōyu to cut; cēyu to do; mēyu to graze; mūyu to close, etc. Corresponding to this vowel some languages show a short grade and some a long one. y proceeds from *c in many cases, and a similar lack of contrast between the short and long vowels does not occur at the c-stage; e.g., mūyu to close, shut (< *mŭy < *muc-); muccu to close; Ta. mūyu id.; Ta. Ka. Tu. muccu to close, cover; Kui muspa; Kuvi muh-; Go. muc- wrap round; Kur. Mlt. muc- to close, shut up; Brah. must adj. closed; cf. Kur. mus$^{u}$g- to envelope; Mlt. musgr- to be closed up; musg- to pack up.

§1.299. Since the weakening of c in the final position and the lack of distinction between short and long grades before y are features common to the whole family, one could assume these developments to have occurred in PDr. itself.

§1.300. There are a few cases in which comparative evidence yields both the grades, short and long, for reconstruction in the radical vowels, even when no vowel derivatives follow; e.g., kanu to see; *kānu, kāncu id.; Ka. kāṇ- (kaṇḍ-); Ko. kaṇ-/kāṇ- (kaḍ-); To. kōṇ- (koḍ-); Ta. kāṇ (kaṇ-ṭ-); Ma. kāṇuka (kaṇ-ṭ-); Pj. Oll. kanḍp- to look for; Brah. <u>kh</u>an-; (< PDr. *kāṇ-/*kaṇ-.). Another such instance occurs in the words meaning to eat, drink, etc. from PDr. *ūṇ-/*uṇ- (for forms see Kolami, Vocabulary No. 977).

In cases of this nature the alternative grades in PDr. can be explained in terms of the Common Dravidian alternation between syllables with a long vowel + a single consonant and those with a short vowel + two consonants. Therefore, we can set up an original alternation of *kāṇ-/*kaṇṇ-. Since single and double consonants behave alike in certain morphophonemic situations (i.e., root finally, or before a vowel or consonantal derivative), *kaṇṇ- has fallen together with *kaṇ-, e.g., *kaṇṇ-t- > kaṇ-ṭ- : *kaṇ-t- > kaṇ-ṭ-; *kaṇṇ-V- > kaṇ-V- : *kaṇ-V- > kaṇ-V-. This situation also explains why contrast has come to be lost between single and double consonants in the root-final position.

## NOTES TO CHAPTER I

[1]A case for separating a native phonemic system from the one introduced by unassimilated loanwords is made by C. C. Fries and K. L. Pike. (See "Coexistent Phonemic Systems," Lg. 25, 1949, pp. 29-50.) They say that a mixture of these two systems is a mixture of approaches, "mixing of purely descriptive analysis with dialect study, comparative work or historical study" (p. 31). Whether all linguists agree to this procedure or not, it is especially serviceable when we are dealing with the phonemic systems of older languages, for which no phonetic data are available. In OTe. one can separate two strata of loanwords, tadbhavas (assimilated loans) which conform to the native phonemic system, and tatsamas (unassimilated loans) which belong to a conflicting coexistent phonemic system. As far as the simple Telugu verbal bases treated in this work are concerned, the native phonemic system is adequate. There is also a clear morphological difference in stem formation between the native Te. verbal bases and those taken directly from Sanskrit, viz., native verbal bases directly enter into inflexion whereas a suffix -incu is added to all Skt. tatsama verbs before the tense-mode suffixes, e.g., Te. kōyu to cut, kōs-i having cut : bhās-incu to shine (Skt. bhās-), bhās-inc-i (past participle) having shone. Also see Uriel Weinreich, Languages in Contact, pp. 8-9, §2.12.

[2]M. B. Emeneau, "The Nasal Phonemes of Sanskrit," Lg. 22 (1946), pp. 86-93.

[3]Bālav. 8.103. "In native forms ai̯ and au̯ alternate with ayi and avu respectively"; ayidu/ai̯du five; avuḍu/au̯ḍu lip.

[4]Bālav. 9.10. (I.e., word-initially ṛ ḷ are equivalent to r l); atāḍu ṛṣi (no sandhi).

[5]Bālav. 1.7, 8, 9. If the tatsama words are taken into account, [ts dz] and [č ǰ] which are allophonic in the native system have to be taken as separate phonemes, since in Skt. /c j/ are palatal affricates [č ǰ] before all vowels, front or back. (Whitney, Skt. Gramm., §44.a). See Bālav., ibid., Commentary to Sūtra 10; Prauḍhav. 1.5, 6.

[6]There is a small class of verbs in final -n/-nu, viz., anu, kanu, konu, tinu, manu, vinu; these, with the present participle -cu, become ancu-/añcu- (añcu represented graphemically aṃcu; [ṃ] = anusvāra, see the following para.); alternatively, anucu- (Bālav. 8.55); this occurs also in certain long-vowelled bases, pūncu/pūñcu to yoke, pūnu to put on (8.77).

[7]The rule goes thus: "In native words, an 'u' of the medial syllable following an n, l, ḍ or r, is optionally omitted," e.g., kinuka/kinka, kānuka/kānka, ciluka/cilka, kāluva/kālva, aḍugu/aḍgu, arugu/argu (Bālav. 9.17). But for this phonological situation, [n] [ñ] and [ṅ] could have been assigned to /n/. In cases with loss of 'u', following this rule [n] freely alternates with [ñ] before /c/, e.g., mancu/mañcu; so it is still an allophone of /n/. (See note 6.)

[8]It is likely that ardhānusvāra meant nasalization (of the preceding vowel), but there is no indication in the traditional grammars for this assumption.

[9]See §§2.5-8.

[10]Burrow, DS III, pp. 128-129.

[11]Emeneau, "Proto-Dravidian *c- : Toda t-," BSOAS XV, p. 112.

[12]In Kur. Mlt. and Brah. k- < *k- only before i and ī; before ĕ they have <u>kh</u>/q; for a detailed formulation of this, see Burrow, op. cit., pp. 132-139.

[13]Burrow shows some cases of reborrowing from IA where the usual rule does not operate; but there are still several forms which are clearly not loanwords or reborrowings from IA, e.g., khap- to cover (see Burrow, op. cit., pp. 138-139).

[14]It may be useful here to remember that Te. /c/ has two allophones in Old as well as Modern Telugu, [t͜s] before back vowels and [č] before the front vowels (§§1.4, .8). A similar distinction in pronunciation characterizes the Modern Kannada speech of the Northern and Northeastern dialects (see T. N. Sreekantaiya, "Affricates in Kannada Speech," Indian Linguistics (1953), pp. 87-90).

[15]Burrow, DS VI, pp. 144-145; Emeneau, Kota Texts Part I, p. 15, §1.

[16]Emeneau, BSOAS XV, pp. 98-112, see p. 112.

[17]Burrow, ibid.; Pierre Meile, "Sur la sifflante en dravidien," Journal asiatique (1943-1945), pp. 87-89.

[18]Burrow, op. cit., p. 142.

[19]Burrow, DS III, pp. 122-139 (see, especially pp. 122, 126).

[20]Op. cit., p. 128.

[21]ceṃceruvu 5th century A.D. (line 13; see QJAHRS I-ii, p. 101); cem- < *kem-ceruvu < *keṟuv-; cf. Ka. keṟe, Ta. ciṟai tank; ceṃceruvu red-tank, name of a village.

[22]DS VII, p. 378, item 136.

[23]Burrow, DS VI, pp. 142, 143.

[24]Items 1 and 3 below occur in Burrow's list (DS V, p. 607).

[25]Burrow, op. cit., pp. 604, 606.

[26]K. K. Pillai, "The Palatal ñ in Tamil," University of Ceylon Review, Vol. I, No. 2 (1943), pp. 67-68.

[27]K. K. Pillai, ibid. Pillai thinks that ñ- forms are original here belonging to pre-Ta., which shifted to y- in the Tolkāppiyam period and again changed to ñ- after ṉ or ṇ; but there is no reason to assume a string of shifts here as *ñ- > y- > ñ-. It is clear that y- > ñ- after ṉ or ṇ is morphophonemic.

[28]E. H. Tuttle, "Some Dravidian Prefixes," BSOS, VIII (1936), p. 815.

[29]For more cases of p-/v- in Dravidian, see L. V. R. Aiyar, "The Initial Bilabials in Dravidian," ER, Vol. 37 (1931, Feb.), pp. 104-105.

[30]More evidence for m-/v- in Dravidian occurs in Burrow, DS IV, pp. 351-352; see also §1.41.

[31]For more information on the history and phonetics of bilabials, see L. V. R. Aiyar, ER (1931, Feb.), pp. 98-105; see note 29.

[32]A. N. Narasimhia, A Gram. of the Oldest Kan. Inscr., p. 54.

[33]L. V. R. Aiyar, "Materials for a Sketch of Tulu Phonology," IL, VI (1936), pp. 434-435.

[34]Free-variation in literature should mean an original admixture of two dialect forms which later writers used as free variants.

[35]Caldwell[3], pp. 138-139.

[36]"Intervocalic Consonants in Dravidian," IA 48, pp. 194-195; BSL XXV, pp. 11-12.

[37]Goda Varma (BSOS, VIII, p. 562); F. B. J. Kuiper (BSOAS, IX, pp. 987 ff.); Alfred Master (BSOAS, IX, p. 1008); S. K. Chatterji (IL, Vol. 14, 1954, pp. 9-15).

[38]DS I, pp. 711-722.

[39]A good example of this is Te. jĕna a span : Ka. Tu. gēṇ, Ta. Ma. cāṇ.

[40]A. N. Narasimhia, A Grammar of the Oldest Kanarese Inscriptions, pp. 52, 55; see p. 252, Inscription No. 7, line 4.

[41]"A Primer of Dravidian Phonology," IA 38 (1909), pp. 193-221.

[42]Comparative Grammar, 3rd ed., pp. 138-139.

[43]BSL XXV, pp. 11, 12; MSL XIX, pp. 88-90 (Engl. trans. IA 48 (1919), pp. 194-195).

[44]History of Grammatical Theories in Tamil (Madras, 1934), pp. 49-58.

[45]"Intervocalic Plosives in Early Tamil," BSOAS IX, pp. 1003-1008, esp. p. 1007.

[46]Jules Bloch, "The Grammatical Structure of Dravidian Languages" (translated into English by R. G. Harshé, Poona, 1954), p. 69; Burrow, DS III, p. 131.

[47]Telugu:

Pogulūra (1.19) 660-661 A.D. (IA 13, p. 137)
Pidena, Kodinki 673 A.D. (EI, VIII, p. 236)
Koḍimuṭi (1.2) (EI, XV, p. 269)
Kanḍukur (1.8) 850 A.D. (EI, XIX, p. 271)

Kannada (see A. N. Narasimhia, Index to the Gram. of Oldest Kan. Inscr.):

Pogevōgi (vb.) c. 675 A.D.
Koḍakaṇi (pr. n.) c. 690 A.D.
Paḍedum (vb.) 692 A.D.

[48]Earlier discussions about -c- [-s-, -ś-]/-y-: Caldwell suspects *-c- as original (3rd ed., p. 153); Subbayya (IA 38, p. 216) wrongly sets up a fronted g [ǵ] for PDr., from which he derives SDr. -s- and -y-; S. A. V. Pillai, Dravidic Studies III (Madras Univ., 1923), pp. 29, 30; E. H. Tuttle, Dravidian Developments, (1930) §10; L. V. R. Aiyar, "A Problem of Dravidic Phonology," JOR VI (1932), pp. 11-21 (in later Tamil -y- > -ś-, earlier -y- < -s- [p. 21]; -g- < -y- suggested in a fn. on p. 20); Meile and Burrow, see notes 17, 18 (of this work); Bh. Krishnamurti, JAOS, 75 (1955), p. 247, §20, fn. 31.

[49]For a detailed description of the developments of this phoneme in all Dr. languages and its phonetic value in modern speeches: Caldwell[3], pp. 161-163; Subbayya, IA 38, pp. 209, 210; A. F. Thyagaraju, "Developments of Dravidian ḻ," Vyāsasaṃgrahamu (Miscellany of Essays presented to Sri G. V. Ramamurti Pantulu, 1933), pp. 75-88; L. V. R. Aiyar, JOR IX (1935), pp. 140-147, 195-210; Bh. Krishnamurti, Saṃskṛti (Telugu Journal, Rajamundry, 1953, Sept., Nov.; 1954, March, May). Phonetics: Tolkāppiyam, Eḻut. 21; Dravidic Studies III, pp. 32-34; J. R. Firth, Appendix to Arden's Progressive Grammar of Common Tamil (Madras, 4th ed., 1934), p. xvi. Burrow and Bhattacharya, The Parji Language, p. 6; Oldrich Svarný and Kamil Zvelebil, "Some Remarks on the Articulation of the 'Cerebral' Consonants in Indian Languages, Especially in Tamil," Archiv Orientální XXIII (1955), pp. 388-391. For a thorough treatment of the developments of this phoneme, see Bh. Krishnamurti, "Proto-Dravidian *ẓ," IL (1958), pp. 259-293.

[50]DS VI, pp. 142, 143; also see §§1.23, .114.

[51]Dravidic Studies III, pp. 28-30; DS VI, pp. 132 ff. See §§1.210 ff.

[52]Caldwell[3], p. 155; S. A. V. Pillai, Dravidic Studies III, pp. 43, 44; Pierre Meile, "Sur la sifflante," pp. 73, 74, 80, 81; K. Godavarma, "Indo-Aryan Loan Words in Malayalam," p. 110.

[53]Tolkāppiyam makes a distinction between two n sounds: n blade-dental, ṉ point-alveolar (Tolk. Eḻut. 93, 94). L. V. R. Aiyar notes that this distinction tended to be lost during the Middle Tamil period and is completely lost in Mdn. Ta. He quotes a few instances from MTa. inscriptions where an alveolar ṉ is used utterance-initially instead of a dental n. These two nasals are still phonemic in Ma. to the present day (L. V. R. Aiyar, A Primer of Malayalam Phonology, Chap. I, p. 10). For the distribution of n and ṉ in OTa., see Tolk. Eḻut. 25, 26, 78, and 82. In Mdn. Te. and Ka. /n/ is an alveolar everywhere except before dental and palatal stops where it has [n] and [ñ] as allophones (see §1.8); in Mdn. Te. [ṅ] is also an allophone of /n/ before velar stops, but Mdn. Ka. /ṅ/ contrasts with /n/ before velar stops and hence should be set up as a separate phoneme; see H. S. Biligiri, "The Nasal Phonemes of Kannada," IL, 16 (1955), §§1.2, 2.3).

[54]-koṇi, -goṇi (1.5, 8; SII X, No. 593, c. 650 A.D.); (cē)koni (1.5, Nellore District Inscriptions II, p. 966, Ongole, No. 39; 850 A.D.).

[55]E.g., mulaga : munaga horse-radish. In the substandard dialect of Viśākhapatnam, an initial l- is regularly replaced by n-, lāgu > nāgu to pull, lēdu > nēdu it is not, etc.

[56]Tolkāppiyam classes ṟ with voiceless stops "vall-eḻuttu" (see Eḻut. 19, 94; L. V. R. Aiyar, "The History of the Tamil-Malayāḷam Alveolar Plosive," JOR VIII, pp. 283-285). L. V. R. Aiyar takes the PDr. phoneme as voiced but there is no particular evidence for this. P. S. S. Sastri interprets Tolkāppiyam to mean that Ta. -ṟ- was an alveolar fricative (Comp. Gram. of the Ta. Lg., p. 64). As in the case of other stops we can attribute the voicing of intervocalic -ṟ- to PSDr. (see §§1.74-.78; also §1.85). A. N. Narasimhaia, Gram. of Oldest Kan. Inscr., pp. 35-41.

[57]L. V. R. Aiyar, op. cit., p. 279 (a table of correspondences given).

[58]In spoken Ta., older -ṟṟ- and -ṉṟ- change to -tt-/-ṭṭ- and -nn-/-ṇṭ- respectively (see R. P. Sethu Pillai, "Tamil—Literary and Colloquial," JOR II (1937-1938), reprint, p. 17. Colloquial Malayalam, with the exception of a few instances, generally preserves the alveolar stop phoneme unlike Tamil (see L. V. R. Aiyar, A Primer of Malayāḷam Phonology, Chap. III, pp. 1, 2).

[59]Earlier, Burrow held the opinion that an -s- (-z-) was probably the original here (DS, IV, p. 346), but recently in a private communication he says that he no longer holds the opinion.

[60]The original phonetic difference between ṟ and r seems to be one of manner of articulation rather than point of articulation, i.e., [ṟ] a trill continuant, [r] a single flap. In Mdn. Te. /r/ is always an alveolar with an [ṟ] allophone in gemination and a flap [r] elsewhere, e.g., /barre/ buffalo [bʌṟṟæ] : /karugu/ to melt [kʌrugʊ], /mārcu/ to change [mārt̮sʊ]. This assumption is based on two facts:

(1). Both Te. and Ka. grammarians defined the distinction (on a phonetic level) between r and ṟ as one of prayatna (manner of articulation). [r] is called laghurēpha (light r) and ṟ alaghurēpha (non-light or heavy r); see Bālav. 1.18; Kittel, Kannada Gram., p. 194, §§238, 239; L. V. R. Aiyar, "Hist. Ta. Ma. Alv. plosive," op. cit., p. 284.

(2). Classical writings preserve the distinction between r and ṟ in all positions except in closed syllables. Even the oldest grammars of Te. and Ka. have approved the merger of ṟ with r when it is immediately followed by a stop (for Ka., see Kittel, ibid., pp. 20, 21, §39); e.g., Te. māṟu v.i. to change, mār-cu v.t. to change, convert. This clearly shows that the shift of ṟ > r is caused by reducing the continuant ṟ to a flap r due to the immediately following stop. Indigenous grammarians from the oldest times have always warned that r, ṟ should never be confused in writing; this is probably an indication that they were being confused even in open syllables.

L. V. R. Aiyar considers Ta. Ma. /r/ as a pre-alveolar, while Kittel describes Ka. /r/ as a post-dental; this is however doubtful in view of the above-mentioned developments.

[61]P. S. S. Sastri notes that "r began to be used in the place of ṟ and vice versa even before the time of Tolkāppiyam" (Comp. Gram. of the Tamil Lg., p. 65). Subbayya also quotes a few forms of ṟ/r alternation (see IA 38, p. 210). In many cases, the occurrence of both ṟ and r in suffix syllables should not be taken as a phonemic correspondence, because they can as well be different suffixes, e.g., Te. ced-aru to be scattered; Ka. ked-aṟu; Ta. cit-ai, citaṟu id.; cit-ar v.t. to scatter; Ma. cit-aṟuka be scattered; cit-ar dust. As is obvious from Ta., -aṟ and -ar are different derivative suffixes just as -ay and -aṟ in the same example. So also Te. kōru to wish; Ka. kōṟu; Ta. kōru; Ma. kōṟuku. This form is from (*koy-ar/aṟ < *koc-ar/aṟ; Te. Ka. kosaru id., see §1.197). Some of the above cases of -ṟ/-r in Te. can be eliminated on this ground, e.g., pāṟu/pāru (see Part II).

[62]In Kui we expect to find an ḷ beside l, since ṇ occurs beside n. But such a distinction is reinforced on a morphophonemic level though not on phonemic, e.g., sil(pa) to shave, past stem silt-, but nol(pa) to lade out, past stem nolt- or noṭ- (< *noḷ-t-); nīl- to be standing (as corn), past stem nīṭ- (< *nīḷ-t-). However, these are not always suggestive of the two sources of l in Kui, e.g., alpa to weave, past stem alt-; here we expect *aṭ- because the base is from PDr. *aḷ- (see s. v. Te. allu to weave, plait, in Part II).

[63]For a detailed discussion on this alternation, see Bh. Krishnamurti, IL (1958), §§17, 18.

[64]Bh. Krishnamurti, JAOS 75, p. 240, §6, p. 247.

[65]Burrow, TPS 1945, pp. 109, 110.

[66]The results presented under this topic and the following one are a thorough reinterpretation of all earlier writings on these developments, especially those of L. V. R. Aiyar (QJMS 22, pp. 448-480) and Alfred Master (BSOAS XII, pp. 340-364).

[67]Most of the Tulu instances show a mere loss of the initial vowel, e.g., ḍambaḍi agreement : Ta. uṭampaṭi id. The metathesis type also occurs, e.g., reṅke wing (of a bird); Te. ṟekka id.: Ta. iṟakkai (see for details L. V. R. Aiyar, "Aphaeresis and Sound-displacement in Dravidian," op. cit., pp. 455-458, 469, 470, 476-478; Alfred Master op. cit., p. 362); Go. rōn house (*ḷōn < *oḷ-an; PDr. *uḷ/*oḷ inside, v. s. v. Te. lõgu, loṅgu in Part II).

[68]Consonants, if any, preceding the radical vowels are not taken into account here, since they have no bearing on this development.

[69]This development is a different source of initial ḍ- in Te. and does not strictly belong to the metathesis type. But since it is a part of the history of initial ḍ- in Te. it is thought best to include it here as a separate section.

[70]Burrow and Bhattacharya, The Parji Language, p. 4, vocab. pp. 171-173. There are numerous examples from Kui, e.g., ṭōṇḍa to begin: Te. toḍāgu; ḍunḍra adj. distended : Te. tuṇḍu a stout piece of wood, stoutness. Examples from the other languages: Kur. ṭiṇḍī strength : Ta. tiṇi strength; Ma. tiṇ firm, strong; Mlt. ṭuṇḍe to look : Ta. tūṇṭu to suggest, bring to notice; Te. cūḍu to see.

[71]Jules Bloch, BSOS V, p. 737.

[72]Subbayya, IA 38, p. 209; L. V. R. Aiyar, op. cit., p. 454; Master, op. cit., p. 351.

[73]L. V. R. Aiyar, QJMS 22, pp. 448-480 (see esp., 470-476); Alfred Master, BSOAS XII, pp. 340-364 (see esp., §§10-15).

[74]Op. cit., pp. 471-472; originally Subbayya, Dravidic Studies II (1923), pp. 44-45; E. H. Tuttle, Dravidian Developments (1930), §§27, 56; Emeneau, Lg. 21, p. 191, §8.

[75]I have discussed this problem in some detail in a recent article in JAOS 75 (1955), pp. 244-246.

[76]It has been concluded earlier in this work (§1.73) that initial voiced stops cannot be set up for PDr. or even for PSDr. due to lack of common evidence among the cognate languages. Initial voicing even in consonant clusters of the type under discussion is shown to be secondary.

[77]It is difficult to date the chronological order of the relative phonemic developments in the reconstructed forms, for instance, the weakening of the medial vowels and the voicing of the suffixes. That which we are certain of here is that both these developments were later than the earliest reconstructed situation of PDr. (as preserved fully in the syllabication of OTa.) in which the medial vowels were still not weakened and the stop suffixes remained unvoiced. It is not necessary, nor is it fully possible, to ascertain the relative chronology of all the phonemic alternations in the reconstructed forms in order to show the structural principle involved in the formation of initial consonant clusters in Telugu. We are in the main concerned

here with the alternations of syllables rather than with those of individual phonemes.

[78]"Vowels retain their full value and are pronounced separately when they come together in a word, so that hiatus is very common in Kui, e.g., lāa young woman, bẽoṭi behind, mliu reed, gii I will do," W. W. Winfield, Kui Grammar, pp. 1, 2.

[79]The only exception to this is Mdn. Te. rāy- (rās-) to write (< OTe. vrāyu) with the loss of the initial member of the cluster. Parallel to this exceptional loss of $C^1$ in the initial cluster $C^1C^2$ (rāy- < vrāy-) is rā- < *vrā- < *vara-, the allomorph of vaccu before back vowel suffixes.

[80]A case in evidence is the Te. form truḷḷu to frisk, jump, be proud, etc., which is used in classical works like KS and Bhr. II. Comparative evidence shows that r in the initial cluster here is not from any earlier stage but created within Te. itself presumably through a tendency to hyperstandardize the form on the basis of the then archaic forms with initial consonant clusters; cf. Ta. tuḷḷu to frisk, etc.; tuḷippu pride, arrogance; Ma. Ka. Tu. tuḷḷu to jump, frisk, etc.

[81]In present day spoken Te., there is clearly such a differentiation on a dialectal basis, for instance, Rāyalasīma dial. minda above : Sarkārs' dial. mīda above, OTe. mĩda < *mīnda. A similar dialectal differentiation could have existed even in the OTe. stage.

[82]In the reconstructions for the following Te. forms, only the immediately preceding stages are given; those belonging to the still earlier stages are mostly obvious from the items of Ta. Ma., etc.

[83]perggaḍa(luṃ) 1.5 (850 A.D.), Nellore District Inscriptions II, No. 31, Classical Te. preggaḍa; Ka. perggaḍe a chief (951 A.D., SII XI-i, No. 39, quoted by G. S. Gai, Historical Grammar of Old Kannada, p. 155).

[84]G. S. Gai, op. cit., p. 12; see Burrow's review of this book (BSOAS XII, p. 467). This writing tradition seems to have been taken from Skt. where a similar situation occurs. For an interpretation of this writing system, see Siddheswara Varma, Critical Studies in the Phonetic Observations of Indian Grammarians (London, 1929), pp. 63-65.

[85]QJAHRS. I-ii, p. 101, line 1.8.

[86]EI XXII No. 429, p. 239, 2.9; also Nellore District Inscriptions, p. 606, 1.14 (Kandukur No. 67); SII VI, No. 250, 1.9.

[87]EI IX, p. 318, 1.11 (seems to be an orthographic error for *pḷakki; Mdn. Te. prakki, pr.n.).

[88]EI XVIII, p. 59, 1.14; EI XV, p. 150, 1.29/30; EI V, No. 27; SII VI, No. 593, 1.6; EI XXVIII, No. 42-G., p. 235, 1.22.

[89]A bibliography of these developments is given in note 56; also see Emeneau, Kolami, pp. 151, 152.

[90]Quoted by L. V. R. Aiyar, JOR VIII, p. 264.

[91]This last one is a case of progressive assimilation in Te., i.e., mp > mb > mm which is not common elsewhere.

[92]In a recent article Emeneau has shown that c/cc in most of these bases is traceable to an original past tense morpheme *c rather than to *t (see "Toda, a Dravidian Language," §§39-56).

[93]Final l̲, r, r̲, and v are rare in free (as opposed to bound) light bases; they occur mostly in bound root-morphemes.

[94]The only exception to this is a small class of seven verbs, all with final -n following a short vowel, i.e., anu to say, kanu to see, etc. (see §§2.16-17; §3.30).

[95]The evidence for this contraction comes from the MI loanwords in Telugu, e.g., Te. divve, diviya, divviya, divya a lamp (-vve < -viya); the -iya forms are earlier; cf. also Te. dīviya id., Pkt. dīvia, Skt. dīpikā f. id.

[96]Te. -r̲r̲ is not from PDr. *ṯṯ. It occurs only within Te. as a result of vowel contraction; cf. Te. gor̲r̲e a sheep, beside gor̲iya; Ta. Ma. Ka. kor̲i id.

[97]Meile, "Sur la sifflante en dravidien," Journal asiatique (1943-1945), pp. 73-89; Burrow, DS VI, BSOAS XII (1947) pp. 132-147. Only Meile discusses the developments of Brahui. Also see §§1.15 ff.

[98]Burrow, op. cit., pp. 142, 143.

[99]Several examples can be shown from the other parts of the vocabulary, cf. Te. cīdu to blow nose, Kui jinja id.: Mlt. īnje, Kur. cīcr-, ījhr-; Te. cīma an ant : Kur. īma a white ant; cf. Ta. īyal winged white ants.

[100]Burrow, DS V, BSOAS XI, pp. 595-603.

[101]A. N. Narasimhia, A Gram. of the Oldest Ka. Inscr., pp. 1-6.

[102]TPS 1945, p. 108.

[103]There is one form in Ka. with a/e after s-, saḷe/seḷe to pull, Kui jelba. Here, the alternation might have taken place in pre-Kannada before c- > s-, and presumably the different vowels were originally represented in different dialects.

[104]Tuttle, Dravidian Developments, §45; L. V. R. Aiyar, ER 37 (1931, Aug.), p. 551; Burrow, DS VI, p. 143, fn. 1.

[105]Tolk. Eḻut. 98; Nan̲. 9; see L. V. R. Aiyar, ER 37 (1931), p. 99.

[106]Op. cit., p. 99.

[107]In colloquial Ta., the change of front vowels to back in the vicinity of bilabials is common, see for examples R. P. S. Pillai, "Tamil—Literary and Colloquial," JOR 2, pp. 7, 8, 12.

[108]For a general treatment of this problem, see Bh. Krishnamurti, "Alternations i/e and u/o in South Dravidian," Lg. 34, pp. 458-468.

[109]This correspondence is not obviously problematical and hence will not be treated here.

[110]Caldwell[3], pp. 136, 137; Subbayya, IA 38, p. 160; T. N. Sreekanthaiya, "The Mutation of i u e and o in Kannada," Proceed. and Trans. of the 8th AIOC, Mysore (1935), pp. 769-800.

[111]Burrow, DS II, pp. 291-296.

[112]For a detailed discussion of this development, see Sreekantaiya, op. cit., pp. 783-797; Burrow, op. cit., pp. 296, 297; G. S. Gai, Historical Grammar of Old Kannada, pp. 5, 6.

[113]R. P. Sethu Pillai, "Tamil—Literary and Colloquial," JOR 2, pp. 6, 7, 9; Sreekantaiya, op. cit., pp. 780, 781; 797, 798.

[114]P. S. Sastri, Comp. Gram. of the Ta. Lg., p. 40, fn. 1; H. G. T., p. 32.

[115]R. P. Sethu Pillai, "Tamil—Literary and Colloquial," JOR 2 (1937-1938), p. 12.

[116]Caldwell[3], p. 136.

[117]Dravidic Studies III, p. 19.

[118]L. V. R. Aiyar, A Prim. of Ma. Phonology, Chap. II, pp. 11, 12.

[119]IA 38, p. 159.

[120]The conclusions presented under this topic are a brief summary of my paper "The History of Vowel-length in Telugu Verbal Bases," JAOS 75 (1955), pp. 237-252.

[121]K. V. Subbayya, IA 38, pp. 160-162, 168; Burrow, DS V, p. 601.

CHAPTER II

# COMPOSITION OF THE VERBAL BASES

## (Etymological Analysis)

### INTRODUCTION

§2.1. This chapter deals with the etymological analysis of the verbal bases, and the history and distribution of the analyzed elements. Here, only the simple bases are taken into consideration as opposed to the compound ones. A simple base may be defined as one which, on a descriptive level, enters directly into inflexion with tense-mode suffixes without the intervention of any verbalizing morphemes. Such verbalizing morphemes are -cu, -incu, -illu, -paḍu, -konu, etc.,[1] e.g., ciguru a sprout, cigur-cu, cigir-incu v. i. to sprout. Sometimes the root to which these suffixes are added is a bound form; e.g., the root *uṅk- in uṅk-incu to attempt, underlies uṅkuva an attempt; so also agapaḍu to appear (*aga + paḍu).

§2.2. Most of the simple bases are Dravidian in origin. However, a few assimilated loans have also been included since they fit into the definition of simple bases and pattern with them in features of phonemic composition; e.g., saḍ-alu to be loose, slack (< Pkt. saḍhila, Skt. śithila-), and prabalu to increase (< Skt. prabala- or a contamination of a Skt. prefix with the Dr. base *val- > bal- to be strong), fit into the large class of verbs with final -al(u), i.e., aḍalu, kadalu, etc. There are twenty-three bases of this type (see Chapter IV, note 17).

§2.3. The verbal bases listed in the etymological index (Part II) can be analyzed into two major categories with canonical forms as follows:

| I. Disyllabic forms:[2] | | | Number of bases | |
|---|---|---|---|---|
| Type A. | 1. | (C)V̆CV̆ | 25 | (Two short syllables) |
| | 2. | (C)V̆CCV̆ | 219 | (A long syllable + a short syllable) |
| | 3. | (C)V̄CV̆ | 238 | |
| | 4. | (C)V̄CCV̆ | 32 | |
| Type B. | 1. | CVCCV̆ | 37 | |
| | 2. | CV̄CV̆ | 22 | |
| | 3. | CCVCCV̆ | 51 | |
| | 4. | CCV̄CV̆ | 25 | |

[1] See p. 187.

| | Number of bases | |
|---|---|---|
| II. Trisyllabic forms | | |
| Type C. 1. (C)V̆CV̆CV̆<br>2. (C)V̆CV̄CV̆ | 565 | (Three short syllables) |
| Total | 1,214 | |

The forms of Type B are peculiar to Telugu while those of Types A and C are common to all the South Dravidian languages. Though descriptively Type B has the same syllable structure as Type A, etymologically and historically it belongs to Type C (see §§1.121-.159).

§2.4. The remaining twenty-two bases out of the total of 1,236 which also fit into our definition of simplexes have different syllable lengths as follows:

I. Non-metathesis type:

1. Eight forms with the syllable structure, long-short-short, viz.
   - (a). ārayu, ēkaru, ēmaṟu, ēsaru, vēsaru
   - (b). mucciru, vanduru, mikkilu
2. Two forms with a single long syllable each, viz.
   - *ūr-, kān-
3. Two forms of four short syllables each, viz.
   - alāduru, alamaru

II. Metathesis type:

1. Four forms of three short syllables each, viz.
   - (a). prabalu, pridulu, braduku
   - (b). ragulu
2. Four forms with long-short-short, viz.
   - (a). krammaṟu, krummaṟu, trimmaru
   - (b). ḍaggaṟu
3. One form with two short syllables, viz.
   - tregu
4. One form with a single long syllable, viz.
   - *lē-

§2.5. All verbal bases fall into two etymological categories: (1) primary, i.e., forms with zero derivatives (no derivative suffixes); (2) secondary, i.e., forms with derivative suffixes. Of the above described three types of bases, B and C are always secondary in that they necessarily include derivative suffixes. Classes 1 to 3 of Type A belong to either of the etymological categories; class 4 is always secondary, e.g.:

| | | Primary | Secondary |
|---|---|---|---|
| Type A. | 1. (C)V̆̄CV̆̄ | vinu to hear<br>(< *vin-) | iḍ-u to place<br>(< *iṭ-u) |
| | 2. (C)V̆CCV̆ | kappu to cover<br>(< *kap-) | cik-ku be caught<br>(< *cil-k-) |

| | | Primary | Secondary |
|---|---|---|---|
| Type A. | 3. (C)V̄CV̆ | āḍu to play (< *āṭ-) | tā-˜ku to touch (< *tā-ṅk-) |
| | 4. (C)V̄CCV̆ | always secondary | ēḍ-cu to weep (< *yāl̠-c-) |

(CC in Class 2 is either a nasal-stop group or a geminated stop, but in Class 4 a consonant cluster.)

§2.6. The etymological boundary, which separates the root element from the rest (derivative suffixes) in a word, is determined on the basis of comparison of related sets of words occurring in cognate languages or sometimes within the same language. The criteria are simple; for instance, comparing such forms in Tamil as tiri to walk about, move, tiruku to turn, twist, tirumpu be turned, wound, tiruppu to wind, tirai a curtain (that rolls up), tiraḷ to become round, one can isolate tir- as the constant element and -i, -uku, -umpu, -uppu, -ay, -aḷ as variables; so also *tir- can be replaced by another such constant as *vir-, Telugu viriyu to separate, virugu to break, vippu to untie (< *vir-pu), vrīlu (< *vir-il) to break open, crack. Therefore, on the basis of "substitution" and the occurrence of "identical differences" in substituted elements, we can set up etymological boundaries in comparative linguistics, just as we can indicate morpheme boundaries in descriptive linguistics. The statistical criterion also holds good here in that the suffixes we set up are far fewer in number than the roots.

§2.7. The Telugu verbal bases analyzable into root + derivative suffix have etymological boundaries occurring as follows:

| | | | Examples |
|---|---|---|---|
| Type A. | 1. | (C)V̆C-V̆ | ag-u to become |
| | 2. | (C)V̆C-CV̆ | cik-ku to be caught (< *cil-k-) |
| | | (C)V̆-CCV̆ | i-ccu to give (< *iy-cc-) |
| | 3. | (C)V̄-CV̆ | tū-r̠u to pierce (cf. tū-pu an arrow) |
| | | (C)V̄-˜CV̆[3] | tā-˜ku to touch, attack (< *tā-ṅk-) |
| | 4. | (C)V̄C-CV̆ | ūḍ-cu to scrape (< *ūl̠-c-) |
| Type B. | 1. | CV-CCV̆ | ḍi-ggu to descend (< *il̠-g-) |
| | 2. | CV̄-CV̆ | ḍā-yu to approach (< *aṭ-ay-) |
| | 3. | CCV-CCV̆ | bru-ṅgu to sink (< *mul̠-$^{u}$ṅg-) |
| | 4. | CCV̄-CV̆ | krā-lu to shake (< *kal̠-al-) |

In forms of 2 and 4 it is difficult to mark precisely the etymological boundary since the long vowel in these forms is a result of contraction of root and suffix vowels of the pre-metathesis stage and therefore represents at the same time both the root and the suffix.

Type C. 1. (C)V̌C-V̌CV̌ al-ayu (< *al-ay-)
kal-iyu (< kal-i-)
2. (C)V̌C-ṼCV̌ aḍ-ãgu (< *aṭ-aṅk-)

One can observe that in all the canonical forms set up above the radical syllables are only of two shapes, viz., (C/CC)V̽- or (C/CC)V̽C- and the suffix syllables of four shapes, viz., -CV̌, -CCV̌; -V̌CV̌, -VCCV̌. The PDr. types from which the classes of the three Telugu types emerge will be described at the end of this chapter.

## ANALYSIS OF THE SUFFIXES

§2.8. The length of a PDr. derivative suffix ranges from a one-phoneme unit to a four-phoneme unit or even more. It can be simply one of the vowel phonemes a i u (generally short, rarely long), or one of the following consonants or consonant groups: -p, -mp. -pp; -t, -nt, -tt; [-ṯ, -nṯ, -ṯṯ];[4] -ṭ, -ṇṭ, -ṭṭ; -c, -nc, -cc; -k, -nk, -kk; -m, -n, -ṇ; -l, -ḷ; -r; -ḻ; -y, -v; or more frequently a combination of both in the order -V(C)C. Vowel derivative suffixes occur after roots with consonantal finals and consonant-suffixes occur after roots with vowel-finals. The suffix sequences may be stated as a formula as follows:

V = vowel admissible in that position (i.e., a i u suffix initially, and u suffix finally)

L = a sonorant consonant (nasal, lateral, flap, spirant, or semivowel)

P = a voiceless stop

N = pre-consonantal nasal which always precedes P (that is to say, N does not mean the nasals of L)

| Root | + | Suffix | |
|---|---|---|---|
| (C)V̽- | + | L | (u)[5] |
| | | P | u |
| | | NP | u |
| | | PP | u |
| (C)VC- | + | V | |
| | | VL | (u) |
| | | VP | u |
| | | VNP | u |
| | | VPP | u |

Before L, V may be any one of the three vowels, as in -al, -il, -ul, -ar, -ir, -ur, etc.; but before -P or -NP sequences the occurrence of i is very uncommon. Therefore, practically the only admissible vowels in this position are a and u. (See §1.142 chart.)

## Initial V of the suffix

§2.9. In general the PDr. system of syllabification in suffixes as represented in the above formula is well preserved in Ta. and Ma.

Telugu has only a few cases among verbal bases in which vowels alone occur as derivative suffixes (§2.124). Even where the other literary languages show a simple vowel derivative, Telugu usually has an extended type with a vowel plus a consonant (§§2.85 ff.); e.g.:

kaḍ-acu to cross : Ta. kaṭ-a, Ma. kaṭ-akka; Ka. kaḍ-e; Tu. kaḍ-apuni.
par-acu v.t. to spread : Ta. par-a to extend; Ma. par-akka; Ka. par-e.
kaṟ-acu to bite : Ta. Ma. kaṟ-i; Ka. kaṟ-i; Tu. kaj-apuni.

This is normally the case with disyllabic and trisyllabic forms where Telugu has a final -cu. It appears that this is a later addition in Telugu through the incorporation into the base of an original past-tense morpheme (§§2.43-.45; 2.86).

§2.10. The only forms where Telugu preserves a one-vowel derivative are those belonging to A (1), i.e., forms with two short syllables, which are only two per cent of all bases, e.g.:

iḍ-u to place, put; Ka. iḍu; iḍuṅke act of putting; Ta. iṭ-u; Ma. iṭ-uka; Kui iṭ-a-.

Here the final -u is not the same as the non-morphemic (non-grammatical, see §1.191) -u which occurs in kaṭṭu to build, etc. These two vowels obviously contrast in their effect on the preceding stop, for before a non-morphemic -u the PDr. final stop following a short vowel is always doubled (§1.191). Therefore, if we reconstruct *iṭ- for iḍ-u and *kaṭ- for kaṭṭu, the different developments in the final consonants can be accounted for only by the different values of the following vowels. Elsewhere we notice that a derivative vowel weakens the intervocalic geminate stop, e.g., kappu to overspread : kaviyu (< *kap-i-). The non-literary languages which show iḍ- (Ko. Tu. Pj. Klm. Nk. iṛ-) have obviously lost the following vowel whose original existence is testified by the voicing of PDr. *ṭ.

§2.11. These three PDr vowels (i.e., a i u) have different degrees of stability in the individual languages. Ta. and Ma. show all the three vowels before L suffixes. Te. has only one case of i occurring before l, viz., udilu to tremble. However, i occurs frequently before y where Ta. has only i, e.g., Te. kad-iyu to be joined, mud-iyu to grow old, kal-iyu to be mixed, to meet, etc. Before the other L suffixes an original i is assimilated to the u of the following syllable.

Te. ed-uru to face, attack : Ka. edir, idir, eduru; Ta. etir; Ma. etirkka.

§2.12. All literary languages furnish evidence to show that a is more stable in this position than i and u, especially in extended suffixes,[6] (i.e., when they are followed by L, P, NP, or PP). It has been shown earlier that the different behavior of the vowels (u as opposed to a) in pre-Te. was the basis for different vowel grades in metathesized forms. An original derivative u was lost leading to simple metathesis in radical phonemes while an a was maintained and contracted with the radical vowel to a long vowel (see §§1.122, .143). Again the loss of derivative u led to a further loss or assimilation of the root final liquid, e.g., po-ndu (< *por-nd) : Ta. por-untu to approach; cok-ku (< *cor-ku) to be intoxicated : Ma. cor-ukkuka id. (PDr. *cŏr : cor-V-; see §§1.167, .173). In literary Te. a derivative u following n, l, ḍ, and r freely alternates with zero, whereas an a does not (§1.144); e.g., vir-ugu v.i. to break : virgu id., but mar-alu, to return; kar-āgu to melt, etc.

Colloquial Ta. has a similar tendency to drop a derivative u in extended suffixes: e.g., OTa. maruntu > Mdn. Ta. mandu.[7]

Old Kannada shows many cases of loss of the derivative u leading to the assimilation of a root-final sonorant with the suffix-stop. This is also probably the reason for voicing of suffixes originally unvoiced; e.g., Ta. āḻ-, aḻ-uttu to immerse : Ka. aḻ-du, ar-du, ad-du (< *aḻ$^{u}$d-).

§2.13. Männer indicates for Tulu a weakened u before r with a subscript [ ̥ ]. He also gives alternative forms where u is completely lost, e.g., adu̥ru̥ni/adruni to tremble. This is not common with i, e.g., adir, adu̥r a limit. Tulu shows numerous examples with a complete loss of u before NP suffixes:

ur-ṇḍe a lump (also u-ṇḍe), a ball : Te. u-ṇḍa a ball; Ta. ur-uṇṭai, u-ṇṭai id.

kar-ṅka state of being burnt : Te. ka-ṅgu vb.

kor-ṅgu a crane : Te. ko-ṅga id.

par-ndu̥ ripeness : Te. pa-ṇḍu (< *paḻunt-)

§2.14. In the other non-literary languages most of the vowel-derivatives are lost whatever their quality, especially in extended suffixes. Kota is a typical example of this: e.g.:

nur-b- (nurby-) to twist (< *nuṟ-ump-)

ur-ṇ- (urḍ-) to roll : Ta. ur-uḷ

er-g- (ergy-) go down : Ta. iṟ-aṅku, Te. eṟ-āgu

ter-v- (terd-) to open : Te. teṟ-acu, Ta. tiṟ-a

or-j- (orjy-) to rub : Te. or-ayu, Ta. ur-aiñcu

Since Ko. shows, in common with Ka., the PSDr. development of *i *u > e o before a, it should be assumed that the loss of a is only later than this shift and even probably later than the separation of Ko. from pre-Kannada-Kota.

§2.15. In Central and North Dravidian we notice similar developments sometimes in different phonological situations. In Parji a derivative u in the environment [C#/C[8] alternates with zero in [CV[9]; e.g.

| | | |
|---|---|---|
| mer-ud | medicine | pl. mer-d-ul, cf. Ta. mar-untu |
| pol-ub | village | pl. pol-b-ul, cf. Te. pol-amu field (< *pol-amp-) |

This is also common with the i vowel:

| | | |
|---|---|---|
| nel-iñ | moon | pl. nel-ñ-il (< *nel-anj-; cf. Kui ḍānju) |
| paḍ-ic | boy | pl. paḍ-c-il |

It is likely that these vowels are only prothetic in origin; but the notable fact is that they developed in the same place where original derivative vowels occurred. Alternatively they may be considered the original derivative vowels themselves, which underwent certain qualitative alternations, being assimilated to the following consonants; note the occurrence of i before palatal consonants and u elsewhere. In most cases there is complete loss of the vowel.

Te. koṟ-uku (alt. korku) to gnaw : Pj. kor-k- id.

Similar loss of derivative vowels in different phonological situations occurs also in Kolami (see Emeneau, Kolami, p. 50).

The following etymologies suffice to show the loss of derivative vowels in Central and North Dravidian:

1. naṟ-aku to cut, hew; cf. aṟ-u to be severed; Ta. naṟ-ukkụ to cut off : Go. naṛ-k- id.; Mlt nar-k- to seratch.

2. koṟ-uku to bite; Ta. Ma. Ka. koṟ-i : Go. kōr-k-, Klm. kor-k-.

3. peṟ-uku to pull out (weeds, etc.) : Go. peh-k- to pick up; Kur. pes$^{e}$g- to weed, pes- id.

4. ad-uku to paste, etc.; Ka. ad-aku/ad-uku; Ta. at-ukku to press down with fingers : Kur. ass-g- to hold together : Mlt. as-g̣- to paste on.

5. ud-uku to wash, clean : Klm. sut-k-; Go. suh-k-.

6. moṟ-ugu to bark : Kui mus-ka; Go. moh-c-.

§2.16. Grignard speaks of auxiliary vowels (inserted within consonant groups) which "are as a rule unstable."[10] In some cases at least these are nothing but assimilated derivative vowels of PDr., e.g.: Kur. mul$^{u}$k͟h-to sink, mul$^u$k͟h͟r- to capsize; Mlt. mulg- id. : Ta. mul̠-uṅku; Tu. mur-kuni; Te. bru-ṅgu.

§2.17. From the above discussion it can be concluded that derivative vowels occurring in extended types of suffixes have a tendency to be weakened and lost. This developed independently in each language or subgroup. Since Ta.-Ma. preserve the full value of these vowels in the literary records, we cannot attribute these developments to PDr. or even to PSDr. The reasons for such a weakening are obviously phonological, i.e., the position of the vowels in question, and hence do not necessarily have to take place at a common period before separation.

§2.18. Burrow incidentally discusses the problem of vowel weakening in -il, -ir, etc. in DS III, pp. 131, 132. He observes: "The original pronunciation of what appears in Ta. -il, -ir is probably most nearly represented in Tu. by forms beduru, madulu." He sets up l̥, r̥, or əl, ər as being original (probably PDr.). This view does not seem to be correct, especially in view of the relative chronology of vowel-weakening in the individual groups of languages. On the basis of the oldest records of the literary languages, we have to set up a i u for PDr. as basic vowel derivatives with extended types by the addition of L or P or NP as the case may be. This fits into the general scheme of the structure of Dravidian suffixes in which the vowels a i u are followed not only by l and r, but also by a whole series of stops and sonorants. Weakened articulation developed in i and u only in certain environments in the old literary languages, i.e., when they are preceded and/or followed by liquids r, l, etc., or certain consonants of types that are observed to assimilate across vowels. A Modern Telugu example is a good case in point:

| Old Telugu | | Modern Telugu |
|---|---|---|
| pag-alu day | : | pag-alu |
| tag-ulu to touch | : | tag-ulu id. |
| saḍ-alu to slacken | : | saḷḷu (< *saḍlu) |
| oḍ-alu body | : | oḷḷu |
| mar-alu turn | : | maḷḷu |

Similarly, the pre-Telugu forms which later developed metathesis had root-final r, r̠, or l̠ (§1.142); where this consonant was a stop the following vowel was maintained; e.g., krandu < *kar̠-unt-, but odũgu < *ot-uṅk-.

§2.19. Apart from the question of the relative stability of these suffixal vowels, they have introduced certain alternations in the radical vowels through assimilative or dissimilative influence. This is another point to support the view that their loss is to be attributed to a post-separation period.

In PSDr. a derivative a lowered PDr. *i *u to *e *o respectively; later, these two vowels underwent dissimilatory change, i.e., *e[-a *o[-a > i[-a u[-a in a vast area of Ta. Ma. (§1.278). In the OKa. period PDr. *e *o were raised to *i *u before a derivative i or u. A similar shift has taken place in pre-Toda.[11] Grignard reports a raising of radical ĕ ŏ to ĭ ŭ under the influence of a following i or u (op. cit., p. 5). The Kuru<u>kh</u> case is different from the former ones since the following vowels need not be derivative; in most cases, as a matter of fact, they are inflectional.

§2.20. Caldwell observed the fact that these vowels are not parts of radical syllables. He calls them "particles of specialization" since they "in some manner specialize the meaning of the root."[12] Though these vowels seem to modify the nuclear meaning of the root, it is no longer possible to assign any semantic value for them. Any attempt at a semantic connection between two word-groups having the same phonemic content of the root-syllable but with different vowel-derivatives has to be carefully judged in the light of comparative evidence and considerations of homonymy; for instance, Caldwell connects Ta. aṭi to beat, with aṭu to come near; unite.[13] This is wrong, since a comparison with the other languages shows two separate series of meanings: (1) to beat, hit, kill, etc.; (2) to unite, come together, join; both are connected with PDr. *aṭ- Thus, when we obtain two such meaning groups throughout the whole family, it is better to keep them separate even though the phonemic content is similar.

1. PDr. *aṭ- to beat, smite, etc. with i, u, a as suffixes: Te. aḍ-ucu to beat, smite, kill; Ka. aḍ-acu to cuff; aḍ-i a blow; Ta. aṭ-i to beat, dash; n. blow, stroke; aṭ-u (past aṭṭ-) id.; Ma. aṭ-ikka v.tr. id.; aṭ-i n. a blow; Pj. aṭṭ-; Oll. aṭ-; KGad. aṭṭ-; Mlt. aṛ-g- to press down.

2. PDr. *aṭ- to be near, to join; with zero, a, u as suffixes: Te. ḍā-yu to approach; ḍā-pu proximity (stem ḍā-); Ka. aḍ-asu to join, be near; unite; aṭṭu closeness; Ta. aṭ-u v.i. to join, to be next; Ma. aṭ-ukka to approach; Kui aḍ-a to be joined to; aṭ-pa to join together (past aṭṭ-); aṭ-u adj. near; Mlt. aṭ-ge near, close.

The second of these is further related to forms with extended suffixes: Te. aḍ-uku to pile up (< to join together); Ta. aṭ-ukku, etc. (see Part II).

Caldwell stated that both the above sets and a few more that he quoted possess aṭ- with the generic notion of "nearness"; but the meaning connection between "beating" and "joining together, approaching" is too flimsy to form the sole basis for such a relationship in the two series. It is likely that *aṭ- to join was related to another group of words which occurs mostly in SDr. with the root element in *aṇ-/*aḷ- (see Part II s. v. aṇṭu to touch, etc.). Through internal reconstruction of the morphophonemics of PDr. we can set up *aṭ- < *aḷ-t-.

§2.21. This is probably the place to point out a morphological difference between the vowel derivatives and the derivatives of L, NP, and PP type that follow them. Vowel derivatives are in function purely derivational; they have no grammatical significance whereas NP and PP suffixes are semi-grammatical. Certain cases of alternation of NP or B (i.e., voiced P) with PP or P are tied up with a change in the morphological functioning of the forms of which they are parts, viz., intransitive > transitive; non-tense > past-tense, etc. (see §§2.72, .73).

## Sonorant Suffixes

§2.22. As far as Telugu is concerned the following sonorant suffixes occur in verbal bases:

| | | | | | | |
|---|---|---|---|---|---|---|
| [L | -lu | -ru | -r̲u | -yu | -vu | -mu] |
| VL | -alu | -aru | | -ayu | -avu | -amu |
| | -ilu | | | -iyu | | |
| | -ulu | -uru | | | -uvu | -umu |

Each of these sets is treated below in detail.

### Lateral Series

-alu, -ilu, -ulu

§2.23. -il(u) is extremely rare. There are only two forms in -ilu, viz., udilu to tremble, shake (Classical; cf. uduru id.), and cikilu to cry (as a child). There are forty-four forms in -al(u) and twenty-two in -ul(u).

Te. -al is traceable to PSDr. -al/-aḷ, -ul to PSDr. -il, -ul and -iḷ/-uḷ. In other words, *i fell together with u and *ḷ fell together with l in Te. (§§2.11, 1.109). Lateral suffixes are rare in Central and North Dravidian. Even where we find cognates in these languages they have either zero or a different suffix corresponding to V + lateral of SDr. Therefore, we can reconstruct this suffix only for PSDr.

§2.24. The following examples point to common lateral suffixes in SDr. while the other Dravidian languages lack them:

1. ag-alu v. i. to break; depart, separate from; fritter away; Ka. ag-al, ag-alu to go away from; go to pieces; Ta. ak-al to leave, vanish,

part : Ma. ak-aluka to part, retire. This can be connected with CDr. *cāy- to leave; cf. Klm. sāy- to leave, let go; Nk. sāy- leave; Pj. cāy-; Oll. sāy-; KGad. cāy-. The SDr. forms are from *ay-al : āy-, with -k- [-g-] < -y- (see §1.79) and vowel-shortening (§1.289). Ta. and Tu. also have forms with a different derivative, Ta. ak-ai to be broken, crumbled; Tu. ag-apuni v.i. to be removed from; to separate; ag-apelụ separation, despatch.

2. aḍ-alu to grieve; n. grief; Ka. a<u>l</u>-al id.; Tu. ar-luni to burn, smart; Ta. a<u>l</u>-al to burn, glow; Ma. a<u>l</u>-aluka to burn with grief : Ta. ta<u>l</u>-al to burn, glow; Go. tar-ī- ṭo be hot (of sun); Klm. tar-i- to burn; Nk. tar-; Pj. taṛ-; PDr. *ca<u>l</u>-; CDr. *ta<u>l</u>-; PSDr. *a<u>l</u>-al : *ta<u>l</u>-al (*c > zero, t-; see Burrow DS VI, p. 142). A form without -al occurs in Tu. ar-atè burning.

Similarly, on the basis of comparison, we can set up V + lateral suffixes for PSDr. for the following forms: kad-alu to move, shake; kan-alu to be angry; ter-alu to increase; swell up; por-alu to roll (on the ground); ur-ulu to roll down.

§2.25. There are more forms in which the suffix -al/-ul is an independent development in Te. and not represented even in the remaining literary SDr. languages, e.g.:

peg-alu to be dug up; be plucked, pulled out (< *piy-al); Ka. pikku to disunite, separate; piñju to divide; Ta. piy to be tattered, torn open; routed; v.tr. to separate, pluck; Ma. pikkuka to pluck; piccuka to tear; PSDr. *piy-.

So also in vaḍ-alu to wither, fade, dry up : vāḍu id.; eḍ-alu v.i. to leave, depart; veḍ-alu to set out, start; med-alu to move slowly, stir, quiver; pag-ulu to break; crack; pig-ulu to burst as seams; neg-ulu to grieve; nog-ulu to grieve; pog-ulu to lament, etc.

§2.26. An alternation of -al, -ul with -ar, -ur occurs within Telugu itself in the following forms, while the other SDr. languages have either of the suffix series:

1. aḍ-aru to burn, shine; n. grief; aḍ-alu to grieve, n. grief; Ka. a<u>l</u>-al; Tu. ar-luni; Ta. a<u>l</u>-al, Ma. a<u>l</u>-aluka.

2. ud-ilu/ud-uru to tremble, shake; Ka. od-a<u>r</u>u to shake, move; Ta. ut-a<u>r</u>u to shake off, shake hands; Ma. ut-iruka to be shed as flowers, etc.

3. kan-alu to burn; to be angry; kan-aru id.; Ka. kan-al id.; kan-i to glow; Tu. kaṇ-akụ firewood; kan-epuni to be afflicted; Ta. ka<u>n</u>-al be hot; glow; grow angry; ka<u>n</u>-i to glow, get angry; Ma. kan-al fire; kan-iyuka to glow.

So also kam-alu, kam-aru to be scorched; vid-ulu, vid-uru to be scattered; other languages have mostly V + r, r̲ suffixes.

§2.27. In a few cases Telugu -al/-ul is originally a part of the radical syllable, shifted to the suffix position through metathesis:

1. ker-alu to increase, rise, swell; Ka. ker-aḷu, keḷ-ar to increase, extend : Ta. kiḷ-ar be abundant; kiḷ-ai to abound; Ma. kiḷ-aruka to rise, grow high.

2. mar-alu to turn back, return (< *mal-ar); Ka. mar-al, mal-ar id.; Go. mall- to return; GoM. mald- id.

3. var̲-alu to shine, flourish; Ta. vaḷ-aru grow, increase; Ma. vaḷ-aruka; Ka. baḷ-e id.; Tu. baḷ-apuni; cf. Te. vālu to increase, grow, etc.

4. pig-ulu, piv-ulu, pīlu to burst as seams; Ka. piḷ-igu id.; Common Dr. *piḷ- to burst, etc.

In the above forms -al/-ul is to be considered a suffix only structurally and descriptively, but not etymologically and historically.

§2.28. In some cases Telugu has -al/-ul corresponding to -ar, ar̲/-ur, -ur̲ of the other SDr. languages.

1. kud-ulu v.i. to shake, jolt; Tu. kus-uruni to shiver; Ta. kut-ar̲uka to become loose; Ma. kut-ar̲uka to shake off.

2. kum-ulu to burn, grieve; Tu. gum-uluni to be hot; Ta. kum-ur̲u to bubble up in boiling; Ma. kum-ur̲uka to be hot.

§2.29.

(a). Cases in which Te. has V + lateral suffixes in common with Ka. (in many cases also Tu.), as against Ta. Ma. : baḍ-alu, saḍ-alu, vad-alu, nam-alu, ker-alu, cer-alu, ar-alu, mar-alu, or̲-alu, peṭ-ulu, mas-alu, tag-ulu, mig-ulu.

(b). Cases where Te. agrees with Ta. Ma. as against Ka. Tu. in this respect: kum-ulu, kud-ulu, ?ig-ulu, pog-ulu (Ma. only), var-alu, kam-alu.

§2.30. While there is no evidence for the occurrence of this suffix, i.e., -al/-ul, in Central and North Dravidian, it is not even regular in SDr. On the whole we can hardly find ten cases where all the literary SDr. languages agree in possessing a V + lateral suffix.

Ko. preserves cases with original -aḷ/-uḷ in the following manner: Ko. ur-ṇ- (urḍ-) v.i. to roll over, urṭ- v.tr. to roll over : Ta. ur-uḷ v.i., ur-uṭṭu v.tr.; similarly, cur-ṇ- (curḍ-) lie in coils : Ta. cur-uḷ; por-ṇ- (porḍ-) roll backwards and forwards : Ka. por-aḷu, Ta. pur-aḷ; etc.

§2.31. On the basis of the foregoing discussion we assume that V + lateral suffixes had their origin in PSDr. and also developed later independently in the individual languages. On the whole cases with -il/-iḷ suffixes are few.

§2.32. Caldwell thinks with Gundert that derivative -il and -uḷ are identical with free forms il house, and uḷ to be (p. 211). This sort of explanation is outmoded in modern linguistics unless it can be demonstrated that all forms with the -uḷ suffix have some feature of distribution (phonemic or morphemic) which can be explained only with reference to the free form uḷ- to be. On the other hand we are still left with -al, -ul, and -aḷ which cannot be so resolved. It can be seen that sometimes different suffixes do not introduce difference in meaning, e.g., Ta. ka<u>n</u>-i to glow, grow angry; ka<u>n</u>al id.

Trill (Flap) Series

-ar(u), -ur(u)

§2.33. Telugu has thirty-three verbs in -ar(u) and seventeen in -ur(u). -ar(u) can be traced to PSDr. *-ar, and -ur(u) to PSDr. *-ir/*-ur. i in -ir fell together with u, being assimilated to the vowel of the following syllable.

§2.34.

(a). Cases for PSDr. *-ar:

1. aḍ-aru to increase; be suitable; Ka. aḍ-ar to rise, come up; Ta. aṭ-ar to attach; aṭ-u to be fit, proper.

2. toḍ-aru to follow, attack; Ka. toḍ-ar to fall in with; Ta. toṭ-ar to follow, pursue; Ma. tuṭ-aruka v. tr. to pursue.

3. am-aru to suit, be proper; Ka. am-ar, am-aru; Tu. am-aruni become quiet; Ta. am-ar be suitable; Ma. am-aruku to rest on.

Similarly al-aru to blow (of a flower); tal-aru to fear, shake, etc.

(b). Cases for PSDr. *-ir/*-ur:

1. ad-uru to tremble, shake; Ka. ad-ir, ad-aru; Tu. ad-uruni; Ta. at-ir; Ma. at-iruka; Kur. as-r- to tremble.

2. kuḍ-uru to settle down; to be cured (as disease); Ka. kud-uru; Tu. kud-ụruni recover from sickness; Ta. kut-ir be settled.

3. mud-uru to grow old (of fruit, etc.), become ripe, mature; advance (in age, time, etc.); Tu. mud-uruni become enlarged; Ta. mut-ir grow old; Ma. mut-iruka id.

4. ed-uru to face, confront; Ka. ed-ir, id-ir, ed-uru that which is opposite; Tu. ed-uru id.; Ta. et-ir be opposed; to oppose; Ma. et-irkka to attack.

§2.35.

(a). It is curious to note that Telugu does not show an alveolar <u>r</u> as part of the derivative suffix after V, even where the other SDr. languages have -a<u>r</u>/-i<u>r</u> suffixes:

1. pad-aru to be overhasty or precipitate; Ka. pad-a<u>r</u>u; Ta. pat-a<u>r</u>u id.; pat-a<u>rr</u>am rashness; pat-ai to be anxious; Ma. pat-a<u>r</u>u be overhasty, etc.

2. ced-aru to be scattered : Ka. ked-a<u>r</u>u; Ta. cit-a<u>r</u>u, cit-ar; Ma. cit-a<u>r</u>uka.

3. bed-aru to startle; fear; Ka. bed-a<u>r</u>u : Ta. vit-a<u>r</u>u, also vit-ir to tremble; cf. Ma. vit-a<u>r</u>uka to scatter; Kuvi (F) ped-ṛ- to be startled.

(b). Sometimes even the remaining three literary languages do not agree in showing only <u>r</u>.

vis-aru, vis-uru to fling, fan; Ka. bis-ur; Ma. vis-aruka : Ta. vic-i<u>r</u>u.

§2.36. There are several forms in which -ar/-ur are exclusively found in Telugu:

1. kod-aru to increase; ? Ka. Ta. Ma. kottu a bunch, collection.

2. tan-aru to flourish; rise, develop; Ka. tan-i thrive, etc.; Tu. tan-è breeding (as cattle); Ta. ta<u>n</u>-i matchlessness; Ma. tan- to extend.

Similarly van-aru to grieve; cam-aru to crush; cem-aru to sweat, perspire; mad-uru to become sweet (etymology not available); nim-uru to stroke the body gently; jav-uru to flog.

There is one form listed in the dictionaries (Śab.R., SAN) with -u<u>r</u>u, viz., giv-u<u>r</u>u with a single usage cited from Āmuktamālyada of the 16th century; even this is doubtful since it has other text versions in the printed books.

§2.37. Even in the Classical language the u vowel preceding r freely alternates with zero in a few forms, viz., aduru, trans. adurucu/adrucu; eduru : edurucu/edrucu; paduru : padurucu/padrucu. In the cases adrucu, edrucu, padrucu, the vowel preceding the consonant group -dr- is treated as a short syllable in Classical verse as well as in grammatical descriptions (see Bālav. 9.20). Though this is an exception to the principles of syllable division (see §1.6), it seems to indicate that weakened -ur- in this position was more like a vocalic r than like consonantal r as in Skt. adri mountain.

§2.38. Another striking feature, which concerns not only V + r, <u>r</u> suffixes but also the V + l, ḷ suffixes is that most of the verbal bases with these suffixes are intransitive in their signification. This is more so with -al/-ul forms. This fact, coupled with the complete absence of these suffixes as derivatives in Central and North Dravidian and their irregular distribution in SDr., suggests that they probably originated in PSDr. as intransitive or middle voice-suffixes, and were later incorporated into the base.

A valuable parallel occurs in Kuru<u>kh</u>. In this language any transitive verb is changed to passive or middle voice by the addition of r which has an allomorph in V + r in certain consonant combinations;[14] e.g., ān- to say : ānr-/ān$^{a}$r- to be said; kam- to make : kamr- to be made. Even in this language, it has two types of signification. The first, "reflexive," can also apply to intransitive verbs, e.g., cī<u>kh</u>- to weep : cī<u>kh</u>r- to weep on oneself, bewail one's private affairs. A second signification is purely neutral or passive; e.g., kickicr- (a) refl., to worry oneself; (b) neuter, to worry; (c) passive, to be worried (op. cit., p. 84). An incorporation of this suffix into the base appears clearly in the form as-r- to tremble : Ta. atir. Here Grignard particularly states that this form is not the middle voice form of ass-.

## Semivowel Series

-ayu, -iyu

§2.39. In Telugu all forms with final -y(u) suffix replace the y by s in past stems, i.e., before front-vowel suffixes, e.g., orayu v. i. to rub : pp. oras-i, past rel. ppl. oras-ina, past tense (3rd. sg.) oras-enu (§§3.29, .45); similarly, kiniyu to grow angry : pp. kinis-i, past rel. p. kinis-ina, past tense (3rd sg.) kinis-enu. This y/s alternation is an important factor in tracing the history of all suffixes ending in y, viz., -y(u), -ay(u), and -iy(u).

-ayu

§2.40. There are fifty-three verbs in Telugu in -ayu. One regular series of correspondences for this suffix in SDr. is as follows: Te. -ay(u), Ka. -e or -a; Tu. -e, -ey(u), or -iyu; Ta. -ai (= ay); Ma. -ay(u), -a, or -e. For this series we can reconstruct *-ay for PSDr. (§1.286, .287); e.g.:

1. or-ayu v. i. to rub, to be scraped, scratched; Ka. or-e v. tr. to touch, rub on; crush; n. friction; Tu. or-e(vuni) to rub, wipe; ur-e(pini) to assay, test, rub, polish; Ta. ur-ai be reduced to powder; to wear away; Ma. ur-e(kka) to rub.

2. ne<u>r</u>-ayu to be full; Ka. ne<u>r</u>-e; Tu. ner-iyuni Ta. ni<u>r</u>-ai; Ma. ni<u>r</u>-ayuka.

3. nar-ayu to become grey-haired; Ka. nar-a, nar-e; Tu. nar-evuni; Ta. nar-ai; Ma. nar-e(kka).

§2.41. Another series of correspondences which applies to a considerable number of cases shows s in the place of y in Ka. and Tu. as well as the regular correspondences; the other languages remain as usual, i.e., Te. -ay(u), Ka. -as(u) or -e/-a, Tu. -es(u) or -e/-ey(u)/-iy(u), Ta. -ai, Ma. -ay(u):

1. en-ayu v. i. and tr. to mix, mingle; Ka. eṇ-asu to add together, make equal; Ta. iṇ-ai v. i. and tr. to unite; Ma. iṇ-ayuka v. i. to agree; iṇ-ekka to unite.

2. ber-ayu to happen; to attain, reach; Ka. ber-asu v. i. to mingle

together; be united; ber-e to be joined; Tu. bir-asuni, bir-āvuni to mix, mingle; ber-asu n. an admixture; Ta. vir-avu v.i. and tr. to be joined; to unite; Ma. vir-aku(ka) to mix (-k- < -y-); Kur. bir-kh- to mix (several seeds); Mlt. bir-g- to mix, add, join.

3. nel-ayu to be established; to remain; Ka. nel-asu v.i. id.; Tu. nel-asu bottom, soil; nil-e(vuni) to be steadfast; Ta. nil-ai id.; Ma. nil-e(kka) to come to stand.

Tulu has actually more s forms than Kannada; e.g.:

1. Te. por-ayu to obtain : Tu. pur-es(uni), pur-eis(uni) v.i. to be satisfied; Ka. por-e.

2. Te. mor-ayu v.i. to sound : Tu. mur-es(uni)/mor-es(uni) to rumble, rattle; Ka. mor-e.

§2.42. The immediate questions that occur on a study of the above cases are: what is the origin of s in Ka. and Tu., and what is its relation to y of the other languages? The problem becomes more complicated when we note the occurrence of c/s also in Ta. and a few languages of CDr. One clear case is the words meaning "to rub."

1. or-ayu (oras-) to rub, test; Ka. or-asu to rub gently; Tu. or-esuni v.i. to wear off; tr. to rub; Ta. ur-aicu to rub; Ma. ur-asuka v.i. to wear off, diminish; Kui rū-sa to crush, grind.

2. al-ayu (alas-) to become weary; al-asaṭa weariness; Ka. al-asu; Tu. al-asuni v.i.; Ta. al-acu be exhausted; al-aicu to be lazy; Ma. al-asuka be tired; Kui laha langor, laziness (< *-lasa-); alāṛi n. fatigue; Mlt. al-esi sweat, heat; > l.w. Skt.' alasa- (Burrow, TPS 1945, pp. 80-83); the regular series for *ay : Te. al-ayu; Ka. al-a fatigue; al-e to shake, roam; Tu. al-eyuni be weary; Ta. al-ai to roam; (alu be weary); Ma. al-ayuka to be wearied.

These two are strong evidence for an s-element which has been added to ay stems or which occurs side by side with the ay forms. That it is a very early element is testified by Kui rūsa, Mlt. alesi and the Skt. l.w. from Dravidian, viz., alasa-. Another important point is that this element occurs as s in all languages including Ma., except that in Ta., where no special symbol for s was used in classical recordings, the c symbol was used instead. This occurrence of s seems to have something to do with the replacement of y by s in past stems in Telugu.

§2.43. The starting point of our inquiry is an examination of related data in Gondi which is extremely useful in this respect. Corresponding to SDr. *-ay (suffixal), Go. regularly shows -ī; e.g.:

1. rāyu to be rubbed, chafed; Ka. ar-e; Tu. ar-eyuni; Ta. ar-ai; Ma. ar-ayuka; Kui rāga : Go. ar-ī-, pp. ar-ī-sī.

2. kal-ayu to join (v.i. and tr.); Ka. kal-e v.i. : Go. kal-ī- to meet, pp. kal-ī-sī.

3. bal-ayu to surround; Ma. val-ayuka id. : Go. wad-ī- to twist or twirl fiber into thread, pp. wad-ī-sī.

4. mal-ayu to wander, roam; Ma. val-ayuka to wander about; Klm.(SR) mal-ay- id. : Go. wal-ī- to roam, pp. wal-ī-sī.

5. cel-ayu, cel-āgu to sound, increase; Ka. kel-e to cry : Tu. kel-evuni; Ta. cil-ai; Ma. cil-ekka : Go. kil-ī- to weep loudly, pp. kil-ī-sī.

6. nav-ayu to languish, sink; Ka. nav-e/nam-e to fall in flesh, emaciate; Tu. nam-eyuni to wear away : Go. naw-ī- to grow crooked (of a rheumatic old woman or of damaged hemp), pp. naw-ī-sī.

7. mor-ayu to sound, resound; Ka. mor-e/mur-e; Tu. mur-esuni : Klm. mur-ay- : Go. mōr-ī- to guggle in the throat (in sleep), pp. mōr-ī-sī.

In all these cases Go. -ī < *-ay. In radical syllables PDr. *ay = Go. ay, cf. *kay hand = Go. kai; PDr. *ey = Go. ī, cf. *ney oil = Go. nī. It may be assumed that suffixal *ay was evaluated as *ey in pre-Gondi; this latter developed to ī similarly to the *ey of radical syllables. A similar difference in the treatment of suffixal (unstressed) ay from the radical (stressed) ay also occurs in the South Dravidian languages, e.g., in Ka. PDr. *ay = ay in radical syllables, but in suffix position *ay = e (< *ey). (For more information on this problem see §§1.283-.286.)

§2.44. Gondi forms the past participles by the addition to verb stems of -sī which has allomorphs -cī and -jī;[15] e.g.:

| | | | |
|---|---|---|---|
| doh- | to bind | doh-cī | having bound |
| tin- | to eat | tin-jī | having eaten |
| kilī- | to weep | kilī-sī | having wept |
| kī- | to do | kī-sī | having done |
| bai- | to catch | bai-sī | having caught |
| witt- | to run | wit-sī or wit-cī | having run |

All forms ending in -ī form their pps. by adding -sī regularly. Trench states it thus, "verbs ending in -ītānā replace -tānā by -sī" (p. 30).

§2.45. Therefore a Go. pp. form wal-ī-sī is traceable to an older *wal-ay-ci; so also kilī-sī < *kil-ay-ci. Juxtaposing Te. mal-asi and cē-si with Go. wal-ī-sī and kī-sī, we can easily see the source of the y/s alternation in verbs ending in -y(u) in Telugu. On a descriptive basis and also on the analogy of past forms with -i, malas- and cēs- have been separated as the alternants of malay- and cēy- (§3.29). This is proved beyond doubt by the fact that the s-alternants occur only in past stems. Ka. has lost even this trace by remaking the stems with final -s(u) for the whole paradigm. Before the incorporation into the root of this s (from *-ci) both Te. and Ka. have lost the original base final y : *mal-ay-ci > *mal-a-ci > mal-asi; with wrong separation of -i, the stem emerges as mal-as-. Loss of y before stops and the spirantization of intervocalic c are features common to all the SDr. languages and therefore go back to PSDr. Loss of y before stops in radical syllables is much older tnan its loss in the derivative position. -ay > -a in derivative syllables before stops occurs in Middle Ta. and Old Malayalam; e.g., Ma. 10th century inscr. amacc- < amaicc-.[16]

This development is also represented in MTa. inscriptions (ibid., p. 22) which can be dated from the 8th century onwards.

According to this discussion Ka. oras-, alas-, nelas-, and the Te. s-alternants of oray-, alay-, and nelay- are to be traced to older *or-a-si < *or-ay-ci, *al-a-si < *al-ay-ci-, *nel-a-si < *nel-ay-ci-. After the loss of y, c of -ci becomes inter-vocalic and hence regularly spirantized. A strong case in evidence for the *or-ay-ci stage is the occurrence in Ta. of the forms alaicu to be lazy and uraicu to rub (§2.42) besides Ka. orasu, Tu. oresuni, etc. To the same conclusion point the Tu. cases oresuni, puresuni, pureisuni, moresuni, in which e < ay (i.e., oresu- < oray-s-). Most interesting of all is the e in Mlt. alesi sweat. Does this e point to an earlier *ey < ay?

§2.46. Another important conclusion which can be drawn from the foregoing discussion is that the Go. past participial morpheme -si belongs to PSDr. or even PDr. Though its history and development are not a relevant question here, it is likely to be originally a combination of two past tense morphemes c and i. c as past morpheme occurs in Kur. Mlt. and Brah.; i occurs in many Dravidian languages. Similarly, the Te. past tense suffix -ti- appears to be made up of two such past tense morphemes *t and *i.

§2.47. Since Go. also shows the reflex of the *ay suffix, it should be assumed that the isogloss for *ay extends beyond SDr.

§2.48. Kolami has six verbs in ay : alay- (alayt-) to become tired; kalay- (kalayt) liquids, etc. are mixed; (SR) malay- to roam; moray- (morayt-) bell, etc. rings; negay- (negayt-) to fly; neray- (nerayt-) to spread (v. i.). (Emeneau, Kolami, p. 86, §5.71). They form transitives by substituting -p- for -ay-: alay- to become tired : alp- to make tired, and so on. It is doubtful whether these are early loanwords from Te., especially in view of the absence of s-alternants in past stems. This does not, however, exclude the possibility of borrowing from non-past forms which, probably, later took an independent past morpheme in Kolami. At any rate, they cannot be modern borrowings, since Mdn. Te. has no longer the old ending -ay; ay shifted to *iy/is, whence in Mdn. Te. ī/is or ē/is in different dialects.

§2.49. Sometimes evidence for the PSDr. *-ay suffix comes only from two or three languages in SDr. while the others either show different suffixes or lack cognates; e.g.:

1. neg-ayu to rise, fly; Ka. neg-e id. (< *nik-ay-); Klm. neg-ay- : Ta. niv-a to rise; Ma. nik-akka id.; ? Mlt. nek-e to get well (? final e < *ay).

2. keḍ-ayu to fall down; Ka. keḍ-e, Tu. keḍ-aguni; Ma. kiṭ-akuka (-k- < -y-) : Ta. kiṭ-a to lie (Kalit.).

3. mor-ayu to sound (of musical instruments); Ka. mor-e; Tu. mor-esuni; Ta. mur-al to make sound; to cry, sing; Ma. muraḷuka to hum.

4. meṟ-ayu to shine; Ka. meṟ-e; Tu. mer-eyuni : (no cognates in Ta. Ma. except l. ws. from Ka., i.e., Ta. Ma. meruku luster).

Similarly for dor-ayu to happen; to meet; kal-ayu to join, mix; bal-ayu to encircle; el-ayu to be pleased, ol-ayu to spread; Ta. does not show ai (= ay) as expected.

§2.50. In many cases Ta. has only -a instead of -ay, even when Ma. shows -ay(u): keḍ-ayu to fall; Ta. kiṭ-a (past st. kiṭa-nt-); Ma. kiṭakuni; bal-aya to surround : Ta. vala (past st. vala-nt-); Ma. vaḷayuka; kal-ayu to mix: Ta. kal-a (past st. kala-ṇṭ-); Ma. kal-ayuka.

This situation shows that, most probably, Ta. lost the y of an original *-ay in these forms, especially on account of the following nasal stop sequences in past tense; therefore, vala-nt- (< *valay-nt-) with stem remade as vala-.

§2.51. In the following cases only Telugu possesses the -ay(u) suffix: sog-ayu to be intoxicated : Kui sōsa (< *sogay-s-); gen-ayu to flourish; cen-ayu to touch, oppose; nen-ayu to adorn, suit; val-ayu to be agreeable, desirable, necessary; mel-ayu to be twisted; to mix; col-ayu/sol-ayu to faint, swoon.

§2.52. Since Telugu is regular in its paradigms it is likely that in some cases -ay(u) forms could be analogical formations on original constructions of -as- (< -ay-c-) : -ay type. Therefore, unless at least two languages agree in possessing -ay, we are not justified in reconstructing it for PSDr.

§2.53. There is one case in which -ayu is historically not a suffix;

it is a separate verb-base which is normalized in Te. to the -ayu stems by adjusting the vowel-quantity: ar-ayu, also ār-ayu to search; consider; Ka. ār-ay, ār-ayu, ār-ai; Tu. āraisuni to expect, look for; Ta. ār-āy to examine, consider, etc.; Ma. ār-āyka id. This appears to be a compound verb made up of two separate bases *āra- (?) fully (cf. Te. āru, Ta. ār to be full) + *āy to examine. Cf. Ta. āy- to choose, examine; sift; Ma. āyka id.; Ka. Tu. āy; Go. āc-; Kui āska; Pj. āc-; Mlt. ād- (see Burrow, DS V, pp. 612, 613). Burrow equates the first element with Ta. Ma. Ka. ōr- to think, consider.

-iyu

§2.54. There are seventy-one verbal bases in final -iyu. The past stem, as usual, is formed by substituting s for y, e.g., tan-iyu to be satisfied, tan-is-i having been satisfied.

§2.55. Only Tu. and Ma. agree with Te. in possessing the suffix. Ta. Ka. have usually -i corresponding to this:

1. tan-iyu be satisfied; Tu. taṇ-iyuni; Ma. taṇ-iyuka to become cool : Ta. Ka. taṇ-i to be satisfied.
2. um-iyu to spit; Ma. um-iyuka : Ta. um-i; Ka. ug-i.
3. er-iyu v.i. to burn, grieve; Tu. er-iyuni; Ma. er-iyuka : Ta. er-i; cf. Go. ēr-ī-, pp. ērī-sī.
4. av-iyu to be broken, spoiled; Ma. av-iyuka : Ta. Ka. av-i id.
5. a-iyu to perish, be effaced; Ma. a-iyuka to go off; Tu. al-iyuni : Ta. Ka. a-i to peril.

In item 3 Go. ī in ēr-ī- indicates an alternative suffix -ay, as in *er-ay-. There is only one instance of -isu in Ka.: kin-iyu to become angry; Ka. kin-isu id.; Ta. ci-a; Ma. cin-ikka.

SR's Kolami has one case of -iy: pul-īy- to get sour; cf. Te. pul-iyu; Ta. Ka. puḷ-i.

§2.56. It is a problem whether there was in PSDr. an *-iy suffix besides *-ay, or not. Considering the pattern of other sonorant suffixes: -al, -il; -ar, -ir, it is likely that there were originally both *-ay and *-iy. In that case, Te. Ma. and Tu. are archaic in preserving *iy which has obviously lost the y-element in base final position in Ka. and Ta.

Alternatively, Ta. Ka. may be archaic in possessing only the -i suffix to which a y is added as an off-glide before vowel suffixes, e.g., Te. teliy-a to know (inf.) < teli-(y)-a. The infinitive morpheme is -a occurring elsewhere, e.g., koṭṭ-a to beat.

§2.57. In many cases the correspondence formulated in §2.55 does not hold good. Different languages have different suffixes:

1. mog-iyu to attempt, undertake; Ka. mog-asu to act zealously for a plan; Ta. muy-al undertake (Kr̲ḷ.).

2. viḍ-iyu to lodge temporarily; Ka. biḍ-u id.

3. kad-iyu to join, be close to; Ka. kad-e; cf. Ta. kat-uvu to seize, grasp.

4. mud-iyu grow old; Tu. mud-iyuni be worn out; Ka. mud-u; Ta. mū-; Ma. mū-kka.

Similarly, in cad-iyu be crushed, kiṇ-iyu be angry; tun-iyu be cut to pieces; mur-iyu to exult; ir̲-iyu be tightened, and so on.

§2.58. In a few cases Telugu itself shows alternative forms in -ay(u) and -iy(u): kal-ayu, kal-iyu v.i. and tr. to mix, mingle; mel-ayu, mel-iyu to be twisted.

§2.59. The other Central and North Dravidian languages do not show any traces of the occurrence of this suffix even where etymologies are available; e.g.:

1. mug-iyu v.i. to end; Ka. mug-i; Tu. mug-iyuni : Kui mūg-a; Kur. mu-ñj$^{u}$r- to end.

2. ur-iyu v.i. to burn; Ka. ur-i; Tu. ur-iyuni; Ta. ur-u̥ : Kui ur-p-a to boil; Kur. ūr- to set fire to.

-v(u), -av(u), -uv(u)

§2.60. This is another series of suffixes whose occurrence is limited in most cases to SDr.

There is one case in which the isogloss unites Te. with the Pj.-KGad. subgroup to the exclusion of all other SDr. and CDr. languages: du-vvu (< ḍuvv- < *ḻuvv- < *uḻ-uv-) to comb; Pj. uṛ-v-; KGad. uḍ-uv-; cf. Ta. uḻ-u to adjust the hair with fingers; Kuvi rū-ss- to dress another's hair; (cf. Kui ṛū-sa to rub, scrape).

§2.61. -v(u) occurs after long radical vowels and -vv(u) after short ones. The -Vv(u) suffixes, as usual, occur in trisyllabic bases.

Whether disyllabic or trisyllabic, the v-element of this suffix series can be traced to two older sources: *(V)v or *(V)g (< *-(V)k).

(a). -(a)v(u)/-(u)v(u) < (V)v:

1. taḍ-avu to grope, feel, search; Ka. taḍ-avu; Ta. Ma. taṭ-avu.

2. od-avu to give; Ta. ut-avu; Ma. ut-akuka.

So also, for ner-avu to assemble, be full, par-uvu to spread, Ta. shows forms with the -(V)v suffix.

(b). -(a)v(u)/-(u)v(u) < *-(V)g:

In most cases of this type there is free variation in Telugu between -v- and -g-; e.g., toḍ-uvu/toḍ-ugu to swear; ta<u>r</u>-uvu/ta<u>r</u>-ugu to chop; al-uvu/al-ugu to be angry; vē-vu/vē-gu to dawn. In most of these and similar cases it is the velar suffix that is more widely distributed among the members of the family, e.g.:

1. pō-vu to go (allom. pō-); Ka. pō-gu to go; Ta. pō to go; pōku id.; pō-kku to send; Ma. pō-ka to go, pō-kkuka to send.

2. vē-vu, vē-gu to dawn; the isogloss of the original velar suffix here includes also CDr.: Ta. vai-ku; Kui vē-ga; Pj. vē-v-/vē-y- (-y- < -g-); Klm. Nk. vē-g-; KGad. vē-g- : Kur. bijj-; Mlt. bīj- The Kur. Mlt. forms yield a reconstruction *vey- (*y = j) without the suffix, whereas for the remaining area we can reconstruct *vayku/*veyku (see §1.285).

In Ka. and Te. the alternation is always between v and a voiced velar stop rather than a voiceless one. Therefore, even where Ta. Ma. also show -k-/-v- alternation, it should be assumed that -k- was phonetically -g-. Additional proof of this comes from the above item Te. vēgu/vēvu, where most of the languages point to a Proto-South and Central Dravidian *g in the suffix position (also see §§1.79-.81).

§2.62. In the following forms Telugu -vv(u) is originally -v(u) doubled on account of the shortening of the radical vowel.

1. ci-vvu to chip off, pare off, scrape, etc.; Ka. ci-vvu, cī-vu, civ-aru, civ-uṭu, id.; sib-a<u>r</u>u a splinter; Ta. cī-vu to pare off, etc.; Ma. cī-vuka scrape, peel, polish; the base *cī- occurs in Ta. cī-rai rags; Ka. cī-ru fragment, etc. (see Burrow, TPS 1945, p. 101).

2. o-vvu to suit, be agreeable (only in negative forms); root *ō-, cf. o-ppu id.; Ta. o-vvu id.: Ma. o-vvā, neg. of o-kkuka to be like, to agree; Kur. okk- to agree with, fit in well.

3. o-vvu to suffer (< ō-vu); this is probably a denominative verb from no-vvu n. suffering, from no-, with the loss of movable n-.

§2.63. The occurrence of -l, -r, -<u>r</u>, and -y as suffixes is not as clear as the occurrence of those suffixes containing sonorants preceded by a vowel, i.e., -al, -ar, etc. In attributing a suffixal status to sonorants in forms like mī<u>r</u>u to exceed, kālu to burn, etc., we are going farther back into pre-historic Dravidian, presumably early Proto-Dravidian or pre-Dravidian. This question can better be reserved for the sections dealing with the analysis of roots, since elements like -l, -r, etc. are no longer distinguishable as suffixes in the same way that -al, -ar, etc. are. In other words, it may be possible to show that they are also originally derivative suffixes, but their distribution and behavior is no longer any different from that of the elements that belong to primary types (§§2.142-49).

## Nasal Series

§2.64. Of the two nasal consonants, viz., -n(u) and -m(u), which occur in the base-final syllables, -n(u) is invariably a part of the root morpheme and hence belongs to forms of the primary type; but -mu can be either a part of the root or of the derivative suffix; e.g., primary type: ammu to sell (< *am-), tummu to sneeze (*tum-); secondary type: nammu to believe < *na-mp-.

§2.65. As a derivative suffix the bilabial nasal occurs in three shapes: -m(u), -mm(u), and -am(u)/-um(u). -m(u) and -mm(u) arise from two sources each, i.e., *-m or *-mp and occur in complementary distribution: -m(u) after a long radical vowel and -mm(u) after a short radical vowel.

-m(u)/-mm(u)

§2.66. Most of the occurrences of the suffix *-mp (= Te. -m(u)/-mm(u)) are confined to SDr. alone; e.g., na-mmu to trust, believe; like; Ka. nambu id.; Tu. na-mbuni; na-mmuni; Ta. na-mpu to long for, desire; confide in; Ma. na-mpuka (PSDr. *nay-mp-, see §§1.190, .188).

§2.67. There is, however, a single case of the isogloss of *-mp enclosing a part of CDr.: nē-mu to winnow; Ta. nē-mpu; Ma. nē-mpuka : Go. ē-m-; Kui ē-mb- (PDr. *yā-mp- : *ñā-mp-, see §1.254, .31).

§2.68. In one case Telugu -m(u) is originally from an older *n-p (where n is part of the root morpheme) which fell together with the sequence *mp in pre-Telugu (see §1.172b.): nō-mu to observe a religious ceremony, n.; nō̃-cu id. (< *nōn-c-); Ka. nōn id.; nōm-pi any religious obligation; Tu. nōm-buni to fast; nōm-u fast; penance; Ta. nōl, nō<u>n</u> to practice austerities; nō<u>n</u>-pu ceremonial fasting, etc. (colloq. nōmpu); Ma. nōl-ka to fast; nōn-pu fasting. In Tu. and Te. the verb is obviously denominative in origin; corresponding to the verb form of the other languages Te. has nō̃cu (< *nōn-c-) with the usual c-suffix.

§2.69. The other forms with -m(u)/-mm(u) include pa-mmu, also pambu (< *pa(r)-mp-) intr. to spread; ve-mmu v.i. to be hot (< *ve(y)-mp-); o-mmu to suit, fit (< *o-mp-); ō-mu to nourish (< *ō-mp-); tō-mu to rub and wash (< *tōy-mp-), etc.

In the following this suffix is peculiar to Telugu: timmu to bless (rhyme word with tiṭṭu to scold; no standard literary usages); pāmu to smear, daub (colloq.); vāmu to make into a heap and lift up (lexical, dial. and colloq.); mēmu to agree (cf. *mē-/*mey agreement, willingness in mēkonu/meyikonu to consent to; lexical).

In cimmu to scatter, strew, -mm(u) can be derived from *ṟm in ciṟumu id., or *mp in *cimp-, cf. Ka. sim-p-isu to sprinkle; cim-aku, cim-iku id.; also cimmu id. It is likely that the base is *cim- here, in which case it is uncertain whether Te. mm < *m-p or *m (geminated).

-am(u)/-um(u)

§2.70. -m(u) in extended suffixes (i.e., in trisyllabic bases) is traceable to three sources, viz., *-Vm, *-Vmp, *-Vv:

(a). Te. -am(u)/-um(u) < *-Vm (*-am/*-um)

1. naṟ-umu to powder : Ta. naṟ-umu to grind teeth; crush between teeth.

2. kra-mmu to overspread, overflow: Ta. kaḻ-umu to grow, be full, overflow, be thick (Tolk.).

There are two cases of exclusive agreement between Te. and CDr. in this type of suffix:

1. us-umu to wash, scour, cleanse: Go. us-ūm- to wipe, clean with a cloth; Klm. us-m- to wipe, apply; (Kuvi shows a form without the -m suffix : ūss- to plaster, anoint).

2. ad-umu to press together; Ka. ad-umu (local, probably l. w. < Te.)[17] : Go. ad-m-; GoM. ad-m-; Klm. Nk.(E) ad-um- id.

(b). Te. -am(u)/-um(u) < *-Vmp:

1. al-amu to spread : Ka. aḷ-umba excess, greatness; with different suffix aḷ-ur to overspread, cover, etc.

2. tuṟ-umu to stuff, cram, tuck in : Ka. tuṟ-ubu, tuṟ-umbu to insert, tuck in; Ta. tuṟ-umpu to be close, crowded.

(c). Te. -am(u)/-um(u) < *-Vv:

This is a case of -m-/-v- alternation, in which it is difficult to decide upon one or the other as historically original except on statistical grounds.

1. kad-umu to seize, occupy, etc.: Ka. kad-ubu to press, seize firmly; kad-uku id.; Ta. kat-uvu to seize, grasp (Tiv ); encroach upon (Jaffna dial.); cf. Ta. kaḻ-umu to join, unite; n. combination; cf. Kur. kajj- to press under weight; probably -ḻ-/-d- points to an original *-c- as reflected in Kur.

2. taḍ-amu to feel gently with hand (KS), seek, search; also taḍ-avu: Ka. taḍ-avu id.; taḍ-a touching; taṭ-avu to stroke, etc.; Ma. taṭ-avuka; Kui dahpa to seek, search for.

§2.71. There are many more forms where Te. alone has the suffix -am(u)/-um(u). In the absence of comparative evidence it is difficult to trace the sources of the suffix in these forms; for instance, cad-umu to crush; cid-umu to pinch, pluck off; tun-umu to cut into pieces; ner-umu to rub or grind; ar̲-umu to attack, tar̲-umu to chase, mer̲-umu to shine (as lightning); ul-umu, tul-umu, pul-umu, etc. Etymologies are available for most of these but the cognate forms have different suffixes.

Again, most of the forms with the -(V)mu suffix are transitive, as opposed to forms in -l, -r, and -y suffixes which are predominantly intransitive. Some cases of this differentiation can be illustrated from the same etyma:

cid-iyu to be crushed : cid-umu to crush

kad-iyu to be put together : kad-umu to join together

From this it appears that these and such other semi-derivational suffixes have had originally a grammatical function, i.e., introducing transitive or intransitive signification in the meaning of root morphemes. (Cf. discussion on -al, -ar, etc., in §2.38.)

## Stop Suffixes

§2.72. Under stop suffixes three types have been set up for PDr., viz., -P, -NP, and -PP, with or without a preceding V. In trisyllabic bases in Te. *-VNP (later *-VNB) freely alternates with -V̌P/-V̌B, and *-VPP regularly with -VP, e.g., *kal-aṅk(u) be disturbed (water, etc.) > Te. kal-aṅg(u)/kal-ãg(u), *nar̲-ukk(u) to cut > Te. nar̲-uk(u). Sometimes the -V- of -VNP/B or -VPP is weakened and lost in the medial position; e.g., *mul̲-uṅk- > Te. bru-ṅgu (< *mul̲-ṅg-); *tir-upp(u) > Te. trippu (< *tir-pp-); see §1.149.

The stop suffixes are not purely derivative. Many times an alternation of -NP/-PP is associated with an alternation between intransitive and transitive forms, etc. (§4.46). Since most of the languages have overt allomorphs for the formation of transitives but not for that of intransitives (i.e., a dental, palatal or labial stop),[18] it may be assumed that historically NP sequences are earlier than their corresponding PP ones, when these sequences are related as intransitive and transitive.

§2.73. As far as Te. is concerned transitive stems are formed by the substitution of a voiceless labial stop or an affricate for the final consonant of a base, especially of those bases that end in -y(u) and -g(u) (§§3.11-20, .53-56):

| Intransitive | | Transitive | |
|---|---|---|---|
| eḍayu | to be separated | eḍapu | to separate |
| aḍāgu | to be suppressed | aḍācu | to suppress |
| perugu | to grow | pencu | to rear (< *per-nc-) |

In the case of bases in -l, -al/-ul, -r, -r̲, or -ar/-ur, etc., transitives are formed by the addition (rather than substitution) of a voiceless affricate:

| Intransitive | | Transitive | |
|---|---|---|---|
| kadalu | to shake | kadal-cu | to shake |
| kālu | to be burnt | kāl-cu | to burn |
| amaru | to be suited | amar-cu | to fit |
| tūr̲u | to pierce through | tūr-cu | to pierce |

From this it may be assumed that where there is substitution the substituted elements are in direct opposition as intransitive and transitive, whereas in cases where there is an addition, the intransitive morphemes (i.e., -al, -ar, etc.) historically have become parts of the root morpheme.

In the remaining cases Te. uses an extended type of this morpheme, i.e., -incu, to form transitives; e.g., puṭṭu to be born : puṭṭ-incu to cause to be born.

Velar Series

-(V)ku/-(V̄)ku, -(V)gu/-(V̄)gu (< *-(V)ṅk-)

§2.74. Voicing of k in the post-nasal position is not uniform either in Te. or in Ka., e.g., boṅku to be; koṅku to hesitate; talāku (< talaṅkŭ) to fear, etc., besides poṅgu to swell, kalāgu to be disturbed. In Middle and Mdn. Ta. post-nasal voicing of stops is regular, and OMa. ṅṅ < *ṅk[19] indicates that post-nasal voicing was widely represented in the Middle Ta. period itself. We can expect a stage of partial assimilation, i.e., ṅg < *ṅk to intervene between *ṅk > ṅṅ. A close parallel development in Te. is *mp > mb > mm/m, where the mb stage is also historical. From this we gather that ṅk > ṅg started in PSDr. and developed independently in the individual languages.

§2.75. Velars are the most widely represented of all Dravidian derivative suffixes and can even be reconstructed for PDr. in certain cases. A few examples suffice to illustrate this:

1. pid-uku to milk, pis-uku to squeeze; Ka. hid-uku, pis-uṅku, pis-uku; Tu. pis-k-(uni); Ta. Ma. pit-ukku; Ta. pic-akku, pic-ai id.; Go. pis-k-; Pj. pī-k- (< *pic-k-); Kur. ped$^{e}$-k̲h̲-, pī-k̲h̲-; Mlt. pī-q- (< *piy-k-).

2. nā-ku to lick; Ka. Tu. Ta. Ma. na-kku; Kui Kuvi Go. Klm. Nk. Oll. nā-k-; Pj. nē-k; Brah. la-kk-; cf. Mlt. naqlu uvula (< *nalq-); cf. Ta. nā tongue.

3. po-kku to blister; a blister; Tu. po-kkè a boil; Ta. po-kku v. i.; Ma. po-kkuḷ n., Kur. po-kkh- v. i.; Mlt. po-k-.

Others of this type are nar-aku, ad-uku, pe<u>r</u>-uku, ve-kku, mu-kku, etc. For these and similar forms it is possible to reconstruct complete sequences, for instance: *pic-ukku/*pit-ukku (item 1); *nā-k- (item 2, *nā tongue); *po-ṅk-/*po-kk- (item 3), and so on.

§2.76. On the basis of the presence or absence of velar suffixes in the other languages for a given item in Telugu, the material can be analyzed into five sets of oppositions:

| | | |
|---|---|---|
| 1. Te. and SDr. | : | Central and North Dravidian. |
| 2. Te. and CDr. and NDr. | : | other SDr. languages. |
| 3. Te. Ka. (and Tu.) | : | Ta.-Ma. |
| 4. Te. Ta.-Ma. | : | Ka. (and Tu.). |
| 5. Te. | : | all other languages. |

§2.77. There are actually very few cases of Set 1. If all SDr. languages agree in possessing the velar suffix, very often we find etymologies also in the other groups with the same type of suffix. However, there are instances which provide isoglosses that enclose all SDr. against the other geographical groups:

1. cek-ku to insert; cer-uvu id.; Ka. ser-ku, sek-ku; Ta. cer-uku; Ma. ter-ukkuka, cer-utuka : Kur. <u>kh</u>err-; Mlt. qer-.

2. e<u>r</u>-ăgu to descend, to bow down; Ka. e<u>r</u>-agu; Tu. er-aguni; Ta. i<u>r</u>-aṅku, ī<u>r</u>-aiñcu, i<u>r</u>-ai; Ma. i<u>r</u>-aṅṅuka : Kui jā-mba to subside (< *<u>t</u>ā- < *e<u>t</u>a-); Kuvi (F) rec- id.; Kur. ett- to descend; Mlt. et- (< *e<u>tt</u>-).

§2.78. Te., Central and/or NDr. : other SDr. languages.

Since Te. is geographically as closely related to CDr. as to SDr., it has numerous isoglosses both phonological and morphological which tie it up with CDr. as against SDr. In the following instances Te. has velar suffixes in common with CDr. and NDr.:

1. ud-uku to wash as a garment; drub, thrash; Klm. sut-k-; Go. suh-k-; cf. Kui jō-ga id. : Ta. ut-ai, cut-ai to kick, beat; Ma. ut-ayuka; Ka. od-e/i; Mlt. ut-es-/us-et- id.; for meaning connection cf. Ma. ma<u>l</u>-akku to beat, wash, cleanse, wipe off.

2. bar-uku to scratch, scribble; Kui ver-ka; Kuvi (F) bakṛ- (< *baṛ-k-) id. : Ka. bar-e, bar-i; Tu. bar-ipuni; Ta. var-ai; var-i a line; Ma. var-ekka.

3. ā̃-gu to stop, be prevented; to prevent; Kui ā-ṅga to intercept;

Kuvi ā-ṅg- to hinder : Ka. ān, ā- be arrested; ā-pu stoppage; Tu. ai-runi to stay, stop; Ta. Ma. ā-ppu wedge.

4. moṟ-ugu to bark (of a dog); moṟ-a a cry; Kui mus-ka; Kuvi mō-kh- (< *moh-k-) : Ka. moṟ-e to cry aloud as a tiger, yell; Ta. moṟ-u moṟ-u to grumble; Ma. mur-aḷuka dog to howl.

§2.79. Te. Ka. (and Tu.) : Ta.-Ma.

Wherever there is disagreement in SDr. in possessing velar suffixes it is usually Te. Ka. and Tu. that form a sub-group as against Ta.-Ma.

1. toḍ-uku to hold, grasp; Ka. tuḍ-uku, tuḍ-uṅku to seize quickly; Tu. toḍ-aṅku a clasp, hook : Ta. Ma. toṭ-u to handle, take hold of.

2. tuṟ-ugu to stuff in, cram, insert; Ka. tuṟ-uku to stuff, cram; tuṟ-ugu be packed, etc.; cf. Mlt. tur-g- to bury the ashes of the dead : Ta. tuṟ-u tr. to cram, stuff; Ma. tuṟ-uttuka id.

3. nik-ku to stand erect, be proud, etc. (< *niḷ-k-); Ka. niḷ-uku, nil-ku, nil-uku to strut, rise up to; be extended to full height : Ta. Ma. nīḷ to extend to full length.

§2.80. Te. Ta. Ma. : Ka. (and Tu.).

There are relatively few cases where Te. agrees with Ta.-Ma. in possessing a velar suffix as against Ka. (and Tu.):

1. per-ugu to flourish, grow; Ta. per-uku id.; Ma. per-ukuka : Ka. per-cu; Tu. per-cuni.

2. mar-āgu, mar-ugu to become familiar, be tamed, trained : Ma. mar-aṅṅuka to be tamed, accustomed, etc.; mar-akkuka to tame, seduce : Ka. mar-cu; Tu. mar-cuni to be tamed.

§2.81. Te. : all other languages.

There are over twenty items in which Te. alone shows a velar suffix while the other languages have different suffixes. There are twenty-five more items in final -ku/-gu without proper etymologies in the sister languages:

1. pal-uku to say, speak : Tu. paṇ-pini; Ta. paṇ-i to ask, say; Kui plā-pa to ask, say, address; Klm. pāna language; Brah. pān- say, speak; (PDr. *pāḷ-/*pāṇ-).

2. cel-āgu to sound (as drum) : Ka. kel-e cry out with joy; Tu. kil-evuni; Ta. cil-ai, cil-ampu; Ma. cil-ekka, cil-ampuka; Kuvi kil-eri howling; Go. kil-ī- to scream.

Other forms of this class include tan-uku, gun-uku, nim-uku, cib-uku, meṟ-uku, tal-āku, par-agu, kas-ugu, mū-gu, etc.

§2.82. Though Te. -g(u) is traceable in most cases to PSDr. *-k or *-ṅk, it is possible that it arose from older *-y- or *-v- in certain instances; (for -g- < *-y-, *-v-, see §§1.79, .81).

(a). -g- < *-v-.

1. mar-ugu to be accustomed, be tamed; mar-upu to tame : Ta. mar-uvu id.; Ma. mar-uvuka.

2. aḍ-ugu to ask; Pj. aḍ-g- id. : Ta. aḷ-avu to enquire after one's health (Tolk.); aḷ-i speak, express.

3. kaḍ-ugu to wash: Ta. kaḻ-uvuka id. (Krḷ.); Ma. kaḻ-ukuka id. (-k- [-g-] < -v-).

(b). -g- < *-y-.

The evidence is not conclusive for this development; but in the following forms, corresponding to Te. -ugu other SDr. languages have -i, for which the expected correspondence in Te. is -iyu (see §2.55). Therefore, it is possible here to derive -ugu < *-igu < *-iyu. The assimilation of medial i to u of the final syllable is thoroughly regular (§2.11); e.g.:

1. med-ugu to be well pounded (< *med-igu < *med-iyu); Ma. met-iyuka id.; Ta. met-i; Ka. mid-i to pound; Tu. med-upuni.

2. tir-ugu to turn, move about; Ka. tir-i, tir-igu; Ta. tir-i; tir-uku to twist; Ma. tir-iyuka. It is interesting to note the -igu (< -iyu) form in Ka.

3. vir-ugu, vir-iyu to break, crumble; Tu. bir-iyuni; Ma. vir-iyuka; Ka. vir-i; Ta. vir-i.

§2.83. It is difficult to draw any historical conclusions from the absence of a given series of suffixes in contiguous languages. It is likely that neighboring languages which do not now have cognates with velar suffixes, might have originally possessed them and lost them sometime during the post-separation period, and preserved only forms having different suffixes. We can assume, for instance, that at a common stage each of the languages (then dialects) possessed several forms derived from the same root but with different suffixes. For some reason or other, certain of these derived forms may go out of use in one language, while a neighboring language may treasure them with especial care. This can even happen at a dialectal stage.

On the contrary, it is possible to deduce certain conclusions from the occurrence of a suffix in nearer or farther languages. In the following example only Mlt. has a velar suffix in common with SDr.; the remaining Central and North Dravidian languages lack correspondences: tin-uku to strain (at stool); Ka. tiṇ-uku; cf. Ta. tiṇ-uṅku to congeal; tiṇ-i to become solid, etc. : Mlt. tin-q- to strain (at stool). This shows that Mlt. inherited this form at a common stage with SDr., and its neighboring Kur. lost it. Similarly if some of the languages, geographically contiguous, and forming part of a sub-group, possess a certain series of suffixes which are altogether absent in other geographically distant groups, then we assume a high degree of probability for the exclusive development of that particular series in that particular group; in other words, such developments have taken place not at the PDr. stage but at PSDr., PCDr., or PNDr. stages.

From the evidence furnished by the distribution of velar suffixes, we gather that Te. occupies a midway position between SDr. and CDr., since it has cases of exclusive agreement with each of the groups (§§2.76-.80).

Palatal Series

-(V)cu, -(V̄)cu

§2.84. Palatal affricates are the most characteristic of all Te. verbal derivatives. In the majority of cases they have no parallels either in the remaining SDr., or CDr. or NDr. languages. A few examples suffice to illustrate this:

1. ēḍ-cu to weep; Ta. Ma. Ka. aḻ-u; Tu. ar-pini; Pj. aṛ-; Kui ṛī-va; KGad. āḍ-.

2. ār-cu to shout, roar; Ka. also ār-cu/ā-cu id.; Ka. Ta. ār- id.; Ma. āṛ-kuka; Tu. ār-kuni; Kui ār-pa; Kuvi(S) ār-; Klm. ar-, Klm.(SR) arr- to cry; Mlt. arr- to call to goats.

3. vēl-cu to offer a sacrifice; Ka. bēḷ, bēḷu; Ta. vēḷ; Ma. vēḷ-ka to marry before fire, vēḷ-vi sacrifice.

Since only Telugu shows -c(u) here, one should reconstruct forms without c for PDr., viz., *yāḻ-, *ār-, vēḷ-, and so on.

§2.85. Similarly, in the case of Telugu trisyllabic bases with derivative -acu or -ucu (with or without an ardhānusvāramu), the final -cu element does not occur in the other languages; e.g.:

(a). -ac(u):

1. vag-acu to consider; Ka. bag-e; Tu. bag-eyuni; Ta. vak-ai.

2. naḍ-acu to walk; Ka. naḍ-e; Tu. naḍ-apuni; Ta. naṭ-a; Ma. naṭ-akka; Kui ḍṛā-pa (ḍṛāt-) to step over; overflow.

3. maṟ-acu to forget; Ta. maṟ-a id.; maṟ-ai to be hidden; Ma. maṟ-akka; Ka. maṟ-e; Tu. mad-apuni; Go. mar-ēng-.

4. teṟ-acu to open; Ka. teṟ-e be opened; to open; Ta. tiṟ-a; Go. tar-ī- (pp. tarīsī).

5. paṟ-acu to run away, flee, flow; Ta. paṟ-a to fly; Ma. paṟ-akka fly, flee; Tu. par-apuni to flow; Go. par-ī- (parīsī) to fly; Mlt. parc- to run away.

(b). -uc(u):

1. kuḍ-ucu to eat, drink; Ka. kuḍ-i; Ta. kuṭ-i; Ma. kuṭikka; Kuvi goh-.

2. pil-ucu to call; Ta. viḷ-i to call; roar; Ma. viḷ-ikka; Tu. buḷ-puni to cry aloud.

3. gel-ucu to win; Ka. gel-i; Ta. vel; Ma. velluka; Ko. gel-c- id.; To. kel-c- be successful.

Examples can be multiplied. Since -c(u) is peculiar to Te. in most cases, internal evidence of Te. may furnish some clues for its reconstruction. There are two homonymous -c(u) morphemes in Te.: -c(u) causal or transitive, with -pu and -incu as alternants, and -c(u) verbalizing, with an allomorph -incu. Both these suffixes are considered inflexional, since a simple base can take tense-mode suffixes without them. Again, these two -c(u) morphemes are opposed to derivative -c(u) occurring in the above instances. Te. grammars separate 'āgama-c' (inflexional) from non-āgama-c, i.e., 'siddha-c' (non-inflexional, lit. original, i.e., derivative). All verbs in final -c(u) (ungeminated) have two stems in conjugation. If it is a derivational -c(u) it alternates with -v- before all back-vowel suffixes (i.e., non-past and non-present), elsewhere it is -c(u), e.g.:

| | | |
|---|---|---|
| pilucu to call: | pres. part. | pilucu-cu- |
| | past part. | pilic-i |
| | infinitive | piluv-a |
| | neg. part. | piluv-aka |
| | imp. 2nd sg. | piluv-umu, pil-umu |

The conjugation is the same even for forms ending in -ac(u), except that -a- is not assimilated to the quality of the following vowel, e.g., te<u>r</u>acu, te<u>r</u>acu-cu-, te<u>r</u>ac-i, te<u>r</u>av-a, te<u>r</u>av-aka, te<u>r</u>av-umu, etc.

§2.86. Here we have the same historical development as in the case of y-ending bases which have alternate stems in s in the past. In all the above mentioned cases, where Te. alone has c corresponding to zero of the other languages, it should be taken as originally a part of the past participial morpheme *-ci, of which the c-element is wrongly incorporated into the base. Consequently in non-past forms the original disyllabic base occurs without c, i.e., *pilu with probably a glide v before back vowel suffixes. Imperative pil-umu (2nd sg.) is a very ancient type of construction which preserves the PDr. base even without the glide v. *-ci in these cases could be traced to an earlier *-cci which was probably a phonologically conditioned allomorph of the morpheme (or morpheme sequence) *-ci; *-si was the other allomorph of *-ci occurring after y-ending stems.

The present tense is historically a later innovation in Te., and is actually a compound construction formed with the verb un- to be. It is therefore likely that the c-stem, wrongly separated from the past tense forms, later formed the basis of the present tense.

§2.87. Even in Gondi where the past participial *-ci is preserved intact, a similar re-formation of the base took place in certain forms through the incorporation of c into the root. We can see this development in verbs ending in c or s in Gondi; e.g.:

1. Go. anc- to press; pp. ancī (historically *aṇ-ci); Te. aṇ-ācu to press down; Ka. aṇ-e to push; Tu. aṇ-epuni to press, push.

2. Go. dals- to pound with fists, thresh with a flail; pp. dalsī (< *dal-ci); cf. Ka. taḷḷu thrust; taḷ-isu to pound; Tu. taḷḷuni to thrust, dash against, etc.

3. Go. (kōr)-kūs- to crow (of cocks), pp. -kūsī (< *kū-ci); Te. kūyu to crow, cry; Ka. kū-gu, kū-ku id., kū a cry; Tu. kū-guni; Ta. kū cooing; kū-vu call, crow; Ma. kū-kkuka; Kui kū-pka; Klm. kū-g-; Mlt. kū-kr-; Brah. kū-k n. cry; (< PDr. *kū-).

§2.88. An alternative source of c in Te. is the past tense morpheme *-t-/*-tt- which is palatalized to -cc- in many cases in Middle Ta. and OMa.; but this solution is less probable for the following reasons:

1. tt > cc occurs only when it is associated with bases ending in i or ai, e.g., Ma. vaccu (inscr.) (< *vaiccu < *vaittu; 10th century; vaiccu also occurs); muṭiccu (< *muṭittu; 13th century); piṭicc- (12th century).[20] This does not, therefore, explain the numerous forms in Te. where -c(u) occurs after ḍ, n, r, l, etc., ēḍcu, ārcu, vēlcu, pīlcu, etc.; besides, there are also forms in which c is originally preceded by neither *ay nor *i, e.g., par̲-acu to fly, flee : Ta. par̲-a; mar̲-acu to forget : Ta. mar̲-a; further, there are also monosyllabic forms, viz., vil-ucu/vil-cu to sell : Ta. vil (past st. vir̲r̲-); nil-ucu/nil-cu to stand : Ta. nil id. (past st. nin̲r̲-); in all these cases the development of a palatal from original *t/*tt is inconceivable.

2. The development of a palatal affricate from the past morpheme t/tt is a Middle Ta. and OMa. development; there was no possibility of Te. inheriting this, since it was not the PSDr. stage.

3. It is only the geminated allomorph *-tt- of past *-t-, but not *-nt- or *-t-, that is palatalized after *i or *ay; but many of the Ta. verbs in final i and ai and even a have for their past the allomorph -nt-, i.e., they belong to the 4th or 12th conjugation;[21] e.g.:

| Telugu | Tamil | | |
|---|---|---|---|
| vag-acu to consider | vak-ai 4 v. tr. | past st. | vakai-nt- |
| kaḍ-acu to pass (as time), to cross, etc. | kaṭ-a 4 v. i. | past st. | kaṭa-nt- |
| naḍ-acu to walk | naṭ-a 12 v. i. | past st. | naṭa-nt- |

This further restricts the possibility of identifying Te. -c(u) with the palatalized variant of the past allomorph which occurs in Tamil.

§2.89. Traces of a similar incorporation into the root of the past morpheme *c or *ci occurs also in a few other languages besides Te.

| | |
|---|---|
| 1. kaḍ-acu to cross | : Kui gṛā-s- pass over |
| 2. paṟ-acu to flee | : Mlt. par-c- to run away |
| 3. par-acu to spread (out a cloth, etc.) | : Kui pra-hpa (< *pras- < *parc-); Go. par-h- (< *pars-); Kuvi pre-ss- (< *pers-) |
| 4. caṟ-acu to slap, whip | : Kui jaṛ-sa to whip; Mlt. taṛ-c- to slap |
| 5. pil-ucu to call | : Kur. piṅ-j- (< *piṇ-j-/-c-) id. |
| 6. gel-ucu to win | : Kuvi gel-h- (< *gels-) id. |
| 7. kol-ucu to measure | : GoM. kōl-s- id. |
| 8. vā-cu to swell, inflame Ka. bā, bāyu; Tu. bāpuni; Ma. vāykka; Pj. vāp-, vāt- | : GoM. wāh-c- to boil |
| 9. vai-cu to throw; Ka. bay; Ta. vai | : Kur. bā̃-c- to throw; Mlt. bā-s- to cover |
| 10. īr-cu to comb out nits | : Mlt. īr-c- to scratch ground as fowls; Brah. ir-is comb |

These cases show the inclusion of c in the base, which does not occur in Ta. Ka. and Ma. It is to be noted that the languages quoted belong to Central or North Dravidian and most of them have a past tense morpheme c/s. In this respect Te. goes closer with Central and North Dravidian than with South Dravidian.

§2.90. The following case evidences the occurrence of a c suffix in all South Dravidian languages: vī-cu to blow, as wind; to fling; Ka. bī-su; Tu. bī-juni, bī-suni; Ta. vī-cu to fling, swing (PN); to blow as wind; Ma. vī-cuka to fan, blow; vī-yuka, vī-śuka id. : Kui vī-ka to blow a wind instrument with mouth, vī-nja to blow, fan.

Comparing the SDr. forms with Kui vī-ka, *vī- can be separated off as the ultimate base. Here all languages form the past participle by adding -i, viz., vīci which can historically be analyzed as *vī-ci. This etymology is one of the fossils of the stage in PDr. when the isogloss of the c-past includes also all SDr. languages, including Ta. and Ma. It is to be assumed that Ta. and Ma. mainly lay outside this isogloss, while Ka. was probably on the border-line, since it possesses several forms with incorporated s or c.

Retroflex Series

§2.91. Of the remaining suffixes of the stop series there come in order of frequency retroflexes, dentals, and labials.

The retroflex series occur as follows: -ṭ(u), -ṇṭ(u), -ṇḍ(u) in disyllabic bases, and -aṭu/-āṭu, -uṭu/-ūṭu, -aḍu/-uḍu in trisyllabic bases:

-ṭ(u), -ṇṭ(u)

§2.92. In most cases the suffixes of the retroflex series can be etymologically traced to dental stops with morphophonemic alternations; for instance, one can set up an incorporated dental stop suffix in the following instances:

1. cāṭu to publish, proclaim; Ta. Ma. cā_rr_u; Ka. sā_r_u to cry aloud, proclaim; Tu. sāriyuni; Ta. cā_rr_ < *cā_t_-t-.

2. nāṭu tr. to fix, plant; Ka. nāṭu id.; Tu. nāṭuni to affect, impress; move, operate upon, as medicine; Ta. nāṭṭu to fix, plant; Ma. nāṭṭuka; Ta.-Ma. nāṭṭ- < *nāṭ + t- or *nāḷ + t-.

Similarly, māṭu to hide, Ta. mā_rr_u id., Kui mārga to take shelter; Kur. mā̃ṛ- (maṇḍ-y-) to hide away, bury. In all these cases it is possible that doubling in Ta., where the original condition of the suffix is preserved, is due to the incorporation of a causal -t- into the base.

§2.93. A similar morphophonemic alternation can be set up for the PDr. or PSDr. stage itself, viz., -ṭ- < -ḷ-t-; *-ṭ- is geminated in all the languages in the root-final position; e.g.:

1. kaṭṭu to tie up, build; Ta. Ma. Ka. Tu. kaṭṭu id.; Go. Klm. kaṭṭ-; Kur. Mlt. kaṛ- to twist together : Ta. kaḷai to tie, fasten; *kaṭ- : *kaḷ-. Since ḷ < ṭ does not occur in open syllables, the course of change is ṭ < *ḷ + t.

2. taṭṭu to pat, slap, stop; Ka. taṭṭu; Tu. taṭṭuni, Ta. taṭṭu knock at, tap, strike, hinder (Kalit.); Ma. taṭṭuka id. (< *taṭ-) : Ta. taḷ (taṭṭ-) to hinder, stop; taḷḷu (taḷḷ-in-) to shrink, etc., Ka. taḷugu to stop; cf. Te. taḍayu to delay.

In these and similar cases the incorporated t-element could be originally a past tense or a causative morpheme.

§2.94. In one instance NDr. has evidence for an incorporated *ṭ, i.e., *-ṭṭ- < *-ṇṭ- :

dā̃-ṭu to jump over, cross; Ka. dāṇṭu, tāṇṭu; Ta. tāṇṭu; Ma. tāṇṭuka, tāṭṭuka id.; Klm. dāṭ- : Ma. tāṭuka to leap; cāṭṭam n. leap; Kur. cāṭak̲h̲- to stride, jump over.

§2.95. The suffix -ṇṭ(u) in most cases is analyzable into *-ṇ-ṭ- of which ṇ is originally a part of the root morpheme (§1.163); e.g., aṇ-ṭu to touch, adhere; Ka. aṇ-ṭu, aṇ-e to touch; Tu. aṇ-ṭuni id.; aṇ-epuni to paste; Ta. aṭṭu to join, paste; aṇ-ai to touch; Klm.(SR) aṇ-ṭ-, Klm.(E) aṭ- to stick; Nk. aṭṭ- to stick to; Pj. an-ḍ- attach string to bow.

-aṭ(u)/-uṭ(u)

§2.96. There are only five forms with suffix V + ṭ(u) in Te.: pag-aṭu to proclaim; baṟ-aṭu to scratch; taṟ-aṭu to beat with a rope; cim-uṭu to wink; por-āṭu to fry. Of these, the suffix can be reconstructed for PSDr. only for two forms: baṟaṭu < *paṟ-aṇṭ-; cim-uṭu < *cim-iṭṭ-, cf. Ta. cim-iṭṭu, cim-iḷi id. (*ṭṭ < *ḷ-t).

-aḍ(u)/-uḍ(u), -ṇḍ(u)

§2.97. In all cases of -aḍ(u), -uḍ(u), ḍ is from an original sonorant suffix -ḻ according to the regular Te. shift of *-ḻ- > -ḍ- (see §1.84).

neg-aḍu to happen, become known; Ka. neg-aḻ; Tu. neg-aruni; Ta. nik-aḻ.

-aḻ/-uḻ is characteristically a SDr. suffix except in one case where Mlt. shows -ol corresponding to SDr. -aḻ:

pog-aḍu to praise; Ka. pog-aḻ; Tu. pog-aruni, vb.; pog-uḷu n.; Ta. puk-aḻ; Ma. puk-aḻuka : Mlt. pog-ole renown, praise, pog-olare to be praised.

In disyllabic forms with a long radical vowel and final -ḍu as in āḍu, kūḍu, etc., -ḍu is part of the root morpheme itself.

§2.98. There are eighteen bases in final -ṇḍ(u), twelve with the suffix after short vowels and six after long vowels. In almost all these instances ṇ is part of the root and ḍ (< *ḏ/*ṯ) is the suffix. The question of the formation of this consonant group has been treated elsewhere (§1.163).

This is a widely distributed suffix-type and the isoglosses involve the whole family of the Dravidian languages. Sometimes the isoglosses enclose only CDr. and NDr., putting Te. with CDr. One typical example is: niṇ-ḍu to be full; Kui nen-ja; Kuvi nen-j-; Go. nin-d-; Klm. nin-d-; Nk. nin-d-; Kur. nīn-d- v.i.; nin-d- v.tr.; Mlt. nīn-d- : Te. neṟ-ayu id; Ka.

ner̲-e; Ta. nir̲-ai; Ma. nir̲-ayuka. The Central and North Dravidian forms proceed from *nin-t̲- : SDr. *nir̲-; for PDr. we can reconstruct alternative bases *nin-/nit̲-. On account of the occurrence of both ninḍu and ner̲ayu in Te. this is a typical example of the position of Te. between South and Central Dravidian with isoglosses from both sides.

Similarly in the case of vaṇ-ḍu to cook, *van-t̲- can be set up only for Central and North Dravidian.

§2.99. One isogloss includes also Ta.: eṇ-ḍu to dry up, eṇ-ḍa sunshine; Ta. en̲-r̲u sun, el sunshine; ell-ai id.; Pj. nen-di sunshine; Go. ad-di heat of sun; ? Kur. iṛ-; Mlt. eṛy- parch grain in sun. The Kur. Mlt. forms seem to arise from a reconstruction without the nasal preceding the suffix, i.e., *et̲- < *el-t-, whereas *en-t̲- < *el-nt-.

§2.100. Another isogloss which ties up Te. and Tu. with CDr. is provided by the words meaning "to ripen": paṇ-ḍu to ripen; Tu. par-nduni; Klm. pan-ḍ-; Pj. pan-ḍ- (plant) to mature; Go. paṇ-ḍ-; Kur. pā̃n- (panj-) to ripen; Mlt. pān- : Ta. pal̲-u; Ma. pal̲-u; Ma. pal̲-ukka; Ka. paṇ. In CDr. there are also forms with different suffixes. Pj. paṛ-ñ- < *pal̲-nc-; probably the Kur. Mlt. suffixes also go back to *-nc. Again, Oll. paṛ-ŋ(g)-, KGad. paḍ-iŋ- show a velar suffix.

§2.101. It is clear from the above instances that the occurrence of a t̲/nt̲ suffix on light syllables is a common Dravidian characteristic which is widely represented in Central and NDr. In many cases Te. goes with CDr. and NDr. rather than with SDr.

§2.102. In forms with -ṇḍ(u) after long vowels there are no parallels in CDr. and NDr. for this suffix.

1. vē-ḍu (< *vēṇ-ṭ-) to request, desire; Ka. bēḍu; n. bēṇ-ḍa longing; Tu. bēḍuni; Ta. vēṇ-ṭu to want, beg, request (Kaliṭ.); vēḷ- to desire, love (PN); Klm. Nk. vēl- to request.

2. tō-ḍu to dig up, pull up; Ka. tōḍu dig out; Tu. tōḍuni; tolluni to pluck out (hairs, feathers); Ta. tōṇ-ṭu to dig, draw; Ma. tōṇ-ṭuka id.: Ta. tōḷ- (tōṭṭ-) to dig out, scoop; perforate (Kr̲ḷ.); ṇṭ < *ḷ + nt.

<u>Dental Series</u>

(V)-t(u), -nt(u), -d(u), -nd(u)

§2.103. There are hardly any clear cases of a -t(u) suffix in verbs (see §1.176). -du/-ndu occur both in disyllabic and trisyllabic bases.

Dental stop suffixes in verbs do not have many parallels in Central and North Dravidian. There are two instances where it is possible to reconstruct the suffix for the whole family:

1. cī̃-du to blow nose; Ka. sīnu (pp. sītu, sī-ntu, sī-ndu); Ta. cī-ntu; cī mucus of nose; Ma. cī-ntuka; Kui jī-nj-a, srī-nd-a; Kuvi si-nd-; Mlt. jī-nj-; Kur. cī̃-cr- : Go. īc-; Mlt. ī-nj-; Kur. ī̃-jhr-. The etymology has problems on account of Ka. sīnu and Kui srīnd- and forms without c/s in Go. and Kur.-Mlt. Even eliminating these, we have evidence for PDr. *cī-nt-, with palatalization of the dental in Central and North Dravidian.

2. ū-du (some dict. ū̃du) to blow through mouth; Ka. ū-du, Tu. ū-duni; Ta. ū-tu; Ma. ū-tu; Klm. Nk. ū-nd-; Pj. ū̃-d-; KGad. ū-nd-; GoM. u-d- : Kur. Mlt. ū-r- id. For South and Central Dravidian a common suffix can be reconstructed, viz., *-t alternating with *-nt; for NDr. *-r̠. Ultimately *ū- is the basis, presumably from *uy- to breathe.

-du

§2.104. Te. -du in disyllabic bases of (C)VCCV type (where CC is geminated stop) is traceable to an earlier extended suffix occurring in trisyllabic form, i.e., *-utt(u).

1. ad-du to immerse, dip; dye; Ka. ad-du, ar̤-du, al̠-du, āl̠ id.; Ta. al̠-untu to be immersed; al̠-uttu to immerse; āl̠-ttu to immerse.

2. did-du to rectify; Ka. tir-du/tid-du; Tu. tid-duni; Ta. tir-uttu to rectify (PN); tir-untu be correct; Ma. tir-uttuka tr. id.

Obviously in these cases the original grade of the suffix is preserved in Ta. and Ma. while the weak grade occurs in Ka. (Tu., Ko., To.) and Te. with (1) loss of the suffix vowel, and (2) simplification and voicing of the stop-geminate.

After a long vowel -d(u) occurs in five verbs: bādu beat; ēdu[1] to reach (< eydu); ēdu[2] to foster, nourish; mōdu to beat; mēdu to smear. Of these, all SDr. languages have *-t(u) suffix for ēdu to reach and mōdu to beat. In the remainder, the suffix is peculiar to Te.

-nd(u)

§2.105. There are ten forms with -nd(u) occurring after short vowels, six forms after long vowels; after long vowels -nd(u) > -˜d(u).

For kandu to be scorched and kundu to reduce, all SDr. forms are traceable to *kan-ṯ and *kun-ṯ with the etymological boundary occurring after the root final n.

§2.106. In two cases Te. -nd(u) is a reduction of an original extended suffix *-unt(u), with loss of the suffix vowel:

1. va-ndu to grieve (< *var-nd-); va-nta grief; Ta. var-untu to suffer, grieve (Kr̠ḷ.); var-uttu affliction (Maturai.); Ma. var-uttam trouble.

2. po-ndu to reach, get; be fit (< *por-nd-); Ka. por-du, hor-du, hod-du; Tu. por-duni; Ta. por-untu to agree, be suitable; por-uttu tr. to fit; Ma. por-unnuka be joined, agreed.

On the analogy of these forms we can reconstruct *cer-unt- for Te. ce-ndu to belong, reach, be within reach (< *cer$^{u}$nd-); cf. Te. cēru to reach, South and Central Dravidian cēr-/sēr- id.

§2.107. -nd(u) after long vowels occurs in six forms: cā̃-du to triturate; ī̃-du to swim; cī̃-du to sneeze; ū̃-du$^{1}$ to hold; ū̃-du$^{2}$ to blow with mouth, cē̃-du to bale out water. Of these, -̄̃du is peculiar to Te. only in cā̃du; in the remaining forms *nt is reconstructable for ī̃du, cī̃du, ū̃du, cē̃du. Except in the case of cī̃du (§2.103), the isogloss of *nt encloses only SDr. Te. ū̃du to hold is from *ūn-t̲- with an original *t suffix, distributed widely:

ū̃du to hold (as a support); ūnu hold, set firmly; Ka. ūr̲u to lean; Tu. ūruni to set firmly, plant; Ta. ūn̲r̲u to be fixed, tr. to fix, plant (Kr̲ḷ.); recline on; to support (Kr̲ḷ.); Ma. ūn̲n̲u to be fixed, firm; to lean; Kui uha to plant; usa to set a post into ground ( ? -s- < *-nt̲); Kuvi ūh- to plant; Go. urs- plant, transplant (rice, etc.); Kur. ūd- to fix closed (door, shutter) by a bolt; to lean upon; udd$^{u}$r- to lean upon a walking stick; Mlt. ūdure to lean upon; all from PDr. *ūn-t-/*ūn-t̲-.

§2.108. As in the case of retroflex suffixes there are no exclusive isoglosses of dental suffixes that include Te. with Central and North Dravidian. In dental suffixes either the isoglosses include all Dravidian languages or simply the SDr. ones. This is one case in favor of Te. being considered a member of the SDr. group.

§2.109. There are only five forms with the suffix (V) + d(u) or (V̄) + d(u), viz., al-ādu tr. to smear, as sandal paste, ey-idu to approach, eg-udu to run, mey-idu to be beside oneself, and sar-udu to distribute equally, to adjust. Of these ey-idu is a later variant of ey-du with an original *-tu suffix shared by all the other South Dravidian languages (see Part II, s.v. eydu); in the remaining forms there are no parallels among the other Dravidian languages for the dental suffix (see etymologies in Part II).

## Labial Series

§2.110. In most of the forms, -p(u), -mp(u) with or without a preceding vowel are inflectional suffixes in that they replace an original derivative suffix to form transitives from intransitive bases; e.g.:

eḍ-ayu to be separated : eḍ-apu to separate

nad-acu to walk : naḍ-apu to drive
cir-ugu to be torn : ci-mpu to tear

For this reason they do not come within the scope of this chapter.

§2.111. There are, however, a few forms in which verbs in derivative -p(u) occur in Te., without clear parallels in the other Dravidian languages.

1. sal-upu to ache, pain (as spasms); n. ache, etc.; Ka. saḷ-e id.
2. cē-pu milk to collect in the udder (of a cow), n.; Ka. cē-pu a gush or spirt of milk; cf. Ta. cē-kku breast milk.
3. ō-pu to be able to, to endure, be capable of; Ta. ō-mpu to guard, protect, etc.; Ma. ō-mpuka; Ka. ō-vu.

In all these cases -pu in Te. appears to derive from the noun-forming suffix *-pp(u) of PSDr., from which denominative verbs were formed later in Te.

-bu, -bbu, -mbu

§2.112. Forms with -b(u) finals are very few and rare in Classical literature. Altogether there are some six of this type, viz., pambu to spread; abbu to accrue; dabbu to tell a lie (18th century); ubbu to increase in size, swell, be elated; gebbu to steal; to seize; rubbu to crush, grind into paste.

Except pambu, abbu, and ubbu, all the other forms are much later and occur in less standard works.

1. pa-mbu (< *par-mp-) to increase, spread; Ta. par-ampu id.
2. ub-bu (< *ur-bu < *ur-vu) to swell, rise; Ka. ub-bu, ur-bu, ur-vu; cf. Ta. ur̲-uvatu that which increases; ur̲-uttu tr. to increase; (the evidence is for PSDr. *-uv- or *-ump-). The Te. form is probably a loanword from Ka. on account of -b- < -v-.

No etymology is found for abbu to accrue, but it may be compared with Telugu arugu to approach, etc.

## ANALYSIS OF THE ROOTS

### Structure of PDr. verb-roots:

§2.113. It has been stated earlier that two main types of root-morphemes can be set up for PDr. with two sub-types for each.

| | Possible number of occurrences |
|---|---|
| Type I (a) (C)V | 44 |
| (b) (C)VC | 760 |

| | | Possible number of occurrences |
|---|---|---|
| Type II | (a) (C)V̄ | 44 |
| | (b) (C)V̄C | 760 |

Roots of Type I can be called light bases, and those of Type II heavy bases respectively, according as the radical vowel is short or long. Alternatively, they may be analyzed as vowel-ending and consonant-ending: I (a) (C)V, I (b) (C)V̄; II (a) (C)VC, II (b) (C)V̄C. Both types of analysis are useful and necessary for historical discussion.

A vowel is the nuclear element of a syllable with or without a preceding or following consonant. An initial consonant, when it occurs, is any one of the PDr. consonantal phonemes except the alveolar and retroflex series; this gives us the following phonemes in the initial position: p, t, c, k; m, ñ, n; y, v. In the second position (i.e., vowel), any one of the short or long vowel phonemes can occur, with the exception that there is no evidence for the occurrence of back rounded vowels after *ñ, *y, and *v.[22] In the root final position any of the consonantal phonemes except *ñ can occur.

§2.114. Other pertinent features of the PDr. structure of radical syllables are as follows:

(1). All roots can occur either free or bound; but there is a steadily rising degree of freedom in radical syllables in the order presented above, i.e., (C)V, (C)VC, (C)V̄, (C)V̄C; in most cases (C)V- occurs bound.

(2). The radical syllables may be bound to derivative suffixes beginning with vowels or consonants. Suffixes with initial vowels occur after bases in final C, i.e., (C)V̄̆C-; suffixes with initial consonants occur after bases in final V, i.e., (C)V̄̆-. There is also evidence for the occurrence of consonantal suffixes after bases in final consonant. This is, however, a marginal class, which mainly consists of roots ending in n or ṇ, e.g., Te. niṇḍu (< *nin-ṯ-).

(3). When vowel derivatives follow, the (C)V̄C- type fell together with (C)VC- in most cases even in PDr. (§1.289). Therefore, in the sequence $(C)V^1C\text{-}V^2\text{-}$, the radical $V^1$ is generally short. Moreover, when (C)VC- is followed by a vowel derivative, the whole sequence, i.e., (C)VC-V-, alternates with a heavy base containing a secondary long vowel. This occurs when the radical final C is y, v, or k [-g-] (§§1.277, .295). Evidence for this latter alternation occurs mainly in South and Central Dravidian.

§2.115. In the following sections the radical syllables of the Telugu verbal bases will be resolved into the PDr. types by setting forth the changes of pattern that they have undergone from the norm.

All bases have been analyzed into two historical categories: primary, i.e., those occurring without derivatives, and secondary, i.e., those occurring with derivatives. The forms of the primary type are directly traceable to one of the PDr. types with the usual phonemic alternations.

## Primary Formations

§2.116. Primary forms occur in Classes 1 to 3 of Type A (see §2.5); they are: (1) (C)V̌CV̌, (2) (C)V̌CCV̌, (3) (C)V̄CV̌.

### (1) (C)V̌CV̌

§2.117. Out of the twenty-five forms of this canonical type (including primary and secondary forms) seven ending in -nu have alternants in -n in inflexion. This sub-class may be called the anu-class in conformity with the traditional nomenclature of native grammars. All these forms go back to PDr. primary forms of the (C)V̌C type where the final C is *n or ṇ/ḷ.

| | |
|---|---|
| anu/an- to say | *an- (vowel quality doubtful, see §1.222) |
| kanu[1]/kan- to see | *kă̄ṇ- |
| kanu[2]/kan- to give birth to | *kan- |
| konu/kon- to give | *koṇ-/*koḷ- |
| tinu/tin- to eat | *tin- |
| manu/man- to live | *man- |
| vinu/vin- to hear | *vin- |

The remaining forms of this class end in -gu, -ḍu, and -ṟu; the final vowel occurs as -u in all SDr. and may be considered a derivative -u on account of the absence of doubling of the previous stops (see §2.10). It may be recalled here that after a radical short vowel a PDr. stop occurs geminated in all SDr. in the root final position. Weakening of this into a voiced stop or spirant occurs only when a derivative vowel follows as in ceḍ-u to be spoiled (< *keṭ-u). The final vowel occurs as -u in all literary languages: Ka. keḍ-u to be destroyed; Ta. Ma. keṭ-u to perish, decay.

### (2) (C)V̌CCV̌

§2.118. The primary forms of this type are all traceable to the PDr. type (C)V̌C, where the final C is a stop or a sonorant. In any case, it occurs geminated in Te. with the usual non-morphemic (u) in the final position. When it is a sonorant, the remaining literary languages are not regular in showing it as a geminate as in Te.; e.g., Ta. uṇ- to drink, eat, etc., pres. un-kiṟ- or uṇṇu-kiṟ-; past uṇ-ṭ-; fut. uṇ-p- or uṇṇu-p-; here, we set up two freely varying basic alternants uṇ-/uṇṇu (< PDr. *uṇ-) as far as present and future tense forms are concerned, but in the past there is a single alternant *uṇ- which actually represents the PDr. type.

A few examples are given below for PDr. (C)V̆C- where the final C is a stop occurring geminated in Te. followed by (u) (see also §§1.191-.200):

1. vekku to sob, hiccough : PDr. *vek- (see §1.192).

2. koṭṭu to beat : PDr. *koṭ- (§1.255).

3. vaṭṭu to dry : PDr. *vaṯ- (§1.195, b.).

4. vittu to sow seed, n. seed : Ka. bittu to put seed; Tu. bittuni/ buttuni; Ta. vittu id. (Aiṅk.); Go. wīt-; Kui vīti scattered; PDr. *vit-.

5. tappu to miss, fail; Ka. tappu : Tu. tappuni; Ta. tappu; Ma. tappuka; Kuvi (F) taph- to interrupt; Kuvi (S) tappahannai to fail; PSDr. *tap-. Forms with weakened -p- occur before vowel derivatives; cf. Ta. tavaṟu to slip, miss; taval failure.

§2.119. PDr. (or PSDr.) root-final sonorants, i.e., m, n, ṇ, l, ḷ, occur doubled in Telugu; e.g.:

1. tummu to sneeze, n. sternutation; Ta. tummu id. (Kṟḷ.); Ma. tummuka; Kur. Mlt. tum- id.; Klm. tum-, Pj. tumm-, Oll. tum-, KGad. tumm-. Though some languages have *mp, for instance, Tu. tumbilu̥ sneezing, it is definitely secondary there on account of the occurrence of the mm form in Ancient Ta. and also in Kur. Mlt.

2. pannu to make, do; Ka. paṇṇu; Tu. paṇipuni to give a shape; Ta. paṇṇu to make; Ma. paṇṇu; (< PDr. *paṇ-).

3. allu to plait, knit; Ka. allu; aḷa joining, Ta. aḷḷu : Klm. al-; Kui alpa; Kuvi (S) all-; Pj. alc- wind around; Nk. KGad. all- to weave; (< PDr. *aḷ-).

4. cellu to fit, suit; be valid as coin; Ka. cellu; Tu. salluni; Ta. Ma. cel; Ko. cal-; (< PSDr. *cal).

Forms with voiced stop-geminates are always involved in secondary formations.

### (3) (C)V̄CV̆

§2.120. Primary forms of this type can be resolved into PDr. (C)VC- where the final C is a stop or sonorant. However, forms where it is a stop are mostly secondary formations with an ultimate root morpheme of

*(C)V̄ type plus suffix C. In some cases this incorporation of root and suffix elements is so ancient that the forms involved appear throughout the family as if they represent the primary type. One good example is: nāku to lick; Ta. Ma. Ka. Tu. nakku; Go. Kui Kuvi Klm. Nk. Oll. KGad. nāk-; Pj. nēk-. This can probably be connected with *nā- tongue, in which case k is a derivative suffix.

Where there are no shorter forms to compare with (as in *nāk- : *nā-) or forms with varying suffixes (Te. cīku to smack : other languages cīp-), we have to decide upon taking the whole form as primary, if all languages show evidence for a single reconstruction. Cases of this type abound in forms with sonorant finals but are much restricted in those with stop finals; e.g., mōdu, mottu to beat, strike; Ka. mōdu id; Ta. mottu id. (Kamp.), n. stroke, blow (Cilap.) : Ma. mōtuka, mottu; Ka. mōdu id. On account of restricted geographical distribution we cannot set up a primary *mōt- for PDr., but it is possible for PSDr.

§2.121. Many of the Te. verbs of this class in -ḍu go back to the PDr. primary type (C)V̄C-; e.g., pāḍu to sing; Ka. pāḍu; Ta. Ma. pāṭu; Go. pāṛ-, GoM. pār-; Klm. Pj. pāḍ-; Nk. pāṛ-; Oll. KGad. pār-; Kur. Mlt. pāṛ-; (< PDr. *pāṭ-).

§2.122. Forms with sonorant finals:

| | | |
|---|---|---|
| vānu to make to shine | : | PDr. *vān- |
| pūnu to put on, wear | : | *pūṇ- |
| kāyu to boil; to shine | : | *kāy- |
| cēyu to do | : | *kĕy- |
| cēru to reach | : | *cār-/*cēr- |
| ūṟu to grow big, to swell | : | *cūṯ- (§1.211, 7) |

For all the above forms except cēru, primary root forms corresponding to the PDr. sequences occur in almost all members of the family. For cēru, NDr. has no cognates; still it can be taken as primary because of the absence of any related forms with variable final consonant.

Many items in -ṟ(u) and -l(u) are either restricted in distribution (mainly to SDr.) or give evidence for the final syllable being a variable. However, it is possible to set up some of these primary formations for SDr.; e.g., pēṟu to condense, solidify; Ka. peṟu, pp. pettu; Ko. pet-; Toda peṟf-; Tu. perpuni; cf. Ta. pirai fermented buttermilk (PSDr. *pēṯ- : *peṯ-V-).

In cases like mīṟu to exceed, pāṟu to run, and tūṟu to pierce through, it is possible to set up complete sequences for PDr. as primary formations on the basis of distribution, but comparison with related sets of etyma shows that the final syllable is a variable here, the roots being *miy-, *pā-, *tū-, and so on. This problem of inner derivation in Common Dravidian will be treated later (see §§2.142-.149).

§2.123. Only these and similar forms in the three classes of Type A are primary; all other Telugu verbal types occur as secondary formations. The occurrence of etymological boundaries in all such classes has been indicated earlier (§2.7). In the following sections each class of forms under the three types will be treated separately.

## Secondary Formations

### Type A

#### (1) (C)V̆C-V̆

§2.124. This is a small class of fourteen verbs with two short syllables. The final -u is taken here as a derivative suffix on structural grounds explained earlier (§2.10). Five bases occur in -g-u, where g is from earlier *y or *k.

| | |
|---|---|
| ag-u to be (allom. ay-, āy-) | PDr. āy (+ u) |
| *eg-u (only inf. eg-a adv. up) *to be high, etc. | PDr. ey-/ē- |
| tag-u to suit | PSDr. *tak-u < *tay-u |
| nag-u to laugh | *nak-u/*nav-u |
| teg-u to be cut, severed | *tek-u |

Five forms end in -ḍ-u from earlier *-ṭ-u: iḍ-u to place (< *iṭ-u); ceḍ-u to perish, be spoiled (< *keṭ-u); toḍ-u to wear (< *toṭ-u); paḍ-u to fall (< *paṭ-u); viḍ-u to leave (< *viṭ-u).

One form with restricted distribution: *oḍ-u *to be together (inf. oḍ-an together, oḍāgūḍu to assemble together (< *oṭ-u).

Three forms with -r̲-u: ar̲-u to be cut off; ur̲-u[1] to fit, suit; ur̲-u[2] to care for, care. These forms are traceable respectively to PSDr. *at̲-V, *ut̲-V, and *ut̲-V; with the last item cf. Ta. uṉṉu to think, consider, ur̲u id.

#### (2a) (C)V̆C-C(V̆)

§2.125. Forms of this class arise from earlier sequences of light bases followed by stop suffixes, voiced or voiceless. The final C of the original root morpheme is either a nasal /m n ṇ/ or a liquid continuant /r r̲ l ḷ l̲/. In the former combination of root-nasals with suffix-stops, certain morphophonemic alternations take place in Telugu which are treated under phonology (see §§1.162-.166, .170). The canonical form of this sub-class can be more specifically re-formulated as (C)VN-P/B(V). A few examples of this combination:

1. iṅ-ku to sink (< *im-k-); cf. Ka. im-uru, iṅ-gu id.

2. vaṅ-gu v.i. to bend (< *vaṇ-k-): Ka. baḷ-ku; Ta. vaṇ-aṅku.

3. pan-cu to send (< *paṇ-); Ta. paṇ-i to order, command; Kui paṇ-ḍ- to send; Klm. pan-k-; the c-suffix is peculiar to Te. (origin treated earlier §2.86).

4. in-cu to be sweet (< *in-); Ta. in̲-i to be sweet.

5. aṇ-ṭu to stick (< *aṇ-ṭ-); Ka. aṇ-e to touch; South and Central Dravidian have the retroflex suffix, originally a dental.

6. daṇ-ḍu to collect (< *taṇ-ṭ-); cf. Ka. taḷ-e to receive; PDr. *taḷ-/*taṇ-.

7. eṇ-ḍu to dry up (< *en-t̲-); cf. Ta. el, en̲-r̲u sunshine.

8. kan-du to be scorched (< *kan-t̲-); cf. kan-alu to burn; Ta. kan̲-r̲u id.

pan-cu is a good example for the divergence of the various languages in suffixes but agreement in possessing the root morpheme: pan-cu to send, commission; pan-upu, pam-pu a commission : Ta. paṇ-i to order, command; Kui paṇ-ḍa to send; Kuvi (S) pan-d-, pan-t- id.; Klm. Nk. pan-k-.

§2.126. The canonical forms for the second type of combination (see §2.7) can be re-formulated as *(C)VR-P/-B(V); here, R is taken as a cover symbol for the liquid type of consonants (viz., r r̲ l ḷ l̲). This canonical form develops in Te. to (C)VP-P(V) or (C)VB-B(V), R being assimilated to the following stop-suffix (for details see §§1.173 ff.). In most of these cases there occurred a u-vowel originally before P/B which was lost in the pre-Te.-Ka. stage of this development; this loss of the derivative vowel later brought about the assimilation of R-P/-B > P-P or B-B; e.g.:

1. cok-ku to be intoxicated (< *cor-k-) : Ka. sok-ku, sor-ku; Ma. cor-ukkuka; (PSDr. *cor-ukku).

2. vic-cu to blossom (< *vir-c-) : Ka. bic-cu, bir-cu; cf. Te. vir-iyu; Ta. vir-i id.

3. ub-bu to swell (< *ur-b-) : Ka. ub-bu, ur-bu, ur-vu id. (PSDr. *ur̲-upp- or *ur̲-uv-); cf. Te. Ta. ūr̲u to increase (as flesh); grow fat, etc.

It has been stated earlier that the isogloss of this combination includes Te. Ka. (Tu. Ko. To.) as against Ta. Ma. and the languages of Central and North Dravidian (§1.185).

(2b) (C)V̆-CC(V̆)

§2.127. In this sub-class the suffixal CC is either an NP/NB or PP sequence, sometimes with a preceding V lost. The root morpheme is traceable to an older (C)VC-. In the latter case the final C is in the proto-form usually y, r, or l̲, which is lost in Te. before the NP/NB or PP sequences; e.g.:

1. bo-ṅku to tell a lie, Ka. bo-ṅku (< *poy-nk-); Ta. Ma. poy id.

2. po-ndu to obtain, get; Ka. por-du; Ta. por-untu; (PSDr. *por-unt-/-und-).

Sometimes the loss of the root final l̲ is accompanied by a morphophonemic alternation in the suffixal nasal that follows: paṇ-ḍu to ripen (< *pal̲-nd-) : Tu. par-nduni id.; Ta. pal̲u.

This development is peculiar to Te., whereas Ka. usually preserves the PDr. light base and denasalizes the suffix-group; cf. Te. po-ndu : Ka. por-du (< *por-nd-). Therefore, these two languages part at the stage of *por-nd- which has a still preceding stage in PSDr., with the derivative vowel occurring before NB; cf. Ta. por-untu; Ma. por-unnuka.

§2.128. Examples for the loss of the root-final C before suffixes of the sequence PP: i-ccu to give (< *iy-cc-); no-ccu to suffer (< *noy-cc-), me-ccu (< *mey-cc-), etc. (see §1.186).

(3a) (C)V̄-C(V̆)

§2.129. This is at least a common SDr. type, if not Common Dravidian. The final syllable is traceable to a stop or sonorant suffix while the root goes back to two PDr. types: (C)V̄-, or (C)VC-; in the latter case the final consonant is of a spirant type (either originally or rendered so by position, i.e., y, v, k [-g-]) and the whole sequence has contracted to (C)V̄-. This is a Common Dravidian development with wide occurrence in SDr. (see §1.295).

Example for Te. (C)V̄- < *(C)V̄-:

pū-cu to blossom; pūvu a flower; Ka. pū-, hū; Tu. pū a flower; Ta. pū to blossom; Ma. pū-kka id. (the c-suffix peculiar to Te., §2.84).

In cases of this type the PDr. root *(C)V̄- is very widely represented in the daughter languages, sometimes with different suffixes.

Examples for *(C)V̄- < *(C)Vy- (y = a spirant):

kū-lu to fall down; sink, drop, die; Ka. kū-lu id.; Kui kū-ra to fall down; Klm.(SR) kū-l- to drop; < *kuy-il; cf. Ka. kus-i to bend, to sink, be lowered; Tu. kus-uruni to shrink; Go. kuss- to fall.

Similarly, sōlu (< *coy-al) to droop (in intoxication), to stagger; cf. Ta. toy (< *coy) to languish; uy-al to wave, shake.

Though not many common etyma are available in the material under discussion, there is sufficient evidence to show that this development is common to many Dravidian languages and unites all South and Central Dravidian by a single isogloss (see §§1.277, .295).

(3b) (C)V̄-˜C(V̌)/(C)V̄̃-C(V̌)

§2.130. [˜] stands for an original nasal phoneme lost regularly after long vowels in the pre-Classical period (see §1.6). Whether or not etymologies are available, the morpheme boundary in the Classical period is always after the radical vowel; this is because the nasal, whether it is a part of the root or the suffix, is regularly lost.

The root morphemes of this class proceed from two PDr. types: (1) *(C)V̄-, (2) *(C)V̄C-. In the latter case the final C is a nasal (N). The suffixes that unite with (1) are of the NP/NB type and those that unite with (2) are of the *P/B type. The canonical forms can be reinterpreted more specifically as: (1) *(C)V̄-NP/NB, (2) *(C)V̄N-P/B. Since both these lost N in pre-Classical Te., we get for Old and Mdn. Te. only (C)V̄-P/B.

(1) Te. (C)V̄-˜P/B < PSDr. *(C)V̄-NP/NB

§2.131. Examples:

tā-˜ku to touch, hit, attack; Ka. tā-ku, tā-gu, tā-ṅku, tā-ṅgu to hit; Tu. tā-guni, tā-kuni; Ta. tā-ṅku to oppose, attack; tā-kku to come in contact, etc.; Ma. tā-kkuka to hit, touch; Kur. Mlt. ta-k- to touch, knock; the root is *tā- which occurs elsewhere with different derivatives, cf. Ka. tā-ṭu to strike against, touch; Tu. tā-cuni to come in collision.

So also sā-˜ku to nourish (< *cā-ṅk-); gī-˜ku to scratch (< *kī-ṅk-); ā-˜gu v.i. to stop; tr. to intercept (< *ā-ṅk-); ī-˜gu, nī-˜gu to abandon, discharge (debts) (< *nī-ṅk-); ī-˜du to swim (< *nī-nt-/*ī-nt-, movable *n-).

§2.132. In many forms of this type the PSDr. root *(C)V̄- is itself a contraction of PDr. *(C)V̌y-. The alternation of a radical vowel + y with a corresponding long vowel in closed syllables (i.e., V̌y-/V̄-) is a Common Dravidian development (see §1.297). In the following cases comparative evidence shows that the PSDr. *(C)V̄- (> Te. (C)V̄-) is originally an alternant of *(C)V̌y:

1. pī-˜ku to pull out, pluck, uproot; Ka. pī-ku id. (probably l.w. < Te.); Ta. piy to pluck off, pull out; pey-ar to uproot (< *piy-ar); Ma. pē-ruka id.

2. cō-˜ku/sō-˜ku to come in contact with, touch; Ka. sō-ku, so-ṅku, so-kku id.; Tu. sō-ṅkuni, sō-ṅguni; Ta. tōy tr. touch (PN); come in contact with; (PSDr. cō-nk- < *cŏy-nk-).

3. kā-˜gu (< *kā-ṅk- < *kāy-ṅk-); Ta. Ma. Ka. Tu. kāy- to grow hot; Kuvi (S) kai kī- to boil; Kur. k͟hāy- become quite dry; Mlt. qeyr- be hot. In the following forms derived from the same root, all languages furnish evidence for the loss of *y before consonants which points to a similar situation in PDr.: Ka. kā-ṅke heat; Tu. kāṅguni become pale; Ta. kā-ṅkai heat; Ma. kā-ntu to be hot; Kui kā-ga to warm oneself by fire; Kuvi (S) kā-th'- to heat; Go. kā-s- become hot (s wrongly added from pp. -sī); Klm. Nk. kā-ŋg- become hot; Brah. k͟hā-k͟har fire.

Other forms of this type include mā-˜gu to ripen (< *māy-ṅg-); vā-˜gu to prattle (< *vāy-ṅg-); vī-˜gu to protrude, be swollen; be proud (< *vĭy-ṅg-); ū-˜gu to swing, rock (< *ŭy-ṅg-); tū-˜gu to swing, wave (< *tūy-ṅg- < *cŭy-ṅg-); mū-˜gu to swarm (< *mŭy-ṅg-); ē-˜gu to go (< *ĕy-ṅg-); vē-˜gu to burn, be fried (< *vĕy-ṅg-); tō-˜gu to bathe, sink in water (< *tŏy-ṅg-); cā-˜du to triturate (< *cāy-nt-); ū-˜du to blow with mouth (< *ŭy-nd), etc.

(2) Te. (C)V̄̃-P/B < PSDr. *(C)V̄N-P/B

§2.133. Examples:

1. tō̃-cu to appear (< *tōn-c-); Ka. tōṟu; Tu. tōjuni; Ta. tōṉ-ṟu; Ma. tōn-nuka; Kui tōn-j- v.i.; tōs- v.tr.; tōm-b- v.i.; Kuvi ton-ja ai- to appear; tōss- v.tr.; Pj. tōn-d- appear; Oll. tōn-d-.

2. mī̃-ṭu to toss, fling, fillip (< *mīṇ-t-); Ka. mī-ṭu to strike the wires of a lute, etc.; mīṇ-ṭu lever up; Tu. mīṇ-ṭuni to force up or out; Ta. mīṭ-ṭu to redeem, fillip; mīḷ to release; Ma. mīṭ-ṭu fillip; mīṇ-ṭu draw out, pull.

Similarly ū̃-ḍu to fix, transplant (< *ūṇ-d-); vē̃-ḍu to ask, desire (< *vēṇ-d-); tō̃-ḍu to draw up, dig up (< *tōṇ-d-); cī̃-du (probably, < *cīm-d-); ū̃-du to hold as a support (< *ūn-ṯ-).

The composition of consonant groups in forms of this class has been briefly stated under phonology (§1.171). This type of composition of root and suffix is not only common in SDr. but also common to the other geographical groups; isoglosses with extensive range of application can be drawn for forms corresponding to ī̃du, cī̃du, ū̃du, etc.

Except for Te. and sometimes Ka. all other languages preserve the nasals occurring after the radical vowels.

### (4) (C)V̄C-C(V̆)

§2.134. The majority of forms of this class have -c(u) as the suffix, i.e., -C(V), which is in most cases peculiar to Telugu. The development of this suffix has been treated earlier (§§2.84 ff.). The radical element (C)V̄C- proceeds from PDr. (C)V̄C-, where the final -C is a sonorant: r ṟ l ḷ ḻ n ṇ, etc. Corresponding to this class of bases, the other SDr. languages show merely the (C)V̄C- forms, thus representing a more archaic condition than Te. as far as the root morpheme is concerned. A few examples will suffice to show this relation:

1. īḍ-cu to drag; Ka. īḻ; Ta. iḻ-u; Ma. iḻ-ukka; Kui ḍri-pa; Kur. īc- (c < *ḻ); Mlt. ic- to take off.

2. ār-cu to cry; Ka. ār, ār-cu, ã-cu id.; Tu. ār-kuní; Ta. ār; Ma. ār-kuka; Kui ār-.

3. tāl-cu to wear, put on; Ka. tāḷ.

4. vēl-cu to offer sacrificial fire; Ka. bēḷ; Ta. vēḷ; Ma. vēḷ-ka to marry before fire.

So also ūḍ-cu to strip off; ēḍ-cu to weep; kān-cu to see; pīl-cu to suck, etc. from *ūḻ-, *yāḻ-, *kāṇ-, *pīl- respectively.

The form kān-cu is one of the few cases where the nasal occurring between the radical vowel and the suffix stop is not lost as in forms of A(3), e.g., nō-˜cu (< *nōn-c-). This is probably due to the occurrence of *kān- to appear, see, in certain verb forms side by side with kān-cu. Some interpret this c as a causative morpheme.[23] This is, however, disputable (see Part II, s.v. *kān-).

## Type B

§2.135. Forms belonging to this type have C or CC regularly in the initial position by metathesis, unlike those of types A and C. This type is peculiar to Te. in SDr., and the developments involved in the formation of initial ḍ-, r-, ṟ-, l-, and consonant groups have been treated in detail under phonology (see §§1.121-.159).

### (1) CV̆-CC(V̆)

§2.136. The root morphemes underlying this type are light bases of VC- type where the C is one of the following phonemes: ṭ ḻ ḷ l r ṟ, e.g., *aṭ-, *iḻ-, *eṟ-, etc. These were followed by consonantal suffixes (P, NP, B, NB). The i/u-vowel preceding these suffixes was lost and metathesis took place in the two radical phonemes.

1. *l̲a-ccu to efface, destroy (< *al̲-c-); Ta. Ma. Ka. al̲- to be effaced.

2. ru-ddu to rub, scour (< *ur-d-); Ka. ur-du, ud-du; Tu. ur-d-; Ta. ur-ai (ur-ai-tt-) rub into paste.

(2) CV̄-C(V̌)

§2.137. These forms have the same sequences of radical syllables as those in (1) except that the derivative suffix commenced here with -a, with which the radical vowel contracted into a long vowel (see §§ 1.125 ff.):

1. rā-yu to rub (< *ar-ay); rā-cu id.; Ka. ar-e/i; Tu. ar-eyuni; Ta. ar-i; Ma. ar-ayuka.

2. ḍā-yu to approach (< *aṭ-a-); Ta. aṭ-aicu to be joined; aṭ-ai joining; Ka. aḍ-asu to join, be near, etc.

(3) CCV-CCV̌

§2.138. The root syllables underlying Te. CCV- of this class are of CVC- type which are traceable to either of the PDr. types *CVC- or *CV̄C-; of these, the latter fell together with the former in PDr. itself when followed by a vowel derivative.

Of the root syllable the final C is r, r̲, or l̲. Metathesis has taken place in this syllable producing CCV- when followed by consonantal suffixes which lost a preceding u-vowel; e.g.:

1. mri-ṅgu to swallow (< *mil̲-ṅg-); Ta. vil̲-uṅku, mil̲-uṅku; Ma. mil̲-uṅṅuka.

2. tro-kku to tread upon; (< *tol̲-k-); Ka. tul̲-i; Tu. tor-puni; Ma. tol̲-ikka.

(4) CCV̄-C(V̌)

§2.139. The original root morphemes had the same sequences as those of class (3), except that the radical vowel is lengthened through contraction with the suffix vowel which is -a in most cases; metathesis as usual occurs in the radical phonemes:

1. mrō̃-gu to sound (as drum, etc.) (< *mol̲-aṅg-); Ka. mol̲-agu; Ta. mul̲-aṅku; Ma. mul̲-aṅṅuka.

2. trō-yu, trō-cu to push (< *tor-a-); Kui trō-pa press forward with fingers; Ta. tur-a to drive away, expel; Ma. tur-attuka id.

As stated earlier, it is difficult to mark precisely the etymological boundary in forms of classes 2 and 4 of this type, since the radical long vowel in them is a "link phoneme" in that it represents at the same time both the root and suffix vowels.

§2.140. To sum up, the sequences underlying the radical syllables of all the four classes in Type B are light bases; for classes 1 and 2 they are of the VC- shape, and for classes 3 and 4 they are of the CVC-shape. In classes 2 and 4 the pre-metathesis forms had a vowel beginning the derivative suffix; in classes 1 and 3 the pre-metathesis forms had a consonant in the same position, having lost, in most cases, a u-vowel preceding it. Etymologically Type B goes back to forms of Type C, i.e., those with three short syllables.

Type C

(1) (C)V̆C-V̆C(V̆). (2) (C)V̆C-V̄C(V̆)

§2.141. Nearly forty-four per cent of the Telugu verbal bases belong to this type. Here the root morpheme is always traceable to a similar sequence of PSDr. or PDr., i.e., (C)V̆C-. This (C)V̆C could be either original, or secondarily derived from a heavy base when a vowel derivative follows (see §§1.289, .290). For examples, see forms under extended suffixes of the sonorant and stop series (§§2.22 ff., .72 ff.).

## INNER DERIVATION

§2.142. Though this topic has no direct bearing on Telugu verbal bases, it will, however, be useful for internal reconstruction of PDr. and for an understanding of word formation in the Dravidian languages.

§2.143. The two main distinguishing features of roots and derivative suffixes in a language are: (1) the higher frequency of occurrence of suffixes in relation to the occurrence of any one root element, and (2) the higher number of roots that can unite with any given series of suffixes. In addition to this there is the criterion of meaning. In many languages the meaning of root elements is more or less perceptible and broadly determinable whereas the semantic conditioning of derivative suffixes is hazy and less definable.

§2.144. In a given form with extended suffixes in Dravidian, it is possible to separate more than one layer of derivation. Proceeding from the outermost layer, we can make our first cut before P, NP, PP (B or NB), or L and separate these elements from the preceding vowel. These elements are derivatives in character in the sense that they occur unchanged along with the root syllables in paradigm; and the inflexional suffixes are always added to them, but not directly to the root element. Notwithstanding this, it is found that some of these suffixes themselves have a grammatical denotation which changes along with certain regular types of alternation in their phonemic content. Thus in Ta., Ma., and Kui, etc., an alternation between NP and PP or between B and P is associated with an alternation between intransitive and transitive. In these cases a covert allomorph of a transitive morpheme is involved which sometimes is represented by an overt alternant, viz., t or p; e.g., Kui puh- to get wet: puh-p- to make wet; but ni-ṅg- to rise : ni-k- to raise, where -ṅg-X- > -k- (X = covert allomorph of the transitive morpheme).

Similarly at this level of derivation, we have seen the possibility of giving some sort of semi-grammatical signification to suffixes in l and r as being originally intransitive morphemes (§2.38). So also the Te. -c(u) suffix in many cases is shown to be a later addition to roots, being wrongly annexed from an original past tense morpheme. On the whole, some functional significance can be given to many of these suffixes out of internal as well as comparative evidence.

§2.145. The vowels (a, i, u) preceeding P, NP, PP, or L constitute the second layer of derivation; these vowels are purely derivative in character insofar as historical linguistics can show. Their suffixal status is based on the fact that they are variable in relation to the root morpheme occurring in the preceding position, e.g., Te. ur-iyu v.i. to burn; Ka. ur-i to burn, smart; Tu. ur-iyuni, but Ta. ur-u v.i. id.; to grow angry (Kalit.); Kui ur-pa to boil; ru-ta to ignite; Kuvi ūr-h- to boil over; Kur. ūr- to set fire to; Te. has a form with a suffix beginning with the a-vowel, ur-alu to be burnt, consumed. All languages point to a reconstruction *ūr- for this set and all the following vowels are variables. Here the word variable is used to mean that the changing vowels do not yield to any interpretation of phonemic correspondence as do the vowels of root syllables.

§2.146. Following these principles of etymological analysis, we have set up four types of roots for PDr.: (C)V-, (C)VC-, (C)V̄-, (C)V̄C-, with an observation that there is a higher amount of freedom (as opposed to boundness) in the latter types than in the former. For any given set of words constituting an etymology, one can easily isolate a root morpheme which will fit into one of the above PDr. types. Comparing such reconstructed roots of PDr. or individual sub-groups among themselves, it seems possible to discover further layers of derivation within the reconstructed elements; thus in some cases (C)VC- can be further analyzed as (C)V-C- and similarly (C)V̄C- as (C)V̄-C-. This is more obvious in the latter set where (C)V̄ emerges as the ultimate root element. One such clear case in Dravidian is the words meaning "to burn." We can set up primarily the individual series as follows:

1. kāyu (sun) to shine, to be heated; Ta. Ma. Ka. Tu. Ko. Koḍ. kāy- id.; Kur. khāy- become quite dry; Mlt. qeyr-; < PDr. *kāy-.

Other series with external derivation:

2. kā̃-gu to be heated; Tu. kā-ṅguni; Ta. kā-ṅk-ai, Ka. kā-ṅke heat; Kui kā-ga to warm oneself; Klm. Nk. kā-ŋg- to become hot; Brah. khā-khar fire; < PDr. *kā-ṅk-.

3. Ma. kā-ntuka to be hot; Kui kā-nda to be hot; Kuvi (F) ka-d- to be burnt (probably *kā-d-), Kuvi (S) kā-th- to heat; < PDr. *kā-nt-.

On the basis of these three series, one can reconstruct for PDr. a root of (C)V̄C- type *kāy-, alternating with *kā- before NP or PP suffixes. This helps us to isolate the final reconstructed consonant as a suffix in the following set:

4. kā-lu to burn, blaze; Ma. kā-ḷuka; < *PSDr. *kā-ḷ-; there are many more forms meaning "blackness" caused by heat, etc., with different suffixes, -r, -ṟ, -l, -ṭ, etc., ultimately yielding *kā- as the original root morpheme.

§2.147. A few more such series are given below:

1. Te. nik-ku to stand erect, be proud, Ka. nil-uku, niḷ-ku, nik-ku to strut, rise up to; < PSDr. *niḷ-ukku.

2. PSDr. *niḷ-ukku : Ta. Ka. Ma. nīḷ to grow long, stretch out oneself; < PSDr. *nīḷ : *niḷ-V-.

3. PSDr. *nīḷ- : Tu. nig-acuni, nī-cuni to stretch out, Ka. nig-uḷ be extended; Pj. nik-ip-/nik-it- to stretch out. This gives a reconstruction *nik- (cf. Pj. Tu.); *nik-uḷ > *nīḷ; at this stage we can abstract ḷ as suffix; this is also substantiated by the occurrence of different suffixes after *nik- in place of *-uḷ.

4. Ka. nig-ur, nim-ir to be stretched forth (< *niv-ir/ur), Ta. nim-ir, niv-ar id. (-v-/-m- alternation); Ma. niv-iruka to stand erect, niv-irkka, nī-rkka to raise (> *niv-ir/-ur/-ar).

Comparing *nik-uḷ and *niv-ir-, an alternation of -v-/-k- [-g-] can be set up for PDr., which is also observed in other sets. At this stage it is difficult to say which is original, *k or *v, though the phonetic likelihood is that *-k- was spirantized in the intervocalic position rather than *niv- > *nik-.

§2.148. This tentatively reconstructed element *nik- to rise up, is seen to be at the bottom of another series: Te. neg-ayu to rise up, fly;

Ka. neg-e id.; Ta. niv-a rise, grow, become high; Ma. nik-akka; Klm. negay-.

Comparing this reconstruction *nik- with Kui ni-ṅg- to rise, stand up; ni-pk- to raise (< *nik-p-), Kuvi ni-ng- to rise; ni-k- to awake; ni-ph- to erect, one can easily isolate *ni- as the ultimate base in PDr. with -k, -nk/-kk as suffixes. A comparison of PDr. *ni-, *ni-k- with the following series is interesting: Te. nilucu to stand : Ta. Ma. Ka. Tu. nil to stand; Go. nill-; Kui nis-, nil-, nīlc- ; Kuvi nī- ; nic- (past nīt-); Klm. il-; Kur. il-; < PDr. *nil-/*il-.

All these forms meaning "standing, etc." can be derived from the base *ni- with the generic meaning of "upward motion," isolating -l as a suffix representing an inner layer of derivation.

§2.149. However, at this stage we are on a more conjectural plane since neither *k nor *l in *nik- and *nil have the same amount of variability and flexibility as the suffixes of outer derivation. In other words, they run through the whole family with as much constancy as the constituent phonemes of the root *ni-. On the whole it is not theoretically possible to set an upper limit for such an analysis except by the aid of the principle that the higher the amount of variability of the outer elements of a sequence on comparative grounds, the better are the chances of their being parts of the derivative suffixes rather than of the roots.

It is, however, to be expected that the inner layers of derivation have a greater degree of constancy than the outer ones, since they have been incorporated into the root for a longer time and new formations arise on them by addition of new derivative elements.

## NOTES TO CHAPTER II

[1]Bālav. 9. 63, 71; it should be noted that -cu, -incu here do not have the same function as -cu, -incu which occur as transitive morphemes added to simplexes, e.g., pūḍu to be buried, pūḍ-cu to bury; kaṭṭu to build, kaṭṭ-incu cause to build, etc. Similarly -paḍu and -konu are bound auxiliaries here mostly occurring after nouns: cēkonu to take, cēpaḍu to be available, from cē-/cēyi hand.

[2]For the definition of syllable, etc., see §1.6.

[3]For an interpretation of this nasal grapheme [ ˜ ], see §1.8.

[4]The formation of this group as etymologically a separate suffix series is still not certain.

[5]For information on the value of base final u, see §1.143 end.

[6]In this work a simple V or C suffix is called a basic suffix and sequences of -VL, -VP, -VNP, -VPP and such similar combinations are called extended suffixes.

[7]arumanta- < arumarunta- (a rare medicine), see A. C. Chettiar, "Aphaeresis, Syncope and Apocope in Tamil," Journal of the Annamalai Univ. IX, p. 52.

[8]I.e., consonant followed by utterance final juncture or another consonant.

[9]The Parji Lg., pp. 2, 3.

[10]A Grammar of the Oraon Lg., p. 7, §§18-20.

[11]Communication from Emeneau.

[12]Caldwell[3], p. 205.

[13]Op. cit., p. 207; also see p. 208.

[14]Grignard, The Gram. of the Oraon Lg., pp. 80-84.

[15]Trench, Grammar of Gondi, p. 30.

[16]A. C. Sekhar, Evolution of Malayalam (Poona, 1953), p. 21.

[17]Ka. has also adapu, adugu, adubu but no literary usages are cited. Kittel notes that they are all dialectal in Mysore Kannada.

[18]Jules Bloch, "Structure grammaticale . . . ," pp. 48-50. Also see §§3.11-19; 4.46 ff.

[19]Sekhar, Evolution of Malayalam, pp. 22, 23.

[20]Op. cit., pp. 25, 122.

[21]L. V. R. Aiyar, "The Old Tamil Verb," QJMS 30 (reprint, p. 6).

[22]There is also no clear evidence for the occurrence of i after *y, though it is possible to reconstruct a form like *yin- to explain the alternation en-/in- to say (< *yin-/*yen-) (see §1.222). Since there is no contrast between e/a after *y-, even an-/en- series (meaning to say) can probably be explained by the same reconstruction. It may be recalled here that there was no contrast between ă̄ and ĕ̄ after *y or *ñ in the period that is possible for reconstruction.

[23]V. China Sitaramaswami Sastri, Ándhra Vyākarana Samhitā Sarvasvamu, p. 1580.

## CHAPTER III

# INFLECTIONAL CLASSES
## (Descriptive Analysis)

### OLD TELUGU[1]

#### Introduction

§3.1. In this chapter the verbal bases of Old and Modern Telugu are analyzed into inflectional classes on morphophonemic grounds. But for one class of irregular verbs, each inflectional class consists of base morphemes whose allomorphs possess one common phonemic alternation of an automatic nature, not shared by the members of the other inflectional classes. Where necessary, sub-classes have been set up within the inflectional classes on the basis of certain morphologically conditioned alternations. Though a complete statement of the verb morphology does not fall within the scope of this treatment, a brief description of the structure of the Telugu verb is given to facilitate a better understanding of stem-formation.

§3.2. The Old Telugu verb may be finite or non-finite. On the syntactic or the outer distributional level, a finite verb may be the only constituent of a sentence while a non-finite verb always occurs as a satellite to a finite verb. On the morphological or the inner distributional level, a finite verb always possesses a morpheme indicating person, which is lacking in the non-finite verb.

#### Finite Verbs

§3.3. A finite verb in Old Telugu may be simple or compound (periphrastic). Each simple finite verb has members belonging to three substitution classes: I stem or inflected root, II tense-mode suffix(es), III personal suffix(es), e.g., vaṇḍ-iti-ni I cooked (vaṇḍ- to cook; -iti- past; -ni 1st pers. suffix).

The following diagram shows the structure of the simple finite verbs in Old Telugu together with the tense-mode alternants (substitution class II) as conditioned by the person-alternants (substitution class III).

[1]See p. 231.

| | I | II | III | | | | | | | |
|---|---|---|---|---|---|---|---|---|---|---|
| | Verb-stem | Tense-mode suffixes | Person-suffixes | | | | | | | |
| | | | 1st person | | 2nd person | | 3rd person | | | |
| | | | sg. | pl. | sg. | pl. | sg. | | pl. | |
| | | | | | | | m. | f.n. | n. | m.f. |
| Past | vaṇḍ | e | | | | | nu | nu | nu | |
| | | i | | | | | | | | ri |
| | | iti | ni | mi | vi | ri | | | | |
| Habitual | vaṇḍu<br>vaṇḍ | ϕ }<br>eḍu } | | | | | nu | nu | nu | |
| | vaṇḍ | eḍi | | | | | ni | ni | ni | |
| | vaṇḍ<br>vaṇḍu | eda }<br>du } | nu | mu | vu | ru | | | | ru |
| (Hortative) | vaṇḍu | d | | amu | | | | | | |
| Negative | vaṇḍ | a | nu | mu | vu | ru | Nḍu | du | vu | ru |
| Imperative- | vaṇḍ | u | | | mu | Nḍu | | | | |
| Benedictive | vaṇḍ/vaṇḍu | eḍu/ta | | | | | nu | nu | nu | nu |
| Prohibitive | | (Neg.) (Imp.) | | | | | | | | |
| (Negative-Imperative) | vaṇḍ | ak - u | | | mu | Nḍu | | | | |

A simple finite verb has only one inflected base or stem in the whole construction belonging to substitution class I. Past, habitual, negative, imperative-benedictive and prohibitive (negative-imperative) are all simple finite verbs; of these, past, habitual, and negative have eight-membered paradigms, i.e., 1st person sg. and pl., 2nd person sg. and pl., 3rd person masculine (m.) sg., feminine-neuter (f.n.) sg., masculine-feminine (m.f.) pl., and neuter (n.) pl.; the imperative-benedictive has a six-membered paradigm, i.e., 2nd person sg. and pl., and 3rd person m. sg., f.n. sg., n.pl., and m.f.pl. The negative-imperative or prohibitive has a two-membered paradigm, i.e., 2nd person sg. and pl.

A compound finite verb is made up of a bound non-finite verb + the finite forms of a verb meaning 'to be.'[2] The present and future tenses belong to this type with eight-membered paradigms like the past, habitual, etc.

§3.4. Paradigms of a simple finite verb:[3] Base: vaṇḍu to cook; vaṇḍ- before vowels, vaṇḍu- before consonants.

1. Past:

| | |
|---|---|
| vaṇḍ-e-nu | he cooked |
| vaṇḍ-e-nu | she/it (f. n. sg.) cooked |
| vaṇḍ-e-nu | they (n. pl.) cooked |
| vaṇḍ-i-ri | they (m. f. pl.) cooked |
| vaṇḍ-iti-vi | you (sg.) cooked |
| vaṇḍ-iti-ri | you (pl.) cooked |
| vaṇḍ-iti-ni | I cooked |
| vaṇḍ-iti-mi | we cooked |

2. Habitual:

| | |
|---|---|
| vaṇḍu-ϕ-nu/-eḍu-nu/-eḍi-ni | he cooks |
| vaṇḍu-ϕ-nu/-eḍu-nu/-eḍi-ni | she/it cooks |
| vaṇḍu-ϕ-nu/-eḍu-nu/-eḍi-ni | they (n. pl.) cook |
| vaṇḍu-du-ru/vaṇḍ-eda-ru | they (m. f. pl.) cook |
| vaṇḍu-du-vu/vaṇḍ-eda-vu | you (sg.) cook |
| vaṇḍu-du-ru/vaṇḍ-eda-ru | you (pl.) cook |
| vaṇḍu-du-nu/vaṇḍ-eda-nu | I cook |
| vaṇḍu-du-mu/vaṇḍ-eda-mu | we (incl. excl.) cook |
| (Hortative) | |
| vaṇḍu-d-amu | we (incl.) cook or let us cook[4] |

3. Negative:

| | |
|---|---|
| vaṇḍ-a-Nḍu[5] | he (does, did, and will) not cook |
| vaṇḍ-a-du | she/it (does, did, and will) not cook |

| | |
|---|---|
| vaṇḍ-a-vu | they (n. pl.) (do, did, and will) not cook |
| vaṇḍ-a-ru | they (m. f. pl.) " " |
| vaṇḍ-a-vu | you (sg.) " " |
| vaṇḍ-a-ru | you (pl.) " " |
| vaṇḍ-a-nu | I " " |
| vaṇḍ-a-mu | we " " |

4. Imperative-Benedictive:

| | |
|---|---|
| vaṇḍ-u-mu | cook! (you, sg.) |
| vaṇḍ-u-Nḍu | cook! (you, pl.) |
| vaṇḍ-eḍu-nu/vaṇḍu-ta-nu | may he cook |
| vaṇḍ-eḍu-nu/vaṇḍu-ta-nu | may she/it cook |
| vaṇḍ-eḍu-nu/vaṇḍu-ta-nu | may they (m. f. pl.) cook |
| vaṇḍ-eḍu-nu/vaṇḍu-ta-nu | may they (n. pl.) cook |

5. Prohibitive (Negative-Imperative):

| | |
|---|---|
| vaṇḍ-ak-u-mu | don't cook (you, sg.) |
| vaṇḍ-ak-u-Nḍu | don't cook (you, pl.) |

§3.5. From the preceding table and the paradigms, one can see that the tense-mode allomorphs are complementarily distributed in relation to the person allomorphs, and are therefore morphologically conditioned. These former allomorphs have again variants conditioned by the preceding stem-features. It is essential to give here a complete account of the allomorphic distribution of the tense-mode morphemes occurring after the stem morphemes since both these classes have mutually conditioned distribution.

Interpretation of symbols:

| | |
|---|---|
| / | free variation |
| ~ | phonologically conditioned alternation |
| ∞ | morphologically conditioned alternation |
| ~/ | phonologically conditioned free variation |
| ∞/ | morphologically conditioned free variation |
| ( ) | enclose the less frequent alternants |
| { } | enclose the morpheme in question |

1. Past: Tentative shape (of the morpheme): {e ∞ i ∞ iti}

After the (C)V̌ṇ- alternants of (C)V̌CV̌ bases in final -nu (Class IV, §3.30-1), -iti- alternates with -ṭi-; e.g., aṇ-ṭi-ni I said; anu to say; allom. aṇ-.

Final shape: {e ∞ i ∞ iti (~ ṭi)}.

2. <u>Habitual</u>: Tentative shape: {ϕ/eḍu/eḍi ∞ eda/du ∞ d}

(a). -du- freely alternates with -d-/-ḍ- after the (C)Vn-/ṇ- alternants respectively of the Class IV bases (see §3.30) before the 2nd person pl. and 3rd person m.f.pl. -ru; e.g., an-du-ru: an-d-ru/aṇ-ḍ-ru you (pl.) or they (m.f.pl.) say; kon-du-ru: kon-d-ru/koṇ-ḍ-ru you (pl.) or they (m.f.pl.) take.

(b). -du- ∞ -d- alternate with -tu- ∞ -t- after the bases ending in -cu (Class II and some of Class VI, see §3.25, Rule 4); morphemes in final -cu have alternants without it before -tu- ∞ -t-; e.g., pilu-tu-nu I (hab.) call; pilu-t-amu let us call; basic alternant pilucu to call.

Final shape: {ϕ/eḍu/eḍi ∞ eda/du (~/d/ḍ) ~ tu ∞ d (~ t)}.

3. <u>Negative</u>: Tentative shape: {a ∞ ak} (-a- in negative tense and -ak- in prohibitive).

(a). -a- and -ak- which occur after stems in final consonants have alternants -ϕ- and -k- respectively after stems in final vowels (always long); e.g., (rā- allom. of vaccu to come, see §3.31, 10; .25, 6).

| | | |
|---|---|---|
| | rā-ϕ-nu | I (do, did, and will) not come |
| | rā-k-u-mu | do not come! (you, sg.) |
| | rā-k-u-Nḍu | do not come! (you, pl.) |
| cf. | vaṇḍ-a-nu | I (do, did, and will) not cook |
| | vaṇḍ-ak-u-mu | do not cook! (you, sg.) |
| | vaṇḍ-ak-u-Nḍu | do not cook! (you, pl.) |

Final shape: {a (~ϕ) ∞ ak (~ k)}.

4. <u>Imperative-benedictive</u>: Tentative shape: {u ∞ eḍu/ta}.

(a). -u- alternates with -ϕ- after monosyllabic stems in final short vowels, e.g., ra-ϕ-mmu come! (you, sg.)

ra-ϕ-Nḍu come! (you, pl.)

ra- allom. of vaccu to come (§3.31, 10); -mmu is the morphologically conditioned alternant of -mu (2nd sg. imper.).

Final shape: {u (~ϕ) ∞ eḍu/ta}.

§3.6. The allomorphic distribution of the personal suffixes is not described here since it is not a conditioning factor in the distribution of the allomorphs of the stem morphemes.

## Non-Finite Verbs

§3.7. Following are the suffix alternants of the non-finite verbs in Old Telugu; the less frequent ones are given in parentheses:

| Grammatical name | Suffix alternants | Examples |
|---|---|---|
| 1. Past participle | -i | vaṇḍ-i having cooked |
| 2. Past adjective | -ina | vaṇḍ-ina that cooked |
| | (~/na ∞/a̧) | an-ina/an-na that said |
| | | paḍ-ina/paḍḍ-a that fell |
| 3. Conditional, etc. | -inaN | vaṇḍ-inaN if cooked, on cooking, etc. |
| | (~/naN ∞/aN) | an-inaN/an-naN if said, etc. |
| | | paḍ-in-aN/paḍḍ-aN if fell, etc. |
| 4. Habitual adjective | -ϕ/eḍu/eḍi | vaṇḍu that cook(s) |
| | | vaṇḍ-eḍu that cook(s) |
| | | vaṇḍ-eḍi that cook(s) |
| 5. Negative participle | -aka | vaṇḍ-aka not cooking |
| | (~ ka) | rā-ka not coming |
| 6. Negative adjective | -ani | vaṇḍ-ani that not cooked |
| | (~ ni) | rā-ni that not come |
| 7. Infinitive | -aN | vaṇḍ-aN to cook |
| | (~ N) | rā-N to come |
| 8. Post-action (meaning 'after') | -ḍuN | vaṇḍu-ḍuN after cooking |
| 9. Present participle | -cuN | vaṇḍu-cuN cooking |
| 10. Bound present participle | -c- (/cun-) | vaṇḍu-c-unnānu I am cooking (or vaṇḍu-cun-unnānu id.) |

Of 2 and 3, -na and -naN occur after the n-final stems (Class IV); similarly, -a and -aN occur after three monosyllabic stems in -ḍ (iḍu to put, paḍu to fall, ceḍu to perish). Of 5, 6, and 7, the alternants without the initial a occur after stems in final vowels. Of the above, 1 to 8 may be taken each as a separate morpheme;[6] 9 and 10 may be assigned to the same morpheme, 10 occurring always bound to the paradigm of un- to be, and 9 occurring unbound.

Final N occurring in the above alternants is a morphophoneme with the following phonemic values in different positions:

(a). /n/ before a vowel;

(b). /n/ or /nu/ freely varying with /ϕ/ before any consonant and in final position;

(c). also (= freely varying with)

/ṅ/ before /g/, /n/ before /d j/, /ṇ/ before /ḍ/, /m/ before /b/ freely varying with /ϕ/ after short vowels, but always /ϕ/ after long vowels.

Morphs having initial /k c ṭ t p/ elsewhere have regular alternants in initial /g j ḍ d b/ after N.[7]

## Compound Verbs

§3.8. The present and future tense verbs are formed through compound construction in Old Telugu.

The present tense is formed by adding the finite forms of the defective verb un- 'to be' to the bound present participle in -c- (and also less frequently -cun- in the older classics):[8]

| | |
|---|---|
| vaṇḍu-c-unnānu | I am cooking |
| -unnāmu | we are cooking |
| -unnāvu | you (sg.) are cooking |
| -unnāru | you (pl. ) are cooking |
| -unnāNdu | he is cooking |
| -unnadi | she/it is cooking |
| -unnāru | they (m. f. pl.) are cooking |
| -unnavi | they (n. pl.) are cooking |

Similarly, the future tense is formed by adding the finite forms of the defective verb kal- 'to be' to the infinitives in -aN, e.g.

| | |
|---|---|
| vaṇḍ-aN-galanu | I shall cook |
| -galamu | we shall cook |
| -galavu | you (sg.) shall cook |
| -galaru | you (pl. ) shall cook |
| -galaNḍu | he will cook |
| -galadu | she/it will cook |
| -galaru | they (m. f. pl.) will cook |
| -galavu | they (n. pl.) will cook |

## Intransitives and Transitives

§3.9. Each verb stem belonging to substitution class I may comprise members of two or three form classes, viz.:

(1) root (with or without an inalienably bound marker of intransitive/ transitive of class 2; when not followed by this marker, the monomorphic root is by itself [i.e., inherently] either intransitive or transitive);

(2) intransitive/transitive marker inalienably bound to class 1;

(3) transitive/causal marker.

The different possibilities of stem composition in terms of the above three classes may be diagrammatically presented as follows.
(R = root unbound; R- = root bound; -intr. = inalienably bound intransitive; -tr. = inalienably bound transitive.)

| Stem | Example: |
|---|---|
| R (intr.) | manu to live |
| R (tr.) | ammu to sell |
| R (intr.) + tr. | manu-cu to nourish, protect |
| R (tr.) + caus. | amm-incu to cause to sell |
| R– + { -intr. / -tr. } | aḍã-gu to be suppressed<br>aḍã-cu to suppress |
| R– + { -intr. + tr. / -tr. + caus. } | aḍã-g-incu to suppress<br>aḍã-p-incu to cause to suppress |

Not all intransitive stems have the corresponding transitives, and not all transitives the corresponding causatives. In the case of many stems, the intransitive or transitive allomorph is covert (i.e., zero) matched by an overt transitive or causative allomorph respectively (see §3.23 b).

There is a large class of intransitive stems related to the corresponding transitive stems through some alternation in the final syllable. Relatively few forms have covert allomorphs in both intransitive and transitive in related sets; in other words, in this sub-class the stem is alike in intransitive and transitive. Cases in which the root parts of the stems have morphophonemic alternants in transitive formation, are described at the end of each such sub-class. The various sets of intransitive and transitive stems are classified below:

| §3.10. Intransitive -$\phi$ | Transitive -$\phi$ |
|---|---|
| ãgu to be obstructed | ãgu to obstruct |
| karãgu to be melted | karãgu to melt (butter, etc.) |
| talãgu to be warded off | talãgu to ward off |
| nĩgu to be given up | nĩgu to give up |
| kuriyu to rain, leak (as roof) | kuriyu to shower, rain (fire, flowers, etc.) |
| teliyu to be known | teliyu to know |

§3.11. Intransitive -$\phi$ Transitive -cu

Bases in final -ru, -r̲u, -lu, -nu, and -ḍu form transitives in this manner. They all have free variants without the final u before transitive -cu. Examples:

| | |
|---|---|
| amaru to be made ready | amarcu/amarucu to make ready |
| kār̲u to leak (of pot, etc.) | kārcu/kār̲ucu to make to leak |
| temalu to come up or out | temalcu/temalucu to take out |
| kālu to be burnt | kālcu/kālucu to burn |
| mānu to cease, stop (a practice) | māncu/mānucu to stop (from doing something) |
| pūḍu to be buried | pūḍcu/pūḍucu to bury |

The transitive alternants of this type are given under the respective bases in the etymological index (see Part II).

In the formation of transitives with -cu, some of the bases of this sub-class have further morphophonemic alternants as follows:

(1) ḍullu/dullu to drop off and ḍollu/dollu to roll over have alternants ḍul(u)-/dul(u)- and ḍol(u)-/dol(u)- respectively:

| | |
|---|---|
| ḍullu to drop off | ḍulcu/ḍulucu to shake off (tr.) |
| dullu to drop off | dulcu/dulucu to shake off (tr.) |
| ḍollu to roll over | ḍolcu/ḍolucu to cause to roll over |
| dollu to roll over | dolcu/dolucu to cause to roll over |

(2) ceḍu to be spoiled and paḍu to fall, suffer, have alternants cer̲u- and par̲u- respectively:

| | |
|---|---|
| ceḍu to be spoiled | cer̲ucu to spoil, kill |
| paḍu to experience, suffer | par̲ucu to let suffer |

(3) āḍu to shake, play, ōḍu to be defeated, kūḍu to be mixed have alternants ār(u)-, ōr(u)-, kūr(u)- respectively (see §1.85).

| | |
|---|---|
| āḍu to play, shake | ārcu/ārucu to cause to play, to shake |
| ōḍu to be defeated, to run | ōrcu/ōrucu to defeat |
| kūḍu to be joined | kūrcu/kūrucu to join, add |

| §3.12. Intransitive -gu | Transitive -cu |
|---|---|

Both -gu and -cu are preceded by a pre-consonantal nasal. /ṅ/ before -gu alternates with /n/ before -cu:

| | |
|---|---|
| aḍẵgu to be subdued | aḍẵcu to subdue |
| alẵgu to be troubled | alẵcu to trouble |
| ā̃gu to be obstructed | ā̃cu to obstruct (late) |
| ū̃gu (a cradle, etc.) to swing | ū̃cu to swing (a cradle, etc.) |
| karẵgu to be melted | karẵcu to melt (late) |
| kalẵgu to be disturbed (of water, mind, etc.) | kalẵcu to disturb |
| kā̃gu to be boiled, etc. | kā̃cu to boil |
| krā̃gu to be burnt out | krā̃cu to burn out |
| cā̃gu to be stretched | cā̃cu to stretch |

| Intransitive | Transitive |
|---|---|
| ḍaṅgu to be pounded | ḍancu to pound |
| ḍā̃gu/dā̃gu to hide oneself | ḍā̃cu/dā̃cu to hide |
| tū̃gu to be weighed | tū̃cu to weigh, balance |
| tō̃gu to sink in water | tō̃cu to sink, dip |
| truṅgu to fall in pieces | truncu to cut into pieces[9] |
| nalā̃gu to be crushed | nalā̃cu to crush, crumple |
| penā̃gu to be twisted | penā̃cu to twine, twist |
| maḍā̃gu/maṇā̃gu to be bent | maḍā̃cu/maṇā̃cu to bend |
| malā̃gu to turn back or to a side | malā̃cu to bend, cause to slant |
| muḍū̃gu to contract, shrink in | muḍū̃cu (? ˜) to fold, hold within |
| rē̃gu to rage, be excited | rē̃cu to incite |
| lō̃gu to be subdued | lō̃cu to subdue (rare) |
| vaṅgu to be bent, to stoop | vancu to bend |
| vē̃gu to grieve, suffer | vē̃cu to trouble |
| sā̃gu to become long | sā̃cu to elongate |

§3.13. In the following, the whole phonemic sequence that occurs after the root-vowel of the intransitive base is replaced by -ncu in transitive:[10]

| | Intransitive | Transitive |
|---|---|---|
| (a) | cirū̃gu/cinū̃gu to be torn | ci-ncu to tear |
| | tunū̃gu to be snapped | tu-ncu to snap |
| | munū̃gu to dive | mu-ncu to sink, drown |
| (b) | ḍiggu/ḍigu, diggu/digu to descend | ḍi-ncu/di-ncu to bring down |
| | perugu to flourish, grow | pe-ncu to breed, nourish |
| (c) | noccu to suffer | no-ncu to make to suffer, to defeat |

§3.14. Intransitive -ḍu — Transitive -cu

Root-final /ṇ/ preceding /ḍ/ alternates with /n/ before -cu:

| | Intransitive -ḍu | Transitive -cu |
|---|---|---|
| (a) | uṇ-ḍu to be, to occur | un-cu to keep, let stay |
| | niṇ-ḍu to be filled, full | nin-cu to fill (alternatively nin-ucu) |
| (b) | magu-ḍu to return, turn back | magu-cu to cause to turn back |
| | mogu-ḍu to close, contract | mogu-cu to fold, close (hands, eyes, etc.) |

Items under (b) have alternative transitive forms, maguḍ-cu/maguḍu-cu, moguḍ-cu/moguḍu-cu respectively, according to the rule given under §3.11.

§3.15. Intransitive -ϕ — Transitive -pu

| | Intransitive -ϕ | Transitive -pu |
|---|---|---|
| (a) | konu to buy, take; to occur; (as an auxiliary) a reflexive morph | kolu-pu to instigate, incite; (as an auxiliary) causal morph |
| | canu to pass, elapse (as time) | calu-pu/cal-pu to pass (time) |
| (b) | kanu to see | kān-pu to show (oneself), to appear before |

The alternations among the root-phonemes of the above three bases reflect a similar situation in PDr., viz., kon-/kol- (< *koṇ-/*koḷ-), can-/cal- (< *can-/*cal-), kan-/kān- (< *kaṇ-/*kāṇ-); see Part II, under items konu, canu, kanu.

§3.16. Intransitive -gu    Transitive -pu

In this sub-class -gu of the intransitives is not preceded by ˜ as in those of §3.12.[11]

| | |
|---|---|
| ar̲ugu to be digested | ar̲upu to digest |
| uḍugu to end, be subdued | uḍupu to end, subdue |
| jarugu to move, proceed | jarupu to move, push |
| tirugu to turn, revolve | trippu to revolve (< *tir-up-, metathesis) |
| medugu to be well-ground | medupu to mix well |

§3.17. Intransitive -cu    Transitive -pu

Most of the bases belonging to the inflectional class II(a) (see §3.27) form transitives in this manner:

| | |
|---|---|
| kaḍacu (time) to pass | kaḍapu to pass time |
| kar̲acu to learn | kar̲apu to teach |
| kuḍucu to eat, drink | kuḍupu to feed, let suck |
| cūcu to see | cūpu to show |
| nil(u)cu to stand, cease | nil(u)pu to set up, stop |
| nēr(u)cu to learn | nēr(u)pu to train |
| mōcu to rest, lean on | mōpu to rest something on |
| lēcu to rise up, rise | lēpu to raise, awake |

§3.18. Intransitive -yu    Transitive -pu

An /i/ vowel occurring before -yu alternates with /u/ before -pu:

| | |
|---|---|
| eḍayu to be separated | eḍapu to separate |
| kaliyu to be close together | kalupu to join, put together |
| keḍayu to fall, perish | keḍapu to fell, kill |
| taḍiyu to become wet | taḍupu to soak, make wet |
| taniyu to be satisfied | tanupu to satisfy (somebody) |
| tar̲iyu to approach, meet | tar̲upu to join together (late) |
| teliyu to be known | telupu to enlighten, tell |
| naliyu to be powdered | nalupu to squeeze between palms |
| nuliyu to be twisted | nulupu to twist, twine |
| nerayu to extend, increase | nerapu to spread, increase (tr.) |
| ner̲ayu to become full | ner̲apu to fill |
| pāyu to be separated | pāpu to separate, divide |
| pogayu to be smoked | pogapu to season (food) |
| māyu to be hidden | māpu to hide, screen, destroy |

| | |
|---|---|
| mēyu (cattle) to graze | mēpu to graze (cattle, etc.) |
| viriyu to burst, blossom | vippu (< *vir-p-) to unfold |

§3.19. Intransitive -yu    Transitive -cu; -ncu in a few cases. On formal grounds there is no way of distinguishing this sub-class from the above one. In one case the radical vowel which occurs short in the intransitive alternant occurs long in the transitive alternant.

| | | |
|---|---|---|
| (a) | kuḍiyu to shrink, decrease | kuḍucu to press into a small place |
| | oliyu to be peeled | olucu to peel, flay |
| | nuliyu to be twisted | nulucu to twist |
| | pāyu to be separated | pācu to separatę, leave (besides pāpu) |
| | penayu to be twined | penacu to twine (alt. penapu) |
| | rāyu to be rubbed | rācu to rub, graze |
| | bigiyu to be tight | bigucu to tighten (rare) |
| | meliyu to mix well with | melucu to twist, join well |
| | vaḍiyu to ooze, be filtered | vaḍucu to strain, filter |
| (b) | eriyu to burn, grieve | ērcu to burn, aggrieve |
| (c) | bigiyu to be tight | bigincu to tighten |
| | treyyu to be cut off | trencu to cut off |
| | bruyyu to perish | bruncu to kill (rare) |

§3.20. The following sets show suppletive base-alternants in the transitive. It is therefore found best to list them as follows:

| | | |
|---|---|---|
| (a) | Intransitive -ϕ | Transitive -incu |
| | agu to become | kāv-incu to make |
| | vaccu to come | rāv-incu/rapp-incu to make somebody come, bring, summon |
| (b) | -ϕ | -ccu |
| | pōvu to go | pu-ccu to send[12] |
| (c) | -ccu | -mpu |
| | ca-ccu to die | ca-mpu to kill |
| (d) | -ccu | -npu/-nupu |
| | co-ccu to enter | co-npu/con-upu to insert |

§3.21. In addition to the foregoing types of transitive formation, one other very common and productive type is by adding -incu to the intransitive bases. Even bases which have transitive alternants through internal modification add -incu in forming alternative bases in transitive. One example from each of the sub-classes treated so far is given below:

| Intransitive -ϕ | Transitive -incu | Alternative transitive (with internal modification, etc.) |
|---|---|---|
| karãgu to be melted | karãg-incu to melt | karãgu (§3.10) |
| amaru to be ready | amar-incu to make ready | amarcu/amarucu (§3.11) |
| adãgu to be subdued | aḍãg-incu to subdue | adãcu (§3.12) |
| perugu to flourish | perig-incu to grow | pencu (§3.13) |
| niṇḍu to be full | niṇḍ-incu to fill | nincu (§3.14) |
| uḍugu to end | uḍig-incu to fill (tr.) | uḍupu (§3.16) |
| naḍacu to walk | naḍap-incu to run (tr.), make someone walk | naḍapu (§3.17) |
| keḍayu to perish | keḍay-incu to cause to fall | keḍapu (§3.18) |
| kudiyu to shrink | kudiy-incu to abridge | kuducu (§3.19) |

No Telugu grammar has precisely stated which and how many of the verbal bases form transitives in this manner; however, they say that almost any verb is eligible to take -incu to become a transitive or causative. But a number of bases do not have transitives in -incu in the literary usage, e.g., cēru to reach: cērcu to let reach, take to, but not *cēr-incu; kālu to be burnt : kālcu to burn, but not *kāl-incu. Though not every verbal base of the intransitive class need have a corresponding transitive in -incu, one can say with confidence that more verbal bases form transitives by the addition of -incu than by any other means.

## Causatives

§3.22. The traditional Telugu grammars have not made any distinction between the transitives and causatives. They use the word prēraṇārthaka- (having the meaning of Skt. prēraṇa- causal) for the whole group of transitive-causative suffixes -cu, -pu, and -incu. However, this is wrong, since, syntactically, it is necessary to distinguish the causals from the transitives; a statement containing a causal verb may have two actor-words as immediate constituents, one in the nominative and the other in the instrumental, whereas, a statement containing a transitive verb may have a single actor-word occurring in the nominative. Morphologically, causals are formed by adding -incu (exception, see the end of this section) to the transitive bases, e.g.:

| Intransitive | Transitive | Causative |
|---|---|---|
| kālu (house, etc.) to burn | kālcu to burn | kālpincu to make somebody burn something |
| aḍãgu to subside | aḍãcu to suppress | aḍãpincu to cause to suppress |
| cirũgu to be torn | cincu to tear | cimpincu to cause to tear |
| jarugu to slide, move | jarupu to move (tr.) | jaripincu to cause to move |
| nilucu to stand, stay | nilupu to erect, to set up | nilipincu to cause to set up |
| keḍayu to fall down, perish | keḍapu to destroy | keḍapincu to cause to destroy |
| caccu to die | campu to kill | campincu to cause to kill |

Before the causal morph -incu, a transitive /cu ~ c/ (cu before a consonant and c before a vowel) alternates with /pu ~ p/ (pu before a consonant and p before a vowel); and /n/ occurring before /cu/ alternates with /m/ before /pu/; -u- occurring in the second syllables of the trisyllabic bases alternates with -i- before -incu. -incu has a variant -ipincu after a small class of bases of the (C)V̌n- type, e.g.:

| Transitive | Causative |
|---|---|
| anu to say | an-ipincu to cause some one to say |
| kanu to see | kan-ipincu to cause (something or somebody) to be seen; to show oneself, to appear |
| konu to buy | kon-ipincu to cause (somebody) to buy |
| tinu to eat | tin-ipincu to cause to eat, to feed through somebody (altern. tinucu) |
| vinu to hear | vin-ipincu to cause (somebody) to hear oneself, to tell (altern. vinucu) |

§3.23. The foregoing discussion of the formation of transitive bases in Old Telugu can be summarized by presenting the intransitive and transitive suffixes in matching sets arranged according to the identity of the suffixes on each side.

(a) Arranged from the standpoint of intransitives:

| Intransitive suffix | Transitive suffix | |
|---|---|---|
| -ϕ | -ϕ | (§3.10) |
| | -cu | (§3.11) |
| | -pu | (§3.15) |
| | -ccu | (§3.20) |
| | -incu | (§§3.20, .21) |
| -yu | -pu | (§3.18) |
| | -cu | (§3.19) |
| | -ncu | (§3.19) |
| -gu | -cu | (§3.12) |
| | -pu | (§3.16) |
| -cu | -pu | (§3.17) |
| -ḍu | -cu | (§3.14) |
| -ccu | -mpu | (§3.20) |
| | -npu | (§3.20) |
| syllables after the root-vowel | -ncu | (§3.13) |

(b) Arranged from the standpoint of transitives:

| Transitive suffix | Intransitive suffix | |
|---|---|---|
| -ϕ | -ϕ | (§3.10) |
| -cu | -ϕ | (§3.11) |
| | -gu | (§3.12) |
| | -ḍu | (§3.14) |
| | -yu | (§3.19) |
| -ccu | -ϕ | (§3.20) |
| -ncu | -yu | (§3.19) |
| | syllables after the root-vowel | (§3.13) |
| -incu | -ϕ | (§§3.20, .21) |
| -pu | -ϕ | (§3.15) |
| | -gu | (§3.16) |
| | -cu | (§3.17) |
| | -yu | (§3.18) |
| -mpu | -ccu | (§3.20) |
| -npu | -ccu | (§3.20) |

## Morphophonemic Criteria for Stem-Classification

§3.24. The verb-bases of Old Telugu are divided into five inflectional classes on the basis of their stem-alternations before the tense-mode allomorphs. For the purpose of economy of statement, the more frequently occurring tense-mode suffixes have been re-classified into three morphophonemic groups, A, B, and C. The other alternants are given in parentheses.

Group A Alternants beginning with a consonant:

| | | |
|---|---|---|
| 1 | -cuN | present participle |
| 2 | -c- | bound present participle |
| 3 | -ta- | imperative-benedictive (before 3pers.) |
| 4 | -ḍuN- | post-action (meaning 'after') |
| 5 | -ϕ- (~n) | habitual adjective (see B-6) |
| 6(a) | -du- (~/d~/ḍ) | habitual tense |
| (b) | ~-tu- | |
| (c) | ∞-d- | |
| (d) | ~ -t- | |
| 7 | -ṭi- | past tense (see §3.5) |

Group B Alternants beginning with a front vowel:

| | | |
|---|---|---|
| 1(a) | -i- | past tense |
| (b) | -e- | |
| (c) | -iti- | |
| 2 | -i | past participle |
| 3 | -ina (~/na ∞/a) | past adjective |
| 4 | -inaN (~/naN ∞/aN) | conditional |
| 5 | -eḍu-/-eḍi-/-eda- | habitual tense |
| 6 | -eḍu-/-eḍi- | habitual adjective |

Group C Alternants beginning with a back vowel:

| | | |
|---|---|---|
| 1 | -aN (~N) | infinitive |
| 2 | -a- (~ϕ) | negative tense |
| 3 | -ak- (~k) | negative imperative (allom. of negative -a-) |
| 4 | -aka (~ka) | negative participle |
| 5 | - ani (~ni) | negative adjective |
| 6 | u- (~ϕ) | imperative-benedictive (before the 2nd person suffixes) |

§3.25. Except in the case of some irregular verbs (Class V, see §3.31), most of the alternations among the verb-stems before the tense-mode suffixes can be described by a few morphophonemic rules of wide application. The stem allomorphs of one or more typical morphemes are described in terms of their arrangement as well as process. In the case of process statements, the verbal bases as listed in Part II and the suffix alternants as listed under §3.7 are taken as the basis for deriving the grammatical forms by certain processes.

Rule 1. Stems having a final vowel before a consonant have alternants without it before another vowel. In other words, $-V^1 + V^2- > -V^2-$ ($V^1$ base-final vowel; $V^2$ the vowel beginning a suffix). E.g.:

| | |
|---|---|
| kaṭṭu-cuN | building (A-1) |
| kaṭṭ-i | having built (B-2) |
| kaṭṭ-aN | to build (C-1) |

Stem morpheme kaṭṭu- ~ kaṭṭ- to build; kaṭṭu- before A-suffixes, kaṭṭ- before B- and C-suffixes.

Rule 2. In trisyllabic bases, u of the second syllable alternates with i, when a front vowel (i or e) occurs in the following syllable, i.e., (C)VCuC-i/e- > (C)VCiC-i/e-; e.g.:

| | | |
|---|---|---|
| | aḍig-i | having asked (aḍugu to ask, -i past participle suffix B-2) |
| Elsewhere: | aḍugu-cuN | asking (A-1) |
| | aḍug-aN | to ask (C-1) |

With the application of this rule and the above any trisyllabic base with a medial u, has at least three allomorphs as in the following example:

| | |
|---|---|
| aḍugu- | before a consonant (A-suffixes) |
| aḍig- | before i/e (B-suffixes) |
| aḍug- | before any vowel other than i/e (C-suffixes) |

Rule 3. Stems which have final yu/y elsewhere, have regular alternants in final s before a front vowel of the B-suffixes, i.e., -y + i/e- > -s + i-/-s + e-; e.g., kās-i (sun, moon) having shone; elsewhere kāyu-/kāy- to shine.

A base ending in -yu has therefore three alternants as in the following examples:

| | |
|---|---|
| kāyu-, kaliyu- | before a consonant (A-suffixes) |
| kās-, kalis- | before i/e (B-suffixes) |
| kāy-, kaliy- | before any vowel other than i/e (C-suffixes) |

Rule 4. All stems having final cu before other consonants, have alternants without it before the alternants /tu ~ t/ of the habitual tense (see §3.5, 2b.); stems having final ccu before the other consonants, have alternants in final t before /tu ~ t/; the alternation may be stated more economically in terms of the following process:

-cu + du- (~d-) > -tu- (~-t-)

-ccu + du- (~d-) > -ttu- (~-tt-)

E.g., pilu-tu-nu I call; pilu-t-amu we (incl.) call or let us call (basic stem alternant, pilucu to call); put-tu-nu I send; put-t-amu we (incl.) send or let us send (basic stem alternant, puccu to send).

Here /-tu---t-/ and /-ttu---tt-/ represent at the same time alternations in two successive morphs.

Rule 5. Stem alternants in final n(u) (preceded by a short vowel) have alternants in ṇ before the past tense allomorph -ṭ- and the habitual tense allomorph -ḍ- (§3.5, 1, 2); i.e., -n + ṭ- > -ṇṭ- and -n + ḍ- > -ṇḍ-.

E.g., aṇ-ṭi-ni I said; aṇ-ḍ-ru you (pl.), or they (m. f. pl.) say; elsewhere the stem is anu- or an-

Rule 6. After monosyllabic stem-alternants in final long or short vowels, all C-suffixes have alternants without the initial vowel (see §3.5, 3, 4).

E.g., rā + i̸N > rāN to come (C-1)
ra + i̸ + mmu > rammu come! (you sg.)
ra + i̸ + Nḍu > raṇḍu come! (you pl.)
rā-/ra- allomm. of vaccu to come (see §3.31).

## Class I

§3.26. This class, which comprises about seventy-four per cent of the Old Telugu verbal bases, may be divided into two sub-classes:

(a) disyllabic bases of the (C)V̄CV̆ or (C)V̆CCV̆ type and trisyllabic bases of the (C)V̆CV̆CV̆ type without u (i.e., with a or i) in the second syllable.

(b) trisyllabic bases of the (C)V̆CV̆CV̆ type with u in the second syllable.

Morphophonemic rule 1 operates in sub-class (a), and rules 1 and 2 operate in sub-class (b). Consequently, a member of sub-class (a) has one alternant in final u before A-suffixes, and another alternant in final consonant before B- and C-suffixes; on the other hand, a member of sub-class (b) has three allomorphs: (1) with final u before A-suffixes, (2) with final consonant before C-suffixes, (3) with final consonant and with i for medial u (which occurs elsewhere) before B-suffixes.

The allomorphic distribution of a member of each of the two sub-classes is given below:

| Basic stem alternant: | Stem alternants before the suffixes: A | B | C |
|---|---|---|---|
| (a) 1. kaṭṭu to build | kaṭṭu- | kaṭṭ- | kaṭṭ- |
| 2. aḍāgu be subdued | aḍāgu- | aḍāg- | aḍāg- |
| (b) aḍugu to ask | aḍugu- | aḍig- | aḍug- |

This is obviously the major inflectional class in Telugu but there are no strict formal features to distinguish it from the other classes. However, it may be said generally that verbal bases which do not end in -cu, -yu, and -nu (preceded by a short vowel) belong to this class. Examples can be noted from Part II, in which all bases unmarked by a suffixed number belong to this class.

## Class II

§3.27. Bases ending in -cu belong to this class. Morphophonemic rules 1, 2, and 4 operate in this class. The alternation characterizing this whole class is the loss of final cu before tu ~ t of the habitual tense (see §3.25, 4).

On the basis of the morphological conditioning of the alternants before C-suffixes, we can set up 4 sub-classes under this class, of which in

(a) the final -cu/-ccu alternate with -vu/-vvu,

(b) the final -cu/-ncu alternate with -pu/-mpu,

(c) the final -˜cu occurs in free alternation with -˜pu,

(d) no alternation occurs before the C-suffixes, or usages with C-suffixes are not available.

The distribution of the allomorphs for each of the above sub-classes is exemplified below:

| Basic stem-alternant | Stem alternants before the suffix-groups A | B | C |
|---|---|---|---|
| (a) kācu to protect | kācu- (1-5)<br>kā- (6b, d) | kāc- | kāv- |
| pruccu to rot | pruccu- (1-5)<br>prut- (6b, d) | prucc- | pruvv- |
| kuḍucu to eat or drink | kuḍucu- (1-5)<br>kuḍu- (6b, d) | kuḍic- | kuḍuv- |
| (b) truncu to kill | truncu- (1-5)<br>trun- (6b, d) | trunc- | trump- |
| anucu to send | anucu- (1-5)<br>anu- (6b, d) | anic- | anup- |
| (c) talācu to think | talācu- (1-5)<br>talā- (6b, d) | talāc- | talāc-/talāp- |
| (d) koncu to hesitate | koncu- (1-5)<br>kon- (6b, d) | konc- | konc- |
| gīcu to scratch | gīcu- (1-5)<br>gī- (6b, d) | gīc- | ... |

The sub-classification of each base belonging to this inflectional class is indicated in Part II by a suffixed (a), (b), (c), or (d) to Class II.

§3.28. In describing the stems of this class of verbs, the Telugu traditional grammarians distinguished between two types of final -cu: (1) āgama-cu, i.e., the -cu that occurs through a grammatical process[13] (transitive or verbalizer) in the bases;[14] this occurs mostly as an additive or replacive morph (see §3.22b); (2) siddha-cu or the original -cu, i.e., that which is an integral part of the verb-base without being derived by any grammatical process. They have further made a rule that siddha-cu is always replaced by -v(u) and āgama-cu by -p(u) before the C-suffixes. In forms where siddha-cu is preceded by an arasunna [˜], the final -c(u) sometimes alternates with -p(u). These rules have many exceptions; for instance, among the bases in sub-class (b) in which -cu alternates with -p(u) before the C-suffixes, there are quite a number of forms for which it is difficult to show that -cu is added by any grammatical process (i.e., as a transitive or verbalizing morpheme), e.g., aḍucu to beat, anucu to send, tālcu to wear, telucu to pacify, panucu to send, etc., all of which belong to sub-class (b); no corresponding intransitive forms or noun stems are attested for these in literature or elsewhere. However, most of the stems possessing a transitive allomorph in final -cu (i.e., -cu, -ncu, -incu) belong to sub-class (b); the only exceptions seem to be ōr(u)cu to defeat, tr. of ōḍu to be defeated (see §3.11 (3)), and vār(u)cu to strain water, tr. of vāru water to be strained, which have ōr(u)v- and vār(u)v- respectively as in sub-class (a), instead of ōr(u)p- and vār(u)p- before the C-suffixes.

Further, the traditional grammars do not speak of the large class of forms in (d), for most of which evidence is not available to show the alternation of final -c(u) before the C-suffixes.

## Class III

§3.29. Bases of this class have final -y(u) or -yy(u) before A and C suffixes and -s(u) or -ss(u) respectively before the B-suffixes. Therefore, morphophonemic rules 1 and 3 operate in this class. Since the trisyllabic bases of this class do not have u in the medial syllable, rule 2 does not operate here. The allomorphic distribution is as follows:

| Basic stem alternant | Stem alternants before the suffixes | | |
|---|---|---|---|
| | A | B | C |
| cēyu to do | cēyu- | cēs- | cēy- |
| jaḍiyu to fear, shiver | jaḍiyu- | jaḍis- | jaḍiy- |
| treyyu to be cut off | treyyu- | tress- | treyy- |

There are 171 verbal bases in -yu or -yyu which belong to this class.

## Class IV

§3.30. This is a relatively small class comprising eight bases of two short syllables ending in -n(u), viz., anu to say; kanu[1] to see; kanu[2] to bring forth; konu to hold, buy; canu to go; tinu to eat; manu to live; vinu to hear.

(1) Final -nu in all these bases alternates with -ṇ before -ṭi- (past) and -ḍ- (habitual) of the A-suffixes (see §3.5; morphophonemic rule 5, §3.25).

(2) Before -cuN∞-c- (present) and -du-∞-d- (habitual), stems of all these bases have free variants without the final u, e.g., anu-cuN/an-cuN saying; anu-du-nu/an-du-nu I say. With the rest of the A-suffixes, stems in final u occur, e.g., anu-ta-nu may he say, etc.

(3) All bases of this class have free variants in final -iy before any suffix beginning with e of the B group (see 1, 5, and 6);

| | | |
|---|---|---|
| e.g., | aniy-e-nu | he said |
| | aniy-eḍu-nu<br>aniy-eḍi-ni | he says |
| | aniy-eda-nu | I say |
| | aniy-eḍi- | that say(s) (adj.) |

alternatively, anenu, aneḍunu, aneḍini, anedanu, aneḍi-, and so on.

The following table illustrates the allomorphic distribution of an- to say.

| Basic stem alternant | Stem alternants before the suffixes | | |
|---|---|---|---|
| | A | B | C |
| anu to say | anu-/an- (1, 2) | an- | an- |
| | anu- (3, 5) | an-/aniy- (1b, 5, 6) | |
| | aṇ- (6a, 7) | | |

## Class V

§3.31. This class consists of bases having irregular stem-alternants, not all of which can be brought under a set of consistent morphophonemic rules. It is therefore considered convenient to list separately the alternants of each base before the three suffix-groups; for the sake of convenience, a sub-classification of the suffixes is made as follows:

a-suffixes: suffixes beginning with a in Group C (1 to 5) with their alternants (§3.25, rule 6)

u-suffix : the imperative (C-6) with its alternant

i-suffixes }
e-suffixes } : suffixes beginning with i or e in Group B

It may be recalled that a short vowel (a or u) of the C-suffixes is lost after stems in final vowels (§3.25, rule 6); the imperative 2sg. is -mmu, 2pl. -Nḍu after monosyllabic stems in final vowels, e.g., ra-ϕ-mmu you (sg.) come; ra-ϕ-Nḍu you (pl.) come (see item 10).

1. agu to become, to be; allomm. agu-/avu-/aṷ-, ay-, āy-/ayy-, kā-

| A | B | C |
|---|---|---|
| agu-/avu-/aṷ- | ay- (i-suffixes) | kā- (a-suffixes) |
| | āy-/ayy- (e-suffixes) | ka- (6); also agu- (6, before 2sg.) |

2. iccu to give; allomm. icc-, it-, ī-, īy-, i-

| A | B | C |
|---|---|---|
| iccu- (1-5) | icc- | ī-/īy- (a-suffixes) |
| it- (6b, d) | | i- (6) |

3. uṇḍu to be; allomm. uṇḍu-, uṇḍ-, un-, uṇ-

| A | B | C |
|---|---|---|
| uṇḍu- (3-5) | uṇḍ- (1a, b, 2-6) | uṇḍ- |
| uṇḍu-/un-/uṇ- (6a, c) | un- (3, 4) | |
| uṇ- (7) | | |

(see §3.5-1, 2; §§3.7, .25-6, .30)

4. *kān- to see

| A | B | C |
|---|---|---|
| | | kān- (a-suffixes) |

5. caccu to die; allomm. caccu-, cacc-, cat-, cāv-/cā-

| A | B | C |
|---|---|---|
| caccu- (1-5) | cacc- | cāv-/cā- (a-suffixes) |
| cat- (6b, d) | | cāv- (6) |

6. cūcu to see; allomm. cūcu-, cūc-, cūḍ-, cū-, cu-

| A | B | C |
|---|---|---|
| cūcu- (1-5) | cūc- | cūḍ- (a-suffixes) |
| cūt- (6b, d) | | cūḍ/cu- (6) |

7. coccu to enter; allomm. coccu-, cocc-, cot-, cor-

| A | B | C |
|---|---|---|
| coccu- (1-5) | cocc- | cor- |
| cot- (6b, d) | | |

8. teccu to bring; allomm. teccu-, tecc-, tet-, tē-/tēr-, te-

| A | B | C |
|---|---|---|
| teccu- (1-5) | tecc- | tēr-/tē- |
| | | (also) te- (6) |
| tet- (6b, d) | | |

9. noccu to suffer; allomm. noccu-, nocc-, not-, nōv-/novv-

| A | B | C |
|---|---|---|
| noccu- (1-5) | nocc- | nōv-/novv- (a-suffixes) |
| not- (6b, d) | | |

10. vaccu to come; allomm. vaccu-, vacc-, vat-, rā-, ra-

| A | B | C |
|---|---|---|
| vaccu- (1-5) | vacc- | rā- (a-suffixes) |
| vat- (6b, d) | | ra- (6) |

11. pōvu to go; allomm. pōvu-, pōv-, pōy-, pō-, po-

| A | B | C |
|---|---|---|
| pōvu- (1-5) | pōy- | pōv-/pō- (a-suffixes) |
| pōvu-/pō- (6a, c) | | po- (6) |

12. valacu to like, to desire; allomm. valacu-, valac-, vala-, valav-, oll-

| A | B | C |
|---|---|---|
| valacu- (1-5) | valac- | valav- (1-6) |
| vala- (6b, d) | | (also) oll- (2-4) |

§3.32. Of the above forms those that end in -cu/-ccu, viz., iccu, caccu, cūcu, coccu, noccu, vaccu, valacu, can be set aside as a subgroup in that their stem-formation is like that of any member of Class II before A and B suffixes; different allomorphs occur only before the C-suffixes. In imperative 2sg., all vowel-ending stems occur long with the person suffix omitted, i.e., kā (1), ī (2), cā (5), cū (6), tē (8), rā (10), and pō (11), besides the usual ka-mmu, i-mmu, cāv-u-mu, cu-mmu, te-mmu, ra-mmu, and po-mmu respectively.

§3.33. The few other forms that come under the head of suppletives are as follows:

(a) poda/pada, podamu/padamu go with me! (you, sg.); podaNḍu/padaNḍu go with me! (you, pl.) or let us go (hortative).

(b) kal- to be occurs only with B-3, as kal-a- (verbal adj.) that has (also see note 8).

(c) inda/indamu take this! (imper. 2sg.) occur in early classics (see Bhāratamu, 5.5.304; UH 1.155); these forms may be analyzed as inda-$\phi$/inda-mu, of which $\phi$/mu is the 2sg. suffix. The stem inda- seems to be a combination of in- and ta-, the latter of which is traceable to the common Dravidian verb tar-/tā- to bring, take, etc.; cf. cognates, Ta. intā "an interjection used in the sense of 'here! take this!'; an exclamation expressive of calling a person's attention to something, lo! behold! (Cīvaka.); come here!" (Tamil Lexicon); Tu. inda, indā, ĩndā 'here it is, take this'; Ma. idā behold here. The first element in- is from PDr. *in- here, now : Ta. in̠i now; in̠r̠u today; Ma. innu id.; innā here (calling cows to feed, etc.); Ka. indu this time, today; Tu. indu, īndu this; ini, inne today; Te. indu here; inka now; Go. ingā now; Pj. ine today, ini here; Klm.(E) indeḍ today, (Kin.) iner̤ id.; Nk. inḍi now, indar̤ today; Olle. ine, inen today; Kur. innā, Mlt. ine today (< PDr. *in-, *in-ṯ-, *in-k-).

(d) In the negative tense, the 3f. n. sg. finite form of agu to be or become is kā-ϕ-du it will not be, it will not become. With the interrogative modal suffixes ā/ē, this form kā-d-ā/ē? (lit. it isn't, is it?; is it?; isn't it?) has several variants in the classical literature: ka-d-ă (4 variants), kă-d-ĕ (4 variants). Forms like kad-ā and kad-ū also occur in modern Telugu utterance-finally, meaning 'isn't it so?'

(e) valayu to be necessary occurs always with the infinitive of a verb in -aN (-a/an) or a nominalized verb (formed by adding -ṭa to any basic alternant), e.g., vanḍ-a- valayu-ϕ-nu (hab. 3sg.) or vanḍu-ṭa valayunu it is necessary to cook. The paradigm of this defective verb is as follows:

| | |
|---|---|
| valayu-ϕ-nu | hab. 3f. n. sg. |
| valayu-ϕ(~n) | habitual adjective (A-5) |
| valas-i | past participle (B-2) |
| valas-ina | past adjective (B-3) |
| valas-inaN | conditional (B-4) |
| valas-e-nu | past tense (3f. n. sg.) |
| valav-a-du/val-a-du | negative (3f. n. sg.) |

(f) paḍ- to fall, ceḍ- to perish, and iḍ- to give of Class I have alternants paḍḍ-, ceḍḍ-, and iḍḍ- respectively before the past adjective -a (B-3) and concessive -aN (B-4), i.e., paḍḍ-a, ceḍḍ-a, iḍḍ-a, paḍḍ-aN, ceḍḍ-aN, iḍḍ-aN respectively; alternatively, paḍ-ina, ceḍ-ina, iḍ-ina, etc. (see §3.7).

(g) konu of Class IV freely alternates with kō- before C-1, 2, 5 and ko- before C-6, i.e., kō-N to take, etc., ko-mmu take (you, sg.)!, ko-Nḍu take (you, pl.)!, besides the regular kon-aN, etc., and kon-u-mu, kon-u-Nḍu respectively.

(h) anu of Class IV has a free variant nā- before C-1 to 4;

| | | |
|---|---|---|
| e.g. | an-aN/nā-N | (C-1) |
| | an-a-/nā-ϕ- | (C-2) |
| | an-ak-/nā-k- | (C-3) |
| | an-aka/nā-ka | (C-4) |

(i) kol(u)cu to measure, nil(u)cu to stand, and pil(u)cu to call of Class IIa have alternants kol-, nil-, and pil- respectively before certain of the C-suffixes besides the regular kol(u)v-, nil(u)v-, and pil(u)v-, e.g., imp.-ben., sg. pil-u-mu, pl. pil-u-Nḍu; regular forms: pil(u)v-u-mu, pil(u)v-u-Nḍu.

## MODERN TELUGU

### Introduction

§3.34. In the following sections the verbal bases of modern standard Telugu[15] are analyzed into inflectional classes applying morphophonemic criteria. We have here a stronger basis for description than in the case of Old Telugu since the material is a standard spoken Telugu dialect which can be easily controlled and is limited in time and space.

§3.35. A Modern Telugu verb may be finite or non-finite. All finite verbs and some non-finite verbs (those that occur before /+/ juncture within an utterance) can occur according to situation before the utterance final juncture /#/ characterized by any of the following terminal contours: /↑/ rising pitch, meaning question; /|/ level pitch, meaning statement; /↓/ falling pitch, meaning command or dismissal.[16] A finite verb does not occur before any of the non-final junctures /- +/. On the morphological level, no non-finite verb contains a morpheme indicating person; this statement should not, however, be taken to mean that all finite verbs necessarily contain a morpheme having reference to person. Since any verb, finite or non-finite, occurs only after some marked juncture, by definition of these junctures, all verbs have phonetic stress or prominence on their first syllable, which invariably forms part of the root.

### Finite Verbs

§3.36. The eight finite forms of the Modern Telugu verb may be arranged into three structural types, which are set up according to the differences in the grouping of the three substitution classes, viz., (I) stem or inflected root, (II) tense-mode suffix, (III) personal suffix(es). The paradigms of the finite forms of a simple verbal base are given below under the three structural types: ammu to sell, with two allomorphs: amm- before a vowel, ammu- elsewhere (a hyphen in the following indicates the morpheme boundary but not any feature of juncture, unless enclosed in / /.

Type I: stem + personal suffix:

1. Imperative: sg. -u amm-u sell! (you, sg.)
   pl. -aṇḍi amm-aṇḍi sell! (you, pl.)

(The plural form can be used in honorific singular.)

Type II: stem + tense-mode suffix:

2. Admonitive or abusive: -a. On account of semantic restrictions, many verbs cannot occur in this mood. A few bases like kālu to burn, kūlu to fall, cāw- to die, pagulu to break, etc., occur; e.g.:

| | |
|---|---|
| nīkaḍupu kāl-a | may your womb (children) burn! |
| nīyillu kūl-a | may your house fall! |

This verb generally occurs in 3rd person sg., but it can also occur with the other persons; in other words, there is no indication of person in the verb forms.

3. Obligative (in all persons): -āli

| | |
|---|---|
| amm-āli | I, we, you (sg. pl.), he, she/it, they (m. f. pl.), they (n. pl.) should sell |

Type III: stem + tense-mode suffix + personal suffix

4. Habitual-future or non-past: -t-

| | | |
|---|---|---|
| ammu-t-ānu | I (habitually) sell, | I shall sell |
| ammu-t-ām | we (habitually) sell, | we shall sell |
| ammu-t-āw | you (sg.) " | , you (sg.) shall sell |
| ammu-t-āru | you (pl.) " | , you (pl.) " |
| ammu-t-āḍu | he " | , he " |
| ammu-tun-di | she/it " | , she/it " |
| ammu-t-āru | they (m. f. pl.) " | , they (m. f. pl.) " |
| ammu-t-āy | they (n. pl.) " | , they (n. pl.) " |

5. Past tense: -i-

| | |
|---|---|
| amm-i-ānu* | I sold |
| amm-i-ām | we sold |
| amm-i-āw | you (sg.) sold |
| amm-i-āru | you (pl.) sold |
| amm-i-āḍu | he sold |
| amm-in-di | she/it sold |
| amm-i-āru | they (m. f. pl.) sold |
| amm-i-āy | they (n. pl.) sold |

(*i-ā is morphophonemic spelling; phonemically, it is ǣ)

6. Hortative: -d-

| | |
|---|---|
| ammu-d-ām | let us sell, or we (incl.) shall sell |

7. Negative tense: -a-

| | | |
|---|---|---|
| amm-a-nu | I (do, did, and shall) not sell | |
| amm-a-m | we " | " |
| amm-a-w | you (sg.) " | " |
| amm-a-ru | you (pl.) " | " |

| | |
|---|---|
| amm-a-ḍu | he (does, did, and shall) not sell |
| amm-a-du | she/it (does, did, and shall) not sell |
| amm-a-ru | they (m. f. pl.) (do, did, and shall) not sell |
| amm-a-w | they (n. pl.) (do, did, and shall) not sell |

8. Negative imperative or prohibitive: -āk-

| | |
|---|---|
| amm-āk-a | you (sg.) don't sell! |
| amm-āk-aṇḍi | you (pl.) don't sell! |

## Non-Finite Verbs

§3.37. There are ten non-finite verbs which may be arranged into two structural types: (I) unbound, (II) bound.

Type I:

| | | | |
|---|---|---|---|
| 1. Present participle | -tū | e.g. ammu-tū | selling |
| 2. Past participle | -i | amm-i | having sold |
| 3. Concessive | -inā | amm-inā | even though sold, etc. |
| 4. Conditional | -itē | amm-itē | if sold |
| 5. Infinitive | -a | amm-a | to sell |
| 6. Negative participle | -aka | amm-aka | not selling |
| 7. Habitual adjective | -ē | amm-ē | that sells (habitually) |
| 8. Past adjective | -ina | amm-ina | that sold |
| 9. Negative adjective | -ani | amm-ani | not selling (adj.), that not sells, sold, etc. |

Of these, morphemes 1 to 4 occur before /+/ juncture and therefore constitute a form class. Morphemes 5 and 6 occur before another verb with an intervening /-/ juncture. Morphemes 7 to 9 occur before /-/ juncture, followed by a noun. Therefore, items 5 to 9 belong to a major form class with two sub-classes on the basis of what morpheme class follows.

Type II:

1. Bound present -t-: ammu-t- occurs with any finite form of the verb un- to be, and also a few non-finite forms (those with suffixes 3, 4, and 8);

| | | |
|---|---|---|
| e.g. | ammụ-t-unnānu | I am selling, etc. |
| | ammu-t-un-nā | even selling (now) |
| | ammu-t-uṇ-ṭē | if selling (now) |
| | ammu-t-un-na | that selling (now) |

Verb forms belonging to this type are used to indicate the present continuous.

## Morphophonemic Criteria

§3.38. As in the case of Old Telugu the more frequent variants of the tense-mode suffixes in Modern Telugu can be organized into three morphophonemic groups, A, B, and C, as follows to facilitate the analysis of the stem allomorphs into inflectional classes; the less common suffix alternants are given in parentheses.

Group A: Suffixes beginning with a dental stop, voiceless or voiced:

| Grammatical name | Suffix alternant | Environment |
|---|---|---|
| 1. Present participle | tū (~ṭū) | before /+/ |
| 2. Bound present | t (~ṭ) | before the verb un- |
| 3. Habitual-future | (a) t (~ṭ) | before other personal suffixes |
| | (b) tun (~ṭun) | before 3rd pers. f. n. sg. |
| 4. Conditional | tē (~ṭē∞itē) | before /+/ |
| 5. Hortative | d | before 1 person pl. (incl.) |

Group B: Suffixes beginning with a front vowel:

| Grammatical name | Suffix alternant | Environment |
|---|---|---|
| 1. Past participle | i | before /-/ or /+/[17] |
| 2. Past tense | i (~n∞in) | before personal suffixes |
| 3. Past adjective | ina (~in~na~n) | before /-/ + N(oun) |
| 4. Concessive | inā (~nā) | before /+/ |
| 5. Habitual adjective | ē | before /-/ + N |
| 6. Conditional | itē (see A-4) | before /+/ |

Group C: Suffixes beginning with a back vowel (a or u):

| Grammatical name | Suffix alternant | Environment |
|---|---|---|
| 1. Infinitive | a (~ϕ~an~n) | before /-/ + V or $N^1$ |
| 2. Admonitive | a (~nu) | before /#/ + /\|/ |
| 3. Negative tense | a (~ϕ) | before personal suffixes |
| 4. Negative participle | aka (~ak~ka~k) | before /-/ + V or $N^2$ |
| 5. Negative adjective | ani (~an~ni~n) | before /-/ + N |
| 6. Obligative | āli | before /#/ + /\|/ |
| 7. Negative (in imperative) | āk | before imperative personal suffixes (see 8, 9) |
| 8. Imperative pl. | aṇḍi (~ṇḍi) | before /#/ + /↓/ or V |
| 9. Imperative sg. | | |
| (a) positive | u (~ϕ~i) | before /#/ + /↓/ or V |
| (b) negative | a | before /#/ and follows C-7 |

$N^1$: two words meaning "necessity," viz., akkara, pani

$N^2$: the noun mundu meaning "front," "before," e.g., ammaka-mundu "before selling" (lit. not selling, before).

§3.39. Among the A-suffixes, the retroflex variants of dentals occur after a small class of n-final stems (see §3.49). The habitual allomorphs tun~ṭun occur before the neuter singular suffix di. Conditional itē occurs after Class I (a) and (b) bases; elsewhere, only tē~ṭē occur.

Among the B-suffixes, all alternants in parentheses with initial n (i.e., B-2, 3, 4) occur after the few monosyllabic stems in final n belonging to Class V (see §3.49). Past -in- occurs after two suppletive stems, viz., ay- to become and poy- to go, before all personal suffixes, and after all bases before the f. n. sg. suffix di.

Of the C-suffixes, all alternants without the initial vowels (i.e., 1-5, 8, 9) occur after monosyllabic stems in final long vowels (see §3.50). Infinitive an~n occur before vowels following /-/, and a~ϕ before consonants, the presence or absence of the initial a being conditioned by the environment in the preceding position (see above). Imperative sg. -i- (9) occurs after stems in final y/yy (Class IIb);[18] after the other classes, only -u- occurs. Imperative sg. a occurs in the formation of the prohibitive (negative-imperative) forms following the negative allomorph -āk- (7).

All suffixes, of whatever group, with final short vowels before consonants, have alternants in final consonants before vowels (see B-3, C-1, 4, 5).

§3.40. Among the A-suffixes the alternants under items 1, 2, and 3 can be grouped into one morpheme, since they all occur in complementation. The alternants under A-4 and B-6 belong to one morpheme. Among the B-suffixes, those under items 1 and 2 are members of the same morpheme. Among the C-suffixes, alternants under 1 and 2 may be grouped into a single morpheme, since they are complementary in their syntactic environments. Prohibitive /āk/ may be put either with the negative tense /a/ or the negative participle /aka/ since it is in complementation with either of them. However, no attempt has been made here to analyze the past adjective /ina/, the negative participle /aka/ and the negative past adjective /ani/ as a sequence of morphemes each (/i/ past + /na/ adjective; /a/ negative + /ka/ participle, /ni/ adjective) on account of the poor productivity of the latter elements in forming fresh combinations (see note 6).

§3.41. The more frequent alternants of the personal suffixes are given with the less frequent ones in parentheses:

| | | | | |
|---|---|---|---|---|
| 1st person | sg. | ānu (nu) | pl. | ām (am) |
| 2nd person | sg. | āw (w) | pl. | āru (ru) |
| 3rd person | m. sg. | āḍu (ḍu) | m. f. pl. | āru (ru) |
| 3rd person | f. n. sg. | adi (du, di) | n. pl. | āy (w) |

Those in parentheses occur in the negative tense and the rest in habitual, past, and bound present. However, -di of f. n. sg. occurs after the habitual /tun ~ ṭun/ and past /in/, and -adi also after the past allomorph /n/ (see §3.39).

§3.42. It is now possible to describe the distinguishing features of each class of bases by giving the allomorphic distribution of one or more (if there are sub-classes) stem-morphemes of that class before the three suffix groups, A, B, and C described above. Generally, in the case of many sub-classes, a given stem morpheme has a single alternant each before B- and C-suffixes, but more than one alternant before A-suffixes; in the latter case, the alternants are phonologically conditioned by the members of group A. It will, however, be noticed that contrast among the alternants of the various inflectional classes set up is mainly reinforced before the suffixes of group C.

## Class I

§3.43. This class consists of four sub-classes as follows:

(a) trisyllabic bases of $(C)^1\breve{V}^1C^2\breve{V}^2C^3\breve{V}^3$ type, in which u occurs as $V^2$ and $V^3$, and $C^3$ is not c or s e.g., toḍugu to wear; kuduru to be settled (in a position, etc.), to be cured, be set right;

(b) disyllabic bases of $(C)\breve{V}C\breve{V}$ or $(C)\breve{V}CC\breve{V}$ type, e.g., āḍu to play; paḍu to fall; ekku to ascend; manḍu to burn;

(c) monosyllabic bases of $(C)\bar{V}C$ type in final n or l, e.g., nān to become wet; cāl to be sufficient; kāl to burn;

(d) disyllabic bases of $(C)\breve{V}C\breve{V}C$ type in final l; the second vowel ($V^2$) is u.

The allomorphic distribution before the three classes of suffixes is as follows:

| Basic stem alternant | Stem alternants before the suffixes | | |
|---|---|---|---|
| | A | B | C |
| (a) toḍugu | toḍugu- | toḍig- | toḍag- (1-8); toḍug- (9) |
| (b) āḍu | āḍu- | āḍ- | āḍ- |
| paḍu | paḍu- | paḍ- | paḍ- |
| ekku | ekku- | ekk- | ekk- |
| (c) nān | nān- | nān- | nān- |
| (d) kadul | kadul- | kadil- | kadal- (1-8); kadul- (9) |

A broader analysis might put (a) and (b) together into one sub-class, and (c) and (d) into another; however, a statement has to be made that $V^2$ of the $(C)\breve{V}^1C\breve{V}^2C(\breve{V}^3)$ bases of this former sub-class is u before A-suffixes (and C-9), i before B-suffixes, and a before the C-suffixes (except 9).

§3.44. As in the case of Old Telugu, this constitutes the major inflectional class consisting of over seventy per cent of the total simple verb-bases in Modern Telugu. A list of more frequent verbs occurring in the author's dialect is included in Part II of this work, in which all bases belonging to this class are left unmarked by a suffixed asterisk and a roman figure.

## Class II

§3.45. Two sub-classes may be set up under this as follows:

(a) Disyllabic bases of the $(C)^1\breve{V}^1C^2\breve{V}^2C^3$ type in which the final $C^3$ is c or s and $V^2$ is u, e.g., piluc- to call; taḍus- to get wet (in rain, etc.).

(b) Monosyllabic bases of the $(C)\bar{V}C$ type in final c or s, e.g., tīs- to take out, rāc- to smear.

The allomorphic structure of the members of these sub-classes is given below:

| Basic stem alternant | Stem alternants before the suffixes A | B | C |
|---|---|---|---|
| (a) piluc- | pilus- (1-3)<br>pilis- (4)<br>pilud- (5) | pilic- | pilaw- (1-8)<br>pil- (9) |
| taḍus- | taḍus- (1-3)<br>taḍis- (4)<br>taḍud- (5) | taḍis- | taḍaw- (1-8)<br>taḍ- (9) |
| (b) tīs- | tīs- (1-4)<br>tīd- (5) | tīs- | tīy-/tiyy- |
| rāc- | rās- (1-4)<br>rād- (5) | rāc- | rāy- |

Sub-class (b) contrasts with sub-class (a) in that the final c or s alternates with y/yy before C-suffixes instead of with w as in (a).

§3.46. Following are the commonest verb bases belonging to these sub-classes:

Sub-class (a):

| | |
|---|---|
| aruc- | to shout, howl |
| oluc- | to peel |
| karuc- | to bite |

| | |
|---|---|
| kuḍuc- | to suck, smack |
| koluc- | to measure |
| gaḍuc- | (time) to pass |
| geluc- | to win |
| tuḍuc- | to wipe off, to clean floor, etc. |
| teruc- | to open door, box, etc. |
| toluc[1]- | to clean plates, etc. with water |
| toluc[2]- | to bore a stone, etc. |
| naḍuc- | to walk |
| niluc- | to stop (as fever); to stop, stand, stay |
| nūruc- | to thresh grain, etc. |
| paruc- | to spread (for drying); to spread bed, etc. |
| piluc- | to call, shout |
| poḍuc- | to pierce, bore; (animals) to butt |
| maḍuc- | to fold (cloth) |
| maruc- | to forget |
| maluc- | to engrave; fashion stone (in sculpture) |
| moluc- | to germinate (bud, sprout, leaves, etc.) |
| viḍuc- | to leave off |
| īḍuc- | to drag, pull |
| ūḍuc- | to clean, sweep (floor, etc.) |
| ēḍuc- | to scream, weep |
| nēruc- | to learn |
| pīluc- | to suck up water, etc., to inhale |
| kalus- | to join, meet |
| kurus- | to rain, to leak |
| jaḍus-/daḍus- | to be scared, to fear |
| taḍus- | to be wet, be soaked |
| nerus- | (hair) to grow grey |
| pulus- | to become sour |
| balus- | to become bulky, fat |
| bigus- | to become tight (as a knot) |
| mugus- | to be over, to end |
| merus- | to shine, glitter |

Sub-class (b):

| | |
|---|---|
| ūs- | to spit |
| ēs- | to throw |
| **kās-** | (tree) to have fruit |
| **kūs-** | **to sing (of birds), to speak abusive language** |
| **kōs-** | **to pluck (fruit, leaves, etc.); to reap, cut** |

| | |
|---|---|
| gīs-/gīc- | to draw lines; to scrape, scribble |
| cēs- | to do |
| tīs- | to take out, to remove |
| tōs- | to push out |
| nēs- | to weave |
| pūs¹- | to daub, smear |
| pūs²- | (mouth) to blister |
| pōs- | to pour |
| mās- | to become dim, (cloth, etc.) be soiled |
| mūs- | to close (a bottle, a door, etc.) |
| mēs- | (cattle) to graze |
| mōs- | to carry (on shoulders) |
| rās- | to write |
| kāc¹- | tr. to boil, as water, etc. |
| kāc²- | to watch; to protect, to wait, waylay (before refl.) |
| tūc- | to weigh |
| pūc- | (plant) to have flowers; to flower, blossom |
| rāc- | to smear; to scrape, rub, assay (metals, etc.) |
| vāc- | intr. to swell[19] |

## Class III

§3.47. Three sub-classes may be set up in this class:

(a) A few monosyllabic bases of the (C)V̄C type in final c, e.g., cāc- to stretch out (limbs, etc.).

(b) Transitive stems in final uc/c, e.g., kāl-uc- to let burn, set fire to (kāl-, v.i. to burn).

(c) Transitive or causative stems in -inc-, e.g., tiṭṭ-inc- to cause to scold (to make somebody scold another) (: tiṭṭu to scold, abuse).

| Basic stem alternant | Stem alternants before the suffixes A | B | C |
|---|---|---|---|
| (a) cāc- | cās- (1-4)<br>cād- (5) | cāc- | cāc- |
| (b) kāluc- | kālus- (1-3)<br>kālis- (4)<br>kālud- (5) | kālc- | kālc- |
| (c) tiṭṭinc- | tiṭṭis- (1-4)<br>tiṭṭid- (5) | tiṭṭinc- | tiṭṭinc- |

This class contrasts with class II stems in that the alternants before B and C suffixes in this class are alike.

Bases belonging to these three sub-classes are as follows:

Sub-class (a):

| | |
|---|---|
| ūc- | to swing (a cradle) |
| kāc- | to boil water, etc. |
| cāc- | to stretch out (hands,. legs, etc.) |
| tūc- | to weigh (in a balance) |
| tōc- | to strike to one's mind, to appear |
| dōc- | to plunder |
| tēc- | to belch |
| wīc- | (wind) to blow |

Sub-class (b):

| | |
|---|---|
| āruc- | to let dry (: āru to dry) |
| imuḍuc- | to make to contain, fit in (: imuḍu to be fit, be contained) |
| kāruc- | to let drip (: kāru to drip, trickle) |
| kāluc- | to burn (tr.) (: kāl to be burnt) |
| kuduruc- | to cure a disease, to settle, establish (: kuduru to be settled, be cured) |
| kaduluc- | to shake, cause to move (: kadul to move, tremble) |
| kūluc- | to fell (a tree, etc.) (: kūl to fall) |
| cimuḍuc- | to let rice overboil (: cimuḍu (rice) to over-boil) |
| cīluc- | to split, slice (: cīl to be torn, split) |
| cēruc- | to take near (: cēru to reach, approach) |
| jāruc- | to let slip, drop (: jāru to slip, slide) |
| tīruc- | to settle (a debt), to put an end to (: tīru to be settled; be ended) |
| tēluc- | to let float (: tēl to be afloat) |
| dūruc- | to insert (: dūru to squeeze through; to steal into) |
| nānuc- | to soak (: nān to get wet) |
| pūḍuc- | to bury (: pūḍu to be buried) |
| pēruc- | to pile up (: pēru to get accumulated, be amassed, to get curdled) |
| pēluc- | tr. to explode (: pēl to be exploded) |
| pōluc- | to compare, make a match to (: pōl to be a match, be equal) |
| māḍuc- | to let burn (rice on fire) (: māḍu (rice, etc.) to be burnt) |
| māruc- | to change, exchange (: māru to be changed) |
| vāluc- | to bring down, cause to bend (: vāl to bend, perch) |

Sub-class (c):

Any verb stem transitive or causative in -inc- (§§3.56b, .57)

## Class IV

§3.48. Sub-class (a): Monosyllabic bases of the (C)V̌CC type in final ṭṭ, e.g., koṭṭ- to beat; and one base in final pp, viz., cepp- to say, speak.

(b) Two bases of the same type, one in final nn, another in ḷḷ, i.e., tann- to flog, weḷḷ- to go. The stem alternants are as follows:

| Basic stem alternant | Stem alternants before the suffixes A | B | C |
|---|---|---|---|
| (a) koṭṭ- to beat | koḍu- (1, 2, 3b) | koṭṭ- | koṭṭ- |
| | koḍa- (3a, 5) | | |
| | koḍi- (4) | | |
| cepp- to say | cebu- (1, 2, 3b) | cepp- | cepp- |
| | ceba- (3a, 5) | | |
| | cebi- (4) | | |
| (b) tann- to flog | tan- | tann- | tann- |
| weḷḷ- to go | weḷ- | weḷḷ- | weḷḷ- |

The commonest bases of sub-class (a) are as follows:

| | |
|---|---|
| kaṭṭ- | to build |
| giṭṭ- | to be gainful, be suitable |
| kuṭṭ- | to sew, prick |
| koṭṭ- | to beat |
| cuṭṭ- | to turn round, roll up |
| taṭṭ- | to tap, slap |
| tiṭṭ- | to abuse, scold |
| neṭṭ- | to push out |
| paṭṭ- | tr. to hold, v.i. to suit |
| puṭṭ- | to be born |
| peṭṭ- | to place, lay |
| maṭṭ- | to crush under heel or foot |
| muṭṭ- | to touch |
| moṭṭ- | to rap with knuckles |

## Class V

§3.49. Seven monosyllabic bases of the (C)V̌C- type in final n, i.e., an- to say; kan-[1] to see; kan-[2] to bring forth; kon- to buy; tin- to eat; win- to hear; un- to be. The stem allomorphs are as follows (un- occurs with all members of A and with numbers 2-5 of the B-suffixes):

| Basic stem alternant | Stem alternants before the suffixes A | B | C |
|---|---|---|---|
| win- to hear | wiṇ- (1-4)<br>win- (5) | win- | win- |

## Class VI

§3.50. This class consists of bases with irregular alternants. It is therefore convenient to give the stem allomorphs of each base separately.

| Basic stem alternant | Stem alternants before the suffixes A | B | C |
|---|---|---|---|
| 1. icc- to give | is- (1-4)<br>id- (5) | icc- | iww- |
| 2. cacc- to die | cas- (1-4)<br>cad- (5) | cacc- | cāw- |
| 3. tecc- to bring | tes- (1-4)<br>ted- (5) | tecc- | tǣ- (1-5, 9)<br>tǣw- (6, 7)<br>tē- (8) |
| 4. wacc- to come | was- (1-4)<br>wad- (5) | wacc- | rā- (1-5, 8, 9)<br>rāw- (6, 7) |
| 5. aw- to become | aw- (1-3, 5)<br>ay- (4) | ay- (1-4)<br>ayy- (5) | kā- (1-5, 8, 9)<br>kāw- (6, 7) |
| 6. pō- to go | pō- | pōy- (1)<br>poy- (2-4)<br>poyy- (5) | pō- (1-5, 8, 9)<br>pōw- (6, 7) |
| 7. cūc- to see | cūs- (1-4)<br>cūd- (5) | cūc- | cūḍ- |
| 8. lēc- to rise | lēs- (1-4)<br>lēd- (5) | lēc- | lǣw- (1-8)<br>lē- (9) |
| 9. *lē- to be | ... | ... | lē- (3-5) |

One more defective verb in Modern Telugu is pad- to go, depart, occurring in two forms in imperative (with hortative-imperative meaning), viz.

| | |
|---|---|
| pad-a | go! (you sg.; I also accompany) |
| pad-aṇḍi | go! (you pl.; I also accompany) |

§3.51. The following table shows the phonemic alternations which form the basis of classification of the five regular inflectional classes (and their sub-classes). The underlined sequences in the canonical forms are the ones involved in alternation in the phonological environment of the tense-mode suffix alternants.

| Class | Canonical form of the basic alternant | Phonemic alternations before the suffixes | | | | | |
|---|---|---|---|---|---|---|---|
| | | A | | | B | C | |
| | | 1-3 | 4 | 5 | | 1-8 | 9 |
| I a. | (C)VCuCu | | uCu | | iC | aC | uC |
| b. | (C)V̌Cu<br>(C)V̌CCu | | u | | ϕ | ϕ | |
| c. | (C)V̄n/l | | none | | none | none | |
| d. | (C)V̌Cul | ul | il | ul | il | al | ul |
| II a. | (C)V̌Cuc<br>(C)V̌Cus | us | is | ud | ic<br>is | aw | ϕ |
| b. | (C)V̄s<br>(C)V̄c | s | s | d | s<br>c | (V̄)y/(V̌)yy | |
| III a. | (C)V̄c | s | s | d | c | c | |
| b. | (C)V̌Cuc | us | is | ud | c | c | |
| c. | . . . . .inc | is | is | id | inc | inc | |
| IV a. | (C)V̌ṭṭ | ḍu<br>(1, 2, 3b)<br>ḍa<br>(3a) | ḍi | ḍa | ṭṭ | ṭṭ | |
| | (C)V̌pp | bu<br>(1, 2, 3b)<br>ba<br>(3a) | bi | ba | pp | pp | |
| b. | (C)V̌nn | | n | | nn | nn | |
| | (C)V̌ḷḷ | | ḷ | | ḷḷ | ḷḷ | |
| V | (C)V̌n | ṇ | ṇ | n | n | n | |

Under the suffixes of Group C, 9 stands for 9a and not 9b, since the latter does not immediately follow the verb-stem but follows B-7 (see §3.38).

## Alternative Analysis by Item and Process

§3.52. Taking the suffixes listed in §3.38, and the stem alternants noted under each inflectional class as basic, the other alternants can be derived from them by a set of morphological processes, automatic and non-automatic, as follows:

Automatic alternations:

Rule 1. u of the second syllable of disyllabic and trisyllabic bases of the (C)VCVC(V) type becomes /i/ before a front vowel and /a/ before /a/ in the immediately following syllable; the same thing stated in a formula is as follows:

(C)VCuC- + (C)i/ē > (C)VCiC-(C)i/ē-
(C)VCuC- + (C)ā̆ > (C)VCaC-(C)ā̆-

| | | | | |
|---|---|---|---|---|
| e.g. | aḍug- + i | > | aḍig-i | having asked |
| | kadul- + tē | > | kadil-tē | if moved, moves, etc. |
| | aḍug + a | > | aḍag-a | to ask |
| | kadul- + a | > | kadal-a | to move |

Rule 2. A stem-final short vowel is lost before another vowel (short or long) beginning the suffix, i.e.

$$\breve{V}^1 + \breve{\bar{V}}^2 > \breve{\bar{V}}^2$$

| | | | | |
|---|---|---|---|---|
| e.g. | ammu + i | > | amm-i | having sold |
| | aḍugu + i | > | aḍig-i | having asked |

(for medial u > i, see Rule 1)

Rule 3. A suffix-initial short vowel following a stem-final long vowel is lost, i.e.

$$\bar{V}^1 + \breve{V}^2 > \bar{V}^1$$

(There are five stems in Modern Telugu, all of which belong to the suppletive class in final long vowels (inflectional class VI, see §3.50), i.e., rā- to come, pō- to go, lē- to be, tē- to bring, kā- to become, after which a short a or u of the C-suffixes is omitted)

| | | | |
|---|---|---|---|
| rā- + aka | > | rā-ka | not coming |
| rā- + u(imper.) | > | rā | come! (you, sg.) |
| rā- + aṇḍi | > | rā-ṇḍi | come! (you, pl.) |

Rule 4. The following consonantal sandhi alternations are automatic:

| | | | | |
|---|---|---|---|---|
| ($\breve{V}$)n+t > ṇṭ; | an + tū | > | aṇ-ṭū | speaking |
| cc/c+t > st; | vacc + tū | > | vas-tū | coming |
| | tūc + tū | > | tūs-tū | weighing |
| cc/c+d > dd; | vacc + d-ām | > | vad-d-ām | let us come |
| | tūc + d-ām | > | tūd-d-ām | let us weigh |

| | | | | | | |
|---|---|---|---|---|---|---|
| s+d | > dd; | kōs | + d-ām | > | kōd-d-ām | let us cut |
| n+Vn | > nn; | kon- | + ina | > | kon-na | that bought |
| nn+t/d | > nt/nd; | tann | + tū | > | tan-tū | beating |
| | | tann | + d-ām | > | tan-d-ām | let us beat |
| ḷḷ+t/d | > ḷt/ḷd; | weḷḷ | + tū | > | weḷ-tū | going |
| | | weḷḷ | + d-ām | > | weḷ-d-ām | let us go |

Non-automatic alternations:

Rule 1. Conditional tē > itē after Class I a, b, verbs, e.g.

ammu to sell, amm-itē if sold, sells, etc.

aḍugu to ask, aḍig-itē if asked, asks, etc.

Elsewhere kōs-tē, viṇ-ṭē, kadil-tē, etc.

Rule 2. Habitual t > tun before 3rd person f. n. sg., e.g.

ammu-tun-di she/it will sell

Rule 3. Past i > in, (a) before 3rd person f. n. sg. of all verbs, and (b) after ay- to become, poy- to go, before all personal suffixes, e.g.

a. amm-in-di she/it sold

kōs-in-di she/it plucked, cut, etc.

b. ay-in-ānu, ām, āw, āru, āḍu, di, āyi, āru

poy-in-ānu, ām, āw, āru, āḍu, di, āyi, āru

Rule 4. Infinitive a > an before a vowel, e.g.

vāṇṇi[1] koṭṭan[2]ē[3] lēdu[4] (lit., (one) has[2] not[4] beaten[2] him[1] at all[3]) he is not beaten at all

vāṇṇi koṭṭa lēdu he is not beaten

After bases in final long vowels, by the operation of automatic rule 3, a > $\phi$ before a consonant, an > n before a vowel: pō- to go: infinitive pō- before a C; pōn- before a V.

vāṇḍu pōn-ē lēdu he hasn't gone at all

vāṇḍu pō lēdu he hasn't gone

Rule 5. Admonitive a > nu after stems in final long vowels, e.g.

nī-kaḍub-bangāran-gānu! may your womb become gold! (kā- allom. of agu to become)

Rule 6. Final ṭṭ and pp of Class IV verbs become ḍ and b respectively before a consonant (suffixes of group A), and a vowel homorganic with that of the next syllable is inserted between these two consonants as follows:

| | | |
|---|---|---|
| koṭṭ | + tū > koḍutū | beating |
| | + tē > koḍitē | if beaten, beats |
| | + t-ānu, etc. > koḍa-t-ānu | I will beat, etc. |
| | + tun-di > koḍu-tun-di | she/it will beat |
| | + d-ām > koḍa-d-ām | let us beat |

Similarly, cebutū, cebitē, cebatānu, cebutundi, cebadām, from cepp- to say.

Rule 7. (a) Base final c/s of Class II(a) verbs is replaced by w before the suffixes beginning with a (group C):

piluc + aka > pilaw-aka  not calling
taḍus + aka > taḍaw-aka  not getting wet

( u > a by automatic rule 1 )

(b) Base final c/s of Class II(b) is replaced by y before the C suffixes:

rās to write + a > rāy-a to write (inf.)
tūc to weigh + a > tūy-a to weigh (inf.)

The paradigms of a given verb can be built by the application of any one or more of the above sandhi rules. The suppletive stem-alternants may be listed as in §3.50.

## Intransitives and Transitives

§3.53. Simple bases in Modern Telugu are either intransitive or transitive. There is no thoroughgoing principle for predicting this on formal grounds.

§3.54. As in the case of Old Telugu, in Modern Telugu also a number of intransitive and transitive stems are related through internal alternation involving the non-radical syllables. In other words, derivative suffixes in certain bases have reference to their intransitive or transitive situation in sentence construction.

§3.55. The following sets of intransitive and transitive stems are related through alternations in the non-radical syllables.

| | | |
|---|---|---|
| (a) | Intransitive -gu | Transitive -c- (6 sets) |
| | ūgu to swing | ūc- to nod (head, etc.) |
| | kāgu to be boiled | kāc- to boil |
| | tūgu to be weighed | tūc- to weigh |
| | maṇugu to be bent (as in sheets, etc.) | maṇuc- to bend, etc. |
| | wangu to bend, bow | wancu to bend |
| | aṇugu to be pressed down | aṇuc- to press down |
| (b) | -ḍu | -cu (1 set) |
| | uṇḍu to be, to occur | uncu to keep, lay, let stay |
| (c) | -gu | -ncu (2 sets) |
| | tegu to sever | tencu to snap, break (thread, etc.) |
| | digu to descend | dincu to cause to descend |

(d) In the following four sets, all non-initial syllables alternate with -ncu in the transitive.

| | Intransitive | Transitive |
|---|---|---|
| | cirugu to be torn | cincu to tear |
| | tunugu to be split, be snapped | tuncu to snap |
| | muṇugu to be immersed | muncu to drown |
| | perugu to grow | pencu to breed, grow, nourish |
| (e) | Intransitive -gu | Transitive -pu (5 sets) |
| | āgu to cease, stop | āpu to stop; to obstruct |
| | ūgu to swing | ūpu to swing, or rock (a cradle, etc.) |
| | jarugu to slide, move | jarupu to move |
| | tirugu to turn, revolve, wander | tippu (< OTe. trippu, < *tirpp-) to revolve |
| | nalugu to be squeezed (as flowers, etc.) | nalupu to squeeze, to mishandle |
| (f) | -c- | -pu (7 sets) |
| | kuḍuc- to drink, suck | kuḍupu to let suck |
| | gaḍuc- (time) to pass | gaḍupu to pass time |
| | cūc- to see | cūpu to show |
| | naḍuc- to walk | naḍupu to drive, run (machine, train, etc.) |
| | niluc- to cease, stop | nilupu to stop, impede |
| | nēruc- to learn | nērupu/nērpu to train, teach |
| | lēc- to rise | lēpu to raise |
| (g) | -cc- | -mpu (1 set) |
| | cacc- to die | campu to kill |
| (h) | -ϕ | -mpu (1 set) |
| | pō- to go | pa-mpu to send |

(pa- is the suppletive alternant of pō- before the transitive -mpu)

| | | |
|---|---|---|
| (i) | -s- | -pu (4 sets) |
| | kalus- to meet, mix with | kalupu to join, to bring together |
| | taḍus- to get wet | taḍupu to make wet, to soak |
| | mās- to become dim, to be soiled | mápu to soil (a cloth) |
| | mēs- (cattle) to graze | mépu to graze cattle |

§3.56. A more frequent way of forming transitives is by the addition of -uc or -inc to the intransitive verb stems.

(a) Most of the intransitive stems in final n, l on the one hand, and ru, ḍu on the other have corresponding transitive alternants with the addition of -c and -uc respectively (see §3.54, sub-class b).

(b) Intransitive stems of Class 1 (a) and (b) have transitives with the addition of -inc. All stems with final u before consonants have alternants without it before -inc and the u of the second syllable of the (C)VCC(V) bases alternates with i. A few examples are given below:

| 1. Intransitive -ϕ | Transitive -inc |
|---|---|
| aṇṭu to adhere | aṇṭ-inc to join together, paste |
| andu to be obtained | and-inc to hand over |
| ān to rest (on a support) | ān-inc to rest (something) with support |
| iruku to be squeezed | irik-inc to insert with difficulty |
| uḍuku (water, etc.) to boil | uḍik-inc to boil (water, etc.) |
| ubbu to swell, be bloated, be elated | ubb-inc to flatter, cause to swell |
| ekku to rise up | ekk-inc to raise, cause to ascend |

2. In two bases intransitive verbs have final -us which alternates with -inc in the transitive.

| | |
|---|---|
| bigus- to be tightened | big-inc to tighten |
| mugus- to end, to be finished | mug-inc to end, complete (an action, etc.) |

3. The final c or s of intransitive stems of Class II in final -uc and -us alternates with p before the transitive allomorph -inc, e.g.

| | |
|---|---|
| moluc to sprout | molip-inc to let a plant grow |
| kurus to rain | kurip-inc to shower, (to let rain) |
| jaḍus to be scared | jaḍip-inc to scare |
| merus to shine | merip-inc to let shine |

§3.57. Certain Modern Telugu bases have two transitive stems each, which occur more or less as free variants.

| | |
|---|---|
| nĕruc to learn | nĕrpu/nĕrp-inc to teach, train |
| cūc to see | cūpu/cup-inc to show |
| naḍuc to walk | naḍupu/naḍip-inc to run, to let walk |
| pō to go | pampu/pamp-inc to send |
| digu to descend | dincu/dimp-inc to cause to descend |

## Causatives

§3.58. A number of transitive stems have causative alternants with the addition of -inc.

(1) Transitive stem alternants which do not end in c or s simply add -inc to form causals. As usual, u of the second syllable alternates with i, e.g.

| Transitive | Causative |
|---|---|
| aḍugu to ask | aḍig-inc to cause (somebody) to ask |
| kaṭṭ- to build | kaṭṭ-inc to cause (somebody) to build |
| tiṭṭ- to scold | tiṭṭ-inc to cause to scold |

(2) Final c of the transitive stems of Class IIa alternates with p before the causal -inc, e.g.

| Intransitive | Transitive | Causative |
|---|---|---|
| | oluc to peel | olip-inc to cause (somebody) to peel |
| | poḍuc to pierce | poḍip-inc to cause to pierce |
| | īḍuc to drag | īḍip-inc to cause to drag |
| kāl to be burnt | kāluc to burn | kālip-inc to cause to burn |
| cīl to be split | cīluc to split | cīlip-inc to cause to split |
| dūr to enter | dūruc to insert | dūrip-inc to cause to insert |
| pūḍuc to be buried | pūḍuc to bury | pūḍip-inc to cause to bury |
| māru to be exchanged | māruc to exchange | mārip-inc to cause to exchange |

(3) Transitive stems of Class V in final n have the causative variant -ipinc, e.g.

| Transitive | Causative |
|---|---|
| an to say | an-ipinc to cause to say |
| kon to buy | kon-ipinc to cause (somebody) to buy |
| tin to eat | tin-ipinc to cause (somebody) to eat |
| kan- to see | kan-ipinc to appear (to cause oneself to see) |
| win- to hear | win-ipinc to tell (cause to hear) |

(4) Final s/c of the transitive stems of Class II alternates with y before the causative -inc, e.g.

| Transitive | Causative |
|---|---|
| mūs to close (bottle, etc.) | mūy-inc to cause to close |
| tūc to weigh | tūy-inc to cause to weigh |

(5) Transitive stems of Class VI (suppletive) have causal alternants as follows:

| Intransitive | Transitive | Causative |
|---|---|---|
| | icc- to give | ipp-inc to cause to give |
| cacc- to die | campu to kill | camp-inc to cause to kill |
| | tecc- to bring | tepp-inc to cause to bring, to get |

## NOTES TO CHAPTER III

[1]The inflectional classification of the OTe. verb contained in this chapter is a restatement on modern lines of the traditional grammatical treatments of the standard Telugu classics. The latest and the most systematic of these grammars is Bālavyākaraṇamu by Paravastu Chinnayasūri (1858). This is however, incomplete, but is supplemented to some extent by Triliṅgalakṣaṇaśēṣamu or Prāuḍhavyākaraṇamu of Bahujanapalli Sītārāmachāryulu (1885). None of the traditional Te. grammars mentions the exact scope of the material taken as basis for analysis, either in terms of time-limit or the writings of certain classical authors. However, the usages of kavitraya (the three authors of Āndhramahābhārata: Nannaya—11th century, Tikkana—13th century, and E͟r͟rana—14th century) are invariably accepted as standard besides those of Śrīnātha (14th-15th century) and occasionally Peddana (16th century). The writings of the Śaiva poets of the 13th century and the prabandha literature of the 16th century and beyond show considerable departure in many cases from the grammatical norms of the kavitraya usage. But, very often, grammatical forms belonging to different strata (probably of different periods) all occur together in the poetic works from the earliest epics down to the later prabandhas, more so in the case of the latter. This state of affairs has necessarily made things difficult for the grammarian, who, not precisely limiting his material to any particular period or authors, has to treat the diachronic data as being synchronic. This explains why there have been in some cases several variants for the same grammatical function, all of which have been taken as received usage (pramāṇa or sādhuprayōga). All such cases are treated in this chapter as cases of free variation, and this, in effect, is treating the historical (i.e., diachronic) data on a purely descriptive (synchronic) level; e.g., the habitual tense has three free variants eḍu/eḍi/$\phi$, complementarily distributed with eda/du and d/ḍ (see §3.5, 2). Nothing better can be done until we have correct and comprehensive grammars for the individual classics taken by author or time. The popular language had all along been undergoing the normal course of change, as is evident from the inscriptions, but the language of poetry did not keep pace with it and became gradually divorced from it to a marked degree.

[2]Similarly, the compound non-finite verbs of the present and the future are formed by adding the non-finite forms of a verb meaning 'to be' to the bound present and infinitive respectively, e.g., vaṇḍu-c-unna- that is cooking (un-na that which is); vaṇḍ-aN-gala- that will cook (lit. that is to cook, vaṇḍ-aN to cook, kal-a that is).

[3]Two possible theoretical objections for the method of morphemic division as presented in the chart and in the paradigms are as follows:

(1). There are no overt differences among the morphemes of 3 m. sg., 3 f. n. sg., and 3 n. pl. in the past and habitual. In the past, the three morphemes occur with the same shape -nu, and in the habitual they have the shape -nu/-ni with phonologically conditioned free variation. Again in the imperative-benedictive all the four 3rd person morphemes (m. sg., f. n. sg., m. f. pl. and n. pl.) occur with identical shape -nu. One may therefore question here the justification for setting up so many different morphemes among which there is no overt differentiation.

The explanation is as follows: The negative categories have the maximal overt differences in the 3rd person and they are taken as the basis for setting up the past and habitual categories: Neg. 3 m. sg. -Nḍu, 3 n. f. sg. -du, 3 n. pl. -vu, 3 m. f. pl. -ru. One can see the allomorphs of each person-morpheme by studying the vertical columns in the chart; 3 m. sg. {nu ~/ni ∞ Nḍu}, 3 f. n. sg. {nu ~/ni ∞ du}, 3 n. pl. {nu ~/ni ∞ vu}, 3 m. f. pl. {nu ∞ ru} (for the interpretation of the symbols, see §3.5).

The alternative analysis would be to set up a single morpheme -nu for all the 3 sg. and the n. pl. in the past and habitual (with an alternant -ni in the habitual when preceded by -i-) and -nu 3 pers. (all genders and numbers) in the imperative-benedictive. The main objection to this analysis would be that many other similar cases in the system are ignored; e.g., the morphemes of the 2 sg. and 3 n. pl. in the negative occur with the same shape -vu; again the 3 m. f. pl. and the 2 pl. occur with identical shapes in the past, habitual, and negative, viz., ru~/ri. The 1 pl. of the habitual and negative -mu is identical in shape with the 2 sg. of the imperative-benedictive and the prohibitive.

The only explanation is therefore that the maximal contrasts in any one paradigmatic series are taken as the basis for setting up the categories of the other series.

(2). Another theoretical objection will be to the morphemic division, vaṇḍu-ϕ-nu (hab.) he cooks, as opposed to vaṇḍ-u-mu (imp.-ben.), you (sg.) cook, with -u as part of the base in one case and as a morph in another.

That -u- in the imperative-benedictive sg. vaṇḍu-u-mu is not the same as u in the stem-alternant vaṇḍu- in the habitual will be clear from a comparison of the former with the prohibitive forms, vaṇḍ-ak-u-mu (stem + neg. + imper. + 2 sg.) where it occurs as a significant element, also in a position other than the stem-final. Further, there is a morphophonemic advantage facilitating description in that the imp.-ben. -u- as a member of the C-suffixes produces certain phonemic alternations in the stem-finals which are absent in the habitual paradigms (see §3.24 A and C, §3.27).

[4]With importance to the party addressed (hortative).

[5]N occurring within a morph (i.e., non-finally) has the same phonemic values as that of the ardhānuswāra ˜ (see §1.4); e.g., imperative vaṇḍ-u-Nḍu is therefore phonemically vaṇḍ-u-ṇḍu freely alternating with vaṇḍ-u-ḍu. Following a non-radical short vowel, N (i.e., = [˜]) has the alternating values of a zero or a nasal phoneme conditioned by the following consonant; but, following a radical short vowel, it is never a zero, e.g., ra-ϕ-Nḍu > ra-ṇḍu come! (you, pl.). The only exception to this, among verbs, is cu-Nḍu (= cũḍu) see! (you, pl.), which is either /cuṇḍu/ or /cuḍu/, cu- to see (allom. of cūcu) (see §§3.5, 4(a), 3.31, 7).

[6]I have not attempted here to interpret the alternants under 2, 3, 5, and 6 as sequences of two morphs each on account of the obvious difficulties in segmenting each alternant into two functional elements; for instance, if we analyze -ina (2) as i (past) + na (adjective), the other alternants of the whole sequence, viz., -na ∞ -a do not yield to two cuts each. This necessarily involves the setting up of several zero alternants, which is a sloppy analysis. The problem may be taken as one comparable to that of English fl-, gl-, hw-, etc. in a series of forms with some theoretical justification for analysis as separate morphemes, which is however not advised as a practical procedure on account of the poor productivity of the residue in forming fresh combinations (see Bloomfield, Language (1933), pp. 244-246; Z. S. Harris, Methods in Structural Linguistics, Chicago (1951), pp. 192-194).

[7]Examples for the different phonemic values of morph-final N:

(a) vaṇḍ-aN + ēgitini > vaṇḍ-an ēgitini I went to cook

(b) vaṇḍ-aN + rammu > vaṇḍ-an rammu come (you, sg.) to cook!
vaṇḍ-anu rammu
vaṇḍ-a rammu

| | | |
|---|---|---|
| rammu vaṇḍ-aN > | rammu vaṇḍ-an | come (you, sg.) to cook! |
| | rammu vaṇḍ-anu | |
| | rammu vaṇḍ-a | |

| | | | |
|---|---|---|---|
| (c) | vaṇḍ-aN + kōritini > | vaṇḍ-an gōritini | I wished to cook |
| | | vaṇḍ-aṅ " | " |
| | | vaṇḍ-anu " | " |
| | | vaṇḍ-a " | " |
| | pō-N + kōritini > | pō-ϕ-gōritini | I wanted to go |

(In the old Telugu manuscripts, the four nasal phonemes /n ṇ ṅ m/ occurring before the stop consonants are indicated by the symbol O called bindu or pūrṇānusvāramu).

[8]It has been pointed out by commentators on Telugu grammar that the present and the future tense forms with -unnānu, etc. and -kalanu, etc. respectively are later developments which do not occur in Nannaya's usage. The present tense forms occur with the declensions of -unnavā̃ḍu and -unnadi bound to the present participles in -cun- or -c- (nos. refer to parvan, canto, and verse of Bhr.):

| | | | |
|---|---|---|---|
| e.g., | cēyu-c-unnavā̃ḍu | (1, 7, 36) | he is doing, or he is the doer |
| | cēyu-cun-unnavā̃ḍu | (3, 2, 26) | " " |
| | perugu-c-unnadi | (1, 3, 93) | she is growing |
| | vedaku-c-unnavāru | (1, 6, 281) | they (m. f. pl.) are searching |
| | agu-cun-unna(y)adi | (3, 2, 26) | she is becoming |
| | navayu-c-unnavā̃ḍanu | (3, 4, 119) | I am suffering or I am the sufferer |
| | kōru-cun-unnavāru | (3, 2, 49) | they are desiring |
| | (āpada-y) āpādincu-c-unnavā̃ḍavu | (2, 2, 44) | you are causing (hardship) |

The immediate constituents of unnavā̃ḍu are unna (verbal adjective of un- to be, i.e., un-na that is) and vā̃du person, of which the latter is declinable as follows:

| | | |
|---|---|---|
| vā̃ḍ-anu | 1sg. | (lit. the person, I) |
| vār-amu | 1pl. | (lit. the persons, we) |
| vā̃ḍ-avu | 2sg. | (lit. the person, you) |
| vār-aru/vā-ru | 2pl. | (lit. the persons, you, pl.) |
| vā̃ḍu | 3m.sg. | (lit. the person, or he) |
| vā-ru | 3m. f. pl. | (lit. the persons, they) |

Similarly, in n. sg. and pl. -adi and -avi occur respectively with -unna bound to the present participle forms (see example above).

In Tikkana's portion of Mahābhārata (13th century) we find present tense forms with the loss of v- of vā̃ḍu/vāru, e.g.

| | | |
|---|---|---|
| noppincu-c-unnā̃ḍu | (2, 5, 44) | he is afflicting (pain upon) |
| (iḍumulā) baḍu-c-unnadi | (5, 3, 136) | she is suffering (troubles) |
| pōvu-cun-unnāru | (4, 3, 138) | they are going |
| unnāramu | (5, 2, 6) | we are |
| cēyu-c-unnā̃ḍavu | (11, 2, 81) | you are doing |

But forms with -unnānu (1sg.), -unnāmu (1pl.), -unnāvu (2sg.) do not occur in the early classics; they may be assigned to the period after the 14th century (see Āndhravyākaraṇasamhitāsarvasvamu, abbreviated AVSS, pp. 1328; 1358-1360).

Similarly, the future tense forms in Nannaya are formed by adding the declensions of -kalavā̃ḍu to the infinitives in -aN (for the different phonemic values of the morphophoneme N, see §3.7, and note 6):

| | | |
|---|---|---|
| ī-galavā̃ḍ(anu) | (2, 2, 174) | I shall give |
| kāv-aṅ-galavāramu | (3, 3, 384) | we shall protect |

Tikkana (13th century):

| | | |
|---|---|---|
| an-ā-galavā̃ḍan(u) | (4, 1, 90) | I shall say |
| pond-aṅ-galavāramu | (5, 3, 80) | we shall obtain |
| kon-aṅ-galavāramu | (5, 3, 142) | we shall take |
| cēy-aṅ-galavā̃ḍan(u) | (6, 3, 286) | I will do |
| gelav-ā-galāru | (6, 4, 11) | they will win |

Errana (14th century):

| | | |
|---|---|---|
| cēy-ā-galaru | (3, 4, 288) | they will do |
| viḍuv-ā-galaru | (3, 4, 289) | they will give up |

kal- is a defective verb in Telugu which is connected traditionally with kalugu 'to have' (see s.v. kalugu in Part II). Intransitively, it means 'to be' occurring as a finite verb with an eight membered paradigm, as follows:

| | |
|---|---|
| kalā̃ḍu | (or kalaNḍu) he is/was |
| kalaru | they are, were |
| kaladu | she/it, is/was |
| kalavu | they (n. pl.) are/were |
| kalavu | you (sg.) are/were |
| kalaru | you (pl.) are/were |
| kalanu | I am/was |
| kalamu | we are/were |

In the post-14th century works, all these forms when occurring with the infinitive stems indicate future tense. However, the 1sg. and pl. and 2sg. are rare in the early classics. Transitively, kal- means to have or possess, inflected in the same way as the intransitive but occurring in a different syntactic situation, in which it is qualified by a noun in the objective case.

(lāvu tempu) galaru (5, 4, 109) they have (strength and courage)
(magaṭimi) galā̃ḍu he has (valor) (AVSS pp. 1367-1370)

The verbal adjective of kal- is kal-a, which occurs before any noun with intransitive or transitive signification, e.g., iṇṭā-gala dhanamu the money that is in the house, telivi gala-mānavũḍu a man possessing knowledge. In Nannaya's poetry, -kala is bound to the verbal infinitive in -aN and followed by the declensions of -vā̃ḍu the person (m.) and -adi (f. n. sg.), these forms denoting the future tense (see examples above). In the poetry of Tikkana (13th century), we find forms with the loss of v in -vā̃ḍu, beside those without the loss; e.g., cēy-ā-galāru, cēyagalā̃ḍu, etc. In subsequent writings, we find forms with shortened vowel, as in kalā̃ḍu instead of kalā̃ḍu, bound to the infinitives in the formation of the future tense.

[9]truncu has been considered the transitive of tunũgu (Bālav. 8.77; AVSS p. 1594), but it is better to put it with truṅgu, which has similarity in form as well as in meaning.

[10]For sub-class (a), we may alternatively state that the final sequence -ũgu of the intransitive stems is replaced by -cu in the transitive.

[11]There are however a few exceptions to this, i.e., intransitive -˜gu alternating with -˜pu in transitive; e.g., ā̃pu (beside ā̃gu, ā̃cu); rẽgu : rẽpu (beside rẽcu, q.v.).

[12]Traditional grammars treat anucu to send, and panucu to commission as the transitives of pōvu to go, besides puccu to send (see Bālav. 8.77; AVSS, pp. 1595-1597).

[13]-cu is said to represent any morph that ends in -cu, i.e., -cu, -ncu, and -incu (Bālav. 8.88, 89).

[14]For the verbalizer -cu cf., e.g., ciguru sprout, cigurcu/cigurucu to sprout; bases of this type belong to sub-class (b). Nouns verbalized by affixation are ex-

cluded from the scope of this work and do not find place here; see §2.1, 2.

[15]The word 'Standard Telugu' is used here in a rather limited sense. The material is drawn from the author's own dialect which is the Brahmin class speech of Guntur District with occasional mixture of some Visakhapatnam dialectisms. In the dialects of the cultured middle class of whatever district, the degree of mutual divergence is much less pronounced than in the case of the speech of the uneducated classes. The author's dialect represents the cultured middle class speech of Central Andhra which has a large amount of 'common core' with the standard dialects of the rest of Andhra. For a list of the Modern Telugu phonemes, see §§1.7, .8, .9.

[16]The analysis of junctures (boundary features) for Modern Telugu has not been worked out with any high degree of clarity. The following is my own analysis based on my speech material.

Modern Telugu has four juncture phonemes, of which three are marked and one unmarked, i.e., /– + #/. The unmarked juncture is the normal transition from one segmental phoneme to another without any pause or allophonic features found along the other (boundary features) junctures.

/–/ Consonants immediately following this juncture have fortis allophones; the first syllable following this has always phonetic stress, e.g.

/ #cūcǣḍu #/ he saw [cṹčǣḍʋ]

/ #cūc-ceppǣḍu #/ having seen, he said [cṹččέppǣḍʋ]

/+/ This is an open juncture with a distinctive pause or break in speech succession accompanied by a non-terminal pitch contour, viz., slow-rising with a sharp fall at the end.

/#/ An open juncture occurring utterance initially and finally, indicating silence at the beginning as well as at the end of an utterance. Utterance finally, this occurs with the following terminal contours: /|/ /↑/ /↓/; the first syllable following any of the marked junctures is always stressed, e.g.

/ #ceppǣḍu|#/ he said [čέppǣḍʋ]

/ #ceppǣḍu↑#/ did he say? [čέppǣḍʋ]

/ #ceppi+weḷḷǣḍu|#/ having said, he went [čéppi wέḷḷǣḍʋ]

/ #cūc-ceppu↓#/ look in and say! [cṹččéppʋ]

A stress-contrast predictable in terms of junctures can be seen from the following minimal pair:

| | |
|---|---|
| / #reṇḍeḍla-banḍlu+tīsuku-rā↓ #/ | bring two-bullock-carts! |
| [réṇḍeḍḷabə́nḍḷu tī́sukurā́] | (number of carts unspecified) |
| / #reṇḍ-eḍlabanḍlu+tīsuku-rā↓ #/ | bring two bullock-carts! |
| [réṇḍéḍḷabənḍḷu tī́sukurā́] | (number of bullocks of each cart is unspecified) |

/–/ is indicative of juncture only when enclosed in / /; elsewhere in this chapter it is only used as the mark of a morph-boundary (that which shows two morphs separately).

[17]Past-participle -i- can also occur before /ϕ/ according to the style used.

[18]y after a long vowel and yy after a short vowel; long and short vowels of all qualities except a/ā freely alternate before y/yy; e.g., ceyy-i/cēy-i do! (imper. sg.); koyy-i/kōy-i cut! (imper. sg.), etc.

[19]There is one more base of the (C)V̌CV̌C-type in final s belonging to sub-class (b), viz., telus- to be known, with the following distribution: telus- (A 1-3); telis- (A-4); telis- (B); teliy-/telē- (C 1-7).

CHAPTER IV

# THE PLACE OF TELUGU IN THE DRAVIDIAN FAMILY

## INTRODUCTION

§4.1. The following sections present a summary of the conclusions reached in chapters I and II and seek to indicate the relative position of Telugu in the Dravidian family. The words South Dravidian (SDr.), Central Dravidian (CDr.), and North Dravidian (NDr.) have been used all along without indicating geographical boundaries or the language membership of each group. So far, they have been used only to suggest broadly the geographical situation of a given member of the family in the South, Center, or North of India. It should be interesting to find out to what extent the contours of linguistic parallelisms (i.e., isoglosses) correspond to the geographical division. The composition of SDr., CDr., and NDr. is as follows:

| SDr. | CDr. | NDr. |
|---|---|---|
| Tamil } } | (Telugu)[1] | Kurukh } |
| Malayalam } } | | Malto } |
| Toda } } | Kui } | |
| Kota } } | Kuvi } | Brahui |
| | Kolami } } | |
| Kannaḍa } | Naiki } } | |
| Badaga } | | |
| Koḍagu } | Parji } } | |
| Tulu | Ollari } } | |
| | Gadaba } } | |
| Telugu | | |
| | Gondi | |

Languages enclosed with a single brace belong to the same minor or major linguistic sub-groups within the family.[2] In other words, members within each sub-group are more closely related among themselves than members across the sub-grouping. The degree of nearness in genetic relationship between any two or more sub-groups is a problem which does not yield to easy solution in the present state of our knowledge of

[1]See p. 272.

Dravidian. More members of the CDr. group have come to light during the recent years and more keep coming; Koṇḍa, Pengu, and Koya are the new additions, but much work needs to be done on these languages before they can be used profitably for comparative study. It is suspected that they connect the Kui-Kuvi sub-group with Gondi, which together will constitute a major sub-group in CDr., vis-à-vis the major sub-group Klm.-Nk.-Pj.-Oll.-Gad.[3] Telugu by virtue of its geographical position and also certain linguistic features (detailed in the following sections) occupies a midway position between SDr. and CDr. A thorough quantitative study of all the relevant comparative material (which, of course, is not attempted here) will probably estimate precisely to which side it inclines more.

§4.2. In plotting the comparative isoglosses for Telugu, the relevant material is treated under three heads, viz., comparative phonology (chapter I), etymology (only insofar as the verbal bases are concerned [chapter II]), and comparative morphology (only certain important features).

## COMPARATIVE PHONOLOGY

§4.3. From a study of the comparative phonology of Dravidian (see chapter I), the following phonemes can be set up for PDr. with a fair degree of certainty:

**Consonants**

| | | | | | |
|---|---|---|---|---|---|
| p | t | ṯ | ṭ | c | k |
| | | | ḻ | | |
| m | n | | ṇ | ñ | |
| | | l | ḷ | | |
| | | r | | | |
| v | | | | y | |

**Vowels**

| | | |
|---|---|---|
| i | | u |
| e | | o |
| | a | |

Long vowels are marked by a superscript phoneme of length /¯/.

In PDr. any vowel can occur root-initially, or any consonant except a member of the alveolar and retroflex series, viz., /ṯ l r ṭ ḻ ṇ ḷ/; in the final position any consonant except *ñ can occur. However, all stops in the final position are followed by a non-morphemic (the so-called enunciative) u.

The phonemic composition and the etymological structure of a word in PDr. with a zero derivative or a single derivative suffix can be formulated as follows (see §1.121, §§2.8, .113, .114):

$(C^1)$ = any consonant admissible root-initially (see §2.113), its occurrence being optional

$(C^2)$ = any consonant admissible in the root-final position (see §2.113)

$\check{V}^1$ = vowel short or long (in the radical syllable, any vowel phoneme, short or long)

$V^2$ = i/u/a

$\phi$ = zero suffix or absence of any suffix

P = a voiceless occlusive (p t ṯ ṭ c k)

N = nasal homorganic with the following stop (phonemically, m n ṇ ñ)

L = a sonorant or a non-occlusive consonant (m n ṇ ḻ l ḷ r v y) (by definition L includes N)

| | Root | + | Suffix |
|---|---|---|---|
| I | $(C^1)V^1$ | + | $\phi$ / L / P / NP / PP |
| II | $(C^1)V^1C^2$ | + | $\phi$ / $V^2$ / $V^2L$ / $V^2P$ / $V^2NP$ / $V^2PP$ |
| III | (C)VN | + | P[4] |

§4.4. The regular developments of the PDr. phonemes in OTe. are treated from the standpoint of Telugu in chapter I. They are presented below as a set of correspondences by reversing the order (i.e., from the standpoint of PDr.):

Symbols:

| | |
|---|---|
| ] | preceding environment |
| [ | following environment |
| ( ) | enclosed in these are the less frequent developments |
| / | developments with unpredictable conditioning |
| (u) | non-morphemic u occurring word-finally is left out |
| FV | front vowels ĭ, ĕ |
| nFV | non-front vowels ă, ŭ, ŏ |
| -C- | intervocalic |
| C- | prevocalic and initial |
| -C | postvocalic and final |

## Consonants

| | Proto-Dravidian Root | Proto-Dravidian Suffix | Old Telugu Root | Old Telugu Suffix[5] |
|---|---|---|---|---|
| *k | *k [nFV | | > k-/(g-) | |
| | *k [FV | | > c- | |
| | *-k- | | > -g- | |
| | *V̌] k[6] | | > V̌] kk | |
| | | *-k | | > -g |
| | | *-nk | | > -ṅg/-ṅk |
| *c | *c- | | > (1) c-<br>(2) (c-/ϕ-)<br>(3) (t-) | |
| | *-c- | | > -s- | |
| | *V̌] c | | > V̌] cc | |
| | | *-ñc | | > -nj/-nc |
| *ṭ | *-ṭ- | | > (1) -ḍ-<br>(2) ḍ- (> d-) | |
| | *V̌] ṭ | | > V̌] ṭṭ | |
| | | *-ṇṭ | | > -ṇḍ/-ṇṭ |
| *ṯ | *-ṯ- | | > (1) -ṟ- > -r-<br>(2) ṟ- > r- | |
| | *V̌] ṯ | | > V̌] ṭṭ | |
| | | *-nṯ | | > -ṇḍ/(-nd) |
| | | *V̌] ṯ | | > -V̌] ṟ/r |
| *t | *t- | | > t-/(d-) | |
| | *-t- | | > -d- | |
| | *V̌] t | | > V̌] tt | |
| | | *-nt | | > -nd/-nt |
| *p | *p- | | > p-/(b-) | |
| | *-p- | | > -v- | |
| | *V̌] p | | > V̌] pp | |
| | | -V̌] mp | | > (1) Ṽ] m<br>> (2) V̌] mm/(mb) |

| Proto-Dravidian | | | | Old Telugu | |
|---|---|---|---|---|---|
| | Root | Suffix | | Root | Suffix |
| *ñ | *ñ- | | > | n- | |
| *ṇ | *-ṇ- | | > | -n- | |
| | *V̌] ṇ | | > | V̌] nn/n | |
| | | | | V̄] n | |
| *n | *n- | | > | n-/(ϕ-) | |
| | *-n- | | > | -n- | |
| | *V̌] n | | > | V̌] nn/n | |
| | | -V̌] n | | | > V̌] n |
| *m | *m- | | > | m- | |
| | *-m- | | > | -m-/-v- | |
| | *V̌] m | | > | V̌] mm | |
| | | -V̌] m | | | > V̌] m/(v) |
| *ḻ | *-ḻ- | | > | (1) -ḍ- | |
| | | | | (2) ḍ- > d- | |
| | | -V̌] ḻ | | | > -V̌] ḍ |
| *ḷ | *-ḷ- | | > | (1) -l- | |
| | | | | (2) l- | |
| | *V̌] ḷ | | > | V̌] ll | |
| | | | | V̄] l | |
| | | -V̌] ḷ | | | > -V̌] l |
| *l | *-l- | | > | (1) -l- | |
| | | | | (2) l- | |
| | *V̌] l | | > | V̌] ll | |
| | | | | V̄] l | |
| | | -V̌] l | | | > -V̌] l |
| *r | *-r- | | > | (1) -r- | |
| | | | | (2) r- | |
| | *V̌] r | | > | V̄] r | |
| | | -V̌] r | | | > -V̌] r |

| | Proto-Dravidian Root | Proto-Dravidian Suffix | Old Telugu Root | Old Telugu Suffix |
|---|---|---|---|---|
| *y | *y- | | > ϕ- | |
| | *-y- | | > -y- (or loss and lengthening of the preceeding vowel) | |
| | *V̌] y | | > V̌] y | |
| | | -V̌] y | | > -V̌] y |
| *v | *v [FV or ā̆ | | > v- | |
| | *-v- | | > -v-/-g-/(-m-) | |
| | *V̌] v | | > V̌] vv<br>V̄] v | |
| | | -V̌] v | | > V̌] v/(m) |
| | *C¹V¹l̠-V²-<br>t̠<br>r | | > (1) C¹rV̄¹- (where *-V̌² is -a)<br>(2) C¹rV̌¹- (where *-V̌² is u or i) | |

<u>Vowels</u>

| Proto-Dravidian Root | Proto-Dravidian Suffix | Old Telugu Root | Old Telugu Suffix |
|---|---|---|---|
| *i [Ca | | > e [Ca | |
| *u [Ca | | > o [Ca | |
| *ñ] ā̆-/ē̆- | | > n] ē-(/ā-)<br>e-(/a-) | |
| *y] ā-/ē- | | > ϕ] ē- | |
| *ay | | > (1) ay-<br>(2) ē-(< *ey) | |
| | -ay | | -ay/-a |

*a in the suffix position is generally preserved, whereas *i in this position preceding any consonant falls together with u (< *u) (§§2.12 ff.).

§4.5. Following the usual procedures of comparison, we need to reconstruct a different phoneme in the proto-language for each different series of phonemic correspondences observed in the daughter languages in the same position. Therefore, in a set of related etyma, we expect a single series of correspondences for each position compared. But in a number of cases in Dravidian, more than one series of reflexes occur for the same position in related etyma. This situation should technically suggest the presence of more than one phoneme in that position in the proto-language, which is not normally expected, unless it is a case of phonemic alternation in the proto-language itself brought about by non-phonetic reasons, i.e., dialect mixture, analogy, etc. A few instances from Dravidian are noted below:

1 (a) c : t (initially and intervocalically, §§1.23, .90 ff., .213)
 (b) -c : -l̲ (§1.191)
 (c) -c : -y (§1.193)

These three series of correspondences along with the retention of *c- in all languages and the alternation of c : zero (SDr.) should indicate the presence of five different phonemes at an older stage of PDr. These five phonemes of pre-Dravidian must have merged with two phonemes each, viz., (1) *c : *t, (2) *-c : *-l̲, (3) *-c- : *-y-, (4) *c : *ϕ, in PDr. whose reflexes turn up in the descendant languages. c-/s- retained in all the languages in certain other etyma points to PDr. *c, which should be obviously different from the above series. If we are to explain these developments as cases of phonemic split in PDr., we should be able to establish complementary distribution of reflexes between the members of each set; for instance, in set (1), *c : *t should occur in complementary environments. But since they occur in the same environment, we may assume that a pre-Dravidian phoneme **X developed into *c in one area and *t in another with dialect mixture following; consequently we cannot now demarcate the boundary line between the c- and t- areas from the evidence of the modern Dravidian languages. Since the conditions leading to the split in each case might have been obscured by subsequent phonetic changes, any speculation beyond this point is likely to be misleading.

A few more alternations of this nature are:

(1) *n- : *ϕ- (§1.218-19) besides the regular *n > n

(2) (a) *-ḷ : *-ṭ (§1.83)
 (b) *-ḷ : *-ṇ (§1.93) besides the regular *ḷ > ḷ/l

(3) *l : *n (§1.95) besides the regular *l > l

(4) alternation of higher and lower vowels, i.e., *i/*e, *u/*o, and *a/*e, before *y and retroflex consonants (§§1.241-9, .255-6, .283-7)

§4.6. The different developments of the PDr. phonemes in the various Dravidian languages along with an indication of the comparative position of Telugu in the whole family is shown in the following chart. Only the regular or widely prevalent phonemic changes are taken into account. Languages from Toda to Gadaba are arranged more or less according to their geographical contiguity. Languages 1 to 7, 5 to 8, and 8 to 15 are geographically contiguous; so also are 16 and 17. Brahui is far removed from the rest. Languages listed to the left of Telugu may be considered to represent South Dravidian, and those to the right represent Central and North Dravidian. A horizontal line running below the names of the languages shows the area of prevalence of a given development for each phoneme or phonemic sequence listed under the PDr. column. A continuous line denotes that the phonemic development in question is a case of retention or continuation of the PDr. feature, and an interrupted line denotes phonemic innovation in the descendent languages. If, for the same PDr. phoneme, a language shows two developments, they are to be considered either diachronic or dialectal; no attempt is made to mark this distinction in the chart. An arrow mark in the Telugu column indicates the direction in which Telugu shares a given phonological innovation with the other languages, i.e., whether it is towards South Dravidian or Central Dravidian.[7]

§4.7. In order to determine the relative position of a language among the sub-groups of a family, we need to eliminate the most inclusive and the most exclusive isoglosses. An isogloss which includes the whole family (at least one member from each minor sub-group) indicates that the change in question has affected all the sub-groups and therefore must have operated at a time before the first split had taken place, e.g., the movable *n in the initial position, and the shortening of radical long vowels before vowel-suffixes are common Dravidian developments shared in some degree by members of each sub-group (§§1.32, .294). On the other hand, exclusive isoglosses like those representing the developments of PDr. *l̠ show that widely divergent reflexes arise from the fact that the PDr. phoneme had been preserved in the sub-groups for a long time after their separation, and phonetic change had occurred in each sub-group or language independently afterwards.

§4.8. Again, distinction should be made between an isogloss representing the retention of a given proto-feature and one representing an innovation. While chance retention is possible, even common to geographically distant languages, several exclusively shared innovations in more than one sub-group provide evidence to establish their closer

## DEVELOPMENT OF PROTO-DRAVIDIAN PHONEMES AND THE COMPARATIVE POSITION OF TELUGU

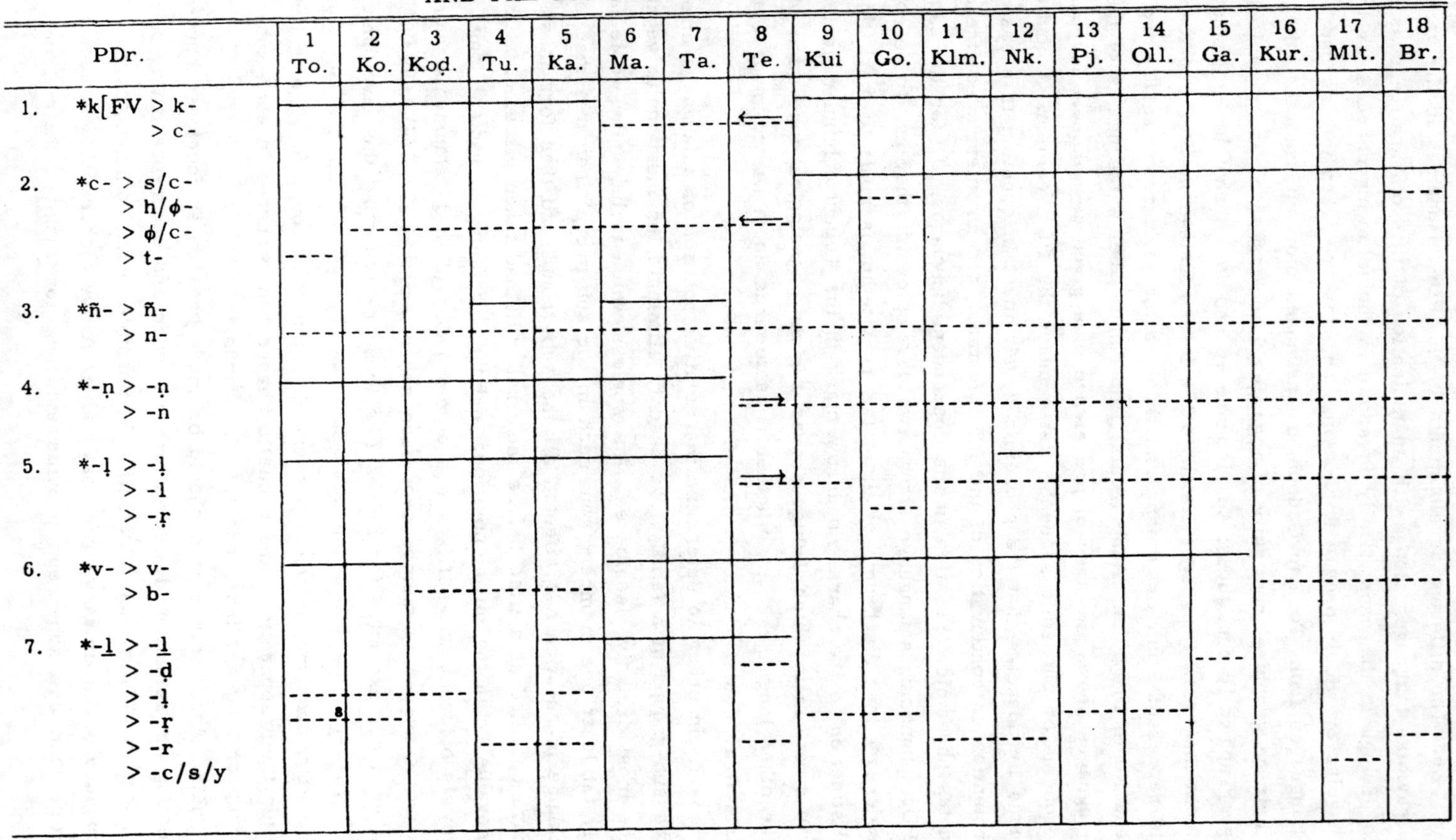

8. *-ṯ > -ṟ (> r)
> -r
> -d
> -j/c/s

9. *ṯṯ- > -ṟṟ
> -ṯ
> -tt
> -ṭṭ

10. *-nṯ > -nṯ (nṟ)
> -ḏ
> -ṇḍ
> -nd
> -nj/-s

11. *(C¹)V¹C²V²-
> (C)VCV-
> (C¹)C²V̆¹-⁹

12. *i/e[-a > e[-a
*u/o[-a > o[-a
> i-
> u-

13. *ñ]ā/ē- > ā-
> ē-

14. *y]ā/ē- > ā-
> ē-

15. *ay- > ay-
> ē/ey-

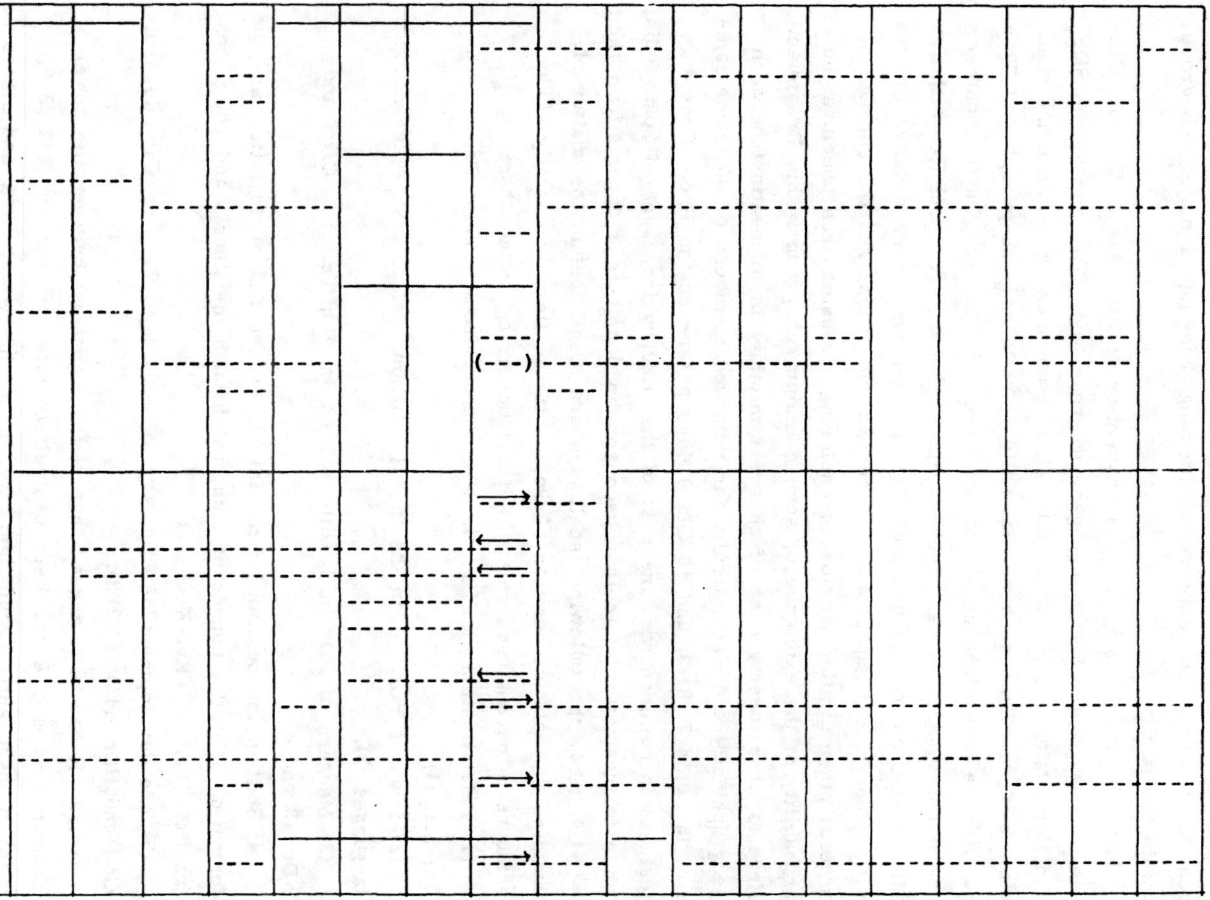

genetic affinity at an early period forming them into a major sub-group within the family.

In the chart, item 6 shows the retention of PDr. *v- in Te. and CDr. and in many of the SDr. languages, whereas Koḍ., Tu., and Ka. in SDr., and Kur., Mlt., and Brah. in NDr. show a common phonemic innovation, viz., b < *v. This does not naturally point to any sub-grouping of Telugu with the other languages that preserve the PDr. *v. On the contrary, one might suspect an early sub-grouping of Koḍ., Tu., and Ka. with Kur., Mlt., and Brah. on the basis of their shared innovation, b < *v. But the wide geographical gap between these two sub-groups and the absence of several other similar isoglosses enclosing the same area preclude the probability of the existence of such a major sub-group within Dravidian. Here is, therefore, a case of chance similarity in 'innovation' between geographically and linguistically far-removed members of the same family. In items 7, 8, 9, and 10 Old Telugu preserves the Proto-Dravidian features in common with the rest of the literary languages of South India, while in the matter of their subsequent developments it departs from them.

§4.9. Only the following isoglosses are significant in the matter of deciding the relative position of Telugu in the Dravidian family. (The numbers in parentheses refer to items occurring in the chart).

(1) Palatalization of PDr. *k- > c- before front vowels; Te. : Ta. Ma. (1).

(2) Loss of PDr. *c in the initial position; Te. : all other SDr. languages (2).

(3) Mergers of PDr. ṇ ḷ with n l (< *n *l); Te. : CDr. and NDr. (3 and 4).

(4) Shift of the position of medial *l, *r, *ṭ and *ṯ to initial and the formation of initial consonant clusters through metathesis and vowel contraction; Te. : Kui-Kuvi (11).

(5) The development of PDr. *ay to ē (< *ey); Te. : CDr. (except Go.) and NDr. (15) (§1.283).

§4.10. It has been argued that in PDr. contrast between the vowel phonemes *ā and ē has been neutralized after *ñ and *y (§§1.28-9, .215). Consequently, some languages show this vowel as ā and others as ē. Even though no phonemic change is involved here in any of the Dravidian languages, the fact that this vowel phoneme (the archi-phoneme *ā/*ē) should be identified in one area with ē and in another with ā, both of which can be clearly separated by marking isoglosses, is in itself significant. Telugu goes with Central and North Dravidian in identifying this proto-Dravidian vowel phoneme with ē.

§4.11. The merger of PDr. radical *i *u with *e *o (< *e and *o) before an a vowel in the following syllable can be shown clearly to have operated throughout the SDr. area;[10] the data from the non-literary languages of CDr. and NDr. are difficult to utilize for this purpose on account of the scarcity of items in them that preserve the quality of the suffix vowel, i.e., the vowel of the second syllable, in disyllabic and trisyllabic forms (§1.272). However, one diagnostic set of etyma shows that this development has covered the whole of the CDr. area besides SDr., viz.,

Ta. Ma. Ka. Tu. Te. uppu salt
Ta. uvar salt; Ka. ogaru astringent
Te. ogaru id.
Pj. cup, Oll. Klm. Nk. sup, Gad. cuppu salt
Go. (Adilabad) sovar (dial. hovar, ovar) id.
Koṇḍa sōru id.
Kui sāru id.
Kuvi hāru id.

We reconstruct for PSDr. *upp- : *uvar and for CDr. *cup- : *cov-ar (< *cuv-ar); Koṇḍa sōru and Go. sovar support the reconstruction *covar for CDr.; Kui-Kuvi forms may be later developments of *cŏr (< *covar) by *ŏ > ā. The etymology and the reconstruction admit of little doubt. Therefore, the developments shown in item 12 in the chart may not point to any exclusive innovations between Te. and SDr.

§4.12. The loss of PDr. *c- (item 2) and the development of PDr. *k > c- before front vowels (item 1) are the two exclusive innovations that put Telugu with SDr. Of these, palatalization of PDr. *k in Te., Ta., and Ma. is not sufficient evidence for constituting these languages into a sub-group within SDr. since this appears to be an isolated case of coincidence in phonetic change not supported by any further innovations exclusively shared between Te. and Ta.-Ma. Even in the distribution of this development Te. and Ta.-Ma. are independent of each other (§1.18).

§4.13. Within SDr. Telugu has several features in common with the Kannaḍa sub-group, Tu., and also to a certain extent To. and Ko.:

(1) Irregular voicing of the post-nasal stops; Te.: Ka. Tu. (§1.77).

(2) Progressive loss of the preconsonantal nasals in trisyllabic bases; Te.: Ka. Tu. Koḍ. To. and Ko. (§1.171).[11] Ka. goes further (also To. Ko.) in losing this nasal even in disyllabic forms, e.g., Ka. mūṟu three (< *mūnṯu), Ta. mūnṟu, Te. mū̃ḍu (inscr. mūnṟu); Ka. kaṟu calf (< *kanṯ-), Ta. kanṟu id.

(3) (a) Loss (through weakening) of the medial vocalic peak (the vowel beginning the suffix) in trisyllabic forms, and (b) assimilation of the root-

final sonorant (trill, lateral, or spirant) to the following suffix stop[12] (§§1.153, .180-5):

(a) Te. : Ka. Tu.

(b) Te. : Ka. Ko.

§4.14. Even in the case of common phonemic changes occurring in a group of contiguous languages, it should be ascertained whether the innovation in question is inherited from a common proto-stage or has developed independently in each language, eventually spreading by accident, as it were, over a wide area covered by several geographically contiguous languages. There are many cases of this latter nature in Dravidian. For the merger of PDr. *ḷ *ṇ with l n (< *l *n), we can now draw a clear isogloss enclosing Te. and the languages to the north of it (i.e., CDr. and NDr.), whereas they are phonemically preserved in the rest of the SDr. languages, viz., Ta. Ma. Ka. Koḍ. Tu. To. and Ko. There is sufficient evidence to show that this merger has occurred independently in each language or sub-group within Central and North Dravidian and therefore cannot be attributed to a common remote past, i.e., the undivided stage (if any) of the present CDr. and NDr. languages.[13]

The merger of PDr. ṯ with a dental or retroflex (voiced or voiceless) stop in gemination and post-nasal position is also a latent development in the different languages;[14] as a matter of fact most of the languages show both the PDr. developments (§1.165).[15] In all the literary SDr. languages /*ṯ/ -ṟ- has fallen together with -r- (< *r) during the historic period, of course independently of one another.

Again, *ñ- > n- has occurred in Tamil during the historic period in the same way that it happened elsewhere in the family during their respective prehistories.

Though palatalization of PDr. *k[FV occurred in a composite area of OTa. (which includes Ma.) and Te., the conditions under which it took place were different in each of them. On the basis of this it has been suggested that these developments in these two languages are independent of each other.

§4.15. Not every isogloss representing a phonemic shift necessarily indicates a language or sub-group boundary, but a bundle of isoglosses enclosing a given area points to an early sub-grouping of the languages of that area as a major dialect area within the proto-language. Isoglosses of common or shared phonological innovations that cut across the modern language boundaries within a family are usually traced to a period when the languages in question were dialects of the undivided parent language.[16] But the cases shown from Dravidian are of a different nature. Here the isoglosses bind composite geographical areas consisting of many languages of the family, but there is evidence to show that phonological innovations have taken place in them independently during their historic period rather than when they were dialects of the proto-language.

§4.16. Assuming that none of the Dravidian languages had available historical data and that we are only dealing with the material of the modern Dravidian languages for comparison, should we not be led to the conclusion that n l (< *ṇ *ḷ) in CDr. and NDr., r < *ṯ in SDr., n- < *ñ- in all the Dravidian languages, and c- < *k[FV in Ta. and Te. took place in PDr. itself, presumably on the dialectal level? The answer will be in the affirmative, following the usual procedures of comparison and reconstruction.

§4.17. The developments involved are too many to be ruled out as possessing uniformity through accidentally similar phonetic changes. The difficulty may be got over if we assume that languages which are contiguous and which show common phonemic innovations independently during their respective histories have inherited a common phonetic tendency or a speech habit from the pre-separation period; for instance, all CDr. and NDr. languages that have now n l (< *ṇ *ḷ) had inherited the tendency to front the positions of *ṇ and *ḷ rather than the accomplished fact of the phonemic change. Similarly, the (phonetic) tendency to change *ñ- > n- could have had its origin in PDr. and operated at a phonemic level in all the languages except in OTa., where it was accomplished only during the historic period independently of the rest. Similarly, Ta., Ma., and Te. inherited a common tendency to front the position of PDr. *k- before front vowels, but palatalization on a phonemic level came about after they developed into independent languages.

A contrasting situation to this is offered by the developments of PDr. *ḻ which are numerous and which do not offer any clear isoglosses separating two or three major dialect areas within PDr. In this case we cannot attribute any common phonetic tendency to the speakers of one area against the rest in the undivided parent language. The phoneme in question remained intact in all the Dravidian languages until recently, and changes in phonetic habits that led to its merger with different phonemes in different languages are independent of one another and should only be traced to their respective historic periods.

§4.18. From the preceding discussion it appears that Te. belongs to a major sub-group including the members of the present Central and North Dravidian languages. Among these, it has much closer genetic affinity with the Kui-Kuvi sub-group, especially judging from the phonological features represented by items 11, 13, 14, and 15 on the chart.

## ETYMOLOGY

§4.19. A quantitative study of the evidence of the presence or absence of cognates in the other Dravidian languages for a given number of verbal bases in Telugu will not be in itself a safe guide to determine its comparative position. No objective criteria have been so far evolved to discover the conditions under which some members of a language family lose certain native etyma that other members preserve intact.

Each set of etyma taken individually may not contribute to determining the various degrees of genetic affinity among related languages. But if a group of languages possesses a preponderantly large number of cognates as against the rest of the members of the family, this fact may be significant in drawing certain historically valid conclusions. If, for instance, of the three geographically contiguous language groups A B C, A B share a large number of cognates and also A C, but not B C, it is very likely that C was contiguous to A rather than to B in the pre-historic (or pre-separation) period, the geographical contiguity between B and C during the historic period being brought about either by a migration of the speakers of B towards the C area or of those of C towards B, i.e.,

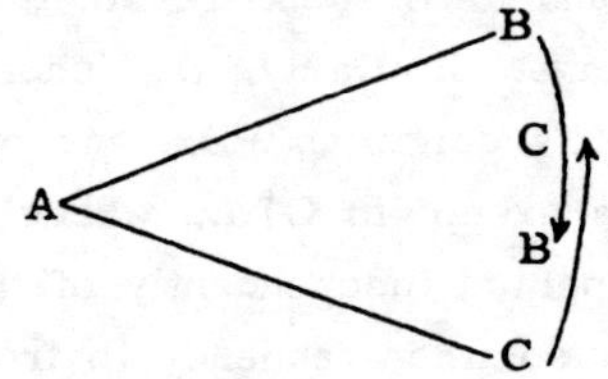


However, this observation can be valid only when we are certain that the etymological data available for comparison from the three language groups A B C are quantitatively comparable.

§4.20. Turning to the approach made here, the eighteen or so recorded Dravidian languages are subsumed under eight sub-groups keeping Telugu apart, since it is the position of Telugu among these sub-groups that we are to decide. The sub-groups are set up partly on tested linguistic data and partly ad hoc. These eight sub-groups are again classed under the three major geographical groups; languages subsumed under each sub-group are given in parentheses.

I South Dravidian:

Ta. (Tamil, Malayalam, Toda, Kota)

Ka. (Kannada, Koḍagu)

Tu.

II Central Dravidian:

Pj. (Parji, Ollari, Gadaba, Kolami, Naiki)
Kui (Kui, Kuvi)
Go. (Gondi, several dialects)

III North Dravidian:

Kur. (Kurukh, Malto)
Brahui

§4.21. Telugu, Old and Modern, has a combined total of 1,236 simple verbal bases listed with etymologies in Part II of this work. Out of these, 23 are suspected to be assimilated loans from Indo-Aryan,[17] of which 8 have corresponding forms in some of the other Dravidian languages. Considering that they are common Dravidian (or common SDr. or CDr.) loans, they have been treated on a par with the native Dravidian items. The remaining 15 which occur only in Telugu are deducted from the total number, i.e., 1,236 — 15 = 1,221. Out of this total, 165 are eliminated as redundant numbered entries[18] in Part II, i.e., 1,221 - 165 = 1,056.

§4.22. Out of the 1,056 verbal bases thus obtained, 106 are native Telugu bases for which etymologies are not available. For the remaining 950 one or more of the Dravidian sub-groups set up in §4.20 possess cognates. Making a check mark under the sub-group in which a cognate occurs for a given verbal base in Telugu, a complete check-list has been prepared for all the items that have cognates.[19] After the completion of this process the 1,056 items have been classified into 8 sets A to H on the basis of no cognation or exclusive cognation between Te. and any one of the three major geographical groups, SDr., CDr., and NDr., or a possible combination of these. Within each of these groups, it is also shown how many cognates the individual sub-groups have for a given number of items in Telugu.

§4.23. The eight possible combinations between Telugu and the three geographical groups, arranged to code, A to H, and the tables of count of cognates are as follows:

A Native items for which cognates are not available in any of the other Dravidian languages.

B Te. + SDr.

C Te. + CDr.

D Te. + NDr.

E Te. + SDr. + CDr.

F Te. + CDr. + NDr.

G Te. + SDr. + NDr.

H Te. + SDr. + CDr. + NDr.

Table 1

| Code | Te. | SDr. Ta. | SDr. Ka. | SDr. Tu. | CDr. Pj. | CDr. Kui | CDr. Go. | NDr. Kur. | NDr. Brah. |
|---|---|---|---|---|---|---|---|---|---|
| A | 106 | | | | | | | | |
| B | 417 | 339 | 300 | 193 | | | | | |
| C | 30 | ... | ... | ... | 18 | 17 | 11 | | |
| D | 9 | ... | ... | ... | ... | ... | ... | 9 | |
| E | 210 | 182 | 174 | 122 | 93 | 120 | 84 | | |
| F | 6 | ... | ... | ... | 2 | 4 | 3 | 5 | 1 |
| G | 69 | 59 | 58 | 32 | ... | ... | ... | 61 | 8 |
| H | 209 | 201 | 117 | 153 | 107 | 150 | 98 | 174 | 58 |
| Total | 1,056 | 781 | 649 | 500 | 220 | 291 | 196 | 249 | 67 |
| Percentage of cognation in sub-groups | | 73.95 | 61.45 | 47.34 | 20.83 | 27.55 | 18.56 | 23.58 | 6.34 |

Table 2
Percentage of Cognation between Telugu and the Other Geographical Groups

| | Total items | A Te. alone | B Te. +SDr. | C Te. +CDr. | D Te. +NDr. | E Te. +SDr. +CDr. | F Te. +CDr. +NDr. | G Te. +SDr. +NDr. | H Te. +SDr. +CDr. +NDr. |
|---|---|---|---|---|---|---|---|---|---|
| Telugu items | 1,056 | 106 | 417 | 30 | 9 | 210 | 6 | 69 | 209 |
| Percentage | | 10.03 | 39.49 | 2.84 | 0.85 | 19.90 | 0.56 | 6.53 | 19.80 |

An item counts under the Telugu column if it has cognates in any one language classed under the major geographical groups SDr., CDr., and NDr., or a combination of these according to the code; for instance, the figure 417 occurring in B denotes that there are 417 verbal bases in Telugu for which some member of SDr. group has cognates, but none of

CDr. or NDr. Out of these 417, Tamil has cognates in 339 cases, Kannada in 300, and Tulu in 193.

§4.24. It is clear from the two tables above that the highest rate of exclusive cognation occurs in B (Te. vs. SDr.) and the lowest in F (Te. vs. CDr. + NDr.). We will also not fail to notice that more cognates occur in G (Te. vs. SDr. + NDr.) than in D (Te. vs. NDr.) or F (Te. vs. CDr. + NDr.). This observation is significant in that Te. has only a few exclusive cognates with NDr. and fewer still that it shares with CDr. and NDr. put together. It is therefore likely that NDr. is closer to SDr. rather than CDr., in spite of the apparent geographical contiguity between CDr. and NDr. Exclusively shared innovations between CDr. and NDr. are rare. On the other hand, in the case of personal pronouns[20] and certain possessed kinship terms[21] Kuru<u>kh</u> and Malto show closer resemblance to Tamil than to any other sub-group.

§4.25. Table 1 also shows how many cognates Telugu has with the individual sub-groups. Among the sub-groups Telugu has the highest rate of cognation with the Tamil sub-group and the lowest with Brahui. However, these figures cannot be taken absolutely, since the number of cognates discovered from each language will be in proportion to the total available vocabulary in that language. Since Tamil, Kannada, and Telugu have recorded material of many centuries, the available dictionaries of these languages have fairly large vocabularies. The CDr. and NDr. languages are only known to us for the last one hundred years or so and it is to be doubted whether any of them has been as exhaustively recorded as could be.

It is therefore necessary that we should study the number of cognates available in each of the eight sub-groups in relation to the total available native vocabulary in that sub-group. Since only the simple verbal bases are taken into account for Telugu and not the compound ones, we need consider here only the native primary vocabulary from the other sub-groups out of the total vocabularies recorded in their respective dictionaries.

§4.26. As far as the Tamil sub-group is concerned, only the vocabulary of Tamil as recorded in the Tamil Lexicon is counted, on the assumption that items exclusive to Ma., To., or Ko. (i.e., without cognates in Tamil) are too few to change considerably the total number of the items occurring in the Tamil language alone. A rough estimate has shown that the Tamil Lexicon records 9,900 (rounded off to 10,000) primary words out of which the available cognates for the Telugu verbs are 781; the primary word-items for the Pj.-Klm.-Oll. sub-group have been estimated at 2,000 and those of Kui at 1,965, of which the available cognates for Telugu are 220 and 291 respectively. Assuming that we had in the CDr. sub-groups as adequate vocabularies as in those of SDr., the rate of cognation between Te. and the Pj. or the Kui sub-groups would present altogether a different picture. In other words, if the Pj.-Klm. sub-group had a recorded vocabulary of, say, 9,000 items drawn from records of about ten centuries as in the case of any literary language of South India, the expected number of cognates for the Te. items out of this total would be 900; this figure registers 93.5 of cognation for the 1,056 verbal bases in Telugu. These figures put the Pj.-Klm. sub-group closer to Telugu than they appear to be from the figures in Table 1. Under the same conditions, the Kui sub-group will naturally have a higher rate of cognation. The Kur.-Mlt. sub-group records a larger number of cognates for Te. than any single sub-group of CDr., because the Kurukh dictionary of Grignard, from which the cognates are drawn, is fairly exhaustive, comparable to Mãnner's Tulu dictionary, and therefore provides a much larger corpus for comparison than the vocabularies of any single CDr. language.

§4.27. The low rate of cognation between Te. and CDr. as shown by the table is therefore illusory. It is clear from the above quantitative study of etymology that Te. is linguistically as close to CDr. as to SDr., if not closer.

§4.28. While treating the distribution of derivative suffixes in Telugu (chapter II), many instances have been shown of exclusive occurrence of a given series of suffixes in Telugu and the different sub-groups. Probably this evidence cannot be exploited with the same justification as that of comparative phonology and morphology, since the question of innovation does not arise in the formation of derivative suffixes. All derivative suffixes, from whatever language, can be traced to the general pattern formulated for PDr., viz., -L, -P, -NP, -PP : -VL, -VP, -VNP, -VPP (§§2.8 ff.). Again, there are a number of examples within the same language for the occurrence of different suffixes with the same root (< PDr. root) in the formation of words, e.g., Te. viriyu, virugu, viccu, vrīlu (see note 18). In short, all derivative suffixes used in word-formation are traceable to PDr. and no innovations attributable to a post PDr. stage in this regard have yet been discovered.

However, if a group of noncontiguous languages show an identical derivative suffix exclusively, this fact is significant in that the whole form, i.e., root + suffix, rather than the mere root, can be reconstructed for that group of languages; even though the suffix in question is not an innovation, a number of cases of this sort pointing to a large measure of exclusive inheritance can furnish evidence for an early sub-grouping of the languages in question. Cases which have already been treated in chapter II are summarized with references:

(1) The velar, retroflex, and alveolar suffixes have a much wider distribution among the various geographical groups than any other series (§§2.74 ff., 2.92-3).

(2) The derivative suffix series of the type V + lateral, viz., *-al, *-ul, -il/*-aḷ, *-uḷ, *-iḷ (> Te. -alu/-ulu), and -V̆y are exclusive to Te. and SDr. in the majority of cases (§§2.23-4, .31, .59).

(3) It is likely that *-Vr suffix is originally a grammatical suffix with intransitive significance in PDr. The majority of verb-bases with this suffix in SDr. have a neuter or passive connotation; Kur. Mlt. still use them on a morphological level, a feature not to be met with in CDr. This provides a case of exclusive inheritance by SDr. and NDr. (§2.38).

(4) One case of sharing the *-uv suffix and two cases of sharing an *-m suffix occur exclusively between Te. and CDr., see s. v. duvvu (< *ul̲-uv-) (§2.50); us-umu to wash and ad-umu to press (§2.70a.).

(5) A case of *-mp suffix shared by Te., SDr., and CDr. is shown under the etymology of Te. nē-mu to winnow (§2.67).

(6) PDr. *-nt̲ suffix (etymologically -n-t̲ or -nt̲) is shown by CDr. and NDr. in several cases including Te. without parallels from SDr.; v. s. v. eṇḍu to dry; (< *en-t̲), niṇḍu to be filled (< *nin-t̲), vaṇḍu to cook (< *va-nt̲) (§2.100).

## COMPARATIVE MORPHOLOGY

§4.29. Though a study of comparative morphology is outside the scope of this work, certain important features of it are discussed in the following to lend additional support to the conclusions already reached in determining the comparative position of Telugu.

### Nouns: Gender

§4.30. There are two major types of grammatical distinction of gender in Dravidian:

Type I: A two-way distinction in the singular as well as in the plural with two sub-types as follows:

(a) male person sg. : non-male person sg. (i.e., female person and non-person) male person pl. : non-male person pl. (female persons, animals, and inanimate objects)

(b) male person sg. : non-male person sg.

person pl. (male and female persons) : non-person pl. (animals and inanimates)

Type II: A three-way distinction in the singular and a two-way distinction in the plural, viz.

male person sg. : female sg. : non-person sg.

person pl. : non-person pl.

All Central and North Dravidian languages including Telugu belong to type I and the South Dravidian languages belong to type II.[22]

Jules Bloch and Emeneau agree that the gender system occurring in the Central and North Dravidian languages represents the PDr. situation;[23] but Burrow and Bhattacharya think that type II is the PDr. situation and type I is an innovation in CDr. and NDr.[24]

Since all the Dravidian languages agree in having only a two-way distinction in the plural, it is likely that there was also a two-way distinction originally in the singular in Proto-Dravidian. The classification of gender by Tolkāppiyam into uyartiṇai 'high class' and aḥriṇai 'low class' and by the traditional Telugu grammars into mahat and amahat conforms to this line of argument. In the case of the plural the only difference between the SDr. group and the Central and North Dravidian group is in the morphological alignment of the female person.

In SDr. the female person belongs to the person group, whereas in CDr. and NDr. she is assigned to the non-person group. This could be an innovation in SDr. arising out of a situation where mixed groups of men and women had to be grammatically denoted.[25]

§4.31. There are in all Dravidian languages several morphological devices to distinguish the female from the male in both the personal and the animal categories; of these, the addition of a derivative of PDr. *āḷ woman to an abstract adjectival stem is a common construction to distinguish the female person in the singular; e.g.

Te. kōḍalu daughter-in-law (cf. koḍuku son)

Go. koṛiāṛ daughter-in-law

Koṇḍa koṛiyā daughter-in-law or younger brother's wife; cf. koṛo a boy; koṛor children

Kui tōṛenju friend (male)
tōṛali a friend (female)

Pj. podal mother-in-law
koṛol bride

Oll. koṛal daughter-in-law

Nk. koraḷ id.

Klm. koral younger brother's wife

This, in fact, is a small class in CDr., and the majority of nouns derived from adjectival stems denoting a female person are formed by means of the non-person suffixes; e.g.

Te. mancivā̃ḍu a good man
mancidi a good woman or thing

Kui neganju a good man
negari a good woman or thing

Pj. viled a white man
viler white men
vilot a white woman or thing
vilov white women or things

§4.32. Finite verbs, demonstrative pronouns, and the majority of derivative nouns show only the two-way distinction of gender. It is possible that in SDr., extending the addition of the free morpheme āḷ woman (< PDr. *āḷ) to the level of finite verbs and demonstratives is an innovation, in the same way that it was extended to numeral adjectives in the Parji-Kolami sub-group in Central Dravidian.[26] Telugu goes with Central and North Dravidian (type I) in gender distinction in the singular but with SDr. in the plural; e.g.

vā̃ḍu he (male person) : adi (non-male person) she, it
vāru they (person pl. men and/or women) : avi they (non-person pl., those animals or things)

§4.33. This is again indicative of the mid-way position that Telugu occupies between South Dravidian and Central and North Dravidian.

## Nouns: Number

§4.34. The number morphemes which can be reconstructed for PDr. are *-V̆r (*-ar/*-ur/*-ir) for the nouns and demonstratives of the 'high class' and *-(n)kV/*-(V)ḷ/*-(n)kVḷ for those of 'low class.'

The qualities of the vowels in the above reconstructions are hardly uniform in the different Dravidian languages on account of their position in unaccented syllables where they are subject to the influence of vowel harmony; this variation is more pronounced in the languages of Central Dravidian. While the 'high class' plural suffix is more or less uniformly prevalent throughout the whole family, the distribution of the 'low class' plural suffix is somewhat complicated:

| | | | |
|---|---|---|---|
| I | *-(n)ka/(-n)ku : | Go. | -k, -sk/-nk, -ng |
| | | Kui | -ka/-ga, -ṅga, -ska |
| | | Koṇḍa | -ku/-gu, -ŋ/-ŋu, -k/-g |
| | | Brah. | -k, -sk |
| II | *-(V)ḷ/*-(n)kVḷ : | Te. | -lu, -kalu/-kulu |
| | | Tu. | -ḷu, -kuḷu/-guḷu |
| | | Pj. | -l/-ul/-il, -kul |
| | | Klm. | -l, -ul, -kul |
| | | Oll. | -l/-ul/-il, -kil/-gil, -kul/-gul |
| | | Gad. | -l/-ul/-il, -kul/-gul, -kīl/-gīl |
| III | *-(n)kaḷ | Ta. | -kaḷ/-nkaḷ |
| | | Ma. | -kaḷ/-ṅṅaḷ |
| | | Ka. | -kaḷu/-gaḷu |
| | | Ko. | -kūḷ/-gūḷ |

Telugu has a majority of nouns with -lu and only a few where an original *-k(V)ḷ could be discerned:

| sg. | pl. | | |
|---|---|---|---|
| ciluka parrot | cilukalu | : | Ta. kiḷi, pl. kiḷikaḷ |
| eluka rat | elukalu | : | Ta. eli, pl. elikaḷ |
| ēnũgu elephant | ēnũgulu | : | Ta. yāṉai, pl. yāṉaikaḷ |
| nakka jackal | nakkalu | : | Ta. nari, pl. narikaḷ |
| mrānu tree | mrā̃kulu | : | Ta. maram/maraṉ, pl. maraṅkaḷ |

The distribution shown above gives us two clear isoglosses, one uniting Go., Kui-Kuvi, and Brah. with pl. *-(n)k(V) and the other uniting Ta. Ma. Ka. and Ko. with pl. *-(n)kaḷ; we can also get an exclusive isogloss for Telugu, where the plural is from PDr. *-V̌ḷ in over 99 per cent of cases. In this respect Telugu is closer to the Parji-Kolami sub-group of CDr. rather than the Tamil or Kannaḍa sub-group of SDr.

§4.35. There is another plural suffix confined only to Telugu and the Parji sub-group, viz., -til/-tul, e.g.

| | sg. | pl. |
|---|---|---|
| Te. | cēyi hand | cē-tulu |
| | nūyi well | nū-tulu |
| Pj. | vār root | vār-til |
| Oll. | supar tamarind tree | supar-til |
| | kaṇīr tear | kaṇīr-til |

In Telugu this type of plural formation is confined to a small class of neuter nouns ending in -yi.

## Nouns: Inflection

§4.36. In all the Dravidian languages, there are certain sub-classes of the noun in which each number has at least two stems in declension, one an uninflected stem used in the nominative and the second an inflected stem occurring in the oblique cases. In the formation of the inflected stems, a class of suffixes intervenes between the nominal roots and the case-markers. *-t- is one such inflectional suffix of pan-Dravidian distribution, e.g.

| | Nominative stem | Oblique stem |
|---|---|---|
| Ta. | kāṭu forest | kāṭ-ṭ- (< *kāṭ-t-) |
| | nilam ground | nila-tt- |
| To. | neln id. | nel-t- |
| Ka. | maram/maravu | mara-d- (gen., inst., abl., and loc.) |
| Go. | rōn house | rō-t- (acc., dative) |
| | kai hand | kai-d- |
| Kui | kōru buffalo | kōru-ti- (acc., dat.) |
| Pj. | mer tree | mer-to of the tree |
| | key hand | key-to of the hand |
| | polub village | polub-to of the village |
| Oll. | ule house | ule-ṭ- of the house |
| | mar/marin tree | mar-t-in- in the tree |
| Klm. Nk. | ūr | ūr-ut |
| | ella house | ella-t (acc., dat.) |
| Koṇḍa | ayli girl | ayli-di- |
| | no<u>r</u>es tiger | no<u>r</u>es-di- |

§4.37. In Telugu a class of neuter nouns ending in -y(u), -l(u), -r(u), -<u>r</u>(u), and -ḍu adds -ti- to form the oblique stem, e.g.

| | |
|---|---|
| nīru water | nīṭi- (< *nīr-ti-) |
| nūyi well | nū-ti- |
| ē<u>r</u>u stream | ēṭi- (< *ē<u>t</u>-ti-) |
| nā̃ḍu town | nā̃ṭi (< *nāṇṭ-ti-) |
| goḍḍali axe | goḍḍaṭi (< *goḍḍal-ti-) |

Addition of -ti- instead of -t- distinguishes Telugu, Kui, and Koṇḍa from the rest of the languages. It is likely that -*ti- is a combination of two Proto-Dravidian inflectional suffixes *t and *i.

## Pronouns

§4.38. A comparative table of the forms of the 1st person singular is as follows:

| | Nominative | Oblique |
|---|---|---|
| Ta. | yāṉ | eṉ- |
| Tu. | yānu̥ | en- |
| OKa. | ām (ān) | en- |
| Te. | ēnu | ... |
| Kui | ānu | ... |
| Go. | anā/annā | ... |
| Pj. Klm. Nk. Oll. Gad. | ān | an- |
| Kur. Mlt. | ēn | en- |
| Brah. | ī | ... |

All these forms can be traced to two PDr. reconstructions *yān/*yēn : *yan/*yen; variation in the quality of the radical vowels ā/ē indicates the presence of a PDr. *y preceding the vowel, because in this position contrast between ă and ĕ was neutralized in PDr. It should be noted that Te. Kui and Go. do not have oblique forms formally related to their corresponding nominative stems in the table.

§4.39. There is also a different series of forms for the 1st person singular:

| | Nominative | Oblique |
|---|---|---|
| Ta. | nāṉ- | ... |
| Ma. | ñān | |
| Ka. | nānu | nan- |
| Te. | nēnu | nan- (acc.)<br>nā- (other cases) |
| Kui | ... | nā- |
| Go. | nannā (Eastern dialect) | nā- |
| Koṇḍa | nānu | nā- |

These forms arise from PDr. *ñān/*ñēn. The occurrence of ñ- in Ma. (< PDr. *ñ-), together with the fluctuation of the vowel quality provide the basis for this reconstruction. We do not know whether *ñān/*ñēn was a later development from *yăn/*yĕn by incorporating an n from certain preceding environments or an innovation independent of *yān/*yĕn.[27] In any case *ñān/*ñēn should be attributed to the PDr. stage since the derived forms represent languages from both SDr. and CDr.

The oblique stem nā- in Te., Go., Kui, and Koṇḍa derives from *ñān, rather than *yān/*yēn, by dropping the final *n, whereas the rest of the languages base their oblique stems on *yan-/*yen-. In the nominative, the Kui form is traceable to PDr. *yān/*yēn and the Koṇḍa form to PDr. *ñān, whereas Te. and Go. have two forms recorded for nominative sg., one traceable to PDr. *yān/*yēn and the other to PDr. *ñān/*ñēn-.

§4.40. First person plural (exclusive):

| | Nominative | Oblique |
|---|---|---|
| Kui | āmu | mā- (incl.-excl.) |
| Go. | ammaṭ/mammaṭ | mā- " |
| Koṇḍa | māp | mā- " |
| Te. | (ēmu)<br>mēmu | mā-/mam- (excl.); mana- (incl.) |

PDr. *yām-/*yēm- explains the nominative forms of all the languages except the forms beginning with m- in Go., Koṇḍa, and Te. The oblique bases in all these languages presuppose a reconstruction *mām/*māmp- for the nominative. ē in Telugu mēmu could be on the analogy of the vowel in the alternative nominative stem ēm- (< *yām-/*yēm-). *mām/ *māmp is therefore a morphological innovation in the area covered by the ancestral forms of these four languages, probably to distinguish this form from the inclusive plural *nām-. Telugu inclusive plural manamu seems to have resulted from a contamination of mā(m) + nām; shortening of the medial long vowel is in conformity with the syllable systems of Telugu.

§4.41. Second person singular:

| | Nominative | Oblique |
|---|---|---|
| Ta. | nī | nin̲- |
| OKa. | nīn | nin- |
| Tu. | . . . | nin- |
| Kur.<br>Malto | nīn | nin- |
| Brah. | nī | nē-/n- |
| Te. | nīvu | nin- (acc.) |
| Koṇḍa | nīnu | nī- |
| Te. | . . . | nī- |
| Kui | . . . | nī- |
| Go. | . . . | nī- |
| Klm.<br>Nk. | nīv (? l. w. < Te.) | . . . |

These forms can be traced to PDr. *nīn : *nin in contradistinction to the following which arise from PDr. *īn : *in-:

| | Nominative | Oblique |
|---|---|---|
| Tu. | ī | ... |
| Kui | īnu | ... |
| Go. | immā | ... |
| Pj. | īn | in- |
| Oll. | īn | in- |
| Gad. | īn | in- |
| Klm. | ... | in- |
| Nk. | ... | in- |

Go. -m is an aberration, presumably the plural morpheme being used honorifically in the singular.

In line with the construction of the other personal pronouns, Te., Go., Kui, and Koṇḍa share the common innovation of forming the oblique stem by dropping the final consonant of the nominative, i.e., nī- (< *nīn). It is mainly in CDr. that loss of initial n occurs, and Telugu by virtue of its forms nīvu/īvu partakes of the characteristics of both SDr. and CDr. However, in the formation of the oblique it aligns itself with the Gondi-Kui-Koṇḍa sub-group of CDr.

§4.42. Second person plural:

| | Nominative | Oblique |
|---|---|---|
| OTe. | īru<br>mīru (Old and Modern) | mim- (acc.)/mī- (elsewhere) |
| Kui<br>Kuvi | īru<br>mīmbu | mī- |
| Go. | (immaṭ) | mī- |
| Koṇḍa | mīr | mī- |

The forms from the other languages can be explained in terms of PDr. *nīm/*īm : *nim-/*im-, the distribution being parallel to that of the singular forms. Since Te., Kui, Go., and Koṇḍa drop the final consonant, which is the plural marker, in forming the oblique stem, it is likely that they all shifted the plural marker *-m in *nīm from its final position to the initial in order to keep it distinct from the 2nd person singular oblique base *nī-.[28]

The divergent nominative forms are apparently independent developments in each of these languages. The m-initial forms in the nominative are probably back-formations from the oblique stem. This explains the existence of doublets in the nominative in Telugu and the Kui-Kuvi subgroup.

§4.43. Telugu has two oblique stems for each of the personal pronouns, viz., nan-/nā- (1 sg.), mam-/mā- (1 pl. excl.), nin-/nī- (2 sg.), mim-/mī- (2 pl.); of these nan-, mam-, nin-, mim- occur in the accusative, and nā-, mā-, nī-, mī- in all other cases.

A more common formation of the oblique stem in personal pronouns seems to be by shortening the nominative stem-vowel; all Dravidian languages except Gondi, Kui-Kuvi, and Koṇḍa retain this type. The formation of the oblique stem by dropping the final consonant of the nominative form is therefore a morphological innovation in this major sub-group of CDr., which is also shared by Telugu as shown by one series of the oblique bases. Besides, Telugu also preserves the common Dravidian type in the other series, viz., nan-, mam-, nin-, mim-. Even here, the initial m- in the plural forms mam- (1 pl. excl.) and mim- is an innovation under the influence of the second series of doublets, mā- and mī-. The weight of evidence of the personal pronouns is therefore in favor of grouping Telugu with the major sub-group of Gondi-Kui-Kuvi-Koṇḍa of Central Dravidian.

§4.44. The distribution of the 3rd person masculine singular forms in the various languages provides two PDr. reconstructions: (1) *avan, (2) *avanṯ. The forms occurring in Telugu and in the Central and North Dravidian languages derive from PDr. *avanṯ; the forms in the SDr. languages derive from PDr. *avan-[29] (-ṯ in avanṯ is probably the nominative singular suffix).

PDr. *avanṯ

| | Nominative | Oblique |
|---|---|---|
| OTe. | vā̃ḍu (< OTe. vāṇḍu, vānṟu) | vān- |
| Koṇḍa | vānṟu | vān- |
| Kui | aanju | aan- |
| Go. | ōl, ōr | ōn- |
| Pj. | ōd | ōn- |
| Oll. Gad. | ōnḍ | ōn- |
| Klm. | amd/avnd (dial.) | amn-/avn- |
| Kur. | ? ās | |
| Tu. | ? āye | |

It is also likely that Ta. and the other SDr. languages lost the nominative sg. suffix -ṯ in PDr. *avanṯ in the same way that Ta. lost the final -n in *nīn you (sg.) in the nominative.

## Numerals

§4.45. The comparative vocabulary for the numeral one yields three reconstructions: *on-ṯ-, *ōr/*or-V- and *ok-. Of these the first two are common to all the Dravidian languages; *on-ṯ- denotes non-personal number and *ōr/*or-V- denotes personal number. The third one *ok- occurs only in CDr. in Go. and the Pj.-Klm. sub-group, with the isogloss also including Telugu; i.e.

| | | |
|---|---|---|
| Te. | okkāḍu | one person (or thing) |
| | okkaṭi | one thing |
| | okkate | one woman |
| | okka-/oka- | one (adjective) |
| Go. | okō, okōrē | one each |
| Pj. | ok- | one |
| | okur/okuri | one man |
| | okal/okali | one woman |
| | okat/okti | one thing |
| Klm. | okkon | one man |
| | okkod | one woman or thing |
| Nk. | okko, okkon | one man |
| | okkod | one woman or thing |
| Oll. | uku | one man |
| | ukuṭ/okuṭ | one woman or thing |
| Gad. | okkur | one man |
| | okkal | one woman |
| | okkuḍ | one (animal or thing) |

This is an exclusive case of relationship between Telugu and the Pj.-Klm. sub-group of Central Dravidian.

## Verbs

§4.46. There are two types of structural relation between the intransitive and transitive or causative verb stems in Dravidian:

Type I: Nasal + stop combination in the final syllable of the intransitive base alternating with stop + stop combination in the transitive (or causative) base; or a voiced stop with or without a preceding homorganic nasal alternating with the corresponding voiceless stop (single or double). This may be shown in a formula thus:

| Intransitive | : | Transitive |
|---|---|---|
| NP | | PP |
| (N)B | | (P)P |

(P = any voiceless stop; B = any voiced stop; N = nasal homorganic with the following stop)

Type II: Addition to or substitution for the final syllable of the intransitive stem of a morpheme of transition or causation, viz., *t, *c, or *p, or one of these with a preceding or following i-vowel: *it, *ip, *ic; *pi. Examples for the two types:

Type I

| | Intransitive | Transitive |
|---|---|---|
| Ta. | aṭaṅku to become compressed | aṭakku to compress |
| Ma. | aṭaṅṅuka to become compressed | aṭakkuka to compress |
| Ka. | aḍagu/aḍaṅgu to be contained | aḍaku to press |
| To. | tïrx- to turn | tïrk- to turn |
| | tïrb- to be twisted | tïrp- to turn the key |
| Ko. | tirg- to turn | tirk- to twist or turn |
| Kui | niṅg- to rise | nipk- (< *nik-p-; past nik-t-) |
| | ḍūmb- to be shrunken | ḍūpp- (past ḍūp-t-) |
| Koṇḍa | niŋ- to rise from bed | nik- to wake up |

The occurrence of the type II construction is more widely prevalent in Telugu and the Central and North Dravidian languages, though traces of its occurrence can also be discerned in South Dravidian.

Type II

| | Intransitive | Transitive |
|---|---|---|
| | *-t | |
| OTa. | vāl̲ to flourish | vāl̲-tt- to cause to flourish |
| | ōṭu to run | ōṭṭ- (< *ōṭ-t-) to cause to run |
| Ta. Ma. | tur̲u to be stuffed | tur̲u-tt- to stuff |
| To. | ōḍ- to move violently | ōṭ- (< *ōḍ-t-) to shake violently |
| Tu. | tirng- to revert | tir-d- to turn |
| Kui | aḍ- to be joined | aṭ- (< *aḍ-t-) to join |
| | sōl- to enter | sōṛ- to usher |
| | tin- to eat | tis- (< *tin-t̲-) to feed |
| Klm. | un- to drink | ur-t- to give to drink |
| | ōḍ- to burst | ōṭ- to smash |
| Kur. | ēg- to go | ēk-t- to send |
| | ōn- to drink | ōn-t- to make to drink |

| | Intransitive | Transitive |
|---|---|---|
| | | *-p |
| Ka. | tirigu to go round | tiri-pu to turn round |
| Tu. | aḍeṅg- to be shut | aḍe-p- to shut |
| Te. | jarugu to slip or move off | jaru-pu- to move, shift |
| Kui | puh- to be wet | puh-p- to make wet |
| Koṇḍa | ḍāŋ- to be hidden | ḍā-p- to hide |
| Klm. | ḍāŋg- to be hidden | ḍā-p- to hide |
| | tari- (fire) burns | tar-p- to light fire |
| Oll. | iṛg- to descend | iṛig-p- to dismount |
| | | *-c/s |
| Te. | kālu to be burnt | kāl-c- to burn |
| | amaru to be ready | amar-c- to make ready |
| Ka. | ba<u>l</u>al to be tired | ba<u>l</u>al-c- to tire |
| | a<u>l</u>i to perish | a<u>l</u>i-s- to cause to perish |
| Kui | kānd- to be hot | kā-s- (past kās-t-) to heat |
| | nōv- to be in pain | no-s- (past nos-t-) to pain |
| | | *-c + *-t |
| Go. | huṛ- to see | huṛ-st- to show |
| | warī- to fear | war-uht- (< *-ust-) to frighten |
| | arr- to fall | ar-hutt- (< *-sutt-) to let fall |
| | | *-is/*-inc |
| Ka. | nagu to laugh | nag-is- to cause to laugh |
| | kēḷ to hear | kēḷ-is- to cause to hear |
| Te. | āḍu to shake or play | āḍ-inc- to cause to play, to move |
| Koṇḍa | piṇḍ- to carry | piṇḍ-is- to cause to carry |
| | | *-ip |
| Pj. | tuñ- to sleep | tuñ-ip- to put to sleep |
| | panḍ- to be tired | panḍ-ip- to tire |
| Klm. | ud- to sit | ud-ip- to seat |
| | | *-pi |
| Ta. | naṭa- to walk | naṭa-ppi- to make to walk |
| | eṇ- to count | eṇ-pi- to let count |
| | kaṭṭu to build | kaṭṭu-vi- to cause to build |
| Koṇḍa | uṇ- to drink | ūṭ-pis- to make to drink |
| Te. | vin- to hear | vin-p-inc- to cause to hear, i.e., to tell; Mod. Te. vinipis- id. |

Telugu, Central Dravidian (except Kui-Kuvi-Koṇḍa), and the North Dravidian languages are characterized by the absence of the Type I construction. This provides us with additional evidence to class Telugu with the Central and North Dravidian group of languages. There is evidence that both types were present in PDr., but Type I mainly was prevalent in the area occupied by the present SDr. languages and Type II in that of CDr. and NDr. including Telugu. Kui is enclosed by both the major isoglosses. There is, therefore, overlapping of the two isoglosses in the CDr. area with NDr. and SDr. outside the overlapping zone.

§4.47. Another isogloss that unites Te. with CDr. is the original use of a c-morpheme in the formation of the past participle in some of the class II verbs (§§3.27 ff.).[30] Gondi, Koṇḍa, Parji, Ollari, and Gadaba, together with Telugu, use -ci as the past participial morpheme.

| | Past participle | Verbal base |
|---|---|---|
| Te. | va-cci having come | war-/rā- |
| Go. | tin-jī having eaten | tin- to eat |
| | wā-sī having come | wāi- to come |
| Koṇḍa | suṛ-zi having seen | suṛ- to see |
| | wā-zi having come | wā-/ra- to come |
| Pj. | nil-ci having stood | nil- to stand |
| Oll. | tin-zi having eaten | tin- to eat |
| Gad. | in-ji having said, being so | in- to say |

The c-past occurs throughout the whole family, but it is more widely prevalent in Kur. Mlt. and Brah. in NDr., and in Pj. Oll. Gad. Go. and Te. in CDr. However, the occurrence of *-ci as the past-participial morpheme characterizes only the CDr. languages, Te. Go. Koṇḍa Pj. Oll. Gad.

§4.48. One more exclusive feature that establishes a closer genetic affinity between Telugu on one hand and Kui-Koṇḍa on the other is the construction of the person morpheme in the imperative plural in verbs:

| | sg. | pl. |
|---|---|---|
| OTe. | -mu | -(ṇ)ḍu or -ḍu |
| | koṭṭu-mu beat (you, sg.) | koṭṭū-ḍu/koṭṭuNḍu beat (you, pl.) |
| Kui | -umu | -tu/-ṭu, etc. |
| | tin-umu | tin-ju (< *tin-ṯ-); tin- to eat |
| | pāṇ-umu | pāṇḍu (< *pāṇ-ṭ-); pāṇ- to obtain |
| | sal-umu | saju (< *can-ṯ-/caṯ-t-); sal- to go |
| Koṇḍa | -ʔa | -du/-ḍu/-ṟu |
| | raʔa | radu; ra- to come |
| | kiʔa | kidu; ki- to do |
| | kolʔa | koṇḍu (< *koṇ-ṭ-); kol-/kon- to buy |
| | sonʔa | sonṟu (< *son-ṯ-); son- to go |

It is clear that the morpheme of the imperative 2nd person plural is historically *tu with several sandhi alternants. It is likely that in pre-

Telugu *-tu (-du), occurring after n-final bases as *-ṉṯu/*-ṉḏu (> Te. -ṇḍu), was carried over to the rest of the system by analogical leveling. An alternative but less likely explanation is that *-nṯ(u) was the original morpheme preserved in Telugu as -ṇḍ(u), of which the preconsonantal nasal was lost in pre-Koṇḍa and pre-Kui. In the imperative singular, Telugu and Kui, but not Koṇḍa, share the identical morpheme -mu.

§4.49. Telugu and Parji share an identical morpheme in the formation of the negative participle, viz., -aka (§§3.7); e.g.

| | | |
|---|---|---|
| Te. | īya-ka | not giving |
| | koṭṭ-aka | not beating |
| | rā-ka | not coming |
| Pj. | cīy-aka | not giving |
| | ver-aka | not coming |

It is likely that this -k- may reconstruct to an older /?/ (glottal stop) occurring in the negative tense formation of Kui-Kuvi and Koṇḍa.

## Conclusion

§4.50. The use of terms 'retention' or 'innovation' is not technically justified in comparative morphology any more than in comparative phonology. With successive changes in the speech habits of people, phonetic changes which have no relation to the phonological set-up of the proto-language can take place even in the individual languages independently, i.e., in such a way that the phonetic changes cannot be predicted from an understanding of the phonemic system of the proto-language. But native morphemes having grammatical functions in the different daughter languages are theoretically a part of the inherited proto-system. Innovations, if any, could be in the structuring or ordering of the morphemes rather than in the morphemes themselves. For instance, in the Telugu-Kui-Koṇḍa-Gondi sub-group of Central Dravidian, the occurrence of *mā- (1 pl. obl.) and *mī- (2 pl. obl.) instead of *nam- and *nim- as elsewhere in the Dravidian languages, is interpreted as an innovation (§§ 4.40-42). But here the innovation is only in shifting the position of the plural marker *m from the final to the initial (§4.42) rather than in the plural marker itself, namely *m, which is admittedly a Proto-Dravidian plural morpheme in personal pronouns.

The following chart is designed to show the distribution of the PDr. morphological features in the different languages. The direction in which Telugu shares a given feature with the other sub-groups is indicated by a small arrow. The weight of comparative evidence discussed in some detail in this chapter is in favor of considering Telugu as an off-shoot of the Central Dravidian branch of proto-Dravidian with very intimate genetic relationship with the Kui-(Kuvi)-Koṇḍa sub-group. Since it has also several exclusive features in common with South Dravidian in phonology rather than in morphology, it may be considered that Telugu has been in intimate geographical contact with the members of South Dravidian from a very remote past. The morphological evidence puts it rather conclusively with Central Dravidian. The relationship between Telugu and North Dravidian has not clearly emerged from this study on account of the limitations on the material taken for comparison as well as the scope of the treatment in this chapter.

## DISTRIBUTION OF PROTO-DRAVIDIAN MORPHOLOGICAL FEATURES

| PDr. | 1 To. | 2 Ko. | 3 Tu. | 4 Ka. | 5 Ma. | 6 Ta. | 7 Te. | 8 Kui | 9 Koṇḍa | 10 Go. | 11 Klm. | 12 Nk. | 13 Pj. | 14 Oll. | 15 Gad. | 16 Kur. | 17 Mlt. | 18 Br. |
|---|---|---|---|---|---|---|---|---|---|---|---|---|---|---|---|---|---|---|
| **Noun:** | | | | | | | | | | | | | | | | | | |
| 1. Gender | | | | | | | | | | | | | | | | | | |
| Type I | | --- | --- | --- | --- | --- | --- | | | | | | | | | | | |
| Type II | | | | | | | ⟶ --- | --- | --- | --- | --- | --- | --- | --- | --- | --- | --- | |
| 2. Number (pl.) | | | | | | | | | | | | | | | | | | |
| i. *-(n)ka/-(n)ku | | | | | | | | --- | --- | --- | | | | | | | | --- |
| ii. *-Vḷ | | | --- | | | | ⟶ --- | | | | --- | --- | --- | --- | --- | | | |
| iii. *-(n)kVḷ | | --- | --- | --- | --- | --- | (. . .) | | | | --- | --- | --- | --- | --- | | | |
| iv. *-til/*-tul | | | | | | | ⟶ --- | | | | | | --- | --- | --- | | | |
| 3. Inflexional suffix | | | | | | | | | | | | | | | | | | |
| *-t | --- | --- | --- | --- | --- | --- | | | | --- | --- | --- | --- | --- | --- | | | |
| *-ti | | | | | | | ⟶ --- | --- | --- | | | | | | | | | |
| **Pronoun:** | | | | | | | | | | | | | | | | | | |
| 4. i. I sg. | | | | | | | | | | | | | | | | | | |
| a. nom. *yān/*yēn | --- | --- | --- | --- | --- | --- | --- | --- | | --- | --- | --- | --- | --- | --- | --- | --- | --- |
| a. obl. *yan/*yen | --- | --- | --- | --- | --- | --- | | | | | --- | --- | --- | --- | --- | --- | --- | |
| b. nom. *ñān/*ñēn | | | | --- | --- | --- | --- | | --- | --- | | | | | | | | |
| b. obl. *ñā | | | | | | | ⟶ --- | --- | --- | --- | | | | | | | | |
| ii. I pl. obl. *mā | | | | | | | ⟶ --- | --- | --- | --- | | | | | | | | |

| | | | | | | | | | | | | | | | | | | |
|---|---|---|---|---|---|---|---|---|---|---|---|---|---|---|---|---|---|---|
| iii. II sg. | | | | | | | | | | | | | | | | | | |
| nom. : obl. | | | | | | | | | | | | | | | | | | |
| *nīn : *nin- | - - - | - - - | - - - | - - - | - - - | - - - | | | | | | | | | | - - - | - - - | - - - |
| *īn : *in- | | | | | | | | - - - | | - - - | - - - | - - - | - - - | - - - | - - - | | | |
| *nī(n) : *nī- | | | | | | | → | - - - | - - - | - - - | | | | | | | | |
| iv. II pl. | | | | | | | | | | | | | | | | | | |
| nom. : obl. | | | | | | | | | | | | | | | | | | |
| *īr/*mīr : *mī- | | | | | | | → | - - - | - - - | - - - | | | | | | | | |
| *nīm : *nim- | - - - | - - - | - - - | - - - | - - - | - - - | | | | | | | | | | - - - | - - - | |
| *īm : *im- | | | | | | | | | | - - - | - - - | - - - | - - - | - - - | - - - | | | |
| v. III m. sg. | | | | | | | | | | | | | | | | | | |
| *avanṯ | | | | | | | → | - - - | - - - | - - - | - - - | - - - | - - - | - - - | - - - | ? | ? | |
| *avan | | - - - | - - - | - - - | - - - | - - - | | | | | | | | | | | | |
| **Numerals:** | | | | | | | | | | | | | | | | | | |
| 5. *onṯ | - - - | - - - | - - - | - - - | - - - | - - - | - - - | - - - | - - - | - - - | | | | | | - - - | - - - | |
| *ok | | | | | | | → | | | - - - | - - - | - - - | - - - | - - - | - - - | | | |
| **Verbs:** | | | | | | | | | | | | | | | | | | |
| 6. Past participle *-ci | | | | | | | → | | - - - | - - - | | | - - - | - - - | - - - | | | |
| 7. Imp. II. sg. *-m(u) | | | | | | | → | - - - | | | | | | | | | | |
| pl. *-t(u) | | | | | | | → | - - - | - - - | | | | | | | | | |
| 8. Neg. participle *-ak | | | | | | | → | | | | | | - - - | - - - | - - - | | | |

## NOTES TO CHAPTER IV

[1]Telugu is included in SDr. as well as CDr. since it is geographically contiguous to both the groups. Linguistically there is more evidence to put it with the CDr. group, though it shares several phonological and morphological innovations exclusively with SDr. Arguments are advanced in this chapter for considering Telugu as an off-shoot of the major branch of CDr.

[2]Many of the linguistic sub-groups tentatively set up here are obvious to scholars working in the field of comparative Dravidian. Evidence for setting up the Ta.-Ma.? sub-group can be found in L. V. Ramaswami Aiyar's The Evolution of Malayalam Morphology (1936) and A. C. Sekhar's Evolution of Malayalam (Poona, 1951). Toda and Kota have intimate genetic affinity and compare as a set with ancient Tamil (see M. B. Emeneau, Toda, A Dravidian Language, TPS 1957, pp. 15-66). Discussion on the problem of Toda-Kota relationship was postponed by Emeneau (see §59), but his evidence in §§31, 38, 52, 65 of the paper points to the possibility of putting these together into a sub-group which compares with pre-Tamil rather than with pre-Kannada (see ibid., §58). The Ka.-Badaga-Koḍ. sub-group is set up rather ad hoc than on tested evidence. My own meagre knowledge of Badaga and Koḍagu materials points to this suggestion. A sub-grouping of Klm.-Nk.-Pj.-Oll.-Gad. is now fairly established (for a detailed discussion, see Emeneau, Kolami, A Dravidian Language, chap. X, pp. 141-163; this was suggested earlier by Burrow and Bhattacharya, The Parji Language, p. xi). The sub-groups Kui-Kuvi and Kurukh-Malto are fairly apparent to comparative Dravidianists, though nowhere has this problem been discussed in earlier writings. Tulu and Brahui stand by themselves. There seems to be considerable justification for considering Tu. as an independent off-shoot of PCDr. (see §§4.34, .41); of course, this problem is of little concern to us here. The position of Go. in CDr. has still to be worked out when more reliable linguistic data on some Gondi dialects and also on the still unrecorded tribal languages of Central Dravidian are available.

[3]See Burrow and Bhattacharya, op. cit., p. xi; Emeneau (review) Language 34. 161 (1958); my own field-notes on a Koṇḍa dialect in Araku Valley (1958) have shown that it is closer to the Kui-Kuvi sub-group than to Gondi.

[4]Relative to the other two types, this type represents only a small class of PDr. forms; e.g., *en-ṯ- sunshine; *on-ṯ- one (numeral); for more information, see §1.161-5.

[5]The non-morphemic u occurring word-finally in Old Telugu is not shown since its occurrence is phonologically conditioned, i.e., -u[C ~ Ø]V̆, where C or V̆ begin the following word.

[6]PDr. stop consonants occurring after a long vowel in root syllables have the same correspondences in Te. as the intervocalic stops, i.e., *pāṭ- to sing: Te. pāḍu, but *kaṭ- to build: Te. kaṭṭu.

[7]Details regarding the phonological developments included in this chart can be found under the history of the respective phonemes of Telugu in Chapter I.

[8]The Toda developments of PDr. *ḻ are too many to be indicated on the chart (see Emeneau, Toda, a Dravidian Language, loc. cit., §§62-64 (pp. 51-57); so also are the developments in Kota.

[9]For the structural details regarding these developments, see §§1.121-.159. The Northern dialect of Koṇḍa also has items with methathesis while the Southern

and South Eastern dialects do not have them; e.g.

| Sovva-Gazba dial. (Orissa border) | Araku Valley dial. |
|---|---|
| mrānu tree, pl. mrāku | maran, pl. marak |
| pṛivu worm, pl. pṛīku | piṛvu, pl. piṛku |
| gr̲ōnu hill, pl. gr̲ōku | gor̲on, pl. gor̲ok |

[10]See §§1.267-.280.

[11]Also see Emeneau, Toda, A Dravidian Language (loc. cit.), §31.

[12]Ibid., §65.

[13]Early Telugu inscriptions (5th to 9th century, A.D.) preserve PDr. *ḻ *ṉ distinctly. Ollari still preserves PDr. *ṉ (see Bhattacharya, Ollari, A Dravidian speech, p. 7); Naiki has ḷ (< *ḻ) after all the back vowels (Emeneau, Kolami, p. 144. §10.19); Gondi has ṛ/r/l for PDr. *ḻ in different dialects; Koṇḍa has ṉ (< *ṉ), and ṛ/l dialectally for *ḻ.

[14]Koṇḍa is the only exception which still preserves PDr. ṯ in all environments, e.g., vānr̲u he (< *avan-ṯ, see §4.44); ēr̲u water (< *yāṯ-/*yēṯ-); vaR- to dry (< *vaṯṯ-). /R/ is a voiceless alveolar trill pronounced [r̲ʰ], which is phonemically distinct from /r̲/ voiced alveolar trill.

[15]A detailed account of the distribution of the reflexes of PDr. *ṯ in different combinations is given by Emeneau, Kolami, §10.25 (pp. 151-153); see also Burrow and Bhattacharya, The Parji Language, §7, pp. 4, 5.

[16]L. Bloomfield, Language, §§18. 11-12, pp. 314-318; C. F. Hockett, A Course in Modern Linguistics (1958); pp. 521, 522.

[17]The items are listed below. The underlined numbers have cognates and the rest occur in Telugu alone. Numbers refer to the serial numbers of items in Part II: takku (521), ḍukku (506), ḍokku (513), saṇugu (1216), saggu (1214), lācu[1] (1107), vācu (1150), saīcu (1227), maduru (940), caduru (407), cemaru (467), saḍalu (1215), prabalu (893), ḍīlu (569), jār̲u (488), moṭṭu (1050), paḍu (784), lōḍu (1117), pagaṭu (779), oḍḍu (119), loḍupu (1115), sarudu (1219), car̲acu (413).

[18]For a given group of more than one etymologically related verbal bases in Telugu (all deriving from a single Proto-Dravidian root but having different derivative suffixes), if one or more Dravidian languages possess a single series of cognates, then the whole group in Telugu is treated under a single etymology. That member of the group in Telugu, which has the closest phonetic-semantic resemblance to the cognates selected from the other languages is the one that counts in the group, the remaining items being considered redundant. E.g. (the number in parentheses refers to the serial number of the item in Part II):

nog-ulu (769) to be afflicted, to grieve;
no-ccu (770) to ache, suffer, to grieve;
nōyu (777) to suffer, etc.

These three bases are obviously members of an etymological group within Te. deriving from a PDr. *nŏy-, followed by the suffixes -ul, -cc in the first two cases and by none in the third. There is only a single series of cognates in the other Dravidian languages corresponding to these 3 forms in Telugu; parallel forms with suffixes -ul and -cc are lacking in the rest of the Dravidian languages. Therefore only one base, i:e., nōyu, among these three counts for comparison and the remaining two entries are considered redundant, since they are presumably independent formations in Telugu on the PDr. base *nŏy-. In other words, the same set of cognates has to be repeated for nogulu and noccu as for nōyu. It is to avoid repetition in the count of the cognates that the two items in Telugu are considered redundant.

On the contrary, among a group of related bases in Telugu, as many items count for comparison as there are structurally comparable series of cognates for them in the other languages, e.g.

(1) viccu (1161), tr. to untie, loosen; intr. to blossom, to break, burst open [Ka. biccu, bircu to untie; be open, broken; Tu. biccuni id.]

(2) viriyu (1172), intr. to open; blossom, as flower; to break, burst; be scattered [Ta. viri, intr. to expand, spread out; tr. to open, split; untie; Ma. viriyuka to blow; virikka to expand; To. pïry- tr. to open; Ka. biri to burst open; to blossom; Tu. biriyuni id.; Kur. bird- to pierce, break; Brah. birr- v.i. to separate out.]

(3) virugu (1173) to break or go to pieces [Kui vriṅga to be loosened; to disperse; vripk- (< vrik-p-; past vrik-t-) to untie; briṅgna to be dispersed by; Pj. viriŋg- to be loosened.]

(4) vrīlu (1210) to go to pieces; to crack [Kui vrīva (vrī-t-) to fall to pieces; Kuvi brī- to topple over.]

These four series of etyma are derivable from a PDr. root *vir- + a number of divergent suffixes. Nevertheless, for each Te. base, there is a parallel series of cognates with much the same structural composition, making it possible to reconstruct a PDr. form for that series. Therefore in this case all the four bases count for comparison.

[19]Even if a single member of a sub-group has a cognate for a given Telugu item, it is assumed that the relationship is between Te. and the whole sub-group. As the members of a sub-group are more closely related among themselves than any one of them and Telugu, the relationship should be traced to the pre-separation stage of each sub-group and Telugu. It is likely that the other members of a sub-group have lost the corresponding forms, if only one member shows a cognate for a given Telugu item.

In evaluating the cognates, all doubtful forms and cross-language borrowings have been meticulously eliminated from the count.

[20]§§4.38, .41.

[21]Emeneau, "Dravidian Kinship Terms," Language 29.345. (§§16-18).

[22]Emeneau, Kolami, §10.17. Toda and Brahui distinguish only number but not gender; they are therefore outside the present analysis; see also "Toda, A Dravidian Language," loc. cit., p. 65.

[23]Jules Bloch, The Grammatical Structure of Dravidian Languages (translated into English), p. 5; Emeneau, Kolami, §10.17.

[24]The Parji Language, op. cit., p. 8, §13.

[25]Jules Bloch, op. cit., p. 7.

[26]The Parji Language, §54, p. 36; Emeneau, Kolami, §10.4, p. 142.

[27]This at least is morphophonemically possible in Ancient Tamil (Tolk. Eḻut. 147), also see §1.31. An alternative suggestion is that the alternative 1sg. form nāŋ in Ta. etc. is a back formation from the PDr. 1st person inclusive form reconstructed as *nām- (see Burrow DS V, p. 597, and fn. 9). The difficulty in accepting this suggestion is the unexplained correspondence of PDr. *n-: Ma. ñ-. We should have therefore, to reconstruct *ñām- for the inclusive plural, but the comparative etyma support only *n- and not *ñ-.

[28]This interpretation equally holds good for the formation of 1 pl. mā- instead of nā-, §4.40.

[29]See Emeneau, Kolami, §10.15, pp. 146, 147.

[30]See §§2.42-.46; .85-87; Emeneau has treated the distribution of PDr. past morpheme *c in the various Dravidian languages, see "Toda, A Dravidian Language," loc. cit., §§39-56.

# PART II
# AN ETYMOLOGICAL INDEX OF VERBAL BASES

# AN ETYMOLOGICAL INDEX OF VERBAL BASES

## A

1 agalu* (1) intr. to leave, depart; to be diminished, to break down (as courage or strength in war) (Bhr.)

[Ka. agal, agalu, (agaḷ, agulu, allu, aḷḷu) to separate from; go away from; to part; become loose; to leave; agalcu to remove from; abandon; Tu. agapuni v.i. to remove, depart; v.tr. to separate, extend; agapelu̥ separation, despatch; Ta. akal v.i. to leave, vanish (PN); part; spread, widen (PN); akar̲r̲u v.tr. to remove, expel; widen; Ma. akaluka become extended; to part; akalca separation; distance; akar̲r̲uka v.tr. to remove, put away; Mlt. ekalare to be separated, to be alone; PSDr. *ay-al- : *ãy-; cf. CDr. *cãy- : Klm.(SR) sãy, Klm.(E) say- to leave, let go; Nk. sãy- leave, abandon; Pj. cãy id.; Oll. sãy-; KGad. sãy-.]

agalu* (2) intr. to break, go to pieces (Bhr. II).

[Ka. agal, agalu to go to pieces; Ta. akai to be broken, crumbled; tr. cut into pieces.]

2 agu V intr. to be, become; prove to be; to be proper, agreeable (Bhr. I); alt. avu, au̯; allom. ay-, āy, *kā-; vb. adj. suffixed to cardinal numbers to form ordinals, e.g., padi(y)agu tenth, with alt. -avu, -ava, Mdn. Te. -ō, pad-ō- (Caldwell[3], pp. 355, 356).

[Ka. āgu, agu (alt. ā, āy-, akk-) id.; Tu. āpini; Ko. āy- (āc-) to become; āk- to make to become, construct, ākc- id. (alt. āy-, ān-, ā-); To. ōx- (ōy-, ōn-, ō-) to become; Ta. ā (āy-in̲-/ā-n̲-); āku v.i., ākku v.tr.; Ma. āku v.i., ākku v.tr.; Kui āva to become, be, happen, be finished, etc.; n. being, etc., Kuvi(F) aiyali (ā-t-) id.; Kuvi(S) ā'- to last, occur; Go. ai- (ā-st-). All these forms point to PDr. *ā-, *āy-; certain languages of CDr. and NDr. point to another base *ǎṇ-, cf. Klm. an- (an-ḍ-) to be in a place, belong to, etc.; imper. ān-; Nk. anḍ- to be (LSI, IV, p. 572), ant- (p. 573); Brah. ann- to be (alt. an-, ar-, as-, a-); see Kolami 18. On account of retroflex d in Klm. Nk., n cannot be a part of past -in, occurring in SDr. Emeneau suggests contamination of ā- with uṇ-/uḷ- to be (see Kolami §2.55, p. 25). All that we can be certain of is that there are two bases here meaning 'to be,' viz., *ā-, *ǎṇ-.]

3 aṅku intr. (colloq.) to come to hand, be obtained (Viśākhapatnam; also listed in SAN).

[Ka. akku v.i. to subdue, to seize, retain possession.]

4 accu[1] intr. to pay (taxes) SII IV, No. 1281 (UH, Vijñ.); cf. ari tax; Mdn. Te. accu to owe, owe unjustly; stand security; appu loan, debt; aruvu id.; v.s.v. aruvu.

[Ka. accu to pay unjustly (as rent for land on which crop has failed); Ko. ark- to use up extravagantly; (father) refuses to repay bride price; Ta. ari tax, duty (Piṅ.); appu loan, debt (l.w. < Te.).]

5 accu[2] intr. to prove auspicious, desirable (colloq., author's dial., always used with the verb 'to come' vaccu), e.g., accirālǣ (a custom, a practice) hasn't turned out to be desirable, auspicious; acc(i)-occindi it turned out to be auspicious, etc.; prob. related to naccu to be agreeable, q.v.

6 aḍāgu/aṇāgu intr. to yield, submit; to be concealed, contained; be suppressed, humbled (Bhr. I, II); to perish (UH, Bhr. II); tr. aḍācu/aṇācu; cf. ḍāgu to be hidden.

[Ka. aḍagu, aḍaṅgu to conceal oneself, be contained; to decrease; aḍaku to press, subdue, control; aḍacu, aḍasu id.; aḍe to be enclosed, shut up; to close, shut in; Tu. aḍeṅguni v.i. to be shut, close; aḍepuni id.; aḍēyuni, aḍēvuni to hide; Ta. aṭaṅku to obey, yield (Kṟḷ.); become compressed; aṭakku to control, hide; aṭai v.tr. to shut, close (PN); Ma. aṭaṅṅuka v.i. id.; v.tr. aṭakkuka; aṭekka to shut; Kui āṭpa/āṟpa to hide, conceal; Brah. aḍ sheltered; shelter.]

aḍācu IIb tr. of aḍāgu; to subdue; hide (Bhr. II, Kāś.), v.s.v. aḍāgu.

7 aḍaru[1*] intr. to be fit, proper (Bhr. I); to be prepared (Bhr. II); to increase, spread (Bhr. II).

[Ka. aḍar to be united with, be joined to; to ascend, rise; aḍarcu to bring together, prepare; aḍavu suitableness; Ta. aṭu to be fit, becoming; aṭar v.i. to be close, thick, crowded (Maṇi.).]

8 ḍaru[2*] to burn, shine; n. grief, sorrow, v.s.v. aḍalu[1].

9 aḍalu[1] intr. to be distressed, to grieve (Bhīm.), n. grief (Bhr. II).

[Ka. aḻal to grieve, be afflicted, n. mental heat, grief; aḻaṭu to be in affliction; Tu. arluni v.i. to burn, blaze; to smart; Ko. aṟc- (flame) shoots up; make a flame shoot up; Ta. aḻal to burn, glow (PN), n. fire, burning (Parip.); aḻi to suffer, be troubled (Tolk.); aḻuṅku to be in distress; Ma. aḻaluka to burn as a wound; burn with grief, aḻal n. heat, fire, grief : Ta. taḻal to burn, glow; Klm.(E) tari- to burn (of fire); tarp- to light fire; Nk. tar-; Pj. taṟ- (Sth. taṟi-, taṟv-) to be hot; Go. tarī-t- to be hot (of sun); tarīst- to be heated over a flame; tarmī a glowing piece of wood ash; cf. Te. trampi a burning pyre; PDr. *caḻ- > PSDr. *aḻ- : *taḻ-. Cf. Ka. aḍalu to grieve; Ta. aṭalai distress (Tēv.); l. ws. from Te. after Te. -ḍ- < PDr. *-ḻ-.]

10 aḍalu² intr. to tremble, shake (Kāś.); to be afraid (Rasika.); n. fear, alarm (Mdn. also).

[Ka. aḍalu to be shaken; n. tremor, confusion of mind (Mdn.); ? l. w. < Te. Ta. aṭi to flap, twitch; Klm.(E) aḍg- (aḍak-t-) (pulse) throbs.]

11 aḍuku tr. to arrange in a set or series; to pile up (as pots); a pile.

[Ka. aḍaku, aḍuku to pile; aḍasu to be joined; be near; unite; aṭṭu n. the state of being joined; Tu. aṭṭi a pile, heap of rice; Ko. aṛk- to be piled in order; To. oḍg- id.; oṛk- to pile up; Ta. aṭu v.i. to join, to be next; tr. to join; aṭukku tr. to pile up (Cilap.); n. a pile; Ma. aṭukkuka to pack up, pile up; aṭukku a pile, layer; aṭuka to come in contact; aṭuttu near, next; Kui aḍa to be joined to; aṭpa to join together (past aṭṭ-); aṭu adj. near; aṭse/aṛse adv. jointly; Mlt. aṭge/i near, close; cf. āṭi pāṭi neighborhood. Cf. Te. ḍāyu.]

12 aḍucu IIb tr. to beat, flog (Bhr. I, II); to smite to death, kill (Bhr. II); āṭu n. a beating, hit (Bhr. II).

[Ka. aḍacu to rap, cuff; aḍi n. beating, a blow; aḍe to strike; throw with fingers; Ko. ayṛ- (aṛc-) to strike (of a ball in game); (lightning) strikes; Koḍ. aḍi (lightning) strikes; Ta. aṭi to beat; slay; dash; n. blow, stroke; aṭu (aṭṭ-) smite, kill, destroy; āṭu n. killing; Ma. aṭikka v. tr. id.; n. stroke, blow, etc.; Pj. aṭṭ- to strike; Oll. aṭ- id.; KGad. aṭṭ- to hit, strike; Mlt. aṛk- to thrust, wedge in; aṛg-, aṛges- to press down; < PDr. *aṭ-. See Emeneau, Lg. 29, p. 351.]

13 aḍ(u)gu tr. to request (Bhr. I), inquire, ask (Bhr. II); beg, solicit (KS); desire.

[Pj. aḍ- (Sth. aḍi-) to ask; Kur. eṛ- (eḍḍ-) to call, summon; to invite, command; Mlt. eṛy- (eṛc-) to speak with fluency; cf. Ta. aḷavu to inquire after one's health (Tolk.); aḷi v.t. to speak, express; v.i. to create desire; n. desire; aḷa v.i. to talk together (Kallā.).]

14 aḍḍu tr./intr. to obstruct (as a vb. Mdn.); to be obstructed, hampered (as a work, etc.); adj. crosswise; aḍḍamu across; n. obstruction, obstacle; aḍḍa-paḍu to stop, block; aḍḍa adj. hampering, interrupting, intriguing; aḍḍagincu to obstruct.

[Ka. aḍḍi an obstacle; aḍe to obstruct, close up; Tu. aḍḍi/aḍḍa obstacle, opposition; aḍḍāpini to hinder; aḍepuni to shut, close; Ko. aṛv- (aṛt-) (door) shuts; v. tr. to shut (hole, door, etc.); aṛv (aṛd-)

become blocked by an obstacle; To. aṟf- (aṟt-) to shut; Ta. aṭai to shut, close (PN); obstruct (Kr̲ḷ.); be obstructed (as the ear, throat, etc.); aṭṭi (l. w. < Ka.) hindrance, obstacle; Ma. aṭayuka to be shut up; aṭekka to obstruct; aṭṭam hindrance; Kui aḍa a screen, an intervening object; Go. (Dawson) aḍām a veil; Pj. aṛñ- to cross; Kur. aḍ- (aḍc-, aḍḍ-) to stop (of children, fighters, etc.); Mlt. aṛatr- to hinder; Brah. aḍkann- to halt, stop; aṛ obstacle, obstruction; (Pkt. aḍḍa- athwart; for IA, vide Nep. Dict. s. v. aṛinu to stop; aṛbhaṅge traverse; Katre, IFK. v. s. v. aḍkhaltā, āḍa; > l. w. Skt. aṭṭa- a defence wall, see Burrow TPS, 1945, pp. 1, 2).]

15 aṇṭu intr. tr. to touch, adhere (Bhr. I); to stick (as glue); v. tr. to anoint, smear (Manu.); aṇṭa- adv. thoroughly, closely, aṇṭā-baṭṭu to hold tightly; aṇṭā-gōyu to cut closely, etc.

[Ka. aṇṭu to touch, embrace; v. i. stick to; n. adhesion; aṇe to touch; come in contact; embrace; aṇke, aṇpu the act of smearing or anointing; Tu. aṇṭuni v. i. to adhere, stick; aṇepuni to paste; v. i. to come in contact; Ta. aṇṭu to approach; aṭṭu to join, stick, paste; aṇai to touch; Klm.(SR) aṇṭ- to stick; Klm.(E) aṭ- v. i. to stick; Nk. aṭṭ- to stick to; Pj. anḍ- to attach string to bow; PDr. *aṇ-, v. s. v. *anāgu- Cf. Skt. aṇṭhati to visit (Buddh.), Burrow, TPS (1946), p. 21.]

16 attu intr. to be attached; to hold fast; join (Bhr. II, Vijñ.); tr. to hold, unite; l. w. < Ka.

[Ka. hattu v. i. to stick to; to join; apply oneself to; Tu. hattuni; Ko. at̲- (ac-) to seize firmly, persist (in doing); Ta. attu v. tr. to unite, apply, lean, etc. (later usages); v. s. v. hattu, paṭṭu; PDr. *pat̲-.]

17 adaru, aduru (alt. adr-) intr. to shake, tremble (out of fear, etc.) (Bhr. I); n. shaking; fear; tr. adur(u)cu.

[Ka. adir, adaru id.; Tu. adu̥runi/adruni v. i. to tremble, quake; Ta. atir v. i. to tremble, shake (as by earthquake); be startled by sound (Kr̲ḷ.); v. tr. to alarm by shouting; atirvu shaking (Cilap.). atirppu id.; Ma. atiruka to fear, tremble; Mlt. adyar to be agitated. *-t- alternating with *-c- : Te. asadu thin, slender; asi(-y-āḍu) to tremble, shake; Ka. asi to move, shake, tremble; asumbu to shake, agitate, cause to move; asi thinness; asa slenderness; Ta. acai v. i. to move, stir; be slender, flexible (Kr̲ḷ.); v. tr. to shake, move; acaivu shaking; ayakku v. tr. to shake; ai slenderness; Ma. aśu thin, slender (loc.); ayavu elasticity; Kur. asr- to tremble, scintillate, shiver, shudder; Mlt. asr-, asrān- to hesitate (ān- to say).]

18 adalu intr. to start, to be alarmed; tr. adal(u)cu to threaten; chide, rebuke; adupu, colloq. hectoring; see forms under adaru, to which may be added the following items.

[Ka. adalu to tremble; adaṭu to scold; adapu to reprove; to tremble; Tu. adarpuni to admonish, rebuke, reprove; cause to tremble; addalipuni to rebuke, etc.; Ta. atir v. tr. to alarm by shouting; to rebuke (Piṅ.); ataṭṭu to rebuke authoritatively; atampu id.]

19 aduku (later, atuku) intr. to hold to (KS); to be attached to; to suit, fit; tr. to join, unite (UH, Naiṣ.); solder, paste; n. junction, union; a joint; seam, patch.

[Ka. atuku, aduku to be joined; soldered; to be fit; v. tr. to join, unite, solder, cement; Ta. atuṅku v. i. to be compressed; atukku to press down with fingers; slap with hand (Cīv.); attu to apply as medicine; n. sewing (Piṅ.); Ma. atukkuka to squeeze; Kuvi (S) atti kī- to paste; forms with -s- < *-c- : Ka. asa fitness, propriety; Kuvi (F) ass- to fit, hold; Kuvi (S) ah'- to hold; Kur. assg- v. i. to adhere, stick; to fit; ass$^a$gta'- to glue, paste; Mlt. asg- to paste; asg-, asgr- to adhere; PDr. *ac-/*at-.]

20 adumu tr. to press, squeeze; put together (as two pieces into one); (Bhr. I); to reprove; subdue (Bhr. I and II).

[Ka. adubu, adumu to press, compress; squeeze, cram; Ta. atakku to subdue, subjugate; control; cram, press softly; Go. (Dawson) adm-, GoM. ādm- to press; Klm. (E) adum-, Nk. adum- to press; ? Pj. ayb- to press; PSDr./PCDr. *at-ump-; for more forms see s. v. aduku.]

21 addu[1] tr. to immerse, cause to sink (BP); to dip, dye.

[Ka. addu, ardu, al̲du v. tr. to immerse, dip, dye; sink in a fluid; also ajju id.; āl̲, al̲- to sink in a fluid; to be immersed; be lowered, be deep (pp. āl̲du/al̲du); Tu. arduni to wash or bleach clothes; Ko. aj- dip into liquid; Ta. al̲untu to be immersed; al̲uttu v. tr. to immerse down; al̲uṅku to sink; āl̲ v. i. to sink; be immersed; āl̲ttu tr. to plunge, immerse; Ma. āl̲uka to sink; āl̲ttuka to immerse, sink; PSDr. *āl̲ : *al̲-V-.]

22 addu[2] tr. to press gently (Kaḷā.); to cause to touch.

[Ta. al̲untu v. i. to be pressed, al̲uttu to press down; impress; n. pressure; al̲uṅku to be pressed, Ma. al̲iyuka to be united; Kur. arb- to press down, keep down; cf. Tu. arkuni to be humbled, depressed; To. ark- (arky-) to subdue; Go. āhc- to massage. There seems to be some confusion in usage between this item and the previous one.]

23 *anāgu* intr. to mix or mingle freely; occurs only as a past participle in the phrase anāgi penāgi closely, intimately, lit., mixing and mingling, v.s.v. penāgu (Bhr. II); cf. anūgu adj. beloved, dear; n. a friend.

[Ka. aṇe to come in contact; to embrace; aṇaka closeness; aṇpu friendship; aḷ contact; aḷke an embrace; Tu. anepuni to touch, embrace; alejuni v.i. to mix, mingle, be united; Ta. aṇaṅku to interlace in growing together (Malaip.); be united; aṇuku to draw near; aṇai v.tr. to approach, touch; come in contact; aḷai v.tr. to mingle; v.i. to be mixed (Tolk.); Ma. aṇekka to embrace, hug; aṇavu closeness, love; aṇayuka to approach; Brah. haning- to copulate (of human beings), also aning- id. Cf. Klm.(SR) yalg- to embrace. PDr. *aṇ-/*aḷ-, v.s.v. allu.]

24 anu IV (past stem aṇ-ṭ-, habitual stem an-ḍ-/an-d-; alt. nā- before C-suff.) to say, express; mind; aux., so, thus; adj. named, called.

[Ka. anu, annu (an-d-); en, ennu (en-d-) to say, speak, tell, call; Tu. anpini, inpini; Ko. in- (i<u>d</u>-) say or be said to be (so-and-so); To. īn- (ī<u>d</u>-) id.; ȫšt- (ȫšty-) to tell; Ta. e<u>n</u> (e<u>nr</u>-) to say, utter, express; Ma. ennuka to sound, say, think; appear thus; be such, etc.; Kui inba (is-) to say, be articulate; Kuvi(F) inj-, Kuvi(S) into say; Go. ind- to say, call; Klm.(E) en- (en-t-) to say or be said; be said to be (so-and-so); Klm.(SR) in- to speak; idd- to tell; Nk. (y)eṇḍ- said, ind- saying; iḍuktēn (he) said (LSI IV, pp. 572, 573); Pj. en- (ett-, end-) to say; KGad. in- (in direct quotation) so-and-so; Kur. ān- to say, tell, point out; designate; Mlt. ān- to think, say or do thus; PDr. *ă̄n-/*en-/*in-, or ? *yan-/*yen.]

25 anucu*, ancu IIb to send away, send officially (Bhr. I, II); transitive of an obsolete verb *an(u)-; also anupu, ampu id. (Mdn. Te. ampak-ālu a ceremony of sending a bride to the groom's place soon after marriage).

[Ta. a<u>n</u>uppu to send, despatch; Ma. anuppuka to send in official style. Cf. Kur. amb- to set free, send away (as wife), give up; give as a gift.]

anupu var. of anucu, q.v.

ancu[1]* IIb to send, delegate, permit to go (Bhr. II), v.s.v. anucu.

26 ancu[2]* IId to oppress, afflict (KS) (< *am-c-).

[Ka. avuṅku/avuku to press or hold firmly, squeeze, trouble; avugu yield to pressure; avucu, amucu v.tr. id.; Tu. avuṅkuni to press down; avumpuni id.; amapuni to press down; Ta. amukku v.tr. to crush, press, squeeze; overcome, repress; Ma. amukkuka id.; Ko. amc- to press hard.]

27 anju* intr. to be afraid, to hesitate (HariV., BP).
[Ka. añju to fear, feel anxiety; n. fear; Tu. añjuni id.; Ko. anj- to fear; anjrc- to terrify; To. oẓ- (oj-) to fear; Ta. añcu to fear, dread (Kṟl.); n. fear, terror (PN); Ma. añcuka id.; Ta. Ma. accam fear, dismay; Kui aja to fear; Kuvi (S) az- (z = j); Kuvi (F) ajj- to fear; PSDr. *ay-nc-/*ay-nt-, PDr. *ay-/*ac-; v. s. v. adaru.]

28 andu tr. to get (difficulties) (Bhr. I); to reach (Bhr. II), get at; gain, intr. to be within reach, be available (Bhr.); and-incu to hand in, hand over; andu-konu (refl.) to reach.
[Ka. andu v. tr. to meet with, reach, get at, obtain (no literary usages, prob. l. w. < Te.); Kuvi (S) and- to join, meet; intermix; ? < *ar$^{u}$nd-, v. s. v. arugu.]

29 annu* intr. to be intoxicated (KS); be beside oneself; n. intoxication, indulgence (Bhr. III).

30 abbu intr. to be acquired; come into one's possession or control (Bhr. II; HariV.); come into one's enjoyment (as wealth, education); to be obtained, caught (as an enemy, Bhr. II).
[Ety. dub. v. s. v. arugu.]

31 amayu* III intr. to be made ready; to be done in advance (UH).
[Ka. save, same to be made ready; to make ready; Tu. ampuni to do; Ta. amai, camai v. tr. to effect, accomplish; (Tolk.); to prepare; v. s. v. amaru.]

32 amaru intr. to be ready, prepared (Bhr. II); to fit, suit (Bhr. I); tr. amar(u)cu to arrange, prepare; make (Bhr. I).
[Ka. amar, amaru be fit, agreeable; amarisu, amarcu to prepare; Tu. amaruni to fit, suit; Ta. amar to be suitable; amai v. i. to agree, submit (Kṟl.); be suitable; be complete, finished (Kalit.); tr. to effect, accomplish; n. fitness; amaivu being suitable (Kṟl.); Ma. ameyuka v. i. to agree; forms with initial c-/s- (< PDr. *c-) occur as follows: Te. sama-kaṭṭu be ready; Ka. same, save be made ready; savasu to prepare; samaṟu, savaṟu to make proper, fit; Ta. camai v. i. be suitable; get ready; be made; tr. to prepare; do, perform; Ma. camayuka to get ready; camekka to prepare; see Burrow, DS VI, p. 137; PDr. *cam-; PSDr. *cam-/*am-; cf. Kur. sam- (samc-) to fit, be of right size; Mlt. sambr- to be cured, mended, come right.]

33 ammu tr. to sell (SII X, No. 58); ammu-baḍi, amm-uḍu selling (KS).
[Go. mamm- to sell; (Dawson) mom- id. No other language shows the verbal form. However, it seems to underlie the following forms: Te. aṅgaḍi a shop; Ka. Tu. Koḍ. aṅgaḍi id.; Ko. aŋgāḍy; To. ogoḏy;

Ta. aṅkāṭi bazaar, bazaar street (Cilap.); Ma. aṅṅāṭi id.; Klm. aŋgaḍi; Nk. aŋgāṛi; < *am-kăṭi a selling place, cf. Te. kaḍa, Ka. kade, gaḍi a place.]

arayu* III (aras-) var. of ārayu, q. v.

34 aralu* intr. to spread (as a creeper) (post-classical and rare).

[Cf. Ka. aral, aralu to expand, open, blow (as a flower); Tu. araluni id.; aravu width, breadth; Ta. alar to increase in size, become large (Kalit.); Ma. alaruka to open as a flower; cf. alaru.]

35 arugu* intr. to go, approach (Bhr. I), to pass (of time); proceed, walk.

[Ta. aruku to approach; n. nearness, border, edge; Ma. aru, aruvu edge, brim; Ka. arugu vicinity, border; Tu. aru brim, border; arupattuni to reach the shore; cf. Ka. (Bucher) arulu to roam; Go. araluk (waiānā) to follow persistently; alternatively from *ār- < *cār- with loss of *c- in SDr., v. s. v. tāru, cēru.]

36 aruvu* tr. to pay as taxes (Vijñ.); colloq. a loan in kind (grain, articles, etc.), v. s. v. accu[1]. SAN gives aruvu; the basic stem can be *arucu (usages only for the vu-ending stem; belongs to the class of kolucu : koluvu).

37 aṟacu IId intr. to cry, cry out, weep (Bhr. I); vociferate, yell, prattle (Bhr. II).

[Ka. aṟucu, aṟacu, arcu id. to cry aloud, etc.; Klm.(SR) arr- to cry, frighten; Kui ṛaspa to ring, make reverberating sound; Mlt. arr- to call to goats. Cf. Ma. aṟai v. i. to sound; v. tr. beat as a drum, speak, declare; n. sound; Ma. aṟayuka to beat (as drum).]

38 aṟu* intr. to diminish, decrease (of strength in war) (Bhr. I); to be destroyed; to decay.

[Ka. aṟu to be severed; aṟe to lose one's form, be defaced; Tu. arpuni to efface, obliterate; To. aṟf- (aṟt-) to cut; Ta. aṟu v. i. to be severed; to become extinct; go to ruin; v. tr. to cut out; root out; Ma. aṟuka to be cut off, to end, be finished; aṟukka to cut off; cf. Tu. areḍuni to destroy, ruin; see also aṟugu, taṟugu.]

39 aṟugu intr. to be digested (Bhr. II); to decay; wear away, decrease (Bhr. II); colloq. to be chafed, worn out; to be digested.

[Ka. aṟave, aṟambe the state of being worn out, decayed or digested; aṟaka, aṟake being broken or injured (as a tile, etc.); Tu. arkuni to become less; Ta. aṟu v. tr. to digest (Cīv.); Go. rokk- to be digested; cf. Kui rāga to be worn away, be chafed; see also s. v. aṟu, taṟugu.]

40 aṟumu, armu* to attack; seize (an enemy), subdue, occupy; n. attack (Bhr. II); to increase (post-classical).

[? Ta. aṟai strategem, wile, trick (Kalit.); n. place of encampment, camp (Patiṟ.); v. s. v. taṟumu; prob. < PDr. *caṯ-.]

41 alāgu* intr. to suffer, lament (Bhg. JBhr.); be afraid (Pāṇḍ.); to be tired; tr. alācu, cf. alayu, alāduru.

[Ka. alugu, aluṅgu be agitated, be unsteady; alañcu to tease; Tu. alaṅkuni, alaṅguni be agitated; alaṅkāvuni to perturb; alacuni to move, shake, agitate; Ta. alaṅku to move, shake; be agitated; ala. to suffer (Kṟi.); alu to be tired; Ma. alaṅnuka be agitated, shaken; alternatively Ta. Ma. allal affliction, distress, grief : celial id. (Burrow, DS VI, p. 137); in this case the series deriving from *al- to shake, etc. has to be separated since it also occurs in CDr. Loss of c- in *cel- (cellal) and a/e alternation after c-. Contamination with the meanings of nalāgu, nalācu possible.]

alācu* IIb tr. of alāgu to afflict, cause to suffer (Bhr. II, BhR.).

42 alādu* tr. to smear, daub, apply (of sandal paste to body, etc.) (Bhr. II).

[No exact correspondences. Cf. Ka. alabu, alambu to wash with water; Tu. alambuni id.; Ta. alampu id.; Ma. alakkuka to wash clothes.]

43 alāduru* intr. to be distressed (Bhr. I); to lament; cpd. base ? *alam + *tur-; *tur- to get, cf. dorayu, doraku; for *alam-, cf. alāgu, alayu; altern. aland-ur.

[Cf. Ta. alantalai trouble, distress, vexation (Lex.); confusion (Tiv.); Ma. alati troublesome; n. misery.]

44 alamaru* intr. to be tired; to grieve, suffer; alamaṭa n. difficulty, trouble (Bhr. I, II), n. sorrow (UH). Cpd. base, ? alam + *ar- (*ar- to get; ? cf. arugu). Cf. alāgu, alayu, alāduru.

[Ta. alamaru v. i. to be agitated (Tolk.); alamaral confusion (Tolk.); sorrow (Piṅ.); alamala v. i. to be confused, be anxious (loc.); alamaru be bewildered (Cīv.).]

45 alamu intr. to spread, extend; enclose, overspread (of smoke over sky) (Bhr. II); prevail intensely (of passions) (Bhr. I, II); to mix with, be one with (Bhr. II); tr. to seize, take hold of.

[Ka. aḷumba excess, greatness; aḷur to enclose, cover, overspread, prevail, fall upon; Tu. alamuni to mix with hand, alavuni id.; Ta. aḷai v. tr. to mix up, mingle; v. i. be mixed up (Tolk.): aḷavu v. i. to blend, mingle (Tolk.); PDr. *aḷ-; v. s. v. allu.]

46 alayu III intr. to be fatigued; be weary (Bhr. I); be disgusted (Bhr. I), to delay (UH); be grieved (Bhg.); der. n. alāta, alayika, alasaṭa.

[Ka. alasu become weary; to loiter; ala fatigue; Tu. alasuni, alapuni, aleyuni id.; alasu old, worn out; alasalu̥ fatigue; Ko. alv- (ald-) to be fatigued walking or searching; Ta. alu v. i. be fatigued (Tēv.); alacu id.; alacal laziness, languor (Piṅ.); alaicu be lazy; Ma. ala-yuka, alasuka be tired; alasal fatigue, agitation; Klm. (E) alay (alay-t-) become tired; Pj. alac illness; Kui alāṛi n. fatigue, distress (< *alahaṛi); laha languor, laziness, adj. lazy (< *lasa); Mlt. alesi sweat, heat (-e- < -ay- ?); Brah. alla commotion. (> l. w. Skt. alasa- lazy, tired, Kittel, IA I, p. 236, Burrow, TPS 1945, pp. 80-83; for Uralian DS IV, p. 350; for Middle and NIA, v. s. v. alasi, Nep. Dict., also Katre, IFK, s. v. ālas). PDr. *al- to be tired, be lazy; to suffer.]

47 alaru* intr. to blossom, flower (Bhr. II); be splendid, shine; to rejoice (Naiṣ.); n. a flower, blossom; splendor; joy; adj. splendid.

[Ka. alar, aral to open, blossom, bloom, rejoice; n. flower; also aral, araḷu, arlu, alarcu to expand, blow, etc.; Tu. araḷuni, araluni to expand, bloom; alaru a flower; Ta. alar to blossom; to increase in size (Kalit.); shine forth; n. flower; Ma. alaruka v. i. id., alar flower; cf. Kui ale n. a dear one, darling (term of affection); alga tidy, clear; Mlt. alkre to be opened; alktr- to open. ? Kur. alkh- to laugh; Mlt. alq- id.; also Kur. all- to become clear.]

aliyu III var. of alayu, q. v. (rare).

48 aluku$^{1}$ tr. to smear the floor of a house or a mud wall, etc. with macerated cow dung and water; n. smearing the floor, etc. (Bhr. II).

[Ka. alambu, alabu (also with -u-) wash with water; Tu. alambuni, lumbuni to wash, rinse; To. as̱py- (as̱py-) to clean; Ta. alampu id. (PN); Ma. alakkuka wash clothes; alakku washing; Kui akali (< *alaki) n. rinsing; < PDr. *al-.]

49 aluku$^{2}$ tr. to sprinkle, scatter (rice, etc., in a net to lure birds, etc.) (Bhr. II, KS).

[Kui lānja to sprinkle, scatter around, disperse; Kuvi (F) lānj-, Kuvi (S) lanz- to scatter (z = j; < *alanj-); Klm. (SR) alk- to sprinkle; Nk. aḷk-; Pj. alk-; cf. Ta. alavu to spill; < PDr. *aḷ-k-.]

50 aluku$^{3*}$ tr. to stick (flowers in braid) (HariV.); to plant seedlings (Pāṇḍ.).

51 aluku$^{4*}$ intr. to dread, to be afraid; to hesitate (Bhr. II); n. fear, dread, hesitation.

[Ka. aḷuku, aḷku vb. and n. id.; aḷaṟu to fear, n. fear; aḷku to be impotent; Tu. aḷkuni, alkuni v. i. id.; alku̥ adj. timid, frightened; Ta. aḷukku v. i. id.; aḷamaru be bewildered (Cīv.); Ma. aḷukkuka start, shrink; aḷukkam awe, fear; c- forms: Ka. caḷi be deprived of one's power; Tu. caḷḷu/callu imbecile, weak; calle a weak man; Ma. caḷuṅṅuka to shake, be frightened; for t- alt., v.s.v. talāku, talaru; cf. Kur. Mlt. elc- to fear; < PDr. *caḷ-.]

52 alugu/algu, aluvu/alvu intr. to become angry with (Bhr. I), to hate, dislike (Bhr. II) (governs dative).

[Cf. Ka. alugu to be agitated; alasu to be vexed, teased, disgusted. Cf. alãgu, alayu.]

53 allu tr. to interweave, plait, braid (Bhr. II), to fabricate; intr. to spread as a creeper, etc.; der. n. allika, allu (also Mdn. Te.).

[Ka. allu join, connect, knit, braid ( ? l. w. < Te.); aḷvaḷ-isu to tie together; aḷa joining; Ta. aḷḷu to be thickly interwoven (Cīv.); aḷavu v.i. to blend, mingle (Tolk.); aḷḷu to weave (loc.); Kui alpa (al-t-) to weave sticks together; interweave, interlace; plait, etc.; Kuvi (S) all- to intertangle, plait; Klm. (E) al- (al-t-), Klm. (SR) all- to weave, dress hair; Nk. all- id.; Pj. alka bowstring (cf. Te. alliya, alle); alc- to wind around a tree (of a snake); alṭ- to be twined around; alṭayt- to wind round; < PDr. *aḷ-.]

54 aviyu III intr. to be broken, burst, break open (of eggs, tank-bund, etc.) (Bhr. I, KS); to be destroyed; Mdn. to be spoiled, rot (food, etc.).

[Ka. avi to be damaged, to perish; be spoiled, rot; avugu to yield to pressure, as the surface of a ripe fruit or tumor; Ta. avi to be subdued; become extinguished (Cīv.); perish, die (Kṟḷ); v.tr. suppress, destroy; avi<u>l</u> v.i. to open, expand (Ci<u>r</u>up.), v.tr. to loosen, cause to open; Ma. aviyuka to rot, spoil as fruit; < PSDr. *av-.]

55 avuku (colloq.) intr. to yield to pressure (bull not being able to pull cart), adj. weak, (of a wall or soil); n. hesitation, weakness. Cf. javuku.

[Ka. avugu, amugu yield to pressure; Ta. ñemuṅku yield to pressure, be squeezed; namuku id.; Ma. ñammuṅṅuka id.; Kuvi (F) nabg- to press down; Burrow DS V, p. 605; PSDr. *nam-/am-, *ñam-/*ñem.]

56 a<u>l</u>iyu* III (a<u>l</u>is-) inscr.; tr. to efface, destroy (as the writing in an inscr. etc.)

[Ka. a<u>l</u>i to be ruined; destroyed; tr. to destroy; Tu. aḷyuni v.i. to perish, decay; arpuni to efface, obliterate, also darpuni; Ko. aḷc- to be erased, to erase; To. oḍy- (oḍc-) to spend; ? a<u>r</u>- to get lost; Ta. a<u>l</u>i v.i. to perish; v.tr. to ruin, efface; n. destruction (Kṟḷ.); Ma. a<u>l</u>iyuka go off, be destroyed; < PDr. *a<u>l</u>-.]

Ā

57 ā̃gu tr. to stop, prevent, resist (Bhr. I), prohibit (Bhr. II), bear (Bhg.); intr. to cease, stop, stay; be suppressed; refrain from; other tr. ā̃cu, ā̃pu; der. n. ā̃ka prevention, check (Bhr. II); restriction, custody (Bhg.); ā̃-kaṭṭu to prevent (< *ā̃ka + kaṭṭu); āpu restraint.

[Ka. ān be arrested, lay hold of, endure, suffer, support, āpu stoppage, restraint; Tu. airuni to wait, stay, stop; Ta. āppu n. wedge, peg; bondage, tie; ācu support, prop (PN); Ma. āppu n. wedge, plug (what stops); Kui āṅga to intercept; Kuvi (F) āng- to check; Kuvi (S) to hinder, defend; āsh- to impede; < PDr. *ā-/*ān-; cf. ānu to lean on. Burrow compares words meaning 'to tie' Ta. yā, ā; Kur. hē'-; Mlt. ey- (ĕc-), but it seems better to keep the two sets of meanings separate, because the meaning 'to stop' implies here stopping something from movement, i.e., obstructing, etc., whereas the meaning 'to tie' is associated with the ideas of tying up together, compose as a poem, stitch, sew, etc. (cf. Ta. and Kur.).]

ā̃cu* IIb tr. of ā̃gu

58 āḍu[1] (1) intr. to move, shake (Bhr. I), function as limbs (Bhr. II); to hover over (as birds over a dead body); tr. ārcu to shake, flutter (wings, etc.).

[Ka. āḍu be in motion, swing, shake; Tu. āḍuni to move, swing, shake, totter; tr. to rock; Ko. āṛ- (āc-) move, move violently; To. ōḍ- (ōḍy-) move violently, ōṭ- to shake violently; Ta. āṭu to swing; Ma. āṭuka to wave, swing, rock; shake, totter; cf. aḍalu[2].]

āḍu[1] (2) intr. to play, dance (Bhr. I); play in water, bathe (Bhr. I, KS); der. n. āṭa a play, dance, game.

[Ka. āḍu id.; āṭa, āṭu n. jest, a dance; Tu. āṭa sport, play; Ko. āṛ- (āc-) to dance; To. ōḍ- (ōḍy-) id.; Ta. āṭu to dance, play in water (Maṇi.); Ma. āṭuka to dance, visit holy baths; Ta. Ma. āṭṭam n. playing, dance; Klm. āḍ- to play; Nk. āṛ- id.; PDr. *āṭ-.]

59 āḍu[2] tr. to say, speak, to abuse (Bhr. II).

[Ka. āḍu to speak, utter, sound (as an instrument); to caluminate, abuse; Ko. āṛ- (āc-) to speak; Ta. āṭu v.tr. to say; < PSDr. *āṭ-. Cf. Ka. āl to cry aloud; ālisu to make oneself heard, cry aloud; mind, be heard; Ta. ālu to sound, make noise, cry aloud (PN).]

60 āḍu[3]* intr. to pierce (as arrows); be fixed, planted (Bhr. II, BhR); alt. of nāḍu with loss of n-, v.s.v. nāḍu, nāṭu.

61 ā̃ṭu (SAN), āṭu (Dh.M.) intr. be adequate, sufficient (of food, money, etc.; post-classical and mdn.), be capable of, endure, withstand.

[Ta. ār̲r̲u be sufficient, become strong, powerful (Kr̲ḷ.), be possible; ān̲r̲al abundant; ān̲r̲a extensive, excellent; Ka. ār̲- (pp. ārtu) be able, possible; be adequate, endure; present participle ārpa, āpa.]

62 ānu[1] intr. to lean, recline, rest on; tr. to touch, reach, carry, support (Daś.).

[Ka. ān, ānu (pp. āntu) be or become contiguous; rest on, lean against, recline; bend; take, receive, bear, support, suffer; Tu. ānipuni make to lean; Ta. ār̲r̲u to bear on head or shoulder (Kallā.), to assist (PN), lead, guide (Kr̲ḷ.); Kui (tlau) ēṇba to recline the head upon; Kur. ānn- (ānc-) cause pain by being pressed against the skin (as gravel on road, etc.); Mlt. ān̲r̲eṭ- to lean or rest on pillows; cf. Ma. aṇa n. support, pillow; < PDr. *ān-.]

63 ānu[2]* to experience, enjoy, taste, drink, eat (Bhr. II).

[Ta. ār v.tr. to eat, drink (PN), experience (Kalit.); ārttu to feed; cause to experience; < PSDr. *ā- with -n and -r as suffixes.]

ā̃pu tr. of ā̃gu to prevent, stop (Bhr. I); keep under control (Paṇḍ.); n. hindrance, obstruction (Mdn.).

64 ārayu* III tr. to seek, search (Bhr. I); investigate; consider, examine (Bhr. I and II); to look after, protect (Bhr. II); to wait, look for.

[Ka. āray, ārayu, ārayyu, ārai to search, consider attentively; ponder, nourish; Ta. ārāy to examine, consider, deliberate upon (Kr̲ḷ.); search for; Ma. ārāyka to seek, search, examine; Tu. āraisuni to expect; wait, look for; āraike n. protection, care of; cf. araṇṭuni to seek, look for; arantuni to feel, grasp at. Probably a cpd. form of *āra- (fully, v.s.v. āru) + āy- to select, choose, examine. Burrow says *ār- in Te. ērcu to choose, pick up; Ka. āriśu + Ta. āy to search, examine, sift; Ma. āyka to select, choose, cull; Ka. Tu āy id.; Go. āc-; Kui āska; Pj. āc-; Mlt. ād-, cf. Kur. ād- to recognize, by feeling with the fingers; to know by touch. (Burrow, DS V, BSOAS XI, pp. 612, 613).]

65 āru intr. to become full; increase (Bhr. II); āraN- (adv.) fully, thoroughly; ārābaṇḍu to be completely ripe (Bhr. II); āragāgu (āraN + kā̃gu) be fully boiled (Rāyalasīma dial.; Mdn.); an intensifier as a second member of compound bases : ēpāru, esalāru, etc.

[Ka. ār be filled; abound, teem; āru n. fullness, abundance; adv. fully; Tu. āruni to distend, grow stout; Ta. ār become full; be satisfied; ārttu to fill, complete (Cilap.); ār n. fullness; Ma. āra richly, satisfactorily : Kui sār to be in excess; n. excess; Kuvi (S) hār- to remain; ? Klm. (SR) ērād enough; Nk. ērāl enough (LSI IV, p. 574); Mlt. ēgr- (< *ērg-) to be abundant; ēgrtr- (< *ērgtr-) to overfill; PSDr. *ār- : PDr. cār-.]

66 āṟu[1] intr. to be calmed, pacified (of sorrow, exhaustion) (Bhr. I); to cool off; to be extinguished (a lamp, etc.) (Bhr. II); to be abated; to become dry, to dry; sweat to dry up (post-classical); to heal (as wound).

[Ka. āṟ, āṟu id.; Tu. āruni to grow cold or dry; ājuni to dry up; Ko. ār- (wound) heals, (dew) dries; To. ōṟ- become dry by heating; āł- (āṯ-) (stream) goes dry; Ta. āṟu be appeased, to abate; to cool, grow cold, be with patience (Cilap.); heal as a wound (Kṟḷ.); āṟṟu to assuage (Maṇi.); cool; dry up hair (Cīv.); Ma. āṟuka v. i., āṟṟuka v. tr. id.; Kui āja to cool down; āspa to make cold; Go. ār- to grow cool, warm oneself; Kur. arta'- (caus. of an obsolete verb *arnā) to spread out in the sun for drying; reduce fire; Klm. Nk. ār- to become dry; Pj. ēd- (NE. ēḍ-) to cool off; to warm onself; PDr. *āṯ-.]

67 *āṟu[2] (in āṟitēṟu) to be capable, be powerful (SAN gives āritēṟu); der. n. āṟ-aḍi adv. (pp. of an obsolete cpd. verb) in vain, powerless, āṟu strength + *adu to abate (aḍi, pp.).

[Ka. āṟ become strong, capable, competent; āṟu n. power, self will; Ta. āṟṟu be strong, powerful, etc. v. s. v. āṭu.]

ārcu[1] IIb (tr. of āḍu[1]) to shake, to cause to dance, play a game (Bhr. II); to cause to bathe.

ārcu[2]* IIb (caus. of āḍu[2]) to cause to say (Bhr. II).

ārcu[3] IIb (tr. of āṟu[1]) to dry something in sun, air (Pārij.); to put off (lamp, etc.) (Naiṣ.).

68 ārcu[4]* IIa intr. to cry aloud, shout, roar (in a battle) (Bhr. I).

[Ka. ār, āru id.; Tu. ārkuni id.; Ko. ār- (āt-) to call, summon; Ta. ār v. i. id.; tr. to slander, vilify (Kalit.); araṟṟu to lament, cry aloud; bewail; pour out one's troubles in lamentation (Tolk.); shout (Piṅ.); Ma. ārkuka, ārttuka to cry aloud, etc.; Kui ārpa to call; Klm. (SR) arr- to cry, frighten; Pj. ār- to sound (bell, etc.); Mlt. arr- a call to goats; PDr. *ār-.]

# I

69 iguru (var. ivuru) intr. to dry up, evaporate (Bhr.); to perish; be absorbed; n. (Mdn.) curry (cooked by boiling); tr. igur(u)cu.

[Ka. igaru be evaporated, dried up; also v. s. v. iṅku, imuru, ivuru.]

70 igul̇(u)cu IId (var. ivul(u)cu, from obs. *igulu/*ivulu) tr. to grin, show the teeth; alt. igil-incu id. (BP) : cf. iguru n. gum or gums of teeth (KS).

[Pj. ikp- (ikt-) to grin, show teeth; Ka. igaru gums; Ta. īṟu gums of teeth; eyiṟu n. tooth, gums (Piṅ.); Ma. ekiṟu tooth, fang; Kur. ij$^{i}$g- (ijg-) to show teeth, scorn; Mlt. igj- to grin, reproach (< *ijg-; -j- < *-y-); PDr. *iy-.]

71 iggu* intr. to bend (backwards); tr. to pull, drag (18th century work).

[Ka. iḻaku to incline, go down; Tu. igguni to draw, pull (< *iḻ-g < *iḻuṅk-); PDr. *īḻ-; *iḻ-V-; v. s. v. īḍcu.]

72 iṅku (var. inuku, rare; also īku, Brown, Śab. R.) intr. to be absorbed, to sink (of water, etc.); evaporate (Bhr. II); to perish (Bhīm.).

[Ka. iṅgu id.; Tu. iṅguni id.; Ta. iṅku, iñcu to abide, stay; sink; cf. Pj. ninḍk- flood to subside; prob. the Pj. form is derivable from *nil- stop; for the remaining, PSDr. *im- is the closest possible reconstruction, considering imuru, ivuru, iguru, etc.]

73 iccu V (allom. ī-, īyu; Mdn. īy-/iyy-, ivv-) tr. to give, offer, grant; aux. with inf. to let, permit.

[Ka. ī (itt-) id.; Ta. ī (īnt-) give to inferiors, give alms, bestow, grant (Tolk.); forms with *c- : Klm. (E) sī- (sīt-); Klm. (SR) siy-; Nk. śī-; Pj. cī- (ciñ-); Oll. sī-; Go. sī- (sī-sī) to give, allow; GoM. hiy-, hint- (hit-); Kui sīva, jīva (sī-t-, jī-t-); Kuvi (S) hī-; Kur. ci'- (cicc-); Mlt. ciy- (cic-); PDr. *ciy-/*cī-.]

inuku rare var. of iṅku (only a single usage cited: post-classical); back formation on the analogy of forms like penucu : pencu; ninucu : nincu; munugu : mungu, etc.

74 incu* IIb intr. to be agreeable, pleasant (Bhr. II, Panḍ.); impu agreeableness, sweetness (Bhr. II), also imbu/immu pleasure, joy (Bhr. I).

[Ka. in- sweetness; ini, ine id.; in cpds. ǐn-, ǐm- īṅgaḍal (-kaḍal) sea of milk; Tu. impu agreeableness; pleasantness; Ta. iṉi (iṉi-tt-) be sweet; iṉ- (in cpds.) sweet (Kṟḷ.); Ma. iniya adj. sweet; PSDr. *in-.]

75 indu* (post-Bhr.) intr. to be tasty, agreeable (Kāś.); prob. denom. vb. from *inidu.

[Ka. inidu that which is sweet; Ta. iṉitu that which is sweet, pleasing, agreeable (Tolk.); v. s. v. incu.]

76 iḍiyu* III intr. to crack; be split, broken (Pāṇḍ.).

[Ka. iḍi be powdered, crumble; Tu. iḍe a split, chasm; Ko. iṛy- (iṛc-) to crush; Ta. iṭi v.i. to break, crumble; become bruised, break into two (Piṅ.); Ma. iṭika, iṭiññuka to crumble, fall to pieces; Klm. (Kin.) iṛ- to strike, fall to pieces; be in ruins (see Kolami, Vocab. 3052); Kur. is$^{i}$g- (isgy-) intr. to open in long slits, to crack; Burrow compares Ka. siḍi burst forth as seeds from a fruit, to bounce, DS VI, p. 138, but Klm. form without s- precludes such a possibility; cf. Kur. es- to crush, break by force; eṭ- (eṭṭ-) to tear to pieces; Mlt. eṭ- to destroy; eṭgr- be broken, defaced; PDr. *iṭ-.]

77 iḍu* I and V tr. to put, place; lay (Bhr. I, II); -iḍu after a subst. to make, e.g., kannam-iḍu to make a hole, etc.

[Ka. iḍu (iṭṭ-) put down, put, place; lay on, keep; perform; Tu. iḍpini id.; Ko. iḍ- (iṭ-); To. īḍ- (īṭ-); Ta. iṭu (iṭṭ-) place, deposit; throw, serve; give, grant; lay eggs; Ma. iṭuka put, place, plant, throw; Kui iṭa place, put, fix, keep; Kuvi (F) itt- to keep; Go. irr-; Klm. (E) īḍ- (iṭṭ-) to put, allow; with nouns 'to do, give'; Pj. iḍ- (iṭṭ-) put, keep, (hen) to lay eggs; to allow; Nk. iṛ- (iṭṭ-); īḍ- keep (imp.) (LSI IV, p. 572); KGad. ir- (iṭṭ-); cf. Kur. id- (idd-) to put in the ground for growth; to plant; Mlt. id- plant, erect, build (< *ild-); also Kur. ic- (icc-) to set, lay (a snare, trap); PDr. *iṭ- ? < *il-t-.]

78 imuḍu intr. to be contained, to fit into a given space; to remain, stay; tr. imuḍ(u)cu to hold in, hide, thrust in (Naiṣ.).

[Ta. imai v.tr. to diminish, shrink (Kallā.); imiḻ v.tr. to bind as by an order; restrain; v.tr. to fasten, tie (Cīv.); cf. Ka. imb-idu to deposit; imbu-goḷ to seize.]

79 imuru (var. ivuru, q.v.) intr. to be evaporated as oil in lamp (RR), v.s.v. iṅku, iguru.

[Ka. imaru, imiru, imuru v.i. to evaporate in boiling, to dry up; disappear, wane, waste away; cf. Ta. imai to diminish, shrink (Kallā.); PSDr. *im-.]

ivuru (var. of iguru, q.v.) intr. (Bhr. II); be absorbed (Bhr. II).

[PDr. *im-V-, v.s.v. iṅku, imuru.]

80 iṟiyu* III intr. to be squeezed, be tight (in embrace) (Bhr. II); to be thick; iṟi- adj. (in cpds. only) tight (embrace) (Bhr. II), narrow (path), slender; iṟiyincu to keep together (as fingers) (Kāś.), to hold tight (UH).

[Ka. iṟi to be closely confined; to compress; Tu. iriyuni tr. to rub or squeeze between hands; Kuvi (F) īri-itt- to dam; for the rest of the forms see s.v. iṟuku; cf. Kur. eṭṭ- to be too tight (of articles of clothing).]

81 iṟuku tr. to close in tight, hold tight, thrust in a narrow place (Bhr. I); intr. to be contained, squeezed in narrow space; n. a narrow place, lane; adj. narrow; cf. iṟumu n. a corner, hiding place; iṟumu-konu to be hidden (BhR).

[Ka. iṟuku intr. and tr. to compress, make tight, iṟuṅku, iṟiṅku id.; n. being close, squeezed; ikku (< *iṟk-) n. being close, narrow, pressed; Ko. irg- become tight or tightly wedged in; irk- to tighten (clothes), pinch, press tightly in crowd; Ta. iṟuku v.i. become tight (Nāl.); iṟukku tr. to tighten (Kamp.), clothe tightly (Cūṭā.); iṟukkam tightness; cf. iṟu v.tr. to pierce through as an arrow (PN); Ma. iṟukuka become tight; iṟukkuka to tie tight; Mlt. eṛg- to shut, imprison; eṛgpo a bar to fasten a mat door with; cf. Kur. eṭṭ- remain stuck at one place, be hindered from coming out (as a ring forced down a finger); (of articles of clothing) to be too tight; cf. Ka. iṭṭu being close, narrow, pressed; PDr. *iṯ- : *iṭ-; *iṯ-uṅk-/*iṯ-ukk-.]

82 iluku* intr. to be sprained (post-classical); n. sprain (as a vb. only listed in SAN).

[Ka. iliku to be squeezed or bruised; iluku n. cramp, sprain, cf. uḷuku, uluku a sprain; ulaku be sprained; Tu. uḷkuni id.; uḷku, ulku n. a sprain; Ta. uḷukku be sprained (loc.), n. sprain, dislocation; uḷai to ache or suffer pain in the limbs; tr. to afflict, torment (Kallā.); Ma. uḷukkuka be dislocated; with *c- : Ta. Ma. cuḷukku id., see Burrow, DS VI, p. 140.]

83 ilugu* (var. of īlugu, also cf. nīl(u)gu) intr. to die, expire (Bhr. II), v.s.v. īlugu/īlgu.

## Ī

84 ī̃gu[1]* (var. of nī̃gu, q.v.) tr. to redeem, discharge (debts) (Bhr. II); to get rid of; abandon.

85 ī̃gu[2]* intr. to enter (Pāṇḍ.); to hide oneself (rare).

86 īḍu[1]* tr. to milk (Nava. N.; Bhg.); adj. īḍu-munta milk-pot; prob. related to words under īḍcu to pull, q.v.

[Cf. Ko. iḷv- (iḷt-) to suck; Ka. īḍu pulling, dragging; Ta. īṇṭu v.tr. to extract, pluck out, dig out (Tēv.).]

87 *īḍu[2]* intr. only as inf. īḍ-aN-, e.g., īḍ-ā-bōvu to withdraw oneself (Bhr. I); lag behind; īḍ-a-viḍucu to leave behind, forsake (KS);

īḍ-ig-ilu to lag behind.

[PDr. *īḻ-, v. s. v. īḍcu.]

88 īḍ(u)cu IIa tr. to pull, drag (Bhr. I); draw, attract.

[Ka. īḻ to pull, drag; Ko. iḷv- (iḷt-) to drag on ground; To. īṣf- (īṣt-) id.; īθ- id.; Ta. iḻu to draw, pull; iḻiccu lower, let down (Tēv.), pull down (SII, III, 93); Ma. iḻekka to drag; iḻukka id.; Kui ḍripa (ḍrit-) to drag away, abduct; Kuvi (S) ren- to drag, Kuvi (F) rej- (rec-) to pull; Kur. īc- (īcy-, icc-/īc-) to draw out, pull out (with friction), alt. īs-; Mlt. ic- to take off, put off; icgṛ- to come off, get loose; PDr. *īḻ : *īc-, ultimately *ī-; cf. Ka. īr to pull, draw; Tu. īruni to rub off; Ko. iv- (ivt-) to pull out; Ta. īr v. tr. to drag, pull; to draw, paint, write (Kalit.); Go. īs- (pp. ī-sī) to draw a picture or line (original base ī- with -sī pp. suffix); Pj. īrp- (īrt-) to pull; KGad. īr- id.]

89 īnu tr. to bring forth the young, yean (only of animals); to produce, yield (crops) (Bhr. II).

[Ka. īn (pp. īdu) id.; ī, īyu to bring forth (also said of the plantain tree); Ko. īn- (īnḏ-) (animal) to bear young; To. īn- (īḏ-) to bear (calf); īṯ- (īṯy-) to bear child (said of goddess); Ta. īṉ (īṉṟ-) tr. to bear, bring forth (Nāl.), produce, bring into being (Kṟḷ.); īṟṟu to bring forth (of animals); n. young one, young plant; īṟṟam n. giving birth; Ma. īṟṟam the womb of animals, iṟṟu the infant, young of animals; Pj. īn- (grain) to produce head; Brah. hīn- to lamb, kid, fowl, calve, etc.; PDr. *ī- : *īn-/*īṯ-.]

90 īdu intr. to swim; tr. to swim across (Bhr. II).

[Ka. īju, īsu id.; Tu. īcuni, ījuni id.; with movable *n- : Tu. nīnduni to swim, float; Ko. nīnj-; To. nīd-; nīẓ- (nīj-); Ta. nīntu swim in water; overflow; swim across (Kṟḷ.); get over, overcome (Maturai.); give up; n. ocean (Cīv.); nīccu swimming, flood; Ma. nīntuka to swim, etc.; Klm. (SR) īnd- id.; PDr. *nī-nt-/*ī-nt-, root *nī-/*ī-; prob. connected with words meaning water from PDr. *nī-r/*ī-r (see Kolami, Vocab. No. 328).]

īyu V (allom. of iccu, var. of ī-) tr. to give (Bhr. I), v. s. v. iccu.

91 īr(u)cu IId tr. to comb out nits (post-classical); prob. denom. vb. from īru nits.

[Ka. īr- to comb out nits (loc.); Tu. īruni to rub off, pick up; Ma. īruka to comb hair; cirakkuka to grate; to comb; Brah. iris n. comb; iris-kann- to comb; cf. Pj. īrc- to rub; Kur. irc- to scratch, poke; Mlt. īrc- to scratch the ground (as fowls do); words meaning nits: Te. īru; Ka. īr, sīr; Tu. tīru̥; Ta. Ma. īr; Go. sīr; Kuvi hīru; Kur. cīr (Burrow, DS VI, p. 139).]

92 īl(u)gu*, also nīl(u)gu intr. to die; perish (Bhr. II, BhR.).
[Cf. Pj. īl- to fall off (leaves, fruits, etc. from tree); KGad. īl (īli-) id.; v. s. v. nīl(u)gu.]

## U

93 ukku intr. to be suffocated through excessive humidity and hot weather (colloq.).
[Ka. ukku, urku to boil excessively; Tu. ukkuni id.; Ma. urukkuka to melt; PSDr. *ur-ukku; v. s. v. uriyu (< *ūr-).]

94 *uggu intr., only inf. ugg-aN-, e.g., ugg-ā-gaṭṭu to fasten tight; ugg-ā-baṭṭu to hold tight (hair), to refrain from food, etc. (Kāḷ.); cf. uggamu a rope tied to anything as handle; probably a back-formed base from uggamu.
[Ka. ugga a rope handle; Tu. uggi id.; uggikaṭṭuni to fasten a hook; (< *uṟ-g-); cf. Ta. Ma. Ka. uṟi a net-work of rope for placing pots and suspended by a cord from the hand, roof of a house, etc.; Te. uṭṭi id.]

95 uccu* IId intr. to pierce through, enter and go out on the other side (as an arrow) (Bhr. II); tr. to pierce (Bhr. II).
[Ka. urcu to enter into and go out the other side, penetrate; tr. to penetrate and pull out; uccu to penetrate right through; to pull out; to fly off as an arrow; Tu. urumbuni, rummuni to bore; cf. urepini v. i. to be penetrated (as with salt); Ta. uruvu tr. to pierce through, penetrate as an arrow (Tiruvāc.); Pj. ucc- to transfix; cf. Ta. ūr v. i. be unloosed, relaxed (Kalit.). PDr. *ūr- : *ur-V-.]

96 uṭṭu[1]* intr. to be born, to occur (cited in a 14th century work); l. w. < Ka.
[Ka. uṭṭu, huṭṭu, puṭṭu to be born; Ko. uṭ- (uc-) (plant, hair) sprouts, to be born; uṭc- to create; v. s. v. puṭṭu.]

97 uṭṭu[2]* intr. to ooze, trickle in drops, flow; uṭṭipaḍu to issue forth suddenly (all classical; Bhr. II, Naiṣ.).
[Ka. oṟe to ooze, spring, exude, flow; oṟate fountain, flow; Tu. uja a fountain, spring; Ta. ūṟu v. i. to spring, flow (as water) (Kṟḷ.); to ooze; uṟṟu v. tr. pour out, spill; PSDr. *uṯṯ-; see s. v. ūṟu, uṟiyu; also cf. Ka. toṭṭu, Ta. coṭṭu, Ma. coṭṭuka intr. to fall in drops, drizzle.]

98 uḍuku intr. to be aggrieved, be unhappy (through jealousy, anger, etc.) (Bhr. II); to be cooked, boiled (Manu.); be angry (Manu.); to

seethe, simmer, bubble with heat (also Mdn.); n. heat, boiling.

[Kur. uṛtūr- (uṛtur-) to be agitated by the action of heat; to boil; be boiled or cooked; fig. be tired up to excitement; Kui uṛgi boiled rice, cooked rice; Go. ukuṛ (ukuḍā; ? metathesis of *uḍk-) the boiling point; ukuṛ (wātā) (the water has come to the) boil (wā- to come); cf. Keikaḍi uḍku hot (Hislop, p. 19, transcribed udku).]

99 uḍugu tr. to give up, stop, desist from (an action) (Bhr. I, II); intr. to sink (as water); shrink, abate (KS, Bhr. II); tr. uḍucu, uḍupu to stop, avert; to block or bar (a way) (Bhr. II); to put an end to (Bhr. I); der. n. uḍukuva rest, interval (Bhr. II).

[Ka. uḍugu to shrink, abate, desist, stop; tr. to remove; Ta. oṭuṅku v.i. to be restrained, to calm down; shrink, be hidden (Kṟḷ.), be inactive (PN); oṭukku to subjugate, reduce (Tiruvāc.); oṭivu cessation (Cīv.); Ma. oṭuṅṅuka to come to an end, die; oṭukkuka to finish, destroy, spend; oṭuka come to an end; oṭuvu n. end; Kui ḍūmba be shrunken; ḍūppa to cause to shrink; pull together; Kur. uṭ$^{u}$r- to be stopped; be intercepted behind; be hidden; uṭ- (uṭc-, uṭṭ-) tr. to close an aperture (by obstructing); to stop a hole, gag; dam a river, bar a way, etc.; Mlt. uṭ- to close, fill up; PDr. *uṭ-/*oṭ-. On account of uḍu- < *oḍu-, probably a l. w. < Ka.; possibly related to PDr. *uḷ-/*oḷ- : cf. Ka. uḷi to conceal oneself; Ta. oḷi v.i. to hide, tr. to conceal; Ma. oḷikka to hide oneself, to conceal, suppress.]

uḍucu* IIb tr. of uḍugu q.v.

uḍupu* tr. of uḍugu q.v., alt. of uḍucu.

100 uṇḍu V (allom. un(u)-) intr. to be, exist, live; remain, stop, stay; reside, dwell; last, endure; wait (class. and Mdn., Bhr. I, etc.); tr. un(u)cu to place, put, deposit, retain, preserve; set apart for a purpose (class. and Mdn.); uniki existence, living.

[Ka. uḷ, oḷ to be, to have, possess; uṇḍu is (also with plural subj.); Tu. uṇḍu there is or exists; Ko. oḷ- (3rd person non-personal oḍō) to exist, be in place; To. wïḷd- (3rd pers. wïḍ-i) exist, be in a place, have; Ta. uḷ to be; uṇṭu to be (all persons, genders, and numbers); Ma. uḷ to be within, to exist; uṇṭu there is; Brah. uṭ I am, pl. un; us (2nd sg.), ure (2nd pl.); ur 3rd pl.).]

utuku free var. of uduku, q.v. (post-classical).

101 udaru, uduru* intr. to tremble, shake; to be startled in fear, anger, etc. (Bhr. I, II); to be angry (Bhr. I); udiri-paḍu id. (intensive) (Bhr. I).

[Ka. odaṟu to move to and fro, to shake, shake off or about; Tu. udēvuni v. i. (hands) to shake as in sickness; tr. to throw out; Ta. utaṟu v. i. to shake (as one's hands through cold, anger, etc.); tr. to shake off, throw off; utai v. i. to tremble with fear (colloq.).]

102 udalu, udulu* intr. to leave off (grip, hold); udalcu (often with -konu) to leave, to release oneself, to shake off limbs, etc. in releasing oneself from other's hold (Bhr. II, III); v. s. v. vadalu/vadulu.

[Ka. udir, udaru to fall, fall off (as fruit from tree); udircu to cause to fall; Tu. udu̥runi to fall, drop off; udruni id.; Ta. utir v. i. to drop off as leaves, etc.; Ma. utiruka id.; Kur. od°kh- tr. to render less tight, to disjoin, to detach; to get rid of, get clear of; PDr. *ut-V-; cf. forms with -ḻ- : Ka. uḻal to swing, be loosened and fly away; uḻi to leave, quit; Ta. uḻal id.; Mlt. urgr- to fall off (as hair). Does the *-t-/*-ḻ- alternation point to *-c-/*-ḻ- in PDr. ? ]

103 udilu* intr. to tremble, shake; udila-gonu to tremble (as heart in fear); to fear (Bhr. I, II); to be in haste, precipitancy (Naiṣ.); udila n. shaking, trembling in fear.

[v. s. v. udaru, uduru; also Tu. uttāṇa haste, precipitancy.]

104 uduku (var. utuku) tr. to wash (as garments) (Manu.); to drub, thrash (BhR); to dash off, destroy (Bhīm.)

[Go. suhk- to wash clothes (Grammar, vol. I, p. 80); sukk- id. (vol. II, p. 130); sukk- id. (Dawson, p. 197); Klm. Nk. sutk- id.; cf. Kui jōga to wash clothes; Ta. utaṟu tr. to shake out as clothes (Kamp.); probably connected with the following series: Ka. ode/odi to kick, spur; Ta. utai to kick, beat, strike; cutai kicking (Piṅ.); Ma. utayuka to kick; uta kicking; utappu striking; Mlt. utes-/uset- to kick. PDr. *cut-, PCDr. *cut-ukku. For meaning association, cf. Ma. maḻakkuka to beat, wash, cleanse, rub off.]

105 uduru* intr. to be proud (UR); der. n. uduṭu pride, arrogance (KS, Bhr. I).

un(u)cu IIb tr. of uṇḍu to put, place, keep, cause to stay.

106 unupu* tr. to dye clothes (dial.); unupulavāḍu a dyer (no literary usages cited).

[Ka. uni to be soaked, lie steeped, to soak (loc.); Kittel compares with Skt. unna- wetted, moist, wet; Ta. ūṭṭu to dye (Nāl.); ? PSDr. *ūṇ-/*uṇ-V.]

107 uppu* tr. to boil (Kāḷ.); adj. uppuḍu boiled; upp-ari that is hot, heated on fire (as a pan) (KS).

[Ta. uvi v. i. to boil away as water in a pot of rice; tr. to boil (PN);

uviyal boiled dish (PN); Tu. ubè steam; To. ub- (uby-) to boil over; -v- < -p- : uv-i < *up-i; PSDr. *up-.]

108 ubuku intr. to swell, heave, rise; jet, bulge, project; n. swell, swelling, bulging (post-sixteenth century).

[Ka. ubiku, ubaku id.; Ta. upukku id.]

109 ubbu intr. to well up (as tears), to swell, be puffed up, to bulge out; be abundant; to be proud; be flattered, elated (Bhr. II, Naiṣ.); n. joy, energy, exuberance (Bhr. II); adj. bulging; der. n. ubbaramu swelling, bloating (of abdomen, etc.).

[Ka. ubbu, urbu, urvu to rise, swell, be puffed up; be full of energy; ur̲ubu violence; ur̲uvu being excessive, large; excellence; ur̲e abundantly; Tu. ubbuni, ubbēruni to swell, be elated with joy; urbi/urbu n. increase as of any disease; Ko. ub- (part of body) swells; Ta. ur̲uttu tr. to increase, spread out open; ur̲uvatu that which accrues, gains; ūr̲u to increase as flesh in a person; to increase; cf. Ma. ur̲uppu a large bag (for clothes); PSDr. *ut̲-uv-; PDr. *cūt̲ : *cut̲-V-, v. s. v. ūr̲u$^{2}$.]

110 umiyu III intr. and tr. to spit (Bhr. I), to spit out remains (KS); colloq. ūyu, ummu, umm(i)ēyu (loc.).

[Ka. ugi, ugul̲ to spit; spit out, emit; Tu. ubbi saliva, ubbiyuni to spit; Ta. umil̲ to spit; gargle, emit as rays of light; reveal news (Cīv.); Ma. umiyuka, umikka, umil̲ka to spit : Kui sūpa to spit; Kuvi hūp- id.; with *c- > *t- : Ka. tūpu to spit; Ta. tuppu id.; Kur. tupp- id.; Mlt. tup- id. PDr. *cup- : *tup-; PSDr. *up- : *tup-; *uv-i < *up-i-; umi- < *uvi-.]

111 uralu$^{1*}$ (also urulu) intr. to roll down (as tears, head cut off) (Bhr. II, KS); fall off; tr. ural(u)cu; ural-aN-drōcu tr. to roll, knock down (classical).

[Ka. uruḷ to roll down; roll, revolve, be turned over; uraḷcu turn round, roll down; Tu. oreṅkuni, reṅkuṇi intr. to roll on the ground, in the dust or mire; Ko. urṇ- (urḍ-) to roll over and over in one direction; To. ūḷ- (ūḍ-) v. i. to roll; tr. ūṭ-; Ta. uruḷ (uruṇṭ-) v. i. to roll, tumble over; uruṭṭu tr. to roll as ball; n. rolling; ūr v. i. to be loosened, relaxed (Kalit.); Ma. uruḷuka to roll, toss, revolve; Kuvi (F) ṛūp- to roll up a rope; Go. urr- to fall (Driberg's vocab. quoted by Hislop, p. 13); Mlt. urgr- to fall off (as hair); orb- to fall in showers (fruit from a tree); cf. urur- to slip off. PSDr. *ur-uḷ, PDr. *ūr-/*ur-V-.]

112 uralu$^{2*}$ (var. urulu) intr. to be caught in a snare (Bhg.); cf. uccu, uri a running knot, a snare, noose.

[Ka. urul, urul, urlu (ural, uralu, etc.) n. a running knot, noose, snare; Tu. urlu a noose, snare.]

113 uralu$^{3*}$ intr. to burn, be consumed by fire (Bhīm.).

[Ka. uralu, urlu aliment of fire, fuel; for other forms, v. s. v. uriyu$^{1}$.]

114 uriyu$^{1*}$ III intr. to burn, be consumed by fire; to be afflicted, to grieve; (Bhr. II).

[Ka. uri to burn from rage, etc.; to smart or itch; uru burning, flame; Tu. uriyuni to blaze, burn; feel pain, become angry; uri n.; Ko. ury- (urc-) pain is felt (dative of pers.), to hate; Ta. uru v. i. to get angry (Kalit.); burn, smart (PN); tr. be angry with; Ma. uruku v. i. to melt, tr. to melt; Kui urpa v. i. to boil, seethe; ruta to ignite, set fire to; ṛuja be scorched, seared; Kuvi ūrh- to boil over; Kur. ŏr- (ōrc-) impers. to be warm weather; ūr- to set fire to; Brah. hush-ing- be burnt, scorched; burn with rage, jealousy; hush- to set fire, burn, scorch. PDr. *ūr- : *ur-V-.]

115 uriyu$^{2}$ III intr. be rubbed; to get friction, rubbing (Bhr. II).

[v. s. v. orayu]

116 uriyu$^{3*}$ III to ripen (as fruits) (Bhr. II); hair to become grey (late).

[Ta. uru to become ripe, mature (PN). Cf. Tu. urve unripe.]

117 uriyu$^{4*}$ III to shake, tremble (as a slender waist) (HariV.).

[Cf. Ta. ūr- be unloosed, relaxed (Kalit.).]

uru$^{1*}$ (var. of uṟu$^{1}$, q. v.) intr. to be excellent, fit (Bhr. II, III); der. n. uravu that is proper, suitable, becoming; propriety (UH).

*uru$^{2*}$ (only in the neg. participle ur-aka; v. s. v. *uṟu$^{3}$ and *ūru$^{2}$) intr. and tr. to speak, utter.

118 uruvu* tr. to abandon, give up (Bhr. II); leave off, throw away unwanted matter (as bones while eating meat) (Bhr. II).

[Ka. uricu to flay, strip off; Ta. uri v. i. to peel (as skin, bark); tr. strip off, as clothes, to divest (Tēv.); v. tr. to slough off, strip off; n. rind, peel (Kamp.); Ma. uriyuka be stripped off; tr. to strip off; urikka to flay; ūruka to strip off, flay; uriyuka, uriññuka be stripped off; Kui ṛuha to lose the skin by peeling; ṛuhpa to squeeze out filth from entrails, etc.; Go. uṛuh-t- to skin (uṛuh-cī); urum- to be skinned, scraped (esp. head of maize); cf. Klm.(SR) uṛp- to leave; uṛp- to undress; Kur. oṛ$^{o}$k- (uṛ$^{u}$ky-, oṛk-) tr. to strip a tree of its bark; Mlt. ōṛy- (ōṛc-) to peel, unveil; oṛku bark, peel. The form occurs in Te. in a general meaning while the remaining languages show it in a specialized sense. PDr. *ūr : *ur-V-.]

urlu* (later var. of uralu[1]/urulu, q. v.).

119 ur̲iyu III intr. (a roof) to leak (Kāś.); to pour (as rain); v. s. v. ūru[1]/ūr̲u.

[Go. urīs- to sprinkle or crumble salt, sugar, sandal powder, etc.]

120 ur̲u[1]* intr. to happen, arise (BhR); to be proper, becoming, suitable, desirable, agreeable (Bhr. I, II; KS); adj. proper, becoming.

[Ka. ur̲u to come about, arise; ūr̲u to be, exist; ur̲e nicely, well; n. abundance; Ta. ur̲u to exist, occur; be desirable, worthy of choice (Kr̲ḷ.); be permanent; adj. copious (Tolk.); Kur. uṛ- (uṛc-) to have one's sufficiency; grow broad; be as thick as required; be filled; Mlt. uṛ- be filled, satisfied; uṛd- to fill, satisfy; cf. Ma. ur̲uka to be firm; Kur. urḵh- to evolve, turn out to be; be a success; (feelings) to come upon.]

121 *ur̲u[2]* (only in neg. ur̲-aka- not minding; ur̲-ā-ḍu he does not care) tr. to mind, to take into consideration, to care.

[Ta. ur̲u v. tr. to perceive by touch (Kr̲ḷ.), to think; v. i. to pass one's mind (Kamp.); cf. Ka. ur̲isu to hold out, bear, suffer, endure; with *-n/*-t̲ : Ta. un̲n̲u to think, consider; Ma. unnuka id.; Kuvi (S) onp- to intend; v. s. v. ũku. PDr. *un-/*ut̲-; PSDr. -t̲- > -r̲-.]

*ur̲u[3]* only in negative participle ur̲-aka not speaking, without word, simply, merely, quietly (Bhr. II); also *uru, ur-aka, v. s. v. *uru[2], *ūru[2]. A case of r/r̲ confusion.

122 ur̲uku intr. to jump down (Bhr. II); to come up (Kāś.); to run (Āmu.).

[Ta. ur̲ukku tr. to jump, leap over (Piṅ.); Go. (Maṛia) uṛtōr (they) came out (LSI IV, p. 535); (Narsingpur) uchchī-kun having run (ibid. p. 494; base uc-); Klm. (E) urki tap- to jump down; Pj. urk- to fall; Mlt. urq- to come out, come forth; Kur. urkh- to come or go out; germinate; break forth (eruption), to succeed. PDr. *ut̲-uk-.]

123 ur̲umu intr. to thunder, roar (Bhr. I); n. thunder, roar.

[Ta. ur̲umu to rumble as a thunder; Ma. ur̲umpuka, urampuka to grumble, roar; ur̲umpal n. roar of a tiger; Kui rūmba, rūma to roar; runja to thunder, reverberate; v. s. v. r̲oppu, r̲ōlu. PDr. *ut̲-u-.]

124 uliyu[1]* III intr. to sound (as calls, drums, etc.); to cry; der. n. ulivu sound, noise.

[Ka. uli to sound, utter, cry, speak; uli, ole a cry, word, sound; ulipu, ulivu id.; Ta. oli to sound (as letters), roar (Kr̲ḷ.); n. noise; thunder; word (Parip.); ulai to make noise; Ma. oliyuka, olikka to sound; oli n.; cf. Tu. uliyuni tr. to instigate. On account of u-i < *o-i, prob. an early l. w. from Ka.; PSDr. *ol-i-. Contamination with the following set possible: Ka. ūḷ, ūḷu to call from distance; cry out, howl; n. cry, howl; Ta. uḷai v.i. to sound, roar (Kamp.); howl as jackal (Maṇi.); tr. call, invite; n. sound; ūḷai howl of a dog or jackal, cry of a person in anguish; ūḷi sound; Te. ūla, ūḷa id.; PSDr. *ūḷ-.]

125 uliyu[2*] III intr. to shake, move (Śab. R.).
[Tu. uliyuni v.i. to tremble; Ma. ulayuka be shaken, agitated, become slack, loose; v.s.v. oluku (evidence for *ol-).]

126 uliyu[3*] III intr. to be removed, be gone; tr. ulucu to remove (rust) (JBh.); ulupu to remove (chains of dogs) (late; rare, with alternative versions).
[Cf. Ta. oli v.tr. to remove, clean (Kalit.); uluppu to shake off, cause to shed as fruit or leaves from a tree.]

127 ¯ul(u)ku intr. to be startled, to fear (Bhr. I); be ashamed (Bhr. II); n. fear, fright, timidity.
[Ka. uluku, uḷuku the body to shake, tremble, be agitated; Ta. uṭku (< *uḷ-k-) to be afraid; stand in awe; show signs of fear (Kr̲ḷ.); feel shy, be bashful; n. fear, dread; shame; Ma. uḷukku to start, be unnerved; uḷuppu shamefacedness; the forms meaning 'to sprain,' etc. may also belong here, v.s.v. iluku. PSDr. *uḷ-k-, *uḷ-ukk-.]

128 ulumu* (rare) tr. to rub (eyelids after sleep) (Bhg.); probably from nulumu, q.v.

129 usugu* tr. to rub; intr. get friction, be chafed (Paṇḍ.).
[Ka. usiku, usigu, osagu, hosagu to rub anything between the hands (doubtful since ose- < hose- < pose-, cf. hose, pose to churn, rub, etc.; probably Ma. ul̲iyuka to rub, stroke, polish, scrape; Mlt. nusg- to rub, clean.]

130 usumu tr. to scour, wash, clean up (rust) (Pāṇḍ.); (clothes) to wash, clean (colloq., Dh. M.).
[Go. usūm- to wipe, clean with a cloth; Klm.(SR) usm- to wipe; apply; Kuvi(F) ūss- to anoint (oneself); ūsp- to plaster (with cowdung); Mlt. nusg- to rub, clean; cf. To. ud- (udy-) to smear on body. PCDr. *uc-V-.]

## Ū

131 ū̆ku* intr. to make an effort (BhR), n. an attempt (Bhg.); ū̆k-incu id. (Bhr. II); der. n. ū̆kuva attempt.
[Ta. ūkku to make an effort (Cīv.); to consider, n. zeal; ūkkal,

ūkkam effort (Cīv.), firm conviction (PN); Ma. ūkku n. strength, exertion; cf. Te. uṅk-incu to consider, attempt (Bhr. II); Ka. uṅk-isu to consider, observe, look at; unn-isu to think; Ko. uny- (unc-) to think; To. uny- (unc-) id.; Ta. un̲n̲u to think, consider; n. effort; Ma. unnuka to think, aim at; Kuvi (S) onp- to intend. PDr. *ūn-/*unn-, *ūṅ-k- < *ūn-k-; *uṅk- < *un-k-.]

132 ū̃gu intr. to swing, rock; to totter, reel, be shaken (Kāś.); tr. ū̃cu, ū̃pu.

[Ta. ūṅku v.i. to swing; ūkku tr. to swing, shake (Kalit.); ūcal moving to and fro (Kalit.); Kuvi (S) ūmp- to swing; Go. ūm- to pull a swing, etc.; ūkāṛ a swing; GoM. ūng- to swing; Klm.(SR) ūŋg- id.; ūp n.; Nk. ūŋg-; Pj. ū̃g- to hang, swing; ūñ- v.i. to swing, shake; ūkip-/ūkit- to cause to hang or swing; KGad. ūyŋ- to swing, rock; Kur. nuk$^{u}$r- to sway to and fro, up and down; nuk- tr. to shake (as wind shakes trees), up and down, to and fro; Mlt. nukr- to swing, rock, be shaken; nuk- to shake; PDr. *ŭ̃y-nk-, *ŭ̃y-; v.s.v. tū̃gu for further forms; for words for 'cradle,' see Kolami, Vocab. 987.]

133 ūcu IId intr. (hair) to fall off (Brown, Śab.R.), colloq.

[Ka. ūcu id. (loc.); Pj. uy- (Sth. uv-) id.; cf. Ta. ūcu, ūy to decay, deteriorate; uku v.i. to shed as leaves; tr. let fall, cast, as leaves (PN).]

134 ū̃cu IIb tr. of ū̃gu q.v., to shake, move (as wind moves the trees), swing, rock (Bhr. I).

135 ūṭu tr. (cattle) to drink water, etc., completely (colloq.; Dh.M.).

[Ka. ūḍu to take a meal, eat; ūṭa taking a meal; Ko. ūṭ- to suck (young of animals); Ta. Ma. ūṭṭu to feed; Kuvi (F) ūnd- to drink; connected with PDr. *ŭ̃ṇ- (see Kolami, Vocab. 977), ultimately *ū-, cf. Ta. ūr to suck (Cīv.), ūmpu id.; Ma. ūmpuka id.]

136 ūḍu intr. to be unfastened, loosened, detached; to fall off, slip, come off, drop (Bhōj., Pāṇḍ.).

[Klm.(SR) ūṛp-, ūrp- (p. 23) to leave; Mlt. urgr- to fall off, slip off; cf. uṭr- to fall, drop off, down; cf. To. wīθ- (waistcloth) slips; Ta. ul̲al to oscillate, whirl; lose condition or status; also ūl̲ to decay, rot; v.s.v. udalu.]

137 ūḍ(u)cu[1] IIa tr. to strip off, take off (clothes, etc.) (Bhr. II); pull off (feathers) (Bhr. II); to clean the floor, field, etc. by sweeping (Bhīm.), to sweep, clean rubbish, etc. (Mdn.).

[To. ušt- to take off (clothes, ring, etc.); Klm.(SR) uṛp- to undress; Go. uṛp- (urp-, p. 137) to clean a threshing floor; Pj. ūṛcip-(ūṛcit-)

to heap up; put together; cf. Kui ūga to be stripped off, ūpka (< *ūkp-) to strip off; Kuvi (S) hukh- to strip; Kur. ur- to rub off the leaves, etc. by passing the hand along. PDr. *ūḻ-; cf. ūrcu, uruvu; probably ultimately *ū- with *-r, *-ḻ as suffixes.]

ūḍ(u)cu$^{2}$ IIb tr. of ūḍu, q. v., to untie, loosen, unfasten (Bhr. II, BhR).

138 ū̃ṭu* tr. to pierce (a weapon through) (late); n. piercing.
[V. s. v. ū̃ḍu.]

139 ū̃ḍu* intr. to be planted, fixed; mostly with aux. -konu to be planted; tr. ūḍucu to plant, transplant (Hara.); ūḍvu nēla (inscr. 12th cent.) field for transplanting (SII, IV, No. 1364).
[Ka. ūr̲u to put in the ground, put down, fix; Tu. ūruni to set firmly, plant seed; Ko. ūṇḍ- (ūṇḍy-) to transplant; ūt- (ūyt-) to fix into ground by pressure; ūv- (ūd-) sink into ground of its own weight; Ta. ūn̲r̲u be fixed, settled, strike root (Cīv.); tr. to fix (as a pole), to plant (Kr̲ḷ.); Ma. ūnnuka to be fixed firm; Kui usa to set a post into the ground, to set up; uṅa to plant, transplant; Kuvi (F) ūh- to plant; Kuvi (S) uh- id.; (h < s < *nṯ); Go. urs- to plant or transplant (of trees, rice, chillis, etc.); Pj. ud- to plant; Kur. ūd- (ūdy-) to fix closed door, shutter, etc., by a bolt, lock, etc. PDr. *ūn-ṯ-; further, v. s. v. ūnu, ū̃du$^{1}$.]

140 ūnu$^{1*}$ intr. to rest, as mind on something; to serve as support; tr. to hold as support, to put on, wear; to let stay on a support (Bhr. I, II); ūn(u)cu tr. to let (mind) rest on something (Bhr. II); to place steadily; ū̃kuva n. a prop, protection (BhR).
[Ka. ūr̲u to lean on; Ta. ur̲uti n. support, leaning; -n̲-/-r̲- alternation in SDr., further v. s. v. ū̃ḍu, ū̃du$^{1}$ (PDr. *ūn-/*ūṯ-).]

141 ūnu$^{2*}$ intr. to happen, occur (Bhr. II); tr. ūn(u)cu to make (Bhr. I); cause to occur (Naiṣ.).
[Ka. ūr̲u to be, exist, settle; for further forms, v. s. v. ur̲u$^{1}$; PDr. *ūn-/ūṯ-.]

142 ū̃du$^{1*}$ tr. to hold, as a support (Bhr. I), to let stay on a support; to strengthen (Bhr. I, II); to press (Nirv.); plant (Kāś.); der. n. ū̃ta a prop, support; v. s. v. ū̃ḍu, ūnu.
[Ka. ūr̲u to lean on; to settle; take up one's abode; n. leaning on; firmness; ūta firmness; Tu. ūnduni to press down, hold firmly; ūdu a prop; ūta weight, burden; Ta. ūn̲r̲u tr. to recline on, to support (Kr̲ḷ.), press down, push; n. prop; Ma. ūnnuka to lean on, ūnnu n. support; Go. uhasc- to lean heavily on a stick (as an old man); Kur. ūd- (ūdy-) to lean upon; udd$^{u}$r- (uddr-) to lean upon a cane or walking stick; also uddur, ud$^{u}$r-, free vars.; Mlt. ūdur- to lean upon; PDr. *ūn-ṯ, the same as for Te. ū̃ḍu.]

143 ū̃du[2] intr. to blow through mouth (Kāś.); become inflated; swollen (BP); tr. blow out fire, lamp, with mouth (Mārk.), to purify or refine metal with the blow pipe (Mdn.); ū̃da adj. swollen; ūdu colloq. swelling.

[Ka. ūdu, ūbu to blow, become inflated, puffed up; n. blowing, swelling; Tu. ūduni tr. to blow as a pipe; to swell; Ko. ūd- become swollen; Ta. ūtu tr. blow, as a wind instrument; blow out, lamp, fire (Kamp.); breathe upon and allay pain; intr. to swell; blow with bellows, blow-pipe (Maṇi.); Ma. ūtuka to blow fire, puff; GoM. ud- to blow; Kuvi(F) ūk- to blow; Kuvi(S) hūt- to kindle; Go. uhuk- puff at, blow, blow a fire; (Dawson) uk- to blow; Klm. (SR) ūnd- id.; Pj. ū̃d-; KGad. ūnd- id.: Kur. ūr- (ūrc-) to blow with mouth; Mlt. ūr- intr. to blow as wind; tr. to blow a fire or trumpet; breathe upon. *uy-nt-/*uy-t- for PCDr. and PSDr.; *uy-t̲-/-r- for PNDr., *uy-k- for Kuvi, Go.; v. s. v. ūrcu, PDr. *uy- to breathe.]

ū̃pu tr. of ū̃gu, q. v.

144 ūyu III (ūs-) (Dh.M., not in SAN or Śab. R.) intr. to spit (colloq.).

[Go. ucc-; Klm.(E) ūs-, Klm.(SR) us-; Nk. ūs-; Pj. ucc-; Oll. us-; KGad. ūc-; PCDr. *ūc-.]

145 ūru[1] to ooze, exude (Manu.); spring, leak out; (mouth) to water (Daśā.); to be soaked, steeped; der. n. ūṭa a water spring (KS); essence (Bhr. II); cf. ur̲iyu to leak (ūru has r wrongly for r̲).

[Ka. ūr̲u leak, ooze, be soaked; Tu. ūjuni, ūsuni to ooze; To. ūr̲- to spring forth, be filtered; Ta. ūr̲u to spring, as water in a well (Kr̲ḷ.), water as mouth, ooze, soak; ūr̲r̲u to pour out; n. fountain (Nāl.), moisture; Ma. ūr̲uka to ooze, spring; ur̲avu n. a spring; ūr̲r̲uka to pour out, strain, filter; Go. ūs- to drip, water; ūsā a flood, spate; Klm. Nk. ūr- to leak (as a house); Brah. hūring- to break out (of boils), to sprout, as crops; Meile (see §1.211) compares Kui sūga a spring, Go. sū-sū a little wet; PDr. *cūt̲- : SDr. *ūt̲-; evidence conflicting on account of no *c- in Go. Klm. Nk.]

146 *ūru[2] (only neg. pp. ūr-aka silently, quietly; not speaking; (Bhr. II), not asking (HariV.); merely, simply, in vain (BhR). Cf. uru[2], ur̲u[3]) intr. *to speak, say, ask.

[Ka. ore to sound, utter, say, tell; Tu. uripuni to sound, play on; Ta. urai to tell, say, speak; n. word; Ma. ura word, expression; PDr. *ūr; also v. s. v. ur̲umu, r̲oppu.]

147 ūru[3] to grow fat, puffed up (later works and also Mdn.).

[For the other SDr. forms, v. s. v. ubbu; Kui sūja to be fat; Brah. ūrēng-, hūrēng-, hūring- to swell up; cf. Kur. uskār- to swell up slightly; PDr. *cūṯ-.]

148 ūr(u)cu[1]* IId intr. to breathe, respire, sigh (Bhr. I, KS); ūrpu n. sighing; ūr-ārcu to console (lit., to cool sighing; Bhr. I) (< *uy-ir-c-).

[Ka. usir to breathe; breath; Tu. usuru, usulu breath, life; usụ, ussane a deep sigh; Ta. uyir to breathe hard; uyirppu respiration, sighing; Ma. uyir n. breath; Kui ūkuri breath, respiration; Kur. ujj- to have life; Mlt. uj- to live. PDr. *uc-/*uy-; PSDr. *uc-ir-/ *uy-ir-.]

149 ūrcu[2] IId tr. to collect with hand or otherwise as what is spread or scattered on the ground, a plate or other surface (later works).

[V. s. v. ūḍcu.]

## E

150 ekku intr. to increase, rise, swell; accumulate, accrue, be acceptable, to prevail, be successful; tr. to climb, mount, get on (class.); ekkuḍu, ekkuva excess.

[Ka. ekku to come up, stand on tiptoe; ekke n. eminence, superiority; Tu. ekkalyuni to spring, jump up; Ta. ekku to be heaped up; to rise, go up (Parip.); Ma. ekkuka to come up; stand on tiptoe; Kuvi (S) eng- to climb up; ekh- to heighten; Kui ekasi adj. rising, ascending; adv. uphill, upwards; Kur. eke-ekā, ekēkā adv. very; adj. very many, very much; cf. Te. ekk-uva id.; Brah. hēf- to raise, lift up (-f- caus.). PDr. *ey-nk-/-kk-; on account of -kk- in Ta. Ma. Ka., not from *eḻ-k-; no assimilation in Ta. Ma. Cf. ēcu.]

151 egayu III intr. to fly up, rise in the air; rise upwards, soar, jump (Bhr. II, UH); cf. *egu.

[Ta. ika (< *ey-a-) to jump over; go beyond (Kamp.); ēntu to rise high, be elevated (PN); eñcu to transgress, go beyond, overstep (< *ey-nc-); cf. Mlt. ite to spring up; Brah. hē-f- to raise (*hē- to rise); PDr. *ey-/ē-.]

152 *egu (only in inf. eg-aN adv. up, upwards; egaṅga digaṅga up and down (BP); prefixed to a number of verbs egā-gaṭṭu to tie up, egā-brāku to creep up; egā-baḍu to pounce upon, smother; also as an intensifier, egā-bāṟu to run away, etc. [all classical]); intr.

*to rise, shoot up, etc.; der. n. eguḍù (Mdn.) elevation (of surface); egumati export; eguva excess. Cf. egayu.

[Ka. egu rising, embarkation.]

153 egucu* (var. evucu) IIa tr. to chase, pursue (Bhr. I, KS); drive away (a chariot, etc.) (Bhr. II); cf. egudu.

[Cf. Mlt. akr- to chase, fly at, drive; aktr- to suspend; Ko. ĕd- to drive away; Klm.(SR) edg- to drive away; probably tr. of a form derived from *ey- to go; see eydu, ēdu to reach.]

154 egudu* intr. to run, come away running (BP); to be obtained (Paṇḍ.) (< *ey-it-); cf. eydu, eyidu.

155 eguru (var. evuru) intr. to fly, jump up; to rise (Manu.); n. flying, flight, a jump (< *ey-ur-/-ir).

[Ka. egaru to fly away; fly, jump; Ta. ivar to rise on high, ascend (Cīv.); leap, rush out (Kalit.); v. s. v. ekku, egayu, eydu[2], negayu; PDr. *ey-/ē-.]

156 eccu intr. to increase; n. increase (late); cf. heccu.

[Ka. eccu, heccu, percu id.; Tu. heccuni to increase; To. ec- (family) increases; Ta. eccu n. increase; Ma. eccu n. id.; all l. ws. from Ka.; v. s. v. heccu, perugu.]

157 eḍayu* III intr. to be disunited, separated (as two parts, lovers, etc.) (post-classical); cf. eḍamu, eḍa space between, interval; tr. eḍapu to separate.

[Ka. eḍa, eḍe place or space between, interval; Tu. iḍè, eḍe n. id.; Ta. iṭai space between; interval (Kṟl.); v. i. to make room, retreat; Ma. iṭakka to widen a place; iṭa n. interval, space between; iṭam id.; cf. Kui espa to pluck; Mlt. eṛar- to keep aloof; eṛatr- to separate, remove; PDr. *iṭ- to break, PSDr. *eṭ-a- < *iṭ-a-; v. s. v. iḍiyu, eḍaru, eḍalu.]

158 eḍaru* intr. to break (Bhr. I; a single usage discovered in the whole literature; different text version occurs as eḍalu).

[< *eṭ-ar < *iṭ-ar. Cf. Te. iḍiyu, etc.]

159 eḍalu* intr. to be separated, as joints (Bhīm.); to diminish, to be destroyed (Bhr. II); to fall off, as leaves (KS); to be discarded, given up (Bhr. II); tr. eḍal(u)cu to remove, take off, as clothes (late) (< *eṭ-al < *iṭ-al).

[Only Te. has the -al suffix; cf. iḍiyu v. i. to break, etc.; Ta. ıṭu to throw, cut off; cf. Mlt. eṛar- to keep aloof; eṛatr- to separate, remove.]

160 enḍu intr. to dry up (as a stream); evaporate wholly (JBh.); to wither, shrivel up, become lean or thin (Mdn.); enḍa sunshine

(Bhr. II); eṇḍamāvi a mirage (KS); eṇḍugulu dried grain (Āmu.).

[Ta. eṉṟu sun; el lustre, splendor (Tolk.); sun, sunshine (Piṅ.); daytime (PN); ellai sun, daytime (Kalit.); Kui ēski thirst; Kuvi (F) eski thirst; (-s < *-nṯ); Pj. neṇḍi (NE nendi) sunshine, heat; Go. addi id.; GoA. eddi; cf. Mlt. eṛy- (eṛc-) to parch grain, season fodd; Kur. iṛ- (iṛy-) to fry, parch; Kur. nēr- to get dry; Mlt. nēr- id.; PDr. *el-, *el-nt- > *en-ṯ-.]

161 ettu tr. to raise, lift up (Bhr. I); to raise, collect money, alms; to cite, quote, mention (Bhr. I); to assume, as an incarnation; (with -konu) carry a child on arms, etc.; intr. to mobilize troops (Bhr. II); to strike, arise, as a feeling (anger, pain, etc.) (Bhr. II); to increase, as zeal (Bhr. II).

[Ka. ettu to raise, lift; collect money; mention other's name, etc.; Tu. ettuni to raise a subscription or tax; ettaruni to climb, ascend; ēpuni to lift; Ko. et- to carry; build (house); ēṯ- (ēc-) place burden on; Ta. ēṟṟu tr. to raise; lift up; praise (Tolk.); ascribe; think, consider (Tolk.); ēntuka v.i. to rise high, be abundant; tr. to hold in hands; to support beam, etc.; Ma. ēṟṟuka to raise; talk, speak; ēntuka to wield; v.i. to rise; Go. att- to take in one's lap; Kui eta, Kuvi (F) et- carry on the hip; Klm.(E) et- to lift up; Nk. ett- id.; Pj. etip-(etit-) id.; edp- (edt-) to lift out. PSDr. and PCDr. *ēṯ-ṯ- < *ēṯ-t- or *ētt-/ēnt-; cf. Ta. Ma. ēntu.]

162 edugu intr. to grow (as a child, plant, etc.); increase in stature (Nirv.); n. growth (Mdn.); cf. ēdu.

[Mlt. it- to spring up, as seed; itr-, itgr- to be hatched; probably from PDr. ēt-, ultimately ē-, cf. ēcu.]

163 eduru intr. to oppose, attack (governs dative); lit. to be opposite to somebody (Bhr. I); tr. (governs acc.) to attack, oppose, resist against (Bhr. II); n. the front; opponent; equal, match (classical); tr. ed(u)rucu/edur(u)cu to oppose, resist (Bhr. II, UH); ediri opponent (Bhr. II).

[Ka. idir, edir, edur, eduru n. (that) which is opposite; opposition; idircu to face, oppose; Tu. eduru, edụrụ the front; that which is opposite; Ta. etir v.i. to be opposed (PN); to appear (Cīv.); tr. to oppose, meet, face, prevent, etc.; etir-koḷ to attack (Kalit.); cf. Te. edur-konu id.; Ma. etirkka to attack, face; etir n. opposite, match; Kur. etthr- to be visible; come into sight (cf. Ta. to appear); Mlt. ētr- to be seen, appear. PDr. *et-ir-.]

164 enayu* III intr. to equal, resemble (Bhr. II, HariV.); to mix, mingle with, unite; to cohabit with (Bhr. II); to suit, fit; ena n. equal,

match (Bhr. I); enayika agreement, union (Bhr. II).

[Ka. eṇe equality, match; couple, pair; eṇisu, eṇasu to add together; to make equal, compare; Tu. inĕ a pair, couple; Ta. iṇai v.i. to agree, unite (Cilap.); be like; tr. join, connect; tie together (Tirumuru.); n. union, analogy (Cīv.); iṇaṅku union; Ma. iṇa a couple; union; iṇayuka to agree; iṇekka to unite; iṇaṅṅuka to agree; iṇakkuka to reconcile; cf. Ta. eḷḷu v.tr. to equal (Tolk.); eḷḷa adverbial word of comparison; Klm.(SR) yalg-, Nk. elg- to embrace; Kui ēṇba to accept, receive; obey; n. acceptance. PDr. *ēḷ-/ĕṇ-.]

eniyu III to be well mixed, as boiled pulses (colloq.); Mdn. Te. alternant of enayu, q.v.

enucu IIb tr. of eniyu, enayu; altern. enupu.

enupu (colloq.; Guntur dial., to mash boiled pulses into dhall; stir so as to make well mixed), tr. of enayu, q.v.

165 encu IId tr. to count, reckon; estimate (Hara.); to praise; to intend; to recollect (Kaḷā.) (no usages cited from Bhr. or other earlier works; all post 14th century).

[Ka. eṇisu, eṇasu to count; estimate, consider, think of. Te. form < *eṇ-c-; v.s.v. ennu.]

166 ennu tr. to count, reckon (Bhr. I, II); to say, mention (Bhr. II); to consider, think, grasp (Āmu., Vasu.); enn-ika consideration, reckoning, estimation (classical); election (Mdn.).

[Ka. eṇ, eṇṇu id.; eṇisu to count, consider, compare, think of; eṇike, eṇṇike n.; To. oṇ- to count; Ta. eṇṇu tr. think; consider (Kṟḷ.); count, value; eṇ n. calculation (Cīv.); thought (Maṇi.); deliberation, counsel (Kṟḷ.); Ma. eṇṇuka to count, esteem; eṇ n. number, thought; Kuvi (S) ezi kī- to count; cf. Kui ēlu mind, reason, sense, thought; elki mind, reason. SDr. *eṇ-; cf. Kui, PSDr. and PCDr. *ĕṇ-/ĕḷ-.]

167 eyidu[1*] tr. to chase (HariV.); cf. egucu (< *ey-).

eyidu[2] free var. of eydu[1], q.v. (classical).

168 eydu[1*] tr. to reach, go to; join (Bhr. I, II); to obtain (Bhr. II); intr. to suit, be proper (Paṇḍ.); alt. eyidu, ēdu.

[Ka. aydu go to, join; approach; obtain; be fit; To. ïc- (ïč-) to reach; Ta. eytu v.tr. to approach (PN), obtain (Kuṟun.), v.i. to be suitable (Kṟḷ.); Ma. eytuka id.; ettuka to reach, obtain; Pj. ēd- to arrive; PSDr. and CDr. *ey-t-; PDr. *ey-; v.s.v. ĕgu.]

169 eydu[2*] intr. to fly (KS) (< *ey-t-; for *ey-, v.s.v. eguru).

[Ta. ēntu to rise high (PN); < *ēy-nt-/*ey-nt-.]

erãgu same as eṟagu (a case of -ṟ-/-r- confusion; -ṟ- original, v.s.v. eṟãgu), intr. to jump down, bow in respect (Bhr. I, II).

170 eriyu* III intr. to burn (KS, Bhr. II), to grieve (Bhr. II, III); to be destroyed, to perish (Bhr. II); der. n. erivu suffering, pain (BP); tr. ērcu to burn, consume; Mdn. Te. erupu, q. v.

[Tu. eriyuni to be hot; eri n. the glare or heat of fire; Ko. erv- (erd-) shine brightly (except of sun); To. er- (erθ-) be very bright; Ta. eri v. i. to flame; tr. ignite, burn (Tiruvāc.); n. fire, burning, flame (Kr̲ḷ.); adj. of fire; Ma. eriyuka v. i. to burn; n. heat; erikka to kindle, torch; Kui ērpa to kindle, ignite; rīva (rīt-) to burn; Klm.(E) erk- to light (fire); Pj. erip- (erit-) (Sth.) to burn the mouth. PDr. *ēr- : *er-V-.]

erupu (colloq., Guntur dial.; tr. of archaic eriyu; often with refl. -ku), tr. to tease, trouble, torture; e.g., enduku pillalni aṭṭā erupuku tinṭāw? why do you torture the children like that?

171 er̲āgu* intr. to descend, dismount, perch, alight (Bhr. I, II); jump down (KS); bend, bow in respect (Bhr. I).

[Ka. er̲agu to bow, be bent; alight; bow, make obeisance to; perch, fall upon; Tu. eraguni id.; Ta. ir̲aṅku bow respectfully (Tēv.), fall from a high state (Cīv.); descend; ir̲aiñcu to bow, bend (PN); fall down (Kalit.); tr. make obeisance to (Tiruvāc.); ir̲ai to bow in respect, worship; Ma. ir̲aṅṅuka, v. i. ir̲akkuka id.; Ko. erg- to go down; erk- to put down (load); Kuvi (S) rē- to descend; Kuvi (F) rec- id.; reph- lift down; Go. ragg-, rai-, raitt- v. i. to descend; tr. ragst-, reht-; Kur. ett- to descend, alight; Mlt. et- go down; PDr. *et̲-ank-, *et̲-V-.]

172 er̲ūgu (also ergu) tr. to know, learn, be acquainted with (Bhr. I, II; governs acc.); der. n. er̲uka knowledge, spiritual wisdom, memory (Bhr. I, II); er̲ukuva wisdom (Mārk.).

[Ka. ar̲i to know, understand; ar̲ipu to inform, let know; Tu. aruhu knowledge, perception; Ko. ayr- (arc-) to know; To. ar̲y- (ar̲s-) id.; Ta. ar̲i to know, understand, perceive by senses (Nāl.); esteem (Kr̲ḷ.); know by practice (Kr̲ḷ.); Ma. ar̲iyuka to know, etc.; Ta. Ma. ar̲ippu, ar̲ivu knowledge, etc.; Brah. harr-if- to enquire, ask (caus. of an obsolete base *harr- to learn). PSDr. *ēt̲ : *āt̲-; v. s. v. ēr̲u, probably PDr. *cēt̲/*cāt̲.]

ergu free var. of er̲ūgu, q. v. (KS).

173 elamu* intr. to be shiny, splendid (KS).

[Ta. el lustre, splendor, light (Tolk.); Ma. ilakuka to shine, twinkle.]

174 elayu* III intr. to be suitable, become favorable; increase (Bhr. I, Nirv.); to be attracted, as to worldly pleasures, etc. (Bhr. II); to happen, be produced (Bhr. II).

[Ta. ēl to be suitable, convenient (Nāl.); happen, occur; be excessive, to abound; n. fitness (Tiruvāc.); cf. iyai v. i. to harmonize with; be agreeable; icai to fit to; iyal (> ēl) to be possible; agree to; draw near (Kalit.); Ma. iyaluka to agree, go fairly; Ma. ēluka to suit, fit; ēl n. preparation. PSDr. *ēl : *el-V.]

175 esãgu* intr. to increase, augment (Bhr. I); flourish; to happen, shine (Bhr. I, II); esakamu abundance, excess; splendor (Bhr. I, II); cf. ēsaru, ēcu.

[Ka. ese to shine, become manifest; esaka splendor, beauty, appearance; Ta. iyakkam greatness, excellence; icai to fit in, harmonize; PSDr. ey/ē- < *ec-, v. s. v. ēcu, esaru.]

176 esaru* intr. to increase, flourish, exceed (Nirv.; Pāṇḍ.); cf. *esal- in esal-āru to shine, flourish, etc. (Bhr.); esa- instigation, esakolpu to instigate.

[< *ēc(u) + ar, cf. esãgu, ēcu; Tu. iyaruni to be enough, sufficient; iyavuni id.]

## Ē

177 ēku tr. to dress cotton (late); colloq. to pick, beat or clean cotton; to expose or publish the faults of; to defame; n. a roll of cleaned cotton prepared for the spindle; ēkuḍu n. picking, beating or cleaning cotton.

[Ka. ekku to dress cotton; to divide, separate; Tu. ekkuni to gin; Ta. eẖku to pull (cotton) with finger (Patiṟ.); to sift, search for, as the true meaning of passage, scrutinize (Tolk.); eẖkuṟu to be pulled thinly with the fingers; Ma. ekkuka to card cotton; ēkku carding cotton; Kui ēspa to separate, pluck, unravel, spin; ēnda to spin. PSDr. and CDr. *ec- (*es-/*ey-) > *ē-.]

178 ẽkaru* intr. to feel or experience a strong desire for anything after long want or privation; to long for (UH); var. ẽkāru (late) to long for, desire ardently.

[Ta. ēkkaṟu tr. to desire (Ciṟup.); ēṅku to long for, yearn after (Nāl.); to pine, languish (Cīv.); ēcaṟu to long for; ēcaṟuvu longing.]

179 ẽgu intr. to go to; inscr. .ēṅgu (c. 9th century) to walk; resort (Bhr. II); to be gone, dead (Bhōj.); ūr-ẽgu to be taken in procession through the city.

[Tu. ekkāvuni to reach; ekkuni to touch; Ta. ēku to go, walk (Nāl.); Ma. ēkuka id.; Kui epa (et-) to reach, arrive at; Kuvi(F) ej- (et-)

id.; Kur. ēk- to walk, manage; ēkta'- to guide; Mlt. ēk- to go, move; ēṛ- to follow. PDr. *ey-/*ē-, *ēk-; for *ey-, cf. Ta. iyaṅku to move, proceed; n. going (Cīv.); Ma. iyaṅṅuka to move steadily; therefore PDr. *ēk-/*ē-nk- < *ey-k-/*ey-nk-.]

180 ēcu* IId intr. to increase; grow (Bhr. I, II); be abundant; be exulted (Bhr. I); ēpu n. excess, abundance (Bhr. I, II).

[Ta. ē n. increase, abundance (Tolk.); ēntu to rise high, be elevated (PN), be abundant (Tolk.); eyta adv. abundantly; eytu to be adequate; be sufficient (Aiṅk.); Kui epa (et-) to extend, to suffice; n. sufficiency. PDr. *ey-/*ē-; see s. v. esāgu, esaru.]

181 ēḍ(u)cu IIa intr. to cry, weep, lament (Bhr. II); der. n. ēḍ(u)pu screaming, weeping (Bhr. II).

[Ka. al̲u id.; Tu. arpini; Ko. ag- (aṛt-) id.; To. oṛ- (oṛy-) id.; Ta. al̲u to cry, weep (Kr̲ḷ.); cf. al̲ivu n. distress, pain of separation (Tolk.); Ma. al̲uka to weep, cry; Kui ṛīva (ṛīt-) id.; Kuvi rī-; Go. āṛ-; Klm.(E) ar-; Pj. aṛ-; KGad. āḍ-. Except Te. Kui Kuvi, all languages give a reconstruction *āl̲- : *al̲-V-; on account of Te. ē- < PDr. *yāl̲-, but *yā- > ā- in CDr. is not expected; Kui-Kuvi -ī- is problematical; could be from *el̲i- through aphaeresis with compensatory lengthening, rather than metathesis, i.e., *el̲-i > *l̲ī- > ṛī-/rī-. Contamination with the etyma under aḍalu is possible.]

ēdu[1]* free var. of eydu, q. v. (KS; HariV).

182 ēdu[2]* tr. to bring up, foster (a child) (Daś.); intr. to grow, flourish as crops; (< *ey-t-/*ēt-).

[PDr. *ey-/*ē- to increase, abound, etc., v. s. v. edugu, ēcu; cf. Ta. ēntu v. tr. to hold in hands; Ma. ēntuka to wield.]

183 ēdu[3]* intr. to diminish, to be lost; to cease, fail (as of memory, glory, strength, etc.) (Bhr. I, II).

[Ta. āy to diminish, be reduced (Tolk.); cāy to be emaciated; cāyvu deficiency; cf. Klm.(SR) sāy- to leave; Nk. sāy- to leave, abandon; Pj. cāy-, Oll. sāy-, KGad. sāy- to leave; the CDr. forms have a transitive signification, whereas Te. Ta. show the intransitive one; ā/ē alternation explained through the preceding *c-.]

184 ẽcu IIIc tr. to harass, torment; trouble (Bhr. II) (SAN notes that there is no conclusive evidence for [ ˜ ]); (probably < *ēm-c-).

[Ta. ēcar̲u to be troubled, feel sorry (Akan.); ēṅku to weep, cry; to be in panic; ēm-ā to be distressed (Maturai.); ēmpu to suffer; or, Ta. ēccu to abuse, insult; ēcc-urai reproach (Cilap.); ēcu rail at; Ma. ēśaṇi back biting; cf. Te. Ka. ēva hatred, disgust; Ka. ē-goḷ to disregard, despise.]

185 ēmaṟu intr. to be forgetful, be careless, without vigilance (Bhr. I, II); var. ēmāṟu (late) id.

[Probably *ēm- protection + *maṟu to forget; cf. Ta. ēmam defence, protection (PN); ēm-āṟṟu to protect, defend (Parip.); cēmam safety, well-being (< *Pkt. chema-, Skt. kṣema-; see Burrow, DS VI, p. 134); for the latter element, see s.v. maṟacu.]

186 ēyu III (ēs-) tr. to throw, fling (Bhr. I); hit with an arrow (Bhr. I).

[Ka. ēy, ēsu to cast, throw, shoot an arrow, etc.; isu, esu (pp. eccu); Tu. eyyuni to shoot an arrow; Ko. iy- (ic-), ey- (ec-) id.; Ta. ey to discharge arrows; n. arrow; ē n. shooting as an arrow (Pu. Ve.); n. arrow (Cīv.); ēcu to hurl, dart (Piṅ., Tēv.); ēvu id.; Ma. eyyuka id.; GoM. ēs- to throw; Pj. ey- (eñ-) to shoot; eyk- shoot (with arrow); KGad. ey- (eṭṭ-) to throw; cf. Kur. iñj- throw (arrows), shoot; sprinkle with jet; Mlt. iṉh- to pelt, stone; ēg- (ēgy-) to throw away, scatter; PDr. *ey-/ē- < *ec-.]

187 ēr(u)gu intr. to pass stool, go to stool (lex.; Mdn., contemptuous); eruvu manure, dung (Vikram., Hara.; also Mdn.).

[Ka. ēru cow dung; erubu dung, muck; eraṇa dung of calf; Ta. eru animal manure (Kṟḻ.); eruku to have loose motions (of cattle) (colloq.); Klm.(E) erŋg-, Klm.(SR) yarg-, yarŋg- to defecate; Kur. erk̲h̲- to suffer from diarrhoea; Mlt. erġ- to go to stool. PDr. *ēr- : *er-V-; *er-uv-, *er-ukk-/-unk-.]

188 ērcu[1] IId tr. to select, choose the best (Bhr. II); ( ? < ēṟ(u) + c-derivative).

[Kuvi (S) ērs- to sort; Klm.(SR) yers- id.; cf. Ka. ārisu to collect, pick out; select, choose; Tu. aripuni to sift; Ta. ari n. sifting, separating; Ma. arikka to sift; ari n. grain of rice freed from chaff; cf. ēṟu; ety. dub.]

189 ērcu[2] IIb tr. to arrange, plan (a war-front), organize (Bhr. II); cf. ērpaḍu to be arranged, be made, formed, prepared (-paḍu, aux.); ērpāṭu arrangement.

[Ka. ēṟ to become fit, suitable; ērpaḍisu to arrange; set in order; ērpaḍu to be arranged; Ta. ēṟpaṭu to become formed; be produced; ēṟpāṭu n. arrangement; ēṟpu fitness, appropriateness; adj. suitable (Cilap.); ēṟ- < *ēl-; cf. Ta. ēl to be suitable; n. appropriateness; Ma. ēluka to fit, suit; ēl n. preparation.]

ērcu[3] IIb (tr. of eriyu q.v.) to burn (Bhr. I), aggrieve (Bhr. I, II); also intr. to suffer (Pāṇḍ.); in this case the base is merely ēr- with c-derivative from an original past morpheme *ci; ety. same as for eriyu, q.v.

190 ē<u>r</u>u tr. to sift; choose, select; cull, glean (Bhr. II).
[Ka. ē<u>r</u>- glean, gather, pick off; select; Tu. sāruni to sift; sāriyuni id.; Kur. cāj- (cajj-) to choose, pick out the best; PDr. *cā<u>t</u>-/cē<u>t</u>-; PDr. -<u>t</u>- : Kur. -j-; alternatively: Kui ēja to become separate from; ēspa to separate, pluck, detach; Go. ēr- to be separate from; eht- to weed; PCDr. *ē<u>t</u>-, including Te.; v. s. v. ēku, ērcu[1].]

191 ēlu tr. to rule, control, govern (Bhr. I, II); to accept as wife, as servant, etc. (Bhr. II); der. n. ēlika ruler; ēlbaḍi rule, government.
[Ka. āḷ to get; possess; rule; Tu. āḷuni to govern, reign; Ko. āṇ- (āḍ-) to possess, own, keep, rule; To. ōḷ- (ōḍ-) to rule, own (buffaloes); Ta. āḷ, āḷḷu (āṇṭ-) to rule, reign (Tiv.), accept as protégé; control; cherish, maintain (K<u>r</u>l.); Ma. āḷuka to possess; PSDr. *yāḷ-.]

192 ēsaru* var. of esaru, q. v. intr. to excel, increase (rare; late); ēsar-incu id. (Nava. N); ēsa- adv. excessively, e.g., ēsa r̄ēgu to rise up vehemently; v. s. v. ēcu, esāgu, esaru.

## O

193 oggu (1) tr. to offer, present, submit, bend towards, e.g., cevi(y)oggu to give ear to (cevi ear); meḍa(y)oggu to bend one's neck in a favorable position to be cut off (BhR., Kaḷā.); intr. to bend towards, incline, e.g., (manas)-oggu (mind) to incline towards (Manu.); to be ready, favorable, be inclined towards; to yield, submit (governs dative).
[Cf. Ka. oggu to bend, turn towards; become submissive; to agree with one's constitution, as water; Tu. orguni to agree with one's stomach, be favorable; Ta. oruṅku v. i. to concentrate (Tiv.); orukku tr. to subdue, control; Ma. oruṅṅuka to be ready; to yield, be settled; orukkuka to prepare; get ready; Kur. oṛ- (oḍḍ-) to put any object in a position favorable for being acted upon, as ears to prick. PSDr. *or-uṅk-/-ukk-; cf. o<u>r</u>āgu.]
oggu* (2) tr. to lay a trap, net (Vikram.); lay a wager, bet (late).
[Cf. Kui oga to trap, snare; Mlt. oktr- to place, put down.]

194 oṭṭu* intr. to occur, arise, as fear (Bhg.); to accumulate, gain momentum, be put together (Bhr. II); oṭṭina-maṇṭalu flames joined together, piled up (Bhr. II; SAN gives the meaning (intr.) to burn, i.e., burning flames; unlikely); tr. to put, as fire.

[Ka. oṭṭu to pile up, put together; to come together, assemble; Tu. oṭṭuni to pile up; further forms, v. s. v. *oḍu.]

195 oḍiyu[1] III (alt. vaḍiyu) intr. to ooze, trickle (Dvi. H.); to be strained, filtered.

[Ka. oḍi to ooze, flow in a gentle stream; Tu. oḍḍuni to flow, run; To. oṭ- (oṭy-) to pour; Ta. vaṭi drip, trickle; tr. to filter, strain; n. filtration; Go. waṟ- to leak, as a house; cf. Kui ōṛa a channel, drain. PDr. *oṭ-/*vaṭ-; cf. ōḍu[2].]

196 oḍiyu[2] III tr. to snatch suddenly (Bhr. II); to wait for a favorable position to snatch (RR); oḍupu hold, grip (Naiṣ., also Mdn.); see also oḍucu.

[Tu. oḍpuni to pluck; oḍpu plucking; cf. Ma. ñoṭi snap of fingers; noṭikka to fillip, snap with fingers; Ta. noṭi v. tr., n. id.]

197 *oḍu (only inf. oḍ-aN- adv. together; oḍā-gūḍu v. i. to join together [Bhr. I]; to accrue; to come together [Bhr. I]; oḍā-gūrcu tr. to unite, to make obtainable [KS., Bhr. II]; to fulfil; oḍā-baḍu to agree to, consent [Bhr. I]; tolerate [Bhr. II]) intr. *to be together.

[Ka. oḍa union; oḍam together with; oṭṭu to come together; become joined; tr. put together; Tu. oḍa with (post position); Ko. oṭ- v. i. to stick; Ta. oṭṭu tr. to stick; tolerate (Cilap.); be appropriate; n. union; oṭṭa adv. closely; ōṭu with, together with; uṭaṉ adv. together with (Pu. Ve.); Ma. uṭan id.; oṭṭuka to adhere, stick; Pj. oṭp- (oṭt-) to apply whitewash; Brah. vaṟ- to suit, become; vaṟ properly; suitable; n. fitness.]

198 oḍucu[1] IId tr. to suppress; defeat, subdue (Bhr. I); to destroy, eliminate (Bhr. I).

[Ka. uḍugu to abate; tr. to remove; Ko. oṛg- be destroyed; To. wïḍg- be crushed; Ta. oṭukku to suppress; restrain; subdue (Tiruvāc.); oṭunku be restrained; shrink; Ma. oṭukkuka to destroy (further forms, see s. v. uḍugu); < PSDr. *oṭ-.]

oḍucu[2] IId tr. to take away by force (Bhr. I); same as oḍiyu, q. v.

199 oḍḍu tr. to lay as a wager, bet (Bhr. I), as a net, trap (Bhr. II); to arrange battle fronts (Bhr. II); to offer, place, extend hand, to receive a gift (Bhr. II), give ear (Mārk.); der. n. oḍḍ-anamu a planned front in battle (Bhr. II); a stake (Bhg.).

[Ka. oḍḍu v. i. lay, place; catch: to array; to resist, oppose; Tu. oḍḍuni to hold or stretch out as the hand; Ko. oḍ- set trap; crouch down behind shelter; Ta. oṭṭu to wager (l. w. < Ka. or Te.); assail, attack (Kṟḷ.); oṭṭam stake (Pārata.); oṭṭ-iṭu to lay a wager; Ma. oṭṭam id. Cf. IA. Dēś. huḍḍā f. wager; Ku. B. H. hoṛ; S. hoḍa f.;

G. M. hoḍ f.; Sgh. oḍapana, stake; oṭṭuwa wager, see s.v. hoṛ, Turner, Nep. Dict.]

200 oṇṭu intr. to fit, suit one's constitution; to be agreeable, friendly; tr. to touch; cf. oṇṭ-ami hatred, enmity (Bhr. II).

[Ka. oṇṭu to suit one's health (l.w. < Te.); Ta. oṉṟu v.i. to unite, agree (PN); cf. oṭṭu to be appropriate (Kṟḷ.); tr. be friends with (Kṟḷ.); Kur. oṇṭam resemblance; equality; oṇṭamnū together; v.s.v. *on-.]

201 ottu tr. to press, squeeze, suppress (Bhr. II); push aside (Naiṣ.); squeeze out moisture, juice, etc. (Naiṣ.); to aspirate letters (Mdn.); to blow conch in war (Bhr. II); to pronounce clearly (Hara.); intr. (gravel, etc.) to press against feet (Bhr. I); to get dimples due to pressure (BhR.); n. a dimple; pressure.

[Ka. ottu to press together, squeeze; push; subdue, harass; take away moisture by gentle pressure with cloth; to stress; aspirate; Tu. ottuni tr. to press; v.i. be close, thick set; Ta. oṟṟu v.tr. bring into contact, press, hug close (Cīv.); wipe away as tears (Cīv.); v.i. to blow as wind (Kalit.); Ko. orv- (ord-) touch or stroke gently; Ma. oṟṟuka to step aside; retire; Kuvi(S) uh'- to press; ōh'- to stick; Kur. oṛ°g- to press, trample out of shape; oṛgō adj. crushed; Mlt. oṭy- (oṭc-) to prick, hurt (as gravel the bare foot); cf. Kur. oth- (utty-) to touch, give a slight stroke. PDr. *oṯ-.]

202 odaru (var. vadaru) tr. to abuse (Bhr. I, KS); v.i. prattle, prate (Nṛs.).

[Ka. odaṟu to sound, cry aloud, howl; Ta. vataru v.i. to chatter, prate; tr. to abuse; utampu to scold, rebuke; utappu id.; to mumble; ōtai, ōcai sound, noise, clamor; ōtu speak, say; persuade clandestinely, whisper; PSDr. *ot-aṯ-/*vat-aṯ-.]

203 odalu* intr. to increase, flourish (rare: Bhg.) (< *ot-al-); v.s.v. od-agu/od-avu (1).

204 odavu* (1) intr. to happen, occur, arise, to originate (Bhr. II); to come handy, be obtained (Bhr. II, Manu.); to flourish (RR); cf. odugu.

[Ka. odagu, odavu to accrue to; be ready for, be at hand; to happen to; to prosper, thrive; Tu. odaguni to be opportune, ready; to prosper; To. ut- to increase (poetical); Ta. utavu to be possible, be of use; Ma. utakuka to be at hand and of use; to prosper, thrive; PSDr. *ot-av-.]

odavu* (2) tr. to give (Acalā.; late).

[Ta. utavu to give, contribute (Nāl.); to help, assist; utavi n. help, gift, assistance (Kṟḷ.); Ma. utakuka to serve; utakkam help; cf. Te. osãgu.]

205 odugu/oduvu* intr. to increase, thrive (Mārk.), n. abundance (also Mdn., Guntur dial.).

[Ka. odugu, v.s.v. odavu (1).]

206 odũgu intr. to shrink, to make room (BhR, RR); to step aside, withdraw oneself, retreat (Bhr. II, Naiṣ.); to hide oneself, to sneak, shrink.

[Ta. otuṅku, v.i. to get out of the way, step aside (Piṅ.); to seek shelter (Kamp.); step, walk (PN); to retreat; otukku tr. to put on one side; push into a corner (colloq.); n. shelter, screen; gait (PN); Ma. otuṅṅuka v.i. to step aside; hide, be contained; otukkuka to compress, restrain; PSDr. *ot-unk-/-ukk-.]

207 onaru* intr. to suit, fit (Bhr. I, II); to be agreeable (Bhīm., Kaḷā.); n. suitability, beauty, elegance; tr. onar(u)cu to make fit, accomplish, do, etc. (classical).

[< *on-; cf. Ta. oṉṟu (< *on-t-) v.i. to agree, be on intimate terms with (PN); to unite; be similar (Tolk.); Ma. oṉṉuka be united, join; Tu. onaru an art, skill; ombuni be suitable, agree with (< *on-p/b); ombu adj. graceful; for Ka. etc. v.s.v. ondu; < PSDr. *on-.]

208 *on- only inf. on-aN-; onã-gūḍu to be fulfilled; tō be obtained, lit. to come closely to (RR); v.s.v. onaru.

209 ondu intr. to be suitable, fit, splendid (Bhr. I, KS); to happen, occur (Bhr. I); tr. to obtain, possess; to touch, unite with; to have sexual intercourse with (Bhr. II, HariV.).

[Ka. ondu to be united; be possessed of; come to meet; be obtained; to be fit; tr. to touch, obtain, get; experience; Tu. onduni v.i. and tr. to gather, accumulate; ondikè uniting; Ko. ond- (things) grow together; be reconciled; intimacy arises (dative of pers.); Ta. oṉṟu v.i. to agree, unite, grow together; be on intimate terms with (PN); oṟṟu tr. to bring into contact; touch (Kalit.); embrace (Kalit.); to approach (Naṟ.); Ma. onnuka to be united; joined; cf. Kur. ond$^{o}$r- (ondr'-) tr. to bring; take along; oṇṭam equality, resemblance; oṇṭanum together (in place or time); < PDr. *on-ṯ; cf. onaru.]

210 oppu intr. to be suitable, fit, elegant (with dative of person) (Bhr. I, II); to agree to (Kalā.); n. elegance, beauty; suitability (Bhr. II, UH); oppu-konu to agree, accept (Bhr. I).

[Ka. oppu v.i. to fit, be beautiful; agree to; n. fitness, elegance; Tu. oppiyuni be fit; to agree to; Ko. op- to accept; To. up- id.;

Ta. oppu n. likeness (Kr̲ḷ.), beauty (Tēv.); v.tr. to agree, concede (colloq.); o (past ott-, fut. opp-) to be suited to (PN); be harmonious; to resemble, equal (Kr̲ḷ.); Ma. oppu agreement; oppikka to equalize; settle; oppam harmony, being together; okkuka v.i. to be together; to agree; okka together; otta agreeable; equal; Kur. okk- to fit in well; to agree with, tally together; PDr. *o-, *o-k-, *o-p-.]

211 ommu (Brown) intr. to suit one's health, as water, weather, etc. (colloq.).

[Ka. ommu to be fit or proper; Tu. ombuni to be suitable, to agree with; cf. oppu.]

oragu same as or̲āgu (UH, Āmu.) (occurrence less frequent).

212 orayu III tr. to rub, test a metal on touchstone (UH); to graze (KS; BhR.); to scratch with nails (KS); intr. to vie with (Naiṣ.); to be rubbed; to be slightly bruised by pressure; der. n. orapiḍi friction, rubbing (Bhr. II); orapu id.; testing (late).

[Ka. ore rub on; to grind; orasu to touch; rub, scour, crush; n. friction, rubbing; teasing; Tu. oresuni to wear off, tr. to rub; orevuni tr. to rub; uresuni, urepuni to rub, assay metals; polish; Ko. or- (ort-) to rub (on stone, etc.); orj- to rub; Ta. ura, urai be reduced to powder, wear away; uraicu, uraiñcu tr. to rub (Kalit.); uriñu v.i. to rub against (as beasts); tr. to grind away; scrape, triturate (Tirumuru.); rub on, smear (Cīv.); uriñcu v.i. to rub; Ma. urasuka v.i. to rub, wear off, diminish; urasuka rub, come in contact; uraṅṅuka to rub, graze; urekka to rub, grate; urummuka id.; Kui rūsa to crush, grind (> Skt. pr-oñc- to rub, wipe out; Burrow, TPS, 1945, pp. 85-87). PDr. *ū̆r-.]

213 oralu* intr. to roll over this side and that in sleeplessness (BhR.) (< *or-al < *ur-al-; v.s.v. uralu[1]).

214 or̲āgu v.i. to lean on one side; incline, bend slantly, recline (KS, Bhr. II); to bow down; n. a bend; a pillow to lean on; adj. reclining (JBh.).

[Ka. or̲agu, or̲aṅgu, ur̲ugu id.; Tu. oraguni to lean the back on; orduni bend, bow, lean on one side; orda adj. bent; Ta. ur̲aṅku to droop as flower; cf. oruṅku to sink, decline; Kui usa, uta to kneel; Pj. org- to lean; Kur. oṭhong$^{o}$r- to lean against, rest upon; cf. Ta. uraṅku to sleep, etc. which are also related here. PDr. ? *ot̲-ank- or *ut̲-ank-; PSDr. *ot̲-ank-.]

215 or̲alu* intr. to lament, cry, scream (Bhr. II, Kāś.); cf. r̲ōlu id.

[Ka. or̲al, or̲aḷu, orḷu, orlu to cry out from pain, n. an outcry;

cf. Kui oṛpa to pine for, long for; Kuvi (F) oṛp- to grieve; oṛh- to groan.]

216 olayu[1*] III to happen, occur (Bhr. II); strike, as a thought (Bhr. I); to increase, spread (Naiṣ.); to shine (UH); to reach, approach, meet (Bhr. I, Mārk.) (< *ol-ay).

[Ka. ole to come to light, appear; Tu. ulevuni to shine; Ta. oli v.i. to shoot forth, be luxuriant; prosper, thrive (PN); oliyal luxuriance (PN).]

217 olayu[2*] III intr. to swing, shake, move, as a heavy braid of hair of woman while walking (Bhr. I).

[Ka. ole to swing, wave, shake; Ta. olku v.i. to shake, move to a side (Cīv.); ulaivu trembling; Ma. olumpuka to move from side to side; cf. uliyu[2]; PSDr. *ol-.]

218 oliyu* intr. to be peeled, flayed (Bhr. I); (stain or bark) to come off; seems to be secondarily formed intransitive of olucu, q.v.

219 oluku intr. to flow, trickle (Bhr. I, II); to spill out (Kāś.); tr. to spill (water), scatter (rice) (Bhr. I, II); cf. ōl-āḍu to sport.

[Ma. ōluka to flow, ooze; inf. ōla in drops; Ka. ōlāḍu to sport in water; cf. Ka. ole to swing in water, shake; Ta. olku v.i. tremble; shake, move, wave; Ma. olumpuka to move from side to side.]

220 ol(u)cu IIa tr. to peel, flay, strip off as clothes (Bhr. I); to skin; to pillage (Bhr. II); der. n. ol(u)vuḍu stripping off; olvu id. (KS); olupu peeling.

[Ka. suli to strip off, flay; plunder; sole skin or slough; snake; Tu. sulipini, sulipuni to peel; suliyuni to pillage; Ta. oli remove dirt, clean (Kalit.); oliyal n. cloth, garment; coli to peel off; Ma. tolikka to skin; Pj. olc-, Nk. ols- to flay (l. ww. < Te.); cf. Kur. chol- clean by scraping; rub off surface; Mlt. chōly- to flay, strip off the bark; Brah. sil n. skin, rind, slough. PDr. *cōl- : *col-; *col-V- > PSDr. *ol-V- : *tol-V-, *col-V-; see Burrow, DS VI, p. 141.]

221 *ovvu[1*] (alt. ōvu; only in neg., ovv-ani unfriendly; ovv-ami hatred, enmity) *to be agreeable, friendly.

[Ta. ovvu to be like, congruous; ovvuṟu to agree; Ma. ovvā- neg. of okkuka to be like, to agree; probably v an off-glide in *ō + a > ō-v-a/ovv-a-. PDr. *ŏ-; v.s.v. oppu.]

222 ovvu[2*] to be spoiled, to perish (Mārk.; rare).

[Probably a denom. verb from novvu suffering, v.s.v. noccu; also cf. Ta. ōvu v.i. to cease, terminate.]

223 osāgu* tr. to give, present, bestow (Bhr. II, Naiṣ.); n. gift (Āmu.).

[Ka. osage a gift, present; Tu. occiyuni to deliver, give charge; Ta. oy to give (Nar̲r̲.); oyyal giving; uy to give, present (Pu. Ve.); direct (Kr̲ḷ.); send; for forms with *-t- < *-c-, see s.v. odavu; PSDr. *oy-, *oc-, *ot-; PDr. *oc-.]

224 osulu (alt. vasulu) intr. to be loose, as joints (colloq.); to slip out (Paṇḍ.).

[Cf. odar̲u to shake, move, etc., v.s.v. udaru; Ko. ucg- v.i. to move slightly horizontally; uck- v.tr.; To. usx- id.]

## Ō

225 ōḍu[1] intr. to ooze, trickle, flow (Mdn.); cf. oḍiyu[1]

[Ka. ol̲ku to flow; Ta. ol̲uku to flow as stream; leak, drop as water, trickle; n. leaking, dripping (Nan̲.); Ma. ol̲ukuka to flow, run down; ol̲ukku current, stream; cf. Ta. val̲i to overflow (colloq.); to flow (Kamp.); tr. shed; Ma. val̲iyuka to flow, overflow. PSDr. *ōl̲- : *ol̲-V-/*val̲-V-; alternatively *ōṭ- : *oṭ-V-, v.s.v. oḍiyu[1]; Ma. ōṭṭam.]

226 ōḍu[2] to run, flee (Bhr. I, II); to hesitate, be afraid (Bhr. I); to be defeated (Bhr. I, II).

[Ka. ōḍu run, flee; Tu. ōḍuni id.; ōṭa n. race; Ko. ōṛ- (ōc-) to run; To. wīḍ- (wīḍy-); Ta. ōṭu to run, flee, retreat; be defeated (Cir̲up.); ōṭṭu to defeat (Kr̲ḷ.), Ma. ōṭuka to run, etc.; Go. sōḍī- to run away; jōḍī- id.; Kuvi (F) hōt- to run (irreg.; fut. hoṛ'i; past st. hot-). PDr. *cōṭ-; see Burrow DS VI, p. 141.]

227 ōpu intr. to be capable of, to be disposed to (Bhr. I, II); as an aux. added to inf. meaning 'can,' 'may,' etc., uṇḍanōpu can/may be, kalganōpu may occur, may have; tr. to carry, bear, tolerate (Bhr. II); n. toleration; ōpika energy, stamina.

[Cf. Ka. oy, oyyu to carry; Ta. uy to carry (Cīv.); Go. woi- (wōsī) to take away; (Nagpur) ōyā̃ to carry (LSI IV, p. 507); GoM. ōy- id.; Kui opa (ot-) to take away; Kur. ho'- (occ-/hocc-) to conduct, master; to convey, carry off, elope.]

228 ōmu* tr. to preserve, cherish, take care of (KS, Manu.).

[Ka. ōvu id.; ō to be attached to, to be fond of; be pleased with; Tu. ōmana darling, dear; fondness; Ta. ōmpu to protect, guard, defend (Kr̲ḷ.); preserve; cherish (Porun.); ōmpaṭu to protect; Ma. ōmpuka id.; Kur. ui- (uyy-) to let grow; keep; watch over; cf. Mlt. oj- to keep; lay eggs, bring forth young; PDr. *ŏy- : PSDr. *oy-mp-/*ō-mp-.]

229 ōrcu[1] IIa tr. to bear, endure, suffer; have patience (Bhr. II); put up with, have patience, forgive (Mdn. also); ōrmi patience; ōrpu id.

[Ta. ōrppu patience, forbearance; ōrmi to be courageous, brave; ōrmai, ōrmam fortitude; Kuvi (S) orh- to endure; ōrh- to sustain; *ōr- < *oy-ir/ar; ultimately from *oy- to carry; v. s. v. ōpu.]

ōrcu[2*] IIa tr. of ōḍu[2], q. v., to defeat (Bhr. I, II). (Points to PDr. *cōṯ- besides cōṭ- on account of Te. ōḍ-/ōr-.)

## K

230 kaggu intr. to fade, lose color or brightness (late).

[Ka. kargu to turn black; Tu. karṇṭuni to fade; be scorched; karṅka being burnt; To. kar̲f- (kar̲t-) to become black; Ta. karuku be scorched; grow dim; Go. karw- v. i. to burn; with different suffixes : Ka. kari be scorched; Tu. kariya black; Ta. kari be charred (Akan.); Ma. kariyuka id.; Klm.(SR) kārī black; Pj. ker- (Sth. kerv-) v. i. to burn; KGad. karid- v. i. to burn away, as rice overcooked; Kuvi (F) karia black; Kur. k̲h̲arai derangement by great heat in bowels during the hot season; Brah. k̲h̲ar angry; (k̲h̲ā)k̲h̲ar fire; forms occur also with radical long vowel and different suffixes, e.g., -l, -ḷ, -ṭ, -r̲, etc. (> l. w. Skt. kāla black, see J. Bloch, BSOS V, p. 738, Burrow, TPS 1946, p. 16; S. M. Katre, IFK, s. v. karapsāṇi). PDr. *kā- with different suffixes, v. s. v. kā̃gu, kālu, krā̃gu.]

231 kaṅku to admonish, scold (colloq., lex.).

[Cf. Ka. kaṅgu displeasure, anger.]

232 kaṅgu* intr. to be scorched, burnt; to fade (later texts) (< *karng-).

[Ka. kar̲aṅgu to turn black; Tu. karṅka the state of being burnt; Ma. kaṅṅuka be singed; v. s. v. kaggu, krā̃gu.]

233 kaccu to move a piece in the game of chess, etc. (lex.).

234 kaṭṭu (1) tr. to tie, bind, dam (BhR); build (BhR); to gather together (Bhr. I); to pay taxes (Mdn.); intr. to get matted, as hair (BhR); to cease, stop, as a disease, the functioning of human organs, etc. (Mārk.); n. composition; tie, knot, bandage (classical and mdn.).

[Ka. kaṭṭu tr. to bind, build; amass; intr. to stop; n. bundle, binding; Tu. kaṭṭuni to bind, build; Ko. kaṭ- (kac-) tie, build; pay (price); To. koṭ- id.; Ta. kaṭṭu to tie (Nāl.); build, wear; n. tie, etc.; Ma. keṭṭuka id.; Kui kaṭru twisted (as rope); gaspa suspended by tying; gāṭi a knot, joint; Kuvi (S) gatti kī- to knot; Go. kaṭṭ- to be shut (of door); Klm.(E) kaṭ- to tie, Klm.(SR) kaṭṭ- id.; Nk. kaṭṭ-; Pj. kaṭṭ- to tie, bind; build house; kaḍk- to bind; Oll. kaṭ- id.; KGad. kaṭṭ- to bind; kaṭ- to cease, as pain, etc.; Kur. kaṛ- to twist together; Mlt. kaṛk- to tighten; kaṛkar- to restrain oneself; cf. Ta. kaḷai to tie, fasten as a tuft of hair (Pu. Ve.). PDr. *kaṭ-, probably < *kaḷt-.]

kaṭṭu (2) intr. to solidify (as a liquid); become hard, etc. (Mdn.).

[Ta. kaṭṭu to coagulate; swell as a boil; Ma. kaṭṭi what is dense, solid, lump; kaṭṭa id.; To. kar̠f- to tighten; Ko. karv- to become tight; Kui kaja be congealed, solidified; ganja id.; become hard, solid; Kuvi (F) kaj- to be congealed; Kur. kaṛ$^a$r-, kaḍr- to congeal, freeze; kaṛ$^a$rt'- to freeze; PDr. *kaṭ- : *kat̠-.]

235 kaḍāgu* intr. to strive, endeavor, undertake (Bhr. I, II); to be zealous of (Bhr. II); be prepared (Bhr. II); to thrive (Bhr. III); der. n. kaḍāka an attempt, perseverance; strength (Kāś.).

[Ka. kaḍagu, kaḍaṅgu make an effort; be desirous of; n. desire, wish; cf. kaḍu firmness; cf. Ta. kaṭan̠ obligation, duty (Kr̠ḷ.); kaṭu v. i. move swiftly (Maturai.); to be full, to pervade (Kr̠ḷ.); Ma. kaṭan n. id.]

236 kaḍacu IIa tr. to cross; exceed, transgress (Bhr. I, II); intr. to elapse, pass (as time); escape from (with accusative) (Bhr. I); die, perish (Bhr. II); tr. kaḍapu to pass time.

[Ka. kaḍe to pass, transgress; Tu. kaḍapuni; Ko. kaṛv- (kaṛd-) go through, across; To. koḍy- (koḍc-) to die, disappear; Ta. kaṭa v. t. to pass through, cross (Nāl.); transgress (Maṇi.); conquer (Perump.); destroy (PN); v. i. go, proceed, pass; kaṭattu to drive, pass as time; kaṭāvu to drive, discharge; Kui gṛāsa step or pass over; gṛāpa (gṛāt-) to cross over, pass by; Kuvi (F) grānc- id.; Pj. kaḍp- (kaḍt-) to cross; Kur. kaṭṭ- cross (river, etc.); pass over; transgress; kaṛta'- take across; Mlt. kaṭ- exceed, pass, cross; kaṭṭr- to spend time, pass; Brah. k̠h̠arr- to proceed; PDr. *kaṭ-.]

kaḍapu (tr./caus. of kaḍacu, q. v.) to send away (without giving), bypass (Bhr. II, Kāś.); to drive, run a boat, etc. (Bhr. I); to pass time (Bhr. II); give up (Bhr. II); transgress (RR); chase, drive away (Manu.); remove (Kāḷ.); Mdn. gaḍapu.

237 kaḍugu/kaḍuvu tr. to wash, cleanse with water as hands and feet, utensils, etc., scrub; bathe, lave (Mārk., Kāś.); n. water in which rice or any other food remnants are washed (colloq., lex.).

[Ka. karcu id.; Ko. kaṛt- (kaṛty-/kayt-) id.; Ta. kaḻuvu tr. to wash (Kṟḷ.); kāḻiyaṉ a washerman; Ma. kaḻukuka to wash; Kui kahpa (kaht-) to plaster, anoint, wash the face; Kur. khajj- to cleanse the head with clay; cf. khajj earth, clay (back formation from the verb); Mlt. kaj- to wash, as clothes. PDr. *kāḻ- : *kaḻ-V-; *kac-; note the alternation between *c/*ḻ; Kui h < s.]

kaḍuvu (var. of kaḍugu, q.v.) (Mārk.).

238 katuku (alts. gaduku, gatuku) tr. to lap, lick up (later texts; Mdn.).

[Tu. gadukuni, gadkuni to lap, jolt; Ta. katukku tr. gorge, glut; cf. katuvu to seize, grasp.]

239 kadalu intr. to move, shake, totter (BhR); be removed, displaced (Bhr. II); set out for journey; n. motion; journey (UH); tr. kadal(u)cu to shake, move (Bhg.); kadal-ika movement, stir (Mdn.).

[Ka. kadalu to move; kadaḍu, kadar be shaken; to stir; n. commotion; Tu. kadeluni/kadaluni become loose, slack; shatter; kadepuni, kadeyuni to disjoin; kadelu̥ loose; cf. gadduni to shake, shiver; Ma. kadartu shaking; PSDr. *kat-. Alternatively, cf. forms s.v. krālu v.i. to shake (< *kaḻ-al; *-ḻ-/*-t- points to older *-ḻ-/*-c-.]

240 kaḋiyu* III tr. and intr. to reach, approach (Bhr. I, Vijñ.); to meet, be united (Bhr. II); to face, confront, oppose (UH); to seize; kaḋiyābaḍu to fall together (Nirv., Daś.); kad-incu to join together; fasten (late); kadupu n. crowd, flock (Bhr. II).

[Ka. kade tr./intr. to join, be contiguous; be pressed; kaduku to press; kadupu a flock; kadale a mass; Tu. kadiya(-puṇṭuni) (to squeeze) strongly; Ta. katuvu tr. to seize, catch; grasp (Tiv.); Kuvi (F) kanj- (kac-) to cohabit; Klm.(SR) gaddiy- to reach. PSDr. and PCDr. *kac-/*kaḻ > *kat- : kay-; v.s.v. kadumu, kaduru.]

241 kadupu to shake, move, as limbs, etc. (colloq.). Somehow connected with kad-alu q.v.

242 kadumu* tr. to seize; to occupy, press down (Kāḷ., Vi.Pu.); n. a swelling, tumor.

[Ka. kadubu to press, seize firmly; kaduku id.; gadu a gather, swelling, tumor; Tu. kadiya adv. tightly (while holding, squeezing); Ta. katuvu tr. to seize, grasp; Kur. kajj- to press down under weight; Ta. kayaṅku be squeezed; kayakku to squeeze (Pu.Ve.); kayakka strain, stress (Maṇi.). PDr. *kac- > *kat-; see kaduru, kadiyu.]

243 kaduru* intr. to be produced (of anger, fear, etc.) (Bhr. II); to increase, spread (Bhr. II); kadupu a flock, crowd.

[Ka. kade to join; kadale mass, multitude; Tu. kadike a granary, deposit; gadaru̥ a lump; Ta. katir to abound; shine, become manifest (Kamp.); kati v. i. to grow high, abound; katippu thickness; katuppu herd (Piṅ.); cf. Ka. kal̲i to be excessive; Ta. kal̲umu v. i. to join, unite; be complete (Cīv.); mix together (Tolk.); n. denseness; kāl̲ to become firm; to increase beyond measure, abound (Kr̲ḷ.); Ma. kayar̲uka to increase, rise; < PSDr. *kac-/*kal̲- : *kȧt-/*kay-; cf. also kadiyu, kadumu.]

244 kanaru* intr. to grow angry (Śakunt.); n. anger; v. s. v. kanalu, which has different suffix, but same base.

245 kanalu* to be angry (UH); to burn (Mārk., HariV.); n. anger (UH, Naiṣ.).

[Ka. kanal id.; kani to glow; Tu. kaṇaku̥ firewood, fuel; kanepuni to be afflicted; kanipuni, kaṇivuni id.; Ta. kan̲al to be hot, glow as fire (Kamp.); boil as hot water (Nāl.); be angry (Kamp.); tr. to burn; kan̲ali fire; kan̲alvu anger (Kamp.); kan̲ar̲r̲u to cause to burn, render warm (PN, Kalit.); kan̲r̲al anger; kan̲ı v. i. to become red hot, glow; kar̲u tr. to resent, get angry (Patir̲.); n. rancor; kar̲uppu anger (Tolk.); Ma. kanal live coals, fire; kaniyuka to glow; Kui kamba ( ? < *kanb-) to be burned; PDr. *kan-/*kat̲- : PSDr. *kan-al; cf. kandu; > l. ww. Skt. kanala- shining; kan- to shine; kanaka- gold; see Burrow, DS VII, p. 369, item 36.]

kanār-ilu* (kan-ār-ilu, same root as for kanalu) to grow angry (late); v. s. v. kanalu.

[Cf. Ta. kan̲r̲al anger.]

246 kaniyu* III intr. to grow ripe, mellow, as fruit (Bhr. III, HariV.); kanikaramu tenderness, pity.

[Ka. kani n. glow, tender-heartedness; pity; Tu. kanikara pity; Ta. kan̲i to ripen (Kamp.), turn mellow; to melt, as heart (Cīv.); be perfect (Parip.); kan̲ivu n. ripeness; kan̲r̲u v. i. to feel compassion (Cīv.); Ma. kaniyuka to grow ripe, mellow; kani ripe fruit; kanivu tenderness; pity; Kuvi (F) kamb- to become ripe; Kur. k̲h̲añj- to bear fruit; be produced; to come forth; Mlt. qanjpe fruit; PDr. *kan-.]

247 kanu[1] IV tr. to see, observe, perceive, understand, experience; fully attain, obtain (all classical); alt. *kānu-; cf. kannu/kanu eye.

[Ka. kāṇ, kāṇu (kaṇḍ-) to see, etc.; to appear; n. seeing; Tu. kāṇusāvuni to show, mention; Ko. kaṇ-/kāṇ- (kaḍ-) to see; To. kōṇ- (koḍ-) id.; Ta. kāṇ- (kaṇṭ-) to see (Nāl.), to discover, consider (Kr̲ḷ.); v. i. to accrue; appear (Tiv.); n. sight, beauty; (Tirumuru.); Klm. (E) kanḍt seen, visible; Pj. kanḍp- (kanḍt-) to look upon; Oll. kanḍp- id.; Kur. k̲h̲an- be pleasant to the eye; Brah. k̲h̲an- to see.

All forms point to two vowel grades in PDr. *kaṇ-/*kāṇ-; for long grade forms in Te. see *kān-; for related words for eye, see Kolami, Vocab. 344; (> l. w. in IA., see Burrow, TPS 1946, p. 22.)]

248 kanu$^2$ IV to bring forth young (of human beings) (Bhr. I, II) (morphologically this base has fallen together with kǎnu to see, but historically it has no connection with it).

[Brah. k̲h̲an- to give birth to; KGad. karr- to yean; Kur. k̲h̲añj- to be produced; bear fruit; k̲h̲añjkā/k̲h̲añjpā result, effect, fruit; cf. Ka. kandu the foetus of beasts; a calf, young plantain trees around the mother plant; kanda a young child, male or female; Ta. ka̲n̲r̲u a calf; Ma. ka̲n̲n̲u id.; ka̲r̲r̲u a boy, calf. PDr. *kan-; der. n. kan-t̲ < *kan-t-.]

249 kandu intr. to be scorched, to redden as a metal in fire (Bhr. I); to grieve, suffer; to lose color, brightness (Bhr. I, II); (flowers) to wither in handling; (face) to become sun-burnt (Naiṣ., Kāś.) (also Mdn.); n. a wart; dark spot, alloy (Bhr. I, II; Bhg.).

[Ka. kandu id.; Tu. kandu id.; Ta. ka̲n̲r̲u become scorched, sunburnt as face; be aggrieved; fade (Tirikaṭu.); Ma. kanekka v. i. to burn as charcoal; also v. s. v. kanalu; PSDr. *kan-t̲-; PDr. *kan-/*kat̲-.]

250 kappu tr. to cover, lay a cover on, hide (KS; Bhr. II); intr. to spread, to overspread, as clouds (KS, Bhr. I); n. a cover; roofing (late; also Mdn.).

[Ka. kappu to cover, spread, surround, overspread; Ta. kappu tr. to overspread, as a cloud; cram, stuff; Ma. kappuka id.; Kuvi (S) kaph'- to outflank; Pj. kapp- to cover, overspread; Kur. kapp- to overspread with limbs; kapr- to hide oneself; khap- to cover exactly, fit upon; be totally lost; cf. Brah. kapp-ī roofless; PDr. *kap-; for forms with -v- < *-p-, see s. v. kaviyu.]

251 kamaru to be singed, charred (Bhr. II, III, Mārk.); n. burning (Bhr. II); n. rancid smell (of burnt objects, oils, skin, hair, etc.) (JBh., also Mdn.); tr. kamar(u)cu (RR).

[Ka. kamaru to be singed, etc.; n. being scorched; stifling smell of burnt oil, etc.; kamuṭu id.; kavaru, kavuṭu id.; Tu. gameluni to be hot; Ta. kama̲r̲u to be excessively heated; feel a pungent smell produced by chillies on the fire (colloq.); Te. kāviri blackness caused by the smoke of fire (BhR, UH); Ta. Tu. kāvu heat, warmth; PSDr. *kā-v- : *kav-V-/*kam-V-.]

252 kamalu intr. to be scorched; singed; to fade, to be blackened (Śakunt.). (*kam-, same as for kamaru with different suffix; v. s. v. kamaru.)

253 kamiyu[1*] III intr. to become mellow (HariV.); see kaniyu (a sporadic alternation of -m-/-n-).

254 kamiyu[2*] III (1) intr./tr. to pounce upon; overspread; to cover completely (KS, BhR); kamiya- adv. all over.

[Ma. kamiyuka to overspread; v. s. v. kaviyu; -v- > -m-.]

kamiyu[2*] III (2) tr. to swallow, gulp down (Mārk.); kami a lump of food; kamikili a handful (to eat) (Bhīm.) (< *kav-i-).

[-m- < *-v- < *-p- : cf. Ta. kappu to cram into the mouth; kavi to seize, grasp with eagerness; kavvu (< *kavivu) id. (Nāl.); n. bite, seizing by mouth, as dog; eating; kavar id.; Ka. kavar to take away by force, seize; Ma. kappuka to snap at, eat as a dog or mad man; Kui kappa (kapt-) to swallow, gulp; further v. s. v. kamucu, kaviyu, kavvu.]

255 kamucu* IId tr. to hold, seize (KS, Naiṣ.); to nibble at; to swallow (Nirv.; UH), occupy, seize by force (Pāṇḍ.).

[-m- < -v-; v. s. v. kamiyu (2), kappu, kaviyu, kavvu (< *kav-i- < *kap-i-).]

256 karãgu intr. to melt, be dissolved; (heart or mind) to soften (Bhr. II); tr. to melt, soften (Bhr. II); another tr. karãcu (Hara.); der. n. kar(u)vu a cast (of metal, etc.).

[Ka. karaṅgu, kargu be dissolved; softened as heart; tr. to melt; Tu. karavuni, karaguni, karambuni id.; Ko. karg- v. i.; kark- v. tr.; To. karx- v. i., kark- v. tr. id.; Ta. karai to wear away, be dissolved; tr. to dissolve in water, etc.; Ma. karakkuka to melt, dissolve; Kuvi (F) karang- to be dissolved, melted; PSDr. and PCDr. *kar-aṅk/-akk-; cf. kaggu, krãgu.]

karãcu* IIb tr. of karãgu, q. v. to melt, soften (HariV., Hara.).

257 ka<u>r</u>acu[1] IIa tr. to bite, as a serpent (Bhr. I, II); gnaw (UH, Bhr. I, II); cut (UH); der. n. kāṭu a bite.

[Ka. karcu to bite; kaḍi bite, sting, cut; Tu. kajepuni to chew; kaḍiyuni to be cut; kaḍepini bite; gnaw; kaḍpuni to fell, cut down; Ko. kayṛ- (kaṛc-) to bite; Ta. ka<u>r</u>i to chew; bite, nibble (Nāl.); n. chewing, eating (Cīv.); kaṭi bite; eat; gnaw (Tiruvāc.); pinch as new shoes (Kalit.); cut into pieces (Nāl.); Ma. kaṭikka to bite; kaṭi a bite; Kui kasa to bite, sting (-s- < *-<u>t</u>-); krāpa to cut, saw; Kur. <u>kh</u>ār- to gnaw, nibble at, eat; Mlt. qār- bite off; qasw- eat greedily; Brah. gaṭ n. bite, gaṭ hall- to bite; cf. Kur. kaṭṭ- cut with teeth, gnaw; kal[a]g- to unhusk by teeth; Mlt. kalk- bite off; there appears to be an original confusion between two series *ka<u>t</u>- to bite and *kaṭ- to cut; or else *ka<u>t</u>- > *kaṭ- before *<u>t</u> > <u>r</u> in the medial position; there are also forms yielding *c in the place of *ṯ; see Kolami, Vocab. 3059.]

258 kaṟacu[2*] IIa to learn, study (Bhr. I); kaṟadulu knowledge (HariV.).

[Kui grāmba to learn, study; grāppa to teach; Go. karī- (karīsī pp.) to learn; kareh- (karehcī-) to teach; GoM. karah- id.; Klm.(E) karp- to learn, teach; Klm.(SR) karīl- to learn; karāp- to teach; Nk. karap- to learn; cf. Ta. kal (kaṟṟ-) to learn, etc.; see Kolami, Vocab. 347; PCDr. *kaṯ- : PSDr. *kal-.]

259 kaṟuku* tr. to rub, scratch (Manu.; rare).

260 kalãgu* intr. to be stirred up, as water in a pond (Bhr. II); (mind) to be disturbed, agitated (Bhr. II, Naiṣ.); tr. kalãcu; der. n. kalãka, kalagūḍu, kalāta agitation (Bhr. II).

[Ka. kalaṅku, kalaku to be agitated; to stir up, shake; Tu. kalaṅkuni id.; Ko. kalg- be mixed; kalk- to mix; Ta. kalaṅku be stirred up, confused (Nāl.), kalakku to confuse (Tiv.); kalakku, kalakkam turbidness (PN); Ma. kalaṅṅuka be mixed, agitated; kalakkuka to mix water; kalakkam n.; Kui glahpa tr. to mix by stirring; confuse; Kur. k͟halak͟h- to disturb, make muddy, as water : Mlt. qalg̣- to disturb (as water); cf. gāly- (gālc-) to stir (water), disturb; (> l. w. Skt. kaluṣa- turbid, see Burrow, TPS 1946, p. 8; DS VII, 371, No. 51). PDr. *kal-; *kal-aṅk-/*kal-akk-.]

kalãcu IIb (tr. of kalãgu, q. v.) to make turbid; to disturb (the mind), confuse (Bhr. II, Manu.).

261 kalayu (var. kaliyu) III intr./tr. to meet, mix, join (UH); become one with (Bhr. II); to copulate (Manu.); kalay-aN- inf. (adv.) thoroughly, completely; tr. kalapu, kalupu; der. n. kalay-ika meeting.

[Ka. kale to join; kalasu to mix, mingle; n. mixed state; Tu. kalaḍuni to be mixed; kalapuni to knead; mingle; Ko. kalv- (kald-) to knead; To. kaṯf- (kaṯt-) to mix (rice and curry, etc.); Ta. kala v.i. to mix, unite (Tiruvāc.); spread as news (Kamp.); tr. to mix, blend, copulate (Kṟḷ.); kalāvu v.i. mix together; kalavu tr. to mix; n. joint of the body (Akan.); Ma. kalaruka be mixed; to mix; kalaṅṅuka v.i. id.; Kui glahpa to mix by stirring; Kuvi (F) kalp- tr. to mix; kalh- to be mixed; Go. kalī- to meet and embrace; GoM. kāliy- id.; Klm. kalay- be mixed; Kur. k͟hal- to mix with water or other liquid. PDr. *kal-; PSDr. *kal-ay.]

kaliyu (same as kalayu) III intr. to meet, join (Hara.); tr. to copulate (Vijñ.).

262 kalugu V (allom. *kal-) intr. to happen, occur, be produced, be born;

tr. to have, possess, aux. can; kala- (forms future tense with inf. in OTe.); der. n. kalimi wealth (all classical and Mdn.).

[Tu. kariyuni v.i. (aux.) to be able or possible; Ta. kali to come into being; appear; grow luxuriously (Neṭu.); increase; n. flourishing, prospering (PN); Klm.(E) kal- aux. may be, possibly be.]

263 kalucu* IIa tr. to like, love, be fond of (KS); kalupu fondness (KS) (probably connected with words meaning 'to meet,' etc. v.s.v. kalayu.)

264 kavayu* III tr. to embrace, copulate (Bhr. I, II).

[Ta. kavai tr. to join with, embrace; kavavu id. (Kalit.); n. embracing, copulation (Tolk.); kavar v.tr. id.; < *kap-V-; v.s.v. kaviyu.]

265 kaviyu* III intr. to spread as flames (Bhr. I); overspread, as darkness (Bhr. II); fall upon, rush against, attack (KS); kavidala, kavi n. an attack (KS).

[Ka. kavi to rush upon; attack, overspread; kavar take away by force, seize, plunder; gavi, gavu n.; Tu. kabiyuni overspread; surround; Ko. kavc- to finish; cover with a garment; Ta. kavi tr. to overshade; kavippu canopy; seize, grasp; kavar to seize, capture, plunder (Pu.Ve.); captivate; Ma. kaviyuka; kamiyuka to overspread; surpass; < PDr. *kap-V-; (> l.w. Skt. kavaca- armor, corset [see Burrow, TPS 1945, pp. 89, 90]). Further related words, kamiyu, kamucu, kavayu, kavvu, kappu.]

266 kavvu* to seize, seize by mouth; take away by force (lex.) (< kaviyu).

[Ta. kavvu (< *kavivu/*kavavu) to seize, grasp with eagerness (Nāl.); kavi id.; v.s.v. kaviyu, kamiyu).

267 kasaru[1] to scold, chide (Manu.); n. anger, displeasure (Āmu.); rebuke (also Mdn.); kasi anger, vengeance (Bhr. I).

[Ka. kasaru ill-humor; gajaṟu to scold; n. angry speech; Ta. katavu tr. to be angry with; n. anger (Kalit.); kataḻ be angry with; be furious; rage as fire; kacaṅku be displeased; kacakku to harass; kaca be disgusted; kā̃y to be wearied, displeased (Tolk.); Ma. kayarka to start up in anger; kayaṟuka to reprove; Kur. kackacr- be vexed; kackac vexation. PDr. *kā̃c-/kā̃y-; PSDr. *kac-V-/ *kat-V-; probably connected with the words meaning 'bitterness' from *kac-, see Emeneau, Kolami, Vocab. 820, for instance Ta. kai be bitter; to vex; kaippu bitterness, vexation, etc.]

268 kasaru[2]* intr. to increase, rise high, be elated (Kāś.).

[Ma. kayaṟuka to grow high, increase; climb up.]

269 kasugu intr. to mutter in vexation (Nava.N.), a rhyme word with

visugu disgust.

[V. s. v. kasaru.]

270 kā̃gu intr. to be heated, grow hot (water, sand, iron, etc.) (Kāś.); to grow angry; (water) to be boiled, to seethe; tr. kā̃cu to boil water, milk, etc. (Naiṣ., Kāś.); der. n. kā̃ka heat; kā̃gu a boiler.

[Ka. kāṅke heat of any kind; Tu. kāṅguni be dejected, become pale; Ta. kāṅku, kāṅkai earthen pot-boiler; Kui kāga warm oneself by fire; Klm. Nk. kāŋg- become hot; Brah. khākhar fire. *PDr. kāy- : *kā-ṅk-/-kk-, v. s. v. kāyu[1].]

271 kācu[1] IIa (1) tr. to protect, preserve (Bhr. I, II); forgive, spare (Kāś.), restrain (Bhr. II); to herd (cattle); kāpu n. protection, watch; kāvali guarding over (property).

[Ka. kā, kāy id.; kāpu protection; Tu. kāpuni to watch, guard; Ko. kāv- (kāt-) id.; To. kōf- (kōt-) id.; Ta. kā to guard, keep, protect (Kṟḷ., Maṇi.); Ma. kākkuka id.; Kuvi (S) kā'- to guard, save; Klm. kay- (kay-t-) to graze (cattle); KGad. kā- id.; Kur. khāp- guard, watch; Mlt. qāp-; Brah. khwāf- to make to graze; khwāh- to graze (back formation); cf. Go. kēp- to guard, watch (crops); Kui kōpa to tend cattle; Pj. kōp- (kōt-) id. PDr. *kā-.]

kācu[1] IIa (2) to wait for, expect; used esp. with refl. -konu (Kaḷā.; also Mdn.).

[Tu. kāpuni to wait; Ta. kā to wait for (no literary usages cited); Ma. kākkuka to wait; Kuvi (S) kā- to wait; Kui kāpa (kāt-) to await; Pj. kāp- (kāt-) id.; Kur. khāp- id.; Mlt. qāp- id. Note that this meaning does not occur with the forms of Ka. Ko. To. Klm. KGad. Brah., whereas two different forms occur for the two meanings in Kui and Pj. PDr. *kā-.]

kācu[2] IId intr. to bear fruit, fruits to develop on tree (Bhr. I); same as kāyu[2] q. v.

272 kā̃ḍu* intr. to pierce through (as arrows) (Bhr. II); to be fixed, settled (Pāṇḍ. and Bhr. II).

273 *kān-* V (only with back vowel suffixes, kān-aN to see; kān-aka not seeing, etc.) tr. *to see (classical).

[Long grade alternant of kanu (< PDr. *kaṇ-/*kāṇ-), v. s. v. kanu.]

274 kāncu* IId and V tr. to see, cf. *kān-; c-suffix peculiar to Te. in many forms, īḍcu, ēḍcu, etc., part of an original past morpheme *ci.

kā̃cu IIb tr. of kā̃gu, q. v.

275 kāyu[1] III intr. (sun or moon) to shine (Kāś., BhR.); to emit rays.

[Ta. kāy to shine, emit rays; Ma. kāyuka to shine; this set is obviously related to those meaning 'to be hot,' etc.; Ka. kāy grow hot; Tu. kāyuni; Ko. kāy-; To. kōy-; Ta. kāy; Ma. kāyka; Go. kās-; Kuvi (F) kaiyu adj. hot; Kur. k͟hāy- to become dry, evaporate; Mlt. qāy- id.; PDr. *kāy-; also v. s. v. kā̃gu.]

276 kāyu[2] III intr. to bear fruit (Dvā.); kāya an unripe fruit.
[Ka. kāy (kāt-, kāyt-); n. unripe fruit; Tu. kāyuni to get ripe; To. kōy- (kōc-) to bear fruit; Ta. kāy v. i. id. (PN); n. unripe fruit (Nāl.); Ma. kāyuka to be ripe; kāykka bear fruit; Go. kaiā fruit; Kui kāu (pl. kānga) fruit, kernel, seed; Kuvi (F) kaiya fruit; Klm. keik id. (Hislop, p. 29). PDr. *kāy-.]

277 kāṟu intr. to ooze, leak; to run in drops (HariV.) (also Mdn.); tr. kār(u)cu to exude (Naiṣ.).
[Tu. kāranji an artificial fountain; underground channel; Kuvi kāda river; cf. Te. kāl(u)va a stream, channel; Ka. kāl, kālive, kāluve, kālve id.; Tu. kālive id.; Ta. kāl- (kāṉṟ-) to flow, issue as blood, leap forth as a waterfall (Ciṟup.); kār n. rain (Kalit.), water (Piṅ.); irrigation channel; kāl river; kāl-vāy a channel; Ma. kālca oozing out; Go. kālum sweat. PDr. *kāl, *kāṯ < *kāl-t-, or *kā + *-l, *-ṯ as suffixes ?]

278 kālu intr. to burn, blaze (KS); be burnt, scorched or baked (Mdn.); tr. kāl(u)cu to burn.
[Ma. kāḷuka to burn, flame; Pj. kāl to smart. PDr. *kā- with -ḷ suffix, v. s. v. kāyu[1], kā̃gu.]

279 kiṭṭu[1]* tr. to kill (Bhr. II, a single usage cited) (< *kiṭ-t-, cf. giṭṭu[1], keḍayu).

280 kiṭṭu[2]* intr./tr. to approach (Bhr. II); draw near, attack (Bhr. II, UH); to be obtained, to fit, suit (Mdn., giṭṭu[2]).
[Ka. kiṭṭu, giṭṭu to touch, reach; kiḍu touching; Tu. kiṭṭa, giṭṭa proximity; adj. near; Ta. kiṭai tr. to approach (Kamp.); meet in battle; v. i. come into one's possession; kiṭṭu v. i. draw near (Kamp.), be attained; obtained; tr. to approach, attack; kiṭṭuka come to hand; Ma. kiṭṭuka to meet, reach; to come to hand; kiṭayuka to knock against; be found, obtained; kiṭekka id.; kiṭa n. approach, equality; Mlt. kiṭe near; kitr- to approach (probably a misprint for kiṭr-). PDr. *kiṭ-.]

281 kiduku* intr. to fret, be cross on waking from sleep, as children (Bhg.); to groan (Mdn.; Rayalasīma dial.).
[Cf. Ka. kittaḍa disagreeableness; disgustfulness; giji, gija a sound denoting confusion; kisuru, kisaru a disagreeable feeling; Brah. kijj- to groan, fret over.]

282 kiniyu[1]* III intr. to be angry, displeased (Bhr. II, UH); kin(u)-vaḍu (-paḍu) to grow angry (Bhr. II, HariV.); der. n. kin(u)ka, kinupu anger (Bhr. II, Kāś.).

[Ka. kinisu become angry; n. anger; Ta. ci<u>n</u>avu be angry (Kalit.); ci<u>n</u>am anger, fury (Parip.); fire (Akan.); Ma. cinam wrath; cinikka be touchy; cinippu anger (see Burrow, DS III, p. 123). PSDr. *kin-.]

283 kiniyu[2]* III tr. to near, approach (16th century work) (Brown, Śab.R).

284 kivvu* intr. to perish (originally, Brown, Śab.R.; no literary usage cited); cf. civuku, cimuḍu.

285 kuṭṭu tr. to sew together (KS); sting (Bhr. I), to pierce, prick, bore (Manu.); n. sewing; seam; sharp pain in the stomach; n. a sting (Bhr. II); a hole caused by piercing.

[Ka. kuṭṭu v.i. to prick, to ache; n. pricking pain; kuṭuku to sting, as an ant; kuḍuku to peck at; Tu. kuḷipini to sting; koḍapuni to bite, peck; Ta. koṭṭu to sting; n. stinging; Go. kōṭṭ- to sew leaves together; to peck at; GoM. kōṭ- to sew; Klm. Pj. KGad. kuṭṭ- id.; Oll. kuṭ- id.; cf. Te. Ka. koṇḍi the sting of a scorpion; Ta. koṭṭu, koṭukku id.; Ma. koṭukku id.; cf. also Kur. Mlt. kuḍ- to pierce (l. w. < IA.); u/o alternation probably on account of the following retroflex stop; PDr. *kuṭ- (< *kuḷ-t-) : *koṭ-.]

286 kuḍ(u)cu IIa tr. to eat (Bhr. I, II); drink (KS); enjoy or suffer, experience (Bhr. II; Kāś.); kuḍ(u)pu eating, food; kuḍiti drinking water for cattle (Mdn.).

[Ka. kuḍi to drink; n. drinking; Tu. kuḍcuni to drink excessively; swallow; Koḍ. kuḍi id.; Ko. kuṛy- (kuṛc-) to drink; Ta. kuṭi to drink from cup; inhale, absorb; n. drinking; drinking water; Ma. kuṭikka to drink; cf. Kuvi (S) goh'- to suck. PSDr. *kuṭ-.]

287 kuṇṭu intr. to limp, (movement) to be hampered (Mdn.); to decrease, diminish (JBh.); (in earlier classics, occurs as a noun) n. kuṇṭu-vaḍu to lag behind, break down; kuṇṭu n. a lame person, cripple (Bhōj., Kāś.).

[Ka. kuṇṭu to limp; n. lameness; kuṇi move in a hopping manner; Tu. kuṇṭuni, kōṇṭuni to limp, halt; Ko. kuṇṭ- id.; Ma. kuṇṭan a cripple; Klm.(SR) kuṇṭ-; Go. kūṭ-; GoM. kūṭh-. < PDr. *kuṇ-t-.]

288 kudiyu III intr. to sink, decrease, shrink (Bhr. II, RR); to be spoiled, perish (Bhr. II); to diminish, abate (RR), withhold oneself (Dvi.H.); kudiyābaḍu to become close or tight; to cease, stop; tr. kuducu to press down (BhR); to hold tight (KS); to tie tight (Daś.); cf. gudi fetters.

[Ka. kusi v.i. to bend; be lowered (hang down from heaviness), to sink, give way, tumble in; Tu. kusiyuni, kusipuni v. i. to contract, shrink; kuṣkuni id.; kusuruni to shrink in, be afraid; cf. Ta. kul̲ai to fade, languish (Kr̲ḷ.); kutai to fasten the bow string at the notch; n. a loop; Ma. kutam tightness; kutekka to make a notch; Ka. kudi become tight; v. s. v. kūlu.]

kuducu* IIb tr. of kudiyu q. v.

289 kudupu tr. to jerk, jolt (as a bullock cart) (colloq., Brown); n. jolting, violent shaking.

[Cf. kudulu.]

290 kuduru intr. to become settled, established, well grounded; to fit, suit (as an ornament); to be well done, as writing, painting; (disease) to be cured; (mind) to be well settled; be adjusted, arranged (as a verb in later texts and mdn. usage; occurs as a noun in older classics); n. place of settlement, abode; stability (Bhr. II, BP); tr. kudur(u)cu; der. n. kudir-ika; refl. kudur(u)konu to be settled; cf. kuduvābeṭṭu to mortgage.

[Ka. kuduru v. i. to settle, be reformed; to suit; recover from illness; n. symmetry, settlement, beauty; Tu. kuduruni to recover from illness; kudi adj. fixed, settled; Ta. kutir be settled, fixed (loc.); n. a granary, shrub.]

291 kudulu intr. to flutter in agony (Nava N., Bhg.); to jolt, shake (as a vessel filled with liquid; a bullock cart, Mdn.); shake, while walking.

[Ka. kuduku to trot; Tu. kusuruni to shiver; Ta. kutar̲u to become loose, dishevelled as hair; Ma. kutar̲uka to shake off; cf. Ta. kul̲ai to wave as a flag; kuti to jump, splash as water; Ma. kutikka id.; Ka. gudi.]

292 kunuku intr. to nod the head, in sleepiness; to doze, to be drowsy; flame of lamp to sink down slowly; n. a doze (all Mdn.).

[Ka. kunuṅgu, kunugu to contract oneself; bend, stoop, crouch; kuni to bend, bow; shrink; Ta. kun̲i to bend (as a bow) (Cīv.); to stoop; Ma. kuniyuka id.: Ka. kūn to bend; Ko. kūn- (kūnd̲-) to be in a bowed position; Ta. kūn̲ to bend; Ma. kūnuka id.; cf. Te. gūni hump-back. PSDr. *kūn- : *kun-V-.]

293 kundu* intr. to decrease, become short (as life-span), abate, as liveliness, etc. (Bhr. II); to sink down (Bhr. I); to grieve, suffer (Bhr. II); n. decrease, smallness, misery (Bhr. II, Bhōj.); cf. kruṅgu.

[Ka. kundu become small, wane, fail; n. decrease; grief; Tu. kunduni to be reduced, to fade, wither; kundelu̥ deficiency; Ta. kun̲r̲u to decrease, fall from high position; droop, languish; n. deficiency. PSDr. *kun-ṯ < *kun-t-; v. s. v. kruṅgu.]

294 kumulu intr. to smoulder, burn slowly underneath without flame; be consumed inwardly, to grieve, pine (Bhg.); kummu smouldering ashes in which vegetables are roasted (ŚivaR; also Mdn.).

[Ka. kome to begin to burn, as fire or anger; Tu. gumuluni to be hot, feel hot (as in a fit of fever); gumulu fire burning in embers; Ta. kumai to be hot, sultry; be overboiled; be distressed; tr. to overboil, annoy (Tiv.); n. distress (Tiv.); kumur̲u to burn with distress (Tiv.); to bubble up in boiling; Ma. kumur̲uka to be hot; < PSDr. *kum-; cf. Te. kumpaṭi a portable furnace; kummu hot ashes; Ka. kumpaṭe a potsherd; kuppaṭe id.; Ta. kumpi hot ashes; kumpu to become overburnt; kummaṭṭi chafing dish (Tiv.); kummāyam well boiled dhal (Maṇi.); Ma. kumpal inward heat; kummal sultriness.]

295 kuriyu III intr. to rain (ŚivaR), to leak, as roof (also Mdn.); tr. to shower, rain (fire, arrows, etc.) (Bhr. I, Nirv.).

[Cf. Klm. kūl- (kūṭ-) to leak (of water from punctured vessel); Nk. kūḷ- id.; (not probable with Ta. cori, curai, etc., v. s. v. torāgu).]

296 kur̲r̲u* intr. to cry, yell, groan (Brown, Śab.R; no literary usages); n. crying (rare; later work).

[Ma. kur̲ukka, kur̲uṅṅuka, kur̲ummuka to coo, purr; kūr̲kka to snore; Ko. kurv- (kurt-) to snore; Kur. gurrār- to roar (as tiger), to snarl, growl; shout in anger.]

297 kuluku intr. to move the body in a graceful and affected manner (later texts and Mdn.); to shine, be graceful; tr. to spill by tilting, to pour (Kāś., Kaḷā.); to shake, move (Kāś.); n. a graceful and affected movement of the body, gracefulness (Manu. and Mdn.).

[Ka. kuluku tr. to shake, as a bottle, as the body in dramatic action or in putting on foppish airs; n. shaking, jolting; Tu. kurkuni v. i. to shake, as a tree, etc.; Ko. kulg- v. i. to shake, as a diviner, etc.; kulk- tr. to shake; Ta. kulukku to put on airs; kuluṅku to be shaken, shake in fear (Tiruvāc.); kulai become loose; tremble; tr. to shake; Ma. kuluṅṅuka v. i. to shake; kulukkuka tr.· Brah. k̲h̲ulkum soft, tremor, quivering; k̲h̲ul- to fear, be afraid.]

298 kusulu to be discontented; to groan in discontentment (Mdn.; Brown, Śab.R.).

[Cf. Ka. kudi to grieve; Tu. kutiyuni to repent, regret.]

299 kūḍu intr. to assemble, to meet, join (Hara.); to be becoming, proper (Bhr. I, also Mdn. in neg., i.e., kūḍadu it is not proper; with infinitives, e.g., vinagūḍadu should not hear (all persons and numbers); to pertain, belong (Mdn.); tr. to join, meet (JBh.); to copu-

late (Bhr. I); to add, as numbers (Mdn.); der. n. kūṭami an assembly; kūḍika addition; inf. kūḍ-aN adv. along with, colloq. kūḍā; tr./caus. kūrcu.

[Ka. kūḍu to join; be possible; be fit; to have sexual intercourse with; n. joining; kūḍa in company with; Tu. kūḍuni v.i. to meet, be mixed; tr. join, unite, cohabit; (with dative) can; kūṭuni, kūṇṭuni to mix; kūṭa assembly; mixture; Ko. kūṛ- (kūc-) v.i. to gather; kūṭ- (kūc-) v.tr. to join with, gather; To. kūṛ- v.i. to join; kūṭ- v.tr. to gather; kūḍ- to marry (others than Todas); Ta. kūṭu to come together, assemble (Tiv.); be possible; tr. to reach; be friends with; Ma. kūṭuka v.i. to meet, join; belong to; be added; aux.v. will become; kūṭa inf. along with; kūṭṭuka bring together; heap up, add; set up; aux. v. to make to pass; kūṭṭu mixture, connection; Kuvi (S) kūdi-kī- to gather; kūrc- to collect; Kur. khōṇḍ- v.tr. to gather, assemble; khōṇḍr- v.i. to meet together, assemble; PDr. *kūṇṭ-/kūṭṭ-; (> Skt. kūṭa- heap, see Burrow, TPS 1945, p. 94).]

00 kūyu III intr. to howl, cry, as animals, birds (Bhr. II, Hara.); to make outcry (HariV.); to shout; call, prate; kūyi n. an outcry for help, an appeal, protection; kūpeṭṭu to crow, cry (Kāś.); kū̄ta a call of an animal or bird.

[Ka. kūgu, kūku to cry out; a cry; kū a cry, call; Tu. kūguni to cry out; kūgu a cry; To. kūx- to crow; Ta. kū cooing; kūvu to crow (Tiruvāc.), call out (Parip.), cry for help; tr. to call, summon (Tiv.); kuyil to utter, tell (Cilap.); Ma. kū- to cry aloud; kūkkuka to cry (esp. of men); Kui kūpka (< kūk-p-; kūkt-) to hail, cry aloud; Go. (kōr) kūs- (cock) to crow; Klm.(E) kuy- (cock) crows; kūg- to call; Nk. kūg- id.; Pj. kūy- (cock) to crow, to call; kūp- (kūt-) to whistle; Mlt. kūkr- to call out; Brah. kūk cry, shout; kūk-kann- to cry out, call out. PDr. *kūy-/*kū-, *kūk-.]

301 kūru[1*] intr. to be abundant, excessive (Bhr. II, Nirv.); to occur; obtain; to be filled with (Bhr. II).

[Ta. kūr to be abundant (Tolk.); n. exuberance (PN); Mlt. qōr- to be in excess, be enough, qōrtr- to provide for abundantly.]

302 kūru[2*] intr. to doze, sleep (Vasu.).

[Tu. kūruni to be drowsy, sleepy; further forms, v. s. v. kūrku.]

303 kūru[3] intr. to sink, be drowned (Bhg.); tr. to stuff, cram, fill up with (Mdn.); push, thrust, penetrate; cf. krukku to stuff in.

[Cf. Kur. kōr- (kōrc-) to enter, go in (as snake into a hole); kōrta'- tr. to introduce; Mlt. kor- to enter, pass through; kortr- to let enter, thrust in.]

304 kūr(u)ku intr. to sleep, drowse (Bhg., Kāś.); n. a nap, sleep.
[Tu. kūruni, kūluni id.; To. kwïx- to take a nap; Kui kōra to lull to sleep; Go. kūrk- to nod in sleepiness; Pj. kūrk- to nod; Kur. kūg- to slumber, to doze; Mlt. kūg- to slumber; cf. Ta. kūr v.i. to bend (Kalit.); Ma. kūcuka id.; cf. kūlu. PCDr. *kūr-k-; PDr. *kū-.]

305 kūr(u)cu[1*] IIb intr. to be lovable, to be attached, become coveted (Bhr. I, II); der. n. kūrmi love, attachment.
[Ka. kūr to love, be attached to mind; kūrme love; Ta. kūr to hanker after; covet; Ma. kūṟuka to love (loc.).]

kūr(u)cu[2] IIb (tr. of kūḍu, q.v.) to unite, join together (Bhr. I), to amass (Bhr. I); to add together (Kāś.); to cause to obtain (Bhr. II).

306 kūlu intr. to fall down, sink (Bhr. II, UH); to perish, fall dead (Bhr. II); to flow down, as blood (BhR); tr. kūl(u)cu to fell, destroy (Bhr. II, UH); kūlābaḍu to fall flat, perish; (colloq.) to sit down suddenly in tiredness, etc.
[Ka. kūlu id.; kūru to sit down; kūntu bending state; Ta. kūr to bend (Kalit.); Ma. kūluka to crouch, bend; Kui kūra to fall down; cf. Ka. kusi to bend, stoop, sink, tumble; Tu. kuskuni give way, sink in; Go. kuss- to drop off or out (of leaves), to fall. PSDr. and PCDr. *kū-l-/*kū-r- < *kuy-il/-ir- < *kuc-il-/kuc-ir-.]

kūl(u)cu IIb tr. of kūlu, q.v.

keḍapu* tr. of keḍayu q.v.

307 keḍayu* III intr. to break and fall down (Bhr. II), to tumble over; to be broken, destroyed (UH); to perish (HariV.); tr. keḍapu to fell (JBh.), to destroy (Kāś.); keḍay-ika destruction, death.
[Ka. keḍe fall down, sink, perish; keḍapu pull down; Tu. keḍaguni to fall; tr. to spoil, ruin; Ta. kiṭa to lie or lie down as in sleep (Tolk.); Ma. kiṭakka to lie; rest, dwell, kiṭakuka id.; kiṭayuka to knock against; (either < *kiṭ-, v.s.v. giṭṭu[1], or from *keṭ-, v.s.v. ceḍu); cf. Kur. kīd- tr. to allow one to lie down for rest or sleep; put to bed; lay in the grave; Mlt. kīd- to lay down (probably with Ta. cē-, etc.).]

308 keralu[1*] intr. to increase, rise, swell (Bhr. II, Manu.); tr. keral(u)cu to increase, spread (Manu.); to encourage, instigate (< *keraḷ < *keḷar).
[Ka. keraḷu, keḷar to expand, extend; blossom, break forth; Ta. kiḷar to rise; be abundant; to increase (Cilap.); kiḷai v.i. to ramify; multiply, increase; abound (PN); Ma. kiḷaruka to rise, grow high; Kui kelja to be distended; PSDR. *keḷ+ar; the Te. Ka. forms are obviously due to metathesis.]

309 keralu[2*] (later also kerlu) intr. to be angry (BhR); to cry, shout (Manu.); cf. ciracira- echo word for anger, ciraciral-āḍu to be irritated.

[Ka. keraḻ id.; Tu. kērle sound, noise; kerepe a prattler; Ta. cirarru to shout, call loudly; tr. to be angry with (Kalit.). PSDr. *ker-al < *kēr-al; cf. the Tu. form for the long vowel.]

310 kelāku tr. to poke, probe (Paṇḍ.); to pluck out (Kāś.); stir, as water (Mdn.); cf. cenaku, cenayu.

[Tu. kilekuni/kelekuni tr. to draw out, pull; provoke, stir, move; Ka. keṇaku to provoke; Ta. kiḷaru to poke, dig up (Tiv.); stir with ladle, etc.; probe; kiḷai tr. to dig up, stir (PN); To. kiḻy-(kiḻc-) to ladle out (food); cf. Kui keṛga to shake, be shaken. PSDr. *keḷ-/*keṇ-; see Burrow, DS III, p. 128; also v. s. v. ceṇḍu.]

311 kelayu* III intr. to rage, increase (RR).

[Cf. Ka. kele to cry or shout with energy; Ta. cilai v. i. to rage (Pu.Ve.); sound, roar; other form, v. s. v. celāgu; < PDr. *kil-; alternatively, may be derived from the root underlying keralu[1] (< *keḷ-ar).]

312 kēru[1*] intr. to be jubilant, chuckle with joy (Manu.); kēr(u)-konu id.; kēr(u)pu jubilance.

[Ka. keraḻ to cry; Tu. kērle sound, noise; Ta. kēru to cackle as a hen; cirarru to shout; v. s. v. keralu[2].]

313 kēru[2*] intr. to laugh loudly; tr. deride, ridicule (Pārij.); kēr-aḍamu disregard (UH); kēr-inta, kēr-aḍamu krē-ṇi n. ridicule.

[Kui grēspa to mock, ridicule; Go(W) kīrī derision; Klm.(E) kayŋg- to laugh; for discussion of alternative etymologies, see Emeneau, BSOAS XV, p. 112. PCDr. kēr- < *kay-ar/*key-ar; Te. krēṇi < *ker-aṇi; Go. -ī- < PDr. *ey-.]

314 koṅku intr. to hesitate, fear (Bhr. II); n. fear (Bhr. II); hesitation, shyness (Mdn.).

[(1) Ta. kon n. fear (Kurun.); uselessness, futility; konnu to stammer; therefore, Te. koṅku < *kon-k-; also cf. koncu.

(2) Metaphorical from an original meaning 'to shrink, bend, become small': Te. koṅku n. shrinking, bending; Ka. koṅku be bent, get curved; kokke n. crookedness; bend; Ko. kok- to become bent; Ta. kōṇ crookedness (Tiruvāc.), hostility (Cīv.); kōṇu to be bent; kōṭu id.; Ma. kōccuka to be contracted; Kui kōga to become small, shrink; gōṛi a hook; Klm.(E) gog- to bend over; Pj. kokor- be bent; Kur. khõṅgh- tr. to bend, etc.; koṅkō adj.

curved; Mlt. kokr- to stoop down; qonq- bend knees; Brah. kōnḍō bent; see for more etyma, Kolami, Vocab. No. 263; all forms yield a PDr. *kō- with different suffixes.]

315 koṭṭu tr. to beat, strike, smite, knock, flog, lash, strike at (usages not cited from the earliest classics like Bhr., KS, etc.; JBh., Bhg., Āmu.); intr. (wind) to blow, (clock) to strike (Mdn.); aux. with infinitives, to do the action denoted by the verb preceding, ceḍãgoṭṭu to spoil (lit. to make to spoil); also with nouns: busa koṭṭu to hiss (busa n. hissing), ū̃koṭṭu to say [ū̃]; many more combinations with different shades of meaning in Mdn. Te.: ītakoṭṭu to swim (īta n. swimming), and so on; koṭḷ-āḍu to quarrel (Bhr. II); n. beat, stroke.

[Ka. koṭṭaṇa beating the husks of paddy; Tu. korpini beat, flog; Ko. koṭk- to strike; To. kwïṭk- to tap; Ta. koṭṭu to beat as drums, strike, pound; n. beat, stroke (Aiṅk.); Ma. koṭṭuka beat (as drum); Kui kospa (kost-) to beat; kōḍu n. pestle; Go. goṭṭ- to thrust at; kohk- to pound chutney; Pj. koṭṭ- to strike (with axe); Kur. khoṭṭ- to break, shatter; khoṭr- be smashed; Mlt. qoṭ- v.t. to break, knock, strike; qoṭr- to be broken; qoṭur- to knock; Brah. goṭ- to pound; koṭ- cut in pieces; forms with both phonetic and semantic contamination and re-borrowing from IA involved; see Kolami, Vocab. 436; IA loans, Burrow DS III, p. 134, TPS 1945, p. 93, Turner, Nep. Dict. s.v. kuṭnu. PDr. *koṭ-.]

316 kodaru[1]* intr. to increase, abound (HariV.).

[Cf. Ka. kudir, kudur to prosper, flourish, v.s.v. kuduru; or, Ta. Ma. Ka. kottu a bunch, cluster.]

317 kodaru[2]* intr. to be scattered, spilt (Brown, Śab.R).

[V.s.v. kudulu; kod-ar- < *kot-ar- < *kut-ar-.]

318 koduku (later kotuku) intr. to hesitate in speaking, mince words (later works); n. a low mumbling speech; hesitation, doubt; cf. koda hesitancy; kodalu adj. stammering, mumbling; kodalincu to lisp as children do; speak softly (KS); cf. koda, kodava shortness, inferiority.

[Ka. kodalu, kodlu to hesitate in speaking; n. stammering; kodaḷ id.; Tu. koddè stammering, lisping; Ta. kutaṭṭu to babble, prattle (Periyapu.); kutalai lisps, prattle of children (Kallā.); soft talk (Cilap.). PSDr. *kot-; prob. related to words meaning 'cut,' cf. Ta. kottu to mince, chop, etc.]

319 kodupu* tr. to turn about in mouth without swallowing; to munch (no literary usages cited).

[Ta. kutappu id.; kutaṭṭu id. (Kallā.).]

320 konu IV irreg. (allom. kon-(aN)/kō-(N) before C-suffixes, caus. kolupu q. v. mostly aux.) tr. to take, hold, take up (Bhr. I, II); to receive, care for (advice, other's words, etc.) (Bhr. II); to take for granted, to suppose, consider (Bhr. II); to buy (Bhr. II); aux. reflexive, e.g., dā̆gukonu to hide oneself; pres. part. kon(u)cu, pp. kon-i, past st. koṇ-ṭ-; aorist kon-d-/koṇ-ḍ-; with suffixes beginning with a/u both kon-/kō- freely vary, but kō- always as an aux.; -kolupu bound caus. suffix.

[Ka. koḷ to seize, take, buy; koḷ, koḷḷu seizing; as a second member in cpds. to get, obtain; Tu. koṇuni to keep, take, hold; aux., as reflex; Ko. koḷ-/koṇ- (koḍ-) to marry, buy; To. kwïḷ- (kwïḍ-) to carry (corpse); Ta. koḷ, koḷḷu (koṇṭ-) to seize, grasp (Cīv.); receive (Kṟḷ.); buy; acquire (Cīv.); marry (Nāl.); consider, think; esteem (Kṟḷ.); accept (Kamp.); endure (Tolk.); Ma. koḷka to hold; receive; acquire; (in Ta. Ma. aux. reflex.); Klm.(E) kor-, allom. ko- (kott-) to bring; imper. give; kos- to take; Klm.(SM) koṛ- to buy; Nk. koy- (kor-) bring; kōrtēn (man) brought (LSI, IV, pp. 573, 574); Kui koḍa to buy, take up, off or away; Kuvi(F) kōd- to buy, take; Kuvi(S) koḍḍ- to take; cf. Mlt. qōj- to take away, shift. PDr. *koḷ-, *koṭ- < *koḷ-t-.]

321 koncu* IId intr. to hesitate, draw back, be afraid (cf. koṅku).

[(1) Ta. koṉ n. fear; koṉṉu to stammer; Ma. koññuka to stammer, hesitate in speaking; (2) v. s. v. koṅku (2), < *kŏ-nc-; cf. Kur. k͟hoṭkā doubt, hesitation.]

322 kondu* tr. to crush, mash, beat into pieces (late).

[Cf. Ta. kontu to peck, mince; gore, pierce (Periyapu.).]

323 koṟalu[1]* intr. to grow angry (Bhr. II); koṟakoṟal-āḍu to bubble with anger.

[Ta. koṟukoṟu to bubble with anger (Cīv.).]

324 koṟalu[2]* tr. to obtain, get (Bhr. II, HariV.).

[Probably *koḷ-aṟ- with metathesis, v. s. v. konu.]

325 koṟalu[3]* tr. to desire, wish (Bhr. II).

[< *kōṟ(u) + al; v. s. v. koru.]

326 koṟuku tr. to bite, gnaw, nibble (Manu.); n. a bite.

[Ka. kuṟuku, koṟuku, koṟuṅku, koṟaku id.; Ta. koṟi to nip off husks, to nibble grain, graze (Kallā.); Ma. koṟikka id.; Go. kōrk- to gnaw; Klm. Nk. kork- to bite; Pj. kork- to cut with teeth, scissors; to gnaw, nibble. PCDr. and PSDr. *koṯ-i-, *koṯ-uṅk-/-ukk-.]

327 kolucu[1] IIa tr. to measure, as grain, etc. (Bhr. II, Naiṣ.); n. grain (Mārk.); kolāta measurement; kolādi limit, possibility; kolapeṭṭu to measure.

[Ka. kuḷa a certain measure; koḷaga a measure of four baḷḷas; koḷake a third crop of rice; Tu. koḷaga a measure of grain; Ta. kuḷakkam a standard grain measure; Ma. koḷakam id.; GoM. kōls- to measure; Klm.(E) kul- to count; all from *koḷ- to seize, grasp, v.s.v. konu.]

328 kolucu[2] IIa tr. to serve, adore (kings or gods) (Bhr. I, II); n. koluvu royal presence or the presence of deity.

[Ta. kolu n. id.; Ma. kolu; ( ? l. ws. < Te. koluvu); cf. Ta. koḷ to esteem (Kuṟaḷ); Te. konu id.]

kolupu[1] caus./tr. of konu q.v., aux. with inf. to cause to do (the action of the preceding verb) (Bhr. II); to add to.

[Cf. Kuvi (F) kōlh- to forge.]

329 kolupu[2]* intr. to be agreeable; (ideas) to suggest themselves; to strike; to pass on.

[V.s.v. konu.]

330 kosaru[1] intr./tr. to hanker after, yearn, request (Manu.); n. wish, desire (UH); cf. kōru.

[Ka. kosaru to hanker after; desire; n. eagerness, lust; v.s.v. kōru.]

331 kosaru[2]* intr. to hesitate, shrink, fear (Kāś.).

[Tu. kūruni to hesitate; kusuruni to shrink; kuskuni id. PSDr. *kuc-.]

332 kosaru[3] tr. to ask for a little extra quantity after purchasing any article; n. the extra quantity thus given by the trader (Mdn.).

[Ka. kosaru id.; Tu. kusuri n. id.; Ta. kocuṟu id.]

333 kõgu* tr. to shave (Brown, Śab.R.).

[Ta. koy to crop as hair; Ma. kōtuka to dress hair; n. dressing hair; kōtu to disentangle hair with fingers, etc.; cf. GoM. kōr- to shave; < PDr. *koy-, v.s.v. kōyu.]

334 kō̃ḍu ([~] is not likely on account of -ḍ- < *-ḻ-) tr. to separate the broken from the unbroken grain, etc.; separate stones by a sidelong motion.

[Ta. koḻi to sift in winnowing fan (Kamp.); to criticize; koḻippu sifting; Ma. koḻikka to winnow, sift; Ko. kod- (koyd-) id.; To. kwīc- (kwīč-) id.; Kui kṛohpa id.; Kuvi (S) kloh'- id.; Kuvi (F) korss- (krōst-) id.; Go. kōss- to sift in a sūpa; Klm.(E) gonjip- to winnow with side-to-side motion; cf. Go. gōenjē kī- id. PDr. *koc-/ *koḻ-. Cf. Ka. koccu to shake flour on a small fan to separate impurities.]

335 kōyu III tr. to pluck (leaves, fruits, etc.) (Naiṣ.), to cut, chop (Manu.); to slaughter; sever, divide; reap (also Mdn.); der. n. kōta slaughter (Bhr. II); reaping, harvest (Mdn.).

[Ka. koy, koyu, koyyu to cut, sever, crop, reap, pluck; Tu. koyipini, koipini, koyyuni id.; koilu̥ harvest; Ko. koy- (koc-) to cut; To. kwïc- (kwïč-) to chop up; Ta. koy- (koyt-) to cull flowers, pluck; cut, reap (Maturai.); to choose; Ma. koyka cut, reap; Kui kōva id.; kōeri harvest; Kuvi (S) koth'- to pick; Go. kōī- (koyīsī) to harvest; gather berries, etc.; GoM. kōid- (kōit-) to reap; Pj. koy- (koñ-) to reap, harvest; Kur. k̲h̲oy-, Mlt. qoy- id. PDr. *kŏy-.]

336 kōru[1] tr. to wish, desire, select (Bhr. II); hope, intend, ask for; der. n. kōr-(i)ka, -(i)ki, -(i)ke.

[Ka. kōr̲u to purpose, wish, think; n.; Tu. kōruni id.; to expect, hope; Ta. kōru id. (? l. w. < Te.; no literary usages given); Ma. kōr̲uka to wish, hope, think; PSDr. kō-r̲ < *koy-ar-/*koc-ar̲-; v. s. v. kosaru[1].]

337 kōru[2] tr. to cut, scratch (Nr̥s.); to grate coconut (Mdn.); n. a share.

[Ka. kōr̲u cutting, portion (related to kor̲e cut); Tu. gōruni to dig up, out; kōruni id.; Ma. kōr̲uka to tear flesh by thorns; cf. Ta. kōr̲ai scratch, as on the body (loc.); cf. gŏku. Probably *koy-ar/r̲.]

338 krakku* intr./tr. to vomit (Bhr. I), to emit (Bhr. II); n. vomiting; (< *kar̲-k-).

[Ka. kār̲ to vomit; Ko. kār- id.; Ta. kār̲u to hawk, bring phlegm up; Ma. kāruka id.; to vomit; Brah. kashsh- to eject; Ka. Tu. kakku to vomit; To. kak- (kaky-) id.; Ta. kakku id. (Piṅ.); eject as a snake (Kamp.); v. i. to overflow as river; shoot out, as ears of corn; ooze out, as oil through pores of skin (no literary usages); kakkal vomiting (Piṅ.); Ma. kakkuka to vomit (esp. of animals); Go. kakk- to vomit. The kakk- forms in the other languages are likely to be l. ws. from early Te.; since Piṅkalanikaṇṭu (c. 8th century) shows the form, it may be assumed that by the time this word was borrowed into Ta. etc., it was not being pronounced with the initial consonant group kr- in Te., or else we would expect to find *karukku or *kirukku by the insertion of an anaptyctic vowel in the consonant group as Ta. usually does. Also v. s. v. krāyu.]

339 kraccu* tr. to surround, overspread (late, rare); occurs often with -konu to spread; etc. (Vasu.; post-classical); v. s. v. krammu.

340 krandu* intr. to lament (Bhr. II); to ring, sound; n. violent noise (of the sea, etc.); clamor, commotion (as of crowded people); excess, abundance (Bhr. II); krand-illu to sound, cry.

[Ka. kare, kari to sound; emit sound, call; Tu. kareyuni, karevuni to crow; Ko. karv- (kard-) bellow, (crow) croons; To. kar- (karθ-)

to bellow; Ta. karai to sound, roar (Tēv.); weep (Kamp.); call (Aiṅk.); tr. to tell (Tolk.); Ma. karayuka to cry, lament; Go. (Bastar) karingi calling (LSI, IV, p. 535); Nk. karūktu calling (ibid., p. 573); Kur. khar͟kh- to ring, jingle; Mlt. qargr- to cry out; cf. Te. kraṅgu the ring of bells (Naiṣ.); Ta. kaṟaṅku v.i. to sound (PN); Kui krāva the tongue of a bell; Go. kuṛūrka a wooden cattle bell; Kur. khaṛū metallic bell (tied under the head of pack-bullocks); > ? l.w. Skt. kránd- (Ṛgv.) to sound, make noise, to call out; (Ratnāv.) to cry piteously, weep, lament; kránda- m. a cry, crying out (AV); krandana- m. crier; -m, n. crying out, calling, lamenting (Pañcat., Hit.).]

341 kṟammaṟu* intr. to return, retreat, go back (Bhr. I, II); tr. kṟammaṟincu/-ucu to cause to go back (Bhr. I).

342 krammu* intr. to spread, be extended; to overflow, swell (Bhr. II); to overspread (Bhr. II), cover completely; hover over (Vasu.); (< *kaḻ-m-).

[Ka. kaḻumu to be full, complete (Cīv.); overflow (Cūṭā.); n. denseness as a tuft of hair (Tolk.); Kui garja to spread out, increase; grow thick and outspreading.]

343 *krayyu* III inf. krayy-aN- in krayyāpaḍu to break in, to pounce upon, to push in, join, meet (Vijñ., Bhōj.); the dictionary meanings are not clear and conclusive; they are "tr. to enter, meet, join closely."

[Cf. krammu.]

344 krā̃gu* intr. to be burnt, consumed in fire (Bhr. I, II), be heated, grow hot; be melted away (Bhr. II); tr. krā̃cu to melt, destroy (Bhr. II); (< *kar-aṅg-); cf. karā̃gu.

[For SDr. see s.v. kaggu, karagu; Kui kara heat of the sun; kāṛa to be hot; be distressed; Kuvi (F) kaṛṛa sunshine; kāṛbi anger; Go. karw- to burn; Kur. k͟hārāba'- tr. to scorch; Brah. k͟har angry; k͟hā-k͟har fire.]

345 krāyu* III intr. to hawk (Kāś.); tr. to vomit (Naiṣ.); to spit out (UH); (< *kaṯ-ay-).

[Ka. kāṟu id.; Tu. kāruni id.; Ta. kāṟu to hawk; kāl (kāṉ-ṟ-) to flow from the mouth, as saliva (Tivā.); kal, kallu (kaṉ-ṟ-) to vomit (Tivā.); Ma. kāruka to vomit; hawk; kāluka to vomit; kāṟuka to retch, spit; v.s.v. krakku.]

346 krālu* intr. to move, shake, tremble (Naiṣ.); wander, roam (Bhr. II); wave, as a banner (BhR., UH); to shine, exist, behave (Bhr. II, Nirv.); cf. krāl-gaṇṭi a damsel (lit. the tremulous-eyed one, corres. Skt. cañcala-akṣi-).

[Ka. kal̲al to slip off, get loose; Ta. kal̲al to become loose, run away (Kalit.); Ma. kal̲aluka to slip; Go. karēng-, kasēng- to be shaken, swung; v. s. v. kadalu for forms with -d-. PDr. *kac-/ *kal̲-; -al in SDr.]

347 kriyyu* III intr. to be reduced, emaciated (Bhg.; no other work); (< *kir̲-y-).

[Ka. kir̲i small; kiriya adj. id.; Tu. kiri id.; Ta. Ma. cir̲u small; Go. kiṛkwāl very thin (of man); cf. cikku[2]; (also Burrow, DS III, p. 123, fn. 1.).]

348 krukku* tr. to press down, suppress (Manu.); press and kill, as lice (Prabhā.); to stuff, cram (Vi. Pu.); thrust food into mouth; penetrate (also Mdn.); (< *kur̲-k); Mdn. kukku.

[Ka. kukku to peck; to destroy lice; gukku mouthful; ? kuṭuku to stuff; Ma. kur̲ummuka to cram in; eat greedily; further Kur. Mlt. v. s. v. kūru. PDr. *kūt̲-, PSDr. *kut̲-V- : *kut̲-ukk-, *kut̲-umm-.]

349 kruṅku intr. to sink in water, go down, to set, as sun (Bhr. II); to die (UH); n. setting (of sun or moon); (< *kur-nk-); Mdn. gunku/ gūku.

[Kui kṛūva (kṛūt-) to sink down, sink into; to set (sun); for other forms, v. s. v. kruṅgu.]

350 kruṅgu* intr. be bent (Bhr. II); to sink (due to heaviness and pressure) (Kāś.); to abate, perish (Daś.); kruṅgābaḍu to sink down, collapse; Mdn. kuṅgu.

[Ka. kuggu, kurgu be bent down, depressed; to decrease; kul̲gu to bend, shrink (l̲ secondary < *r̲); Tu. kugguni be humbled; Ta. kuraṅku v. i. to bend, incline, droop (Cīv.), diminish (Kamp.); n. bending (Cilap.); kūr v. i. to bend (Kalit.); Kui kṛumba to sink beneath, dive, die out; kṛūva to sink, etc.; Kuvi (F) krūi(y)- (krūt-) to sink; verra krūpu sunset; cf. Kur. gorrē/goreā adj. abnormally bent one way; kōr- to shrink in, lose volume. PDr. *kūr- : *kur-V-; contamination possible with etyma meaning 'to become short,' Ta. kur̲u, kur̲uku, etc. v. s. v. kruyyu.]

351 *kruccu* IIa only in vā-kruccu to say in detail, lit. to knit words together < *vā word(s) + kruccu to bore and knit together as beads on a string; cf. gruccu.

352 krummaru* intr. to wander, roam, ramble (in a forest, garden, etc.) (Bhr. I, II).

[Cf. Ta. kur̲avan̲, Ma. kur̲avan a wandering tribe; Ka. kur̲uba, kur̲umba a shepherd, nomadic; Tu. kurube id.; Te. kor̲ava id.; Ta. kur̲umpu a village in a desert tract.]

353 krummu* to butt with horns, etc. (UH); n. butting with head or horns, stroke; (< *kuṟ-m-); Mdn. kummu.

[Go. kurum- to pound in a mortar; Ka. gummu id.; Tu. gummu cuff; n. a stroke; Ta. kuṟṟu to pound, strike, butt; kuṟu to pound (Kalit.). Ta. kumai to pound, etc. point to PDr. *kum-; Ka. Tu. g- is taken to presuppose mm < *rm; v. s. v. gruddu. Also cf. Kur. kuc- to pound, crush; Nep. kucinu be crushed, q. v. Nep. Dict.]

354 kruyyu* III intr. to diminish, droop, be emaciated (KS); decrease, abate (Bhg.); to shrink, withhold (HariV.); (< *kuṟ-iy-).

[Tu. kureyuni to be worn out; Ta. kuṟai v. i. to diminish, dwindle, decrease; droop in languish (Kamp.); be destroyed (Kamp.); Ma. kuṟayuka to dwindle; Kui kṛōpka (< kṛōk-p-; kṛōkt-) to lower, reduce (tr. of obsolete *kṛōg-); Brah. kurr- to keep back, withhold; shrink from; PDr. *kūṯ-.]

355 kruḷḷu* intr. to grieve, suffer agony within (Bhg.; none from earlier classics); to rot, decay (no literary usages cited with this meaning); Mdn. kuḷḷu to grieve, rot; adj. rotten, decomposed; n. decay.

[Ka. koḻe to become rot; pine away in grief; koḻaku n. being worn out; Tu. kuripini, kuriyuni to decay, rot; kurè filth, dirt; Ko. koḷv- (koḷd-) (flesh) putrifies and falls apart; To. kwaḍ- (kwaḍθ-) to rot; Ta. kuḻai become soft, mashy (Tiv.); become spoiled (Kṟḷ.); Ma. kuḻayuka id.; kuyumpu, kuyimpu, kuśumpal mustiness, decay; Kur. k͟hoss- to decay, rot; be worn, wasted; cf. Mlt. gojnār- be or become dirty. PDr. *koc-/*koḻ- or *kŭc-/*kŭḻ-; cf. Ta. kūḻai mire. Ety. for the Te. form is dubious, either *kuḻ-ḷ < *kuḻ-uḷ, or else kuḷḷu < *kuḷ-iy(u) with contraction of -ḷ-iy(u) > -ḷḷ(u) and kruḷḷu as a hyper-correct formation; ḻ > ḷ indicates borrowing from Ka. (Cf. Pkt. kuṇima- rotten, see Burrow, DS VII, p. 373, No. 81).]

356 krēṭu* intr. to clear the throat by coughing (Manu.; rare).

357 krovvu* intr. to become proud (Bhr. II); to grow fat, to increase (Kāś.); n. fat, pride, arrogance (Bhr. II; Naiṣ.); (< *koḻ-v-); Mdn. kovvu.

[Ka. kobbu, korbu n. id.; korcu to brag; Tu. kommè n. fat; To. kȫw, kwaḷp n. fat; Ta. koḻu to grow, flourish (Nāl.); grow fat; n. fat (Nāl.); koḻuppu n. fat (Piṅ.); impudence; Ma. koḻu, koḻuppu n. fat; Kui krōga id.; Kuvi (F) korowa fat (of animals); GoA. koṛvinj fat; Klm. Nk. koru id.; Pj. koṛ- (Sth. koṛv-) to be fat; Kur. k͟hōr- to thrive; cf. korrā fresh, pure; PDr. *kōḻ : *koḻ-V-.]

358 krōyu* III tr. (fire) to shoot up flames; (serpent) to spread out tongues (Bhr. II, BP); (? < *kor-ay-).

[Cf. Ta. kūr- to be enraged, furious. (Nāl.); be excessive (Tolk.); be sharp pointed (Tēv.).]

359 krōlu* to drink (Bhr. II, Hara.); eat (Manu.); (< *kor-al).

[Cf. Ma. kōruka to eat greedily; to draw water; Ta. kōlu bale, draw up water (Kalit.); Kuvi (S) goh'- to drink; cf. krōl(u)cu.]

360 krōl(u)cu* IId intr. to sing, chirp (as birds) (Kāś., Hara.); tr. to read out, recite (Pāṇḍ.); (< *kor-al-).

[Ka. koralcu to call or cry out; koral, koraḷ, korḷu, koḷḷu sound, voice; throat, neck; Tu. korejuni to make noise; kurelu̥ nape of the neck; Ta. kural n. voice, word (Kalit.); throat (Kuṟun.); kurai to shout, jubilate; Ma. kural sound, throat; Kui guruguru purring; Go. guṛngā throat; Kur. gurrār- to roar; growl, snarl.]

## G

361 gaṇṭu* tr. to wound, cut (Nr̥s.); a wound, a notch, cut; gaṇṭi hole, cut, wound (Bhr. II); gaṇṭivaḍu (-paḍu) to be wounded (BhR); -vaṟucu (-paṟucu) tr. to wound.

[Ka. kaṇḍi, gaṇḍi, kaṇame a hole, opening; Tu. kaṇḍi, gaṇḍi id.; kaṇi a ditch, trench; Ma. kaṇṭi gap in a wedge, breach in a wall; Klm.(SR) gaṇḍ- to prick; Brah. kanḍ gap, breach, opening; hill-pass (also Te. kanuma hill-pass, etc. is related); < PDr. *kaṇ-t-. Te. gaṇṭu appears to be a back-formed verb from the noun gaṇṭi.]

gatuku (free var. of gaduku, katuku) to lick, lap, as a dog (late), eat food defiled by others.

[V. s. v. katuku.]

gaduku (same as gatuku, katuku, q. v.)

362 gadumu tr. to rebuke, scold, check (late); gadd-incu id. (late).

[Ka. gadamu to push away; gadaṟu to thunder, roar; gaddisu to cry; Ta. katavu, katam anger (PN); kataḻ be angry with; v. s. v. kasaru, kadumu.]

363 giccu IId to pinch, squeeze with fingers or pinch with nails (colloq., no literary usages cited).

[Kui kisa id.; Kuvi (F) kic-; Go. kisk-; kidī- to shred chillies; Klm. (SR) kism- to pinch; Pj. kīk- id.; kicc- to pluck; Oll. kisk- pinch; KGad. kicc- to pluck; Kur. kicc- to break into small pieces with fingers (as greens, etc.); Brah. kishk- to pluck, etc. PDr. *kic-.]

364 giṭṭu[1] intr. to perish, die (Bhg.); be destroyed (also Mdn. in proverbial phrases: puṭṭinā giṭṭinā whether born or dead).

[Klm.(E) kiṭ- to be extinguished; Klm.(SR) kiṭṭ- to extinguish; Nk. kiṭ- id.; with irregular palatalization, Pj. ciṭ- (fire) goes out; Oll. siṭ- id.; KGad. ciṭṭ- id.; cf. giṭṭu to kill; < *kiṭ-t-.]

365 giṭṭu[2] intr. to suit one's constitution (as food, water, weather, etc.); to be agreeable; to accrue (as profit), come into one's possession (Mdn.); ety. same as for kiṭṭu[2], q.v.

[Ka. giṭṭu, gīṭu to be obtained; Ko. gicg- be a suitable person (to do); Ta. kiṭṭu, kiṭai id.; Ma. kiṭayuka id.; v. s. v. kiṭṭu[2]. PDr. *kiṭ-.]

366 ginju (mostly with refl. -konu) tr. to writhe, struggle, move the limbs convulsively (HariV., Naiṣ.).

[Cf. Go. winj- to pull with a jerk, as a patwari's chain; or < *kiḻ[i]nj- : Ka. kīḻ to draw, pull off, etc.]

367 giṟuku to scribble (Mdn.); to erase (Śab.R.).

[Ka. kiṟuku to scratch; Ta. kiṟukku to scribble; score out; kīṟu to draw line (Piṅ.); Ma. kiṟukkuka to erase, strike out; kīṟuka draw lines; < *kīṯ- : *kiṯ-V-; v. s. v. gīṟu, gī̃ku.]

368 giṟupu[1]/girpu, also giṟuvu/girvu tr. to wink, as in making a sign or conveying a hint (Bhr. II, Nirv., Bhīm.); cf. gī̃ṭu id.

[Ta. kīṟu to hint at; kiṟi stratagem, artifice; playful mischief, practical joke (Tiruvāc.); v. tr. to play pranks (Tēv.); Go. gir-gir (huṛ-) to wink jocularly at anyone, as a signal (huṛ- to see).]

369 giṟupu[2]* tr. to shake, move, as body (Nirv.), ears (as an animal) (Mārk.).

[Ta. kiruṅku v. i. to move, stir, shake, stagger (loc.); Tu. girpuni v. tr. to loosen, untie; v. i. be loose, pulled down.]

370 giṟupu[3]* to pass fingers through, as feathers of a bird, etc.; to pat, stroke (Nr̥s.).

[V. s. v. gīṟu.]

giṟuvu/girvu* same as giṟupu[1], q. v.

371 giluku (colloq. Guntur dial.) tr. to scribble, write illegibly.

[Cf. giṟuku.]

372 gilupu tr. to wink as a signal (Appak.); to shake, as the pigtail (Paṇḍ.).

[V. s. v. giṟupu[1], giṟupu[2].]

373 gilubu* tr. to steal, rob (Dvā.); n. theft; gil(u)b-āḍu to steal (Daś.); to deceive (Paṇḍ.).

[ ? Ta. kiṟi n. falsehood (Tĕv.); deceit, fraud; Tu. guḷumu̥ loss;

cheating, fraud; Ka. kīḻ to draw, pull; rob; kīḷ base, low, mean; < *kīḻ- to be below; ety. dub.]

374 gillu tr. to nip off with the nails (as greens, chillies, etc.); to pinch with nails (Bhīm.); n. a pinch, nipping.

[Ka. giṇḍu to pinch with the nails; Tu. kiṇkuni, kiṅkuni tr. to pinch; Ta. kiḷḷu to pinch, pluck as a leaf (Nāl.), n. pinching; Ma. kiḷḷuka nip, pinch, pluck; cf. Go. kidī- to shred chillies with finger nails; < PSDr. *kiḷ-, ultimately *ki-, v. s. v. giccu.]

375 givuṟu* tr. to scratch (Āmu.) (disputed version; Śab.R. gives nivuru; -ṟ(u) not likely in the third syllable); may be a contamination of gīṟu and civvu, q. v.

376 gīku tr. to scrape, scratch (Dvi.H.) (also Mdn.).

[Ka. gīku id.; Ma. cīka, cikkuka to scratch, scrape, etc.; further v. s. v. gīcu, gīyu, gīṟu. PDr. *kī-.]

377 gīcu IId tr. draw, as a line on a surface, scrape, scratch (late); to tap as a palm tree for drawing toddy (Mdn.).

378 gīṭu ([˜] unlikely because of derivation < *kīṯṯ-) (1) tr. to gnash teeth (Dvi.H.); to tear, rend; n. a stripe, line, scratch; v. s. v. gīṟu; (2) to wink as a signal (UH; Bhg.); cf. giṟupu id.; Ta. kīṟu id.; v. s. v. giṟupu.

379 gīyu III tr. to scrape (Hara., Naiṣ.); to draw a line on a surface (Manu.); to scratch; tap, as a palm tree for drawing toddy (Mdn.).

[Ka. kīsu, gīcu id.; Tu. gīcuni, gīsuni to scrape, etc.; v. s. v. gīcu, gīṟu.]

380 gīṟu tr. to tear, rend (Bhr. I, Nr̥s.); to scrape, scratch; to comb with fingers (late); gīṟa n. a stripe, scratch.

[Ka. gīṟu to scrape, scratch, draw lines or streaks; rub off with hand; kīṟu id.; Tu. kīruni to scratch, split; gīruni tr. to scratch, wound; Ko. kīr- to tear; Ta. kīṟu to tear, rend; cut, slice (Kamp.); n. a slice; Ma. kīṟuka to scratch; rend; v. i. to be split, torn; Kui gīra n. a line mark or stripe; Klm. kīra stripe; Pj. kir-, kirv- (kirc-) to scratch; kirp- (kirt-) id.; gīru n. line, mark; cf. Mlt. qerc- to scrape. PDr. *kī-ṯ-.]

guccu Mdn. Te. var. of gruccu[1], q. v.

guddu Mdn. Te. var. of gruddu, q. v.

381 guniyu* III intr. to dance (Paṇḍ.); to wave, shake (as hair) (Bhg.) to frisk (KS).

[Ta. kuṉi to dance; kuṉippu a kind of dance (Tiruvāc.); Ma. kunikka to dance, jump; Ko. konc- (calf) frisks; Kuvi (F) gūṛka dance (of female); gūṛk- to dance; probably from *kūn- to bend, v. s. v. kunuku; PDr. *kūn-/*kūṯ- ]

382 gunuku* to run slowly (Dvi.H., Manu.); n. a slow run. Cf. gunaguna imit. of slow run; gunukuparuvu n. slow run (Rāyalasīma dial.).

[Cf. Ka. guḍugu to run when playing a tip-catball; a run; v. s. v. kunuku, guniyu; no exact correspondences.]

383 gunju tr. to draw, pull forcibly; to beat, as clothes in washing (Kāś., Bhōj.).

[Ka. guñju to pull; v. i. to contract (muscles), move convulsively; GoM. gunj- to drag; (*kum-c-/-j-?). Cf. Ta. kum-ukku to wash clothes by wetting and gently pressing with hand; kumai to mash out; v. s. v. gumuku.]

384 guppu[1] tr. to discharge, shower as arrows (Nirv.); to fling, sprinkle something contained in the fist; lay down abundantly (Bhōj.); gupp-eḍu adj. a handful; gupp-ili a fist; cf. kuppa a heap.

[Contamination possible between two series: (1) etyma meaning heap, etc.; Ka. guppu, kuppu to lay in a heap; guppe, kuppe a heap; Tu. guppe id.; for other languages vide Kolami, Vocab. 2174; (2) etyma meaning to hold in hand (and fling, spill, etc.); cf. Go. guht- to seize, snatch; koṛop double handful; Tu. guppuni, gūcuni to pour, shed, spill; Brah. k̲h̲umb the two arms, embrace; v. s. v. gruccu[2] for evidence of base final -ṟ- < *-ṯ-; gupp- < *kuṯ- and *kup-.]

385 guppu[2]* to butt with head, etc. (as a calf does while sucking) (Bhōj.); to pound heavily with a pestle (late); (< *kuṟ-p-).

[V. s. v. krummu, gruddu.]

gubuku* same as gumuku, q. v.

386 gumuku* to cuff, box, pommel (infrequently in later literary texts); gummu a hit, stroke (Rāyalasīma dial.); cf. krummu, kummu.

[Ka. kummu, gummu to cuff, box, strike; Tu. gumusuni to box, strike; gumusu, gumuṭu cuffing; Ko. To. kum- to pound with light strokes; Ta. kumukku to pommel; beat with fists; kumai to mash out, beat in a mortar (Tēv.); n. blow (Tiv.); Ma. kuma bruising; kumekka to beat, bruise; kummu beat in a mortar. PSDr *kum- ]

387 *guṟucu, only as a pp. guṟic-i aiming at, adv. about, regarding; alt. forms *guṟ-incu, *guṟi-(y)-incu tr. *to aim at, regard (Bhr. II, Kāś.); guṟi n. aim, mark, ideal (Bhr. II, Daś.).

[Ka. guṟi a mark, etc.; kuṟi to mark, mark out, take note of; regard (pp. kuṟitu); n. a mark, sign, aim; Tu. guri an aim, mark; guri-tūpuni to aim, mark; Ta. kuṟi tr. to design, intend, think (Akan.); n. mark, aim; kuṟittu adv. with the intention of; Ma. kuṟikka to note, attend to; point at, refer to; towards, for the sake of; kur̲i n. mark, sign, etc.; cf. Ka. kūna, kūnu a mark, sign; PSDr. *kut̲-V-/*kūn-; Kui goṛpa to aim at.]

388 geṇṭu tr. to drive out, expel, push (Dvi.H.); to discharge (arrows, etc.) (JBh.); intr. to withhold, hesitate (Dvi.H.; JBh.); be shaken, as determination (Kaḷā.); geṇṭ-incu to remove, shake off (Kāś.); destroy; cf. geṇṭ-asamu abusive words of expression; angry speech.

[Cf. Ka. geṇṭu distance, removal.]

389 gedumu* to push away, suppress, to scold (late and rare; single usage cited).

[V. s. v. kadumu, gadumu.]

390 genayu* III intr. to increase, flourish (rare; Vi.Pu.).

[Cf. kiḷai to increase, abound (PN); v. s. v. keralu[1]; ? < *kiḷ-/*kiṇ-.]

391 gentu intr. to hop, jump (not listed in dict.; colloq., Viśākha dial.); n. a jump; cf. gantu a hop, jump.

[Ta. kenti- to hop, skip; Kui geha to run, flee; Kuvi (S) gent- to spring; gett- to jump.]

392 gebbu* tr. to steal, take away.

393 gelucu IIa tr. to win, defeat (Bhr. II); der. n. gelupu victory (Bhr. II); gelavamu, geluvaḍi id. (later forms).

[Ka. gel, gelu, geli, gellu to win, conquer; gelavu n.; Tu. gelpuni, genduni to win; Ko. gelc- win and secure; To. kelc- (kelč-) be successful; Ta. vel, vellu (ven̲-r̲-) to subdue, overcome (Mullaip.); destroy; v.i. to excel, prosper; keli to conquer; kelippu success (late; l. w. < Ka.); Ma. velluka to overcome, to kill; ver̲r̲i victory; Kuvi (S) gelh- to upset, win; Klm.(SR) gell-, Nk. ghel- id. ?PSDr. and PCDr. *gel-/*vel-; for a similar case of g-/v- alternation, see s. v. ginju.]

394 goḍāgu, goṇāgu intr. to murmur, mutter (late); (pigeons) to coo.

[Ka. goṇagu grumbling; murmuring; goḍa, goḷa an imit. sound; guḍu, guḍi, guṇa, gul̲a growling; guṇa, goṇa a sound in imitation of grumbling (Mdn.); cf. Ta. kul̲aku to prattle playfully (Tiv.), to coax, wheedle; kun̲aku id.; To. kuḍx- to buzz; further see Kolami, Vocab. 2116.]

goṇāgu var. of goḍāgu, q. v.

395 gor̲ugu tr. to shave (head) (Bhr. III, Kāḷ.) (also Mdn.).

[GoM. kōr- to shave; Go. kōrī- to shave, cut; Brah. kargh̲- to shear, mow down, crop down; cf. Klm. (SR, p. 20) guṛip- to cut grass; v. s. v. kōgu, kor̲uku; traditionally connected with Skt. kṣurá-; Pa. khuro razor; Pk. khura- id., but not likely on account of o instead of u; Te. and other languages point to *kōt̲- : *kot̲-V-, ultimately from *koy-/*kō-, v. s. v. kōyu.]

396 gõku tr. to scratch with nails (Bhr. II), to scratch, scrape (Dvi.H.); gõkuḍu pāṟa (Mdn.) a small hoe, a turf-spade; v. s. v. kōru[2].

[Ka. gōṟu to scratch; Klm.(SR) kōk- to scratch; itch; (Kin.) kōk- id.; Nk. kokk- to itch, scratch; Kui grōpa (grōt-) to scratch, claw; cf. Te. gōru nail; Klm. Nk. gōr; Kui gōra a claw, talon, nail; Kuvi (F) gōrū id.; Go. kojji claws; Keikaḍi koikāl id. (see Hislop, p. 9, Vocabulary); Brah. hōr finger (h = ?); these forms yield the reconstructions, *kō-, *kō-ṯ-/-r-; Te., etc. gõku < *kō-ṅk- or even *kōr-ṅk-; obviously the connection with Ta. ukir nail, etc. is not likely (see Burrow, DS IV, p. 343; Master, BSOAS, XII, p. 355; Emeneau, Kolami, Vocab. 278). Nep. kornu to scratch has a doubtful etymology in IA.; see Nep. Dict.]

397 grukku* tr. to gulp liquid (Prabhā.); grukka a draught of liquid, a gulp (Hara.); (< *kuṟ-k-); grukk-ili id.; grukk-eḍu adj. id.; grukka-konu to gulp down (Paṇḍ.); Mdn. Te. gukka n. a swallow; cf. guṭaka id.

[Ma. kuṟummuka to eat greedily, cram in; Kui guhpa (guht-) to swallow, swallowing; Kuvi (S) guh'- to devour; Kuvi (F) gūss- (gūst-) to swallow. PDr. *kuṯ-; also v. s. v. krukku, kūru[3]; association with IA. only for forms with ṭ, e.g., Te. guṭaka a gulp; Ka. guṭaku; Tu. guṭuku id.; cf. Deś. ghuṭṭaï drinks; M. ghuṭka- gulp; H. ghūṭnā, etc.; see Nep. Dict., s. v. ghuṛko; but this does not explain *ṟ (< *-ṯ-) in Dravidian.]

398 gruccu[1*] IIa (gruvv- before C-suffixes) tr. to pierce, prick, fix, stab, as with pointed instruments (Bhr. II, UH); to thread the needle (Mdn.); to string (beads) together, (flowers) into a garland, (fish) on a rope to carry (Bhr. II, Vikram.); a different shade of meaning occurs in the following phrase: grucci grucci aḍugu to ask point by point (i.e., in extensive detail; aḍugu to ask; grucci pp.); intr. to be pierced (Bhg.); (< *kuṟ-c-).

[Tu. kutṭuni to bore, pierce; To. kut- id.; Ta. kuṟṟu to puncture, prick, pierce; kuttu id. (Tiv.), to stab, wound; plant, set, fix in the ground (Mullaip.); Ma. kuttuka id.; Kui kuta to prick (thorn); Kur. kuḍ- (kuḍḍ-) to thread, string; fix on any pointed instrument; also kuṛ- id.; Mlt. kuḍ- to pierce (as with a needle); Brah. k͟hull- to pierce, stab; to thread the needle. Correspondences conflicting in phonology; in Ta. Ma. etc. *ṯ > t; in Kur. Mlt. *ṯ > *ṭ > ḍ; Brah. *l/*ḷ; PDr. *kuṯ-/*kuṭ- : *kul-; ? *kuṯ- < *kult-; contamination with forms under kuṭṭu, q. v.]

399 *gruccu[2*] IId (only as a pp. grucci in grucci kaũgilincu to embrace

tightly, lit., having held tight, to embrace; Bhr. II, Hara.) *to hold tightly, closely (with hands).

[Go. guht- to seize, snatch; koṛop a double handful; cf. Brah. k̲h̲umb n. embrace, the two arms; k̲h̲umb-kann- to embrace; k̲h̲uṛk close, close to hand; cf. Te. gupp-eḍu a handful; gupp-ili fist; < *kuṟ-p-, v. s. v. guppu.]

400 gruddu* tr. to cuff, give a blow with the fist (Manu.); a blow, cuff (< *gur-d- < *kuṟ-d-); Mdn. guddu.

[Ka. gurdu, guddu id.; kuttu (< *kuṯṯ-) to strike, pound; Tu. gudduni to cuff; Ko. gud-, To. kud- id.; Ta. kuṟṟu to strike, hit, butt; kuṟu to pound (Kalit.); Te. Ka. Tu. Ko. To. forms presuppose a reconstruction *kuṯutt- (> *kuṟ-t/d- > *gur-d-); also v. s. v. krummu.]

401 gremmu* tr. to elongate a heated metal on anvil (rare; Vasu.)

[ ? Tu. kerpuni to prop, support.]

402 groccu* IIb (Śab.R. notes that this form occurs with kr- instead of gr- in written records; why changed ?) tr. to dig up (KS, Bhr. I); to tear open (Bhg.); to dig and pull up, to rout (Dvi.H.).

[Ka. kuḻi to become low or deep; to dig; n. a pit; Tu. kurepini to bore, drill; korepuni, korapuni to be excavated; gōruni to dig from, out, or up; Ta. koḻutu to drill through, hollow out; pluck out (Naṟṟ.), rend, tear (Kalit.); Kui goru adj. holey; gorna id.; Kur. koṛ- (koḍḍ-) to dress soil; khoḍṛā hollow, full of holes; Brah. kōnḍ hole; kōḍ id.; cf. also with radical u : Ta. kuḻi to form pits (Nāl.); to be hollowed out; tr. to excavate, engrave (Kalit.); Ma. kuḻiyuka to become hollow, deepened; kuḻikka to dig a hole; dig out; Ta. Ma. Ka. kuḻi a hole; Tu. guri id.; To. kud̲y- (kud̲c-) to make a hollow; Kui kurṛagiva dig out a rice field, etc.; Kuvi kūrgi a hoe; for o-forms, PDr. *kōḻ-; *koḻ-V-; for IA see s. v. kornu, Nep. Dict.]

## C

403 caccu V (allom. cā-/cāv- before back vowel suffixes, e.g., cā-ka/ cāv-aka not dying, etc.) intr. to die, perish (Bhr. I, KS); campu tr. to kill (Bhr. I).

[Ka. sāy, sāyu (satt-) id.; Tu. saipini; To. soy- (sot-); Ta. cā- (cett-) to die (Kṟḷ.); Ma. cāka (cett-) id.; Kui sāva (sāt-); Kuvi hā'- id.; Go. sai- (pp. sāsī); Pj. cay- (cañ-); Oll. say- (sad-, san-); KGad. cay-; PSDr. and PCDr. *cāy-/*cay-; connection not likely with forms with initial k- < *k-.]

404 cadiyu III intr. to be crushed (Bhr. I, KS); to be destroyed, to die (Bhr. II); tr. cadupu to smash, crush (Bhr. II); cf. cadunu adj. levelled (RR).

[Ka. sade to crush, bruise, strike, beat; be powdered, bruised; tade to strike; Tu. sadevuni to wear away; sadi beating; cade destruction of life; Ko. cac- to hammer with blows; To. toθx- to be smashed flat; Ta. catai to crush, bruise; cati to destroy; catāvu to be shattered; broken; tatai to be shattered (Patir̲.); tatar to be crushed (Tiv.); Ma. catayuka to be squashed; catekka to squash; cata a bruise, catuṅṅuka be crushed; catukkuka to bruise; catukka a bruise, compressing; Pj. cacip- (cacit-) to trample, kick; catip- (catit-) id. PDr. *cac-/*cat- : PSDr. *cat-/ *tat-.]

cadupu (tr. of cadiyu, q.v.) to break, crush (Bhr. II; UH), to kill, beat.

405 cadumu* tr. to crush (RR); strike, beat, cuff (Dvi.H.); (< *cat-ump-).

[V. s. v. cadiyu; different derivative.]

406 caduru intr. to crack a joke (colloq. Viśākha. dialect) also occurs as catur-āḍu/cadur-āḍu to play jokes.

[< Skt. catura- clever.]

407 caduvu (cadvu in Paṇḍ., SII, IV 975) tr. to read, study, recite (Bhr. I, KS, Paṇḍ.); n. study, knowledge (UH); cadiv-incu to announce gifts at the marriage ceremony (through the priest); Mdn. Te. caduvu, in fast speech cawu.

[No exact correspondence in the other languages; Burrow derives Skt. catura- clever from Dr., connecting it with Te. caduvu, etc., DS VII, p. 378, No. 136; Kuvi (S) caḍiv- (? l. w. < Te.); cf. Ka. Tu. ōdu, Ko. ōd-, Ta. Ma. ōtu to read, etc.]

408 canu IV intr. to go (Bhr. I); to be gone, to perish (Bhr. II); to be suitable, to pass for right (Bhr. I, II); tr. to obtain, get, reach (Bhr. I, II); aux. with inf. to be becoming, suitable, can, e.g., cēyājanu it deserves to be done, can be done, etc. (Bhr. I, II); der. n. canupa a way; a ç̣aravan (Bhr. I).

[Ka. ṣal, saliu to join, enter; be proper; pass; depart from life; Tu. salluni to be fit, valid; sanduni to pass as time, to die, be paid; come to pass; Ta. cel, cellu (cen̲-r̲-) to go, pass (Tolk.); be suitable; pass away; lapse, as time (Nāl.); diminish (PN); be due, as money; (fame) to spread (PN); n. payment of loan; loan; celavu going (Tolk.); Kui salba to go, depart; Kuvi (S) han- id.; Kuvi (F) hajj- to go; Go. hand- (pp. han-jī) to go; Pj. cen- (cend-) id.; KGad. cen- (cey-); Kur. calr- to go away; be current, as coin; have value; to behave; calâ adv. off; cf. Mundari sen to go, start, go away. PDr. *cal-.]

409 cappu* tr. to smack, suck, smack with noise (BhR, BP); capparincu id.; cf. cavi taste.

[Ka. jabbisu to sip, suck; Tu. capparipuni to smack the lips; sabipuni to taste; Ko. cap- suck repeatedly; To. sop- to suck; Ko. ayv- (avc-) to chew; Ta. cappu to masticate; chew, as betel; munch, mumble; sip; Ma. cappuka id.; cavekka to chew; cf. Kur. cab- (cabc-) to chew, masticate; Burrow says pp- < -rp-, but not likely on account of -p-/-v- alternation; -pp- (< -rp-) is not weakened to -v- as is *-p- or *-pp-, see DS VII, p. 378, No. 138.]

410 camaru* (also camuru) tr. to crush under foot (Bhr. I); to slap with the open hand (Bhr. I, UH); to kill, destroy (Bhr. III, BhR). (< *cav-ar < *cap-ar); cf. cappar-incu to pat, stroke with hand (KS).

[Ka. capparisu to slap; cappalisu id.; Tu. cappalipuni id.; Ko. cavr- to slash down a collection of standing plants; Ta. capp-āṇi clapping of hands (Ilak.); cappu v.i. to be pressed in, become flat; to subside; there are also forms with the loss of *c-; (> Skt. capēṭa- a slap with the open hand, see Burrow TPS 1945, No. 21, pp. 99, 100); PDr. *cap- : *cav-V-.]

411 camuru tr. to smear, apply, as oil, ointment, etc. (Vijñ., HariV.); n. oil (RR, Daś.; also Mdn.).

[Ka. savaru to apply to, as water, oil or medicine; prob. the same root as for camaru, q.v.; Ta. timir smear as sandal paste (Maṇi.), rub (PN), and Ka. temar to rub do not belong to this set on account of the difficulty in radical vowel.]

carumu* same as camuru, q.v. (metathesized) tr. to rub over gently (BhR).

412 caṟacu IIa tr. to slap or strike with the open hand (Bhr. I), to slap upper arms (as in wrestling) (Manu.); to beat the drum, etc. (Bhr. II); intr. (wind) to blow hard; (fear) to come upon (Bhr. I, Hara.); n. caṟapu a slap, etc.

[Ta. aṟai to slap, strike; beat as a drum (Kṟḷ.); intr. to beat upon, as wind, waves (Cīv.); n. slap; blow, beat; dashing; Ma. aṟayuka to beat hard, as drum; Kui jaṛsa n. a whip; Mlt. taṛc- to slap; Kur. taṛ- (taṛc-) to flog, dash, whip; PDr. *caṯ-; PSDr. *caṯ- : *aṯ-; there are also similar forms in IA: A. sar slap; B. caṛ id.; M. caḍ-caḍ slapping; v.s.v. carkanu, Nep. Dict.]

calupu* (tr. of canu q.v., also salupu[1]) to pass (as time) (Bhr. I); to drive a boat, etc. (Bhr. I); to do, perform (Bhr. III).

413 callu tr. to sprinkle, scatter, as water, seeds, etc. (Bhr. II, UH);

to give in large quantities (Bhr. II); to spread, extend (Nr̥s.); (also Mdn.); callupōru water fight (Bhr. I, Nirv.); cf. jallu a shower of rain.

[Ka. callu, cellu id.; calanku, celaṅku to scatter; cel to throw as water; seḷaku a shower; caḷe, caḷeya, caḷaka sprinkling; Tu. celluni tr. to sprinkle, spill, shed; intr. to drop, shed; calluni id.; Ta. callu to sprinkle (late); Pj. cal- (rain) to fall in a shower; Kuvi (S) jall-; with t- < *c- : Ka. taḷi to sprinkle, strew; Tu. talipuni id.; Ko. teḷc- to sprinkle (liquid); teyḷ- (teḷc-) id.; Ta. taḷi v. i. to drip as rain (Aiṅk.); tr. to sprinkle; n. drop of water (Kalit.), first shower of rain (Parip.); teḷi (< *ceḷi) tr. to strew, scatter, sprinkle, as water (Akan.); n. sowing seeds (loc.); Ma. taḷikka to sprinkle. PSDr. *caḷ-/*ceḷ- : *taḷ-/*teḷ-; cf. Kur. cā̃k̲h̲- to sow, scatter seed; Mlt. cāk the issuing of water from a spout.]

414 cāgu* (also sāgu) (1) intr. to go, move; to flow (JBh., ŚivaR.); to continue (Śakunt.); cāgan-ampu to send off; (bantulu) sāgu to form into (rows) (Kāś., JBh.); SAN separates this from cā̃gu/sā̃gu to be stretched, to extend, lengthen, fall prostrate (Nirv., Bhr. II); kona-sā̃gu to succeed (to continue to the end); tr. cā̃cu q. v.

[Ka. sāgu to go, move forward; n. advance, improvement; Tu. sāguni to proceed, progress; cācuni tr. to bow; Ko. cāg- (time) passes, to be possible (to do); cāgc- pass one's life; Ta. cāy to march in a crowd, to flee (Pārata); to succeed; v. s. v. cā̃cu.]

cā̃gu same as cāgu, q. v. (SAN separates the two, but it does not seem to be necessary); cā̃g-ilu to prostrate; cā̃g-ilā-baḍu id.; tr. cā̃cu, q. v.

415 cāṭu tr. to proclaim aloud; make to be known; declare, announce, publish (Bhr. II); cāṭuva fame, publicity (NavaN.); cāṭincu id.; to proclaim with drums, etc.

[Ka. sār̲u to proclaim aloud, cry out; Tu. sāriyuni id.; Ko. cār- to tell news at all places; Ta. cār̲r̲u to publish, announce (Parip.); explain in detail (Kr̲ḷ.); to beat, as a drum (Kamp.); n. proclaiming; sound (Kallā.); cār̲u festival; worship (Cilap., Parip.); Ma. cār̲r̲uka tr. to speak loud; call on gods and sing. PSDr. cāt̲t̲- < *cāt̲-t-.]

416 cātu* tr. to wear, put on (as holy mantle, caste mark, etc.) (BP, Āmu.); cf. sātāni a Vaiṣṇavite sect among non-Brahmans who render service in temples.

[Ta. cāttu v. tr. to put on (used of idols, great persons) (Cilap.), wear a caste mark; daub, anoint (Piṅ.); cf. cāttan̲ an Arhat, Buddha; cāttān̲i id. (same as Te. sātāni).]

417 cā̃cu IIb (also sā̃cu; tr. of cāgu/cā̃gu q.v.) to extend, stretch, lengthen (Bhr. II); to stretch out (glance, hands, body, etc.) (Bhr. II, Hara.); cā̃pa a mat (that stretched), a sail (Bhr. II, Daś.).

[Ka. cācu id.; cāpu n. stretch, length; cāpe mat; Tu. cācuni to stretch out; Ta. cāṭu to stretch out as the arms or legs (different suffix); cāppai mat; Ma. cāmpu n. length, stretch; Kui sāhpa tr. to stretch out, lengthen out (limbs); stretch across; sāspa id.; Kuvi (S) hāh'- to stretch (hands, etc.); jānj- to outstretch; sāpa a mat; Go. sāh-at- (sāh-cī) id.; PDr. *cā-/*cāy-, trans. *-c-; cf. Kur. chāh- tr. to spread far and wide; Mlt. cāql- to stretch the legs apart.]

418 cā̃du tr. to rub into paste, to triturate on a slab with water, etc., to rub closely (KS); to sharpen a blade on stone; n. a fragrant substance (smeared on the body) (Hara., Kāḷ.); paste (Mdn.)..

[Ka. tē, tēy, tēyu to triturate in water on slab; caccu/ceccu to grind, crush; Tu. tēpuni to rub, polish; Ta. tēy to rub off (Cīv.); Ma. tēyuka be rubbed off; PDr. *cāy-/*cēy; PSDr. *cāy : *tēy (< *cēy-); v.s.v. tēyu; *cāy occurs in noun forms in the other languages; Ka. sādu, sāndu a fragrant substance; Tu. sādike; Ta. cāttu to smear, daub (see Burrow, TPS 1946, p. 14; DS VI, p. 143; ? > l.w. Skt. śāṇá whet-stone, v.s.v. sā̃d-, sān- Nep. Dict.).]

cā̃pu (same as cā̃cu, tr. of cāgu/cā̃gu, q.v.) to stretch out the hand (Naiṣ.); n. stretch, length (HariV.); long vowels or consonants (Appak.).

419 cāru (Śab.R.) tr. to sweep the threshing-floor with a broom (Mdn., loc.).

[Ta. cār̲u tr. to sweep the threshing-floor and gather scattered grain.]

420 cālu intr. to be capable or competent (Bhr. I), be enough, to suffice (Bhr. II); to be suitable, fit (Bhr. I); cāl(u)vaḍu to be completed (Bhr. I); cāl-incu to stop (Mdn.); to make enough (Bhr. II); cālami incapacity, insufficiency (Bhr. II); cālu (hab. 3sg.) enough; inf. cāl-aN-; Mdn. cālā, śǣnā, adv. sufficiently, abundantly.

[Ka. sāl, sālu to be required, to fit; to suffice; Tu. sākụ (defective vb.) to suffice; Ta. cālu (cān̲-r̲-) to be full, abundant (Cīv.); suitable (Kr̲ḷ.); be finished (Kamp.); adv. cāl-a- (Tiruvāc.); Ma. cāla- richly (inf. of *cāl-); Kuvi (S) hāl- be sufficient, can (taken from Emeneau's Kolami, 2304); cf. Kui sāra to be in excess; Kuvi (S) hār- to remain; Brah. sār satisfied, sated; Mlt. sāry-

(sārc-) to finish; PSDr. *cāl-; further, v. s. v. ā̆ṭu, āṟu[2]; Burrow, DS VI, p. 138.]

421 cikilu* intr. to cry tenderly or fondly, as a child (winking the eyes frequently) (late, rare).

422 cikku[1] intr. to become lean, thin; be emaciated (16th century work); to perish (late); (also Mdn.); (< *ciṟ-k-).

[Two possibilities: (1) Go. sīr- to grow thin, emaciate; Ta. cikku id. (Pārata.) (? l. w. < Te.); cikka thinness; ciṟuku to be stunted in growth; to shrink, diminish (Kṟḷ.); Burrow, DS VII, p. 379, No. 141. (2) Go. kiṛk-wāl very thin, of a man; probably connected with the SDr. words from *kil-, *kiṯ- mean, small, little, etc. See Burrow, DS III, p. 122; Emeneau, BSOAS XV, p. 100.]

423 cikku[2] intr. to be caught, in a trap, in battle by enemies, thieves, etc. (Bhr. II, Naiṣ.); to be lost (as in woods); (mind) to be attached to, to be available, be obtained; n. a twist, tangle (Kāś.); capturing (Bhīm.); a difficulty, trouble (Bhr. II); < *cil-k-; also Mdn.

[Ka. sikku, silku, siluku id.; Tu. sikku, silkuni id.; also tikkuni id.; Ko. cik- id.; cikc- to obtain; To. tik- to be caught; Ta. cikku id. (Pārata.; late, probably l. w. < Te./Ka.); Ma. cikkuka id.; Kui sinḍu (pl. siṭka) a snare; cf. sehpa to be caught, entangled; Kuvi (S) cikkukī- to snare (transcribed chickukīnai); Go. hilk- to be entangled, stuck; Pj. cirŋg- to get stuck; be trapped; cf. Go. kirk- to be caught on thorns. PSDr. and PCDr. *cil-, *cil-k-/*ciṯ-k-.]

424 ciṭuku* tr. to snap the fingers (lex.); n. a snapping sound (Bhōj., Manu.); ciṭṭa a snap of fingers; ciṭukar-incu to snap, etc.; ciṭike a snap of fingers, a pinch (of snuff, etc.).

[Ka. ciṭiku, ciṭaku; ciṭike n. id.; ciṭiki, ciṭi a little pinch, as of snuff; ciṭuṅkisu to snap, etc.; Tu. ciṭuku, ciṭiki, ciṭka n. snap of fingers, pinch (of snuff); Ta. ciṭṭikkai id. (Madras); < *ciṭ-, imit.]

425 ciṭ(u)lu, also ciṭilu intr. to crack, break, as a pot, ripe fruit, etc. (Bhīm.), to be dispersed (Bhr. II); tr. ciṭ(i)lincu to break, to disperse; cf. ciṭṭa, ciṭika a snap of fingers.

[Ka. siḍil to be scattered in different directions, become loose; ciṭil, ciṭi an imit. sound; Pj. ciṭṭ- to split, cut; < *ciṭ-, onom.; see s. v. ciṭuku.]

426 cidiyu III intr. to be crushed, smashed or broken, to break (BhR., HariV.); tr. cidupu.

[Ta. citai be injured (Akan.); tr. to injure (Kaiit.); further, v. s. v. ciduku.]

427 ciduku (also cituku) intr. to be crushed, smashed, thresh grain (Bhr. II); Mdn. citak(a)goṭṭu to smash, crush; pound.

[Ka. ciduku, cidaku the state of being freed from its skin by squeezing; Ta. citaku to strip off (Piṅ.); erase; Mlt. cithg- to squeeze out the seed or stone from a fruit. PDr. *cit-.]

cidupu (tr. of cidiyu, q. v.).

428 cidumu tr. to nip with nails, as flowers, etc. (Kāś., Manu.); to cut off (Bhr. II); to make into pieces, divide into shares (KS).

[Ka. kittu to pluck out or up; other forms see s. v. giccu. PDr. *kic-/*kit-.]

429 cin(u)ku intr. to fall in drops (UH, Kal.); tr. to spill in drops; to shower (Manu.); n. a drop of rain (Vēm.).

[Ka. jinugu, jinuṅgu id. (late); Ma. cinaṟuka to be spilt, scattered; cinaṅkuka to drizzle; Ta. ciṇuṅku to drizzle (loc.) (l. w. < Ka.); ciṇukku v. i. to issue in drops; Pj. cinkip- (cinkit-) to drip; cf. Ka. eṟacu, ercu to sprinkle; Ta. iṟai to scatter, disperse, strew; Ma. iṟuka v. i. to drip, drop. PSDr. *cin-/*ciṯ- : *iṯ-.]

430 cin(ū)gu intr. (same as cir(ū)gu; probably back formation from cincu tr. of cirūgu) to be torn, as clothes; to break, burst (RR); to form holes in clothes; n. a tear in clothes, etc.

cincu IIb (tr. of cirūgu/cinūgu) to tear open (Naiṣ.); to break, chop (ŚivaR.).

431 cindu intr. to be spilt, to ooze (Naiṣ., Hara.); to spread (Manu.); to be shed, as flowers (Manu.); tr. to shed, spill; n. a drop; a dancing step; cindulu spray.

[Ta. cintu to be spilled; to trickle, stream; tr. to scatter, strew (Tiruvāc.); spill, sprinkle; expand (Cīv.); cīntu to cast, scatter (Cīv.); Ma. cintuka, ciñcuka, cinaṟuka be spilt, scattered; tr. to scatter; cinnuka id.; either < *cin-t-, or more likely < *cim-t-; cf. Ka. simpaṇi sprinkling; simpaḍisu to sprinkle; cimaku, cimiku to sprinkle; Ta. civiṟi a kind of syringe, squirt (-v- < *-m-); civiṟu to spread, as water; Ka. sīṟu to be sprinkled (< *civiṟ-); PSDr. *cim-, v. s. v. cimmu; cf. Mlt. cicy- to sprinkle.]

432 cibuku* tr. to smack, suck (JBh.); in Mdn. Te. civuku id. (Rāyalasīma dial.); (< *cip-ukku).

[Ka. sīpu to suck; Ko. cip- to suck repeatedly; Ta. cīppu to suck; Kur. Mlt. cīp- id.; v. s. v. cīku.]

433 cimuṭu* tr. to wink as a signal (no literary usages cited).

[Ka. cimuṭu, civuṭu, civaṭu to twinkle the eye; Ta. cimiṭṭu to blink; make signal with eyes; Ma. cimiṭṭuka id.; cimpuka, cīmpuka to twinkle with the eye; cīṇṭuka to give a secret sign; PSDr. *cim-: *im-; for other forms, etc., see Burrow, DS VI, p. 138; DS IV, p. 332, No. 2; DS VII, p. 395, No. 307.]

434 cimuḍu intr. to be overboiled (Dvi.H.), cf. cimacima or simasima imitative representation of heat (later works and Mdn.); tr. cimuḍ(u)cu to overboil (as of rice).

[Ma. cīka to be overboiled as rice; ? Ka. kimuḻ the state of being crushed; kimuḻcu to crush; shrivel.]

435 cimpu (same as cincu; Mdn.), cf. cimpi rag, torn cloth (JBh.); destruction, ruin (Bhr. II).

436 cimmu tr. to fling, throw, cast (BhR., Bhīm.); to brandish a weapon; to spurt, butt with horns, to sweep the floor (Mdn.); intr. to squirt, gush forth, as water, etc.

[Ka. cimmu to shoot with the fingers; cast, fling; squirt; to brandish a weapon; cf. Ta. cintu tr. to cast on all sides (Cīv.), to scatter (Tiruvāc.); v. s. v. cindu (< *cim-); alternatively, cimm- < *ciṟ-m-, v. s. v. ciṟumu.]

437 cirūgu intr. to be torn or rent, as clothes (UH, Kāś.); fruit to be punctured by birds (Pāṇḍ.); see cinūgu.

[Cf. cīru; Kui siri torn, split; Brah. cīr- to slit, tear open; Ka. siguru to cut; cf. Ka. kiri to shave; Ta. cirai to shave; cut with a sickle; Ma. cirekka id.; v. s. v. civvu, cīru, cekku.]

438 ciṟumu* tr. to fling, throw (Bhr. III, BhR.); to increase, extend (Dvi.H.).

[Ka. sīṟu to be sprinkled; To. sīr spray; Kui sīrpa to shake out, sprinkle; Go. jīriā fountain (Dawson); v. s. v. cindu, cimmu; ? < *cīṯ- < *civ-iṯ-.]

439 ciluku[1] intr. to spill or issue in drops (Bhr. II); to ooze; to spread; to be laid out, made public (Mārk.); tr. to spill; to shower (something), to extend, spread; cf. cilacila imit. of flowing; cilupa a pond.

[Ta. cilucilu to rain gently; cilumpu to flow out, gush out; cf. tiḷai to flow, fall unceasingly (Cīv.); v. s. v. cinuku.]

440 ciluku[2] tr. to churn, as buttermilk, etc. (Śakunt.).

[Ka. cilku the noise of milk in churning; Ta. ciluppu tr. to churn (colloq.), stir, agitate.]

441 civuku intr. to become rotten due to wetness; to rot (Bhr. I, II, KS); to grieve, pine (Bhr. I); cf. cīku[2].

[Ta. ciḻ, cīttai rottenness; Ma. cīka, cīṅṅuka to rot, be spoiled; cīkku adj. rotten; Ko. kit- to rot; Kur. kitt-; Mlt. kit- id.; Klm.

sivk- id. (l. w. < Te.). PDr. *kiv-/*kī-; for a similar contraction, see s. v. nil(u)gu; also see Burrow, DS III, p. 123; Emeneau, BSOAS XV, p. 100.]

442 civvu tr. to pare, peel, scrape, as the end of a stick, etc. (Kāḷ.); to make a pointed shape, as pencil, etc. (Mdn.).

[Ka. civvu, cīvu cut thin, scrape, pair, trim; burnish, etc.; sippe the rind of fruits; siguṟ, sibaṟu, sivaṟu, sivuṟu that is pared off; rind; Ta. cīvu to pare off, smooth, polish, comb hair (late); cīval parings; Ma. cīvuka to scrape, peel, etc.; cīka id.; cf. cīru.]

443 cīku[1] tr. to suck, smack (BhR).

[Contraction of cibuku, q. v. (also see Krishnamurti, JAOS 75, p. 242, fn. 18); alternatively < *cī-k-, cf. Pj. cūk- to suck.]

444 *cīku[2] (mostly in cīk-i- with the aux. -pōvu to go, cīkipōvu to rot away); contraction of civuku, q. v. Mdn. only as a verb; adj. rotten (later texts).

445 cī̃du tr. to blow the nose, sneeze (Kāḷ.).

[Ka. sīnu (sīt-, sīnt-, sīnd-); Ta. cīntu to blow the nose; cintu id.; Ma. cīntuka, cīṟṟuka id.; Kui jīnja, srīnda id.; siho a sneeze; Kuvi (F) sind- to blow the nose; Kur. cī̃cr- id.; cf. Go. īc-; Kur. ī̃jhr-; Mlt. īnj- id. PDr. *cī-nt-/*cī-nc-, more probably < *cīm-t-; cf. Ta. cī mucus of the nose (Maṇi.); Te. cīmiḍi, etc.; see Emeneau, Kolami, Vocab. 848; these point to PDr. *cīm-, ultimately *cī-m-; the *kī- forms may be separated.]

446 cīru (1) tr. to tear, rend (Bhr. II, III); to cut down (a banner in battle) (Bhr. II).

[Ka. siguṟu, sibaṟu, sivaṟu, sivuṟu a splinter; rind; sigi to tear, rend with teeth, split wood; sību bamboo-slit; Tu. tiguruni, tigruni to split; tigụtè a chip, piece; splinter; Ma. cīntuka to tear as paper; cīttu strip, shred; Kui sīki a fine strip of bamboo; siki inba to be torn, split, broken; Kuvi (F) sīpla chip; Go. sinder a splinter of wood or bamboo; GoM. hik- to tear; Pj. cīk- to tear; cīŋg- to be torn; all these forms yield PDr. *civ-/*cik- with contraction when a vowel suffix follows, *civ-i-/*cik-i- > *cī-. The NDr. forms are likely to be l. ws. from IA: Kur. cīr- to rend, split; Brah. cīr- to slit, tear open; cf. H. cīr strip; cīrnā to split; for others, v. s. v. cirnu, ciro, Nep. Dict.]

cīru (2) to scratch softly with nails (Bhr. I).

[Ka. cīru, civuru, civaru to scratch with nails or claws; Ma. cīka to scratch, scrape, smooth, polish; to comb; cīntuka to comb; cīr a line, cīpu a comb; Kur. cīr- to scratch, Mlt. circ- id.;

*cīr- < *civur-. Burrow derives the IA forms from Dravidian, and it is very likely to be so; see TPS 1945, pp. 101, 102; also v. s. v. civvu.]

447 cīṟu* (also cīru) tr. to call (Bhōj.), intr. to prate, cry, weep (Daś.).
[Ka. kīṟu to cry out from pain, scream; gīḷ a roar, yell, scream; Ko. kiry- (kirc-) to shout; To. kiṟc- (kiṟč-) to shout; Ta. cīṟu to roar, hiss, as a serpent; ciraṟṟu to shout, call loudly; cf. Ka. cīṟu to scream, cry out; jīṟu screaming (l. ws. < Ta.); ? Mlt. cirq- to shout, make noise; Kur. ciṛā-ba'- to shout, jeer at; ? PDr. *kī-ṯ-/-r- or *cī-ṯ-/-r-.]

448 cīlu intr. to break, split, crack; be torn, rent, split (BhR); tr. cīl(u)cu to tear with knife, teeth, etc.
[Ka. gīḷu tr. to rend, as cloth; Ko. kiv- (kivd-) to become torn; (kivt-) to tear; To. kīṟ- (kīṟy-) to tear; Ta. kīḷ; kīḷḷu (kīṇ-ṭ-) tr. to rent, split, tear (Kamp.); intr. to burst, as the bund of an overfull tank (PN); n. part, portion, piece of cloth (Cīv.); kīḻ v. tr. to rend, split; destroy, demolish (Kṟḷ.); Mlt. kithr- to split wood; PSDr. kī-ḷ- < *kiv-uḷ-; l. ws. with s- occur in Ka. Tu. and Ko.]

449 cuṭṭu tr. to surround, besiege (Bhr. II, Nirv.); roll up as a mat, to pass round; wrap as a thread, cloth, etc. (Naiṣ., Bhīm.); to wind, make into a ball; n. a turn, circuit, side, circle, etc.; adv. all around, on all sides (Bhr. II); also all Mdn.
[Ka. suttu id.; Tu. suttuni id.; Ko. cut-; To. tūṯ- id.; Ta. cuṟṟu intr. to revolve, roam; tr. to go round; coil up, entwine; circle (Nāl.); n. coil, revolving; Ma. cuṟṟuka tr. to roll round, surround; v. i. lie round, be about; cuṟayuka to turn round; Kui sursuri curly; Kuvi (F) sūt- to roll up (cloth); sūtū around (p. 13); Klm.(E) suṭ- to wind (turban); (Kin.) cuṭ- id.; Nk. suṭṭ- wind; KGad. cuṭṭ- to roll up; Pj. cutt- intr. to wind; < PSDr. and PCDr. *cuṯ-ṯ < *cuṯ-t-; ultimately *cuṯ- is analyzable into *cu + ṯ-, cf. Ta. curuḷ to be coiled up, cuḻi become curled, etc., yielding *cu- as the original root. Cf. Kui grūpa (grūt-) to surround; Kur. guruñjta'- to twirl; Brah. kūr- to roll up; a case of irregular palatalization?]

450 cuṇḍu* (Brown; Śab.R.) intr. to be evaporated; (leaves) to dry up through excessive heat (no literary usages cited); prob. l. w. < Ka.
[Ka. suṇḍu v. i. to evaporate; suṇḍisu reduce in boiling (loc.); Ko. cunḏ- v. i. to boil away; Ta. cuṇṭu v. i. to dry up, as water, tr. boil, stew, simmer (loc.); cf. cuḷḷi dry twigs; cuḷḷai/cūḷai potter's kiln (Tolk.); Ma. cuṅṅuka (< *cuṅk- < *cuṇ-k-) to grow dry; cuḷḷal

fuel stick; Go. sūr dry pulled stalks of san hemp; PSDr. *cuḷ-/ *cuṇ-; v. s. v. cū̃ḍu.]

451 cūcu V (irreg. verb, allom. cūḍ- before back vowel suffixes, e.g., inf. cūḍ-aN- to see; neg. pp. cūḍ-aka not seeing, neg. rel. pp. cūḍ-ani that which does not see, or is not seen; in imperative cū-/cu- and cūḍ- freely vary, e.g., cū, cu-mmu, cū-ḍu, cūḍ-umu 2nd pers. sg.; cū-ḍu, cu-ṇḍu, cūḍ-ūḍu 2nd pers. pl.; these and cu-mī, cu-mā, cu-˜ḍī also in exclam., warning, etc., i.e., look!) tr. to see, observe, look at, view; call upon; to meet, note, attend to; to consider, think, perceive; watch, guard, inspect; to taste, experience; (all classical and Mdn.); der. n. cūpu sight; look, vision; cūḍ(i)ki glance.

[Ka. cūṭi/sūṭi aim; cūpu sight, look, vision; suṭṭu to show with the fingers; sūṭi, cūṭi aim; Tu. sūpini, tūpini, hūpini to see, look; observe; examine; visit; consider; take care; cūṭi aim, perception; Koḍ. tuḍuku to examine; Ta. cuṭṭu to point out, show (Parip.); have in view, consider (Malaip.); n. indication (Cilap.); that intended (Tolk.); tūṇṭu to bring to notice; Ma. cūṇṭuka to point at; cuṭṭu pointing out; Kui sūṛa to see; sūṭa to point with the finger; Go. sūr- to expect; huṛ- to look, expect; GoM. huḍ- to see; GoA. sūṛ- to see; Pj. cūṛ- id.; Kur. tuk- (tukc-) to aim at; Mlt. ṭunḍ- to see; Brah. hunn- (hur-, neg. past hutt-) to look, wait, watch; PDr. *cū-/*tū- with different suffixes.]

452 cū̃ḍu* ([˜] is unlikely on comparative grounds; but SAN quotes one clear case in JBh. in which this form rhymes with vī̃ḍu this person; other cases are not conclusive; since JBh. belongs to the early 14th century we cannot take the evidence to be unquestionable) tr. to burn, as fire (Bhr. II, JBh.); to light a lamp (Bhr. II, Manu.); brand with a burning stick (JBh.).

[Ka. suḍu (suṭṭ-) tr. to burn, roast; consume; v. i. be very hot; n. burning; Tu. suḍpini v. i. to burn; tr. bake, roast; cūḍu n. heat; sūḍu, suḍu burning; Ko. tuṛ- (tuṭ-) to roast, bake; burn (corpse); To. tuṛ- (tuṭ-) tr. to burn; Ta. cuṭu v. i. to be hot, burn (Nāl.); tr. to heat (Kṟḷ.); to roast, fry, bake, toast; inflict pain, ruin (Kṟḷ.); cūṭu burnt, roasted; heat; anger; brand (Nāl.); v. tr. to brand, as cattle (loc.); Ma. cuṭuka to be hot; to roast, etc.; cūṭu heat, etc.; ? Kui soḍu a fireplace; Kuvi (S) hūt- to burn, kindle; Go. surr- to cook bread; Brah. hush-, ush- to set fire, burn, scorch (h-/zero- < *c-); cf. Kur. kuṛ- (kuṭṭ-) become hot; bake; Mlt. kuṛ- (kuṭ-) to burn, roast; see Emeneau, BSOAS XV,

p. 102. Excepting Kur. Mlt., PDr. *cǔṭ- probably < *cuḷ-t-, v. s. v. cuṇḍu.]

cūpu (caus. of cūcu, q. v.) tr. to show, etc. (classical and Mdn.).

453 cūru intr. (occurs only with poga smoke); (smoke) to coat walls, roof, etc. inside a house (Mdn., Guntur dial.), e.g., illantā poga cūrindi the whole house is smoked.

[V. s. v. tūr̲u; also probably Ta. cūr v. i. to revolve, whirl round, etc.]

454 cekku[1] to insert (flowers in the braid), to tuck in (of clothes) (Manu.); to set diamonds, etc. in jewels (late); cf. ceruvu.

[Ka. sekku, serku to shove in, tuck in; To. teg- to fasten loin cloth; Ta. ceruku to insert; ceruvu tr. to stuff in (Jaffna dial.); Ma. terukkuka to tuck; gather up the cloth; cerutuka to shove in, put; Kur. k̲h̲err- to insert; stick a comb; (flowers) to be stuck behind the ear; Mlt. qer- to thrust in, tuck in. PDr. *ker-, Ta. Ma. Te. > *cer-; the Ka. form is obviously a l. w. from pre-Te. before rk > kk; Emeneau sets up PDr. *c- instead of *k-, on account of To. t- (BSOAS XV, p. 103), but the Kur. Mlt. evidence is unquestionable; To. t- could arise secondarily from an early l. w. with c-, i.e., cekk-; again To. -g- suggests -kk- rather than -rk- as part of the underlying loan; Emeneau states that early borrowings conform to the regular shift of *c- > t- in To. (op. cit. p. 109).]

455 cekku[2] to cut off, break (HariV., BhR.); to pare, cut the side or rind of; to cut the turf of grass with hoe; to engrave, carve, cut out idols in wood, stone, etc. (Daś.); to chip a pencil to a point: to scrape, polish wood, etc. (Mdn.).

[Klm.(E) kerk- to shave; cf. Brah. karg̲h̲- to shear, crop down; Te. > l. ws. Klm.(E) sek- to make pointed; Nk. śekk- to chip, scrape; Pj. cekk- id.; Tu. cekki/cekke a chip, split; Kuvi (F) sek- to scrape (with a hoe); all these forms can be traced to *ker-k- The PDr. root *ker- underlies a number of forms meaning 'to shave, scrape, etc.,' e.g., Ta. ciṟai, Ka. kere-, etc., see Emeneau, Kolami, Vocab. 379; BSOAS XV, p. 100; Te. cekku < *cetk- is not likely as Burrow assumed (DS III, p. 124) on account of the absence of evidence for -kk- < *-tk-.]

456 ceṅgu* tr. to abandon, give up (JBh.); intr. to leave, move away, to withhold oneself (Rasika.); to lose a game (not given by SAN; found in Śab. R. and Śankaranarayana's Dict.).

457 ceḍu I and V (alt. ceḍ-/ceḍḍ- in ceḍḍ-a-/ceḍ-ina- past rel. pp.; allom. cer̲u-, tr. cer̲u-cu) intr. to perish, be destroyed (Bhr. I), be ruined, become bad, useless, rotten (classical); adj. spoiled,

ruined (Bhr. II); tr. ceṟucu to destroy, defeat (Bhr. I); to make worthless (Hara.); to spoil a virgin (Mdn.); ceṟupu tr. to erase writing (Mdn.); der. n. ceṭṭa, cēṭu evil (classical); ceḍugu id.; ceḍipa a woman of bad character.

[Ka. kiḍu, keḍu (keṭṭ-) to go to ruin, be destroyed, become bad; keṭṭe evil, ruin; Tu. keṭṭa adj. bad, spoiled; keḍaguni tr. to ruin, spoil; Ko. keṛ- (keṭ-) be lost, ruined; to die; keṛc- to ruin; To. kȫṛ- (kȫṭ-) to die, be ruined; kȫḍc- tr. to destroy; kȫṛc- to kill; Ta. keṭu (keṭṭ-) to perish (Nāl.), decay, rot; be elided (gram.) (Tolk.); tr. (keṭutt-) to destroy; remove (Cilap.); lose, drop (Maṇi.); n. peril, risk; kēṭu id. (PN); poverty (Kṟḷ.); Ma. keṭuka v.i. be extinguished; ruined, spoiled; keṭukka to damage; quench; keṭṭa bad, lost; Go. kaṛī- (pp. kaṛīsī) to be rotten; Mlt. qerm- to destroy, massacre; qermr- to die in numbers; cf. Kur. gẽj- (gejj-) to smash, crush; cf. Kuvi(S) hēḍ- to mar; hers- to destroy, pollute (l. ws. < Te.). PDr. *keṭ-.]

458 ceḍḍu (Śab.R.) to slap the thigh in wrestling (no literary usages cited; probably local, colloq.).

459 ceṇḍu tr. to cut, chop off (Bhr. II), to kill (late); ceṇḍ-āḍu to cut into pieces.

[Ka. kiṇḍi a chink, opening, cleft; Ta. keṇṭu to cut and eat (Perump.); Klm.(E, SR) kink- tr. to break into pieces (intr. kini- [kinit-]); Go. kiḍḍī an axe-cut; Mlt. kinḍ- to cut flesh or fish; cf. Go. kiḍrī-pittē a woodpecker (pittē bird); Kui genja to secede; gespa (gest-) to cause schism; Kuvi(S) geh'- to rend; < PDr. *keṇ-/*kiṇ-; (> Skt. khaṇḍ- tear, break to pieces [see TPS 1945, p. 98]; Burrow also connects the words meaning 'to dig' etc. with this group [DS III, p. 128]).]

460 cedaru intr. to scatter, disperse, be splashed (Bhr. II); (mind) to be disturbed (RR); to spread, extend (Manu.); (eyes) to be dazzled; ceduru (late) to escape.

[Ka. kedaṟu v.i. to be scattered; to disperse; tr. throw or toss about; expand as wings; Ka. kedaruni to burst forth; Ta. citar to be strewn; tr. to scatter; separate, slit; citaṟu tr. to be shed; tr. to scatter; citai to be scattered (PN); cetiḷ dust (Cīv.); Ma. citaṟuka to be scattered, split; citar n. dust, a drop of ghee; Kur. k͟hetr- to be thrown off; fall out or off; k͟hett- to shake off by a jerk; k͟hed- to cast out, expel; < PDr. *ket-; cf. Kuvi(F) sedṛ- be dispersed; Ka. cedaṟu, cadaṟu id. (l. ws. < Te.).]

461 cenaku* (also cen(u)ku, but late) tr. to meet in battle (Bhr. II); to

touch (Kāś.); to have sexual intercourse with another woman (HariV., Pāṇḍ.); to provoke by words (Daś., Kaḷā.); to pinch with teeth; n. a hit, touching, impression of teeth or finger nails after pinching.

[Ka. keṇaku to provoke by words or deeds; prod, poke with a pointed instrument; Tu. keṇkuni to provoke; Kur. khen- to have intercourse with (obscene). The basic meaning seems to be to poke with an instrument, etc., to dig: v. s. v. kelāku; PDr. *kiṇ-/*kiḷ- or *keṇ-/ *keḷ-; cf. Ta. kiṇṭu, Ko. kelv- (kelt-) to dig with hands or paws.]

462 cenayu$^{1*}$ III tr. to touch, to meet in battle, oppose (Bhr. II, Nirv.) (< *keṇ-ay-).

[v. s. v. cenaku.]

463 cenayu$^{2*}$ III intr. to vie with, be comparable (Bhr. II, Hara., Bhg.); to be suitable (Paṇḍ.); to reach, obtain (Kāś.).

[Cf. Ka. seṇasu to be envious or jealous, to envy, seṇas-āṭe unwillingness to be excelled; alternatively v. s. v. enayu.]

464 cendu intr. to occur, happen, abide, dwell (Bhr. II); to pertain, belong, refer, tr. to obtain (Bhr. I), reach, meet (Bhr. II); der. n. centa neighborhood, proximity (Bhr. II).

[(1) Mlt. qēnd- (qēndy-) to take along with, to have with, possess; or (2) < *cer$^{u}$nd- < *cēr-unt-, v. s. v. cēru.]

465 ceppu (in imper. alternatively cepu-, e.g., ceppumu/cepumu 2nd sg.) to praise, describe (Bhr. II); to scold, reprove (Bhr. II); to read, recite (Kāś.), to teach lessons (Naiṣ.); to tell, inform (JBh., Kaḷā.); n. word, direction (KS); cepp-i pampu to send a message (Bhr. II); ceppuḍu māṭa words heard secondhand, words of a telltale (Mdn.).

[Ta. ceppu to say, speak in reply; tell (Parip.); n. answer, reply (Tolk.); Ma. ceppuka v. tr. id.; Kur. keb- (kepp-, keb-) to scold, upbraid; lecture; to abuse; < PDr. *kep-. It is likely that this is the underlying root in the words meaning "ear" from PDr. *kev-i, for which alternants in p also occur, cf. Ma. ceppi ear; the association of meaning is common enough in Dr., i.e., *kep- to hear; *kepp- to cause to hear, i.e., to tell; cf. Te. vinu to hear: vinucu to tell (cause somebody else to hear). It may be noted that the meanings of Te. ceppu, etc. presuppose the attention of the listener. For "ear" words, see Kolami Vocab. 384.]

466 cemaru* intr. to melt; to become wet with sweat (HariV.); cemar(u)cu to sweat, perspire; cemma wetness (RR, Manu.); adj. that which is wet; cemmaṭa/cemaṭa n. sweat, perspiration (Bhr. II); tēma wetness, dampness.

[Tu. simma, temma cold, caught; Ta. cemmal water (late); *cimis from IA sim-, cf. Skt. tim- (stim-) to become wet; tēma becoming wet (Lex.); Nep. sim marsh, bog; P. simmṇā to ooze; S. simaṇu, sima f. ooze; M. simpa(ṇem) to sprinkle, v. s. v. sim Nep. Dict.; cf. Kur. simdhār- to become damp. The form is assimilated into Te. by the addition of a native suffix -ar(u).]

467 ceralu* intr. to be in great glee, be jubilant (BP); n. jubilance.
[See keralu[1], with c < k.]

468 cerugu to sift, winnow (Daśā.; not in early texts); der. n. cēṭa winnowing basket (Naiṣ., also Mdn.); (< *ket̲-V-).
[Ka. kēr̲u id.; Ko. kēr- id.; To. kȫr̲- id.; Ma. cēr̲uka id.; Klm.(E) kēd- (kētt-) id.; Pj. kēd- (NE. kēḍ-) id.; Oll. KGad. kēy- id.; Kur. kẽ̄s- id.; kẽ̄t$^{e}$r a shovel basket; Mlt. kēs- to sift; PDr. *kēt̲-; see further, Emeneau, Kolami, Vocab. 391.]

469 ceruvu* tr. to fix, plant, as arrows, etc. (Bhr. II); to stick in flowers, etc. (UH, Naiṣ.); to mend, pat over; n. an insert of leaves, etc. to fill space (UH).
[v. s. v. cekku[1].]

cer̲ucu IIb tr. of ceḍu q. v.

470 celagu, celavu (also selavu) to cut, chop (late); to cut off a fence (Mdn. loc.).
[Cf. Tu. sele a chink, crack; Mlt. calg̣- to split or break open; calg̣ro torn asunder; Kur. calk̲h̲- to uncover; Brah. cal- to be split.]

471 celāgu* intr. to sound, as drums (Bhr. I); to roar (JBh.); to be jubilant, swell with joy (Bhr. II).
[Ka. kele to cry out with energy or for joy, vociferate; Tu. kilēvuni to whistle, resound; Ko. kilc- to cry out in joy; To. kis̲- (kis̲θ-) to crow; kilk- to neigh; Ta. cilai v. i. to sound, roar; to rage, tr. beat as drum (PN); n. sound, roar (Patir̲.); cilampu v. i. to sound, echo (Kalit.); Ma. cilampuka to tinkle; cilappu n. sound; cilekka to rattle, chatter, chirp, tinkle; Kui klāpa to crow; Kuvi (F) kilevi howling, shouting; kilevikī- to shout, yell; Kuvi (S) kileḍikī- id.; Go. kīlī- to scream; GoM. kil- id.; cf. Mlt. gēla a small drum. PDr. *kil-.]

celayu III (Śab.R.; same as selayu, q. v.; no usages cited for this form).

472 celuku* to pull out, as eyeballs (late); butt or gore with horns (late).
[Ka. seḷa, saḷe to pull, take off, n. pulling; Tu. seḷè strong; saḷe force; Kui jelka to pull (plural action of jelba); jelba to pull, draw. PDr. *ceḷ-.]

473 celupu* to daub, anoint (KS) (single usage cited).

[Tu. selipuni to cleanse; seliyuni, selliyuni to become clear, pure; or Ko. keṛc- to smear (liquid).]

474 cellu intr. to suit, be fit; to pass for right (Bhr. II); (money) to be paid off towards debt (Dvi.H.); (time) to pass (Bhr. II); (coin) to be valid, (words or acts) to be proper, valid (Bhr. II); to perish (Bhr. II).

[Ka. sal, sallu (sand-) id.; Tu. salluni id.; Ko. cal- (cad-) (prayer) is acceptable to god; (coin) is genuine; (wife) is suitable; calc- to pay; To. sal- (sad-) to belong to (property, etc.); Ta. cel (ceṉ-ṟ-) be suitable; to perish; pass as coin; be due as money; lapse, expire; Ma. celka id.; further forms v. s. v. canu. PDr. *cal-.]

475 cē̃du tr. to pull up, uplift (Paṇḍ.); to pull up (as a bow) (Āmu.); draw up as water from a well (Daśā.); draw or pull, as a string; with -konu to suffer spasms of muscles (Mdn.); cēda (Mdn.) a bucket for drawing out water.

[Ka. sēdu, sē̃ndu to draw up water (by means of a rope), draw in with the mouth; sēdu drag, pull, suffer spasms, to throb and pain; Ta. cēntu to draw as a rope running over a pulley (colloq.); cāmpu tr. to pull by jerks, pump; draw in; Ma. tēkuka, tēvuka to draw water, empty a well, bale out for irrigation; < PSDr. *cē-/*tē-, suffixes -nt, -k, -v, etc.; v. s. v. dēvu.]

476 cēpu (Śab.R. has [˜]) (milk) to be filled in the udder (of cow) or breasts (of woman) before milking or suckling; milk to be secreted, flow, rush as at the sight of the child (Bhr. II, III); to let milk flow; n. a spirt of milk (Hara.).

[Ka. cēpu a gush or spirt as of milk; Koḍ. cēpu (milk) to secrete (communication from a Koḍagu teacher); Ta. cēkku breast milk; cēkkai woman's breast (Piṅ.). PSDr. *cē-.]

477 cē̃yu III tr. to do, perform, make, fulfill, render (into a language); (all classical and Mdn.); intr. (Mdn.) to occur, happen, e.g., (oḷḷu) cēyu (body of a child) to grow, (jalubu) cēyu (cold) to be caught; der. n. ceydi, ceydamu, cē̃ta act, action (class.).

[Ka. key, gey to do, make, perform, etc.; Tu. gei id.; Ko. gey- (gec-) id.; To. kīy- (kī̃s-) id.; Ta. cey to do, perform, make, create (Tolk.), n. deed; Ma. ceikka to do, etc.; Kui giva (gi-t-) id.; Kuvi (S) kī-, kēp- id.; Go. kī- (pp. kī-sī); neg. kē̃w-; GoM. kiy- (kitt-), imp. kē̃-; KGad. key- (ken-) id.; (Klm. kak- and Brah. kan-, ka- may well be put together with the *kā- allom. of Te. agu, q. v.). PSDr. and PCDr. *key-.]

478 cēru intr. to draw near; to be obtained, to accrue (Bhr., UH, JBh.); (a letter) to be received (Mdn.); to be united with, to join; tr. to reach, approach (Bhr. II, Naiṣ.); to touch (Vikram.); to enter, as a class, party, be enrolled (Mdn.); tr. cēr(u)cu to join, unite (as two parts, etc.) (Bhr. II), cause union between two persons; to lay; cause to be obtained; der. n. cēr-uva nearness; cēr-ika union, meeting; cf. *-tēṟu$^2$, tāru.

[Ka. sēr to go to, approach, enter, reach; sār to be obtained, go near; Ko. cēr- (cẹ̄d-), cẹ̄d- (cēdy-) to arrive, enter, join; cēt- to make to enter a place; To. sȫr- (sȫd-) to arrive; sȫt- to make join with others; Ta. cēr to fit; arrive; reach; go (Kṟḻ.); be in contact with (PN); become united (Kamp.); tr. to join (Nāl.), associate with, obtain (PN); to join, combine; Ma. cēruka to join, approach, belong, suit; cērkka make to arrive or join; Kuvi (S) hēr- to reach; herp- to deliver; Go. sēṛ- to enter or occupy a house; Klm.(SR) sēr- to go; Nk. seddēn (he) went; sērtan I go (LSI IV, p. 572). PSDr. and PCDr. *cēr-, PSDr. *cēr-/*cār-, v. s. v. *-tēṟu$^2$, tāru; cf. Brah. kēb nearness, vicinity, kēbkan- to draw near, approach.]

479 cokku (also sokku) intr. to be intoxicated, be beside one's self, infatuated (Nirv., Naiṣ.); n. ecstasy, trance; infatuation (Bhr. III); fainting, swooning (Bhr. II).

[Ka. sokku, sorku to become intoxicated, mad; sōr be or become loose or slack; Tu. sorkuni to become lustful, insolent; sorku rankness, lust, insolence; sorkelu̥ narcosis; cokku stupid, silly; Ko. cok- to take a nap; Ta. cokku to become enchanted, sleepy; cōr to languish, droop, be relaxed (Kalit.), to faint, swoon (Kamp.); to totter; cōmpu sloth, idleness, inactivity; Ma. corukkuka to feel dizzy; corukka slight intoxication; ccrukuka to be stupefied; Kui sōsa to be intoxicated. PSDr. and PCDr. *cō-, *cō-r- : *cor-V-, v. s. v. sōlu, sogayu; see Emeneau, BSOAS XV, p. 110.]

480 coccu V (irreg., allom. cor- before back-vowel suffixes, e.g., inf. cor-aN-, imp. 2nd. sg. cor-u(mu), pl. cor-ũḍu, etc.; tr. allom. conu- in conu-pu) tr. to enter, penetrate, get in (Bhr. II); intr. take refuge (KS), to happen, occur; aux. with inf. to begin, to be ready for, e.g., cēyājoccu to begin to do, etc.; tr. con(u)pu to insert (Bhr. I), to cause to enter, pierce, as arrows (Bhr. II); insert (head in a noose) (Daśā.); n. coppu way, means (Bhr. II); a trace, vestige (Bhr. III).

[Cf. Kui sōlba (sōṭ-) to enter; sōṛpa (sōṛt-) to cause to enter; Kuvi (S) hō-, hōḍga han- to enter (han- to go); horg- to interfere; Go. sōṛī-, sōḍī-, jōḍī- to enter; GoM. ōḍi- id. (loss of h-); Klm. sōŋg- to enter; Nk. sōŋ- id.; Pj. cōŋg- v.i. (thorn) to pierce; KGad. sōŋg- id. PCDr. *cō-ḷ-, cō-l-, cō-r-, cō-ṅk-; cf. Ka. curcu, cuccu (< *curucu < *corucu) to insert, cause to enter, to pierce as with a thorn, etc.; Ta. tura (< *tora < *cora) to go; drive in; also cf. Kur. kōr- to enter; Mlt. kor- id.; kortr- to thrust in.]

conupu* tr./caus. of coccu, q. v.

colayu* (also solayu) III intr. to hesitate, shrink (Bhr. I).

[V. s. v. solayu, sōlu.]

481 cō̃ku* (also sō̃ku) tr./intr. to touch, come in contact with (KS, Bhr. II); to be possessed (by evil spirits); be caught as a disease; n. touching, contact (Bhr.); sōku a demon; touch (Bhr. II); Mdn. sōku (air) to touch, (evil spirits) to possess; n. infection, possession by evil spirit, an evil spirit; also n. sō̃kuḍu id.

[Ka. sōku, soṅku to touch, come in contact; infect, taint; sokku to touch, infect, attack; sokku, sōku n. touch; coitus; Tu. sōṅkuni, sōṅguni tr. to affect, as a disease; touch, infect; also sōkuni id.; sōṅku an epidemic, etc.; Ta. cōku devil (Piṅ.); Ma. cōku demon; Ta. tōy tr. to come in contact with, touch (PN); unite, copulate (Kṟḷ.); approach, resemble; Ma. tōyuka to unite; Tu. tōku collision. PSDr. *cōy-/*tōy-, *cō(y)-ku/-nku.]

482 cōpu (jōpu, Dh.M.) tr. to drive away, chase (as birds, flies, etc.) (Bhr. II, Daśā.); send away (KS); to thrust in (Mdn.; Rāyalasīma dialect).

[Ka. sōvu to drive off; sō (sōd-) to chase away, drive off, scare away; Ta. ōccu tr. to drive away; cause to go; ōppu to drive away, cause to flee, scare away, as birds (PN); cf. oy- to be off, go away from (Cilap.); Pj. codp- to send; KGad. cōy- to send away; cf. Kuvi (F) hōc- to go. PSDr. and PCDr. *cō-, *cō-p-: PSDr. *ō-p-.]

## J

483 jaṅku to fear (Bhr. II, Hara.); to shrink, hesitate; to shake, be shaky (as a mud wall) (Mdn.); n. fear, shrinking from, hesitation; jaṅkena scolding (Bhr. II).

[Ka. jaṅkisu to scold, chide; jaṅke, jaṅkaṇe scolding, chiding; Ta. caṅku be dispirited (loc.); Kuvi (F) dang- to stagger; < *caṇ-k-; see jaḍiyu, daḍiyu, talãku, talaru; cf. Kur. janka'- to startle, affright; Mlt. janq- to be jerked.]

484 jaḍiyu[1] III intr. to be afraid (Paṇḍ., RR); to shake, tremble (UH); to shrink, to be startled (Bhr. II); cf. daḍiyu; n. jaḍupu, jaḷupu fear (Nav.N.).

[Ka. jaḍi, jaḍe to threaten, menace, chide; caḷi to be deprived of one's power; Tu. jaḍu fright, shyness; jaḷḷu instability; jaḷḷuga a weak, feeble man; Ma. caḷuṅṅuka to be frightened, shake. PSDr. *caḷ-/*caṭ-.]

485 jaḍiyu[2]* III tr. to ward off (arrows by means of a shield) (Bhr. II); to fly, brandish, as a weapon (Bhr. II, UH); to beat, hit (Bhg.).

[Ka. jaḍi to wave, brandish a sword, etc., to beat; Tu. jaḍiyuni to drive cattle; daḍiyuni, daḍipuni to drive away; Kui jaṛpa to shake a cloth, hand, or foot; Go. jaṛhutt- to shake violently; Klm.(E) zaḍp- to flick away; Ma. cāṭuka tr. to throw; cāṭṭuka to throw darts, hurl; cāṭṭu a hurl; cāṭṭa a whip; prob. l. w. < IA : Cf. H. jhāṛna to sweep off, Nep. jhārnu shake off, vide Nep. Dict. s. v. jhārnu[1].]

janukụ* intr. to fear, be scared (late; rare).

[Same as jaṅku, q. v.]

486 jarugu intr. to slide, glide, creep (Bhr. II); move about, ramble (UH); (time) to pass (Bhīm.), to expire, happen, occur, take place (KS, UH, Bhg.) (all Mdn. also).

[Ka. jaragu, jarugu to slip, slide; move; to pass, elapse; jari to slip, fall from; sari to move, go, run away; Tu. jariyuni fall or slip down; Ko. jarv- (jard-) id.; Ta. cari to slip, incline; tr. cause to slip; caṟukku v. i. to slip, slide; n. slipping, sliding; Ma. cariyuka to slide; carikka to move, walk; Kuvi (S) jarg- to occur; Klm.(SR) jarag- to slip; Kur. jarap- to move to and fro, march; Mlt. jarq- to be dropped, fall. PDr. *cār- : *car-V-, v. s. v. jāṟu.]

487 javuku (also jaụku) to be shaky, loose; (wall) to become weak before falling; to lose courage; to be marshy; javajava echo-expression of softness, weakness.

[Ka. javugu, jōgu swampy ground; Ta. cavu to become weak; cavuṅku to faint, droop; be disheartened; Ma. cavaḷuka to be flexible, look disfigured. PSDr. *cav-.]

488 jāṟu to ooze (Hara.); to slide, glide (JBh.); (time) to pass slowly, to elapse (Nṛs.); to run away, flee (Kaḷā, Vasu.); to sneak away (Āmu.); to perish (Manu.); to slip (as pen, tongue, etc.; Mdn.); to slip off from hands; tr. jāṟucu/jārcu to let slip; adj. loose; jāṟumuḍi a slip knot; jāṟuḍu adj. liquid, oozing; flabby (Hara.).

[Ka. jāṟu to slip, slide, steal away; shrink, run, ooze out, flow down from a hill, (knot) to slip open; n. slipping, sliding; Tu. jāruni to slide, slip down; flee; Ta. cāṟu to slip off (Kamp.); flow, issue; caṟukku v.i. to slip, slide; caṟuku id.; Ma. cāṟuka to run off or out; drizzle; Go. saṛ- to drip (of water from wet clothes); dribble (of saliva); Klm.(E) zār- (water) leaks from pot; Kur. cāṛ- to overflow (said of the liquid and the vessel); < PDr. *cā-ṯ-; also v.s.v. jarugu; these words are somehow related to NIA., see H. jharṇā to fall, etc., Pkt. jhaḍai falls, vide Nep. Dict. s.v. jharnu[1], jhārnu[1,2]. This explains j- in SDr.; also v.s.v. ibid. sārnu.]

489 jilugu (Śab.R.) intr. to write letters illegibly without leaving spaces; n. chain-line writing, i.e., jilugu rāta (Mdn.).

[v.s.v. giluku.]

490 jīru* (1) intr. to hang down loose, as the ends of a saree or garment (Bhg.); often occurs with -āḍu to move, shake, jīrāḍu id.

[Probably words meaning to rub, scratch, i.e., rub the ground, etc. related; v.s.v. cīru (2).]

jīru* (2) (Śab.R.) tr. to scratch, scrape (no usages cited).

[Ka. civaru to scratch with the nails or claws; further v.s.v. cīru (2), gīṟu, gīku, etc.]

491 juḍūgu* (juṇūgu, junūgu) intr. to shrink, withdraw (RR); to hide oneself out of fear (late); tr. to deceive (Kaḷā.); n. deceit, theft (l.w. < Ka.).

[Ka. juṇugu to shrink, withdraw; retire; decline action; n. state of being shrunk; Ta. cuṇuṅku to be jaded, to loiter, be hindered; interrupted; n. reduction; cf. cuḷḷi smallness (Kamp.).]

juṇūgu* same as juḍūgu, q.v.

junūgu* (same as juṇūgu) intr. to shrink, hide oneself (late); tr. junūpu, q.v.

junūpu* (printed junupu in the text; SAN corrects to junūpu) tr. of junūgu (i.e., juṇūgu, juḍūgu) (late and rare) to drive away (flies).

492 juṟṟu tr. to drink, sip or sup with noise, as a liquid or semi-liquid food (Pand., Bhīm., Bhg.); (< *juṟ-iyu).

[Ka. juru, jurujuru imit. sound when a child sucks with force (colloq.);

Ta. uṟi, uṟiñcu to sip, suck up, as liquids (late); Ma. uṟiñcuka id.; Kur. sur$^{u}$p- (surpy-) tr. to drink with a noisy sucking of the lips. PDr. *cuṯ-, PSDr. *cuṯ-V- : *uṯ-V-.]

493 jeḷuku* to roll over on the bed (late; single usage found).

494 jōku[1]* (Śab.R.) to revile, abuse; n. reviling.

[Cf. Ka. jaṅku to scold, chide, etc., v.s.v. jaṅku.]

495 jōku[2] intr. to tremble, totter, reel.

[Alternant of javuku, q.v., with contraction of avu > ō.]

## D

496 ḍakku* intr. (> dakku) to accrue, to come into possession of (Bhr. II); to remain, to be saved from being lost (Bhr. II); to be spared or saved (Bhr. II).

[Ka. dakku to accrue, be acquired; to remain, preserved; n. acquirement; Tu. daksuni to be retained, as food or medicine in stomach; dakkāvuni to take charge of; To. tok- to last long; Ta. taṅku to remain, be under control (Kṟḷ.); takku to come to stay, become permanent as a possession (Taṉip.); Ma. taṅṅuka to come into possession; takkuka to be obtained; cf. Go. tagg- to last (of clothes), (servants) to remain in one's service; Klm.(E) tak- to live (in a place), remain; Nk. tak- to stay; < PDr. *taṇ-k-; alternatively, v.s.v. aḍāgu; cf. Te. takku.]

497 ḍaggaṟu* (> daggaṟu) intr. to approach, draw near (Bhr. II); Mdn. Te. daggara in the vicinity, in the presence of.

[ḍagg- < *aḍg-, v.s.v. ḍāyu; -aṟu is a separate morpheme which occurs in forms like krammaṟu, trimmaru, etc.]

498 ḍaggu* (> daggu) to cough (no early usage cited for the ḍ- form, v.s.v. daggu; but it occurs in the compound ḍag-guttika a faltering voice, low voice.).

[GoM. ḍag- (ḍagt-) to cough; Klm.(SR) ḍagg-, Klm.(E) dag- id., (Kin.) ḍag a cough; Nk. ḍhag- id.]

ḍaṅgu* intr. to be pounded, v.s.v. ḍancu.

[Listed as a verb, probably back-formed from the transitive ḍancu, but there is no evidence for its occurrence as a verb; it occurs as a nominal adjective in inscriptions; e.g., daṅguṃbrālu (-prālu rice) pounded rice (SII IV, No. 1114). Here ḍaṅguṃ- should be an adj. formed from a noun *ḍaṅgu on account of -ṃ- connecting the two words as a compound; if it were a verb, the form would be *ḍaṅgu prālu; see Bālav. 2.35.]

499 ḍancu* (> dancu) IIb tr. to pound, as grain in a mortar; (< *taṇ-c-).
[Kui ḍāmba to pound, crush; Ka. taḷisu to pound, beat; Tu. talpuni to thrash as paddy; Go. dals- id.; Mlt. daly- (dalc-) to grind; (> l. w. Skt. taṇḍula- husked rice; J. Bloch, BSOS V, p. 737); alternatively from *ḍānc- < *aḍanc-, cf. aḍā̃gu, aḍā̃cu.]

500 ḍayyu* (> dayyu) III intr. to be weakened, to be emaciated (KS), to be tired, fatigued (Bhr. I, II); der. n. ḍappi destruction, ruin (Bhr. II).
[Klm.(E) ḍay- (ḍay-t-) to become thin; Kuvi (F) dah- to become weak; Kuvi (S) daiyū-ai(yali) to lag behind. The meaning 'to be fatigued' seems to be an extension of the original meaning 'to diminish,' etc. as preserved by Klm.; the root is *al̲-, v. s. v. al̲iyu.]

501 ḍā̃gu* (> dā̃gu) intr. to be hidden, concealed (KS, Bhr. II); to disappear (late); tr. ḍā̃cu/dā̃cu.
[Klm.(E) ḍāŋg- intr. to hide; ḍāp- tr. to hide; (Kiṇ.) ḍāŋg-; Nk. ḍhāp- to cover : Kui ḍāpa (ḍā-t-) to lie in wait for; GoM. tās- to keep; < *aṭ-a-, v. s. v. aḍā̃gu.]

ḍā̃cu* IIb (> dā̃cu) tr. of ḍā̃gu, q. v.

502 ḍāyu* (> dāyu) III intr./tr. to approach, near (Bhr. I); to obtain, to reach (< *aṭ-ay-).
[GoM. dāy- (dāit-) to go; Ka. aḍasu to be near, enter closely; Ta. aṭu tr. to approach, approximate to, come in contact with (Pārata.); aṭai tr. to reach, arrive at (Pārata.); to get, obtain; take refuge in; Ma. aṭuka to come into contact; aṭukka to approach; be proportionate to; Kui aṭu adj. near; aṭse/aṛse jointly; aḍa to be associated with; to accompany; aṭpa to join together; Mlt. aṭge/aṭgi close, near; āṭipāṭi neighborhood; further v. s. v. aḍuku; PDr. *aṭ-.]

503 ḍiggu/ḍigu* (> diggu/digu) intr. to descend, dismount (Bhr. II); be lowered, to sink (UH); to lodge, stay; to decrease (Vasu.); tr. ḍincu/dincu.
[Ka. il̲i to descend, become less; il̲iku to cause to go down; to lower; To. īx- to descend; Ta. il̲i to descend, dismount (Akan.); fall, be reduced; tr. to lower (Tiruvāc.); il̲ittu, il̲iccu to lower; il̲ukku v. i. to slip down from height (Cīv.); Ma. il̲ika to descend; il̲ikka to lower; Kui dīva to drop, descend upon; fall down; Kuvi (F) rī- to fall; GoM. ḍig- to descend; Go. (Nandgaon) ḍīkt- felled (LSI, IV, p. 522); Klm.(SR) ḍigg-, Klm.(E) dig- to descend, come down; Pj. iṛ (Sth. iṛv-, iṛi-) to descend; iṛk-ip- to make to descend; KGad. iḍg- to descend. PSDr. and PCDr. *il̲-i, *il̲-k-; PDr. *īl̲-; further see Kolami, Vocab. 161.]

ḍincu* IIb (> dincu) tr. of ḍiggu/ḍigu, q. v.

504 ḍindu* to be lowered, reduced (Mārk., Bhr. III); to sink, be suppressed (Daś., Mārk.); to be absorbed, to disappear (Bhr. II; Naiṣ.); n. a defeat, submission, yielding, fall (KS); ḍindu-paḍu to be reduced, as grief.

[Ta. il̲i (il̲i-nt-) to fall, be reduced; tr. (il̲i-tt-) to lower (Tiruvāc.); same etymology as for ḍiggu, q. v.]

505 ḍīlu (> dīlu; later than ḍ > d of the other forms of the class) intr. to grow tired or weak (no literary usages quoted); cf. ḍilla-paḍu, -pōvu to be unnerved (l. w. < IA).

[Ka. ḍiḷḷa, diḷḷa unnerved, tottering state; ḍiḷḷisu to become agitated, totter; Tu. ḍīlu̯ adj. loose, not tight; also ḍīla, ḍīlu id.; < Pkt. ḍhilla-, cf. Dés. ḍhella- poor?; Turner says connection improbable with Skt. śithila-, Pkt. siḍhila-; cf. Nep. ḍhilo adj. slack, slow; H. ḍhīlā, M. ḍhilā, G. ḍhīlū, further v. s. v. ḍhilo, Turner, Nep. Dict.]

506 ḍukku* to lie hidden (Kāḷa., and later works); probably l. w. < IA.

[Nep. ḍhuknu v. i. to lie in wait, lurk, H. ḍhūk- to crouch; vide Turner, Nep. Dict. v. s. v. ḍhuknu.]

507 ḍuṅku* to be lowered, to diminish (late); be subdued.

[Connection not probable with uḍūgu.]

508 ḍuṅgu* (disputable text versions) intr. to be afraid, to shrink (KS, Bhr. I) (< ḍūng- < *uṭ-ung-).

[Kui ḍūmba to be shrunken, contracted, shrivelled; ḍūppa to cause to shrink; v. s. v. uḍugu.]

509 ḍuyyu*/ḍūyu (> duyyu/dūyu) III tr. to pierce through, as an arrow or bullet (Bhr. II); to draw as a sword out of the scabbard (UH, BP); to strip off leaves, etc. of a twig by drawing it through the hand or between fingers (Mdn.); (< *ul̲-u-).

[Kui ḍunja to break over; spring forth; v. s. v. ūḍcu[1], duvvu.]

ḍulucu* IIb (tr. of ḍullu, q. v.) to let fall, as leaves, fruit, etc. (KS, Bhr. II); to empty; to scrape off, remove, as rust (JBh.).

ḍulupu* (> dulupu), alt. of ḍulucu, q. v. (Bhōj.).

510 ḍullu to fall off, to roll down (Bhr. II, Kāś.); (dried leaves) to fall off (< *l̲ūl-/l̲ull- < *ul̲-ul-).

[Kui ḍuṛi adj. rolling, tossing; ḍuṛiāva v. i. to roll, writhe, toss; cf. Ka. ul̲al to be unsteady, loosened; to swing, whirl round; Ta. ul̲al v. i. to swing, be in motion (Kallā.); to whirl, revolve; v. s. v. ūḍu.]

ḍūyu* (> dūyu) III same as ḍuyyu, q. v. (most of the literary usages are for ḍuyyu).

511 ḍeppu* (> deppu) tr. to taunt, gibe, gibe at (late); n. a taunt; Mdn. deppu.

[ ? < *l̲ēpp- < *el̲app-; cf. Ka. il̲i to be humbled; il̲ipu to humiliate; cf. Kur. ḍeg- (ḍegc-) to speak with effrontery.]

512 ḍẽku (> dẽku) (no literary usages; both ḍ- and d- forms occur even in colloq. Te. dialectally); tr. to creep or slide along the ground on the posteriors; (< *el̲aṅk-).

[Ma. il̲ayuka to trail, creep, crawl, as infants; to rub as two branches.]

513 ḍokku* (Śab.R.) to grow old (lex.); adj. old (lex., also Mdn.) (prob. < NIA).

[H. ḍhoknā to lean against, dhoknā to bow down; Nep. ḍhoknu to bow down before, q. v. Turner, Nep. Dict.]

514 ḍoṅku* intr. to diminish, decrease (Manu.), to dry up, sink, of water (Bhr. II, Nr̥s.); to shrink, hesitate (Daś.); (< *ḍōnk- < *oṭ-ank-).

[V. s. v. uḍũgu; cf. Ka. ḍoṅku to shrink, retreat; Ta. oṭuṅku to be hidden, sink; oṭukku to reduce, subjugate (Tiruvāc.); oṭukkam gradual sinking, reduction.]

515 ḍoṅgu* (> doṅgu) intr. to hide oneself, to bend, crouch (as a thief) (Panḍ.); ḍoṅga/doṅga a thief.

[Ka. ḍoṅku to bend, be crooked; doṅka n. curved; Tu. ḍoṅku crookedness; adj. curved; Ta. ṭoṅku n. id.; v. s. v. uḍũgu; < *ḍōng- < *oṭang-; for words for thief, see Kolami, Vocab. 172.]

ḍol(u)cu* IIb (> dolucu) tr. of ḍollu, q. v., to cause to roll (Kāś.).

516 ḍollu intr. to die, perish (Bhr. I); to slip off, as a garment (Panḍ.); to fall off, as a head cut off, etc. (Bhr. II); to roll down (Kāś.); to dangle (late); (< *l̲ōl-/l̲oll- < *ol̲-al-).

[Kui ḍoḍga to roll on the ground, sprawl, wallow; Ta. Ka. ul̲al to whirl, revolve; Klm.(E) ḍol- to be felled; ḍolp- to fell tree, pull down (wall); cf. Kur. ol$^{o}$ṇḍār- to roll one's body on the ground; v. s. v. ḍullu.]

517 ḍõku[1] (also dõku) tr. to dig slightly so as to loosen the soil for weeding; to pare or shave the ground, cutting up the turf (colloq.; both ḍ- and d- forms occur in Mdn. usage).

[Ka. dōkari an instrument for grubbing up grass; doge, ḍoge to dig or excavate with an instrument; Ma. ? tōkkuka to bore a hole into any fruit containing liquid; v. s. v. tõḍu; probably < *tōṇ-k-.]

518 ḍõku[2] ([˜] unnecessary) intr. to vomit; make an effort to vomit; n. vomiting.

519 ḍõgu* (> dõgu; Mdn. Te. dōgu) intr. to crawl or move on the hands and knees; to go on all fours, as an infant (ŚivaR.).
[Kui ḍōpa (ḍōt-) to lie down, recline; Klm.(E) dol- to lie down; further v. s. v. ḍoṅgu.]

T

520 takku[1]* tr. to give up, leave, refrain from, omit (Bhr. I, II); intr. to remain, be left, to be excepted or omitted (Bhr. I, II, RR); n. remainder, what is left over (Bhr. II); inf. takka adv. excepting, Mdn. dakka.
[Ka. dakku to remain, be preserved; Ta. taṅku to remain (Kṟḷ.); to be kept back; takku to come to stay; Ma. taṅṅuka to stop, remain; tañcuka id.; PSDr. *tank-/*takk-, v. s. v. ḍakku, dakku.]
521 takku[2]* to pretend; tr. to deceive (Kāḷ., Āmu.); n. pretence, deceit.
[Ka. takku deceit, trickery; Tu. ṭakku, takku dodge; Ta. ṭakku trick, pretence; (l. w. < IA; cf. H. ṭhagnā to deceive; M. ṭhakṇẽ to be deceived; G. ṭhagvũ, etc.; v. s. v. ṭhagnu, Turner, Nep. Dict.).]
522 tagu (also tavu) intr. to be proper, becoming, fit, just, right (Bhr. I); to be worthy, deserving, competent (Bhr. I); der. n. tagavu propriety, justice; settlement (Bhr. II); Mdn. quarrel (over justice), quarrel.
[Ka. tagu (takk-) to be fit, proper; takka adj. fit, proper; good; Tu. takka adj. id.; Ta. taku (takk-, taku-nt-) to be fit, proper (Kṟḷ.); be excellent, deserved; tr. to resemble; takku v. i. to be fit (loc.); takavu n. suitability (Maṇi.); justice (Kṟḷ.); Ma. taku (takk-) to fit, etc.; Kui sãnja to be fitting, proper, be beautiful. PSDr. and PCDr. *cāy-/*cay-V- > *tāy : *tak-V-. In Ta. Ka. etc., pp. takk- < *takuk- through contraction.]
523 tagulu (also tavulu) intr./tr. to touch, come in contact with (Bhr. I, II); to strike against (Bhr. II), to be caught, as in a noose; (fever) to attack, (a hit) to reach, to catch (fire), to be attached (in mind); to be found, met with; tr. to follow, pursue (Bhr. II); to be fond of, to love (KS); to reach, obtain (Bhr. I); n. attachment; tr. caus. tagul(u)cu.
[Ka. taguḷ, taguḷu to be joined; to approach; to run after; taguḷcu to join, attach; get to; tagu to be joined; Tu. tagaruni to draw near; Ta. takai to seize, take hold of; check, bind (PN); n. love, affection; Ma. takaruka to be crushed; takarkka to crush, smash;

taikka to strike against, hit; Kur. tak- to give a very slight knock : Ta. tai (= tay) to sew, join; tie (Aiṅk.); set, place, put; taivā to touch (Tolk.); Kuvi (F) tac- to sew; Brah. taf- to tie up; bind by enchantment; ? root *ta- to come together. PDr. *tay- : *tak-V-.]

524 taggu intr. to bend, be lowered, as banners (Bhr. II); to decrease, become less, be diminished; shrink, draw back (ŚivaR.); n. decrease, abatement, shrinking.

[Ka. taggu, targu, ta<u>l</u>gu to become low, less; stoop; decrease, fall in price; tā<u>l</u> being low, sinking; Tu. tagguni be humble; to incline, lean; Ko. tag- to draw back from fight; To. tog- to be humbled; tōy- (tōs-) to be lowered; Ta. tā<u>l</u> (tā<u>l</u>-nt-) to fall, be lowered, fall down (Nāl.); decline, sink, decrease; bend, bow down (Pu. Ve.); become subdued (Maṇi.); (tā<u>l</u>-tt-) tr. to decrease, let bow down (Tiv.); to lower, etc.; Ma. tā<u>l</u>uka to sink, come down; bow, subside; tā<u>l</u>ttuka to lower; Kui tāli adj. less, reduced in quantity; Kuvi (F) taleni below (p. 13); Kur. tarkā adj. silent, quiet, calm; cf. Kur. Mlt. tār- to fell, cut off; Brah. dar- to get down, descend; ? tamm- to fall, lie down; Kur. tamm- (of fever, etc.) to cease, be assuaged. PDr. *tā<u>l</u> : PSDr. (Ka. Tu. Te., etc.) *ta<u>l</u>-unk-/*ta<u>l</u>-ukk-.]

525 taṭṭu tr. to knock, strike (Kāś.); to pat, slap, clap; to play cymbals (Bhg.); to occur, strike (to mind) (Āmu.); n. stroke, touching.

[Ka. taṭṭu to tap, touch, beat, knock, drive; n. touching, slap, flatness; tāṭu to strike against, touch; Tu. taṭṭuni to hit; Ko. taṭ- (tac-) to pat, strike with flat of hand; (grief) strikes (with dative); Ta. taṭṭu to knock, tap; beat drum (Pu. Ve.); intr. to suggest, as a thought; n. patting (Cilap.); Ma. taṭṭuka to strike, hit, tap, dash; taṭṭu a blow; taṭakkuka to dash against; Kui tahpa to smooth off, level down; Kuvi (F) tass- to slap; Kur. taṛ- to flog, whip; Mlt. taṛc- to slap; (> l. w. Skt. taḍ-, tāḍayati beats, Pkt. tāḷa- musical time; Av. tāḍa a stroke, see Jules Bloch, BSOS V, p. 737); PDr. taṭ-, prob. from earlier *taḷ-t-, v. s. v. taḍayu.]

526 taḍayu* III intr. to delay, lose time (Bhr. I, II, Kāś.); taḍay-aka without delay, soon (Bhr. I); der. n. taḍavu time, period, delay (Bhr II, BP); cf. taḍābaḍu to falter in steps, be impeded (Bhr. II); taḍa obstruction (late).

[Ka. taḍe to delay, stop; tr. to check, detain; n. an obstacle; taḍe n. stop, delay; taḷ(u)vu to delay; stop; n. delay; taḍa id.; check; Tu. taḍeyuni, taḍevuni to halt, stop, tarry; taḍepuni to hold off, hinder; taḍevu a halt, obstruction; taḍavu n. delay, hindrance; Ko. taṛv- (taṛt-) to obstruct; To. taṛf- (taṛt-) to delay; to prevent; cf. toṛ- (toṭ-) to bump foot; Ta. taṭu tr. to detain (Piṅ.); n. hindrance; taṭṭu to obstruct, hinder (Kalit.); taṭai tr. to hinder, stop; n. obstruction; taḷ (taṭṭ-) to hinder, stop (PN); Ma. taṭayuka be obstructed; taṭekka to stop; taṭa, taṭavu obstruction, what resists; Kur. ṭaṇḍ- to prevent, impede (< *taṇ-t-); PDr. *taṭ- < *taḷ-t-, *taḷ-/*taṇ-; (> l. w. Skt. taṭa bank, Pkt. taḍa- id., see Burrow, TPS 1945, pp. 102-104).]

taḍamu, same as taḍavu, q. v. with -v-/-m- (KS, Bhr. II); colloq., taḍumu id.

527 taḍavu (also taḍamu) intr./tr. to grope, feel about with the hands (Bhr. II); to seek, search (Bhr. II, III); to touch, handle, stroke; to broach, bring up a topic in conversation (Kaḷā.).

[Ka. taḍavu to rub or touch gently with the hand; taḍa touching, groping; Ko. taṛk- to search for; Ta. taṭavu tr. to stroke (Kamp.); grope, feel one's way (Periyapu.); Ma. taṭavuka to stroke, pat; Kui dahpa to seek, search for, desire, want; n. a search, longing; PSDr. *taṭ-av-, PDr. *taṭ-; alternatively, *taṭavu by metathesis < *tav-aṭu, cf. Ma. tappuka to grope, feel about.]

528 taḍiyu III intr. to be soaked, get wet (Bhr. I); tr. taḍupu to make wet (Bhr. I); taḍi wetness, moisture; adj. wet, damp; further v. s. v. taniyu.

[Ka. taḍi damp; moisture; To. toṇy- (toṇs-) to become damp, cool. The other forms occur with -ḷ/-ṇ meaning coolness, etc.: Ka. caḷi coldness, cold; taṇi to grow cool; taṇ coolness; Tu. saṇi-puni, saṇiyuni to grow cool; cali, caḷi cold, chilliness; Ko. tayṇ- (taṇc-) (body) becomes cool (before death); To. toṇc- (toṇč-) to cool, calm; Ta. taṇ coolness; taḷi drip as rain; n. rain (Parip.); coolness; caḷi cold, chillness; Ma. taṇiyuka to cool, calm; taṇekka id.; caḷi mud, mire; Te. cali chill; tanu- adj. cool, cold (KS); tanupu cool, coolness (Bhr. II); Pj. talla coolness; cf. Kur. caĩd- to drench, dip; caẽ- (pp. cĩka, caĩka) to get wet; PDr. *caḷ-/*caṇ- : *taḷ-/ *taṇ-; Te. *taṭ-V- < *caḷ-V-; (> l. w. in NIA, H. N. ṭhaṇḍā adj. cold, see Turner (with Bloch), Nep. Dict. s. v. ṭhaṇḍa).]

taḍupu tr. of taḍiyu, q. v.

529 taṇḍu (also daṇḍu) tr. to collect dues, subscriptions, etc. (later works and modern); cf. daṇḍugu, daṇḍuga, daṇḍuvu, daṇḍuva payment of penalty (Daś., Vijñ.); loss in business.

[Ka. taḷe to obtain, receive, take; talapu, talupu to come to hand, be received; taṇḍakār̲a one who amasses, who has a large amount of; Tu. daṇḍ(i)yuni to stretch the hand to receive anything; Ko. taṇḍ- to pay off (debt); win in contest; (debt) is paid; daṇḍ- to work off (debt); Ta. taṇṭu to collect taxes, debts, etc. (inscr.); Ma. teṇṭuka to obtain; intr. to wander about, as for alms; to seek, as insects; teṇṭi a beggar; cf. Go. taṇḍ- to take out, extract, as oil. PSDr. *taṇ-d- : *taḷ-/*taṇ-.]

530 tanaru* intr. to flourish, be accomplished as in art, education, etc. (Bhr. I); to increase, be full-grown (Bhr. II, Mārk.); be well or excellent; tanar(u)pu n. height, elevation, expansion, width, spread (Bhr. I, KS); tanar(u)cu, v. i. same as tanaru.

[Ka. tani to thrive, develop, become full-grown; n. the state of having thriven; abounding in agreeable qualities; adj. full, matured, rich, big; Tu. taneyuni (cattle) to be big with young; tanè breeding, as cattle, sheep, etc.; Ta. tan̲i uniqueness, matchlessness; taṇi to abound, increase in size (ṇ < n̲; usages from later texts); Ma. tan- to extend; Mlt. tān̲ṛy- (tān̲ṛc-) tr. to spread out, stretch out; tān̲ṛgr- to be spread out; tanyar- to become rich; PDr. *tān- : *tan-V-.]

tanar(u)cu* IId intr. same as tanaru, q.v. (Bhr. II).

531. taniyu III intr. to be satisfied, satiated (Bhr. I, II); tanivu/-vi satisfaction (Bhr. II); (Mdn.) tanivi id.; tr. tanupu to satisfy (class.).

[Ka. taṇi to be satisfied, satiated; taṇipu tr. to satisfy, appease; Tu. taṇiyuni to become calm; taṇu quenching; Ta. taṇi to be allayed, satisfied (Kalit.), fulfilled (Maṇi.). PSDr. *taṇ-; this group is associated with the etyma meaning "coolness" etc., v. s. v. taḍiyu; cf. Kur. tarkā calm, quiet.]

532 tanuku[1]* intr. to burn, smart as body in sun; (fuel) to burn (Bhr. II); to grieve (Bhr. II); (sun) to shine (Bhr. II).

[Cf. Ka. taṇal glowing coals; Ta. taṇal live coals, embers; ? PSDr. *taṇ-.]

533 tanuku[2]* intr. to touch, to reach, to occur, befall (governs dative); (fear) to arise (in mind) (Bhr. II); (evil) to befall (Bhr. I); n. fear, loss of courage (Bhr. II).

[Cf. Ta. tan̲n̲u tr. to approach (non-Sangam text); Ka. tar̲u (tatt-) v. i. to join, tr. to approach; to come about, come to pass; ? < *tan-/*tat̲-, v. s. v. tar̲iyu.]

534 tannu tr. to kick, beat (Bhīm.); to strike against (Hara.); to flog (Mdn.); n. a kick (Daś.); beating; with -konu (refl.) to flutter in agony; -paḍu (refl.) to suffer a hit (Naiṣ.).

[Ka. taḷḷu to thrust, throw, reject; taḷisu to beat; Tu. taḷḷuni, talluni to push in; talpuni to knock, thrash; Ko. taḷ- (tayḷ-) to push; To. toḷ- (toḷy-) id.; Ta. taḷḷu tr. to push; expel; reject; press down (Kamp.); taṇi to punish; Ma. taḷḷuka to push, thrust; v.i. to dash against; talluka to strike, beat; knock against; tannuka to be bruised; Go. (Dawson) taṉḍ- to expel; cf. Kuvi tah'- to quash; Kur. taṛ- (taṛc-) to flog, whip; PDr. *taḷ-/*taṇ-; also v.s.v. taṭṭu.]

535 tappu intr. to miss, fail, err, go wrong, be disloyal (Bhr. II); to be unfavorable, as destiny (Bhr. II); tr. to transgress, violate, to say and not fulfill (Bhr. I); to forsake (Bhr. II); as an inf. in various shades of meaning with other verbs, e.g., tappā-jūcu to disregard (cūcu to regard; Bhr. I, II); -drokku (-trokku), -drōcu (-trōcu) to abandon, expel; -baluku to tell a lie (paluku to speak), etc.; neg. ppl. tappaka adv. without fail, necessarily, must (Naiṣ., Bhīm.); n. error, impropriety (all classical and Mdn.).

[Ka. tappu id.; Tu. tappuni id.; Ko. tap- (tapy-) to make mistake, be lost, escape; tavr- (tavry-) make mistakes, omit; To. top- (topy-) to postpone, fail to come; Ta. tappu v.i. to err, mistake, be fruitless (Kṟḷ.); go wrong, be omitted (Kamp.); tr. fail to do, offend (PN); n. fault, slip (Tiv.); escape; tavaṟu to slip, miss; fail, be lost; be unsuccessful; tr. to pass over; n. failure, mistake (Nāl.); taval failure (Kalit.); fault (Nāl.); Ma. tappuka to escape; tappu a blunder; Kuvi (F) taph- to interrupt; tapk- tr. to quiet; Kuvi (S) tapp- to misdo; tappahan- to fail (han- to go); Klm.(E) tap- to turn upside down; < PDr. tap- : *tav-V-.]

536 tamaku* intr. to hesitate, draw back, be afraid; to fail, recede (late).

[Ka. tavu, tavuṅku to decrease, diminish; n. decrease, drooping, humbled state; Ta. tavaṟu to miss, fail; tavaṅku be in distress; v.s.v. tappu.]

537 tarapu[1]* tr. to lower, reduce, deduct (Bhr. II); to remove, destroy (late).

[Cf. Ka. taragu sinking, diminishing; Ta. taṟuvu v.i. to diminish; v.s.v. taṟugu.]

538 tarapu[2]* tr. to exceed the limits, to cross (Varāhapurāṇamu, late).

[Cf. Ma. tāram crossing, pervading.]

539 taralu[1] (also -ṟ- in some cases) intr. to shake, tremble in fear (Prabhā., Vasu.); be lost, perish; tr. to lose (Dvi. H.); (< *taḷ-ar).

[Ka. taḷar to move, tremble, totter; Ta. taḷar to grow slack, become flabby (Nāl.); perish; droop; v.s.v. talāku, talaru.]

540 taralu$^2$ (> tarlu) intr. to walk, go, proceed, set out (Vēm.); to be lost, gone; to step aside (UH); (< *taḷar); Mdn. taralipōvu to set out as a group (pōvu to go).

[Ka. taḷar id.; Ta. taṇa id. v. s. v. talaru$^2$.]

541 tar(u)cu IIa (also traccu, q. v.) tr. to churn, as buttermilk (Bhr. I); to rub two pieces of wood or metal for fire (HariV.); to examine thoroughly (ŚivaR.); to do woodwork (Mdn.); tarupu churning (Hara.); tari- adj. pertaining to churning; tari-kambamu churning post, etc.

[Pj. terip- (terit-) to churn; cf. Go. tarc- to scrape; Ka. tar̲i to be grazed; Tu. tarepuni to assay metal, grind, rub; Ko. tarv- (tart-) to abrade by moving over a rough surface; PSDr. and PCDr. *tar-.]

542 tar̲āku$^{1}$* intr. to be reduced; to diminish, as brightness of sun, etc. (KS); tr. to lose lustre, boldness, etc. (KS).

[V. s. v. tar̲ugu; different suffix (< *tat̲-aṅk-).]

543 tar̲āku$^{2}$* intr. to abound, spread, spread all over, as sweat (usages only in KS).

[V. s. v. tanaru.]

544 tar̲aṭu* (variant taraṭu) tr. to whip (late); n. a whip, whipping.

[< *cat̲-, v. s. v. car̲acu; Kuvi (S) tah'- to press; Kuvi (F) tass- to slap.]

545 tar̲iyu* III intr. to enter in, approach (Bhr. II, UH); to attack; to go beyond, exceed (Mārk.); tr. to meet, join (Bhr. II); tr. tar̲upu to join together, amass, save wealth (late).

[Ka. tar̲, tar̲u (tatt-) v. i. to join, approach, enter in; to come about; tar̲u the state of being joined; tar̲i id.; vb. to put in or down, fixed or settled; Ma. tar̲ekka v. i. to enter, be fixed; tr. to drive in; tar̲ayuka to be fixed; Kuvi dari adv. near; ? Mlt. dāry- (dārc-) to suit, agree, to remain, live; cf. Ta. tan̲n̲u to approach, v. s. v. tanuku$^2$; PSDr. *tat̲-.]

546 tar̲ugu/targu (tar̲uvu/tarvu) intr. to become less, diminish, decrease (UH); tr. to slice, cut, as a fruit (KS); tear a cloth into pieces (Bhr. I, Kāś.).

[Ka. tar̲i, tar̲e to cut off; to be abraded; Tu. taripuni to lop off, as branches; tajapuni to chop, cut in pieces; Ko. tayr- (tarc-) to cut with an implement; Ta. tar̲i tr. to lop, chop off (Tiruvāc.); intr. be cut off, broken; Ma. tar̲ikka to cut down; Kui tahpa to chip off, smooth off; Klm. Nk. targ- to cut off; Kur. Mlt. tār- to fell, cut down; Brah. taṛ- to cut off, slaughter, etc.; PDr. *tat̲-.]

547 tar̲umu tr. to pursue, chase, drive (Bhr. II); to overpower, pounce

upon (Bhr. II); to force (Mārk., Bhr. II); intr. to come too close to; ? increase, abound (Bhr. II); to stress, emphasize (Bhr. II).

[Kur. caṟ- (caḍḍ-) to expel, turn one out of the village; cf. Kui tāja to wipe; PDr. *caṯ-/*taṯ-; also v.s.v. aṟumu, taṟiyu.]

taṟuvu var. of taṟugu, q.v. (Naiṣ.).

targu var. of taṟugu, q.v. (KS).

tarvu var. of taṟuvu, q.v.

548 talãku* intr. to tremble, shake (Bhr. II, UH); to overflow, to drizzle (KS, Nirv.); to tremble in fear; be afraid, hesitate (Bhr. I, II); n. motion, fear (Bhr. II, KS); hesitation (Kāḷ.).

[Ka. taḷḷaḻa, taḷḷaṇa, taḷḷaṅka fear; taḷar to tremble, etc.; Mlt. talqro weak, tender, delicate; v.s.v. talaru, aluku[4]. PDr. *caḷ-/ *taḷ-; *caḷ- > PSDr. *taḷ- : *aḷ.]

549 talãgu* I and V (irreg. vb., allom. tal-; imp. sg. tala(mu), talagu(mu); pl. talã-ḍu) intr. to be lost, as wealth, kingdom, etc. (Bhr. I); way to be cleared of crowds, esp. imp. tala(mu) (sg.), talãḍu (pl.) get out of the way! ; to be spared; tr. to remove (Bhr. I, II), rescue from (Bhr. II).

[Ka. Ta. Ma. taḷḷu to push; Tu. taḷḷuni id.; (v.s.v. tannu); Ta. taḷḷu intr. to be removed (Tēv.), be lost, fail (Kṟḷ.); to diminish (Kṟḷ.); tr. to reject; Go. (Dawson) ṭanḏ- to expel; < *taḷ-; only Te. has the *-aṅku suffix; also see talũgu.]

550 talãcu IIc intr./tr. to consider, regard, think, reflect, imagine; intend, praise, adore, worship (all classical); talāpu intention, idea, wish, etc. (Bhr. I, III).

[Only Te. has the verb connected with the noun tala head; all other languages have forms for head deriving from PDr. *tal-, for which see Emeneau, Kolami, Vocab. No. 883; Burrow, DS IV, p. 332.]

551 talaru[1]* intr. to tremble, shake (Bhr. I); to withdraw, hesitate; be agitated, disturbed (Bhr. I).

[Ka. taḷar to tremble, totter; n. trembling; taṇi, daṇi to be fatigued; daṇu, daṇuvu fatigue; Tu. taḷabaḷa alarm, agitation, exhaustion, weariness; Ta. taḷar v.i. to droop, grow weary (Tiruvāc.), become flabby (Nāl.); taṇi to slacken; Ma. taḷaruka to grow slack, faint; n. tottering, weariness; Mlt. talqro weak, delicate. PSDr. *taḷ-ar-; PDr. *caḷ- : *taḷ-; for forms with c- and zero- (< *c-), v.s.v. aluku[4], also see s.v. taralu[1], talāku.]

552 talaru[2]* intr. to set out, start (Bhr. I); see taralu[2].

[Ka. taḷar to start off, set out, depart; taḷarcu to go away from a place; Ta. taṇa to depart, go away, to go, pass; to put away; to leave, separate from (Kr̠ḷ.); tāḷ leg, foot (Kr̠ḷ.); Ma. tāḷ id.; < *tāḷ-, prob. the same as the one underlying talāgu, tannu.]

talūgu* (> talgu) tr. to remove, dismiss, shove away, expel, as sorrow, fears, etc. (Bhr. I); intr. to be lost, removed (Bhr. I, Kaḷā.).

[V. s. v. talāgu.]

tavu* same as tagu q. v. (Bhr. I).

tavuḍu metathesized var. of taḍavu, q. v. (Mdn. Te. dial.).

tavulu* (var. of tagulu, q. v.) to be caught, obtained (Bhr. I), etc.

553 tasuku* (Śab.R.) intr. to coquet (no usages given for the verb); n. coquetry; tasukari a pretentious person (UH).

554 tā̃ku intr./tr. to touch, hit, attack, oppose in battle (Bhr. I, II); to occur, as hunger (Daś.), come in contact; n. an attack in war; a stroke (of sun) (Bhr. II).

[Ka. tāku, tāgu, tāṅgu, v. i. to join, hit; tāṭu to touch, strike against; to strike; Tu. tākuni, tāguni tr. to touch; tācuni to come in collision; Ko. tāk- id.; Ta. tākku come in contact; attack (Kalit.), strike (PN); touch (Kamp.); n. fight; tāṅku tr. to oppose, attack (Tolk.), hinder (PN); Ma. tākkuka to hit, touch; takkuka, taykkuka to strike; taikka to strike, hit; Kur. tak- to give a slight knock; Mlt. tak- to touch, hurt, as a sore. PDr. *tāy-nk-/-kk-, v. s. v. tagulu.]

555 tācu IId tr. to set, encase, as precious stones (NavaN.); to decorate.

[Ta. tai (taitt-) tr. to stitch, tie (Aiṅk.); string; decorate (Kalit.); set, encase (Kalit.); put on; Ma. taikka to sew; Kuvi (S) tāj- to sew; Kuvi (F) tac- id.; Brah. taf- to tie up, bind (*ta- + caus. -f-); < *tāy-, v. s. v. tagu, tagulu.]

556 tā̃cu IIc tr. to hit, strike, kick (Bhr. I); hit with the fist, to press against (BhR); tā̃pu a kick, stroke (Kāś.).

[Tu. tācuni to come in collision; To. toc- (toč-) to beat; Ma. taykkuka (pp. taycc-) to strike; further v. s. v. tā̃ku, tagulu; different suffix.]

557 tāru* intr. to move about, stroll, wander (KS, HariV., Kāś.); tr./intr. to approach, go near (Prabhā.); caus. tār(u)cu to conduct, take to (Bhr. II); n. tār-as-amu vicinity; tār-as-illu to approach; tār(u)-konu to attack; meet.

[Ka. tarisu to lead, conduct near; sār to come or go near; sārcu to make to go near; put to, in; come near to; Tu. sārluni to proceed; Ta. cār tr. to reach, associate with (Nāl.), to unite (Kalit.); joining; cārttu cause to join; Ma. inf. cāra adv. nigh, close; there are also forms with the loss of *c-, see Burrow, DS VI, p. 138. Te. tār- < *cār- ]

558 tāṟu[1]* intr. to lurk, lie in wait.
[Ta. taṟuku to linger, loiter.]

559 tāṟu[2]* to diminish, be reduced (Bhr. II, BhR); to descend, alight (UH).
[Ma. tāṟuka to sink, decline, droop; tāṟṟuka to kill, let sink or fall; Ka. tāṟu to wither, become emaciated; Tu. carmeri adj. thin. Prob. PDr. *tā-ṯ-; the same root also occurs in tā-ḻ-, v. s. v. taggu.]

560 tālu* intr. in tālābōyu to season food by pouring in fried spices (Hara.); Mdn. tālincu; n. tālupu (Bhīm.).

561 tāḷu tr. (with dative) to bear, suffer, endure, be patient, forbear; to wait, pause (Daśā. and other later works; none in Bhr.); l. w. < Ka., cf. tāl(i)mi patience.
[Ka. tāḷ, tāḷu to forbear, hold; suffer patiently, wait; taḷe to hold, bear, sustain; Tu. tāluni to endure, bear, suffer; tāḷmè endurance; Ko. tāḷ- to stop and wait; Ta. tāḷu tr. to bear, suffer, tolerate; intr. be possible; tāl to stay, rest, stop, halt (Cilap.). PSDr. *tāḷ-/tāl.]

562 tāl(u)cu[1]* IIb to put on, wear (Bhr. I), to bear, as a burden (Bhr. I).
[Ka. tāḷ to wear well; bear with; taḷe put on, as clothes; for the other languages, this meaning does not occur, v. s. v. tāḷu.]

563 tāl(u)cu[2] IId tr. to winnow small grains from flour.
[Ta. tāṟṟu to sift, winnow; n. winnowing; < *tāl-ṯ- or *tāṯ-t-; cf. taṟi to sift by a winnowing fan, v. s. v. ēṟu.]

564 tāl(u)cu[3] IId to twist, twine threads into a strong rope, etc. (UH); n. tāl-ika a twist, twining (Bhōj.).
[Ka. taḷe a tie, tether, halter; Tu. taḷe a rope for climbing trees; Ta. taḷai to fasten, bind, chain; n. tie, fastening, cord, rope, shackles (Tiruvāc.); Ma. taḷekka to fetter, shackle; taḷa fetters, a foot-rope, etc. All these are derived from *taḷ- to stop, according to Ta. Lexicon and Gundert; PSDr. *tāḷ : *taḷ-V-.]

tigiyu* III (also tiviyu, tivvu, tivu; tigucu, tivucu, tīyu).
[V. s. v. tigucu.]

565 tigucu* (also tivucu) IIa tr. to pull, attract (Bhr. I. KS), pull towards oneself; take off, draw, pull as an arrow; v. i. to be taken away, diminish or disappear.
[Ka. tege, tegi, tegu to pull; to be reduced; to disappear; Ko. tev- (tevt-) to pull along or out of; Klm.(E) tiv- to pull; Klm.(SR) tivv- id.; Nk. tivv- id.; cf. Ta. tikai to be taken aback (Tēv.); to subside (Kallā.); tr. to come, be settled; ticai id.; tekku tr. to receive, take (Tēv.); tevvu to take (Maturai.), to seize, grasp; Ma. tikayuka to be finished; PSDr. *tik-/*tiv- : *tek-/*tev-; cf. Mlt. tisg- to lift the latch.]

566 tiṭṭu to abuse, scold, curse; to reprove, censure, find fault with (Bhr. II); n. scolding, curse, blame.

[Ka. tiṭṭu to abuse, scold; siḍuku id.; n. abuse, scolding; siṭṭu, siḍuku anger, wrath; Ta. tiṭṭu to abuse; n. reviling; Brah. jhiṛk- to rebuke, scold. PDr. *tiṭ- or *ciṭ-.]

567 tinu IV (past tiṇ-ṭ-, hab. tin-d-/tiṇ-ḍ-) tr. to eat (Bhr. I); to consume, enjoy; to spend, use up (Mdn.); to get, suffer, undergo, e.g., tiṭlutinu to suffer rebuke; to eat away, destroy little by little, as white ants (Mdn.); der. n. tiṇ-ḍi food (contemptuous in colloq. Te.).

[Ka. tin, tinnu (tind-) to eat (things requiring teeth, as flesh); occasionally also rice (abusive); Tu. tinpini to eat, consume, destroy, waste, receive as bribes, blows, etc.; tindruni to eat all; Ko. tin- (tiḏ-) to eat; To. tīn- (tīḏ-) id.; Ta. tiṉ (tiṉ-ṟ-) to eat; feed (PN); Ma. tinnuka id.; Kui tinba (tis-) id. (-s- < *-ṯṯ-); Kuvi (F) tinj- (tic-) id.; Kuvi (S) tinn- id.; Go. tind- (tinjī) id.; GoM. tīnd (tit-) id.; Klm. Nk. tin- (tin-d-) id.; Nk. tinc- eating (LSI IV, p. 572); Pj. tin- (tind-) to eat; Oll. tin- (tiy-, tinḍ-) id.; KGad. tin- (tiy-) id.; Kur. tind- (tindc-) to put into another's mouth; Mlt. tind- to feed by hand; PDr. *tin-, past *tin-ṯ-.]

568 tinuku (Mdn. tiṇuku, Viśākha. dial.) tr. to strain, as at stool (BP; also Mdn.).

[Ka. tiṇuku, tiṇaku, tiṇiku to use strain in childbirth or easing nature; Mlt. tinq- id.; Ma. tikku n. straining, pressure; cf. Ta. tiṇuṅku to congeal; tiṇi become solid; to stuff; PDr. *tiṇ-ukk-.]

569 timuru* intr. to abound, increase (Dvi. H., Śakunt.); to bubble with desires, to hasten; n. haste, anxiety, exuberance, pride (Manu.).

[Ka. timbu to fill, n. fullness; Ta. timir to grow, increase, become more intense; timiṟu to grow full, big; Ma. timuruka to swell, grow; be mad with joy or rage; tikayuka to become full; tika fullness. PSDr. *tim-, *tim-V-/*tiv-V- : *tik-V-; also see s.v. tivuru.]

570 timmu rhyme-word with tiṭṭu, as in tiṭṭu timmu to abuse, etc., (late, also Mdn.); tr. to bless, or blame?

571 tiriyu* III to wander for alms, to beg, ask alms, live by alms (Bhr. II); n. tiripamu alms (Dvi. H.); tiripa, tiripādu a beggar.

[Ka. tiri to wander in quest of alms; tirapa wandering about for alms (loc.); tiraki, tiruki a female beggar; Tu. tirapa, tirape alms, charity; Ma. tirekka to seek. PSDr. *tir-i, *tir-a-, v. s. v. tirugu.]

572 tirugu intr. to wander, roam (Bhr. I); turn, turn back (Bhr. II); to change, alter (Bhr. II); tr. to surround, encircle (Bhīm.); n. a turn, change of direction, reversal; tiri turn, revolving (Bhr. II); tirugaN inf. (adv.) again, Mdn. tiragā; tr. trippu.

[Ka. tirigu to go round, turn, roll, whirl, go back, etc.; tiri to turn round, roam; tirugu to go round; tiruvu, tirivu, tiripu to cause to go round; to turn; Tu. tirṅguni v.i. to turn, revert, shift, move, travel about; tirduni v.i. to turn; Ko. tirg- v.i. to turn; tirk- tr. to turn; tiry- (tirc-) to change in nature for the worse; tirc- tr. to change; To. tïrx- v.i. to turn; tïrk- tr. to turn; tïrp- tr. to turn key; tïrb- to twist; tïry- (tïrc-) to twist; Ta. tiri v.i. to walk about, move about (Nāl.); tr. cause to wander; tiruku tr. to twist, turn; Ma. tiriyuka v.i. to turn round; tirikka tr. id.; tiri a turn; tirikkuka tr. to turn in, twist; Kui tirga to shiver; terpa to wind round; trēba to wander, travel; trehpa to cause to wander; trikna adv. in a startled manner; Kuvi (F) trig- to shiver; tiṛv- to turn oneself around; tṛic- to twist; tēṛmb- to wallow; Kuvi(S) termp- to roll; Go. tirī- to revolve; caus. tiruht-; GoM. tirh- to revolve; Klm. tirg- (tirik-t-) v.i. to turn, wander; Nk. tirg- id.; Pj. tir- (Sth. tirv-, tiri-) to tremble; tirk- to writhe; Kur. tīr- (tīrc-) tr. to turn on one's heels, etc., to make pirouettes (upon someone's stomach); to disfigure, cripple; tir'ū looking obliquely, squint; tir'ū <u>kh</u>annas squint-eyed man (cf. Te. tiruguḍu kaṇḍlu squint eyes); Brah. sīrr- to recoil; trikk- to wither up. PDr. *tīr-, *tir-V-, *tir-uk-, *tir-uv-; v.s.v. tiriyu, trippu.]

tiviyu*, same as tigiyu, q.v.; for ety. v.s.v. tivucu, tīyu.

tivu* var. of tivvu, q.v.

tivucu var. of tigucu, q.v.

573 tivuru* (1) intr. to be zealous of, to desire (Bhr. I); to start, undertake, be ready to do (Bhr. I); to increase, abound; swell, spread, increase, as the sound of war drums, conches, etc. (KS, Bhr. II), to rage (late).

[The meanings 'to desire, etc.' may be secondary to 'to swell, increase, etc.' Cf. Ka. tīvu to become full, abound, spread; for others, v.s.v. timuru.]

tivuru* (2) intr. to hasten to do (Bhr. I).

[Cf. Ta. tīviri- to hasten, expedite; tīvaram n. speed, celerity (colloq.); fury, rage (Piṅ.); < Skt. tīvra-.]

574 tivvu* (also tivu) tr. to draw, pull, as the string of bow (Bhr. I, KS); to pull down (Bhr. I).

[< *tiv-iyu with -vv < *-v-iyu through contraction, or < *tiv- through the doubling of the final; v. s. v. tivucu; other alts. tigiyu, tiviyu.]

575 tīḍu* tr. to sharpen; gnash teeth (Dvi.H.), to tear, twist (late); with -konu to be sharpened (Naiṣ.); cf. tīṭa itching.

[Ka. tīḍu to rub as to sharpen, kill by pressing; to touch; Tu. tīḍuni to rub, press; tīṇṭu, sīṇṭu to rub, scrape; Ko. tīṭ- (tīc-) to rub on (as liquid), paint; teṛv- (teṛt-) to clean up (mess) by rubbing (< *teṭav-); Ta. tīṇṭu tr. to feel, contaminate by touching; catch hold of (Kr̲ḷ.); tīṭṭu tr. to sharpen, polish, rub, smooth hair, paint; n. whetting, plastering; touching, defilement; Ma. tīṇṭuka to touch, infect; Klm.(SR) dīṭ- to rub, rub teeth; Nk. dhīṭ- to wipe. PSDr. and PCDr. *tīṇṭ/*tīṭṭ-.]

576 tīyu/tiyyu III tr. to pull out, draw (BhR); to take out or away, remove; with nouns in different shades of meaning; rāgamu tīyu to sing a tune; talupu tīyu to open the door; goyyi tīyu to dig a trench; pālu tīyu to draw milk, etc.; also to deduct (in mathematics) (Mdn.); intr. to subside, as a tide; to be reduced (16th century); to withdraw, grow lean, etc.; cf. tigucu.

577 tīru (1) intr. (an action) to be accomplished (Bhr. I, II), (desires) to be fulfilled (Naiṣ., Manu.); to be rectified, set right, to be finished, completed; tr. tīr(u)cu to finish, complete, fulfil (Bhr. II, Kāś., JBh.); to straighten; to decorate, as hair, etc. (KS); to settle quarrel, problem, etc. (Bhr. II); tīru n. beauty (HariV.); manner, fashion, style; tīr(u)pu, tīr(u)vu settlement, arranging, completion (Bhr. II); tīraN thoroughly, Mdn. tīrā id.

[Ka. tīr be finished; cease; be decided; n. end; manner; beauty; Tu. tīruni to be finished, settled; tīra entire, whole, wholly; Ko. tīr- to be finished, settled; tīrc- to finish an undertaking; To. tīr- (dispute) is settled; to settle; tīrc- (tīrč-) to finish; Ta. tīr (tīrnt-) to end; be non-existent (Kalit.), to leave, be cleared, as a doubt (Kr̲ḷ.); be settled, as a quarrel; (tīrtt-) to quit, solve; to leave (Tolk.); to finish, clear off debt; to remove, cure, relieve as pain, etc. (Akan.); to solve a problem; Ma. tīruka to be finished; tīrkka to complete, settle; tīra completely; Klm.(E) tīr- (work, food) to be finished; Nk. tīr- id.; Mlt. tīr- to be off, go away; cf. Kur. tīr- lag behind, arrive late; PDr. *tīr-.]

tīr̲u (2) intr. to perish, be ruined (KS); be settled; to be possible (Bhr. II); to cease, be removed (Bhr. I), to perish, end (Bhr. II,

Kāś.); SAN separates this from tīru but comparative evidence does not warrant such a separation. This is probably one of the cases of hyper-standardization of the form by substituting ṟ for r, which again indicates that contrast between these two phonemes was no longer clear even at the classical period.

[Ka. tīr to be possible, accomplished; Tu. tīruni (with dative) to be able; tīrandi incapable, unsettled; Ta. tīr v.i. to pass, to die, be spent; Ma. tīruka to become; others v.s.v. tīru.]

578 tuḍ(u)cu IIa tr. to wipe, rub, sweep, clean as a surface (Bhōj., Naiṣ.), wipe off; erase (Mdn.); n. tuḍ(u)pu cleaning, rubbing, erasing.

[Ka. toḍe to wipe, remove by rubbing, efface; to smear; Tu. tuḍepuni, toḍepuni to rub, paint, anoint; Ta. tuṭai to wipe, scrub (PN); polish; destroy; rub, apply, dispel (Kṟḷ.); toṭai tr. to wipe, wipe off dust; Ma. tuṭekka to wipe, rub off, v.s.v. toḍayu; PSDr. *tuṭ-, *tuṭay.]

579 tuniyu III intr. to be cut off, to sever, as a body-part (Bhr. I, II); to be torn, as a cloth (UH); to perish, be ruined (HariV.); tr. tuncu to cut off, break (HariV.); to tear (Āmu.); to nip off flowers, fruits, etc.; n. tuṇḍamu a piece (Bhr. II); tuniya, tuṇṭa id.; cf. tunũgu, tun(u)mu.

[Ka. tuṇḍu a fragment; tuṇḍisu to go or cut into pieces; Tu. tuṇḍu a bit; Ta. tuṇi to be cut (Akan.); be torn; tr. to cut, sever, cut off (Tiv.); n. piece, slice; tuṇṭi to cut; be cut off; tuṇṭu a piece; Ma. tuṇiyuka to cut short; n. a piece; Go.(W) tūs a part, share; Pj. ṭunḍa strip of cloth used as bandage; Kur. ṭuṇḍū end, termination; further forms quoted under tunũgu, q.v.; cf. Brah. tuṛing- v.i. to become undone, esp. of stitches; to separate, of milk, etc. PDr. *tuṇ-.]

580 tunũgu to be cut off, be broken, to perish (late); tun(u)ka a slice, piece.

[Kur. tonkh-, tokkh- (tunkhy-, tõnkh-) to break any part of a plant with the fingers, pluck a leaf, a flower; prune a tree, cull greens or fruit; Mlt. toq- to nip off, cut off; toqr- be cut off, to die; toqro broken; (< kk- < *nk- < *-ṇ-k-); Ka. tuṇuku, tuṇaku a piece, bit; other languages have forms without the k-suffix, v.s.v. tuniyu, tunumu.]

tunucu IIb tr. of tuniyu (late).

581 tun(u)mu tr. to cut off, cut into pieces (Bhr. II, UH); to tear, kill; (< *tuṇ-ump-/-um-).

[Ety. same as for tuniyu, q. v., different derivative suffix; other languages do not show the *-mp/*-m suffix.]

tuncu IIb tr. of tuniyu, tunũgu q. v.

582 tummu intr. to sneeze; n. sneeze, sternutation (Bhr. II).

[Tu. tumbilu̥ sneezing; Ko. tub-, To. tüb- to sneeze; Ta. tummu to sneeze (Kr̲ḷ.); tr. emit, let go; n. a sneeze (Kr̲ḷ.); tummal id. (Kr̲ḷ.), breath (Piṅ.); tumpu (later development of tummu); Ma. tummuka, tumpuka to sneeze; tummal n. sneezing; tumekka cattle to snort; Kuvi (F) tūhm- to sneeze; Klm. (E) tum- to sneeze; Nk. tum a sneeze; Pj. tumm-, Oll. tum-, KGad. tumm- to sneeze; Kur. tum'- (tummy-, tumm-) id.; Mlt. tum- id.; PDr. *tum-; *tump- is the basis for Tu. Ko. To., Emeneau, Lg. 29, p. 352, but -mp- < -m-, attested by the Ta. case; for intrusive p on final m, see P. S. S. Pillai, AOR Vol. 2, p. 23. Connection possible with Ka. sumilu breath, sumiyu to sob, cf. Ta. tummu; then *tum- < *cum-; cf. Ma. cumekka to cough, cuma cough.]

583 tur̲ugu* tr. to cram, stuff in, tuck in a loin-cloth (Bhr. II, Mārk.).

[Ka. tur̲uku to cram or stuff; tur̲ugu to be thronged or packed; Ko. turg- to be pushed into a hole; sink into swampy ground; turk- to push through a hole, cram into mouth; Ta. tur̲u to be thick, full, closed (Cilap.); tr. bedeck as flowers (Tiv.); to cram, stuff; Ma. tur̲uka to be stuffed, thronged, tr. cram, push in; tur̲uttuka to cram; tur̲u a heap; Klm. turk- to put (fuel) on fire; Pj. tutt- to be blocked up; Kur. turd- to pass through any narrow aperture; Mlt. turg- to bury the ashes of the dead; Brah. trujj- to choke; < PDr. *tūt̲- : *tut̲-V-; *tut̲-uṅk-, tut̲ukk-; *tut̲-utt-; also v. s. v. tūr̲u, tur̲umu.]

584 tur̲(u)mu[1] to tuck flowers in the braid (Kāś.); to insert, put in (Bhr. II); n. a braid (Bhr. II).

[Ka. tur̲ubu to insert, tuck in as flowers; n. knot of hair; tur̲umbu id.; Tu. turṭu female's hair tied into a knot; Ta. tur̲umu, tur̲umpu to be close, crowded (Tēv.); Kuvi (S) turp- to oppress; cf. Kur. tub- (tubc-) to press, cram into; < PDr. *tut̲-ump-/*-upp- : *tūt̲; v. s. v. tūr̲u, tur̲ugu.]

585 tur̲umu[2] (Brown, Śab.R.) to grate coconut, etc.; make into small pieces; n. (coconut, etc.) grated into small pieces; a piece (colloq.).

[Ka. turuvu to grate; cf. Mlt. tuṛgr- to be broken; tuṛgro broken; also v. s. v. truṅgu.]

586 tulucu* IId (Brown; rare) tr. to shed, as fruit, powder, etc. (late); cf. tulumu.

[Ka. tuḷuku to shed, throw an arrow.]

587 tulumu* tr. to cause leaves to fall through cutting or plucking (late); cf. tulucu.

588 tū̃gu intr. to shake, swing (Paṇḍ., Nirv.); to droop (Bhr. II); to be weighed in a balance (Mārk.); to be equal, comparable (late); to ṇod in sleep, doze (Vikram.); adj. swinging, rocking (Naiṣ.); n. doze; tr. tū̃cu to weigh (Bhr. II, III, Naiṣ.).

[Ka. tūgu tr. to weigh, swing or rock; nod as in sleep; tūṅku to dangle, wave; tūṇa violent agitation; Tu. tūṅkuni, tūṅguni v. i. to reel, doze; tr. to swing, toss; tūkuni to weigh, rock; Ta. tūṅku v. i. to hang (Kṟḷ.), swing (Kalit.); to sleep (Kamp.); tūkku tr. to weigh; compare; tūkkam sleep, weighing; tuñcu to sleep, doze; be drowsy (PN); to hang (Pu.Ve.); Ma. tūṅṅuka to be weighed, be drowsy; tūkkuka to suspend, weigh; Kui sunja to sleep; Kuvi (S) tūng- v. i. to swing; tū- (tutt-) to throb; tūkh'- to weigh; Kuvi (F) tūng- v. i. to sway; tūkh- to swing; hūnj- to lie down; GoM. hunj- to sleep; Go. (Seoni) suncī sleeping (LSI IV, p. 518); Pj. tuñ- to go to sleep; KGad. tuy- v. i. to swing; Kur. jokh- to weigh, compare; Mlt. joky- to measure, weigh; jokar- to be compared; jokartr- to compare; Brah. tugh n. sleep; ? tingān sleep; ? Kur. Mlt. related to IA, vide Turner, Nep. Dict. s. v. jokhnu. PDr. *tŭ̄y-/*cŭ̄y-; *tŭ̄y-nk/-kk-, *tŭ̄y-nc-; v. s. v. tūlu.]

tū̃cu tr. of tū̃gu. q. v.

589 tūncu* IIb tr. of obsolete *tūṇu to weigh (KS); n. tūn(i)ki balance, weighing (Bhr. II); (< *tūn-c-).

[Cf. Ka. tūṇa violent motion; tone (< *tunay-) to swing, wave; tūn- < *tuy-l/n, v. tūlu[1].]

590 tūru[1]* to drizzle, as rain, (spray) to fall (no literary usage cited); n. tūra a drizzle, also tuvvara (JBh.), tuppara id.; (Mdn.); (< *tuv-ar-).

[Ta. tūvu to sprinkle, shower, as arrows (Cīv.); v. i. to rain; tūval drizzling (PN); Ma. tūkuka, tūvuka to spill; Klm.(E) tūk dust; Ta. tuvaṟṟu to scatter drops; tuvaṟal, tuvaḷai drizzle, drop (Akan.); tuval to drip; tukaḷ dust (Maṇi.); tūḷ id.; Ta. Ma. tūṟṟu to scatter, strew; Ka. tūru to drizzle; Go. tūr- to fly away, dust, etc. in wind. PDr. *tūv- : *tuv-V-; alternatively, root *tuv- : *tū-, in which case *tūv is *tū-v-.]

591 *tūru[2] (only in inf. tūr-an-, tūran-ettu to winnow grain) tr. to winnow by pouring down in wind (KS); n. tūr(u)pu winnowing; tūr(u)p-ettu to winnow (late; ettu to raise).

[Ka. tūṟu id.; Tu. tūpuni to winnow, fan; tūpu winnowing; Ta. tūṟṟu to winnow; Ma. tūṟṟuka id.; Go. (W) tureh- id.; Klm.(E) tūrp-et- id. (l. w. < Te.); (> l. w. Skt. sūrpa- a winnowing basket, see Burrow, TPS 1945, p. 118). This series is connected with the one under tūru[1], q. v.]

592 tūṟu* intr./tr. to enter, penetrate (Bhr. I, II); tr. tūṟucu, tūrcu to pierce into, as an arrow; penetrate (Bhr. II, Naiṣ.); cf. tū-konu intr. to enter, etc. (KS).

[Ka. tūṟu to enter, penetrate, pierce; n. penetrating; dūkonu to penetrate; Ta. tuṟu to reach, enter (Kamp.); tūr (tūrtt-) tr. to fill, close, insert; Ma. tūruka to cram, push in; Kui tuspa to make a breach, pierce; Go. durs- to fit one thing in or on to another; Kur. tūr- (tūrc-) to pierce through any soft matter; make a passage into. PDr. *tūṯ- : *tuṯ-V-; ultimately *tū-; cf. Te. tūpu an arrow, tūmu a sluice, canal, etc.; v. s. v. tuṟugu, tuṟumu.]

593 tūlu[1] intr. to swing, dangle, as dishevelled hair (Bhr. I); to hang down, droop (UH); to be fatigued (Bhr. II, Bhīm.); to bend down, perish (Bhr. II); tr. tūl(u)cu, tūlincu to let hang down, dangle; to aggrieve, make tired (BhR); tūlikonu to fall down; cf. tūl-āḍu intr. to shake, tremble (Bhr. II); to reel in intoxication (Naiṣ.).

[Tu. tūluni to totter, reel, nod, be drowsy; Ta. tuyal v. i. to sway, swing (Ciṟup.); to hang; tūr to perish, disappear; tuyar to grieve; tuyaṅku v. i. to faint; tuyakku n. fatigue (Kamp.), sorrow; Kuvi (S) tū- to throb. PDr. *cuy- > PSDr. *uy : *tuy-; cf. Burrow, DS VI, p. 142; cf. Brah. tūl- to alight, dwell, sit.]

594 tūlu[2]* intr. to be scattered, as army in battle (Bhr. II); to be chased, run away (Bhr. II); tr. tūl(u)cu, tūlincu to chase.

[Ka. tūḷ, tūḷu to go off or backward; to chase; n. tūḷdu to chase, remove; Ta. uḷai to be defeated (Tiv.); to disperse, scatter (Patiṟ.); cf. Kui tūspa to bend down and turn the back upon a person; Klm. tūl- to run; Nk. tūḷ- to run, flow; Pj. tūl- to run, run away. PSDr. and PCDr. *tūḷ : *uḷ-V- < PDr. *cūḷ.]

595 tegacu* IId intr. to grieve, to be disturbed (Pāṇḍ.).

596 tegaḍu* (tevaḍu) tr. to disregard, neglect, slight, censure, blame (Bhr. II); to excel, rebuke; n. abusing (Bhr. II).

[Ka. tegaḻ to rebuke, blame; n. blame; tevaḻdam n. id.; Tu. teguni to revile, abuse; tegelè reviling; cf. Ta. tevvu enmity, hostility (Tolk.); tev id. (Kamp.); teviḷ to loathe, dislike. PSDr. *tev- : *tek-V-.]

597 tegu (allom. te- in tr. tencu, q. v.) to be ended (Bhr. II, Mārk.); (work) to be finished, ended (Bhr. II); to dare, rush forth (Bhr. II);

der. n. tegudala end, completion (Nirv., Bhr. III); teguva courage; also as an inf. teg-aN- in many combinations, e.g., tegā-gōyu to cut off; tegā-baḍu to rush forth, dare; tr. tencu[1], q.v.

[Ka. tege, tegu to be removed, diminish, disappear; tr. to put out or extinguish; Tu. tekkuni to be extinguished; Ma. tikayuka to be finished; tikekka to complete; Klm.(E) tik- to die; Klm.(SR) tigtā deceased; Nk. tikk- to die; Mlt. teqr- to burst, as a boil; teqro damaged; teq- v.i. to open, as a boil; come or break forth; cf. To. tïx- (tïxθ-) to take to one's heels. The nuclear meaning seems to be 'to end'; PDr. *tek-, ? *tik-.]

598 teccu V (allom. tē-/tēr- before back vowel suffixes) tr. to bring, get (Bhr. I); to gain, obtain (Bhr. II); to cause, produce, bring about (Bhr. II); teccukonu to cause for oneself, bring upon oneself (Bhr. II).

[Ka. tar, taru (tand-) to bring, lead or conduct near; give; Ta. tā (tant-) to give, cause to get; Ma. taruka to give; Kui tapa (tat-) to bring; tapka (< tak-p-; takt-) to fetch; Kuvi(S) tā-, Kuvi(F) tāc- to bring, fetch; Go. tatt- id.; Klm. -ta, -tar; further, see Emeneau, Lg. 21, pp. 184-213, to which may be added Kur. tai-, tēy- to send, allow one to go; Mlt. tey- to send; cf. Kur. taṇḍ- to take for oneself; occupy, buy up. PDr. *tay-/*tey : *tă-; irreg. phonological developments.]

tencu[1] IIb tr. of tegu, to cut off (Bhr. II, Śakunt.).

599 tencu[2] IId (before back vowel suffixes, allom. tē-/tēr-) (1) occurs bound with verbs meaning 'to go,' and changes the meaning to 'to come,' e.g., canu to go, canudencu to come, canudẽ-ka/canudēr-aka not coming; (2) bound aux. with reflexive meaning, sometime intensifies intransitive meaning, e.g., agudencu to pass, as time, cf. agu to become; cottencu to enter (by oneself), cf. coccu to enter, and so on; also with tr. in puttencu to send, cf. puccu.

[Probably related to teccu to bring, etc. q.v.; in Kolami -ta, -tar occur bound in a similar way, see Kolami, Vocab. No. 414.]

600 teṭṭu* to gather together into a mass on water (late); probably a back-formation from the nouns teṭṭe, teṭṭuva a mass of rubbish which collects on the surface of water (Nr̥s.).

[V. s.v. tēlu, tēṟu.]

601 teṇḍu* (also tẽḍu, q.v.) to lie down, sleep (Āmu.); cf. tenn-uṇḍu to lie down (KS, Kāś.); cf. tēnu.

[Kui ṭēra to sleep; ? Ka. sēḍu bending, shrinking; seḍe to grow crooked, shrink.]

602 temalu intr. to set out, stir, get ready to go (KS); to go away; to slip, slide (Daś.); to shake, tremble; (Mdn.) to feel nausea, be stirred in stomach; tr. temal(u)cu to pull up (Bhr. II), to loosen, dishevel (Naiṣ.); to shake off violently (Bhr. II); (< *tev-aḷ).

[Ka. tē, tege to go away, walk off; tege to remove, extract, pull; be removed; further v. s. v. tiviyu; cf. Ka. tevaḷu to creep along on the ground; Ta. tivaḷ to move as on ground.]

603 teralu$^{1*}$ intr. to stir, move (Bhr. II, III), to be shaken, to fall off (KS); to set out, depart (Bhr. I); tr. teral(u)cu to shake, move; to remove, rout (Bhr. II); to cause to start.

[Ka. teraḷ to move, stir; to depart; teraḷcu to cause to go; either from *tir-aḷ-, *tir-a as in tirugu, etc. q. v., or *tēr-al, v. s. v. cēru, *-tēr̲u$^{2}$. Burrow confuses Te. teralu$^{1}$, taralu, and Ta. taḷar, etc., TPS 1945, p. 106; v. s. v. talaru.]

604 teralu$^{2*}$ intr. to abound, increase (Bhr. I), swell up (KS); teralaN inf. in plenty; teral(u)konu v. i. to increase, augment.

[Tu. tirle a full-grown man; Ta. tiraḷ to assemble, swell up; Ma. tiraḷuka to grow full.]

605 teralu$^{3}$ (> terlu) intr. to boil, simmer with sound (RR, Pāṇḍ.); to overflow in boiling (Vikram.); also Mdn.

teral(u)cu IIb tr. of teralu$^{1}$ q. v. to remove, stir, cause to go (Bhr. II).

606 ter̲acu IIa intr. to be opened (KS); to open, unclose, uncover (Kāś., Vikram.); ter̲api opening, space (Bhr. II), interval (Nirv.), clearing of clouds (Mdn.).

[Ka. ter̲e to be unclosed, to open; tr. make open; ter̲a an opening; Tu. terapu space, room; Ko. terv- (terd-) tr. to open; To. ter̲- (ter̲θ-) tr. to open; Ta. tir̲a tr. to open (Kalit.), cut or lay open; tir̲appu cleft, open place; tir̲avu way, gate; Go. tarī- to be opened (of door); Kui trēppa to lay out; dari adj. opened out, spread forth; cf. Kur. tāṛ- to put out of the way; clear of obstruction; cf. Ma. tur̲akka v. i. to be opened; tr. to open door; clear (a gutter); tur̲appu opening. PDr. *tet̲- : tet̲-V-.]

ter̲alu* (Śab.R.) (smell) to arise, come out (no literary usages cited).

[V. s. v. teralu$^{1}$.]

607 teliyu III intr./tr. to be known, to know (Bhr. II); to become clear for comprehension (Bhr. II); to wake up from sleep (Bhr. II, BhR); to gain consciousness after fainting (Bhr. I); to blossom, shine; tr. telupu to make clear, tell, explain (classical); der. n. telivi knowledge, comprehension, clarity, perspicacity (Bhr. II), brightness.

[Ka. tiḷi to become clear; come to light; to know, learn; n. clearness, knowledge; tiḷisu to inform; Tu. tiḷi clear; tiḷuvaḷikè understanding, knowledge; Ko. teyḷ-/teḷc- (teḷc-) to regain consciousness; To. tüḷy- (tüḷs-) to become clear; Ta. teḷ (teṭṭ-) to become clear; teḷi become clear as water (Akan.); tr. to know, investigate (Kuṟun.); to clarify, make known; n. clearness; teḷḷu be clear (Tiruvāc.); Ma. teḷiyuka become clear; teḷi clearness; Kui ? tispa to awaken; Kuvi (F) tell- id.; Kuvi (S) telh- to know; telp- to interpret; Kur. tiltil adj. of a fresh appearance; Brah. tipp-, titt- allomm. of chā- to understand, know; neg. base tir-; cf. Mlt. teṉg- to tell, relate. PDr. *teḷ; e > i before retroflex consonants.]

608 telucu[1]* IId (tr. of teliyu with restricted range of meanings) tr. to pacify, console (Bhr. II).

[Ta. teḷi tr. to pacify, make up as a love quarrel (Tolk.); etymology same as for teliyu, q. v.]

609 telucu[2]* IIb tr. to praise, worship (Bhr. II); to bow in respect (Bhr. II); to request, pray (Kaḷā.).

[Cf. Go. talehk- to beg, ask for anything; Go. (W) talahk- id.; Kur. temb- to beg for alms.]

telupu tr. of teliyu, q. v., to make clear for understanding (Bhr. I); to tell, point out (Bhr. II); to enlighten, teach (Bhr. I).

tevaḍu* same as tegaḍu, q. v. (Bhr. II).

610 tẽgu* to be afraid, to shake, tremble (Paṇḍ.).

[Probably related to tēyu, q. v.]

611 tẽḍu* to lie down, sleep (Krīḍ.).

[Cf. teṇḍu, tēnu; ? Ka. tēlu to sink into a fainting fit, to faint.]

612 tēnu* intr. to sleep (Pāṇḍ.).

613 tēyu* III (Śab.R.) to be worn or wasted; to wear by use, handling or rubbing (no literary usages cited; prob. l. w. < Ka.).

[Ka. tē, tēy, tēyu tr. to waste by use; Tu. tēpuni to rub, polish; tēpu rubbing, polishing; tēmǎna loss in assaying metals; Ko. tēy- (tēc-) to become worn out; tr. to rub, wear down; Ta. tēy to wear away by friction, become weak (Kṟḷ.); be effaced by rubbing, wane (Kuṟun.); tr. to waste by rubbing, reduce (Kṟḷ.); Ma. tēyuka to be rubbed off; tēkkuka tr. to waste. PSDr. *tēy- < *cāy-/*cēy-, v. s. v. cā̃du.]

tēru (same as tēṟu (1), (2), q. v.) to be appeased, (mind) to become clear (late); to appear, become visible (Naiṣ.).

614 tēr̲u$^{1}$ (1) to regain consciousness from sleep or swoon, etc. (Bhr. I); water or mind to become clear (KS); to be appeased, consoled (Bhr. II); (sediment) to be settled (Manu.); to become successful (Kaḷā.); tr. tēr̲(u)cu/tērcu to make clear, as water, etc.; to be better, improve; ter̲apu n. gaining consciousness.

[Ko. tēr- (day) dawns; tērc- to make (day) dawn; To. tȫr̲- to become better (health or wealth); tȫṯ- to make improve, etc.; Ta. tēr̲u to be made clear, as water (Kalit.); recover from swoon, etc.; be mature, as mind; cheer up; tēr̲r̲u to make clear, enlighten (Kalit.); console; cure, give relief; tēr̲aḷ clearness (PN); tēr̲r̲am assurance (Tolk.), consolation (Tolk.); clearness (Nāl.); thriving; Ma. tēr̲uka to recover, thrive; tēr̲r̲uka tr. to clear, make strong; tēr̲al clearness; Go. tēḍ- to rise, especially from sleep; cf. Kui tija to awake from sleep; cf. To. tēl- (tēd̲-) to slowly recover after swoon. PDr. *tēṯ-; the Go. and To. forms show evidence for separating *ṯ as a suffix, thus yielding *tē-l-, *tē-ṭ-, *tē-ṯ-.]

tēr̲u$^{1}$ (2) to appear, become visible, occur, originate (HariV., Manu.) (probably < to become clear, etc.).

[Ko. tēr- (tēry-) to be visible; cf. tēru; Ta. teri to be seen, perceived.]

615 *-tēr̲u$^{2}$, occurs bound in (kaḍa)-tēr̲u to reach (the end), to perish; to be fulfilled, as a desire; to be finished, be completed (all Bhr. II); (kaḍa)-tēr̲(u)cu/-tērcu to cause to reach (the end), to finish, to fulfill; to destroy, kill.

[Prob. < *cēr-, v.s.v. cēru; Ka. tērisu to cause to reach as an end; Ta. tēr v.i. to mingle, combine; cf. Ta. Ma. Ka. tēr, Te. Tu. tēru car, chariot (< that which goes).]

616 *tēr̲u$^{3}$, occurs as pp. with cūcu to see, e.g., tēr̲i cūcu to look at attentively, closely (Bhr. II).

[Ta. tēr to examine, investigate (Kr̲ḷ.); Ma. tēruka id.]

617 tēlu intr. to be afloat; to swim, bathe (UH); to arise as a result of; to stare upwards (as at death) (Śakunt.); to be settled (Mdn.).

[Ka. tēl to be afloat; stare upwards as at death; tēku, teṅku to float, swim; tekku cause to float; Tu. tēluni to float; Ta. teṅku to rise to the brim; to stay, stagnate (Kamp.); Pj. tēl- to float; tev- (scum) to rise on the surface. PSDr. and PCDr. tē-l/ḷ < PDr. *tev-iḷ/-aḷ; PSDr. tēṅk- < *tev-ṅk-; cf. Kui tlēpa (tlēt-) (water) to stand in depression.]

618 toṅgu intr. to bend, recline (Bhr. I); to lie down; with -uṇḍu (to be) toṅguṇḍu to sleep (Kāḷa.); toṅgi cūcu to peep (Mdn.); cf. toṅgali pendent, falling.

[Ka. toṅku, toṅgu to stoop, hang down; Ta. toṅku to hang down, hang, be suspended; toṅkal hanging (Cīv.); Ma. toṅkuka to hang, be pendent; toṅṅal hanging; Mlt. tonq- to bend, knees, etc.; tonqro bent; cf. Kur. tolong adj. hanging down to heels, loose ends of loin cloth; PDr. *tonk-.]

619 toṭṭu[1]* intr. to be joined, to come in contact with, put on, hold (Mārk.), to commence (governs the accusative) (Bhr. I).

[Ka. tuḍu, toḍu (toṭṭ-) to join, put on; Tu. toṭṭuni tr. to embrace, hug, hold fast; Ko. toṛv- (toṛd-) to put arms around; Ta. toṭu to put on (Kalit.); to begin (Kamp.); toṭṭu touching; concerning, beginning with; Ma. toṭukka to put together; commence a work; < PDr. *toṭ-; further, v. s. v. toḍāgu, toḍu, toḍuku, toḍugu.]

620 toṭṭu[2]* intr. to ooze, flow (Bhr. III, Bhōj.); to spread, extend (Vasu.); with -konu (refl.) to spread, extend.

[Ka. toṭṭu a drop; Ta. coṭṭu intr. to fall in drops, drizzle (Tēv.); n. drop; Kui sṛohpa v. i. to issue from; Go. cōḍ-cōḍ (saṛ-) (to drip slowly) drop by drop; < PSDr. and PCDr. *coṭ-/*toṭ-.]

toḍāku* intr. (tongue) to slip (Dvi.H.); to drop, drip (late, rare), v. s. v. tonāku, tolāku.

621 toḍāgu* (also toṇāgu, Naiṣ.) to undertake, begin, commence (Bhr. I, II); intr. to begin with (Bhr. III).

[Ka. toḍaku, toḍagu to engage in; tr. to undertake, commence; toḍaṅku to be begun, begin; toḍavu the beginning; Tu. toḍaguni v. i. to begin, undertake; toḍagelu̥ commencement; To. toḍ- (toḍy-) to have the ability or strength to; Ta. toṭaṅku v. i. to begin (Aiṅk.); to undertake; toṭu tr. to begin; Ma. tuṭaṅṅuka to begin; toṭuka tr. to commence; Kui ṭōṇḍa to begin; cf. Brah. durr- to dare, venture. PDr. *toṇṭ-/*toṭṭ-, PSDr. toṭ-V-, toṭaṅk-.]

622 toḍayu* III tr. to wipe; to wash (Bhr. II); to scrub (KS); to stroke gently with the hand, pat (Bhr. II); to wipe off, destroy (Kāś.).

[Ka. toḍe to smear, rub on, apply; wipe, remove, efface; Tu. toḍepuni tr. to anoint, smear, rub; Ta. tuṭai to wipe, scrub (PN), to polish (Kalit.), rub, apply; sweep, brush, dispel (Kṟḷ.), ruin (Tiruvāc.); toṭai to wipe, wipe off, dust (late); tuṭu to wash, as clothes; Ma. tuṭekka to wipe, rub off; Kui tuhpa to cast away, throw off (< *tusp-). PSDr. and PCDr. *tuṭ-, PSDr. *toṭay- < *tuṭay-; v. s. v. tuḍucu.]

623 toḍaru[1]* (1) intr. to attack, confront in battle (Bhr. I).

[Ka. toḍar to meet, fall in with; tōṭi a conflict, fight; Ta. toṭar tr. to assail, attack.]

toḍaru[1]* (2) tr. to follow, accompany, pursue (Bhr. I, II); to reach, obtain, copulate with (late); to hold (Bhg.).

[Ka. toḍar, toḍru to be linked to; Ta. toṭar v. i. to follow uninterruptedly (Patir̲.); tr. to pursue (Kamp.), to seize (Pu.Ve.); to be near, close to; n. following, succession; cf. tuṭu to come in contact with, be joined; to begin; Ma. tuṭaruka to pursue; tuṭarccu continuation.]

toḍaru[1]* (3) tr. to undertake (Bhr. III).

[Ma. tuṭaruka to undertake, v. s. v. toḍāgu. All (1) to (3) from PDr. *toṭ-, sometimes alternating with *tuṭ-, o/u on account of the following retroflex stop.]

624 toḍiyu* III intr. (arrows, etc.) to be fixed, to pierce (a single usage cited from a post-classical text); v. s. v. toḍu, toḍugu.

625 toḍu* tr. to put on, wear (clothes, etc.), to put arrow on bow (Bhr. II).

[Ka. tuḍu, toḍu id.; tuḍisu, toḍisu id.; Ta. toṭu (toṭṭ-) to put on, as clothes, ring, etc. (Kalit.); (toṭutt-) id.; to fix an arrow; tuṭu (tuṭṭ-) to put on; Nk. toṛ- (toṭṭ-) wear shirt, etc.; KGad. tuṭṭ- to wear, as a caste-mark, etc.; Kuvi (S) turh'- to wear; PDr. *toṭ-/ *tuṭ-, also v. s. v. toḍugu.]

626 toḍuku* tr. to hold, grasp (late); toḍik-ilu to seize, hold tightly, snatch (JBh., BP).

[Ka. tuḍuku, tuḍuṅku to seize quickly; Tu. toṭṭuni to embrace, hug; Ko. toṛv- (toṛd-) to put arms around; Kod. toḍu (toṭṭ-) to feel; Ta. toṭu (toṭṭ-) to handle, besiege; Ma. toṭuka to touch, handle; Pj. ṭoḍ- (ṭoṭṭ-) to touch; Kur toṛs$^{o}$g- (tuṛsgy-) to touch slightly with the foot; Brah. tor-, ton- to hold (imp. to, tor); PDr. *toṭ-.]

627 toḍ(u)gu (also toḍ(u)vu) tr. to wear, put on, as clothes, etc. (Bhr. II), put an arrow on the bow. (Bhr.I); to dress others (Naiṣ.); n. an ornament, armor, etc. (JBh.); toḍupu a cover, roof, scabbard (lex.); toḍavu a jewel, an ornament (Bhr. II).

[Tu. toḍigè clothes, dress; Ka. toḍige, tuḍige certain clothing, ornament; KGad. toḍg- to wear clothes, etc.; other forms v. s. v. toḍu, also cf. Kolami, Vocab. 938.]

toḍ(u)vu same as toḍugu, q. v. (Bhr. I, II).

628 tonāku intr. (water) to spill, overflow (Vasu.); n. trembling (in fear) (Bhr. II).

[Ka. tuṇuku, tuṇaku v. i. to be agitated, to shake (loc.); cf. Kur. tund- tr. to spill, pour into; tundr- be poured into; Mlt. tund- to spill, shed, throw out, as water. PDr. *tuḷ-/*tuṇ-, v. s. v. tolāku[1].]

629 torãgu[1] intr. to drop, fall (Bhr. I), to be shed, as flowers (Bhr. I), to ooze, flow down (Bhr. II), to rain (Dvi.H.).

[Ka. suri (< *cori) to flow, rain, pour down; tr. to pour out; sōr to drip, trickle, flow as water drops; to leak; n. dripping, leaking; Tu. sōruni, tōruni to leak, ooze, run; sōrtè, tōru oozing, leaking; Ko. corv- (cord-) (milk) streams from udder; jōr- to run in streams (of tears, etc.); To. twar- (twarθ-) (buffalo) to be ready for milking; Ta. cori v. i. to flow down, rain; tr. to shed, as leaves, pour out; cura to spring forth, gush, flow (Kamp.); tr. to pour forth (Cilap.); Ma. coriyuka to flow down; curakka (milk) to gush; Kui tōṛa to flow, trickle; Kuvi (F) tṛōkh- to drop; Go. tōr- to pour water into a vessel; Kuvi (F) torg- to fall; Pj. cōṛ- to trickle; cōrp- (cōrt-) to strain off water from boiled rice; KGad. cōr- to pour (of water, etc.); cf. Kur. curkh- v. i. to leak, ooze, fall in drops; Mlt. curg- id.; Brah. trump n. drop of water; curr- to flow, gush. PDr. *cōr-/tōr- : *cor-V-, *tor-V-.]

torãgu[2] to abandon, give up (late); later form of toṟãgu, q. v.

630 toralu* to meet, join, meet in battle (RR), v. s. v. dorayu.

torũgu (var. of torãgu, q. v.) to fall, drop, to flow down (UH).

631 toṟãgu[1*] tr. to abandon, quit, give up, renounce (Bhr. II, Naiṣ.); n. separation (UH).

[Ka. toṟe to abandon, quit, renounce, give up; toṟavi abandoning; Tu. torepuni to abandon; torelu̥ abandonment; Ta. tuṟa tr. to renounce worldly pleasures (Nāl.), relinquish (Kalit.), leave, quit; Kui tuhpa (< *tusp-) to leave, abandon; < PSDr. and PCDr. *tuṟ-.]

toṟãgu[2*] intr. to ooze, drop, flow down (same as torãgu[1], confusion between r and ṟ).

632 tolãku[1] intr. to spill, scatter, as water (KS), overflow (Bhr. II); to spread, increase (Kaḷā.); n. shaking; a wave (Āmu.).

[Ka. tuḷaku v. i. to spill, be scattered in drops; tuḷuku, tuḷuṅku tr. to agitate; Ta. tuḷaṅku v. i. to shake (Kalit.); be perturbed (Maṇi.); tuḷakku tr.; tuḷi v. i. to drip, trickle, to rain (Akan.); tr. to sprinkle; n. rain; tuḷumpu to be agitated, to shake, overflow; Ma. tuḷaṅṅuka to be shaken; tuḷumpuka to fluctuate; tuḷi a drop; tuḷikka to drip; Pj. tolk- v. i. to spill; tolc- to spill (water out of pot); cf. Tu. tuḷukuni tr. to loosen. PSDr. and PCDr. *tuḷ-, v. s. v. toḍãku, tonãku, truḷḷu/tuḷḷu.]

633 tolãku[2*] to shine, be splendid (Vasu., Kaḷā.).

[Ka. toḷagu to shine, be full of splendor; toḷapu shining, luster; Ta. tuḷaṅku to shine, be bright (Tēv.); tuḷumpu to sparkle; Ma. tuḷakkam splendor; tuḷakkuka to make bright.]

634 tolãgu (imperative 2pl. tolãḍu, freely alternating with tolãgūḍu) intr. to be removed (Bhr. I), step aside (Bhr. II); to retreat, recede, vanish (Bhr. II); to be lost, be made extinct (Bhr. II); to fail (Bhr. I); tr. to abandon, give up, lose (HariV.); tr. tolãcu to remove (late).

[Ka. tolagu, tolaṅgu to go away, aside; to fail, be excluded; Tu. tolguni to depart, move away, leave; Ko. tolg- to be released from debt; tolk- to release from debt; Ta. tolai to become extinct (Patiṟ.), to depart for good, be lost (PN); tr. to destroy, spend (Cilap.), remove, finish; tolaiccu to destroy, exhaust (PN); pay as debt (Perump.); Ma. tuḷayuka intr. to end; tulekka to finish; cf. Kur. dolkh- to deflect from straightness. PSDr. *tol-a-, PDr. *tol-.]

toluku intr. to be spilt, to overflow, to increase (later variant of tolãku).

635 tolãcu[1] IIc to wash, cleanse (Naiṣ.), to scrub in cleaning (Bhōj.), to bathe (late).

[Ka. toḷe, toḷi to wash, remove by washing; Ko. toḷg- to wash (one's hands with tears); cf. Ta. tulakku to clean, cleanse (late, after l < ḷ), polish; Ma. tulakkuka to polish, burnish; Go. tuṛūpst- to rinse out a cup or vessel which has some food at the bottom; cf. Brah. sill- to wash. PDr. *tuḷ-.]

tolãcu[2] IIb tr. of tolãgu, q.v.; late.

636 tol(u)cu IIa tr. to hollow out (Bhr. II); to gore, scoop (UH).

[Ka. toḷe, toḷḷe a hollow, a hole, cavity; joḷḷu emptiness, being pithless or without stuff, etc.; Tu. toḷu adj. empty; tolpuni tr./intr. to prick, open, as a boil', toluvè a hole; Ko. toyḷ- (toḷc-) to pierce; To. tūḷy- (tūḷc-) to make a hole in stone or tree; Ta. toḷai to perforate (Kamp.); n. hole; tuḷai to make a hole; n. aperture (Akan.); toḷkal, toḷḷai id.; Ma. tuḷekka to bore; tuḷayuka to be bored; cf. Ta. toṭu to dig, scoop out (PN), pierce through (-ṭ- < -ḷ-); Go. tull- to be bored or pierced; tulhutt- tr. to bore, etc.; Mlt. tuṉḍa, tuṉḍra hollow of a bamboo or bridge, a tube, tunnel; cf. Kui trupka to pierce; truspa make a breach; Kuvi (F) tūth- to bore; PDr. *toḷ-.]

637 tõgu* intr. to become wet, be soaked (Bhr. II); to bathe, sink in water (Bhōj.); tr. tõcu to sink, bathe, dip in (HariV.).

[Ka. tō, tōyu, toyyu be or become moist (pp. tōdu); to be dipped; Tu. toipuni to wash, as clothes; Ko. tōy- (tōc-) to wash clean (a cloth); To. twīy- (twīc-) to wash; Ta. tòy v.i. to bathe in cold water, be soaked; tr. dip, soak; tuvai to be dipped, moistened;

tr. to dip, soak; toyyil cultivated moist land; toyaḷi a washer woman; Ma. tōyuka to dip, soak; tōyttuka to dip in; tuvekka to steep; Kui jōga to wash clothes; dōpa (dōt-) to plunge into; cf. Kuvi (S) jū- (jutt-) to soak; Go. sū-sū a little wet (of clothes, etc.); Mlt. ḍuṉg- to be drowning, be dipped, lost; Brah. cōsh- to wash by rubbing. PDr. *tō̆y-/*tō- < *cō̆y-/*cō-; v. s. v. torāgu, Ta. cōr-, etc. (> l. w. Skt. toya- n. water, see Burrow, DS VII, No. 169).]

638 tō̆ḍu to pull or draw up or out, scoop out (Bhīm.), ladle out, bale out (Mdn.); der. n. tō̆ṭa a garden.

[Ka. tōḍu to take water out, dig out, excavate; Tu. tōḍuni to dig, burrow; toḷu a hole; adj. empty; tolluni to pluck out, as hair, etc.; Ko. tōḍ- (tōj-) dig a deep hole; To. twīṟ- to dig with fingers; Ta. tōṇṭu to dig, scoop out, draw or fetch (Perump.); tōḷ, tōḷḷu (tōṭṭ-) to perforate (Kṟḷ.); dig out, scoop; remove; Ma. tōṇṭuka to scoop out, draw aside; toḷḷi cavity; Pj. ṭōḍ- to draw water from well; KGad. tōnḍ- to bale out, as water; cf. Kui ṭuṭa a garden; < PSDr. and PCDr. *tōṇ-ṭ- < *tōḷ-nt-, or *tōḷ-/*tōṇ- + t, v. s. v. tol(u)cu.]

tō̆cu[1] IIb tr. of tō̆gu, q. v.

639 tō̆cu[2] IIc to appear, seem, be manifest (Bhr. II), to occur to mind (Bhr. II), to be born, originate (Bhr. II), to arise, as feelings; der. n. tō̆pu manifestation, appearance (Bhr. II).

[Ka. tōṟ, tōṟu to appear, be visible, to occur; tōcu to cause one's self to appear, to occur to; tōcike appearing; Tu. tōjuni, sōjuni to appear; Ko. tōr- id.; tōg- (intuition) comes to person; To. twīṯ- to be foreseen; twīṟ- to be visible; Ta. tōṉṟu to be visible, come to mind (Nāl.); to be born; to exist (Kṟḷ.); tōṟṟu to cause to appear; tōṟṟam appearance (Kamp.), origin, beginning (Maṇi.); tōṉṟal id. (Maturai.); Ma. tōnnuka to appear, come to mind; spring up; tōṟṟuka to produce; tōnnal imagination; Kui tōnja, tōmba to appear; tōspa (tōst-) to show; Kuvi (S) tōnj- to seem; ? tuh'- to manifest; Kuvi (F) tōss- to show; Pj. tōnd- to appear, be got; ṭōṭip- (ṭōṭit-) to show; Oll. tōnḍ- to appear; Klm. tōt- (neg. stem of an obsolete root) to be not, see Kolami, §5.66. PSDr. and PCDr. *tōn-ṯ-; pre-Telugu *tōn-c-.]

640 tōmu tr. to scrub, clean, polish (Krīḍ., Hara.; also Mdn.); n. tōmuḍu scrubbing (Mdn.).

[KGad. dōm- to rub and wash; < *tō̆y-mp-, v. s. v. tō̆gu.]

641 tōlu tr. to drive, as a chariot, etc. (Bhr. II), to chase, drive away (Bhīm.), to dispel, as sins (Bhg.).

[Ta. tōl (tōr̲r̲-) to be defeated, to yield; tolai to be defeated; Ma. tōlka to be defeated; Ka. sōl id.; Tu. sōpuni id.; sōla defeat, failure; v. s. v. tolãgu, trōlu.]

642 traccu* IId tr. to churn (Bhr. II), to produce fire by rubbing two pieces of wood, etc. together (Bhr. II, Manu.), to plane wood, etc. into artistic shapes (HariV.), to rub, sharpen; (< *tar-c-); n. traccana churning (late).

[V. s. v. tarucu.]

643 travvu* (> Mdn. tavvu) to dig, excavate (HariV.), to rout (UH), to bring to recollection (Bhr. II), publicize, bring up a matter in conversation (Naiṣ.); der. n. travv-aṭamu digging (Kaḷā.).

[Kui tāṛa to burrow, scratch or dig out, excavate; Go. taṛ- to dig, scratch up, as pigs, etc.; tarr- to root up; Kur. caṛ- (caḍḍ-) to root, root up, pull out; destroy; < PDr. *caṭ-/*taṭ-.]

644 trāgu* (alt. trāvu; > Mdn. tāgu) tr. to drink, as water, etc. (UH), to swallow, gulp, eat (KS); to smoke (Mdn.); trāguḍu (trāvuḍu) n. drinking (Āmu.); drinking liquor (Mdn.); (< *tar-av-).

[Pj. tār- to swallow; KGad. sark- (ox) to drink water in the tank; Ta. ār to eat, drink (PN) (< *cār-); ārvu eating and drinking. PDr. *cār- : *tār, PSDr. *tār-, ār; cf. Mlt. sorkey- to suck.]

645 trikku* intr. to remain, be left over (Bhr. II).

[Ma. tirikka to separate, distinguish; Ta. tiri tr. to leave (Cīv.); prob. connected with etyma under tirugu, q. v.]

trippu* (tr. of tirugu, q. v.; > Mdn. tippu) to turn, change the direction (Vikram.), to revolve as a weapon (Prabhā.); to fan (Naiṣ.), to make to retreat; n. turning (Dvi.H.), revolving (Bhr. II), twist, difficulty (Bhr. II).

[Ka. tirumpu to cause to go round, turn; tirupu id.; Tu. tirpuni to twirl round; To. tīrp- to turn key; Ta. tiruppu (tr. of tirumpu) to turn, send back, twist, revolve; Klm.(E) tip-, Nk. tipp-; Kui terpa to wind round and round; Kuvi(F) tip- to turn round. PSDr. *tir-upp-; also v. s. v. tirugu.]

646 trimm-aru* intr. to wander, roam, ramble (Bhr. I); to encircle (Bhr. I); der. n. trimm-aṭa wandering, strolling (Bhr. II), trouble, difficulty (Kaḷā.).

[< *tirm-at̲- or *tir-mat̲-; the root is the same as that in tirugu, trippu, q. v.; for the latter element v. s. v. mar̲alu; -ṭ- in the der. n. points to an original *t̲ rather than *r.]

647 truṅgu* intr. to break, fall in pieces (Bhr. II), to perish, die, be destroyed (UH, BhR); tr. truncu to cut or tear into pieces (Bhr. II, Kāś., UH), to kill (Bhr. II); trumpu n. a piece.

[No exact correspondences found; cf. Ka. turuvu to hollow, drill; Ṭu. turuvuni to be bored, perforated; Ta. turuvu id.; n. burrowing, a hole; Kui truṅga, trūva to be pierced; trukpa, truspa to make breach, to pierce; Kuvi (S) turp- to oppress; Mlt. tuṛgr- to be broken; Kur. tuṛukh- to strip, denude; Brah. trukk- to pluck off, strip. Alternatively, may be a hypercorrection of tunugu, tuncu, q. v.]

truncu* IIb tr. of trungu, q. v.

648 truḷḷu* (Mdn. tuḷḷu) to jump, frisk (Bhr. II), be vain, arrogant (Bhr. II); n. vanity (Bhr. II), a jump, leap, conceit.

[Ka. tuḷḷu to frisk, leap; Tu. tuḷḷuni id.; Ta. tuḷḷu to frisk (Nāl.), be haughty, arrogant; n. leap, arrogance; tuḷḷal frisking, leaping (Kalit.); cf. tuṭi be rude, roguish; tuṭippu pride, arrogance; Ma. tuḷḷuka to frisk, leap, jump; tuḷḷal jumping, etc.; PSDr. *tuḷ-. This is a clear case of hyper-standardization in Telugu by introducing an r in the form. The evidence of Tamil is clinching on account of the occurrence of tuḷḷu in a Sangam text.]

649 tregu*, v. s. v. treyyu.

[A contaminated form of tegu and treyyu, q. v.; no literary usages cited.]

trencu* IIb (tr. of treyyu, q. v.), Mdn. tencu to cut into pieces, kill, slay, tear, divide, break (Bhr. II, UH).

650 treyyu* III intr. to be chopped, cut off (Bhr. II); (< *teṟ-y-).

[Ka. tiṟi (< *teṟi) to cut, cut off; Tu. terpuni to separate; Ta. teṟi v. i. to break, be split, broken (Kamp.); tr. to cut, break; teṟu tr. to bruise, crush (Piṅ.); teṟal ruining (PN); Ma. teṟikka to fly in pieces, cut off; teṟukka to pull up the cloth.]

651 treḷḷu* to fall, fall down (Bhr. I), to be broken, routed (Kāś.), to perish, die; (< *teṟ-ḷ < *teṟ-uḷ).

[Cf. Ta. teṟal ruining (PN); v. s. v. treyyu.]

652 trevvu* intr. to be cut off, be snapped, as a rope, etc. (Bhr. II, Pāṇḍ.); (< *teṟ-v-).

[V. s. v. treyyu.]

653 trēcu* IIc (> Mdn. tēcu) intr. to belch (Bhr. I, Bh.R); der. n. trēpu belching.

[Kuvi (F) dreb- to belch; Go. dēr- a belch; obviously Ta. tēkku to belch, etc. do not belong here on account of the absence of r; but prob. Ta. teṟi to be complete, full (PN).]

trēncu* IId (same as trĕcu) to belch (BP, Naiṣ.); (< *trēn-c-); n. trēnpu a belch.

[*trēn- < *teṟam-; prob. *teṟam- was a noun, made into a verb by the addition of the verbalizing c; or *trēn- or *trēṇ- was the original verb-base from *teṟaṇ/*teṟaḷ, with c added from an original past tense morpheme, cf. īḍcu to drag < *īḻ-.]

654 trokku* (> Mdn. tokku) tr. to trample or tread upon (HariV., Kāś.); intr. to walk, behave (Bhr. II); n. treading upon, pressing with foot (KS, BP); oppression (Bhr. II); (< *toḻ-k-).

[Ka. tuḻi to tread on, crush; be trodden (< *toḻi); Tu. torpuni to kick, tread; torpu a kick; Ma. toḻikka to kick; Kui troju inba to tread on the side of something so as to slip; cf. Ta. uḻakku to trample down, tread upon (Kalit.); < PDr. *coḻ-, *toḻ-; in Ta. loss of *c-.]

655 trōcu* IIa tr. to push out, shove, thrust (Bhr. I, II), to throw off, remove (Bhr. II), to expel (UH); der. n. trōpu pushing, felling (Bhr. I); cf. trōyu (< *tor-ac-).

[Kui trōpa (trŏt-) to press forward with fingers; Ta. tura to drive, as an elephant (PN), disperse, scatter; turattu to drive away, expel, remove, reject; Ma. turattuka to drive away; Pj. turkip- (turkit-) to push, shove; KGad. turus key- (ken-) to push in, shove PDr. ? *tur-a-/*tor-a, PSDr. *tor-a-.]

trōyu* III (> Mdn. tōyu, tōsu) same as trōcu, q. v. (< *tor-ay-) (UH, Bhg., Manu.).

656 trōlu* (> Mdn. tōlu) to chase, pursue (Dvā.), drive away, expel (Kaḷā.); (< *toṟ-al).

[Cf. Tu. torelu̥ abandonment, v. s. v. toṟāgu.]

## D

dakku intr. to accrue, be obtained (Bhr. II), subdue, become under one's control or possession (Bhr. II, Kāś.); to remain, be left over; (< ḍakku).

[V. s. v. ḍakku, takku[1].]

daṅgu* (Śab.R.) intr. to be well-pounded (of rice, grain, etc.); adj. well-pounded; daṅguḍu id.; (< ḍangu, q. v.).

[V. s. v. ḍaṅgu, ḍancu.]

657 daḍiyu III to tremble, to fear (< jaḍiyu). No literary usages cited; also Mdn.; cf. daḍa palpitation, imit. sound of heartbeat in fear or in haste (Dvi.H.).

[Ka. daḍa an imitating sound indicating trembling, quivering, palpitation, or hurry; Tu. daḍadaḍa the noise of fast walking or talking; daḍabaḍa n. hurry; v. s. v. jaḍiyu, aluku[4], talāku, talaru[1]. PDr. *caḷ- > *caṭ-V-.]

daṇḍu (same as taṇḍu, q. v.) to collect money, as of subscription, alms, etc. (late and Mdn.); cf. daṇḍugu, daṇḍuvu penalty, fine (Vijñ., Daśā.).

658 daniyu* III (Śab.R.) tr. to join, to copulate; der. n. danivu copulation (Bhr. II).

[Cf. Ta. ta̱ṉṉu to approach; Ka. ta̱ṟu (taṭt-) to approach, come about, etc.; v. s. v. tanuku[2], danuku.]

659 danuku* (also danku) tr. to get, obtain, reach (Bhr. II, Bhg.), to suffer, experience (HarīV.).

[Usages are not conclusive for initial d-; could be tanuku[2], q. v.]

dancu IIb tr. to crush, smash (Kāś.), to pound with pestle (Daśā.); (< ḍancu, q. v.).

660 dabbu* tr. to tell a lie (late), n. deceit, lying. Cf. dabbaṟa falsehood.

[Tu. ḍabbu a lie, falsehood; a boast, brag; Kui dapa falsehood, lie; adj. false; dape adj. id.; Ta. tappaṟa lie, falsehood, deception; tappal fault, crime (Kuṟun.); Ma. tapra a lie; tappal mistake; v. s. v. tappu.]

661 dā̃ṭu tr. to cross (Dvi.H.), to go beyond, pass over (UH); intr. (drive) to pass, to leap, jump (Bhr. II); n. jumping, crossing over.

[Ka. dāṇṭu, dāṭu, tāṇṭu to jump; to pass, elapse; tāgu to jump, leap over; Tu. dāṇṭuni to cross, ford, pass by; Ko. dāṭ- to cross (stream, mountain, etc.); To. tōṭ- id.; Ta. tāṇṭu v. i. to skip, jump; tr. to leap across, surpass, excel (Piṅ.); n. leap; tāvu v. i. to jump up, leap, skip over (Maturai.); tr. to cross, leap over (Kamp.); n. jumping, leaping; Ma. tāṇṭuka to jump, cross; tāṭṭuka to get over; cāṭuka to leap; cāṭṭam, cāṭṭu leap, jumping; Klm. dāṭ- to cross; Kur. cāṭak̲h̲- to stride, tr. to stride across, jump over; cf. Go. ḍai- to leap, hop (of horses, birds, etc.). PDr. *cāṇṭ-/*cāṭṭ- > *tāṇṭ-/*tāṭṭ-.]

dāyu* III intr./tr. to approach, to go near (KS), to occur, happen (RR); to be joined, to attach oneself to (Naiṣ.); (< ḍāyu, q. v.).

digu intr. to descend, dismount (Hara.), to drop or hang down (Bhg.), to lodge temporarily (Manu.), to occupy a house, etc. (Mdn. Viśākha. dial.); to become reduced, to diminish (UH); (a thorn, etc.) to pierce into foot, etc.; inf. dig-aN- adv. down, e.g., digābaḍu to sink down, diminish (Bhr. II), digamriṅgu to devour, gulp down (Dvi.H.), digābeṭṭu to forsake, to save, digājāṟu to flow down, and so on; cf. diguva the low side, bottom (Bhr. II); (< ḍiggu/ ḍigu, q. v.).

digucu* IIb (tr. of digu, q. v.) to lower, to pierce (Vijñ.).

diggu* (free var. of digu and from older ḍiggu, q. v.) to descend (Mārk.); v. s. v. ḍiggu, digu.

662 diddu tr. to set right, to correct, rectify (Āmu.); to train, discipline (Kaḷā.); to make embellishments, to decorate, to do make-up (late); to erase, rectify (Mdn.); n. correction.

[Ka. tiddu, tirdu to make right, correct; to settle a debt; Tu. tidduni to correct, mend; Ta. tiruttu to rectify (PN), mend; arrange; tiruntu to be correct, perfect, be trained, disciplined; tittu to correct, etc.; l. w. < Ka. or Te.; Ma. tiruttuka to mend, erase; Kuvi (S) did- to reverse; PSDr. *tir-utt-, v. s. v. tirugu.]

dincu IIb tr. of digu, q. v. to cause to descend, get down (late).

[V. s. v. ḍiggu, ḍincu.]

dimpu tr. of digu (Mdn.); also tr. to reduce, diminish, v. s. v. ḍindu.

663 dīṭu* (1) to set right, mend, as hair with fingers, etc. (Nṛs.).

[Ta. tīṭṭu to purify, polish (Piṅ.); tīṟṟu to polish (Kamp.), clean a wall, etc.]

dīṭu* (2) to rub or gnash teeth (RR, Bhg.).

[V. s. v. tīḍu.]

dunu* var. of dunnu, q. v.

664 dunnu (dunu) tr. to plow a field (Āmu.); earlier texts show the form dunu (Bhr. II, Vijñ.); cf. dunna a he-buffalo (Manu.); dukki tillage; (< *ḍu-nn- < *ḻu-nn- < *uḻ-n-); the Te. form presupposes an original *uḻ-un(u).

[Ka. uḻ (uḻt-/utt-) to plow; Tu. ūḍuni id.; ura plowing; Ko. ug- (uṛt-) to plow; To. uṣf- (uṣt-) id.; Ta. uḻu (uḻut-) id.; Ma. uḻuka id.; Klm.(E) ur- (urt-) to harrow, Klm.(SR) ūrr-/urr- to plow; Nk. ur- id.; Pj. uṛ-; Go. uṛ-; Kui ṛūva (ṛūt-); Kuvi (F) ruiyali (rūt-), Kuvi (S) lūnai id.; Kur. uy- (uss-) id.; cf. Pj. ḍukki n. (l. w. < OTe.).]

665 dumuku (also dū̃ku) intr. to leap, jump down (later texts); n. a jump, leap.

[Ka. dumuku, dumiku id.; dumikku, dummikku vb. id.; dum, dhum a sound in imit. of body going or coming down suddenly from above; Tu. dumukuni to jump down, alight quickly.]

duyyu (free var. of dūyu < ḍūyu, q.v.) III intr. (an arrow, etc.) to enter and pass through (Āmu.); to draw out (a sword from scabbard; late); to snap, break, as a thread (HariV.).

dulupu tr. of dullu (< ḍullu, q.v.) to let fall off, to shake off a cloth, etc., to let dust, etc., fall off (Mdn.; no literary usages cited).

dullu (< ḍullu, q.v.) intr. to fall off, as leaves, fruit, etc. from the tree (no literary usages cited).

666 duvvu (< *ḍuvv- < *ul̲-v-) tr. to comb, as hair (Śakunt.); to pass fingers gently over in fondling (Bhg.); also Mdn.; der. n. duvv-ena a comb (Mdn.).

[Ta. ul̲u (fut. ul̲u-v-, past ul̲u-t-) to arrange or adjust, as the hair with the fingers (Cīv.); Pj. uṛ- (Sth. uṛv-) to comb; KGad. uḍuv- id.; Kuvi (F) rūss- to dress (another's hair); rūca a comb; Tu. dūbina a comb; cf. Kui ṛūsa to rub, scrape. PDr. *ul̲u-, *ul̲uv-, v.s.v. ḍūyu/dūyu.]

667 dusuku intr. to slip, slide, as a tied knot, something held in hand, or foot in clay, etc. (late); dusik-ilu id. (Āmu.); onomatopoetic.

[Kur. tus$^{u}$g- (tusgy-) tr. to loosen threads that are knit, to undo a piece of plaited straw, to derange, unsettle; Ka. ḍosak, dosak, tosak an imit. sound used when one's foot treads in mud, clay, etc.; dosakk-ane id.]

668 dū̃ṭu$^{1*}$ to peck at (Āmu.); (calf) to butt against the udder of the cow while sucking (Bhg.); to thrust, push (late); n. a thrust, butting, push (late); cf. dūḍa a calf.

[Ka. dūḍu to push, thrust, shove away; Tu. dūḍuni id.; Ta. tūṇṭu to pound, push, force forward, to excite, instigate (late).]

669 dū̃ṭu$^{2*}$ intr./tr. to jump over (Kāś.); run away (late).

[Ka. dūṭu to hop, bound; dūṇṭu to walk on one leg, hop; rock; dūṇṭu n. having uneven legs; unevenness.]

dū̃ku to jump (Daśā.); der. n. dū̃kuḍu jumping, rush.

[V. s. v. dumuku.]

dūyu III (same as duyyu; < *ḍūyu, q.v.) to enter and pass through, as an arrow, etc.; to strip off leaves; to bruise by pressure, as something tied tight to body (late); to form a hole (Bhg.).

670 dūr̲u* tr. to reproach, blame, censure (Bhr. II, BhR); n. reproach, censure (Bhr. II, Nirv.).

[Ka. dūr̲u to blame, abuse, etc.; n. blame; Tu. dūruni to accuse, blame, censure; n. id.; Ta. tūr̲u to slander (loc.); n. calumny, evil (late); tūr̲r̲u to defame, slander (Kr̲l.); n. slander, abuse; Ma. tūr̲r̲uka to abuse; Mdn. Ma. dūr̲u n. blame, slander; cf. Tu.

tūpuni to blame, abuse. PSDr. *tūṯ-/tūṯṯ-, ultimately *tū + ṯ-; v.s.v. *tūru².]

671 deṅgu tr. to copulate (late); n. copulation (Krīḍ.; also Mdn., but obscene); n. scolding, chiding (colloq., sub-standard).

[Klm.(E) deŋg- id.; Ka. deṅgu sexual union; prob. Klm. Ka. forms are l.ws. from Te. Cf. Ka. tekke embracing; Go. ? ḍing- to become erect (obscene). Cf. Nep. ḍhiṅ, ḍheṅ vulva of a cow; anus (of male or female); vagina; pudenda muliebria of an old woman; a term of abuse.]

deppu (< ḍeppu, q.v.) to taunt, gibe at (late and Mdn.); deppu, deppuḍu n. taunting.

672 dēvu tr. to search and take out (BP); search or grope for anything (in water or other liquid, or from a mass) and take out; to search; intr. (nausea) to be caused in stomach (Mdn.).

[Ma. tēkuka, tēvuka to draw out water, bale out; tēṇṭu, tēṭu to search; Ka. tēku to feel nausea; breathe upwards; Tu. tēpuni to throw water with a bucket or trough, to irrigate; To. tōṟk- to search for; Ta. tēṭu to seek, search for (Tēv.); tēṇṭu id. PSDr. *tē-v-/*te-k-, *tē-ṇṭ-/*tēṭṭ-, v.s.v. cēdu.]

doṅgu* (Śab.R) intr. to hide oneself, crouch like a thief (< *ḍongu, q.v.); cf. doṅga a thief (Manu.).

673 dottu* tr. to hit on the head, beat (late and rare).

dobbu tr. to copulate with; to steal, snatch and take away (all colloq., sub-standard); to push (Rāyalasīma dial.); < drobbu, q.v.

674 doraku intr. to be obtained, to accrue (Āmu.); to occur, happen (BhR); to become possible (Bhg.); to come into hand, be available (also Mdn.); cf. dora-konu to be obtained (Bhr. II), occur, happen (Bhr. I), be or become possible (Bhr. I, II); tr. dorapu to cause to occur (late), cf. dorayu, doṟayu.

[Ka. dore to come or draw near, suit, be obtained, to accrue; dore coming near, gain; dorekoḷ to come near, be obtained; Tu. dorakuni to be obtained, procured, found; doraṅkuni id.; Go. (Maṛia) doroktōr was found (LSI IV, p. 535).]

675 dorayu* III tr. to resemble (Bhr. II), to reach, approach, touch (late); intr. to be comparable (Bhr. II, HariV.), to adhere oneself to (Mārk.); to be suitable (Naiṣ.); to occur, happen.

[Ka. dore to resemble, draw near, suit; n. coming near; resemblance; propriety; cf. Kur. dhurᵘr- v.i. to concur, agree together, match; to happen to meet, fall in; dhur- (dhurc-) v.i. to tally with, fit on; v.s.v. doraku, doṟayu.]

676 doralu[1]* (1) to occur, happen (Molla Rāmāyaṇam, 17th century); doralu[1]* (2) to join, mix with (Kāś.); to accrue (Dvi.H.).
[V. s. v. dorayu, doraku (< *tor-); also cf. toralu.]

677 doralu[2] (> dorlu) intr. to roll, turn over (Āmu.); to fall off, drop as snow (Manu.); fall down, as a child from a raised place; to wallow, roll over (Mdn.); tr. doral(u)cu to cause to roll over.
[Kui troṅga v. i. to roll; tropka (< trok-p-) to roll something over and over; torga to writhe; cf. Kuvi (F) dūṛli-kī- to roll (kī- to do); Ta. curi to whirl round, wrinkle; to lie in circle (Kamp.), whirl; n. whirling, curl (Tiv.); cūr- to revolve; ? < *tor-al-, *tor- occurring in the Kui form, or < *cor-al- < *cur-al-, with t- < *c-.]

doral(u)cu IIb tr. of doralu, q. v.

678 dor̲ayu* III tr. to obtain, reach (Kāś.); to copulate with (Vijñ.); intr. to meet, join (late).
[Cf. Ta. tun̲n̲u to be fitted, joined (Nāl.); tr. to approach (PN), adhere to; to join, undertake (Kr̲ḷ.); to gain, reach (Nāl.); tur̲u tr. to reach, enter; Ma. tur̲a a frequented place. PDr. *tut̲-/*tun-, v. s. v. dorayu, doraku.]

dol(u)cu[1]* IIb tr. of dollu < ḍollu tr. to cause to roll over (Bhr. I); v. s. v. ḍollu.

679 dol(u)cu[2]* IIa tr. to make a hole (HariV.).
[Tu. doḷpuni id.; v. s. v. tolucu.]

dolupu* tr. of dollu, q. v.; another form of dolucu[1].

dollu (< ḍollu, q. v.) intr. to roll over, etc. (late); tr. dolucu, q. v.

dõku[1]* (< ḍoṅku, q. v.) intr. (water) to sink down (Śakunt.; rare).

dõku[2] same as ḍõku[1], q. v.
[Tu. dōguni to grub up grass.]

dõgu[1] (< ḍõgu, q. v.) to crawl on all fours, as an infant (ŚivaR.).
[Tu. dōguni to crawl on hands and knees or in a sitting position.]

680 dõgu[2]* intr. to enter into; make a passage in the wall; cf. dõpu.

681 dõgu[3]* (Dh.M.) to become wet, v. s. v. tõgu.

682 dõgu[4]* (skin) to be peeled off (late), cf. dõku[2].

683 dõṭu* (Śab.R.) tr. to give (cited as colloquial usage, not known to the author).

684 dõcu IId tr. to pillage, plunder (HariV.); rob (Kāḷa.); take away by force (BhR); der. n. dõpu plundering, pillage (Vēm., Āmu.).
[Ka. dōcu to plunder; Kuvi (S) tuh- or tuha tūh'- id.]

685 dõpu to tuck in, as a loin cloth, or as flowers in braid (Dvi.H., Manu.).

[Kui dōpa (dōt-) to put within, insert, plunge into; cf. Kur. job- to thrust so as to penetrate; also v. s. v. cōpu.]

686 dōru* (Śab.R.) to perish, die (late); (head) to reel; to fall, incline; tr. dōr(u)cu to move head to and fro (Bhr. II), to fell (KS).

[Cf. Ka. jōl to hang down, to droop, become downcast; Ta. cōr v. i. to fall, drop; to die (Cilap.), see s. v. cokku.]

dōr(u)cu* IIb tr. of dōru, q. v.

687 drobbu* tr. to push, thrust (BhR), to fell (Bhg., Āmu.); n. pushing out, expelling (Bhg.).

[(< *tor-b- < *tor-upp-/-uv-; v. s. v. trōcu, trōyu; but the following are confusing: Ka. ḍobbu, dobbu to shove, push, thrust; Tu. dobbuni id.]

## N

688 nakku intr. to hide oneself, to crouch, lie in wait (Dvā.).

[Ka. nakku id.; ? l. w. < Te.; there are two possible explanations: (1) that this is a back formation from nakka a jackal (< *nar-kaḷ) with k annexed from an original plural suffix; (2) < *naḻ-k-, cf. Ta. naḻukku v. i. to evade, slip away; naḻuvu v. i. to steal or skulk away, escape; ? Klm.(E) naḍ-i- intr. to hide, (tiger) crouches; Klm.(SR) naḍas- id.]

689 nagu* intr. to laugh, to laugh at (Bhr. I); der. n. nagavu/navvu laughter, jocular remark (Bhr. II, III, BhR); adj. surprising, ridiculous; cf. navvu.

[Ka. nagu, nage (nakk-) to laugh, smile, laugh at; nage n. laugh, derision; Tu. nakeruni to tittle, giggle; nakali n. ridicule, satire; adj. spurious; Ta. naku (nakk-) to laugh, smile (Kṟḷ.), to shine, blossom; tr. to despise (Tirikaṭu.); nakai intr./tr. id.; naku n. laughter, smile, grinning; KGad. nagg- to laugh; Pj. nav- to laugh; Brah. mak̲h̲- id. PDr. *nav-/*nak-V-, v. s. v. navvu; Burrow connects this set with words meaning chin, etc., Ta. namuṭu lower lip, etc., see The Parji Language, s. v. nav-.]

690 naggu* intr. to be powdered (BP; a single usage available); cf. nakku a piece, chip (BP); najju that dimpled, crushed; a piece.

[Ka. naggu, nakku to become bruised, as a metal vessel; neggu to crush, smash, destroy; neggu/nekku to get a bruise; Tu. narguni to be crushed, bruised; naggu̥ stunted; Ko. nag- to become dented; nagc- to dent; Ta. ñeri v. i. to break, be crushed; n. broken piece

(Naṉ.); naruṅku v.i. to be crushed, smashed; be deficient in growth; neri v.i. to be crushed; to crack (Tēv.); tr. to crush; n. crack, bruise; Ma. ñeriyuka, neriyuka to be crushed; ñerikka to smash; ñeruṅṅuka to be pressed; Go. nāṛ a crack in a pot; see Burrow, DS V, p. 605. PDr. *ñār-/*ñēr- : *ñar-V-/*ñer-V-; > PSDr. *ñar-i-/*ñer-i-, *ñar-uṅk-/*ñer-uṅk- > *nar-uṅk-/*ner-uṅk-.]

691 naṅgu to speak with a twang, speak through the nose (colloq.); adj./n. naṅgi speaking with twang (in the author's dialect, this verb is always used as a noun or adjective); v.s.v. nattu.

692 naccu[1] to be agreeable, be lovable (Mārk.); to be trusted (Nirv.); tr. to confide in, trust (Bhr. II), to like, (mind) to be attached (Bhg.); v.s.v. nammu, *accu[2].

[Ka. naccu, neccu to confide in; to desire, love; n. confidence, desire, love; (narcu is analogical on the basis of many forms related through the alternation rc > cc, cf. meccu; nanasu given by Kittel does not belong here, cf. Ta. naṉṟu [< PDr. *nal-, *nan-] ); Ko. nac- to like (governs dative); Ta. nacai to love (Kṟḷ.), to desire (Maṇi.); n. desire, hope; naccu to long for, love (Kṟḷ.); n. liking; naya (naya-nt-) to long for (Kṟḷ.); be glad, rejoice (PN), be agreeable; nayam desire; tenderness (Kalit.); nampu to long for; trust in; Ma. nayam gentleness; nampuka to confide, desire; Ka. naya pleasantness, fineness; Tu. naya id.; nase soft, gentle; Te. nayamu liking (Nirv.), excellence; cf. Go. nēm- to obey instruction regarding diet, etc.; nacc- < *nay-cc-, PDr. *nay-/*ney-, v.s.v. nammu.]

693 naccu[2]* tr. to tease, trouble (late); n. troubling, adj. troublesome (Mdn.; Śab.R.); naccukāḍu, naccukuppa, naccugoṭṭu a troublesome person (Śab.R.); naccu slowness, procrastination (author's dialect).

[Ta. naccu tr. to trouble, harass; n. trouble, worry (colloq.); ? cf. nai to crush, destroy (PN).]

694 naccu[3] tr. to move a piece in a game (only in Sankaranarayana's Dict.; not found in SAN, Dh.M.); see nappu[2]

695 naṭṭu intr. to be hindered, stopped, as of progress in movement, etc.; n. hindrance, that which blocks; delay (colloq.).

696 naḍacu IIa intr. to walk, go, pass, proceed (Bhr. II, Kāś.), to behave (Bhr. II, Hara.); (an action) to prevail or progress (Bhr. II), continue, be in effect; tr. naḍapu to let pass, proceed (Bhr. II), make to prevail (Bhr. II), to nourish, bring up (Bhr. I), to run, drive (Mdn.); der. n. naḍa, naḍaka walk, gait (Bhr. II); naḍata

behavior, means of living (late); naḍa adj. walking (Bhr. II); naḍava a way, corridor.

[Ka. naḍe, naḍi to walk, be current, succeed; n. walking; Tu. naḍapuni to walk, behave; naḍake walking; gait; Ko. naṛv- (naṛd-) to walk, proceed, happen; naṛt- tr. make to walk; To. naṛ- (naṛθ-) to walk; naḍt- to conduct; naṛt- to make to walk; Ta. naṭa to walk, pass (Nāl.); to behave, happen; naṭattu tr. to lead, cause to walk; naṭai walk (Nāl.), way, gait; naṭappu behavior; Ma. naṭakka to walk, succeed, behave; tr. carry on work; naṭa, naṭaccu n. walking; naṭattuka to drive, arrange; Kui ḍṛāpa (ḍṛā-t-) vb. to step over, overflow; n. a step, threshold (< *nṛā- < *naṭa-); Klm.(E) aḍg- to walk; Nk. aṛg- id.; Brah. narr- to run away, flee; PDr. *naṭ-a-.]

naḍapu tr. of naḍacu, q. v.

697 naḍūku* intr. to shake, tremble from fear (Bhr. I, II); to fear, shrink (Bhr. II, Naiṣ.); n. trembling, fear (Mdn., Śab.R.).

[Ka. naḍugu to tremble, shake; naḍuka trembling; naḍa tremblingly; Tu. naḍuguni to tremble, quake, totter, shiver; Ko. naṛg- v. i. to shake from cold or fright; To. noḏx- (noḏxy-) to tremble; Ta. naṭuṅku v. i. to shake, quiver, nod head (PN), shake through fear (Maṇi.); naṭukku v. i. id.; tr. to shake; naṭuṅku/naṭukku trembling (PN); naṭunaṭuṅku to tremble greatly (Cīv.); Ma. naṭuṅṅuka v. i. to tremble; naṭukkuka tr.; naṭukkam tremor; naṭam dancing; cf. ñaḷuṅṅuka to shake from damp, fear; Tu. nalikĕ dancing, jumping; Kur. nal- to dance, jump about, move frequently. PSDr. *naṭ-; ? PDr. *ñaḷ-/*ñaṭ-V-; if the etyma meaning 'cold' are separated (see Burrow, DS V, p. 606), we get only *naṭ- for PSDr.; but if the Kur. word belongs here, the Ma. form should be taken as the basis for reconstruction on account of *ḷ.]

naḍucu var. of naḍacu, q. v. (Daśā., Naiṣ.).

naḍupu tr. of naḍucu, q. v. (Vijñ.).

698 nattu to stammer, stutter (no literary usages cited; Mdn.); natti stammering.

[Ka. nattu, nettu to stammer, stutter; Tu. nattiṅge a man partially dumb; Ma. nattuka, nettuka to stammer; prob. *naytt-/*neytt- on account of a/e alternation.]

699 nanayu* III intr. to flower, sprout (rare, so says Śab.R.), v. s. v. nanucu.

700 nanucu[1]* IId intr. to blossom, to sprout (Naiṣ.), to flourish (RR); to arise, appear (Pāṇḍ.); nan(u)pu tr. to cause to blossom (Daśā.);

adj. excessive (Naiṣ.); n. nana a flower (Bhr. II), a sprout (Āmu.), cf. nanalettu to sprout; ṅanabōḍi a damsel (tender-bodied); nanuvu beauty, elegance (RR).

[Ka. nane to bud; n. a flower, bud; Ta. naṉai to bud (Aiṅk.), to appear; n. flower bud (Naṟ.); nāṉam fragrant substance, perfumed oil (Piṅ.); cf. nāṟu to emit sweet smell, give forth perfume (Tēv.), appear, arise, to sprout; Mlt. nan-nanki anew, afresh; Ka. Ma. naṟu fragrance, odor; Ma. nāṟu to yield a smell; Tu. nāduni id.; Ko. nār- to smell bad; Ta. naṟavu fragrance, odor (Nāl.). PDr. *nān-/*nāṯ- : *nan-V-/*naṯ-V-.]

701 nanucu[2*] IId tr. to like, love, be fond of (BhR, Bhīm.); cf. nan(u)pu adj. n. loving, love (KS, Daś.); agreeableness, pleasantness; nanuvu agreeableness (Bhīm.).

[Ka. naṇpu, neṇpu friendship, affection, love, intimacy; naṇpu delightfulness, charm, agreeability; naṇṭu friendship; naṇṭa, neṇṭa a friend; Ta. naṇpu n. love, attachment (Tiruvāc.), friendship (Kṟḷ.); naṇpaṉ lover (Cīv.), friend (Piṅ.); naṇmai proximity (PN); naṇuku, naṇuṅku to become attached (Tiruvāc.); naḷ, naḷḷu (naṭṭ-) tr. to befriend (Kṟḷ.); to like, accept (Kamp.); naḷivu attachment (Kalit.); Ma. naṇṇuka to remember with love and gratitude; cf. KGad. nənn- to enter (< *to be close). PDr. *naṇ-/*naḷ-; a/e in Ka. is probably analogical; the kinship terms from *naṇ- may belong here, cf. Kui Go. Kur. Mlt., etc.]

nancu free var. of nanju, q.v.

702 nanju tr. to eat in small bits, as a relish to the principal food (Bhr. II); take a lick; nanjukonu, nancukonu id.; n. nanjuḍu a relish, pickle, etc.

[Ka. nañju, nañcu to take a little lick; prob. from *nā-, v.s.v. nāku to lick, q.v.]

703 nappu[1] intr. to suit, to fit in size, etc. (colloq. Viśākha. dial.), probably related to naccu, q.v.

704 nappu[2] tr. to move a piece in a game (not found in SAN, Dh.M., given in Śab.R. and Sankaranarayana's Dict.).

705 namalu tr. to chew, chew and eat (KS, Bhr. II); to masticate, munch.

[Ka. namalu, nevaru id.; n. chewing the cud; Tu. nauntuni to chew; nauntu chewing, crushing; naumpuni to chew; Ta. namukku to yield under pressure; ñemunku to be pressed, squeezed (Akan.); Ma. ñamuṅṅuka to yield under pressure. PSDr. *ñam-/*ñem- > *nam-/ *nem-.]

706 nammu tr. to confide, believe, trust (Bhr. I); rely on, depend upon; intr. to believe, think, suppose (Mdn.); der. n. namm-iga, namm-ika trust, confidence, belief (Bhr. II, Daśā.).

[Ka. nambu to confide, believe, rely on, suppose; Tu. nambuni, nammuni id.; Ko. namb- id.; To. nob- id.; Ta. nampu to trust, believe, rely on; hope, accept (Tiv.); to desire, long for (PN); n. desire, hope (Tolk.); Ma. nampuka to confide, desire; Kuvi (F) nām-, Kuvi (S) namm-. PSDr. *na-mp- < *nay-mp-, v. s. v. naccu; alternatively < *nan-p-, cf. Ka. nanni truth, certainty; nanasu certainly, truly; Ta. naṉavu truth, reality (Patiṟ.); certainty; a merger likely in Ta. Ma. forms, of *nay-mp- 'to like' and *nan-p- 'to trust.' V. s. v. naccu[1].]

707 narayu, naṛiyu III intr. (hair) to grow gray (RR, Hara.); nara n. grayness of hair, a gray hair (Bhr. I); narapu grayness; narapa- adj. gray (of hair) (Manu.); nerayu (Mdn., dialectally).

[Ka. nara, nere to become gray, as hair; n. grayness, hoary age; Tu. narevuni to grow gray; narĕ grayness, hoariness; Ta. narai to become gray-haired (Tirikaṭu.); to fade, be pale in color; n. gray hair (PN); whiteness (Kuṟun.); Ma. narekka to grow gray; nara grayness; cf. Ta. nārai white stork; nārai-(kkompaṉ) (ox having) white (horns); Ma. ñāra a heron. PSDr. *ñār-/*ñēr- > *nār-/*nēr- : *nar-V- : *ner-V-. Cf. Kuvi (F) thṛāyū-kamb- to become gray-headed (kamb- to become ripe; prob. thṛāyū- hair < *nrā-).]

nariyu III same as narayu, q. v. (Nṛs.).

narku var. of naṟaku, naṟuku, q. v. (Paṇḍ.).

708 naṟaku to cut, hew (UH), chop off, lop off (Bhr. II), to kill; n. a cut, stroke of knife (UH).

[Ta. naṟukku tr. to cut off, chop (Pu.Ve.); n. a piece; narukku tr. to cut into pieces; Ma. naṟukkuka to cut off; n. a bit of palm leaf; Go. nark- to cut wood, etc.; GoM. naṛk- to cut; cf. Mlt. nark- to claw, scratch (PDr. *naṯ-ukk-); cf. forms without the movable *n- : Ka. aṟu be severed; To. aṟf- to cut; Ta. aṟu to be severed; tr. to cut off; Ma. aṟuka to be cut off; aṟukka to cut off; Go. ask- to cut up or divide meat; Kur. aṛya'- tr. to cut (of overgrown grass, etc.); Mlt. asy- (asc-) to chisel. PDr. *naṯ- : *aṯ-.]

naṟuku (also narku) var. of naṟaku, q. v. (Bhr. II, Bhg.).

709 naṟumu* tr. to harass, trouble (Appak.).

[Tu. narpuni, nerpini to be disgusted; narguḍuni to torment; Ta. nari tr. to torture, torment.]

710 nalāgu (1) intr. to fade, wither, diminish, as brightness (Bhr. II); to be crumpled, as flowers, clothes, etc. (Āmu.); be crushed, powdered (Āmu.); nali n. powder (RR); tr. nalācu to crush with hands, crumple (Daś.); to mash together, to kill, destroy (late); nalapu to crumple, as flowers, etc. (KS); to harass (16th cent.); cf. naliyu.

[Ka. nalagu, nalugu to become rumpled, droop as vegetable, etc., to faint, become feeble from sickness; Tu. nalaguni to fade, wither; be reduced from sickness; Ta. nalaṅku to grow faint, to suffer, pine, become crumpled; nalakku to crumple, soil; Kur. nal$^{a}$b- (nalby-) to clean by rubbing a little water on a moist cloth; rub oil, etc. (cf. Te. nalucu id.). PSDr. *nal-aṅk-/*nal-akk-; PDr. *nal-.]

nalāgu (2) intr. to suffer, pine, to be tired (Vi.Pu.; Kaḷā.); tr. nalācu to torture, harass (UH); nali suffering, sickness (Mdn.).

[Ta. nali v.i. to waste, pine away; be in distress (Tiv.); nalivu distress, suffering; Ka. nalavu, naluvu weakness; v.s.v. alāgu, alayu. PDr. *nal-/*al-.]

nalācu IIb tr. of nalāgu.

711 naliyu* III intr. to be crushed (KS); be powdered (Bhr. II); be broken to pieces (UH); nali powder, obtained by crushing (RR); naliguli that which is reduced into bits, fine pieces, powder (Bhr. II), that destroyed.

[V.s.v. nalāgu.]

nalūgu (var. of nalāgu) to be reduced, emaciated (late); nal(ū)guḍu suffering (Vēm., also Mdn.).

nal(u)cu (later var. of nalācu, v.s.v. nalāgu) to crush, shampoo; rub nose, body, etc. (Daśā.); to rub off dirt on body (Mdn.).

nal(u)pu another form of nal(u)cu, q.v. (late).

712 navayu III intr. to suffer, sink in distress (Bhr. I, III); to suffer from sickness, poverty, etc. (Bhr. I, II); der. n. navāta distress, difficulty, sickness (RR).

[Ka. nave, name to wear, fall in flesh, become poor; Tu. nameyuni to wear away; become poor; Ta. namuku to yield under pressure; namai tr. to vex, trouble; Kuvi (F) nabg- to press down; Go. nawī- to grow crooked, of a rheumatic old woman or of damaged hemp. Other Ta. Ma. forms v.s.v. namalu; cf. Ka. nāmbu to be slack, devoid of energy, slothful or idle; Ta. nāmpu to grow lean. PSDr. *nām- : *nam-V-/*nav-V-; alternatively, *ñam-/*ñem-; cf. namalu.]

713 navvu tr. to laugh, smile, laugh at (Bhr. II), to joke, ridicule (Bhr. II); n. laughing, smiling, ridicule (Bhr. II).

[V. s. v. nagu. Three possibilities: (1) PDr. *nav- : *nak-V-; (2) < *nav-iyu with contraction of -iyu > -u doubling the preceding consonant; (3) < *nav-avu < *nak-avu. In the last case navvu (< *nav-avu) is primarily a noun secondarily employed as a verb. More probability for (2) or (3).]

714 nasuku tr. to smile slyly (colloq. Guntur dial.); a secret smile.

715 nasugu intr. to murmur, utter indistinctly; n. murmuring, indistinct utterance.

*nā-* Freely varying allom. of anu before suffixes beginning with a, e.g., inf. an-aN, altern. nā-N, neg. ppl. an-aka, altern. nā-ka, an-aru they would not say, altern. nā-ru; v. s. v. anu.

716 nāku tr. to lick (Dvi.H., Manu.); cf. nanju to take a little lick; nāl(u)ka tongue.

[Ka. nakku, nekku to lick; Tu. nakkuni id.; Ko. nak-, To. nok- id.; Ta. nakku id. (Nāl.); nā, nākku tongue (Kṟḷ.); Ma. nakkuka to lick; Kui nāka id.; Kuvi nāk- id.; Go., GoM. nāk- id.; Pj. nĕk- id.; KGad. nāk- id.; Klm. Nk. nāk- id. PSDr. and PCDr. *nā-k-/*na-kk- Cf. Brah. lakk- to lap like dog; Mlt. naqlu uvula (< *nalq-); for related words meaning tongue, see Burrow, DS IV, p. 337; DS V, p. 604.]

717 nāḍu$^{1*}$ intr. to enter, penetrate, as an arrow (late); cf. āḍu$^{3}$ id.; tr. nār(u)cu to cause to pierce (Āmu.; rare).

[Ka. naḍu, neḍu (naṭṭ-, neṭṭ-) to fix firmly, plant, pierce; Tu. naḍpini, neḍpini id.; naḍiyuni to be planted; Ko. naṛ- (naṭ-) to fix upright in ground; Ta. naṭu (naṭṭ-) to set up, as a pillar (Tēv.), to place; to establish, as fame (Tirikaṭu.); Ma. naṭuka id. PSDr. *ñaṭ-/*ñeṭ- > *naṭ-/*neṭ-; see Burrow, DS V, p. 607; also v. s. v. nā̃ṭu.]

718 nāḍu$^{2*}$ tr. to torment, harass (late).

719 nā̃ṭu (Śab.R. without [˜]; usages cited in SAN from the earliest classics, i.e., Bhr. I, II, are not conclusive for [˜]) tr. to plant, fix, pierce; insert, thrust (Bhr. II, Bhīm.); intr. to be pierced (Bhr. III); (words) to be impressed on mind, to be convinced (Bhr. II); (mind) to settle upon; to be planted; n. a dent, wound (late); transplanting (Mdn.).

[Ka. nāṭu to enter, as a thorn; tr. to fix in ground, to pierce into; n. planting, being deeply entered; Tu. nāṭuni tr. to impress; intr. to take effect, as medicine; Ta. nāṭṭu tr. to fix, plant (Tiruvāc.);

establish rules (Cilap.); Ma. nāṭṭuka to fix in ground, plant. PSDr. *nāṭ- v.i., *nāṭṭ- v.tr. (< *nāṭ-t-; cf. Ka. nā-gal (a rock) that sticks out of ground; also v.s.v. nāḍu$^{1}$).]

720 nā̃cu* IId tr. to take away by force, snatch, steal (Āmu., Daśā.); in earlier texts occurs with refl. -konu, i.e., nā̃c-i konu to steal, take away (Bhr. II, Mārk.); to enchant mind, to subjugate kingdom, etc. (Nirv., Bhr. III); nā̃cikōlu stealing, usurpation, an unjust seizure, enchanting of mind (Bhr. II, III); ā̃cikonu to steal, seize, etc. (HariV., Bhg.).

721 nānu intr. to be soaked, steeped, get wet (BhR, Āmu.); (oil) to sink into the pores of skin (late and Mdn.); tr. nān(u)cu to soak (Āmu.); nān(u)pu id. (Mārk.).

[Ka. nān (nānd-) to get wet, be soaked; nāṟu to moisten; nāndu to make damp; to liquify; Ko. nān- (nānḏ-) to become wet in rain; nāt-, nānc- to make to become wet; To. nōṯ- to make to get wet in rain; Ta. nāntu to become wet (late); Ma. nāntuka id.; Go. nānd- to be wet; nāht- to make wet; Mlt. nāṉye the cold season; cf. Brah. namb adj. moist, damp. PDr. *nān-, *nāṯ-, *nānṯ-; there is another series with the short grade of root-vowel: Ka. nane, nene to become wet; Tu. naneyuni id.; Ko. nanv- (nand-) id.; Ta. naṉai id. (Kṟḷ.); Ma. nanayuka id.; cf. Kui nenja to water plants; < PSDr. *nān- : nan-V-.]

nār(u)cu* IId tr. of nāḍu$^{1}$, q.v. (Āmu.; disputed version; single usage cited; rare).

722 nikku to rise up straight, stand erect (HariV.); to grow long (Bhīm.); to increase, extend to full length (UH); to be proud (BhR); n. height, increase, erection, pride, etc.

[Ka. nilku, niḷku to strut, rise up to, be extended to full height; < *niḷukk- < *nīḷ-ukk-, v.s.v. nīl(u)gu.]

723 niguḍu intr. to extend, stretch, spread (Bhr. II), to become erect, rise up (Bhr. II), to pounce upon, as in battle (Bhr. II); to increase, swell with joy (BhR, Dvi.H.); to be straightened, fulfilled, as an action (Bhr. II); to become long (Naiṣ.); tr. niguḍ(u)cu to extend, stretch out (Bhr. II, Naiṣ.); hurl arrows, etc. (Bhr. II).

[Ka. nigur, niguru, niguḷ, nimir to be extended, stretched forth; to spread, rise, swell, etc.; Tu. nigacuni v.i. to stretch; nīcuni id.; Ta. niva v.i. to rise (PN); to grow, spread, be exalted; to swell (Parip.); nimir to be outstretched; exceed the limit, as a stanza in a poem (Tolk.), be excessive, far (PN); Ma. niviruka to rise, stand erect; nivirkka to raise, etc.; nīrkka id.; Pj. nikip-

(nikit-) to stretch out. PSDr. and PCDr. *niv-/*nī-; *-v- > -m-, -k- [-g-]; v. s. v. negayu, negaḍu.]

724 ninḍu intr. to be full, be packed to the full (Bhr. II); be fulfilled (HariV.); to increase, spread (Naiṣ.); (span of life) to be over (Kāś.); adj. full, complete (Bhr. II); n. fulness, splendor (Mdn.); tr. nincu to fill (Bhr. II), to spread (Bhr. I); to fulfil, as desires; nimpu id. (KS); n. fulness; adj. full.

[Kui nenja to be full; nehpa (neht-) to fill; nespa id.; neppa (nept-) to finish, bring to an end; Kuvi (S) nenj- to fill; Kuvi (F) nenz- become full; Kuvi (S) neh'- to plenish; Go. nind- to be filled; niht- tr. to fill; GoM. nīh- (nīht-) to fill; Klm. ninḍ- to become full; Klm.(SR) ninḍ-p- to fill; Kur. nīnd- to be filled; nind- to fill; Mlt. nind- to fill; nindgr- be filled. PCDr. and PNDr. *nin-ṯ-; PDr. *nin-/*niṯ-, v. s. v. neṟayu.]

ninucu IIb (alt. of nincu, q. v.) tr. to spread (BhR), to fill (HariV.); ninupu n. fulness, excess (Nirv.), cf. nimpu.

nincu IIb tr. of ninḍu, q. v.

725 nimuku* tr. to suck (Dvi.H.; a single usage cited).

[See Burrow, DS V, p. 611.]

nimuru same as nivuru, q. v. (UH, Bhg.).

726 nilugu* (1) tr. to stretch one's body after sleep (UH, Manu.).

[Ka. niluku, niḷku to stretch one's self upwards, to rise up to full height.]

nilugu* (2) intr. to be proud, conceited (late).

[Ka. niluku to strut, v. s. v. nikku.]

nilugu* (3) intr. to perish, die (Mārk.); cf. nīl(u)gu, īl(u)gu.

727 nilucu IIa intr. to stand, rise, get up; to last, continue; to remain, exist; to stop, halt; to live, survive; to cease (all classical and Mdn.).

[Ka. nil, nilu, nillu (nilt-, nind-) id.; Tu. nilpuni to stay; cease; become quiet; Ko. nil-/nin- (ninḏ-) to stand; To. nīl- (nīḏ-) id.; Ta. nil (niṉ-ṟ-) to stand (Nāl.), stop; continue; cease, remain, etc.; Ma. nilka id.; Kui nisa to stand still, stop; nilpa to stand, be set up; nīlba id.; nīmba to live, survive; nīṛe living; alive; Kuvi (F) nīd- to live; nīc- to stand; Kuvi (S) nī- to stand, halt; Go. nill-, nitt- to stand; Klm.(E) il- id.; Pj. nilp- (nilt-) to stand; KGad. nil-, nilk- (nilt-) id.; Kur. il- (ilc-, ill-) to get up, rise; ild- tr. to erect, set up; Mlt. il- (ij-) to stand; ild- to make to stand. PDr. *nil-/*il-.]

nivuḍu var. of niguḍu, q. v. (KS, BP, Bhr. II).

728 nivuru to stroke, pass the hand over gently and caressingly (Bhr. II, Naiṣ.); to touch, feel (late); to adjust hair with fingers (late).

[Ka. nivaru, nīvu id.; nīvu to make straight or smooth by stroking, as the hair, beard, cloth, etc.; Tu. nimuruni to become straight; nigiyuni to be levelled; nigipuni tr. to level; Ko. niv- (nivd-) to stroke, massage, comb hair; To. nīf- (nīfy-) to stroke; Ta. nīvu to stroke, rub gently (Kalit.), to smear. PSDr. nīv-; *niv-V-/ *nim-V-; also v. s. v. nimuru.]

729 nīgu* (also īgu[1], q. v.) tr. to remove, get rid of, ward off (Bhr. II); discharge a debt (BhR).

[Ka. nīgu to quit, abandon, get rid of; intr. to vanish, be got rid of; Ta. nīṅku tr. to leave, depart, separate from (Kṟḷ.); give up (Cilap.); intr. to turn away, be dismissed, to go; nīkku tr. to remove, abandon (Nāl.); n. separation; nī (nītt-) to separate from (Aiṅk.); to renounce, put away (Kṟḷ.); intr. to be removed (Kṟḷ.); Ma. nīṅṅuka to go off, retire; nīkkuka to put off, remove. PSDr. *nī-nk-/*nī-kk-; *nī-.]

730 nīl(u)gu (1) intr./tr. to stretch one's body to full length (Bhr. I, II); to be proud, stand erect (late).

[Ka. nīḷ, niguḷ to grow long or high, to extend oneself, be stretched out, to spread; nīḍu id.; Tu. nīṭuni, nīḍuni id.; Ko. nīṭ- (nīc-) to stretch out (limbs), lengthen (iron); nīṛ- (nīc-) (iron) becomes long by expansion; To. nīḷ- (nīḍ-) to be stretched out; nīṭ- (nīṭy-) tr. to stretch out; Ta. nīḷ (nīṇ-ṭ-) to grow long; n. length; nīṭu to grow long, be lengthened (Tolk.); spread, extend; Ma. nīṭuka to be long; Kui ḍrīnja to be elongated (< *nṛī- < *niṭi-). PSDr. and PCDr. *nī-ḷ-/*niv-uḷ; *nī-ṭ- : *niṭ-V-; also v. s. v. nikku.]

nīl(u)gu (2) intr. to perish, die (late); prob. a metaphorical extension from the idea of stretching out the body to full length; also v. s. v. īl(u)gu; alternatively from *īl-, cf. Pj., KGad. īl- to fall off, as fruit from tree.

731 nuggu* intr. to be powdered (Nṛs.; a single usage cited; rare); n. bits, fragments, powder (Bhr. I).

[Ka. nuggu, nurgu, nuṟugu to be crushed; to crush, reduce to powder; Tu. nuggiyuni to press; nuggu adj. small, little; nukkuni to bruise; Ko. nugc- to pound (chilies, etc.); Ta. nuṟuṅku to be powdered; nuṟukku to crush; n. grit (Tolk.); nukku to grind, powder (prob. < nuggu, l. w. from Ka.); nuṟuṅṅuka be pulverized; nuṟukkuka to crush. PSDr. *nuṯ-unk-/*nuṯ-ukk- : *nūṯ-, v. s. v. nūṟu, nuṟucu.]

732 nuccu* IId (Śab. R.) tr. to tie a cloth around the udder of goats or sheep; n. a cloth so tied.

733 nuḍuvu* (also nuḍugu, noḍuvu, noḍugu) tr. to say, speak (Dvi.H.); to read, teach (late); n. a word, expression (Bhr. I); nuḍi id.; nuḍikāramu idiom.

[Ka. nuḍi to utter, speak, say; n. sounding; speech; nuḍiha telling; Tu. nuḍiyuni to utter, pronounce; nuḍipuni to speak, talk; nuḍi a word, speech; Ta. noṭi to say, tell (Malaip.); to declare, tell; n. word, phrase; Ma. noṭikka to speak hastily (loc.); noṭiyuka to lisp as fools; on account of u-i < *o-i, the Te. Tu. forms are likely to be l. ws. from Ka.; PSDr. *noṭ-i.]

734 nur̲ucu IIb tr. to crush, destroy (KS, Mārk.); to thresh, as corn (late).

[Ka. nur̲i to be crushed; nurcu, nuccu to crush; Tu. nuriyuni v.i. to go to pieces; nuripuni to powder; Ta. Ma. v. s. v. nuggu; further, v. s. v. nūr̲u, nuggu, nur̲upu, nur̲umu.]

735 nur̲upu tr. to powder, smash, destroy (HariV., Bhg.), make into pieces (BhR); to thresh grain (Mdn.).

[Kuvi (F) nūṛp- to thresh out; Kuvi (S) nurp- to thresh; Klm. (Kin.) norp- to thresh; further cf. Te. nur̲umu, nūr̲u.]

736 nur̲umu tr. to powder, to harass (late); n. powder, grits (Bhr. I).

[< *nur̲ump-; PSDr. *nūt̲- : *nut̲-V-, v. s. v. nūr̲u, nur̲upu.]

737 nuliyu$^{1*}$ III intr. to be twisted (SAN gives only the meanings of nuliyu$^{1,2}$); nulivu a twist; tr. nul(u)cu to squeeze, twist (Bhr. II, Daś.); nul(u)pu id. (late).

[Ka. nuli to twist, wring; n. a twine; nūl to make thread, to spin; nūlu (nū-t-) id.; Tu. nūpuni, nuppuni tr. to twist, spin; Ko. nurb- to twist, wring (< *nur̲ump-); To. nūs̲f- (nūs̲t-) to join ends of thread by rolling them together; Ta. nūl (nūr̲-r̲-) to spin; Ma. nulekka to soften by squeezing; Kui nōlba to twist, spin thread; Kur. nō̃ẽ- (nō̃ẽc-) to wind or twist anything flexible, twist grass, rope, etc. PDr. *nū-l-/*nō-l < *nuy-l-/*noy-l-); cf. words for 'thread,' Kolami, Vocab. No. 604.]

738 nuliyu$^{2*}$ III intr. to be broken, shattered (late, rare).

[Ka. nuḷgu to be powdered; Tu. nuliyuni id.; nuli a bit, fragment; Ta. nuṇi tr. to powder; intr. to waste away; nuṇuṅku to be powdered; n. powder; < *nuḷ-V-/*nuṇ-V-.]

739 nuliyu$^{3*}$ III intr. to shake, tremble, due to weakness.

[V. s. v. uliyu$^{2}$; or cf. Ta. nuṇaṅku v. i. to shake (Kalit.); be flexible.]

nulucu$^{1}$ IIb tr. of nuliyu$^{1}$, q. v.

740 nul(u)cu[2] IIb tr. to pinch, nip off (KS), to squeeze (late).
[Ko. nuḷy- (nuḷc-) to pinch; Ta. nuḷḷu to pinch, nip (colloq.); Ma. nuḷḷuka to pinch, pluck; crop off a bird's head; nuḷḷal a pinch; PSDr. *nuḷ-.]

nul(u)pu alt. of nul(u)cu[1], tr. of nuliyu[1], q.v. (late and Mdn.).

741 nulumu tr. to rub the eyelids (Bhg.); to twist, twist and pluck off; clip off, feather, head, etc.; to uproot a tree; to kill.
[< *nuḷump-; v.s.v. nul(u)cu[2]; contamination with nulucu[1] probable.]

nusalu[1]* same as nusulu[1], q.v. (Dvi.H.).

nusalu[2]* (same as nusulu[2], q.v.) to evade (Dvi.H.); to tell a lie (Bhg.).

742 nusũgu* intr. to slink, slide away, escape (Naiṣ., Vikram.).
[V.s.v. nusulu[2]; cf. Kur. nũkhr-, etc.]

743 nusumu* to draw, pull (Vasu., rare).

744 nusulu[1]* (also nusalu) intr. to shake, tremble (Paṇḍ.); to stir out.
[Tu. nugupuni tr. to loosen; nuguruni tr. to loosen, slacken; Ta. noci to be too slender to bear weight (Tolk.); nukai to become lax, loose; tr. to soften; Kur. nuk- tr. to shake, cause to oscillate; nukᵘr- intr. to sway oneself to and fro; Mlt. nuk- tr. to shake; nukr- to be shaken. PDr. *nuc-/*nuy; *nuk-V- < *nuy-V-; the etyma meaning 'small, slender' from *nuy-/*noy- also belong here.]

745 nusulu[2]* intr. to shrink, withdraw, hide oneself (Bhr. II); n. shrinking one's limbs, hiding (Bhr. II, UH); to tell a lie (Bhg.); cf. nusũgu.
[Ka. nusuḷ to retreat, hide; n. subterfuge, evasion, falsehood; Kur. nũkhr- to hide oneself, be kept secret; nũkh- to keep (eyes) down, defeat (< *nuy-k-); nuṛ- (nuḍḍ-) tr. to hide, conceal; Mlt. nũg- to droop; nuḍgr- to be hidden, to disappear; nuḍ- to hide, conceal. PDr. *nuc-/*nuḻ-; *nuy-.]

746 nusulu[3]* tr. to rub over the eyelids after sleep (late).
[Mlt. nusg- to rub, clean; v.s.v. usugu.]

747 nũku tr. to shove, push away (BP), to fell, thrust (Bhg.); adj. that which pushes (late); nũkuḍu pushing; (Mdn. colloq.) to take away by force or cheating.
[Ka. nũku, nũgu, nũṅku to shove, push away; to pass, as time; dash; nũku, nũṅku n. push; Tu. nũkuni to push, thrust, reject; Ta. nũkku to thrust aside (Nāl.); throw, as a weapon (Tolk.); break, cut down (Parip.), shut, close; PSDr. *nũnk-/*nũkk-; cf. Tu. nurkuni to elbow, push; Mlt. nokkuka tr. to pierce, pass through.]

748 nūr̲u tr. to crush, grind (Bhr. II), to powder; to sharpen knife on a whet-stone (Manu.); tr. nur̲ucu, nūrcu, q. v.

[Ka. nūr̲u that which is powdered; Ta. nūr̲u to pulverize (Akan.), kill, strike; n. powder, dust; Ma. nūr̲uka to be powdered; n. powder; Go. nōr- to grind grain; Kuvi (S) nūi- to mill; Kuvi (F) nui(y)- id.; Brah. nus- to crush, grind, etc.; nusk̲h̲al hand mill; nut flour; also cf. Te. nusi fine powder; Ka. Ta. Ma. nuccu fragments; Te. nūka (< *nuy-k-) grits; Go. nūs-ī a flour weevil (*ī fly). PDr. *nuc-/*nuy, *noy-; *nuy-it̲-/*noy-it̲- > *nū-t̲-/*nō-t̲-; also cf. Ta. nor̲ukku to crush, nor̲uṅku to be powdered; further see s. v. nur̲ucu, nur̲umu, nur̲upu.]

nūr̲ucu/nūrcu IIb to thresh grain in field (Mdn.; prob. a var. of nur̲ucu); nūrpu threshing grain with cattle.

[Kuvi (F) nūṛp- id.; v. s. v. nur̲ucu, nur̲upu.]

749 negaḍu* (also nevaḍu) to occur, happen (Bhr. I, II); to increase, extend, as fame (Bhr. II); to improve, progress; be published, be well known (Bhr. II); der. n. negaḍ(i)ta fame.

[Ka. negal̲, negal̲u to become manifest, known; to shine, be finished; negal̲ke fame; Ta. nikal̲ to happen, occur; to be current, as time (Tolk.); to continue; to shine (Patir̲.); nikar to be visible, to shine; Ma. nikaḷuka to be full; nikal̲ttuka to fulfil. PSDr. *nik-al̲ < *nival̲-; cf. niguḍu.]

750 negayu* III intr. to fly, rise in the air (Bhr. I); to arise, come up (KS); to soar, jump, bound.

[Ka. nege, nese id.; tr. to raise, lift; negepu to raise, etc.; Tu. negiyuni to rise, come up; negipuni to leap; Ta. niva to rise, become high (PN), grow (Kalit.); spread; swell, overflow (Parip.); Ma. nikakka to rise, as in water; Kui niṅga to rise; nipka (< nik-p-) to raise; Kuvi (S) nik'- to awake; niph'- to erect; Kuvi (F) ning- to rise; nikh- to arouse; Klm. Nk. negay- to fly. PSDr. and PCDr. *niv-/*nik-V-; ultimately *ni-v-; cf. niguḍu, nikku, nīl(u)gu, negaḍu; also see s. v. egayu; cf. Mlt. neke to get well, recover.]

751 negucu* IId (var. of egucu, q. v.) tr. to chase, pursue (Bhg.; rare).

752 neggu[1] intr. to be successful, to be fulfilled (Molla Rāmāyaṇamu, 16th cent.); to thrive, prosper, live (late); (< *ner-g- < *ner-unk-).

[Tu. neggi, neggya adj. full, complete; cf. Ta. neruṅku v.i. to prevail, increase; nerukku id.; nēr to be complete (Tolk.).]

753 neggu[2]* intr. to become weak, to droop (late); (< *neg-iyu).

[Ka. naggu/neggu to be bruised; neggu to sink; tr. to crush;

nekku to be depressed, to sink; Ta. neku to become relaxed; be distressed; be ruined; nekil̲ to become loose (Akan.), be injured; tr. to relax, crush.]

754 neṭṭu tr. to push away, thrust, expel (Śakunt., Bhg.); to reject; n. a push.

[Ta. neṭṭu to thrust, push (colloq., l. w. < Te.); ner̲r̲u to thrust, dash; ner̲i to press firmly with hands; Ma. er̲r̲uka to throw, as with sling, propel; beat hard; Tu. nesipuni to press down, make tight; Kui nasa to press, push; Go. natt- to dash or throw down; Mlt. nerm- to clear away anything which adheres; cf. Kur. nepp- to seize with a sweeping movement; to brush up, while sweeping; Kuvi (F) ness- to load, heap up. PDr. *net̲-, *net̲t̲-.]

755 nenayu* III intr. to fit, suit, to adorn (RR; rare).

[V. s. v. enayu.]

756 neppu* tr. to push out, thrust (late and rare); (< *ner̲-p-).

[Kur. nepp- to brush up, while sweeping; see s. v. neṭṭu.]

757 nemaku tr. to seek, search (Bhr. II; also Mdṅ. in the Viśākha dial.).

[< *niv-akku, see *nīv-, s. v. nivuru; Ta. nīṭu to seek, search (< *niv-uṭ-); for a similar meaning association, v. s. v. taḍavu.]

nerapu* tr. of nerayu, q. v.

758 nerayu* III to increase, be full (Bhr. I, II), spread, extend (Bhr. I); tr. nerapu to increase, spread (Naiṣ.), to scatter all over (BhR); n. excess, abundance (UH); cf. neravu.

[Tu. neriyuni to be full; Ta. nirai to swarm; tr. to make full; nira v. i. to spread, expand as water (Cīv.), be full; nirattu to fill; Klm.(E) neray- v. i. to spread; contamination in meaning possible between two series, v. s. v. neravu, ner̲ayu.]

759 neravu* intr. to assemble together (Paṇḍ.); neravu an assemblage (KS), battalion (Bhr. II); spread, abundance.

[Ka. nere v. i. to assemble, be united; n. union; neravu a crowd; Tu. neriyuni to assemble; be attached; Ta. nirai to be crowded, to swarm (Tēv.); tr. to crowd (Maturai.); niravu to be filled, nirampu to abound; neruṅku to be close together, grow excessive; nerukku to set thick; PSDr. *ner-.]

760 nerumu tr. to rub with body parts, etc., crush under foot (late); to move on posteriors (Mdn.).

[Ta. neri tr. to rub or crush with hand; to be crushed; Ma. niraṅ-ṅuka to drag the tail or feet along the ground; to creep, crawl; nirakkuka to push, shove; Ko. nerk- to rub between hands; Kui nēra to rub, stroke, scrape; massage; Kur. nīṛ- to rub, scrape. PDr. *nēr- : *ner-V-.]

761 neṟayu* III intr. to become full (Bhr. I), to spread (UH); to be fulfilled, as desire (Bhr. I, UH); to be accomplished; tr. neṟapu to increase, spread; to make full; to fulfil as promise (Bhr. II); to accomplish (Bhr. II); neṟavu fulness; neṟa adj. full, complete (classical).

[Ka. neṟe to become full; to prevail; neṟa completeness; Tu. neriyuni to be full; To. neṟ- (neṟθ-) id.; neṟf- (neṟt-) tr. to fill; Ta. niṟai to be full (Tiruvāc.); tr. to fill (Tolk.); n. completeness (Nāl.); niṟaivu id.; Ma. niṟayuka to be full, niṟekka to fill; niṟa fulness. PSDr. *niṯ-, PDr. *nin-/*niṯ-; v. s. v. niṇḍu.]

neṟapu* tr. of neṟayu, q. v.

762 nelayu* III intr. to be established, to stay (KS); nelavu a place to stay, an abode, hold, etc. (classical); nelakonu to be established, be set, stay, remain.

[Ka. nelasu to become established; to settle, stay; nele a place, abode; Tu. nilevuni to be steadfast; nilevu residence; Ta. nilai to remain permanent, to stay (Tolk.); n. standing, staying (PN); Ma. nilekka to come to stand; nila place, position, a stop. PSDr. < *nilay, v. s. v. nilucu.]

nevaḍu* alt. of negaḍu, q. v.

nevayu* free var. of negayu, q. v. (Bhr. I).

763 nevulu* to grieve, be distressed (KS); n. regret, grief (Bhr. I); evil, difficulty (Bhr. I); enmity (Kāś.); n. (also negulu) regret, grief; cf. nevva poverty, indigence; grief, difficulty (Bhg.).

[Ko. neg- to suffer reverse of fortune; negc- to make to suffer ill-fortune; Ta. neku to be distressed, to suffer, be ruined (Cīv.); cf. Ta. evvam affliction, distress (PN), pestilence, wretchedness (Kṟḷ.); dislike, aversion (Cīv.); ēval poverty, want. PSDr. *nēv-/ *nevv- : *ēv-/*evv-; *nev-V- : *nek-V-.]

764 nēmu tr. to winnow, sift by moving the basket in a side-long motion (no literary usages cited; Mdn.).

[Ta. nĕmpu id.; Ma. nĕmpuka id.; Kui ēmba tr. to separate rice grains from straw by shaking; Go. (y)ĕm- to sift out husks of rice, pulses, etc. PSDr. and PCDr. *yāmp-/*ñāmp-; cf. Ta. nōmpu to separate by winnowing; Ma. nāvuka cleanse rice from stones.]

765 nēyu III tr. to weave (Naiṣ.); nĕ̄ta weaving of cloth (late).

[Ka. ney, neyi, nĕ, nĕy, nĕyi, nēyu (nĕd-) to weave, entwine; Tu. neyuni to weave, as spider; neyipuni to weave, plait, as braid; nĕpini, nĕyuni, neipini id.; Ko. nec- to weave; To. nīθ- id.; nes-

(nesθ-) id.; cf. nic- (nič-) to darn, spin; Ta. ney tr. to weave (Cīv.); link together (Parip.); necavu texture, web; Ma. neyka to weave, plait; Kuvi (S) neh'- to interweave; nēh'- to weave; Kui ēspa (ēst-) to spin; Kur. ess- to weave; entwine into fabric; plait; Mlt. es- to plait, do mat-work. PDr. *nec-/*ec- > *nĕy-.]

766 nēr(u)cu IIa and V (allomm. nēr-, nē-) (1) tr. to know, learn (Bhr. I, II); to study (Bhg.); (2) intr. to be able, capable (Bhr. I), to be willing, be prepared (Bhr. II); nēr(u)pu to teach; n. skill, ability (Naiṣ.).

[No correspondences for meaning (1) except Ta. nērpaṭu to learn well (Tiv.), but the following are probably related for (2): Ka. nēr to agree to, to yield; nērpu propriety; Tu. nērè straightness, justice, agreement; adj. true, just; Ta. nēr to be fit, appropriate (Tolk.); nērmai harmony; Ma. nēruka to agree. PSDr. *nēr-, *nē-.]

767 nokku tr. to press, pinch (Kāś.), to mend bendings (Vijñ.), to make a dent with teeth, fingernails, etc.; to stresṣ, emphasize (Mdn.); n. a dent, depression, dimple, pressure; a fold, bend (JBh.).

[Ma. okkuka to indent; cf. nokkuka to pierce, bore through. Connection not likely with Ma. ñekku to press, etc.; see Burrow, DS V, pp. 604, 605.]

768 nogulu[1*] intr. to be afflicted, to grieve (KS, Bhr. II); n. ache, suffering.

[< *noy-ul, cf. s.v. noccu, nōyu; alternatively < *nov-ul, formed from the noun novvu affliction, suffering.]

769 nogulu[2*] intr. to be pressed, squeezed, suffer under physical pressure (HariV.); to wither in sun (KS); tr. nogul(u)cu to crush (UH, Bhg.).

[V. s. v. nokku.]

770 noccu V (before back-vowel suffixes, allomm. novv-/nōv- freely alternating with nō-) intr. to ache, suffer, be grieved, to be sorry (all classical); to perish, die (Daśā.); (< *noy-cc-); tr. noñcu to cause to suffer, afflict (Bhr. II); kill (late).

[Ka. noy, nō, noyyu, nōyu (nond-) to feel or suffer pain, be afflicted; Tu. nōpini, nōpuni to beat, flog; nōyipini to ache, pain; Ta. nō to suffer (Nāl.); n. pain (Kṟḷ.); no (nont-) id. (Tolk.); noci id.; tr. to distress (Cī♦.); Ma. nōka v. i. to pain, smart; Kui nōva (nōt-) to be painful; nospa (nost-) to give pain to; Kui Kuvi (F) nōmeri fever; nōhi pain; Go. noi- v. i. to hurt; nokk- to writhe in death, or in a fit; Pj. noy- (noñ-) to hurt; Klm. Nk. oy- (wound) to hurt; Kur. nuñj- to smart, pain; Mlt. nunj- id. PDr. *nŏy-/*nō-; further cf. nogulu[1], nōyu.]

771 noḍucu* IId (Śab.R.) tr. to find fault with; noḍupu n. finding faults (no literary usages cited).

[Ta. noṭi tr. to insinuate.]

772 noḍuvu* (var. of nuḍuvu, q.v.) tr. to say, speak (Bhr. I, II); to utter, pronounce (Bhg.); praise, extol (Bhg.); n. an expression; noḍi id.

[V. s. v. nuḍuvu; PSDr. *noṭ-uv-.]

noncu* IIb tr. of noccu, q. v.

773 nollu[1]* tr. (children) to suck fingers (Nirv.).

[Ka. noṇe to swallow; clean with tongue the substance lodged between the teeth; Ta. noḷ, noḷḷu (noṇṭ-) to swallow, devour.]

774 nollu[2] tr. to scrape and gather into heap, as dried grass (colloq.).

[? Ta. noḷḷu to bale out, as water (Cilap.), measure out, as grain; noḷku id.; Kui nolpa (nolt-, noṭ-) to ladle out; Kur. noll- to scoop out, as paddy with a winnowing basket, etc.; Mlt. lol- to take out with a spoon. PDr. *noḷ-.]

novulu* var. of nogulu, q. v.

775 nõcu IId tr. to perform an act of religious merit (Bhr. I, UH); (< *nōn-c-); see s. v. nōmu.

[Ka. nōn, nōnu (nōnt-) to observe a vow, religious obligation, perform austerity; nōmpi, nōmpu n. a vow, etc.; Tu. nōmpu any meritorious act of devotion; nōmbu fast, penance; Ta. nōl (nōr̲-r̲-) to endure, do or practice austerities (Maṇi.); nōn̲ (nōn̲-r̲-) id. (Akan.); nōn̲pu ceremonial fasting, nōmpu id. (colloq.); Ma. nōlka to fast; nōnpu penance, fasting. PSDr. *nō-l-/*nō-n-, cf. noccu, nōyu, nōmu.]

776 nōmu* tr. to perform a religious ceremony (Kāś.), to worship (JBh.); n. a vow, act of religious merit (Manu.).

[Prob. a denominative verb, v. s. v. nõcu; Tu. nombuni to fast.]

777 nōyu* III intr. to suffer, grieve (Bhr. I, II).

[V. s. v. noccu.]

## P

778 pakku* (Brown) intr. to burst out in laughter; cf. paka paka or pakkuna imit. sound of laughing aloud.

779 pagaṭu* tr. to proclaim, announce (Kaḷā.); adv. openly (RR).

[Prob. < Skt. prakaṭa-.]

780 pagulu (< *pay-ul) intr. to break to pieces (Bhr. II); to burst, crack; to be rent (Bhīm.); n. a crack, rent; cf. pancu to divide into shares; paṅga a forked branch.

[Ka. bagi, bagaru to cleave, separate; n. dividing; pasu, pancu, hancu to divide; paṅga a forked branch; Tu. pagiyuni v. i. to split, to crumble; pagipuni tr. to rend, split; To. pax- (paxθ-) to be divided; paxf- to divide; Ta. paku (pakk-) to be split, separate (Kṟḷ.); tr. to divide; (pakutt-) to distribute (Kṟḷ.), classify; pakir tr. to divide into shares; paṅku a portion; Ma. pakayuka to divide; pakuka to be separated; pakukka to divide; paka separation; pakuppu a portion; Kui paṅga to be split; papka (< pak-p-) to split, to crack, divide; Kuvi (F) pakh- to gash; Go. pai(y)- (paī-sī) to be split, of wood with an axe, etc.; pakkī n. split bamboo; Klm.(SR) pai- to divide; Pj. payp- (payt-) to divide, share; Nk. payk- id.; KGad. pay- id.; Kur. pāk̲h̲- to force open; paṅgē adj. open (not covered by trees, etc.), clear; Mlt. pakme a division of a house; cf. palk- (? < pak-l-) to cut up (as fruit); palka a division of people. PDr. *pay, *pay-k-, *pay-ṅk-; *pay- < *pac-; v. s. v. pancu.]

781 paṭṭu tr. to hold, catch, seize (Bhr. I, II); to hold in, restrain, memorize (Bhr. II); to accompany, approach, obtain (Bhr. II, Kāś.); to receive, accept; blow as a conch, etc. (late); intr. to suit, fit (Bhr. II); to be settled at a place (Bhr. II); to be contained, go into; to adhere; n. a hold, grasp; an abode, settlement; propriety; handle, prop; reason, basis; adherence, care.

[Ka. pattu to seize; be contained; come to mind; Tu. pattuni to hold; v. i. to adhere, stick; Ko. paṯ- (pac-) to catch; be suitable; pat- become stuck fast; To. paṯ- to seize; Ta. paṟṟu to seize; receive, embrace (Kṟḷ.); touch; intr. to hold as color, to stick, be suitable; n. grasp, adherence (Kṟḷ.); paste; resting place (Parip.); support (Kṟḷ.); Ma. paṟṟuka v. i. to adhere; tr. to seize; paṟṟu adhesion; Pj. patt- to take hold of, to buy; KGad. patt- to hold; stick up; Go. padd- to be contained; Kur. paṭ- (paṭc-) to suit; Mlt. paty- (patc-) to catch up, as liquid in a vessel; paṭyar- to be settled; parctr- to take effect, as medicine when applied (cf. Te. paṭṭu id., colloq.). PDr. *paṯ-; alternation in PDr. itself with *paṭ- is possible, cf. Kur. Mlt. forms and Ta. paṭu to catch, trap (Cīv.); smear (Kalit.); be caught; see s. v. paḍayu).]

782 paḍacu* IId (in ĀVāc.) tr. to obtain, get; to beget; v. s. v. paḍayu.

783 paḍayu* III tr. to obtain, acquire, earn; to enjoy or suffer, experience; to bring forth, beget; intr. to accrue, happen (all Bhr. I, II); cf. paḍu$^2$.

[Ka. paḍe, haḍe id.; paḍu (paṭṭ-) to get, obtain; experience; Tu. paḍeyuni to suffer, experience; paḍepuni to obtain, bring forth;

Ko. paṛ-, To. poṛ- to experience; Ta. paṭai to obtain (PN); to create (Tiruvāc.); to acquire; n. means (Kṟḷ.); Ma. paṭekka to create (of gods); paṭuka to be obtained, to happen; Kui paha (paht-) to take form, come into existence; Pj. paḍ- to acquire; cf. Kui pāṇba to obtain, receive, attain. PDr. *paṭ-; *pāṭ-/pāṇ-; v. s. v. paḍu².]

784 paḍu¹ I and V intr. to fall, drop, die (Bhr. I, II), (sun, etc.) to set (Bhr. I), to be subdued, to be thrown down (Bhr. I, Kāś.); to lie, sleep, recline (Bhr. III, Kāś.); tr. paṟucu to let fall (Bhg.); to punish (Bhr. II); also parcu id.

[Ka. paḍu to lie down; go down, set as sun, fall in battle, die; Ko. paṛ- (paṭ-) to lie down, sleep; To. paṟy- (paṟs-) (child) dies; poṛ- (poṭ-) to lie down; Ta. paṭu (paṭṭ-) to perish, die (PN); to rain (Kalit.), set as a heavenly body (Kalit.); lean over (Kṟḷ.); (paṭutt-) to lie down, sleep; tr. to fell; Ma. paṭuka to fall; paṭiyuka to settle, sink; peṭuka id. (post-inscriptional, see Sekhar, Evol. of Ma., p. 19); Go. paṭṭ- to crouch; paṭsuht- cause to lie down; Pj. paḍ- (paṭṭ-) to fall; set (as sun); Klm. paḍ-, Nk. paṛ-, KGad. paṭ- (parr-) to fall; PDr. *paṭ-/*paṯ-; cf. IA. H. paṛ- to fall, Nep. parnu, Pkt. paḍaĩ fall; Skt. pátati, in RV. to fly; see J. Bloch, BSOS V, p. 739; Turner, Nep. Dict., s. v. parnu.]

785 paḍu² I and V tr. to experience, suffer (Bhr. I, II); intr. to occur, happen (Hara., Kaḷā.); to be possible; tr. paṟucu, parcu to cause an experience, to distress somebody (Bhr. II, Paṇḍ.); pāṭu difficulty, experience.

[Ka. paḍu tr. id.; Tu. paḍeyuni id.; paḍibāṭlu straits; Ko. paṛ- (paṭ-) to experience; To. paṟy- to be possible; Ta. paṭu (paṭṭ-) v. i. to come into existence (Kṟḷ.), rise, as a heavenly body (PN); to suffer, endure; further v. s. v. paḍayu. PDr. *paṭ-; also *paṯ- on account of To. and Te. tr.]

786 paḍucu IId intr. to prostitute oneself, earn money through prostitution (late); paḍupu prostitution; paḍupūgatte a prostitute.

[Cf. Ka. paḍupu getting wages; paḍupugārti a woman who acquires; see s. v. paḍayu.]

787 paṇḍu¹ intr. to become ripe, to ripen (Paṇḍ., Dvi.H.); intr. to be completed (Bhr. II), to grow old; n. a ripe fruit; adj. ripe, old, complete (Bhr. II).

[Ka. paṇ to ripen; a ripe fruit; Tu. parnduni to be ripe, hair to turn gray; parnduͅ fruit; pandaḍe productiveness of a tree; Ta. paḻuṉu to grow ripe (Maturai.); Ma. paṇṭu antiquity; Go. panḍ- to become ripe; Klm. Nk. panḍ- id.; Pj. panḍ- to mature (of plants); Kur. pā̃n- (pañj-, pān-) to ripen, have a yellow appearance; pañjkā fruit; peṇḍ-ō yellowish (fruits ripening); paṇḍ-uār-' take a yellow-red appearance (as fruit in ripening); Mlt. pān- (pānj-) to ripen. PDr. *pa\l-nt- > *paṇ-ṭ-; for forms with different stop derivatives, see Emeneau, Kolami, Vocab. No. 634; > IA l. ws., see Burrow, TPS 1946, p. 10.]

788 paṇḍu[2] intr. to lie down, sleep (Daśā.); in Mdn. usage, occurs with the refl. -konu to sleep.

[? Pj. panḍ- to be tired; KGad. panḍ- id.]

789 padaru* (also paduru; Appak. has padaṟu) intr. to be overhasty (Bhr. I), to be agitated, be shaken, to get angry (Bhr. I, UH); tr. to censure, reprove; n. a hasty word (Nṛs.); padrucu, padur(u)cu same as padaru.

[Ka. padaṟu to be overhasty; speak unadvisedly; pase a meaningless word; Ta. pataṟu to be overhasty; be confused; pataṟṟam rashness; patai to throb in sympathy; to shake; be anxious (Kamp.); Ma. pataṟuka to be overhasty, be confused; Mlt. padrar-, padkar- to prattle. PDr. *pat-aṯ-; *pat-/*pac-.]

790 panavu* intr. to lament, recollecting the past, to weep (KS, Bhr. II); tr. to recollect and point out (Bhr. II).

[Cf. Ko. pany- (panc-) to think; Ta. paṉi to suffer, be in pain; tr. cause to suffer; n. distress, suffering, sorrow; cf. paṉuvu, paṉṉu to say, utter (Tēv.); also v. s. v. palavu.]

791 panuku* intr. to be angry (UH).

792 panucu* IIb (also pancu, q. v.) to command, to commission (Bhr. I); to send, let go (Bhr. II); (rā̃)banucu to send (word to come), to let (come) (Bhr. I); (piluvā̃)banucu to let (to call), etc.; pancu, pampu same as panucu; pampu n. a command, commission, also panupu.

[Tu. paṇpini to teach, instruct; Ta. paṇi to order, direct (Maṇi.); n. command (PN); paṇippu id.; paṇikkaṉ teacher (Piṅ.), instructor; Kui panḍa to send; Kuvi (S) panḍ- to remit, transport; pant- to send; Klm.(E) pank- id.; Nk. pank- id.; PSDr. and PCDr. *paṇ-; cf. Ka. panavu a place appointed for meeting.]

pancu[1]* IIb same as panucu, q. v. (Bhr. I).

793 pancu[2] IIb tr. to distribute, divide into shares (Bhr. II).

[Ka. pañcu, hañcu id.; pasu (pacc-) id.; Tu. pasal the share of a fisherman; Kui pahpa id.; also see s. v. pagulu, esp. Ta. paku, Ma. pakayuka; Pj. payp-, Nk. pay̆k-, KGad. pay-; (< *pay-, *pay-nc-, PDr. *pac-/*pay-.]

794 pannu intr. to be ready, prepared for action (Bhr. II); tr. to make ready (Bhr. II), to contrive, plan (Pāṇḍ.); to create (BhR); n. suitability (Bhr. I); der. ~~n.~~ pannugaḍa a scheme, device.

[Ka. paṇṇu to make ready, prepare, equip; Tu. paṇipuni to give a shape; Ta. paṇṇu to make, effect, accomplish (Nāl.); make suitable (PN); Ma. paṇṇuka to make, work; Pj. panḍp- (panḍt-) to make, do. PSDr. and PCDr. *paṇ-; related etyma occur with the meaning 'action,' see Kolami, Vocab. No. 2249.]

pampu (var. of pan(u)cu, q. v.) tr. to command (Bhr. I); to send away (Vikram.), to hurl a weapon (Manu.); to despatch, to send off formally (Mdn.); pampincu id. (Mdn.); n. a command, commission (Bhr. I, Nirv.).

795 pambu* (alt. pammu[1], q. v.) intr. to increase, abound (Bhr. I), to spread (BP), to occur, exist (Bhr. II); (< *par-mp-).

[Ka. parbu v. i. to spread, to prevail; Tu. parbuni v. i. to spread, multiply; Ta. pampu to be thick (Kamp.), be full; spread like vegetation, water, darkness, etc. (Kamp.); parampu to extend, spread. PSDr. *par-amp-, *par-ump-.]

pammu[1]* intr. to increase, abound (Bhr. I); to occur, happen (Bhōj.); v. s. v. pambu.

796 pammu[2]* tr. to fold the ends of a garment and stitch (ĀVāc.)

797 paragu* (Śab.R. has [~], i.e., parāgu, but classical usages contradict this) intr. to spread like water, to increase, abound; shine (Bhr. II, III); to occur, be, fare, be agreeable.

[V. s. v. paracu; cf. Mlt. parc- to shine brightly, to be seen clearly.]

798 paracu IIa tr. to spread out (as a cloth, grain in sun, etc.), extend; cf. par̲acu, prā̃ku.

[Ka. pari, pare v. i. to spread out or run; Tu. paraḍuni, partaruni to extend, spread; Ko. pard- v. i. to spread; part- tr.; Ta. para v. i. to spread, extend (PN); Ma. parakka id.; Kui prahpa (praht-) tr. to spread out grain, etc.; Kuvi (F) press- id.; GoM. parh- id.; Pj. parp- (part-) id. PDr. *pār- : *par-V-; v. s. v. par̲acu, pār̲u.]

parapu* (alt. of paracu, q. v.) tr. to cause to flow (HariV.); n. extension, width; extensive (Bhr. II); cf. par̲acu.

799 pariyu* III (Brown, Śab.R.) intr. to miss; slip; to wear away, be spoiled; (plastering of a wall) to fall away in slits.

[Ta. par̲i to be loosened, as bonds (Tiruvāc.); par̲ai to vanish, be wasted, worn out (Perump.); Ma. par̲iyuka to get loose, come off; par̲ikka to weed; Ta. par̲i to weed; To. par̲y- (par̲c-) to pluck forcibly.]

800 paruṇḍu intr. to lie down, recline; repose, sleep (Mdn.; no literary usages cited).

[Prob. *par- as in paracu, and uṇḍu to be; cf. Tu. parkĕ sleep, rest; bedding.]

801 par(u)vu* intr. to extend, spread; n. spreading, running (Bhr. II), a type of gallop.

[Ka. parvu, parbu to spread, be diffused; Tu. parbuni id.; Ta. paravu v.i. to spread; tr. lay open. PSDr. *par-uv-/-av-; v.s.v. paracu, paṟacu, pāṟu, pambu, prabbu.]

parcu var. of paṟucu, q.v.

paṟãgu* (ĀVāc.) intr. to spread (HariV.); v.s.v. paragu, paracu, paṟacu.

802 paṟacu[1]* IIa intr. to fly, flee, run (Bhr. I), to flow, as water (Bhr. II); tr. to cause to flee (Bhr. II).

[Ka. paṟi, paṟu flying; jumping; pari to run; Tu. parapuni to flow, as water; Ko. parn- (parnd-) to run fast; To. pary- (parc-) horse gallops; Ta. paṟa to fly (Kṟḷ.), be scattered; paṟi to run away, as horse, flow out quickly (Tēv.); Ma. paṟa to fly, flee; Go. parī- to fly (of birds); par(ĕnḍlī) flying (squirrel); Mlt. parc- to run away. PDr. *paṯ-V-, *par-V- < *pā-ṯ-, *pā-r-; ultimate root *pā-; v.s.v. pāṟu, prãku, paracu.]

paṟacu[2] IIb tr. of paḍu[2], q.v.; var. of paṟucu.

paṟacu[3] IIa tr. to spread (Bhr. II); same as paracu.

paṟapu[1] (var. of paṟacu[3], cf. paracu) tr. to spread, stretch out, extend (Bhr. II); n. spread, width, extension (Mārk., Bhr. II); n. a bed (that is spread; Bhr. I).

paṟapu[2]* (var. of paṟacu[1]) to chase, cause to run away (Bhr. II).

paṟucu IIb tr. of paḍu[2], q.v.

803 palãku* (ĀVāc.; Brown, without [˜]) intr. to ripen, produce a crop.

[Cf. Tu. palu n. ripening, as of fruit; palkuni to be very soft, as an overripe fruit; ? < Skt. phala- n. fruit.]

804 palavu* (also palumu) intr. to lament (Bhr. II, JBh.); cf. panavu.

[Ka. palumbu, halubu to lament; Tu. palambuni id.; cf. Ta. pulampu to wail, cry out (Tiv.); pulampal grieving over one's loneliness (Tolk.); lamenting; pula to suffer pain; Ma. pulampuka to lament; PSDr. *pal-/*pol-, a/o alternation common after bilabial consonants; cf. Skt. pallavana- n. useless speech.]

805 paluku[1] intr./tr. to say, speak (Bhr. I, II); to rebuke, censure (Bhr. I); to praise; to utter; reply (Bhr. I); to sound; (birds) to sing (Naiṣ.); n. a word, utterance, a word of praise.

[Tu. paṇpini to say, tell, relate; Ta. palukku to be pronounced clearly (loc.), to boast; to speak (Tēv.) (prob. l. w. < Te.); To. poṇθ- to talk in assembly; Ta. paṇi to say, declare (Tēv.); n. saying, word; Ma. paṇikka to speak; Kui plāpa (plāt-) to ask; say; Klm.(E) pāna language; Brah. pān- to say, speak, tell. PDr. *pāḷ-/*pāṇ- : *paḷ-V-/*paṇ-V-; altern. cf. Ta. pan̲n̲u to praise (Tiruvāc.), to speak, talk, declare (Kamp.); to read; talk, as a parrot; to sing; PSDr. *pāṇ-/*pāḷ-.]

806 paluku² to become pale, to fade (HariV.); see pālu id.

palumu (SN) (var. of palavu, q. v.) intr. to cry, lament (Brown), to mutter, prattle; n. prattling.

pavulu var. of pagulu, q. v. (Bhr. II, UH).

807 pasā̃gu* (Brown, ĀVāc.) to become evident (no literary usages cited).

pācu IIb (tr. of pāyu, q. v.) to remove, release, discharge a debt (Bhr. I); (ĀVāc.) to be disentangled, as hair; see Kolami, Vocab. No. 657.

808 pāḍu (1) intr. to sing, chant (Bhg., Daśā.); tr. to praise (Nṛs.); n. pāṭa song.

[Ka. pāḍu, hāḍu to sing; Ko. pāṛv- (pāṛd-) make noise, as bees, crow, etc.; To. pōṛ- to sing; Ta. pāṭu to sing, chant (PN); to praise; Ma. pāṭuka to sing; Kuvi(F) pacū song; Go. wāṛ- to sing (p. 77); GoM. pār- id.; Klm. pāḍ-, Nk. pāṛ-, Pj. pāḍ-, Oll. pār-, KGad. pār- id.; Kur. Mlt. pāṛ- id.; Kur. pāṛus a singer. PDr. *pāṭ-; for further words meaning 'song,' see Kolami, Vocab. No. 662.]

pāḍu (2) (Brown) to sing, tell or bid at an auction (colloq., Mdn.).

809 pā̃cu IId (Dh.M.; not in Śab.R. or SAN) intr. (food, etc.) to be spoiled after some time; in the author's dialect pāy-/pās- id.; cf. pāḍagu to become spoiled.

[Klm.(SR) pās- to get sour, of food; cf. Ka. pal̲asu to decay, be spoiled; Ta. pāl̲ to become useless; n. putrification; pal̲utu anything rotten; Ma. pal̲acōr̲u boiled rice of yesterday; pal̲akka having a musty smell; pal̲ukka to decay. PDr. *pāl̲-/*pāc-; [˜] in the Telugu form is spurious.]

810 pā̃tu to bury (Bhr. II), to plant, fix in the ground; n. the roots of anything buried under earth (Bhr. I); cf. pādi, pādu a garden bed (Mdn.).

[Ka. pāti a garden bed; basin for water around the foot of a tree; Tu. pāti a nursery for plants; Ta. pāntu n. cavity, deep hole; pātti pan; patukku to conceal; Pj. pend- to bury; Mlt. páthe the root of a tree, patur- to take root. PDr. *pā-nt-/*pā-tt-; or related to Skt. pāda- foot?]

pāpu (tr. of pāyu[1], q. v.) to remove, separate (Bhr. I, II); to break.

811 pāmu tr. to daub, smear, as wet clay, etc.; to clean a drain (Viśākha. dial.) (late and also Mdn.).

812 pāyu[1] III intr./tr. to be separated, leave, quit (Bhr. I, II), to miss; to perish, be ruined (Bhr. I); tr. pācu, pāpu, q. v.

[Cf. Kui pēnja to split, as wood; Ta. pā (pā-nt-) to divide, share (Tolk.); v. s. v. pagulu, pancu; alternatively, Ka. pāy- to jump over, advance; Tu. pāyuni be diffused; Ta. pāy to leap (PN); run, flee; Ma. pāyuka to rush out, flee; Go. pasī- to come out or go out; GoA. pesī- id.; Kui pāga to pounce upon; Pj. pēp- (pēt-) to arise; see also Kolami, Vocab. No. 657.]

pāyu[2] to be addled, spoiled, as food (Bhr. II, UH).

[V. s. v. pācu.]

813 pāru[1] (same as pār̲u[1], q. v.) to run, fly (Manu.); creep or crawl; to grow (cf. Brown).

814 pāru[2] intr. to purge, have loose motions (Mdn., vulgar).

815 pār̲u[1] intr. to run, flee (Bhr. I); to flow, spread (Bhr. II, UH); to fly (Āmu.).

[Ka. pār̲u, hār̲u fly about, run; Tu. pāruni to run, fly, escape; To. pōr̲- to fly; pōx- to flow down completely; Ta. pār̲u to be scattered (Akan.), to run, flee; Ma. pār̲uka to fly, spread like wings; Kui pānja to fly, leap; for forms with shortened radical vowel see s. v. par̲acu[1]. PDr. *pāt̲- : *pat̲-V-.]

816 pār̲u[2] intr. to occur, happen (KS), to suggest, as an idea (Kaḷā.); to become, grow, e.g., er̲r̲a vār̲u to become red (Mdn. errabāru id.), tella vār̲u to dawn, lit. to become white; paṇḍābār̲u to become ready for harvest; prob. related to paḍu[2], q. v.

817 *pālu (only with front vowel suffixes, pāl-i-, pāl-ina-, etc.) intr. to become pallid, turn pale (Brown, also Mdn.), e.g., oḷḷu pāl-i pōyindi body has become pale.

[V. s. v. paluku[2].]

818 pikku[1] (Śab.R., Brown) intr. to draw back, withhold; to be miserly (Viśākha. dial.).

[Ka. piṅgu to go back, retreat; Tu. pinci adj. miserly; n. stinginess; Ta. pintu to go back; pin̲r̲u to retreat; < PDr. *pin- back, etc.]

819 pikku[2] to cheat (late); n. cheating, clue; trick, deceit.

[Cf. Tu. pikilāṭa cheating (āṭa play, action).]

pikulu later var. of pigulu, q. v. (Pārij.).

[Ka. pikilu id. (Bucher).]

820 pigulu (also pivulu, pikulu) intr. to burst, as seams; be torn (late); cf. pikulu.

[Two etymologies possible: (1) < *piy-ul-, with -g- < -y-; for *piy-, v. s. v. pīku; also cf. Ka. pikku, pinju tr. to separate; (2) < *piḷ-ig-; with metathesis > *pig-iḷ- > pig-ul-; see Ka. piḷigu to burst, break; Ta. piḷ, piḷḷu (piṇṭ-, piṭ-ṭ-) v. i. to burst open; piḷa to be disunited; Ma. piḷaruka v. i. to burst; Kui plinga id.; Go. pink- v. i. to break up, of stiff things; Pj. pil- to crack; KGad. pilicen- (cen- to go) id.]

821 piḍucu IId tr. to squeeze, wring, press out (Śakunt., Āmu.); to press into a lump (HariV.); piḍuca n. a small lump of any semi-solid thing.

[Ka. pil̲i to squeeze out; become dry, sapless; Tu. purñcuni to squeeze, as a lemon; pureñcuni, purecuni id. (< *pil̲-unc-); Ko. piṛc- to clench (hand); Ta. pil̲i (pil̲int-) tr. to squeeze (Cīv.); to drip, as oil from hair; Ma. pil̲iyuka to wring out; Kui pṛihpa (pṛiht-) to squeeze out; Go. pīr- to squeeze, wring, to milk; Mlt. pilq- to squeeze; Brah. princ- to squeeze, massage, press hard. PDr. *pil̲-, also v. s. v. pisuku (< *pic-), piṇḍu.]

822 piṇḍu tr. to milk, squeeze for juice (later texts); wring a wet cloth, pinch ears (Mdn.); cf. piṇḍi, piṭṭu oil-cake (Mdn.).

[Ka. piṇḍu, hiṇḍu to squeeze out, wring, pinch, as ears; Tu. piṇḍi what is squeezed; hiṇḍi remnants after squeezing; purñcuni to squeeze; puṇṭuni to wring, as a wet garment; press for juice; Klm.(SR) pinḍ-, Klm.(E) pīnḍ- to squeeze, twist; Brah. princ- squeeze out. PDr. *pil̲-nt-/*pil̲-nc-; cf. piduku, pisuku, piḍucu.]

pituku var. of piduku, q. v. (HariV., Kāś.); the d-form is historically earlier.

823 pittu intr. to fart; a fart (late and Mdn., vulgar).

[Ka. hūsu a fart (< *pū- < *pī-); Tu. pūpuni to fart; pūki a fart; Kui pīt- to fart; Go. pitt- id.; Kur. pīt- (pitty-, pīt-) id.; Mlt. pīt- id. PDr. *pīt-/*pitt-, prob. related to words meaning 'excrement' from PDr. *pī-, see Kolami, Vocab. No. 2260.]

824 piduku (also pituku, q. v.) tr. to draw milk from cows, etc. (Bhr. II); to squeeze; intr. (cows, etc.) to give milk (Manu., Kāś.).

[Ka. hiduku to squeeze; To. pïθk- id.; pïθx- to be squeezed; Ta. pituṅku to protrude; to gush out (Tēv.); pitukku to press out (Nāl.); pitukkam projecting; Ma. pituṅṅuka to be squeezed; pitukkuka to crush, squeeze; Klm. (Kin.) pidk- to press; Pj. pīd- to squeeze, to milk; Kur. ped$^{e}$k̲h̲- (pedk̲h̲-) to squeeze, press hard, strain; cf.

Gȯ. piḍūk- to strain at stool; try hard at anything. PDr. *pit-uṅk-/*pit-ukk-, also see s.v. pisuku, piḍucu.]

825 pilucu IIa tr. to call, invite (Bhr. I), to point out, name (RR); to call, shout; der. n. pilupu call, invitation (late and Mdn.).

[Tu. buḷpuni to shout, exclaim; buḷpu a cry; To. piły- (piłc-) to utter cry of triumph; Ta. viḷ, viḷḷu (viṇ-ṭ-) to say, tell; viḷampu to speak, say; viḷar to call; viḷi to call, summon (Kr̲ḻ.); say, speak (Kamp.); to sing (Aiṅk.); to roar (Kamp.); n. sound (Perump.), word, speech (Tiv.); piḷippu calling, sound; piḷir̲u great noise; piḷir̲r̲u to make a roaring noise; cf. vīḷai shrill sound (Akan.), noise (Pu.Ve.); Ma. viḷikka to call, invite; viḷi n. a call, cry; Kui pṛī a cry of agony, a scream; Kur. piñj- tr. to give a name; Mlt. pinj- id. (< *piṇ-c-); Brah. pin name; pinī named. PDr. *pīḷ-/*pīṇ- : piḷ-V-/*piṇ-V-; PSDr. *piḷ-V-/*viḷ-V-, *vīḷ-.]

826 pisuku tr. to squeeze, knead with hand (Bhr. II), to press hard (Paṇḍ., Dvi.H.); to shampoo.

[Ka. pisuku, pisuṅku id.; hisaku, hiciku id.; Tu. piskuni, pīsuni to press, squeeze; Ko. pick- to squeeze, pinch; picg- to be soft so that it can be squeezed; Ta. picakku tr. to press between fingers and squeeze (Tiv.); picai id. (Tiruvāc.), to rub, apply on skin (Parip.); Kuvi (S) pic- to wring; Go. pisk- to knead flour; Kur. picka'- to press and bruise; pickār- refl.; PDr. *pic-uṅk-/*pic-ukk-; cf. Pj. pīk- to crush; pīc- to grind; Kur. pīkh- to press, squeeze; Mlt. pīq- id. (< *piy-k-); (> l.w. Skt. picc- to squeeze, see Burrow, TPS, 1945, pp. 109, 110; Skt. cc is more likely to be from PDr. *c than from *rc as Burrow assumed; also v.s.v. piduku. PDr. *pic-, pit-V-, *piḻ-.]

827 pīku tr. to pull out, root up, pluck out (no literary usages cited in Śab.R.); (< *piy-ṅk-).

[Ka. pīku id.; pinju, pikku to separate, disunite; Ta. piy tr. to pluck off, pull out; be drawn apart; peyar (< *piyar) to be separated (Tolk.); tr. to remove, dislodge (Kr̲ḻ.); to uproot; pĕr v.i. to separate; tr. to remove; Ma. pĕruka to come off, be plucked. PSDr. *piy-/*pī-; cf. Ta. puy tr. to pull, uproot (PN), be pulled, torn; i/u alternation common after bilabials.]

828 pīru (Brown, Śab.R.) to burst, as seams (< *pig-ur-), v.s.v. pigulu, pīlu; different derivative suffix.

pīr(u)cu same as pīl(u)cu, q.v (no literary usages).

829 pīlu (alt. of pīru) to be torn, (seams) to come off; contraction of pigulu, q.v. (lex.; no literary usages cited; Mdn.).

830 pīl(u)cu IIa tr. to suck in or up (Naiṣ.); to inhale, take in with breath (Āmu.); absorb, as water by soil (Mdn.).

[Ka. pīr, hīr, hīcu id.; cf. pīcu to squirt, syringe; Tu. pīruni to ooze; Ta. pīrccu, pīccu tr. to squirt; v. i. to purge, as motions; pīr n. abundant flow; pīl quantity of milk that gushes out at a single squeeze (loc.); Ma. pīccuka to squirt, syringe; Brah. pōsh- to suck, absorb; < PSDr. *pīr-c-/*pīl-c-; PDr. *pī-; also cf. Kur. phecka'- to throw by a syringe; phec'e adj. gushing out.]

831 puccu[1] IId and V (1) tr. to pull out, remove, as a thorn, an arrow, etc. (Bhr. I, II, KS); to abandon, give up (Bhr. II).

[Ta. puy- (puytt-) to pull out, extract (PN); be pulled out; Go. puck- (shoe, ring, etc.) to become loose; Klm.(E) pus- to pull out, take off (clothes); Nk. pus- id.; Pj. pucc- to extract, take off; Oll. puskir- pull off (clothes); KGad. pucc- to pull out; Mlt. puc- to undress. PDr. *puc- < *puy-c-; cf. Kur. pud$^u$g- (pudg-) to pluck out hair, etc.; to strip by plucking.]

puccu[1] IId and V (2) tr. to release, as a sigh; to send away, let go (Bhr. I); often occurs with *-tencu (tĕ-, tēr-); pu-ttencu, pu-ttĕ-N-, pu-ttēr- id.

[This is either connected with the same etyma as those in (1) above, also cf. parallel usages in Klm. (Emeneau, Kolami, Vocab. No. 732); or, it may be related to the following: Ta. puku (pukk-) to go; (pukutt-) tr. to cause to enter (Tolk.), insert, etc., v. s. v. pōvu.]

puccu[2] (< pruccu, q. v.; Mdn.).

832 puṭṭu intr. to be born, produced or created (Bhr. I); to occur, arise (Bhr. II); to accrue (HariV.); to form, come into existence; to manifest (Vasu.); adj. congenital; der. n. puṭṭuka, puṭṭuvu birth, origin (classical).

[Ka. puṭṭu, huṭṭu, uṭṭu to be born, spring up; Tu. puṭṭuni id.; Ko. puṭ- v. i. to grow; uṭ- to sprout, be born; To. uṭ- be born (only in poetry); Go. puṭṭ- to be born, of a child; to occur; Klm.(SR) puṭṭ- to be born; Nk. Pj. KGad. puṭṭ- id. PDr. *puṭ-.]

833 puḍuku (also puṇuku) (1) tr. to hold with finger-tips (RR); to feel with hand (Dvi.H.); to give in small quantities (Daśā.); to feel or grope in darkness (quoted by ĀVāc.); n. giving, bestowing (lex.); der. n. puḍikili holding, taking (Bhōj.); a handful (with all fingers held together to make it bowl-shaped to hold things); puḍisili id.; puḍisil-incu to hold a handful (Bhr. I).

[Ka. puḍuku, puḍuṅku, huḍaku to search or feel with hand; to seek for; Tu. puḍu, puḍa n. holding, grasping; Kuvi (F) brūc- (brūt-) to snatch; Klm.(E) puḍk- to touch; Nk. puṛk- id.; cf. Pj. piḍk- to embrace. PSDr. and PCDr. *puṭ-uṅk-/*puṭ-ukk-; also cf. forms from *piṭ- to hold, grasp, Kolami, Vocab. No. 688.]

puḍuku (also puṇuku) (2) tr. to pluck off, nip off (Kāś.); to squeeze, press (Bhg.).

[Ta. piṭuṅku tr. to extract, pull out or off, etc.; Ma. piṭuṅṅuka id.; Kui pṛuṅga to be snapped, plucked; pṛupka (< pṛuk-p-; pṛukt-) to pluck; cf. Ta. puṭai tr. to snap, as carpenter's string.]

834 punũgu* (other versions punugu/pungu) to withdraw, retreat, hesitate (Āmu. and later works).

[Cf. Ka. piṅgu to retreat, go away, fail; from PDr. *pin- back, behind, v. s. v. pikku[1]; ī̆/ū̆- alternation after bilabials common, see s. v. pittu, pī̃ku, puḍuku, etc.]

835 puliyu III intr. to become or turn sour, to ferment; der. n. pulusu, pulupu acidity, sourness; puli, pulla, pullani adj. sour.

[Ka. puḷi (> huḷi, uḷi), puḷḷa, puḷu, pulla acidity, sourness; puṇise, huṇise tamarind; Tu. puliyuni, pulipuni to become sour; puḷi, puli sourness; Ko. puḷy- (puḷc-) be sour; puḷc- id.; To. pūḻy- (pūḻc-) id.; Ta. puḷi to ferment, turn sour (Cīv.); n. acidity (Akan.); puḷippu n. id.; Ma. puḷikka be sour; puḷi sourness; Kuvi (S) pulla adj. sour; Klm.(SR) puliy- to get sour (of teeth); Klm.(E) pulle adj. sour; Pj. pulp- (pult-) to turn sour; pul adj. sour; KGad. pullā adj. id. PSDr. and PCDr. *puḷ-; PSDr. *puḷ-i-.]

836 pulumu (Śab.R.) tr. to rub and wash with the two hands; to scour; to smear or plaster in lumps; to beat, thrash; n. pulumuḍu (no literary usages cited; Mdn.).

837 pūcu[1] IIa intr. to blossom, flower, bloom (Bhr. I); pūvu/puvvu, pū flower.

[Ka. pū (> hū) to flower, bloom; To. pūf- (pūt-) id.; Ta. pū (pūtt-) to blossom (Aiṅk.); tr. to produce as flowers; Ma. pūkka to blossom; Kui pūpa (pūt-) id.; Go. pōī- (pōī-sī) id.; Pj. pūp- (pūt-) id.; KGad. pūk- (pūt-) id.; Kur. pū̃d-, puỹd- id.; Mlt. pūth- id. PDr. *pū-/*puy-; Go. pōī < *poy-; for related etyma meaning 'flower' see Emeneau, Kolami, Vocab. No. 736.]

838 pūcu[2] IId intr. (tongue) to blister or become sore, discolored.

[Tu. pū agra a sore mouth; Ko. pūv- (pūt-) (mouth) becomes dry with fever.]

pūcu[3] (Mdn. Te. alternant of pūncu, tr. of pūnu; Viśākha. dial.).

839 pūḍu to be buried, filled; tr. pūḍ(u)cu tr. to fill up, bury; pūḍ(u)pu burying, burial; a treasure-trove.

[Ka. pūḻ, pūḻu (> hūḻu, hūṇu) to wrap in, bury; Ma. pūḻuka to be buried; be lost in the ground; pūntuka to sink in the ground; pūttuka to bury; Klm.(E) pur- (hole) becomes filled in; Nk. purp- to bury; Kur. putt- to set (of sun only). PDr. *pū-, *pū-ḻ-; cf. Ta. pūḻi soft mire or mud (that is dug out); Ko. pūṭ- to fit into a sheath.]

840 pūnu (1) intr./tr. to undertake, engage in, assume; to bear; to attempt, endeavor (HariV.); pūn(u)cu to cause to undertake (Bhr. II).

[Ka. pūṇ to vow, to begin; pūḍu to prepare, arrange, begin; pūn to attempt; Tu. hūṇè a vow; puṇepini to compete, vie; Ta. pūṇ, pūṇṇu (pūṇ-ṭ-) to undertake (Kamp.); pūṇi to make a vow; Ma. punayuka to undertake.]

pūnu (2) to wear, put on; pūn(u)cu tr. to yoke bullocks, etc.; to fasten horses to chariot (Bhr. I).

[Ka. pūṇ to fix an arrow; pūḍu to put to; tie, fasten; Ko. pūṛ- to yoke; To. pūḷ- (pūḍ-) to wear around the neck; pūṭ- to tie around the neck; pūf- (pūt-) to wear; pūc- (pūč-) to put (garment) on someone else; Ta. pūṇ (pūṇṭ-) tr. to put on, wear (Tiruvāc.); be yoked with (Kṟḷ.); be yoked; pūṭṭu to yoke bullocks (Patiṟ.); to place, put; Ma. pūṭṭuka to yoke, put to carriage; pūṇuka to be yoked; put on clothes; Kui pūnḍa to meet; pūṭpa to yoke; Go. puht- to plow, lit. to press upon; weigh heavily, of a burden; Kur. pund$^{u}$r- to pass round one's neck; pūn necklace; Mlt. pūn- to put on one's neck (as necklace); pund- put on another's neck. PDr. *pūṇ-, *pūṇ-t- > *puṭṭ-; Te. pūncu (< *pūṇ-c-); cf. Ta. pūṉai to put on, as clothes (Tēv.); to decorate (PN); to string, bind (Kalit.); Ma. punayuka to put on; Go. pōnḍ- to put on a dhoti, of men only. This latter set of etyma indicates either that -ṇ/-n are suffixes, or that there was a merger of these two phonemes in PDr., thus yielding *pūṇ-/*pūn-.]

pū̃cu* IId (ĀVāc.) to undertake, v.s.v. pūnu; der. n.; cf. pū̃pu an endeavor, undertaking (HariV.).

841 pūyu III tr. to apply, smear, besmear, daub.

[Ka. pūsu to smear, apply, spread over; Tu. pūjuni id.; Ta. pūcu id. (Cīv.); to clean, wash with water; Ma. pūcu, pūyuka to smear whitewash; Kur. pot- (potc-) to whitewash, plaster.]

pekalu (same as pegalu) to set out on a journey (JBh.); (word) to come out from mouth with difficulty, out of hesitation, etc. (Mdn.); tr. pekal(u)cu to remove, rout (late).

842 pegalu (also pekalu) intr. to be plucked, pulled out (Bhg.); come up to surface, turn up; issue, be dug up; tr. pegal(u)cu to pull out, rout.

[< *pey-al < *piy-al; *piy-, v. s. v. pīku; also Ma. pikkuka to break in pieces; piccuka to pinch, tear.]

pegal(u)cu IIb tr. of pegalu, q. v.

peṭilu same as peḍulu, q. v.

peṭ(u)lu var. of peḍulu.

843 peṭṭu[1] tr. to place, put, keep, deposit; give, serve, as food; put on or in (Bhr. II, HariV.); to hit, beat; n. a blow, stroke.

[Ka. peṭṭu to beat with a hammer; push in; heṭṭu to put, put into; Tu. peṭṭu̥ a blow; Ma. peṭṭu a blow; veṭṭu id.; Klm. (Kin.) peṭṭa id.; < PSDr. *peṭ-/*veṭ-.]

844 peṭṭu[2] to lay eggs, of birds; bring forth young, of small animals, like cats, dogs, etc.; (< *peṯṯ-).

[Ka. peṟ, peṟu (pett-) to beget; Tu. pedpini, peddüni id.; Ko. perv- (perd-) to be born; To. pēr- (pēd-) id.; Klm.(E) peṭ- to bear young (of animals); Nk. peṭṭ- to give birth to; cf. Pj. ped- to obtain. PSDr. and PCDr. *peṯ-.]

845 peḍulu* (also peṭulu, peṭlu) to break with a cracking sound (Bhr. I); explode; to open in chinks. Onomatopoetic.

[Ka. peṭal, peṭṭalu, peṭlu imit. sound of a gun; cracking, as rocket; Ta. veṭi intr. to crack, break, split; explode; n. explosion, noise, thunder; veṭil explosion; Ma. veṭi n. id.; veṭikka to explode; cf. Go. piṛ- to burst, as an ant-eaten mud wall, or cotton bolls; Pj. piḍ- (piṭṭ-) to explode. PSDr. and PCDr. *peṭ-/*veṭ- : piṭ-.]

846 penāgu intr. to be twisted; to struggle, fight, wrangle (Bhr. II); tr. penācu to twist (Bhōj.); penāgonu to join, be intertwined (Bhr. I).

[Ka. peṇagu (> heṇagu), peṇasu to wrangle, fight; Ta. piṇaṅku to be at variance; be intertwined (Maṇi.); piṇakku to fasten, intertwine (Parip.); piṇaṅṅuka to be entangled; to quarrel; piṇakkuka to entangle; GoM. piṛaṅg- to entwine. PSDr. and PCDr. *piṇ-aṅk-/ *piṇ-akk-, also v. s. v. penayu.]

847 penayu* III (Śab.R., ĀVāc.) intr. to be joined, intertwined (Vēm.); tr. penapu to link together, join; n. difference, dispute.

[Ka. peṇe (> heṇe) to intertwine; be joined; piṇil a braid of hair; Ko. pīṇ- (pīṇḍ-) to become entwined; pīṇḍ- tr. to entwine; To. pīn- (pīny-) (hair) is matted; to weave basket; Ta. piṇai v. i. to entwine, unite (Cīv.); tr. to fasten, tie; piṇi to tie (Malaip.); Ma. piṇayuka to be entangled; piṇekka to yoke; Kuvi (F) pet- to thread; Brah. pinn- be twisted. PDr. *piṇ-; PSDr. *piṇ-i, *piṇ-ay-; cf. Ta. piṉṉu to plait, braid (Cīv.); become united (another case of ṇ/n alternation in the ancient language; also v. s. v. pūnu).]

848 penucu* IId tr. to foster, rear, grow.

Ta. pēṇu tr. to cherish, foster, send; to protect (PN).]

pencu IIb tr. of perugu, < *per-nc-; alternatively var. of penucu, q. v.

pempu* (Śab.R.) (tr. of perugu (2), q. v.) tr. to destroy, ruin (Bhg., Vasu.); n. damage, destruction.

849 perayu* III (ĀVāc.) tr. to obtain.

[Ka. peṟ, peṟu to get, gain; Ta. peṟu to obtain, possess (Nāl.); Ma. peṟuka id.; Pj. ped- id.]

850 per(u)gu (Śab.R.), also per(u)vu (HariV.); ĀVāc. gives perũgu (1) to grow, increase (Mārk., Pāṇḍ.); to accumulate, be augmented; to advance, extend, expand.

[Ta. peruku to increase, become full; swell, overflow (Tiv.); Ma. perukuka to grow large; perukkuka to multiply; Klm. perg- to grow; Nk. perg- id. PSDr. and PCDr. *peruk-; forms without the velar suffix: Ka. piri abundance; percu to grow, increase; Tu. percuni, perjuni id.; Ta. peru to grow large; SDr. peru-/pēr- adj. big; Go. pirr- to grow, germinate; GoM. pērs- to extend; Pj. berto big; KGad. *ber- big (in berbul tiger: Te. bebbuli); Kur. pard- to grow in number, size, etc., thrive; parica'- to rear, breed; Brah. pir- to swell, of body; PDr. *pēr-/*per-V-.]

perugu (2) intr. to break or snap, as the marriage-thread of woman (elegant, to avoid the taboo).

[Cf. Ta. peruku to be injured, ruined, used euphemistically (Tolk.); be put out, extinguished.]

851 peṟuku[1] (also perku; ĀVāc., also peruku) tr. to pull out, pluck up (BhR).

[Tu. porpuni to pull, pluck off, root up; Ko. perṭ- to dislocate (joint, by force); Ta. piṟaḻ to be dislodged, dislocated; GoM. piṛaṅg- to pull; pēs- to expel; the words meaning 'to pick up, weed' may belong here, see Emeneau, Kolami, Vocab. No. 3107.]

852 peṟuku[2]* to carry loads (Bhr. I); peṟika a bullock (which carries loads).

[Ka. pēṟu to lift up, load, pile up; n. bullock-load; Tu. perikè a bullock's load; burden; To. pīṟ- (pīṯ-) to carry; Ta. piṟakku to heap, pile up; peṟṟam a bull; pile; buffalo (Tolk.); Kuvi (F) pērh- to lift; Kuvi (S) perh- raise, lift. PSDr. and PCDr. *pēṯ- : *peṯ-V-.]

853 per̲ūgu (Śab.R.) intr. to swell, rise; (body) to swell in rage, joy, etc.; to be possessed.

[Ta. pir̲aṅku to become high, lofty (PN), to grow full (PN), be exalted; grow large in size (Malaip.); per̲r̲u bigness (Tolk.).]

854 pē̃ḍu (ĀVāc.; Śab.R. gives as pēḍu) tr. to twine, twist; cf. pēnu.

[Kuvi(F) pet- to thread; Brah. pēṛ- to twine round.]

855 pēnu to twine, twist; cf. pē̃ḍu id.

856 pēru (Śab.R.; Dh.M., as pēru, pēr̲u) intr. to curdle, solidify (HariV.); pēruḍu n. curdling; perugu curdled milk.

[Ka. per̲, per̲u (pett-) to curdle, coagulate; heppu curdling agent: Tu. perpuni to be curdled; perpu curdling agent; Ko. pet- to solidify; To. per̲f- (per̲t-) id. (milk); pešf- (pešt-) id.; cf. Ta. pirai buttermilk used for curdling milk; Ma. piriyuka to coagulate, as milk; piraṅṅuka to curdle; Klm.(SR) perag curd. PSDr. *pēt̲- : *pet̲-V-; r-forms are later.]

857 pēr(u)cu$^{1*}$ IId intr. to increase, rise, swell (Bhr. II).

[V. s. v. perugu; cf. Tu. pērcuni, percuni rise, increase; Ka. percuni.]

858 pēr(u)cu$^{2}$ IId tr. to pile or heap up, to arrange in a column; pēr(u)pu n. a pile, heap (that is arranged) (JBh.).

[Ka. pēr̲u to lift up, load, pile up; Tu. pēruni to load; bēruni to be lifted up, as hand; other forms, v. s. v. per̲uku$^{2}$.]

859 pēlu$^{1}$ intr. (gun, etc.) to explode; to break; to be fried or parched; (body) to be covered with eruption; to have pimples on body through prickly heat; to pop up when fried or parched.

[Klm.(E) pēl- (grain layel) pops when parched over fire; Emeneau connects with Ta. piḷa, etc., but those etyma point to a PDr. *ī̆, i.e., *pīḷ-/*piḷ-V-, whereas the Te. form presupposes *pēḷ-; alternatively, < prēlu$^{2}$, q. v.]

860 pēlu$^{2}$ (< prēlu$^{1}$, q. v.) intr. to prattle, babble, talk nonsense.

861 pokku$^{1}$ intr. to be blistered (Bhr. II); n. blister.

[Ko. puglc- (hand) becomes blistered from heat; To. pïg- to get blistered; Ta. pokku to be blistered; po- (pott-) id.; Kur. pokkh-, Mlt. pok- id.; for words meaning 'blister' n., see Emeneau, Kolami, Vocab. No. 3114.]

862 pokku$^{2*}$ intr. to grieve, be sorrowful (Bhg.).

[V. s. v. pogulu; < *pok-.]

pogacu IIb (tr. of pogayu, q. v.) to cause to smoke, to season food (Bhīm.).

863 pogaḍu (also povaḍu) tr. to praise, applaud (Bhg.); compliment, flatter; der. n. pogaḍ(i)ta praise, worship, compliment (Bhr. II, UH).

[Ka. pogal̲, pogal̲u to praise; n. praise, renown; Tu. pogaruni, pogaḷuni, pugaruni to praise, flatter; pugatè, pogatè praise; Ta. pukal̲ to praise (Tiv.); n. eulogy (PN); pukai to be made public; Ma. pukal̲uka to praise, be praised; pukal̲ttuka to praise; pukal̲ n. renown; Kui pōnga to be praised, made known; become known; n. fame; pōpka (< pōk-p-; pōk-t-) to make known; Mlt. pog̣olar- to be praised; to extol; pog̣ole renown; praise; cf. Pj. KGad. pokk- to speak, tell; Ta. pukal to say, declare, state (Kamp.); n. word; fame; pōr̲r̲u to praise, applaud (< *pok-ar̲r̲-); Ma. pukaluka to speak. PDr. *pō̆-, *pok-; PSDr. *pok-al̲.]

864 pogayu* III (also povayu) intr. to smoke, emit smoke; be smoky, smoulder (Bhr. II); poga n. smoke; tr. pogacu to cause to smoke; pogacu, pogapu to season food (Naiṣ.).

[Ka. poge to be smoked; Tu. pogeyuni id.; pogepuni to fumigate; Ta. pukai (pukai-nt-) v.i. to smoke, steam (Tiruvāc.); (pukaitt-) intr. to fume with anger; tr. to cause to smoke (PN); Ma. pukayuka to be darkened by smoke; be smoked; pukekka to fumigate; Mlt. mog̣- to emit smoke; mog̣j- to fumigate; mog̣tr- to cause to smoke; almost all languages possess etyma for the corresponding noun form, see Emeneau, Kolami, Vocab. No. 704; *pok-V- < *poy-V-, cf. esp. GoA. poya smoke.]

pogucu* IIb (Brown; same as pogacu, q.v.).

865 pogulu* (also povulu) intr. to be sorrowful, afflicted, to smoulder (Bhg.).

[Tu. buguḷuni to be grieved; Ta. pukai to burn, as heart, to grieve; cf. Te. pokku id. PSDr. *puk-, altern. *po-ṅk-/*po-kk-; *po- to burn is the ultimate root, cf. Tu. potta adj. hot, burning; pottuni v.i. to burn; pod(u)puni to broil; poyilu̥ an abscess; Kuvi(S) puiya spark; also v.s.v. pokku, poṅgu.]

866 poṅgu intr. to bubble up, boil; overflow in boiling; to be elated, jubilant; be proud; be puffed up; (stomach) to be bloated; n. boiling, bubbling, overflowing, increase (Āmu.); elation, joy; pride (HariV.); adj. overflowing, boiling.

[Ka. poṅgu to boil over; swell; be elated; Tu. boṅguni to be distended; Ko. poŋg- to spring forth magically; (anger) increases; pog- (pogy-) v.i. to boil over; To. pïg- (pïgy-) to bubble up; (stomach) swells; Ta. poṅku to boil up by heat; to foam (Nāl.); swell with joy (Tiruvāc.); be swollen; n. prosperity; Ma. poṅṅuka v.i. to boil over; rise; pokkuka to raise; Kui poṅg- to be spilt; Kuvi(S) poṅg- to overswell, to swell (body); Kuvi(F) to inflate;

pōng- to swell; Kuvi(S) boi(y)- (bōt-) to overflow (a vessel, etc.); Go. pōng- (a river) to overflow; pōht- to drown a man; cf. pōṛ- to swell, of dough; grow big physically and socially; Mlt. poṉgj- to be increased, be abundant; Kui pō̃j- to spread along by degrees (as swelling, an infection or sore). PDr. *po-ṅk-/*po-kk-; pre-Kur. *po-nc-; ultimately *poy-/*pō-, *poy-/*puy-, o/u alternation common before y; cf. Kur. pūkh- to swell (as soaked rice); tr. to boil vegetables; Mlt. pūg- to swell, boil; pūgr- to be swollen; pūgpe boiled grain; < *puy-k-.]

poṭamu* intr. to be born, to spring up (Vikram.) (-ṭ- could be a wrong version in the text instead of -ḍ-; var. of poḍamu, q.v.; a single usage cited).

867 poṭ(u)lu[1] (Dh.M) intr. (paint or plaster) to come off in slits.

[Ta. poṭu-poṭu v.i. to snap, as cords; wamble, as bowels; Ma. puṭṭuka to burst, explode; Kur. poṭpoṭr- to crackle several times in succession; also see s.v. peḍ(u)lu, peṭlu.]

868 poṭlu[2]* (Śab.R.) intr. fungus to form (rare).

869 poḍamu* (also poḍmu, Bhr. III) intr. to arise, be born (Pāṇḍ.); be produced, caused or engendered.

[Ka. poṇmu, puṇmu to rise, spring up; be produced; Tu. poṭṭè a tender ear of corn; cf. pojilu̥ a germ, sprout; Ta. poṭi to spring up, arise, appear (Cīv.); puṭai to come to light, rise; Ma. poṭiyuka to spring up; appear in every minute particle; < PSDr. *poṭ-/ ? *poṇ-); also see poḍucu[2].]

870 poḍugu* intr. to grow high, lofty: to increase; n. height, loftiness; adj. lofty; cf. poḍavu height, length.

[Ka. poḍe extension, height, length; etymologically connected with forms meaning 'to rise,' etc.; v. s. v. poḍamu, poḍucu[2].]

871 poḍucu[1] IIa intr. to quarrel, fight a battle (Bhr. I, II); tr. to pierce, prick, stab (Bhr. I); to punch; to bore, make a hole with a pointed instrument; (scorpion) to sting; der. n. pōṭu fight, piercing,. hit; poḍi powder, dust (Bhr. I).

[Ka. poḍe to strike, beat; shoot arrow, fell, cut off; poṭṭare, pōṭi a hole or hollow of a tree; also hōṭi, hoṭri id.; Tu. poḍiyuni to pulverize; poḍi powder; puḍapuni to break, burst; puḍipuni to quarrel, fight; poṭṭu adj. injured; Ta. poṭi to be broken to pieces; perish; to puncture; be perforated (Maṇi.); puṭai to thrash, beat, (Kamp.); n. blow (Cīv.); Ma. poṭiyuka to be pulverized, destroyed; poṭikka to pulverize; poṭi powder; Kui pospa (post-) to pierce, bore; bojo wood dust; Kuvi(S) plū-, pluph'- to hit; Kuvi(F) poth-

to hollow out; Go. pohpī a chisel (-h- < *-s- < *-ṭ-); cf. Kur. phoṭ- to hit with a stick; Mlt. puṛg- to break up flooring. *poṭ- < *poḷ-t-; many languages show root-final ḷ with the nuclear meaning 'to make a hole,' etc. from *poḷ-, < *po-ḷ-, cf. Ta. po-, pottu.]

872 poḍucu[2] IIa to rise, as heavenly bodies (Bhr. II); poḍupu n. rising of sun or moon.

[V. s. v. poḍamu (< *poṭ-); Ta. poṭi, Ma. poṭiyuka, poṭikka to rise, spring up.]

873 podalu* intr. to prosper, thrive, flourish, increase (Bhr. III, HariV.); podalu konu to increase, grow big (Nirv.).

[Ka. podal̠ to rise; become conspicuous; Tu. podaluni to come up, rise up; Ta. potir v. i. to increase, swell, become large (Parip.); poti fulness, stoutness; Ma. potiruka be enlarged. PSDr. *pot-.]

874 podugu (also poduvu) (1) to cover, surround; set as precious stones; lay in covering; embed; n. covering.

[Ka. poduṅku to hide; pudugu, hudugu id.; to be covered; tr. to insert, shelter; pode, hode to put over, inwrap, cover; Tu. pudepuni to put on clothes; podepu wearing apparel; Ta. potukku to conceal; poti tr. to hide, cover; n. pack, bundle; putai to be covered (Maturai.); tr. to bury, cover (Cilap.), inlay, as jewels; pottu to bury, cover (Kamp.); Ma. potiyuka to cover; potukka to inwrap; poti a bundle; putayuka to be covered; putekka tr. to cover, bury; Kui poja to pack, make a bundle; Kuvi (F) pŏj- to tie in a cloth; Kur. pojj- tr. to wrap around (paper or cloth); Mlt. poj- to wrap, twist; Brah. putunk bundle; puc clothing. PDr. *poc- > *pot-; PSDr. *poi-, *pot-i, *pot-ay, *pot-uṅk-/*pot-ukk-); (> l. w. Skt. potikā cloth; Pkt. potta- garment; see Burrow, TPS, 1945, pp. 112, 113; No. 41).]

podugu (2) tr. to hatch, as a hen; to sit on or over.

[Tu. podepuni, pudepuni to brood, as a hen her chickens.]

875 poduru* intr. to blossom, flower (late).

[V. s. v. podalu.]

poduvu* (alt. of podugu, q. v.; Bhr. II).

876 ponaru* intr. to suit, be agreeable; to happen, occur; n. agreeableness, fitness; tr. ponar(u)cu to cause to fit, to make, accomplish (Bhr. II, Mārk.).

[Ka. poṇar to be joined, to couple; poṇarcu to join; Ta. puṇar tr. to associate with (Nāl.); to undertake; intr. to suit, fit (PN); be possible; (puṇar-tt-) tr. to bring about, do, make (Kamp.); Ma.

puṇaruka to be joined. PSDr. *poṇ-ar < PDr. *puṇ-ar-, v. s. v. pūnu.]

877 ponalu* intr. to burn, be ablaze (Paṇḍ.).

878 poncu IId intr. to waylay, lurk, lie in wait; n. lurking, lying in wait; poncika id.

[Ka. poncu (> honcu) to be in wait, lurk; honcu to look after, wait for expectantly; Kui pōrpa (pōrt-) to watch for, lie in wait; Kuvi (F) pōrh- id. Te. Ka. forms from *por-nc- < *por-unc-; PDr. *pōr- : *pār-; cf. Ta. Ma. Ka. pār- to look for, wait for; Kuvi (F) par- to search; see Burrow, DS V, p. 613.]

879 ponju (same as pō̃ju, q. v.) intr. to split into filaments, draw out in threads.

880 pondu tr. to obtain, gain, get; to reach; to suit; to feel, experience, enjoy, suffer; to undergo, sustain, bear; to copulate; n. fitness (Bhr. II), harmony, suitability, aptness, friendship; obtaining; copulation; pondika n. id. (< *por-nd-); ponta adv. near.

[Ka. pondu, hondu to join; pordu, poddu, hoddu to join, approach; obtain, fit; Tu. porduni to approach; be accessible; be in harmony; Ta. poruntu v. i. to agree, be suitable; come in contact; tr. to combine with; reach (PN); cohabit with (Maṇi.); poruttu tr. to fit; Ma. porunnuka to be joined, to suit, agree; poruttuka to join together; Go. (Bilas.) pōrī̃ near (LSI, IV, p. 489); Pj. porc- to get; KGad. pōrc- to be found, obtained; Kur. pur$^{u}$m- to mix; unite two or more ingredients into one compound; Mlt. purm- to mix parched and ground grain with water; cf. Kui pomba to embrace (? *por-mb-). PDr. *pōr- : *por-V-; PSDr. *por-unt-/ *por-utt-; also *por-u, *por-ay, v. s. v. porayu.]

881 porāṭu* to fry (as curry), to cook vegetables by allowing the water to evaporate in the pot itself (Āmu.); cf. proyyi a potsherd, Mdn. poyyi.

[Ka. puri to dry, parch, roast; Tu. poriyuni to be broiled; poripuni to broil, parch; purkuni to be half-baked; Ko. poyr- (porc-) to parch grain; Ta. pori to be parched, baked, fried, roasted; tr. to fry (PN), parch, toast, as grain; Ma. porikka to fry, parch; Go. pōṛ-pōṛ-(ai-) to be nicely cooked (of jaori); Kur. porchō adj. (of grains only) to be half-cooked, not sufficiently boiled. PDr. *pōr- : por-V-.]

882 porayu* III (Śab.R. quotes also por̲ayu) intr. to occur (Bhīm.); accrue; tr. to gain, obtain, get (Bhr. II).

[Ka. pore to be joined; tr. to join, come near; Tu. puresuni, pureisuni v.i. to complete, fulfil, be satisfied; Ta. purai v.i. to be appropriate (Tolk.), to occur (Parip.); poru tr. to reach, join, extend, unite (PN); Ma. poruka to meet, vie. PSDr. *por-ay, *por-u-; v.s.v. pondu.]

883 poralu (also porlu) intr. to roll on ground, wallow; to overflow; roll over; n. rolling (of tides, etc.), overflowing; n. poralika id.; tr. poral(u)cu to roll over.

[Ka. poraḷ, poraḷu (> horaḷu, horaḍu) to roll, welter, wallow; Tu. poreluni id.; porepuni, purepuni tr. to roll, turn over; porṅkuni tr. to roll, run over; Ko. porṇ- (porḍ-) to roll backwards and forwards; Ta. puraḷ (puraṇ-ṭ-) v.i. to roll over (Kr̲ḷ.); revolve; abound; Ma. puraḷuka v.i. to roll; Kuvi (S) pŏrh'- to swim. PSDr. *por-aḷ- < PDr. *pur-aḷ; cf. Ta. puri to be twisted, to curl (Malaip.); Ma. puriyuka id.; etc.]

884 polayu* III intr. to wander, move about (Bhr. III), to spread, to approach (Āmu.); to enter (Vikram.).

[Cf. Ka. poḷe to roll about, move to and fro; Ma. puḷayuka to twirl about; puḷekka to roll oneself.]

885 poliyu* III intr. to be spoiled, destroyed (Bhr. II); to die, perish; der. n. poliyika destruction, death.

[Ma. poliyuka to be extinguished; polikka to end; Pj. pŏl to finish, complete; Kur. pol- to be unable, to fail; polpolr- to yield to pressure; Mlt. pol- to be unable, helpless; poltr- to tire out. PDr. *pŏl; cf. Ka. pondu to die; Ta. pon̲r̲u to perish, be ruined (Kr̲ḷ.); to die (Nāl.); to be reduced, wearied by exertion (< *pon-t̲- < *pol-nt-).]

886 polucu* IIa intr. to appear, arise (Pāri.); to shine; to be steady, suitable; to be beautiful; der. n. polupu elegance, grace; manner, steadiness (Bhr. II).

[Tu. poli increase, abundance; Ta. poli to increase (Maturai.); shine; be great or celebrated (PN); live long and prosperously (Tolk.); occur; polivu n. bloom, beauty, prosperity, greatness; por̲pu n. beauty, gracefulness (Kamp.); excellence (Tolk.); cf. Mlt. pulpulr- shine through whiteness. PDr. *pol-/*pon-; also cf. Ta. pon̲ splendor, sun; pular to dawn, clear up; Ma. pularuka (light) to appear; to dawn; to subsist, live.]

povaḍu* (var. of pogaḍu, q.v.).

povayu* (var. of pogayu, q.v.).

povulu* (var. of pogulu, q.v.).

887 posāgu to be favorable (Bhr. II), be agreeable, consistent, just

(Bhr. II); to suit one's constitution; to be got, obtained; to accrue; to happen, befall; (friendship) to prevail.

[Ka. posayisu, posavisu to join, unite, apply to, attach; To. pōc- (pōč-) to be becoming; (dress) suits; Ta. pocuṅku (prob. l. w. < Te.) to be united, to agree. Connected with etyma from *pot- meaning 'relationship,' cf. Te. pottu, Tu. podu; PSDr. *pōc- : *poc-V-; *poc-/*pot-.]

888 pō̃cu IId, pō̃ju (Dh.M as pōcu, pōju; Śab.R., also prō̃ju) tr. to split into filaments, draw out in threads (UH); cf. pō̃ca a blade of grass; prō̃gu, pō̃gu a bit of thread, etc.; (< *poḻ-anc-, *poḻ-aṅk-).

[Cf. Ta. pōḻ to be cleft, split (Tiv.); tr. to split, cleave open (Patiṟ.); n. cleft, piece (Perump.); leather strap (PN), sheet (Cīv.); Ka. pōḻ, pōḻu to cleave, split into two parts; n. a split, slice; any artificial ornamental fabric; Pj. pōṛ- to split, cleave. PDr. *pōḻ.]

889 pōyu III tr. to pour, as liquids; cast in metal; to fling; release bow-string; intr. (sweat or pus) to form, arise; n. pō̃ta casting metal into mold.

[Ka. poy to pour, cast; pōcal pouring water; Ta. poḻi to pour forth, as rain (PN); v. i. to flow, overflow; Ma. poḻiyuka v. i. to pour down; tr. to shower; poḻikka to shower down; Kui popka (< pok-p-; pok-t-) to spill, scatter; Kur. poē̃- (poññ-, pō̃yy-) (rain) to fall; poē̃d- to cause rain to fall; posskā amm rain (amm water); Mlt. poy- (pos-) to rain. PDr. *poc-/*poḻ-; *poc- > *pō̆̃y-.]

890 pōru tr. to fight, combat, struggle against, rival, quarrel (Bhr. II); n. a battle, fight (Bhr. II); pōr-āḍu to fight.

[Ka. pōr, pōru (> hōr, hōru) to wrestle, fight; Tu. pōriyuni to wrestle, quarrel; pordu battle; Ko. pōr a fight; Ta. poru to engage in a battle (PN); strive against; compete, vie with (PN); n. fight, battle (Kṟḷ.); Ma. poruka to meet in battle, to vie; pōr battle; Kui prohpa (proht-) to fight, scold; pōru a quarrel, contention. PSDr. and PCDr. *pōr- : *por-V-.]

891 pōlu tr. to resemble, to be like or similar to (Bhr. II); intr. to be, to exist; to be beautiful; be suitable, possible (Bhr. II); adj. suitable (HariV.); pōl(i)ka comparison, similarity.

[Ka. pōl (> hōl) to be like, to resemble; pol to agree with, liken, be fit, proper; Ta. pōl (pōṉ-ṟ-) tr. to resemble, be like (Kṟḷ.); a particle of comparison (Kṟḷ.); Ma. pōluka to resemble; Kuvi (S) poli'- to compare; < PSDr. *pōl-.]

892 pōvu V (allomm. pō-/pōv- freely before suffixes beginning with a; before u, pō-; before the front-vowel suffixes pōy-; e.g., inf. pō-,

pōva-; imp. pō, po-mmu, po-ṇḍu; pp. pōy-i) intr. to go, proceed, pass, be over; to perish (Bhr. II); to be lost, ruined; to begin, be on (with the inf. of verbs) (Bhr. I); be about to (with inf., e.g., paḍābōvu to be about to fall, etc.); der. n. pōka going, departure.

[Ka. pōgu to go; hōgu id.; Tu. pōpini to go; be lost; to pass, depart, start; To. pīx- (pī-) to go; Ta. pō (pō-nt-) to go, proceed (Maṇi.); pōkku to send, spread; to cease (PN); Ma. pōka to go away; to go; be lost; pōkkuka to make to go; < PSDr. *pō-, *pō-k- < *pok-a- < PDr. *puk-a-; cf. Ka. pugu to enter in; Ta. puku to reach, enter (Kṟḷ.); go, proceed; pukavu, pukal entering (Aiṅk.); Ma. pukuka to enter; cf. Kuvi (S) hō'- to go.]

893 prabalu intr. to grow, increase, become great or powerful; to predominate; (disease) to aggravate.

[Prob. l. w. < Skt. prabala- strong, powerful.]

894 prabbu[1*] intr. to increase, flourish (Bhr. II); spread, thrive; to prevail; (< *parb-).

[Ka. parvu, parbu, habbu v. i. to spread; prevail; Tu. parbuni, habbuni v. i. to spread, multiply; parambuni id.; Ta. parampu v. i. to spread, as water, extend. PSDr. *par-ump-/-amp-; further v. s. v. par(u)vu, paracu, prā̃ku.]

895 prabbu[2*] (Śab.R.) tr. to abuse, blame, censure; n. blame (Kāś.); (< *paḻ-b- < *paḻ-v-); cf. prayi n. censure, blame.

[Ka. paḻi revile, scold; scorn; n. blame, rebuke, fault; paḻivu n. id.; Ko. paḷc- to abuse; Ta. paḻi (paḻitt-) to blame; ridicule (Kṟḷ.); n. blame, reproach, ridicule (Tolk.); fault; guilt (Tēv.); Ma. paḻikka to scold, blame; paḻi a false accusation.]

896 prā̃ku* (> Mdn. pāku) intr. to creep, crawl; n. a pole set up as a support for a creeper; (< *par-aṅk-); cf. pakul-āḍu to grope with hands, as in darkness (Mdn.).

[Ka. pare to spread, as creepers or roots; Tu. parapuni to creep or crawl on hands; spread as a creeper; Ta. para to spread; for other forms meaning 'to spread,' v. s. v. paracu; also cf. Ma. paratuku to seek gropingly at night; Kui parmba to grope, search blindly; Kuvi (F) pṛāk- id.; Go. (Dawson) park- to seek, search.]

897 prāmu* (> Mdn. pāmu) tr. to daub, rub, smear, scour (Kāś.); to beat into pieces (Mārk.); to wipe (Bhg.).

[Cf. Kuvi (S) prāk- to palm.]

898 pridulu* intr. to become loose, get slack, as joints (Bhr. II); to slip, fall off (as garment); to separate; be dislocated; (flower) to bloom (Manu.); (< *pir-d-il-).

[Ko. piry- (pirc-) to separate part from part; pirnj- to separate oneself from; pīṭ- (? < *pir-uḷ-) to separate (joints of carcass); Ta. piri to become parted, be split (Tolk.); tr. to sẹparate (Kr̲l.); n. separation (Tolk.); Ma. piriyuka be separate, part with; pirikka to sever, dismiss; Kui prīva (prīt-) to be cracked, opened out; Go. piṛ- to burst, of cotton bolls or ant-eaten mud wall; Klm.(E) pirs- to slip, slide; Brah. pirg̲h̲- to break. PDr. *pir-.]

899 pruccu* IIa (> Mdn. puccu) intr. to be worm-eaten; to rot; (< *pul̲-c-); cf. der. n. pruvvu, pur(u)vu, pur(u)gu a worm; pruṅguḍu leukoderma.

[Ka. pul̲i to be eaten by worms; putrefy; purcu n. ruin; Tu. purkuni to rot, decay; purṅguni, purkuni to decompose; Ta. pul̲u to breed worms; be worthless as rotten; Ma. pul̲ukka to putrefy, rot; Go. puṛī- to breed worms (of a foul wound); Kuṛ. pocc- to engender worms; to be rotten. PDr. *pul̲-/*puc-; nearly all languages have related forms for the meaning 'worm' from PDr. *pul̲-, *puc-; see Emeneau, Kolami, Vocab. No. 731; KGad. puḍut a worm; Kur. put$^{u}$ṅg a midge.]

900 prēlu[1]* (> Mdn. pēlu) intr. to prate, prattle (Bhr. II); (< *pel̲-al).

[Cf. Ka. pēl̲, pēl̲u (> hēl̲u) to speak, tell; command; pēl̲ike talk, rumor; Ko. pēc- to talk to oneself; Ta. pēcu to speak, roar (Tiv.); repeat many times (Tiv.), abuse (colloq.); pitar̲r̲u to chatter, prate (Nāl.); Ma. pēcuka to speak, chatter, as birds; Mlt. peṛq- to talk, speak; hiss; Kur. perperer- to prate, prattle; parparer- id.; cf. pēs- to command. PDr. *pēc-/*pēl̲-; *pēc-/*pēt-.]

901 prēlu[2]* (> Mdn. pēlu) intr. to explode (as gun); burst, crackle, break, pop up due to heat (Bhr. I); tr. prēl(u)cu to cause to explode; (< *per-al- < *pir-al-).

[Go. piṛ- to burst (cotton bolls, etc.), v.s.v. pridulu.]

902 prŏcu* IIa tr. to nourish, protect, preserve, support, save (Bhr. I); prŏpu n. protection; prŏdi preserving, saving; (< *por-a-).

[Ka. porcu (> horcu) to nourish, support, sustain; be nourished; Ko. porv- (port-) to endure; Ta. poru tr. to bear, sustain (Kr̲l.); bear with, forgive (PN); pura to keep, preserve, cherish (Patir̲.); Ma. porunnuka to hatch, brood; Klm.(SR) puray- to tame, maintain; Pj. porip- (porit-) to rear, foster. PSDr. and PCDr. *por-V-; cf. Kuvi (S) pōhi-kī- to tend.]

prŏ̃ju* (> pŏ̃cu, pŏ̃ju, ponju).

[V. s. v. pŏ̃ju.]

B

903 baḍalu intr. to be tired, fatigued; n. fatigue (Bhr. I); baḍalika n. id. [Ka. baḻal, baḻalu to become weary, fatigued; Tu. baḷalike tiredness; Ta. vaḻalikkai weariness; Kui vaha to be tired; Kuvi (F) vwah- id.; Kuvi (S) wah- id. PSDr. and PCDr. *vaḻ-/*vac-; Kui Kuvi h presupposes an older *s < *c.]

904 baḍiyu III tr. to sweep away the influence of evil spirits on a person (Naiṣ.).

batuku (< baduku, q. v.).

baduku (< braduku, q. v.; also batuku) intr. to live, survive; to be saved. [Ka. baduku id.; Tu. badu̥kuni to live, exist; recover; survive; Ko. vadk- to prosper; To. poθk- id.; Kuvi (F) batk- to live; Go. (Maṛia) badktōr lived (LSI IV, p. 535); Klm. (E) bat- to live in a place; Klm. (SR) badk- to subsist; Pj. badk- to live; all these are likely to be borrowings from Te. or Ka. on account of b- < *br-, see s. v. braduku.]

905 baruku tr. to scratch, claw, lacerate; to scribble. [Ka. bare, bari to draw, write; n. lines, writing; Tu. baripuni to gash, cut, scratch; barepini to draw; Ta. varai to write, inscribe; to limit (PN); vari a line; Ma. varekka to make lines; write; variyuka to draw lines; Kui verka to scratch a part that itches; Pj. varc- to scratch. PSDr. and PCDr. *var-, also v. s. v. vrāyu.]

906 baṟaṭu* tr. to scratch, as a signal (Bhr. II), to scratch (Bhōj.). [Ka. paraḍu (> haraḍu) to scratch with the fingers or nails, to claw; beraṇṭu, beraṭu id.; Tu. parṅkuni, parkuni id.; Ta. paṟaṇṭu, paṟāṇṭu id. (loc.); paṟi to pull, pluck; vaṟaṇṭu to scratch with nails; vaṟuku to scratch, paw; Ma. paraṇṭuka to scratch, scrape; Kui paṛja to be burred over (metal or wood); Kuvi (F) pac- to scratch; bakṛ- to claw (< *baṛk-); Klm. (E) pars- to scratch; Pj. parc- id. PSDr. and PCDr. *paṯ-/*vaṯ-; contamination with etyma deriving from *var-; see s. v. baruku.]

907 balayu* III tr. to surround, encircle, besiege.

[(1) Tu. balepuni to enclose, surround, besiege; Ta. vala (vala-nt-) to encircle, surround (PN); (spider) spins web (PN); ? Go. wadī- to twist or twirl fibre into thread.

(2) Ka. baḷasu to go in a circle; turn round; be surrounded, wrapped up; Ko. vaḷc- to walk in a circle; Ta. vaḷai (vaḷai-nt-) tr. to surround, encompass, besiege (Cīv.); (vaḷai-tt-) id. (Mullaip.); Ma. vaḷayuka tr. to surround; vaḷekka to coil up; PSDr. *val-, *vaḷ-; (> l. w. Skt. valaya- circle, see Burrow, TPS 1946, p. 11).]

908 baliyu III intr. to grow fat, stout, become corpulent; to increase, grow, be augmented; to multiply; balupu n. fatness, increase.

[Ka. bal, bali to grow strong, be full-grown, to increase; bal, balu strength; Tu. balāpini to gain strength, recover health; Ko. valc- (man) becomes stout; (grain) becomes solid lump when boiled; To. paly- (pals-) to become strong; Ta. vali to become hard (Tēv.); tr. to force (Tiruvāc.); n. strength, power (Kr̲ḷ.); valam strength (PN); Ma. valluka to be strong; val adj. strong, powerful; Kui bara strength, influence; Go. (Seoni) vallē much (LSI IV, p. 518); Mlt. balcne large; bale-bale large one; Brah. balun big, large, elder as opposed to younger. PDr. *val-.]

909 bā̃du (Śab.R.; bādu, Dh.M.) to beat, thrash, flog.

[Tu. bāda torment; distress; Ta. vāti to torment, afflict (Tiv.); < Skt. bādhā- affliction.]

910 bigiyu III intr. to become tight, be tightened (Mārk.); tr. bigucu; bigi, biguvu tightness.

[Ka. bigi to become firm; be tightened; be proud; to bind, fasten; n. tightness; Tu. bigiyuni to become tight; bigipuni to fasten; bigipu, bigu, bigi tightness; adj. stubborn; Ko. vigv- (vigt-) to become tight, as tool-handle; To. pïxy- (pïxs-) to become tight; Ta. vici (< *viki) to bind tightly (Malaip.); intr. to become swollen, outstretched (PN); viku to be tight, stiff; piku tightness; piki to be hard knit (l. ws. < Ka.). PSDr. *vik-i- < *viy-i-, v. s. v. vī̃gu, vikku; cf. Kuvi (F) pikh-ni adj. heavy.]

911 bijugu* tr. to say or report falsely; speak lies (late).

912 biddu* (Śab.R., ĀVāc.) intr. to die, perish; (Dh.M.) to ooze, as water.

[Ka. bīl̲, bil̲- (bil̲d-, bird-, bidd-) to fall, slip; bil̲tu a fall; Tu. būruni to fall; to die; Ko. vig- (vir̤t-) to fall; Ta. vil̲u (vil̲u-nt-) to fall, fall down; flow down (Patir̲.); to die; (vil̲u-tt-) tr. to fell, cause to die (Tēv.); vīl̲ to fall, etc. (Kr̲ḷ.); Ma. vīl̲uka to fall; vīl̲ttuka to cause to fall. PSDr. *vīl̲- : *vil̲-V-.]

913 bir̲r̲u* (Śab.R.) intr. to become stiff, as hair (Bhōj.; rare); n. tightness, firmness; bir̲usu n. roughness.

[Ka. bir̲r̲u to become stiff; n. hardness, roughness; adj. whirring; bir̲asu, bir̲ubu hardness; Tu. biru violent, strong; birusu̥ stiff, rough; Ko. verv- (vert-) to become numb from exposure; Ta. ver̲i to stand stiff; vir̲ai to grow stiff, as from cold; be dense; n. stiffness; Ma. vir̲akka to become stiff, as from cold; Kur. beṛh- to be or become hard. PDr. *vet̲-.]

914 buliyu* III intr. to be in great glee, exult, chuckle, rejoice (Kaḷā.); bulupu n. enjoyment, glee, chuckling.

[Cf. Tu. bulpuni, buḷpuni to cry about, shout, exclaim.]

915 begaḍu/beggaḍu* to be afraid of, to dread; n. fear; cf. beggaḍ-ilu to fear, lose courage; begg-alamu fear, alarm.

[Ka. begaḍu to be amazed; to fear; n. fear, amazement; bigur to fear; get amazed; Tu. begaḍuni to be alarmed; be bewildered; bekkasu̥ surprise; Ko. vekar- (vekat̲-) to be puzzled; see s.v. vegaḍu, vegacu.]

916 beḍā̃gu* intr. to be beautiful (Manu.); n. beauty, handsomeness; strength.

[Ka. beḍagu, beḍaṅgu novelty, beauty, grace; showiness; Tu. beḍage a charming man; Ta. viṭaṅku beauty (Pārata.); veṭippu splendor; Ma. veṭippu neatness; < PSDr. *veṭ-V- < *veḷ-V-; cf. velũgu.]

917 beḍiyu III intr. (an action or endeavor) to be spoiled, unsuccessful; to have a difference or misunderstanding, be on bad terms.

[Cf. Ta. veṭi v.i. to crack, as earthenware; to explode (Kamp.); n. hate; viṭai tr. to prevent; intr. to droop, be angry; become disjointed, split; find fault with.]

918 beṇā̃ku (also beḍā̃ku, beṇū̃ku, beḷā̃ku[1]) (1) intr. to move, tremble (Kaḷā.).

[Ka. beḷapaḷa trembling, agitation; beḷkar̲ to become afraid; meḷ bewilderment; Ta. viṇviṇai v.i. to throb, as eye (Tolk.); veṭku, veḷku to be afraid, ashamed.]

beṇā̃ku (2) to be removed, be sprained; n. a sprain.

[Cf. Ka. beṇe a stopple, cork; Tu. buṇpu heel tendon.]

919 bedaru (also beduru) intr. to be startled; be afraid; n. fear, alarm, panic.

[Ka. bedar̲, bedar̲u to be agitated, bewildered, alarmed; n. fright, alarm; Tu. bedaru̥, beduru̥ id.; Ta. vitar̲u v.i. to tremble, be afraid, agitated; n. agitation; vitir v.i. to tremble (Parip.); Kuvi (F) pedr̥- to be startled. PSDr. *vet-ar̲-/-ir-; v.s.v. vidulu.]

920 berayu* III intr./tr. to occur, happen, to join, mix, attain, reach (Bhr. II, HariV.).

[Ka. bere to be joined or united, be mingled; to associate; berasu to mingle together, be united; n. union; Tu. berasuni tr. to mix, mingle; birasuni id.; beravuni to be mixed; berasu̥ admixture; Ta. viracu v.i. to join; tr. to unite (Kamp.); viravu v.i. to be joined, keep company (Tēv.); tr. to join, unite; Ma. virakuka to mix; Kur. birk̲h̲- to mix several kinds of seeds (esp. for sowing);

Mlt. birg̣- tr. to mix, add, join; birg̣r- be mixed, etc. PDr. *vir-, PSDr. *vir-a-, *vir-ac-.]

921 belayu* III (ĀVāc.) intr. to spread, increase (cf. velayu).

beḷāku[1] intr. to stir, move.
[V. s. v. beḍāku (1).]

922 beḷāku[2]* (also beḷuku) intr. to glitter, gleam, shine; n. shining.
[Ka. beḷagu to shine; Tu. beḷaguni id.; Kur. bilc- id.; Mlt. biḍy- id.; < PDr. *veḷ-; v. s. v. velũgu.]

923 besuku (colloq.: Viśākha. dial.) intr. to shake, stir, move; cf. medalu.

beḷuku* (var. of beḷāku[2], q. v.) intr. to shine, glitter.

924 bokku tr. to eat greedily, gobble up, stuff the mouth and eat voraciously.
[Ka. mukku to stuff the mouth and gobble; Tu. mukkuni id.; Ta. mukku to eat in large mouthfuls (PN); Ma. mōval a gulp; mōkuka to sip for tasting; Kui muka to cast food into mouth with hand; mukal a mouthful; cf. muhpa to munch, chew; Kuvi (F) būrca-kōd- to grab for oneself; Kur. mŏkh-, mŏ̃kh- (mokk-, mokkh-, mŏkh-) to eat (anything except rice); prey on; Mlt. mōq- to eat (as meat or fruits). PDr. *mŭk-/*mŏk-; cf. Go. mōrsī-mānāl (tind-) to eat to the vomiting point.]

925 boṅku intr. to lie, speak falsehood; n. a lie; adj. false, untrue; (< *poy-ṅk-); cf. pocc-emu deceit (HariV.).
[Ka. boṅku to lie; pusi (< *poci) to prove untrue, to lie; n. falsehood; pusiga a liar; Tu. boṅkuni to deny; adj. hollow, empty; puskaṭe useless; pōka adj. mischievous; To. pīk- to tell lies; Ta. poy (poy-tt-) v. i. to prove false (Kamp.), fail, as prediction (Kṟḷ.); to lie (Kṟḷ.), to cheat; poykka falsely (Cīv.); pokkam n. lie, deceit (Tēv.); poccai fault; poccamu lie, fault (< *poy-tt-); Ma. poy a lie, cheat; pokkam falsehood; pokkar low people; GoM. bus- to lie. PSDr. < *poy-ṅk-/*poy-kk-.]

926 bollu* intr. to tell lies; to lie; n. a lie, falsehood; adj. false; bolli id.; cf. pollu empty.
[Ka. poḷḷu emptiness; poḷḷumātu an empty word; Tu. pollu adj. empty, void; poṭṭu id.; stupid; Ta. poḷḷal n. fault, defect; Ma. poḷḷu empty, hollow; Brah. pōlō hollow, empty. PDr. *poḷ-; see Burrow, DS VII, No. 216, p. 385.]

927 braduku* (> baduku, batuku, q. v.) intr. to live, subsist, survive, be saved (Bhr. II, Hariv.); n. life, existence; brad-imi existence, livelihood.

[Ka. barduku, barduṅku, to live, remain, be saved; ba_l, bā_l to live, be alive; Ko. vāḷ- to live prosperously; To. poḷc- (poḷč-) to live; Ta. vā_l (vā_l-nt-) to be, exist; to live (Kr_l.), flourish; vā_lccu living; Ma. vā_luka to be, live, flourish; Kui bārti longevity, long life. PDr. *vā_l-; pre-Ka. Te. *va_l-ud-uṅk- > *va_l-d-uṅk-; for forms in other languages with br > b, v. s. v. baduku.]

928 bruṅgu* (1) intr. to be immersed in water, to be hidden (Bhr. II, Mārk.); (< *mu_l-ng-).

[Kui bṛuḍga to sink completely in; Kuvi mrūkh- to drop into; Ka. mu_luṅgu, mu_lgu, mu_l(u)cu to sink under water; dive; Tu. murkuni to sink, immerse; Ta. mu_luku be immersed; mū_lku v. i. to plunge; be hidden (Ci_rup.); be thrust; Ma. mu_lukuka to sink under water; Go. murung- be drowned; GoM. muṛand- to sink; GoM. muṛand- to sink; GoM.(W) murī- (sun) to set; Pj. būṛ- to sink; Kur. bōr- to immerse. PDr. *mū_l- : *mu_l-V-; also see s. v. munūgu; (> l. w. Skt. mruc- to go down, see Burrow, TPS 1945, p. 116).]

bruṅgu* (2) intr. to perish, die (Bhr. II).

[Kui mrūva (mrūt-) to die; Ka. mu_lku to be ruined; Tu. murkuni to be ruined; To. muḷk- to destroy.]

929 bruyyu* III intr. to be destroyed, to perish (Bhr. II); tr. bruncu to kill; (< *mur-y-).

[Ta. muri v. i. be spoiled (Kr_l.); tr. to ruin; alternatively from *mu_l-u-, v. s. v. bruṅgu (2).]

## M

930 makku* (< mrakku, q. v.; alternatively < *ma_lk- or *maḷk- with assimilation) to lose lustre, become dim; to emaciate in sickness (Bhōj.); to perish; n. dimness (Āmu.); adj. dusky (lex.).

[Ta. makku to die, perish; become dull; decay (late); n. sluggishness; a dullard; cf. maṭku to be dim, dusky (Kamp.); lose strength (Pārata.); become dirty; maḷku to be deficient, defective; maṇṇai n. bluntness (Akan.), stupid person. PSDr. *maḷ-/*maṇ-, also v. s. v. mrakku, maggu, māyu.]

931 magucu* IIb tr. to turn back, cause to return (late).

[Ka. magucu, mogucu v. i. to turn round, return; turn, as a book-leaf; to fall upside down; Tu. magucuni, magapuni to draw and turn over; magupuni to turn, upset; magupu a turn; cf. maguḍu.]

932 maguḍu* intr. to turn back, return (Bhr. II); turn toward (Bhīm.);

to step aside (Bhr. II); tr. maguḍ(u)cu to cause to turn (Bhr. II); magiḍi pp., maguḍa(n) again, next (Bhr. II).

[Ka. magul̲ to turn round; return, retreat, recede; magul̲cu to cause to turn round; Tu. magaru̥, maguru̥/magru̥ adj. next; adv. again; magpu, magrane adj. next, following; Ta. makkaḷi v.i. to return, (disease) to relapse; makiḷi id.; makiṭi to be overturned; cf. Te. makkaḷ-incu to put or set back in the same position; to turn back. PSDr. *mak-, *mak-V-; prob. *mā- in mār̲u is a contraction of *mak-a-, v.s.v. mār̲u; also see Emeneau, Kolami, Vocab. No. 480.]

maggu$^{1}$ (alt. of mā̃gu, q.v.; Mdn.).

maggu$^{2}$ (< *mraggu, q.v.; colloq.) intr. to be boiled in steam; to perish, die; be spoiled by heat or sweat.

933 maccu* IIa tr. to attract, enchant (Paṇḍ.); n. something that enchants, intoxicates (Bhr.); (< *mar-c-); cf. macc-ika taming, familiarity.

[Ka. marcu, maccu to be greatly devoted to; maccu to like, be pleased; n. attachment; Tu. marcuni to be enticed, tamed; marca enticement; other forms: v.s.v. maragu, marugu.]

934 maṭṭu$^{1}$ tr. to tread, trample, crush under foot (HariV.), to trouble, torment (KS); cf. maḍama heel (KS); maṭṭamu level, that which is levelled; lowliness (UH, KS).

[Ta. maṇṭu to thrust in, press upon (PN); maṭu to thrust (Kalit.); maṭṭi to destroy; mix and knead; Mlt. maḍy- (maḍc-) to trample, tread. PDr. *maṇṭ-/*maṭṭ-; also v.s.v. maḍãgu; cf. Ka. maḍu to put firmly together.]

935 maṭṭu$^{2}$* to besiege, surround; be thronged (UH), to spread.

[Ta. maṇṭu to be crowded; n. thronging; maṭu to unite, join; Brah. maṭ thick, dense (of weaving, hair, jungle, buttermilk).]

936 maḍãgu (also maṇãgu, maḍũgu, maṇũgu) intr. to be bent, to shrink, be reduced (Mārk.); to be submissive (UH); to be destroyed (Bhg.); tr. maḍãcu to bend, fold (Hara.); to destroy, kill (KS); to contain, fit in (Bhr. II); maḍãta n. a fold; maḍũcu tr. to bend, fold, etc. (Naiṣ.); press down (Daśā.).

[Ka. maḍi tr. to bend, fold; maṇi v.i. to bend, bow; tr. to bend; Tu. maḍiyuni become folded; maḍipuni to fold; māṇāvuni tr. to lessen, decrease; Ko. maṛk- tr. to fold; To. moṛy- (moṛc-) v.i. to fold; moṛk- tr. id.; Ta. maṭi be bent, folded (Kamp.); droop, shrink (Akan.); tr. to fold, kill (Kamp.); maṭaṅku to become bent; be diminished (Cilap.); Ma. maṭaṅṅuka to be bent; maṭakkuka to bend; maṭiyuka to be bent; maṭukka to fold; overcome; **Pj. maḍkip-**

(maḍkit-) tr. to fold, roll up; GoM. maḍp- (maḍap-t-) to fold. PSDr. and PCDr. *maṭ-/*maḷ-, *maṇ-; also v. s. v. vaṅgu for alternants in ṇ.]

maḍācu/maṇācu IIb tr. of maḍāgu/maṇāgu, q. v.

937 maḍavu* intr. to become useless, worthless; to hesitate, shrink; to dislike (all Bhr. I).

[Cf. Ma. maṭukka to loathe; maṭuppu dislike; altern. *maṭ-, s. v. maḍāgu, q. v.; Ta. maṭi to shrink (Akan.), droop, as head.]

938 maḍiyu* III intr. to die, perish (Bhr. II), to be broken, destroyed (Bhg.).

[Ka. maḍi id.; maḍipu to kill; Ta. maṭi to perish, be destroyed (Kṟḷ.); also see s. v. maḍāgu.]

maḍūgu (alt. of maḍāgu, q. v.; [UH, Bhr. II]).

maḍuvu var. of maḍūgu, v. s. v. maḍāgu.

maṇāgu (alt. of maḍāgu, q. v.; late).

maṇūgu (alt. of maḍūgu).

939 maṇḍu intr. to burn, blaze; shine (KS, Bhr. II); (lamp) to burn (HariV.); (wound) to smart (Manu.); to burn with anger (Bhr. II); der. n. maṇṭa a flame, blaze (Bhr. II), anger (Dvi.H.).

[Ta. maṇṭu to blaze up (Pu.Ve.); maṭu tr. to kindle (Nāl.); GoM. maḍg- to blaze; Mlt. mānḍ- to roast in hot ashes; altern. < *manṯ-, v. s. v. maṟāgu.]

940 maduru intr. to be fully ripe, to ripen (Kāś.).

[? < Skt. madhura- sweet; Tu. madura adj. sweet, agreeable.]

941 manu IV (allomm. man-/maṇ-, hab. man-d-/maṇ-ḍ-; past maṇ-ṭ-) intr. to live, exist (Bhr. I); to act, behave (KS, Bhr.); tr. manucu to let live, nourish (Bhr. II); mancu to nourish (Bhr. I); to regard, respect (Bhr. I); manu-gaḍa living, means of living (Bhr. II); man(i)ki living, existence; abode.

[Ta. maṉṉu (maṉṉ-iṉ-) to live long (Kṟḷ.); maṉ abundance (PN); prosperity; maṉai house, wife (Cīv.); Kui manba (mas-) to be, exist, remain; Kuvi (S) man- to be; Kuvi (F) manj- (mac-) id.; Go. mand- (pp. man-jī) to remain; Pj. men- (mend-, mett-) to be, stay, remain; KGad. man- (irreg. allomm. meyy-, manḍ-, manj-) to be; Kur. man- (mañj-) to become, occur, happen; man'- (manc-) to consider; Mlt. many- (manc-) to obey, love; Brah. mann- to be, become (allomm. ma-, mar-); mann- to obey. PDr. *man-; cf. Mundari menā to exist, to be.]

942 manūgu/manuvu* to die, perish (late).

[Prob. related to forms s. v. malugu, q. v.]

man(u)cu* IIb tr. of manu, q.v. (Bhr. I, II, Kāś.).

man(u)pu* (alt. of man(u)cu, q.v.).

mannu (var. of manu, q.v.) to flourish, live long (Vasu.); also occurs in Viśākha. dial. in Mdn. Te.: to last long (as an object).

mappu (tr. of marugu [< *mar-p-]; colloq. Viśākha. dial.) to teach, train, tame; v.s.v. maragu.

943 maragu, marugu (SAN; maragu Śab.R.; marãgu, marugu Dh.M.) intr. to become attached to (governs dative) (KS, Bhr. II); to be accustomed to (Bhr. II); take to, be addicted to; tr. to accustom oneself to, to learn (Bhr. II, BhR); to like, desire, love (Bhr. II, Naiṣ.); tr./caus. marapu, marupu to train one's self (or mind) to; to cause to be accustomed to; to train, teach (Bhr. II, Daśā., Bhg.); to arouse desire (BhR, RR); marupu to tame, train bullocks to plow (Rāyalasīma dial.); mappu to train, teach, tame (Viśākha. dial.); cf. macc-ika, macc-iga love, enchantment, taming, familiarity (Mārk.).

[Ka. marcu, maccu be greatly devoted to; to like; marcu, mercu attachment, fondness; maccu illusion; maccike, meccike liking; Tu. marcuni to be tamed, enticed; marcelụ tameness; marka languor; Ta. maruvu to arise or be evolved as a custom (Tolk.); tr. to come near, embrace (Nāl.); be accustomed with (Kṟḷ.); Ma. maruvuka to become familiar; marańńuka, meruńńuka to be attached to, be accustomed; tame; marukkuka to tame, domesticate; maruttuka id.; Kui mrāspa (mrāst-) to train; Kuvi(S) mrih'- to teach, tame; Kuvi(F) mrīh- be accustomed; mrīss- tr. to accustom; Go. maṛs- to visit frequently, come again and again, as pigs to a field; Pj. mercip- (mẹrcit-) to teach; mer- to learn; KGad. marr- to learn; Kur. maṛ- (maṇḍ-, maṛ-) tr. to select or take for oneself; (of brute animals) to stay habitually, to keep or lodge in a certain place; Mlt. maṛ- to will, wish, love; ? mīnj- to become familiar; Brah. marrī tame, domesticated. The root-vowel is difficult to reconstruct: PDr. *mār- : *mar-V-; *mīr- : *mir-V-; *mēr- : *mer-V-.]

marapu/marupu (tr. of maragu/marugu, q.v.; also cf. mappu).

944 maralu (later works write maṟalu) intr. to turn back, go or come back (Bhr. II, Naiṣ.), to retreat, return (Bhr. II); cf. malãgu, malãcu.

[Ka. maral (also maraḷ, maraḷu), malar to turn back, retreat; happen or do again; Klm.(SR) malāy- to return; Go. mall- to return; GoM. mald- id.; Pj. mell- id.; PSDr. and PCDr. *mal-, PSDr.

*mal-ar-; alternatively, Ta. maṟi to return, recede, retreat; tr. turn about; maṟivu n. return; Ma. maṟiyuka to turn back, turn over; maṟiccal turning over, returning; Go. māṛk- to turn the head and glance quickly. More probability for the former solution.]

945 maṟacu IIa to forget (Bhr. II); to neglect, give up, ignore (Bhr. I); maṟapu inadvertence, ignorance (Bhr. II); tr. maṟapu to cause to confuse (HariV.); maṟap-incu id.

[Ka. maṟe be unmindful of, be forgotten; Tu. madapuni, marapuni to forget; Ko. marv- (mard-) to be forgotten; to forget; To. maṟ- (maṟθ-) id.; Ta. maṟa (maṟant-) to forget (Kṟḷ.), neglect, give up; Ma. maṟakka id.; Go. marēṅg- id.; Go.(W) margīnā to err; GoM. mārand- to forget; Klm.(E) mad- (mat-t-), Klm.(SR) madd- id. PSDr. and PCDr. *maṯ-V-; also v. s. v. maṟũgu².]

maṟalu (same as maralu, q. v.; Dvi.H., Pāri.).

946 maṟũgu¹ (Śab.R.; marũgu SAN; maṟãgu, maṟugu Dh.M.) intr. to be distressed, to grieve (KS, RR, BhR); to boil (Bhr. I); (water) to seethe, bubble; marukuva (SAN) grief (Bhr. II, III).

[Ka. maṟugu, maṟagu to burn; be inflamed with passion; to grieve; love; maṟuka sorrow; Tu. ? maji coal; Ko. maṛv- (maṛd-) (water) bubbles and boils; Ta. maṟuku to be distressed (Akan.); maṟi n. boiling; Ma. maṟukuka to flounder, welter; Kui mṛahpa (mṛah-t-) tr. to burn; Go. maṛūst- to cook in oil; cf. mās- to burn (a corpse, etc.). PSDr. and PCDr. *maṯ-.]

947 maṟũgu²* (Śab.R.; maṟũgu, maṟuvu, maruvu SAN) intr. to be concealed, hidden; be invisible; (SAN) maruvu id. (Dvi.H.); maṟuvu id. (KS); n. shelter, protection, privacy (Bhr. I); armor (Bhr. II); adj. hidden, concealed (Bhr. I).

[Ka. maṟasu to hide, conceal; maṟa secrecy, cover, shelter; maṟavu hiding; Tu. madeyuni be out of sight; madepuni to shelter, hide; make a retired place; madepu id.; Ko. marc- to keep a secret in mind; Ta. maṟai to be hidden (Kṟḷ.); disappear; tr. to hide (Kṟḷ.); protect from danger; n. concealment (PN); Ma. maṟayuka to hide oneself; maṟekka to conceal; maṟeccu n. shelter; maṟa id.; Kui mārga v. i. to take shelter, to hide; Kur. mā̃ṛ- (maṇḍ-, mā̃ṛ-) tr. to intercept view; cover off, hide away. PDr. *māṯ- : *maṯ-V-, v. s. v. māṭu, maṟacu; the Kur. past stem presupposes *man-ḏ-, from *man-/*maṯ-.]

948 malãgu¹* intr. to turn back or to the side, turn around (Bhr. II, Daśā.); turn with a bend (Bhr. II), become crooked; tr. malãcu to turn back or to the side; to bend, cause to be slanted (Bhr. II, Mārk.); malaka a twist.

[Ka. malagu, malaṅgu to incline, bend, as full ears of paddy; mālisu to look obliquely; bend to one side; mālu id.; n. slanting; Tu. maleṅguni to lean against; To. malf (malt-) (buffalo) looks sideways; Ta. malar (malar-tt-) tr. to turn the face or mouth upward, as of a pot (PN); mallā, malkā to fall or lie on the back; Ma. malaruka to be concave; lie on the back; other etyma v. s. v. maralu; PDr. *mal-; cf. Kui malga to fall flat on the face, be prone; Kur. marmar$^{a}$r- to move the body to and fro with short turns.]

949 malãgu$^{2*}$ intr. to wander, roam about (Nirv.).

[V. s. v. malayu$^{1}$.]

malãgu$^{3*}$ to cease, stop, as birth and death, (sins) to diminish (Bhr. II, RR); (< *maḷ-aṅk-); v. s. v. malugu.

[Ka. māḷ, māṇ to stop, cease; be rid of; Ta. māḷ (māṇ-ṭ-) to die, perish, be expended; v. s. v. mālu, mānu.]

950 malãgu$^{4*}$ intr. to burn, blaze (KS); cf. malayu$^{3}$.

[V. s. v. maṇḍu, prob. < *maṇ-/*man-.]

malãcu$^{1}$ IId (Śab.R.; SAN also gives mal(u)cu, q. v.) to carve, engrave, carve idols (UH); malãpu to excavate, make a hole (RR).

951 malãcu$^{2}$ IId (Śab.R.) tr. to winnow grain, clear stones, etc. from rice.

952 malãcu$^{3*}$ IId intr. to flower, blossom (KS).

[Ka. malar a flower; Ta. malar v. i. to bloom (Nāl.); tr. to cause to flower; n. a blossom, flower (Kṟḷ.); Ma. malar n. id.; note that Te. has only the verb form.]

malapu (tr. of malãgu$^{1}$, q. v.) to cause to retreat (late).

malãpu (tr. of malãgu$^{3}$, q. v.; also v. s. v. mal(u)gu) tr. to remove, extinguish.

953 malayu$^{1*}$ III intr. to wander, roam (UH, Kāś.).

[Ma. valayuka to wander about; Go. walī- to roam, wander; walist- cause to roam; Klm.(SR) malāy- to roam. PSDr. and PCDr. *val-/*mal-; also cf. maralu.]

954 malayu$^{2*}$ III tr. to wrestle, fight (UH, Dvi.H.); mallũḍu a wrestler (Bhr. II).

[Ka. male tr. to oppose, fight against; Tu. mallè, malla a wrestler, boxer; Ta. malai to take upon oneself (Kṟḷ.); to oppose; fight (Cīv.); (malaitt-) v. i. to fight (PN). PSDr. *mal-, *mal-ay.]

955 malayu$^{3*}$ III intr. to be distressed, to grieve (Mārk.).

[Ta. malai (malai-tt-) tr. to afflict, distress (PN); Ma. valayuka to be distressed; valaccal n. distress; valekka to distress, also v. s. v. valiyu. PSDr. *val-/*mal-.]

956 malayu[4]* III to increase, spread, expand (KS); to rage (Bhr. I); to move, as wind.

[Ta. mali to abound (Cīv.); be crowded (Tolk.); spread, expand (Pu.Ve.); move swiftly; malku v.i. to increase, be filled with, abound (Cīv.); Ma. malka to abound; malika id.; malekka grow thick, swell.]

957 malayu[5]* III to be; occur, happen (UH, BhR, Daśā.).

[Cf. Ta. malar to appear, rise in view; to happen, befall.]

958 malugu* intr. to be extinguished, as lamp, fire (Bhr. II); to be reduced; to diminish, as hunger, etc. (RR); (lamp) to go down due to lack of oil (Mdn., Rāyalasīma dial.); tr. mal(u)pu to put out, destroy (Nirv., KS).

[Ka. māḷ, māṇ v.i. to be checked; to cease, subside; māṇ id.; Tu. māṇāvuni tr. to lessen, decrease, abate; Ta. māḷ (māṇ-ṭ-) to die (Tiruvāc.); perish; be finished; cf. māntu to be ruined, to perish; be extinct; < PSDr. *māḷ- : *maḷ-V-; also v.s.v. mālu, mānu.]

959 mal(u)cu (var. of malācu) IIa tr. to make, fashion (Bhīm.), to engrave, fashion, carve (Bhr. I, RR, Naiṣ.).

[Ka. māḍu to do; māḷd(am) did, 10th century inscr. (G.S.Gai, p. 217); Tu. maḷpuni to do, make, perform, frame.]

malupu tr. of malugu, q.v.

960 maḷḷu (< maralu, q.v.; also Mdn.) to turn back (Bhg.).

961 masāgu* intr. to increase, rise, swell (KS, Bhr. II, Daśā.); to be extended; (wrath) to increase, etc.

[Ka. masagu, mosagu to rise, expand; break forth; be urged on by passion; to rage; tr. to display; masaka passion, vehement emotion; mā id.; Tu. mastu̥ adj. abundant; fat; masti lust, pride; Ta. maintu desire, infatuation; pride; strength (Tolk.); matar to flourish; increase, abound (Cīv.). PSDr. *mac-/*mat-, *may-; v.s.v. masaru.]

962 masaru* intr. to grow frenzied, arrogant, proud (late); n. arrogance, frenzy, pride (Nirv., Mārk.); cf. masāgu.

[Ta. matar to be affected by frenzy, as bull (Pu.Ve.); be arrogant, full of joy; n. pride, arrogance (Kalit.); matam n. id. (Parip.); strength (Parip.); madness, frenzy (Parip.); mata<u>n</u> strength (PN); cf. Pkt. maccaï is excited; Skt. macate (DhātuP.) is arrogant; H. macnā to be excited, probably from PDr. *mac-; for other IA forms, v.s.v. mācāunu, maccāunu, Turner, Nep. Dict.]

963 masalu intr. to delay (Bhr. I), to stay, stroll about (Bhr. I); to remain, to be.

[Ka. masal delaying; masuḷ to hide oneself; Tu. madaḍu̥ adj. slothful, indolent; Ta. macaku to linger, loiter, hesitate; macakkam dullness, indolence (loc.); maḻuppu to protract, delay in coming to a decision; maḻuṅku to be dull or blunt (PN); Ma. maḻakkuka to delay, protract. PSDr. *mac-/*maḻ-.]

964 masulu intr. (water) to boil, bubble.

965 mā̆gu intr. to ripen fully, to mellow (NavaN.).

[Ka. māgu id.; to grow mature or seasoned, as medicine or snuff; Tu. māguni id.; Kui māja to ripen (off the tree); KGad. māng- id.; < PSDr. and PCDr. *mā-nk- < *māy-nk-; Kui j < y; PDr. *māy-.]

966 māṭu tr. to conceal, hide (16th century); to patch up, holes in vessel, etc.; n. shelter, concealment, protection (Bhr. II); n. a patch (KS); (< *māṯṯ-).

[V. s. v. maṟūgu$^{2}$; Ta. māṟṟu to hide, conceal; Kui mārga v. i. to take shelter; Kur. mā̆ṛ- to cover off, hide away. PDr. *māṯ-, *māṯṯ- < *māṯ-t-; PSDr. *māṯ- : *maṯ-V-.]

967 māṭu$^{2}$ to press down, destroy (late); cf. maṭṭu.

968 mā̆ṭu* (Śab.R.) tr. to hanker after; n. hankering after (late).

969 mā̆ḍu (SAN, Śab.R.; māḍu Dh.M.) intr. to be burnt, scorched black (BhR, HariV.); to suffer from hunger (Bhg.); to be spoiled, ruined (Bhr. II); to be burnt, as rice under excessive fire; tr. mā̆ḍ(u)cu to burn; mā̆ḍu n. burnt rice (Pāṇḍ.).

[Ta. māṭu v. i. to burn; māṭṭu to kindle, as fire; light, as a lamp (Kuṟun.); to burn (Ciṟup.); Ko. māṭ- (māc-) to make fire burn; To. mōṭ- to put fuel on fire; Kui māka to grill, bake by placing on hot ashes; Go. mās- tr. to burn; light a lamp, burn a corpse, wood; Mlt. mānḍ- to roast in hot ashes. PDr. *mā-, māṇṭ-/*māṭṭ, or *māṭ-.]

970 mānu$^{1}$ intr. to cease, stop, subside, diminish (Bhr. II); to stop, stay (Bhr. III, Kāś.); to be extinct; tr. to give up, abandon; retire from (Bhr. II); tr. mān(u)cu to diminish, reduce, remove (Bhr. II), mān(u)pu id. (Manu.).

[Ka. māṇ, māṇu to stop, subside; cease from; be got rid of; māḷ v. i. to cease; tr. to abandon; Tu. māṇ-āvuni to lessen, decrease, abate; mān-āvuni id.; Ta. māḷ, māḷḷu (māṇ-ṭ-) to die, perish; be finished; < PSDr. *māṇ-/*māḷ-; also cf. mālu, malūgu.]

971 mānu$^{2}$ intr. to be healed or cured.

[Ta. māṟu to be cured; māṟṟu to cure; Ma. māṟuka to be healed; māṟṟal curing; Kui māṛa v. i. to be healed; Go. wars- to cure pain; PDr. *mān-/*māt̲-; alternatively, Ka. māṇ, māṇu to be healed, get better; Kuvi (S) mānikī-, mānp- to cure; it may be that Ka. māṇ < *mān-, or that Te. Ka. forms are from PSDr. *māṇ-; v. s. v. mānu[1].]

māpu tr. of māyu, q. v.

972 māyu III intr. to become dim, dirty (KS, Bhr. II); to perish, vanish (Bhg.); tr. māpu to destroy; cause to disappear (Bhr. II, UH); to make soiled or dirty; n. dirtiness, getting soiled.

[Ka. māy (mād-, māyd-) to grow dim; disappear; māju, mānju, mācu, māsu to cause to grow dim; to hide; māsu to grow dim, to fade, decrease; tr. to dirty; Tu. māyuni to be extinguished, put out; mājuni to wear away, vanish; be put out; māsuni v. i. to fade, to soil; mājuni, majakuni to become dim; Ko. mānj- to hide (one's mind); Ta. mā n. paleness through love-sickness (PN), blackness (Cilap.); mācu n. stain, defect (Kr̲ḷ.), dust, darkness (Kr̲ḷ.); māy v. i. to hide, vanish (Maturai.); to perish (Kr̲ḷ.); die (Malaip.); become lustreless, as setting sun (Kalit.); (māy-tt-) tr. to hide, forget (PN); kill; macaṅku to become dim, dull; Ma. māyuka to wear away, grow dim, vanish; māyttuka to wipe off; māccu n. dirt; Kui māsi filth, dirt; sin; Kuvi (F) maci dirty; Kuvi (S) māsk- to mask; Pj. māy to get lost, disappear; Kur. māk̲h̲- to grow dark; Mlt. masg̣- to vanish (of person); masekār- id.; māqu night; Brah. masnāk̲h̲ scarred; maun (< mā + un) black; cf. Go. makk- to disappear; maksuht- to hide; GoM. mak- to conceal. PDr. *mā-/*māy; *māc- : *mac-V-; here c can be taken as a derivative suffix; cf. Ka. mal̲a dimness; Ta. mal̲uṅku to be dim (Kalit.); mal̲uku id. (Parip.); mal̲ai cloud, blackness (Nāl.); Ma. mal̲uka to grow dim; Kur. maṛk̲h̲- to get dirty, lose brightness; Mlt. maṛgro black; maṛgtr- to blacken; PDr. *mac-V-/ *mal̲-V-.]

973 mār̲u (1) intr. to be changed, altered, turned into a new form, be transformed (Hara.); tr. mārcu to change (Bhr. II), change shape (Manu.); mārpu a change, alteration.

[Ka. mār̲u v. i. to be changed into another form; n. being different, opposite, hostile; Tu. māduni v. i. to turn about; Ko. mār- v. i. to change; māt- tr. to change; To. mōr̲- v. i. to change; mōt̲- to change (way, etc.); mōt- to change (clothes); Ta. mār̲u to be altered; Ma. mār̲uka id.; n. a change; Kui māru adj./adv. deferential, deferentially; Go. māṛk- to turn the head and glance quickly (as crane); maṛī-maṛī in different ways; Brah. ? maṭṭēṅg- to be changed (as season). PDr. *māt̲-.]

māṟu (2) to be exchanged, to be current, cashed, as money; mārcu tr. to exchange (Bhr. II).

[Ka. māṟu to barter, sell; to be sold; n. a barter, sale; māṟisu to cause to sell; Tu. māruni to sell, dispose of; Ko. mār- to sell; Ta. māṟu tr. to sell, barter (Perump.); Ma. māṟuka tr. to exchange; Kui māska (māsk-i-) to exchange; Kuvi (S) mask- id.; Go. māṛ- to be spent; māht- to spend; GoM. mārh- tr. to finish; mār- to exhaust. PDr. *māṯ-.]

māṟu (3) to be destroyed, to perish; tr. mārcu to kill.

[Ta. māṟu tr. to forsake; n. death (PN); māṟuka to cease, subside; māṟṟuka to remove; Ko. mār- (sun) to set; Kui mrāpk- (< mrāk-p-; mrāk-t-) to lose, obliterate; GoM. mār- to lose; Mlt. māry- (mārc-) to overcome, subdue; this is further related to etyma meaning 'to be hidden,' etc., v. s. v. maṟugu. PDr. *māṯ-.]

974 mālu to be spoiled, destroyed (UH); to be devoid of (Bhr. II); to fail, miss (Bhr. II); tr. to give up, abandon (Bhr. II).

[Ka. māḷ to cease; to abandon; māṇ, māṇu to stop, cease; subside; Ta. māḷ (māṇ-ṭ-) to die, perish (Tiruvāc.); be exhausted; finished. PSDr. *māḷ- < *mā-ḷ; v. s. v. māṟu (3), malũgu, mānu.]

975 māl(u)gu* intr. to grow lazy; n. laziness (late).

[Ta. māḻku to grow lazy; Ma. māḻkuka to languish, grow faint; Tu. māluni to reel, stagger; prob. Te. is a l. w. from a Mdn. Ta. dialect where ḷ < *ḻ.]

976 mikk-ilu* intr. to increase, be in excess (UH); mikk-ili abundance, the best (Bhr. I, II); adj. abundantly, excessive; v. s. v. migulu.

977 migulu intr. to remain over; to be in excess, to occur excessively (Bhr. I, II); to exceed, go beyond (Bhr. II); to be left unspent; to elapse, pass; tr. to increase (Bhr. II); n. remainder, excess; balance, rest, surplus.

[Ka. migu (mikk-) be in excess; go beyond; migilu abundance, remainder; Tu. mikkuni to exceed; intr. to remain, be left; migi, migilụ surpassing; migiluni to excell, surpass; Ko. mik- to be left over; mikc- to save (money, life, etc.); To. mik- to be left over, remain; Ta. miku (mikk-) v. i. to exceed, be in excess (Nāl.); to increase; be left over; (miku-tt-) to make large (Kṟḷ.), to surpass, increase; adj. great; mikattu to save, spare; mikai (mikai-tt-) v. i. to increase (PN); Ma. mikuka (mikk-) to abound; mikekka to exceed, increase; miñcuka to remain, exceed. PSDr. *mik-, ultimately *mi-k-, v. s. v. mincu[1]; PDr. *miy-/*mī-.]

978 miṭṭu intr. to leap, jump (Naiṣ.); mostly in pp. followed by paḍu to fall, i.e., miṭṭ-i paḍu to jump, leap, bounce (KS, Bhr. II).
[Klm.(E) miṭ- to leap; Nk. miṭṭ- id.; others, v. s. v. miḍiyu. PSDr. and PCDr. *miṭ-.]

979 miḍiyu III intr. to fly off, jump, leap; to swell up (KS, BhR); to be proud; miḍi n. pride, vanity (Bhr. II); adj. proud (Daśā.); projected, protruded (as eyeballs) (Dvi.H.).
[Ka. miḍi to leap, hop, bounce; tr. to make fly; also v. s. v. miṭṭu; (> l. w. Skt. maṭacī a grass-hopper, cf. Te. miḍuta, see Burrow, DS VII, p. 389, No. 247; Emeneau, Kolami, Vocab. No. 534).]

980 miḍuku[1] to be proud, leap, jump (Bhr. II).
[V. s. v. miḍiyu, miṭṭu.]

981 miḍuku[2]* to grieve (Bhr. II, JBh.).
[Ka. miḍuku, miḍugu id.; miḍa, miṭṭane in a sorrowful manner; Ma. muṭukuka to be distressed; cf. Ta. viḷi to suffer, be disgraced.]

982 miḍuku[3] intr. to move, wander (Mārk.); to shake, move (Nirv.).
[Ka. miḍuku v. i./tr. to move, urge on, push; cf. Ta. muṭuku to hasten, move quickly (Pu.Ve.); muṭukku to drive, urge; Ma. muṭukkuka to urge on, drive, as cattle; Go. miḍḍing-miḍḍing-ai- to wander about at a loss; miṙhutt- to seek or hunt for.]

983 miḍucu* IIa tr. to flick with fingers (Daśā., Naiṣ.).
[Ka. miḍi to fillip; Pj. miṭkip- (miṭkit-) to flick; miṭṭ- to flick with finger; v. s. v. mīṭu.]

984 min(u)ku[1] intr. to glitter, shine (Daśā.); n. flash, a ray of light.
[Ka. minu shining; minuku, minugu to shine, glitter; mīn glittering; Tu. minukuni, miṇkuni to twinkle, glisten, sparkle; Ta. mi<u>n</u>uṅku to glitter, shine (Tiv.); to appear bright (Tiv.); mi<u>n</u>ukku to polish; mi<u>n</u> n. flash, glitter (Kamp.), lightning (Maṇi.); mi<u>nn</u>u to shine, glitter; Ma. minukka to glitter, be fine; minnuka to flash, shine; minnal lightning; minukkuka to polish; Pj. minnal spark. PSDr. and PCDr. *min-/*mi<u>t</u>; for *mi<u>t</u>-, v. s. v. me<u>r</u>ayu; also see mincu.]

985 minuku[2]* intr. to murmur within oneself (Paṇḍ.).
[V. s. v. *minnu.]

986 mincu[1] IId intr. to excel, exceed, increase; go beyond (Naiṣ.); be great, high; (time limit) to exceed; be gone by; to be too late.
[Ka. miñcu id.; Tu. miñjuni to exceed; spare; overcome; Ta. miñcu to exceed, surpass (colloq.); v. i. to increase (Cīv.), become proud; n. excess; Ma. miñcuka to exceed, superabound. PSDr. *mi-nc-, cf. migulu.]

987 mincu$^{2}$* IId intr. to shine, as lightning (Kāś.), to shine; n. lightning, brilliance (BP, BhR); (< *min-c-).

[Ko. minc- to flash, glitter; To. mic- (mič-) it lightens; for others, v. s. v. minuku.]

988 *minnu* only as neg. ppl. minn-aka adv. simply (Bhr. II), without a word (Naiṣ.), easily (Hara.); without attempt, merely (Bhr. II); intr. to murmur, say in a low voice; to speak, say; (< *miṇṇ-); cf. minuku$^{2}$.

[Ta. miṇu-miṇu v. i. to mumble, speak with a low reiterated voice; murmur; miṇṭu tr. to talk harshly or arrogantly (Tēv.); Ma. miṇumiṇukka to mumble, mutter; miṇṭuka to utter, speak low; miṇṭādĕ without utterance; quietly; imper. be silent; don't stir!]

989 misuku intr. to move, tremble, quiver (in fear); to stir (later works).

[Ka. misuku to move, stir, quiver; Tu. miskuni to move, meddle with; To. misx- v. i. to move slightly vertically. PSDr. *mic-/ *mit-, v. s. v. medalu.]

990 mī̆ṭu (SAN; Śab.R., Dh.M. mīṭu) (1) tr. to toss or fling with the tip of a finger (Bhr. II), to play a stringed instrument; to fillip (Bhīm., Manu.).

[Ka. mīṭu, miḍi id.; Ta. mīṭṭu id.; Ma. mīṭṭuka, miṭikka id.]

mī̆ṭu (2) to pull or pluck out (Bhr. I, BhR); to remove.

[Ka. mīṇṭu to pull up by the roots; raise with lever; Tu. mīṇṭuni to force up or out, sustain, as with lever; mīṭuni id.; Ta. mīḷ (mīṭṭ-) to liberate, release; mīṭṭu to redeem; Ma. mīṇṭuka to draw out, pluck up; miṭantuka, miṭaṟṟuka to wedge in, force open. PSDr. *mīḷ-/mīṇ-, *mīṭṭ- < *mīḷ-t-.]

991 mīṟu tr. to cross over, exceed; excel, surpass (Bhr. II, UH, Kāś.); intr. to increase, swell with joy, etc. (UH), to pass, elapse (Prabhā.); to grow proud, disobedient (Mdn.).

[Ka. mīṟ, mīṟu to go beyond; transgress, exceed; elapse, as time; be elated; Tu. mīruni to transgress, violate; exceed; Ko. mīr- to be extreme in anything, refuse to heed; mīṭ- to be successful in fight; To. mīṟ- become uncontrollable; Ta. mīṟu tr. to transgress, exceed; intr. to remain over, be great; grow lofty; be haughty, as a person; Ma. mīṟuka to exceed, transgress; to rage; Kui mīja to exceed, excel; overtake; mīnja to pounce upon, attack; Go. wīr- to surpass, outstrip. PSDr. and PCDr. *mīṯ-/*vīṯ-; cf. Ta. vīṟu to increase; To. wīr- to emulate, which show initial v- besides Go.; ultimately *mīṯ < PDr. *mik-uṯ-, v. s. v. migulu.]

992 mukku[1] intr. to strain, as in child-labor or at stool; to moan, groan, grumble; cf. mukk-aṭ-incu to hold breath (Paṇḍ.).

[Ka. mukkar̲i, mukkare to strain; make violent efforts in pain, etc.; Tu. mukkuru snorting, grunting; mukkuruni to snort, growl; Ko. muk- to strain oneself; Ta. mukku to strain, as a woman in travail; make great effort; mur̲ku inarticulate sound (Tolk.); mur̲uku to wriggle; mur̲ukku tr. to twirl; n. convulsion; Ma. mikkuka, mukkuka to strain, grunt; mur̲ukku writhing agony; Kuvi (S) mūrū-kī to growl (kī- to do); Brah. mukk- to stammer; būkh̲- to grumble, groan, moan. PDr. *mŭt̲-k- < *mŭl-k-; v. s. v. mŭlugu.]

mukku[2] (< mrukku, q. v.) to be spoiled, as grain; become musty (Vēm.).

993 mugiyu III intr. to end, be completed (Kāś.); to perish (lex.); tr. mug-incu to complete, to end.

[Ka. mugi v. i. to end, terminate; close, shut; Tu. mugiyuni v. i. to end; close, shut up; mugipuni to finish; Ta. muki v. i. to end; tr. to finish, conclude (Kur̲r̲.); Kui mūga to be finished, completed; mūpka (< mūk-p-; mūk-t-) to finish; mūpa (mūt-) to complete; mugse completely; Kur. muñj- to finish off; spend completely; muñj$^{u}$r- to come to an end; to die. PDr. *muy-/*mū-; PSDr. muk-i- < *muy-V-.]

994 mucciru* intr. to grieve, be distressed (KS, Bhr. II); mucciri one who is sorrowful.

[Ta. muci (muci-nt-) v. i. to be tired; (muci-tt-) v. i. to be distressed (Tiv.), to grow thin, perish; mucippu thinness, languor, fatigue.]

995 muccu* intr. to close, tr. to cause to close; inf. mucc-a (muḍūgu) to (shrink) completely, closely together (KS).

[Ka. Tu. Ta. Ma. muccu to close; Ko. muc- to cover; To. mūc- (mūč-) id.; Kui muspa (must-) to cover, immerse; Kuvi (S) muh- (must-) to peg; mucc- to siege; Go. mucc- to wrap round; Kur. mucc-, Mlt. muc- to close; Brah. must adj. shut. PDr. *muc-; also v. s. v. mūyu.]

996 muṭṭu[1] tr. to touch, reach (Bhr. I, II); intr. to be obtained, (money) to come to hand, be paid; n. touching (Bhr. II).

[Ka. muṭṭu tr. to touch; v. i. to come to hand (as dues); to reach, arrive, as a letter; Tu. muṭṭuni to touch, reach, attain; to arrive at, come to hand; Ko. muṭ- (muc-) to touch; To. muṭ- (muṭy-) id.; Ta. muṭṭu tr. to dash against (Nāl.), to meet (Tolk.); Ma. muṭṭuka tr. to touch, dash against; Go. (Bilaspur) muṭṭis near (LSI IV, p. 489). PSDr. and PCDr. *muṭ-.]

997 muṭṭu[2] to besiege, attack (Bhr. II), to surround, inclose; to spread over (Bhr. II), to abound (Bhr. II), be crowded.

[Ka. muttu to inclose, cover; attack, shut in; v.i. to swarm, throng; Tu. mutṭuni to surround, besiege, hem in; Ta. mur̲r̲u tr. to surround (PN), besiege, blockade (Tolk.); v.i. to abound; Ma. mur̲r̲uka to be close, crowded; cf. Go. mūṛ- to be blocked, of a bamboo or gun barrel; Brah. mūṛk stopper; mūṛk-tinn- to stop up. PDr. *mut̲-.]

998 muḍūgu (also muṇūgu) intr. to contract, become closed; to shrivel up (Dvi.H.); to refrain from (Mārk.); to diminish; tr. muḍūcu, q.v.

[Ka. muḍuku (also muḍugu, muḍubu) to shrink, become crooked; n. bending; Ta. muṭaṅku to contract, bend; muṭakku to bend, as knee (Tiv.), wind round, wrap (Tēv.); n. curve; Ma. muṭar̲uka to be twisted; muṭam contraction of members, as by wind. PSDr. *muṭ-uṅk-/-aṅk-.]

muḍūgu[2] intr. to sink, plunge (late); cf. munūgu.

999 muḍūcu IIb (also muṇūcu; tr. of muḍūgu[1], q.v.) tr. to cause to shrink (Bhīm.); to tie into a bundle (Daśā.); to set flowers in braid (UH); to save money (i.e., tying into a bundle) (Kāś.); der. n. mūṭa a bundle (Hara.); muḍi a knot, of hair, etc.

[Ka. muḍi to bind, as hair; set flowers in hair; muḍu, mūṭe a knot, bundle, as of hair; Tu. muḍeyuni to be folded; muḍepini, muḍepuni to plait, braid, bind; muḍiyuni be knotty; muḍipini/muḍipuni to dress hair with flowers; muḍi bundle, knot; muḍipu bundle; Ta. muṭi tr. to fasten, tie (Tiv.), put on flowers (Kalit.); n. knot, coil of hair, bundle; Ma. muṭikka to tie up; muṭi a knot; Go. muḍhutt- to fold blanket; muṛhutt- to cover with a cloth; Brah. muṭṭukh̲ knotted; cf. Kur. mul- to dress hair; Mlt. mund- to tie up in a cloth; make a knot; mulur- dress hair. PDr. *muṭ-, ? < *muḷ-t-.]

1000 mudiyu III intr. to become or grow old (Bhr. II, RR), to become worn away (Bhr. II); muduka an old man (BhR); mudi adj. old; mudimi old age (Bhr. I); musali old, old man (Manu.).

[Ka. mudu (mutt-) to advance in years, become full grown; become old; Tu. mudiyuni be worn out; adj. old; To. mūf- (mūt-) become old; Ta. mū to become old (Kr̲ḷ.); mutir id. (Maṇi.), become mature (PN); Ma. mūkka to grow old; Kuvi (S) mū'- to outgrow; Kuvi (F) mūssela an old man; Pj. muttak old man; Brah. mutkun old; old thing. PDr. *muc-/*mut-, *mū-.]

1001 muduru to become ripe or mature, become full grown (of leaves, fruit, trees, men, etc.) (Kāś., Bhōj.); become aggravated, as disease; adj. that which has lost freshness, grown-up (Bhr. II); cf. mudiyu.

[Tu. muduruni v.i. to expand, become enlarged; muduru̥ expansion; Ta. mutir to grow old (Maṇi.); become mature or ripe (PN), be saturated, to excel; mutirpu excess; Ma. mutiruka to grow up, grow mature; mutu old; cf. Ta. muṟṟu (< *mū-ṯ-) to become mature, ripen (Nāl.), be advanced in age (Piṅ.), to abound, increase (Pu.Ve.); become hardened, as the core of a tree, come to end; Ka. muduḍu, muduru, mudru to contract, shrivel up; muduke an old man. PDr. *mut-/*muc, *muc-/*mū- < *muy-.]

1002 mun(u)ku$^{1*}$ intr. to be aggrieved, distressed, be displeased (BhR, Naiṣ.); n. displeasure, grief.

[Ka. muni become angry or be displeased; munipu passion; Tu. muniyuni to be in a passion, to hate; munipu n. anger, hatred; Ta. muṉi tr. to dislike (Tolk.), be angry with (Parip.); muṉivu n. anger (Kamp.), dislike (Tolk.); fatigue, suffering (Ciṟup.); muṉai tr. be angry with, to resent, dislike (Perump.); muṇai be angry with, to dislike (ṇ < *n); Ma. muniyuka to look sullen; abhor; munikka to incite; Go. mung-sāng (yē-) to be more angry than sulky (yē- to take); cf. Mlt. mūly- (mūlc-) to tease; munḍ- to bring into difficulty. PDr. *mŭn-/ ? *mŭl-.]

1003 mun(u)ku$^{2*}$ to mutter, grumble (Mārk., RR).

[Tu. muṇkuni to cry as a ghost, to say 'ham' expressing disapproval; muṇumuṇu muttering; Ta. muṉaṅku to mutter, grumble, moan. PSDr. *mun-; also cf. *minnu.]

1004 mun(ū)gu (dial. also muṇugu) intr. to sink, plunge (Bhr. II); to bathe (Kāś.); be drowned; (sun) to set; to perish, be spoiled (Paṇḍ.); to end, be finished (KS, Bhr. II); n. bathing (lex.); munuka a dip, bathing; tr. mun(u)cu to immerse, cause to sink.

[Ka. muṇugu, muṇigu to sink under water; Tu. muḷuguni, muṇuguni to sink; Ko. muḷg- be lost to one completely; To. muḷx- be destroyed; Ta. muṅku v.i. to sink, plunge into water (Maṇi.) (< *muṇ-k-); Ma. muṅkuka to dive, sink; Kui munja to sink beneath; Kuvi (S) munj-, Kuvi (F) mūnj- to sink; Klm.(E) muŋg- to submerge oneself under water, (sun) sets; Nk. muŋg- id.; Pj. mulg- (Sth. muli-) to dive; Kur. mul$^{u}$kh̲-, mun$^{u}$kh̲- v.i. to sink; disappear, get lost; Mlt. mulg̡- tr. to dip in; mulgr- v.i. to dive; < PDr. *mŭḷ-/mŭṇ-; this set may be separated from the one under bruṅgu (< *muḻuṅk-) mainly on phonological grounds).]

1005 munucu* IId intr. to go or appear before; tr. munupu to cause to appear, show.

[V. s. v. monayu; PDr. *mun-.]

muncu[1] IIb (tr. of munugu, q. v.; historically < *muḻ-nc- or *mu-nc-, with *mu- as the ultimate root) to plunge in, dip, immerse (Bhr. I). [V. s. v. munugu, bruṅgu.]

1006 muncu[2*] IId (< *muy-nc-) tr. to cover, envelop (Kāś., JBh.). [Klm.(SR) muns- to cover, close, see Emeneau, Kolami, Vocab., No. 2222; also v. s. v. mūyu, muccu.]

1007 muncu[3*] IId intr. to increase, excel (late). [Ka. muñcu to precede, excel; v. s. v. mincu, i/u after m-.]

1008 muriyu[1] (also muṟiyu SAN) III intr. to be graceful or affected while walking (Bhr. II); to be proud (Bhr. II); to exult, be in great glee; der. n. muripamu, muripemu grace, beauty (Bhr. II, Naiṣ.); pride; mur(u)vu beauty, grace, splendor, pride (Dvi.H., JBh.). [Ka. ṃurku, muṟuku pride; muṟuku, muṟaka making foppish airs, showiness, pride; Ta. muṟai to become stiff, haughty; n. order, arrangement; muṟuku to be haughty; muṟamuṟa to be neat and crisp; muṟamuṟappu cleanness; muṟuval happiness (Tolk.), smile; cf. Kur. mur$^{u}$kh impulsive; adv. recklessly; Mlt. murgtr- to satiate, cloy. PDr. *muṯ-.]

1009 muriyu[2*] (SAN, Śab.R.; muṟiyu Dh.M.) III intr. to be cut off; to break, crumble (KS, Bhr. II); muṟiyu to be broken, severed (RR, HariV.); cf. muṟiya (lex.), mukka (< *murk-) a piece, crumb; cf. muṟugu[2].

[Ka. muṟi to break, sever by fracture; tr. break off, as trees; Tu. mūruni to mince, cut up, as vegetables; murkụ a piece, bit; Ko. mury- (murc-) tr. to break, a stick, etc.; To. mūry- (mūrc-) tr. break in two; müry- (mürs-) to be broken; Ta. muri v. i. to break off, perish (Kṟḷ.), separate; (muri-tt-) to ruin, defeat; muṟi to break away; tr. to break; n. a cut; Ma. muṟikka to cut; break; muṟi n. a fragment; adj. wounded; mūruka to cut up; reap; Kui muṛpa to split wood; Klm.(E) murk- to break; Nk. mur- v. i. to break; murk- tr.; Kur. mur$^{u}$k- to amputate; cut in pieces; murc- to twist and break; Mlt. murk- to cut into bits; Brah. bur- to crumble. PDr. *mūr- : *mur-V-, also mūṯ- : *muṯ-V-; note confusion between *r and *ṯ.]

1010 muṟugu[1] intr. to rot, putrefy (Mārk.); become dirty, rancid. [Ka. muṟikil impurity; muggu to be musty or moldy; Tu. murguni to mold; mugga moldy; ? Ta. muri to be spoiled, perish, be ruined (Kṟḷ.); Go. muṛkst- tr. to rot achar berries in a pot; Klm. (Kin.) murr dirt; Pj. mur, murru dirt; cf. mara, maraṭ rotten; v. s. v. mruggu. PSDr. and PCDr. *muṯ-/*mur-.]

1011 muṟugu[2*] intr. to be crushed (Mārk.).

[V. s. v. muriyu; PDr. *muṯ-uṅk-/-ukk-; also see Emeneau, Kolami, Vocab., No. 2225.]

mulugu (var. of mūl(u)gu, q. v.) intr. to groan as in pain (UH); to sound (Krīḍ.).

1012 musaru (also musuru) intr. to overspread, surround, crowd, swarm, pounce upon (KS, Bhr. II); to settle upon, as flies, etc.; cf. mū̃gu; musuru cloudiness, being overcast.

[Ka. musuṟ, musuṟu id.; n. a cover, veil; Ta. mūcu to swarm about (Neṭu.); n. swarming, thronging (Cīv.); moy (moy-tt-) v. i. to crowd, as flies, ants; throng, swarm (PN); tr. to crowd around; moci to swarm; Go. moi- (moīsī) to rush at, close with; moitt- id.; further v. s. v. muccu, mū̃gu, mūyu. PDr. *muy-/*moy- < *muc-.]

1013 mū̃gu intr./tr. to collect or gather around (HariV.); to overspread (UH); to swarm and settle upon, as flies (Mdn.); to increase, spread (Bhr. II, UH); mū̃ka an army, crowd (Bhr. I, II), a mob of people (Mdn.).

[Ka. mukaṟu, mukkaṟu to come and fall upon; Ta. mūy v. i. to surround closely; mūcu to swarm about; mūḻ tr. to swarm round (Parip.), surround; Go. moi- to rush at. PDr. *muy-/*mū-; v.s.v. musaru, mūyu, muccu.]

1014 mū̃ḍu[1] intr. to happen, occur (Hara.); to befall, as an evil (Bhr. II, BhR).

[Ka. mūḍu to arise, originate, become apparent; Tu. mūḍu to rise, be born; Ta. mūṭu n. root (Kuṟṟ.), cause, origin.]

1015 mū̃ḍu[2*] (Śab.R.; mūḍu Dh.M.) intr. to end, terminate; (death) to approach (Mdn.).

[Ka. muḍi to come to an end; Tu. muḍusuni to consume, eat up; Ko. muṛc- to finish (work); Ta. muṭi v. i. to end (Tolk.); mūṭu v. i. to reach a critical stage, as a disease; come to an end; Ma. muṭiyuka to come to an end, be extinct; muṭikka tr. to finish. PSDr. *mūṭ- : *muṭ-V-.]

1016 mūyu III tr. to close, cover, cover up (Naiṣ.); to conceal, screen, hide; intr. (a flower) to shrivel, close its petals (Dvi.H.); to be shut, closed (Bhr. I); mū̃ta a cover, lid.

[Ta. mūy (mūy-nt-, mūy-iṉ-) tr. to cover (Parip.), fill; intr. to surround closely; n. cover; mūḻ intr. to close, as a bud (PN); To. mōz- (mōǯ-) to hide (news, etc.); Kui muspa (must-) to cover, bury; Kuvi muh'- to bury; Go. moi- to close with; Klm. muy- to cover oneself; Nk. muy- id.; KGad. mūy-/mūyk- (mūy-t-) tr. to close, cover; Kur. mundh- to stop, shut, close; muṇḍh- to lay a cover over; Mlt. musgr- to be closed up (as bag). PDr. *mŭy-/mū-, in morphophonemic situations mu-/mū- with loss of y; ultimately *mŭ-; also evidence for *mŭy-/*mŏy-; v. s. v. muccu, mū̃gu, musuru, muṭṭu$^{2}$, moguḍu, mogucu.]

1017 mūru* intr. to increase, abound, to swell in joy (later texts); mūrī bōvu to increase, be full, swell, etc. (Bhr. II).

[Ta. mūri strength (Piṅ.), greatness (Pu.Ve.).]

1018 mūl(u)gu (also mulugu, q. v.) to sound, to groan, moan as from pain, murmur, grumble (later texts); to stay long (as a treasure, wealth, unused for years) (Bhōj., also Mdn.); n. groan, moan, grumbling.

[Ka. muluku, mūlugu to groan when lifting; Ma. mūḷuka to groan, moan, mumble; Kuvi (S) mūlg- to sulk; Kuvi (F) mūrū-kī- to growl; Klm.(SR) mūlg-, mulg- to groan. PSDr. and PCDr. *mūḷ-, *muḷ-V-; alternatively *mŭl-/*mŭn-, v. s. v. mukku, munuku$^{2}$; then Ma. ḷ < l; note Kuvi (F) r < *l rather than ḷ.]

mūvu* (var. of mū̃gu, q. v.).

1019 mekku to eat greedily or excessively, gobble up, swallow (Āmu.).

[Ka. mel, meli, mellu to eat with sound, chew, masticate; melku bringing up for rumination; Ta. mel, mellu (meṉ-ṟ-) to masticate (Cīv.); Ma. melluka id.; Kui mrēḍa to chew.]

1020 meccu IId tr. to respect, regard (Bhr. I); to care for, like (Bhr. I); to praise, applaud, commend (Bhr. II); intr. to rejoice, be glad (Bhr. I, Naiṣ.); n. rejoicing (Bhr. I, III); approbation, praise (Daśā., Bhīm.); love, liking (Bhīm.); adj. praiseworthy, admirable (Bhr. II, Kāś.); meppu n. appreciation, praise.

[Ka. meccu/maccu to be pleased; to like; n. approbation, pleasure; Tu. meccuni to approve; be pleased; Ko. mec- to praise; Ta. meccu to praise (Tēv.), to esteem; admire; n. approbation; meyccu = meccu, q. v.; < *mey-cc-; PDr. *mey-/*miy- high, above; elsewhere we have the meaning association between 'to raise' and 'to praise,' cf. Ta. eṭu to raise, to praise (Tolk.); Ka. ma- form is due to contamination with marcu/maccu liking, v.s.v. maragu; e/i before y in PDr.; alternation between higher and lower vowels before y common in PDr.; cf. Ta. mē excellence (Maturai.), mī- greatness; mī-kkūṟu to praise (Kṟḷ.); mīkūṟṟam praise (PN); mī-kkoḷ to esteem; cf. Go. maitt- to surpass; Kur. maitā highest; metā id.; meccā adj. high (in position), tall, lofty; Go. Kur. forms < *mey-/*may-.]

1021 meṭṭu intr. to dance (KS); tr. to step on, lay the step on (Naiṣ.), to enter, step in (UH); to press under foot, trample on (Āmu.); to put on (shoes) (Vikram.); n. trampling; a step (of a staircase) (Bhr. II), a mound; a step of a stringed instrument.

[Ka. meṭṭu to step, walk, trample on; put on a shoe; n. a step, a step of a stair, stringed instrument, etc.; Ko. meṭ- (mec-) to tread on; To. mōṭ- (möṭy-) to trample on; Ta. meṭṭu to spurn with foot; cf. Ma. mēṭuka to knock, as with finger, to drive in, strike. PSDr. *meṭ- (vb.); etyma meaning 'mound, hillock' may belong here, see Emeneau, Kolami, Vocab., No. 2209.]

1022 meḍuku* (SAN; not in Śab.R. or Dh.M.) intr. to frisk, leap (single usage cited from a later work).

[V. s. v. miḍuku.]

1023 meṇḍu tr. to lever up (colloq., Rāyalasīma dial.); n. a turn, twist (Āmu.); meṇḍuveṭṭu to turn, twist.

[Ta. mennu to lift with a lever (loc.); prob. < *meḷ-/*meṇ-, v. s. v. meliyu; alternatively *men-/*met-, v. s. v. meruku; cf. Ma. miṭantuka to jerk with a lever to remove something; miṭarruka to wedge in, force open (loc.) (? < *meḷ-V-).]

1024 mettu tr. to apply, plaster with mud or the like (Vikram., Manu.); n. plastering, filling up uneven spots with mud, etc. (Pāṇḍ.); support, protection (late).

[Ka. mettu to coat walls, plaster; press into; Tu. mettuni to fill up with earth; repair, as a dam; mettigè ceiling of house; Ko. met- to plaster (semi-liquids) in handfuls; Ta. mettu tr. to pad, pack, plaster (Cīv.); to fill; intr. to be filled; Klm.(E) met-, Klm.(SR) mett- to plaster; Nk. mett- id.; Pj. mett- to smear; < PSDr. and PCDr. *met-; tt < *l-t not likely (cf. mrēgu) on account of assimilation in PCDr., Ta. Ka.; however, it is possible if we posit borrowing in all these languages from Te., which is less likely but not unlikely.]

1025 medapu (tr. of an obsolete *medayu) to stir, move, make to shake (later text, also Mdn. as medupu).

[V. s. v. medalu.]

1026 medamu* (SAN quotes as an alt. of meramu$^{2}$, q. v.); also cf. medalu.

1027 medalu (also medulu, late) intr. to shake, move slightly (Bhr. I, II), to stir out, wander, roam (BhR, Bhr. III); to exist (Dvi.H., Bhōj.); tr. medal(u)cu, medapu (later works).

[Ka. misuku to move, stir; Tu. miskuni to move; interfere with; medukuni/medkuni to move, be in motion; Ta. miti n. gait. PSDr.

*mic-/*mit-, v.s.v. misuku; alternatively < *mec-/*mey-, cf. Ta. mēy to roam (Tiv.); KGad. meyk- to roam, wander.]

1028 medugu intr. to be pounded, ground (JBh.), to become weakened (Vi.Pu.); to be reduced to fine powder or paste; be trained or practiced, be accustomed (Mdn.); meducu, medupu to mix or pound well (Manu.); cf. metta a cushion; meduku, metuku a boiled grain of rice, etc.; mett-ani, meduvu adj. soft.

[Ka. midi (< *medi) to pound, beat, kill, grind, rub, triturate; Tu. medpuni, medupuni to clean by pounding, as rice, etc.; to mill; medu adj. soft, pliant; Ma. metiyuka to be bruised; metikka to trample, tread, thresh; meti treading on; Kuvi (F) med- to push; Mlt. medg̣r- to discolor, to blacken; medg̣o adj. discolored by bruise; cf. Kui meda a scar, blotch on skin. PDr. *met-; the same root underlies etyma meaning 'softness,' Te. metta, mettani, etc.; Ka. medu, mettane; Ta. metu, metten̲al, etc.]

meducu IIb (tr. of medugu, q.v.) to grind (RR); to mix well, powders and liquids, perfumes, etc. (Kāś.); also medincu, mēd-incu to mix well (Rasika.).

medupu (tr. of medugu, q.v.; [Pāṇḍ.]).

1029 menupu* (Śab.R.) tr. to mix or stir well with churning rod.

1030 meppu* intr. to leap, jump (later text).

[Ma. mettuka to jump; Ta. mettu to increase; < *mey-pp-/-tt-; v.s.v. meccu.]

1031 mempu* intr. to face, encounter (Vi.Pu.).

1032 mey(i)du* intr. to be beside oneself, be infatuated, intoxicated (KS).

[Cf. Ta. maintu n. infatuation of love (Parip.); stupidity (Parip.); maiyal id.; madness (Kr̲ḷ.). PSDr. *may/*mey-; cf. Mlt. mēca an intoxicating beverage made of corn; also v.s.v. masaru.]

mer̲acu* IIa intr. to shine, flash (Bhr. I, II; HariV.).

[V.s.v. mer̲ayu.]

1033 mer̲amu[1]* (also mer̲umu) tr. to pierce, thrust in as a knife and stir (UH, Dvi.H.); to cause pain to mortification; afflict; harass (Vasu.).

[Ta. mir̲ai to oppress, harass; to trouble (Kr̲ḷ.).]

1034 mer̲amu[2]* intr. to stir, move (Nṛs.); tr. to cause to move, stir (Bhg., Manu.).

[? Ka. mere to wander, roam about; Ma. miraḷuka to start, be shaken; Go. mirr- to swarm, of insects in the rains; mirst- to splash, scatter; (of lice) to swarm in head; cf. Tu. mijipuni, mijiluni be full of worms.]

1035 meṟayu III intr. to shine, glitter, to be splendid, beautiful (Bhr. I, II); to be made public, be known (Hara.); to appear; meṟay-incu to make known, to disclose (Bhr. I); meṟ(ũ)gu n. flash, lightning (Bhr. I, II).

[Ka. meṟe to shine; appear; display; miṟugu to glitter; miṟu shining; Tu. mereyuni to go in a procession, to shine; merè n. display; Ta. miruku n. glitter, polish (l. w. < Te./Ka.); Ma. meruku, verukku n. lustre; Go. miḍst- to flash, of lightning; GoM. miṛk- id.; Klm.(E) merp- to lighten; Klm.(SR) to flash; Nk. merp- to flash; lighten; Pj. marp- (mart-) to lighten; KGad. merc- to glitter; cf. Mlt. merg- to thunder; merġe, merġu sky, heaven. PDr. *miṯ-/*min-; also v. s. v. minuku; PCDr. evidence, excepting Go., is for *e in the root syllable, but they may be considered l. ws. from Te.]

1036 meṟuku* tr. to pull or pluck out, break (Kāś.).

[V. s. v. meṇḍu; ? Ko. marṭ- to overturn by levering; cf. Ka. meṟe tossing, meṟekōlu a staff with a hook used to toss the straw that has been trodden out by oxen, and remove it to one side.]

1037 meṟumu[1] intr. to shine, glitter (Bhr. I, II).

meṟumu[2]* (alt. of meṟamu[1], q. v.) to pierce (UH); beat, flog (late).

1038 melaku* intr. to burn, blaze (Bhg.; rare).

1039 melãgu intr. to behave, conduct oneself (Bhr. II), to wander, move about (Bhr. II), to spread, extend (Bhr. II, Bhg.); tr. melãcu to cause to move (Bhr. II); melapu id.; n. care in behavior, mannerly behavior, skill (Nirv., Bhr. II).

[Klm.(SR) melãg- intr. to move; melãp- tr. to wag, move; Klm.(E) melg- intr. to shake; cf. Ka. miḷir to move, move about; to prosper, flourish; v. s. v. melayu/meliyu.]

1040 melayu (also meliyu) III intr. to be twisted, as thread; be entangled; to mix closely (as with friends); to be, behave; to wander (usages quoted from later texts); n. melika a twist, turn, loop, entanglement; meli id.; melivẽyu to twist, twine; tr. melucu to twist, entwine.

[Ka. miḷir v. i. to roll; Tu. meliyuni to become mixed; melipuni to knead; Ta. miḷir v. i. to turn, be upset; tr. to roll, turn over; Ma. miṭayuka to plait, twist (ṭ < ḷ); Kui mliṅga to be turned over; milpa (milt-, miṭ-) tr. to turn over; mlipka (< mlik-p-; mlikt-) id.; Kuvi (F) mriph- to invert; Pj. milkip- (milkit-) to overturn; milŋg- be overturned; Nk. miṭī embrace (LSI IV, p. 572); Kur. miṇḍrī adj. coiled, convoluted; n. coil. PDr. *miḷ-/*miṇ-; cf. Kur. mẽr thread, twine.]

meliyu III (var. of melayu, q. v.).

1041 mesāgu* (also mesavu, Kāś.) tr. to eat, swallow (Naiṣ.); to experience.

[Ta. micai tr. to eat a meal (Kṟḷ.), taste, enjoy; n. food (Aiṅk.); boiled rice; micaivu n. eating, food (PN); < PSDr. *mēc- : *mec-V-; other languages, v. s. v. mēyu.]

mẽgu* (< mrēgu/mrēvu, q. v.) to apply, smear (Dvi.H., ŚivaR.).

[Ko. mek- to cleanse floor with cowdung water; Kim. mēg- id.; Nk. mēgh- (mēkt-) to apply; prob. Klm. Nk. are l. ws. from ancient Te. after m < mr-; in the Ko. form, k < *kk < *ḻk; see Emeneau, Kolami, Vocab. No. 521; Telugu usages point to an early loss of r in mr-, v. s. v. mrēgu/mrēvu.]

1042 mēdu* tr. to smear, daub; mix together (Bhōj., Kāś.).

[V. s. v. mettu; contamination with the meanings of medugu, meducu, q. v. ]

1043 mēmu* intr./tr. to agree, concede (lex.).

[Cf. mē-konu, meyi-konu id.; Ta. mey-kkoḷ to believe to be true; mey-kkōḷ acceptance as truth; meymmai truth, reality (Tiruvāc.); natural state (Tolk.).]

1044 mēyu III intr./tr. to graze, feed on (Naiṣ., Manu.); tr. mēpu to graze cattle.

[Ka. mē, mēy (mēd-) to graze; Tu. mēpini v. i. id.; mēpuni tr. id.; Ko. mēy- v. i.; mēc- tr.; To. mīy- (mīs-) v. i.; mīc- (mīč-) tr.; Ta. mēy (mēy-nt-) v. i. to graze, feed on; gnaw, as white ants (Kṟḷ.); drink (Cīv.); (mēytt-) tr. to feed, graze; mēyal n. grazing (Aiṅk.), pasture (Akan.); Ma. mēyka v. i. to graze; mēyttuka tr.; Kuvi (F) mey- v. i.; Kuvi (S) mē'- to feed; me'- to pasture; Go. mēī- (mēī-sī) v. i.; meht- tr.; GoM. mēh- v. i.; Klm.(E) mī- v. i.; mīp- tr.; Nk. mīy- v. i.; mīp- tr.; Pj. mēy- v. i.; mēpip- (mēpit-) tr.; Mlt. med- to eat food with something to give a relish; Kur. Mlt. men- to eat grass; cf. Brah. bei grass fit for grazing. PDr. *mĕy- < *mec-, v. s. v. mesavu.]

mokku (< mrokku, q. v.) to bow down in respect; n. salutation.

1045 mogiyu[1]* III intr. to attempt, try, be ready for action (BhR); mogi n. attempt, contrivance (UH).

[Ka. mogasu to begin to exert oneself ready for work; to act zealously for a plan; exert oneself; n. desire; Ta. muyal, muyallu (muyaṉ-ṟ-) to practice, make continued exertion (Kṟḷ.), begin, undertake; muyaṟci n. effort, activity, application (Kṟḷ.); muyaṅku to do, perform; < PSDr. *moy-.]

1046 mogiyu$^{2}$* III intr. to overspread; attack, close with (BhR); cf. moguсu tr. to cause to close, contract.

[Ka. mogasu to fall upon, attack; moge to cover, close with; further v. s. v. moguḍu.]

1047 mogucu* IIb tr. to close, shut up (Bhr. II); to fold, contract; prob. tr. of mogiyu.

[Ka. mugi to contract, as eyes; v. i. to contract, as a flower; v. s. v. moguḍcu, mōḍcu.]

1048 moguḍu* (also mogaḍu) intr. to contract, as a flower, (eyes) to close (KS, Bhr. II, UH); tr. moguḍ(u)cu/mōḍ(u)cu to close eyes; join hands in respect (Bhr. II, Kāś.); tuck flowers in braid (Bhr. II).

[Ka. mugi to contract, as flowers; close, as eyes; join hands together; muguḷ to close eyelids, to bud, sprout; Tu. mugiyuni v. i. to close, shut up; Ko. movc- (priest) prays waving his hands; mūv- (mūd-) to raise hand in salute; Ta. mukil̲ v. i. to bud (Cīv.), fold or close up, as flowers, eyelids; Ma. mukaḷikka to close, as a flower; mukil̲ a bud; Kui mogo a bud. PDr. *muy-, *muk-V-; (> l. w. Skt. mukula- bud, see Burrow, TPS 1946, p. 11).]

moguḍ(u)cu* IIb (also mōḍcu) tr. of moguḍu, q. v.

1049 moggu (1) intr. to undertake to do, be prepared for action (Mdn.) (< mogiyu through contraction of -giyu > -ggu).

[V. s. v. mogiyu$^{1}$.]

moggu (2) to incline towards, as the point of a balance (later texts).

1050 moṭṭu tr. to rap, to strike with knuckles, esp. on the head (no literary usages cited; Mdn.); n. a rap.

[Ka. moṭṭu v./n. id.; Ta. muṭṭu to butt (Nāl.), hit; n. battering; Ma. muṭṭuka v./n. id.; Pj. muṭṭ- to batter; Kur. muṭga'- to deal a heavy blow with fist; muṭka'- to hit or hammer upon with the fist; Mlt. muṭi fist; Brah. muṭi id.; muṭrī shampooing with fist. On account of o in Te. Ka., contamination is likely between Dr. mottu and IA muṭh-, cf. Pkt. muṭṭhi fist < Skt. muṣṭi-, see Turner, Nep. Dict. s. v. muṭh, muṭhi; also v. s. v. mottu, mōdu.]

1051 moḍucu* IId tr. to smear, daub (KS).

1052 mottu tr. to strike or beat with something heavy, beat, smite (Bhīm., Bhg.), to suppress (Śakunt.), to crush (Kāś.); n. hit, stroke.

[Ta. mottu to strike, beat (Kamp.); n. stroke, blow (Cilap.); Ma. mottuka id. PSDr. *mott-/*mōt-; also see s. v. mōdu.]

1053 monayu* III intr. to begin, commence, start, attempt, undertake (Bhr. I, II); to prevail (UH, Nr̥s.); to be ready for (Bhr. I); intr./tr. to attack, meet in battle (Bhr. I, II); tr. to effect, do (Bhg.); mona n. a front in war.

[Ka. mone n. fight, battle; Ta. muṉai to be deeply engaged in; to fight; tr. to attack (Kallā.); n. battle (Patiṟ.); muṉṉu to meet (Cīv.), approach, follow; Ma. munakka to go before; munnuka to overtake. PSDr. *mun-, *mun-ay-; PDr. *mu-, *mun- 'before, front'; see Emeneau, Kolami, Vocab. No. 559.]

1054 morayu III intr. to sound (Hara.), resound; (birds) to produce noises (Manu.).

[Ka. more/mure to hum, buzz; to sound, as instruments, tingle, ring as bells; moraḷ to sound; Tu. moresuni/muresuni to rumble, rattle; Ko. morv- (mord-) to mumble; Ta. mural (muraṉ-ṟ-) intr. to make sound, cry (Maturai.); tr. to sing (Kalit.); morumoru to murmur, grumble; Ma. muraḷuka to hum, grunt, buzz, howl; Klm. (SR) muray- to sound; Klm.(E) moray- to make musical sound; Nk. moray- id.; Go. mōrī- (morī-sī) to guggle in the throat in sleep; cf. Brah. marrām n. shout, call, fame. PDr. mor-, PSDr. (including Go.) *mor-ay-, *mor-aḷ; also see s.v. mrōyu.]

moṟayu III (same as morayu; later text).

1055 moṟāgu (SAN morāgu) intr./tr. to deceive (Bhr. II, III); to hide, lurk (UH, Bhg., Kāś.); n. cheating, deceit; occurs mainly in the phrase kanu moṟāgu lit. to hide the eyes, i.e., to escape notice, to deceive and so on; Mdn. to be inattentive (Guntur dial.).

[V. s. v. maṟũgu[2]; cf. Ka. maṟe, moṟe concealment, disappearance; a/o after bilabials common, see s. v. poncu.]

1056 moṟugu intr. (dog) to bark; n. bark of a dog; moṟa, moṟṟa lamenting, complaint.

[Ka. moṟe cry aloud, as tiger, etc.; clamor, bawl; n. lamenting, roaring; Tu. mure a cry; muri yeḍuni to weep, lament; Ko. murg- to growl; To. muṟx- id.; Ta. moṟumoṟu to grumble; muṟai(y)iṭu to complain (Tiruvāc.); Ma. muraḷuka (dog) to howl; Kui muska to bark; Kuvi (F) mōkh- to bark; Pj. mur- to growl (tiger, etc.), to hoot (owl); Go. mohc- to bark, of dog. PDr. *moṯ-, *moṯ-uṅk/ -kk-.]

1057 molacu (SAN quotes also molcu; Śab.R. molucu, molacu) IIa intr. to germinate, arise in mind (Bhr. II, Nirv., Naiṣ.); to sprout, bud, shoot, grow (KS, Daśā.); molaka, mokka a sapling; an offshoot.

[Ka. moḷe to bud, sprout, grow, arise; muḷi a shoot, a cause, germ; Tu. muḷeyuni, muḷevuni, muḷiyuni to germ, sprout; muḷe n. a shoot; Ta. muḷai v. i. to spring, sprout (Tiruvāc.), rise, come to light (Maṇi.); n. shoot; muḷari n. lotus (Aiṅk.); Ma. muḷekka to shoot, grow up, to rise; muḷa n. a shoot; GoM. mōḍiy-

(mōḍit-) to sprout; Kur. muī̃-muī̃r- v.i. to germinate, as in soil, etc.; mulndā the offshoot of a species of grass which grows up amidst paddy. PDr. *mūḷ- : *muḷ-V-/*mūṇ-; (> l.w. Skt. mūla- root, see Burrow, DS VII, p. 391, No. 269).]

1058 mōcu IIa (also mōyu) tr. to bear, carry (Bhr. II, HariV.); intr. to rest, rest on, lean on (KS, Bhr. II); mōpu n. weight, burden, a bundle of sticks, hay, etc.; mū̃pu shoulder.

[Ka. mōr̲(u) to carry on the head; mōpu a load, burden; muy, muybu, muyvu shoulder-blade; Ta. mō to undertake; moympu shoulder; mōtu bundle of straw (loc.); Kuvi mōc- to over-labor; mōpa wīth'- to shrug; Klm.(E) mōp load. PSDr. and PCDr. *muy-/*moy-.]

1059 mōḍcu (contraction of mogaḍ(u)cu, q.v.) IIb tr. to close (eyes, hands) (Bhr. II, Kāś.), to set flowers in braid (Bhr. II); mōḍpu closing (hands, eyes, etc.); adj. joined or closed (hands) (Bhr. II).

[V. s.v. mogaḍu, mogaḍ(u)cu.]

1060 mō̃du ([˜] not likely on account of the existence of the alternative development in mottu, q.v.) tr. to strike, beat (Bhr. II, UH); beating, knock (Daśā.).

[Ka. mōdu to strike, beat, strike against; mōhu id. (? < *mōpu); Ta. mōtu to hit, strike, butt (Piṅ.); blow, dash against with force (Cilap.); n. blow, stroke; cf. mōttai ram (Tolk.); Ma. mōtuka to dash against; mōta a surge of waves; < PSDr. *mōt-/*mott-; v. s.v. mottu.]

mōpu (tr. of mōcu, q.v.) to cause to rest slowly, as a foot on slippery floor (Bhr. II); to join together (Bhr. II, Kāś.); n. resting (Bhr. II), a bundle, as of hay, etc.; burden; responsibility (all Bhr. II).

mōyu$^1$ III (var. of mōcu, q.v.) intr./tr. to carry, bear (Hara., Āmu.), v.i. to rest, touch (late).

1061 mōyu$^2$ (Mdn.) III intr. to be widowed (non-elegant); mōpi a widow.

[Ka. mōcu to become a widow, put a covering (on the head) as the sign of being a widow; Ta. mōppi widow (loc.; disrespectful).]

1062 mrakku* tr. to lose lustre, become dim (no usages quoted from the early classics); to become pale, to wither (Bhg.); (< *mal̲-k-); cf. makku.

[Ka. mal̲gu to grow wan, become pale; mal̲a dimness; mal̲al (eyes) to become dim; Ta. mal̲uku to become dim or obscure (Parip.); Ma. mal̲uka id. PSDr. *mal̲-; v. s.v. māyu for further reconstructed alternants.]

1063 mraggu$^{1*}$ (margu KS; > Mdn. maggu) intr. to perish, die, disappear (Bhr. II); adj. decayed; (< *mal̲-g-).

[Ka. maggu, maḻgu to be destroyed, perish; become strengthless; vanish; Tu. margu̥ adj. dead; Ta. maḻuṅku to be deprived of glory.]

1064 mraggu$^{2*}$ (< *mar-g-) to fall down (Bhr. II).
[V. s. v. mraṅgu.]

1065 mraggu$^{3*}$ (> Mdn. maggu) to be distressed (< *maṟ-g-).
[V. s. v. maṟūgu$^{1}$, maggu$^{2}$; Ta. maṟuku to be distressed (Akan.).]

1066 mraṅgu* intr. to decrease, be abated (Bhr. I, II), to fall down, perish (HariV.), be humbled.
[To. maṟy- (maṟs-) to fall; (maṟc-) to fell; Ta. maṟi (maṟi-nt-) to be turned upside down; recede (Kalit.), fall down (Cīv.); be ruined (Kallā.); tr. to destroy (Tēv.); maṟivu n. ruin (Aiṅk.); Ma. maṟi-yuka to turn upside down; Kui mrānga to be lost; mrāpka (< mrāk-p-; mrāk-t-) to obliterate; Kuvi(F) mṛakh- to obliterate. PSDr. and PCDr. *maṯ-V-.]

1067 mrandu$^{1*}$ intr. to perish, die (Bhr. II); to be afflicted (Mārk.); to be crushed (Bhr. II); to droop; (< *maṟ$^{u}$nd-).
[V. s. v. mraṅgu; esp. Ta. maṟi (maṟi-nt-) be ruined; tr. to destroy, etc.]

1068 mrandu$^{2*}$ intr. to be consumed by fire, burn (Mārk.); (< *maṟ-$^{u}$nd-).
[V. s. v. maṟūgu$^{1}$; cf. mraggu$^{3}$.]

1069 mrāncu* IIb tr. to close, as eyes in intoxication (Pāṇḍ.); cf. mrālu.

1070 mrālu* intr. to droop (Mārk.), (eyes) to close in ecstasy.
[Ka. maruḷ to be bewildered; maraḷu confusion, frenzy; mara intoxicant; mara, marave torpor, bewilderment; Tu. maramara adj. drowsy; marlu̥ madness; marluni to be restless; Ta. maruḷ n. intoxication, bewilderment of mind; v. i. (maruṭ-ṭ-) to be bewildered (Kṟḷ.); Ma. maruḷ frenzy; alternatively < *maṟ-al, v. s. v. mraṅgu.]

1071 mriṅgu* (> Mdn. miṅgu) tr. to swallow, devour (KS, Bhr. II); to kill (UH); to mince words; suppress grief (Mdn.).
[Ta. viḻuṅku to swallow, gulp (Kṟḷ.); to seize, capture (Cīv.); kill; viḻukku n. gulp, swallow; miḻuṅku/muḻuṅku (colloq.); Ma. miḻuṁṅuka to swallow; mince; > l. ws. Ka. miṅgu, muṅgu, Ko. miŋg-, Klm. (SR) miŋ-, Nk. miŋg- id.]

1072 mrukku* (> Mdn. mukku) (food, etc. being kept too long) to become musty, spoiled (KS); mrukka adj.; mugga n. mold, mustiness; adj. moldy, etc.
[Ta. murañcu to be old, ancient (Tolk.); < PSDr. *mūr-; *mur-V-; also v. s. v. mruggu, muṟugu.]

1073 mruggu* (> Mdn. muggu) intr. to ripen, become over-ripe.
[Ko. mut- to become ripe, (person) becomes old and wise; Ta.

muṟuku v.i. to ripen, mature; muṟṟu v.i. to grow ripe; become expert in (Cīv.); n. perfection (Tēv.); muruku to be ripe or mature (Kamp.); marañcu to mature; n. maturing (Malaip.); mūḻ to be mature (Patiṟ.); Ma. muḻukkuka to grow ripe, mature; mūkka to ripen; Go. mūṛ- v.i. to ripen, of a boil, etc.; Pj. muṛ- to ripen after being plucked. PSDr. and PCDr. *mū-ḻ : *muḻ-V-, *mū-ṯ- : *muṯ-V-, *mū-r- : *mur-V-; obviously *mū- is the ultimate root with different derivatives, connected with the etyma meaning 'oldness' etc.; v.s.v. mudiyu.]

1074 mrē̃gu* (also mrēvu; [˜] doubtful) tr. to smear, daub body with perfumes, etc. (Kāś.).

[To. mōšk- to smear buffalo dung on floor for cleaning; Ta. meḻuku to cleanse floor with cowdung water (Tiruvāc.), smear body with sandal paste (Kamp.); n. cowdung; meḻukku n. substance to smear; Ma. meḻukuka to anoint; Kui mrāṇḍa to plaster, smear over; Go. māc- to plaster mud on wall, etc.; cf. maṛhutt- to paint cattle for festival; Mlt. mānḍr- to apply something to one's own body (? < *mār-ṇḍ- < *māḻ-ṇḍ-, cf. Kui); cf. Malayan mĕlēpa, mĕleśter to plaster. PDr. *mēḻ- : *meḻ-V-; Kui and Mlt. go together, < *meḻ-aṇḍ-/*mēḻ-ṇḍ-.]

1075 mrokku* (> Mdn. mokku) to bow in respect (JBh.); n. salutation (Hara.).

[Ka. moḻgu to bend, bow; muḻgu to make obeisance; Ko. aḍmug- (aḍmuṛt-) bow before god or godlike person; To. moṛx- v.i. to bend; Kui mrōṅga to crouch over; Go. murs- to stoop forward; Go. (Dawson) to bow; Pj. moṛk- to salute; murg- to be bent; muṛd- to lie flat on face; Nk. mokk- id.; Mlt. murgr- to lie with face down; murgtr- to turn upside down, put under a cover. PDr. *moḻ-aṅk-/*moḻ-akk-.]

1076 mroggu* (> Mdn. moggu) intr. to kneel, incline or lean, bend forward (Bhr. II, BhR); to kneel before (Nirv.); be weighed down under a weight or burden; (< *moḻ-g-).

[V.s.v. mrokku.]

1077 mroṅgu* intr. to spring, leap up (Bhg.); mrompu n. jumping, leaping, as of snakes (Nṛs.).

1078 mrō̃gu* (also mróvu, Kāś.; > Mdn. mōgu) intr. to sound, ring, as bells, trumpet, etc. (Bhr. II); to reverberate; to cry, shout (late); mrō̃ta sound, ringing (Bhr. II); (< *moḻ-aṅg-).

[Ka. moḻagu intr. to roar, thunder; sound, as musical instruments; tr. to play instruments; n. thundering, roaring; Tu. muresuni to rumble, rattle, as thunder; Ta. mul̲aṅku intr. to roar, thunder, make loud noise (Nāl.); mul̲akku tr. to sound (Kamp.); n. noise; Ma. mul̲aṅṅuka intr. to roar; mul̲akkuka to play an instrument; to thunder; make resound; Kur. murr- to thunder; utter threats. PDr. *mul̲-; PSDr. *mol̲-aṅk-/-akk- < *mul̲-aṅk-/-akk-.]

1079 mrōyu* (> mōyu) III intr. to sound, as drums, musical instruments (Bhr. I, II); to make noise (Daśā.); to spread, as fame (Daśā.).
[< *mor-ay-; v. s. v. morayu.]

R

rakku (Dh.M.; r̲akku Śab.R.).
[V. s. v. r̲akku.]

1080 ragulu (also ravulu) intr. to be kindled, to take fire, to burn, flame (later works).
[Prob. formed from ravva a spark (cf. Ta. ravai a small particle) with the -al suffix; alternatively < *rāv-ul < *arav-ul; *rā- < *ara, v. s. v. rāju.]

1081 rajju* intr. to prate, talk nonsense (Bhr. II); to praise one's own self (Bhg., HariV.); n. a useless talk (Bhr. II), abuse (Bhr. II); boasting (Bhr. II); vanity (KS); rajj-ul-āḍu to abuse, prate; (< *ar-j- < *ar-c-).
[Klm.(E) raz- (ras-t-) to say, speak, talk nonsense; Kui ṛaspa (ṛas-t-) to ring, make a reverberating sound; cf. Ka. arcu to cry aloud; racce, raṭṭu crying aloud, noisy clamor; also v. s. v. ar̲acu.]

1082 ranju intr. (a wound or quarrel) to spread; to gather momentum (colloq., Rāyalasīma dial.).
[Prob. rāju.]

ravulu (var. of ragulu, q. v.) ravul-konu to catch or take fire (Manu.).

1083 rācu[1]* IId tr. to investigate, enquire (KS).
[< *ar-a-, v. s. v. arayu; alternatively this meaning could be a metaphorical extension of the one under rācu[2], rāyu, q. v.]

rācu[2] IId (tr. of rāyu, q. v.) to crush, grind; rub, smear (Āmu. and later works).

1084 rāju intr. to take fire (KS, Āmu.); (smoke) to come out as an indication of the forming of fire (16th century); to grieve (UH).
[< *ar-anj- < *ar-anc-; v. s. v. rāyu.]

1085 rāyu III intr. to be rubbed, to graze, touch closely, get friction (KS, Bhr. II); (throat) to become hoarse (RR); to oppose in war;

to quarrel, fight (Bhr. II, UH, Kāś.); tr. rācu to rub, smear, etc. (q. v.); rāpiḍi friction, worrying, pressure (Mdn.).

[Ka. are, ari to grind, crush; arayisu, arisu to cause to grind; Tu. areyuni, arevuni, arepuni, arepini tr. to pulverize by pounding or grinding; to oppress; arepu, arepelu̥ n. what is ground; Ko. arv- (art-) to grind (chillies); To. arθ- (arθy-) to sharpen; Ta. arai (arai-nt-) to become worn out (Periyapu.); (arai-tt-) tr. to grind, pulverize, destroy by rubbing, mash; arakku to rub with the palm of the hand; Ma. arayuka be bruised; arekka to grind to powder; Kui rāga to be rubbed or worn by friction; rāpka (< *rāk-p-; rāk-t-) to cause to rub together, wear by friction; Kuvi (F) rāc- to clean; Go. arī- (arī-sī) tr. to drag along the ground; Klm.(SR) rāk- to rub teeth. PSDr. and PCDr. *ar-a-.]

1086 rālu to fall or drop down, as fruit, leaves, etc. from tree (Bhr. II), to be severed and fall off; (teeth) to fall out (< *r̲āl- < *at̲-al-); tr. rālcu to shed, cause to fall off.

[Ta. ar̲al becoming detached by cutting; ar̲r̲am loosening (Kr̲ḷ.), separation; ar̲u to be severed; tr. cut off, sever (Cīv.); Go. arr- to fall (from cart, etc.); ar-hutt- caus. to fell, cause to fall; Klm.(SR) rāl- (rāṭ-) to fall; rāp- to fell; Nk. rāl- (rāṭ-) fall out, rālp- to make to fall out; v. s. v. ar̲u.]

1087 runju* (Dh.M.) tr. to draw in through nose.

1088 ruttu* (Śab.R.; not in Dh.M.) tr. to strike, beat.

1089 ruddu (Śab.R.) tr. to rub, scrub, scour, clean (< *urd-; no literary usages cited).

[Ka. ruddu to beat soundly (l. w. < Te.); uddu, urdu to rub, make fine by rubbing; ujju (< *ur-uñc-) id.; Tu. urduni to rub, polish; Ko. uj- to rub; To. warf- (wart-) to rub into paste; ud- (udy-) to smear on body; Ta. urai (uraitt-) to rub (Kalit.); Kui rūsa to crush, grind; Kuvi (F) rūb- to smear; Kuvi (S) rubb- to rouge. PSDr. *or-a, *ur-V-, PCDr. *ur-a-/-u-; Proto-Te.-Ka. *ur-utt-; v. s. v. orayu, rubbu for further forms.]

1090 rubbu (Dh.M.) tr. to grind into paste in a mortar; rubbuḍu n. grinding in mortar; rubbu(ḍu)guṇḍu grinding stone.

[Ka. rubbu id.; n. grinding; Klm.(SR) rubguṇḍ pounding stone; < *urb- < *ur-v-/*ur-pp-, *ur-upp-; v. s. v. ruddu, orayu.]

1091 reccu IId (Śab.R.) intr. to rise, swell, increase (later texts); (Dh.M.) cattle to become uncontrollable; (*r̲ecc- < *er̲-c-).

[< *ēt̲- : *et̲-V-; v. s. v. rēgu; Ta. ir̲a (ir̲a-nt-) to go beyond, pass over (PN).]

rejju (colloq., Viśākha. dial.) (cattle) to be uncontrollable; see reccu.

1092 remmu* to snatch, pull out, pluck out, as hair (late; 18th century).

1093 rẽgu (also rēgu Śab.R.; rēgu Dh.M.) intr. to increase, rise (in vanity, pride) (HariV.); be excited (Bhr. II); be roused, provoked, be angry; cela rẽgu to increase, swell (for cela, v. s. v. celãgu); (< *r̲ē-ṅk- < *et̲-aṅk-).

[Ka. rēgu to rise, as dust, be excited, become angry; rēgisu to irritate, make angry; Tu. rēgiyuni to be excited; Ta. rēṅku to rage, be angry (loc.); all l. ws. < Te.; Kuvi (S) re'- to ascend; Klm.(SR) selārēṅg- to quarrel (l. w. < Te.); v. s. v. rēyu.]

rẽcu IIb (tr. of rẽgu, q. v.) to excite, rouse, stir, provoke, irritate (Bhr. II); another tr. form rēpu id. (Mdn.).

rēpu tr. of rẽgu/rēyu, q. v. (Mdn.).

1094 rēyu (SAN; r̲ēyu Śab.R.) III intr. to increase, swell in joy, pride, etc.; to rage (Bhr. II, JBh.); (< *r̲ēy- < *et̲-ay-).

[Ta. ir̲a (ir̲a-nt-) to excel, go beyond, pass over (PN); Ta. Ma. Ka. ēr̲u to rise, increase; To. ēr̲- to rise high; cf. Te. r̲ẽḍu king, ruler; Ta. ir̲aivan̲, Ma. ir̲ān, Ka. er̲e (< *et̲-ay-); v. s. v. rẽgu, reccu.]

roppu[1] same as r̲oppu, q. v.

1095 roppu[2] (Śab.R.) tr. to chase (Bhg.).

1096 rollu intr. to prattle; rolluḍu prattling.

[V. s. v. or̲alu, r̲ōlu; or < *r̲ōl-/*r̲oll- < *or̲-al, v. s. v. *ūr[2] to speak.]

1097 roḷḷu (Mdn., Guntur dial.) tr. to pick up, make into a heap (as greens on the floor) and take up.

[Kui rūṭpa (rūṭt-) to scrape into a heap.]

1098 rõju intr. to pant, breathe quickly or in a labored manner, to respire, gasp (Bhr. III); (< *or-anj-); cf. rõjuḍu prattling.

[Cf. Ta. ura (ura-tt-) to become hard, as voice, become harsh, as noise; to rage, be boisterous, as the sea; altern., < *or-anj- < *ur-anc-; *ūr- to breathe, see s. v. ūrcu[1].]

1099 rōyu[1]* (Dh.M. also r̲ōyu; Śab.R. says it is wrong) III to seek, search, look for (usage quoted from a later work but there are usages even in the early classics).

[< *or-ay-; cf. Ka. ōru to inquire; Ta. ōr to examine, investigate; ōrccu investigation, research; Ma. ōrka to expect.]

1100 rōyu[2] (Śab.R.; r̲ōyu Dh.M.) III intr./tr. to hate, dislike (obj. in dative); be disgusted with; give up (worldly pleasures, etc.), discard; to despise, rebuke, censure (Bhr. II); rōta disgust, hatred; (r̲ōy- < *ot̲-oy-).

[Ka. rōsu to dislike, feel disgusted; rōte filth; Ta. oṟu to punish, chastise (PN); reprove (PN); to dislike, be disgusted with; ridicule (Kṟḷ.); oṟuppu rebuke, aversion, disgust; bridling of passions; uṟai to rebuke (Piṅ.), disgrace (Tiv.); also cf. oruvu to renounce (Kṟḷ.), to escape (PN); prob. Te. rōyu is a pool of *oṟay to hate and *oray to give up, as attested by the Ta. etyma.]

## Ṟ

1101 ṟakku (Śab.R.; rakku Dh.M.) to rend with nails, claw, scratch with nails so as to lacerate; n. clawing; (< *aṟ-k-).

[V. s. v. aṟu, naṟaku; cf. Go. ask- to cut up; Kur. aṛya'- id.; Mlt. asy- (asc-) to chisel.]

1102 ṟimmu* (Śab.R.) tr. to spurt, squirt water with a syringe, etc.; to cast, fling, toss; butt, as with horns; n. spurt, thrust, butt.

[< *iṟ-m-; ? ciṟumu with loss of *c-, v. s. v. ciṟumu; altern. Ka. iṟi (< *eṟi), Ta. eṟi, Ma. eṟiyuka to throw, fling, but the radical vowel is difficult.]

ṟuppu (Dh.M., same as ṟuvvu, q. v.); (< *uṟ-p-).

1103 ṟuvvu (also ruvvu Śab.R.) to pelt a stone with force, to fling, toss (Āmu.); n. the sound of wind produced by the fluttering of wings (Bhōj.); onomatop. word for falling down.

[< *uṟ-v-; cf. Ka. uṟubu, uṟuvu, uṟvu violence of wind, rapidity, speed, force; Klm.(E) ruv- (ruv-t-) to throw.]

ṟūvu var. of ṟuvvu, q. v. (Āmu.).

1104 ṟoppu (Dh.M.; roppu Śab.R.) to roar, as a tiger; to shout; be angry with (Manu.); to whoop (Mdn.); (< *ṟōppu < *oṟ-app-).

[Ka. ṟoppu to grunt, roar like a hog; Ta. urappu to whoop, vociferate; shout so as to intimidate (Tiv.); to bluster, roar (Piṅ.); tr. frighten (Tēv.); n. shout, roar, threat; ura to become loud, as voice; alternatively from *ūṯ- underlying uṟumu, q. v.]

ṟōyu[1] (var. of rōyu[1], q. v.; Dh.M.).

ṟōyu[2] (var. of rōyu[2], q. v.; Dh.M.).

1105 ṟōlu* intr. to cry, scream (Bhr. II); (< *oṟ-al-).

[V. s. v. oṟalu.]

## L

1106 lāgu tr. to pull, drag, attract, draw; n. pulling.
[Cf. Ko. aṇ- (aṇḍ-) to pluck; Kuvi (F) rānj- to bale out. On phonological grounds, no connection likely with Ka. eḻe (< *iḻay) to pull, etc.]

1107 lā̃cu[1]* IId intr. to pounce upon, attack (late), to lie in wait.
[? Te. lā̃gu n. jump, leap (Bhr. II); Ka. lāgu a leap; Tu. lāguni to leap, jump, skip; Ma. lākuka to leap; l. w. < IA, cf. Pkt. laṅgheī, Pa. laṅghati, Skt. laṅghayati jumps over, H. lā̃ghnā, nā̃ghnā id.; v. s. v. nā̃ghnu/nā̃gnu, nāṅnu, Turner, Nep. Dict.]

1108 lā̃cu[2]* IId (Dh.M.) to long for, desire; (< *aḷ-a-).
[Ka. aḷipu, aḷupu to hanker after, long for; n. love; aḷaviga friend; Ta. aḷi (aḷi-nt-) to be attached; (aḷi-tt-) tr. to create desire, love; n. desire (Kamp.).]

1109 lāyu* (Dh.M.) III intr. to approach; (Śab.R.) to rage (HariV.); (< *aḷ-ay-).
[Ka. aḷa proximity; Ta. aḷ closeness; aḷa (aḷa-nt-) to extend, to reach; further v. s. v. aṇṭu, allu. PDr. *aḷ-.]

1110 *lē- V (occurs only in negative forms lē-du [it] is not, lē-ni adj. [that] not; lē-ka not being; occurs often with the infinitive forms) to be; cf. -iḍi a neg. agentive suffix, mukk-iḍi (he) who has no nose, etc.
[Ka. il to be, exist; ili not being; illa no, not; Tu. ijji id.; Ko. il- to be not; Ta. il, illai not; illatu id. (Kṟḷ.); Ma. illa id.; Kui siḍa neg. aux. not to be; Go. (p. 47) hallē, hal; GoA. sile; Pj. cila indecl. id.; Mlt. cil- to forbid. PDr. *cil-, PSDr. *il-: see Burrow, DS VI, p. 138.]

1111 lēcu V intr. to rise, get up, wake up; to shoot up, come up; (< *el-a-).
[Ta. ēl (ēṟ-ṟ-, ēṉ-ṟ-) to awake from sleep (Kalit.); ultimately *ē-, v. s. v. ēcu, ekku, ēdu; Klm.(SR) lēs- to get up; Klm.(E) lēp- to arouse; begin to compete.]

1112 loggu (Dh.M.) to be humbled, subdued (colloq.), v. s. v. loṅgu.

1113 loṅgu (also lō̃gu) intr. to yield, submit, surrender, be humbled, become low or humble, be cowed down; lō̃kuva subordination to somebody; (< *ḷōṅg < *oḷ-aṅg-).
[Kuvi (S) lōki kī- to subordinate; lug- to hide; Ka. oḷavu authority, control; oḷagu that is within; Ko. oyḷ- (oḷc-) v. i. to hide; To. wïḷy- (wïḷc-) v. i./tr. to hide; Ta. oḷi to be hidden; to conceal; Ma. oḷikka to conceal, suppress; Ka. uḷi be hidden; oḷ what is

hidden; the meaning connection is clear, i.e., to be within (one's might); PDr. *uḷ-/*oḷ- within, inside; for related etyma, see Emeneau, Kolami, Vocab. No. 476.]

lō̃gu (same as loṅgu, q.v.) to be suppressed, be subdued (later texts); to withhold (Āmu.); cf. lōnu inside (Bhr. II); lōn-agu to come under one's control (agu to become [Bhr. II]); v.s.v. loṅgu.

1114 loḍupu (Dh.M.) tr. to ladle, stir with a ladle (colloq.).
[Cf. Skt. (Dhātupāṭha) loḍati stirs; Pa. loleti shakes; Skt. loḍyate is set in motion; āloḍayati stirs up; Pa. āloḷete mixes; Pk. āloḍeī churns, v.s.v. lurkan, Turner, Nep. Dict.]

1115 loḷḷu/ḷoḷḷu (Dh.M.) to sound, as dog's barking (noted as colloq.).
[Ka. loḷ/ḷoḷ imitation of the sound of dog's barking.]

1116 lōṭu (Dh.M.) to accomplish all domestic jobs (noted as colloquial).

1117 lōḍu (Dh.M.; lō̃ḍu Śab.R.) to stir with fingers.
[V.s.v. loḍupu.]

lō̃cu (tr. of lō̃gu, q.v.) to subdue.

## V

1118 vakku* (ĀVāc.) intr. to emaciate; grow lean (Vēm.); cf. bakka lean, thin.
[< *vaṟ-k-; Ka. bakka, bakkaṭa empty; baṟe to grow lean; Tu. bargaṭṭụ adj. reduced, weak; v.s.v. vaṭṭu.]

1119 vagacu* IIa intr. to grieve, lament, regret, repent (Bhr. I, II); to think, ponder over, consider (Bhr. I); der. n. vagapu distress; vagalu id.
[Ka. bage to think, consider, mind; suppose; Mdn. Ka. ogapu sympathy (Bucher); Tu. bageyuni, bagevuni to think, guess, imagine; Ta. vakai to consider; vai (vai-tt-) to consider (Kṟḷ.); meditate upon (Cilap.); vaittu-kkoḷ tr. to suppose, take for granted. PSDr. *vay-; *vak-ay- < *vay-ay-.]

1120 vagar(u)cu* IId intr. to sigh (Daśā.).
[Ka. ugarisu to gasp, breathe hard, respire with difficulty; < *uy-ar-; v.s.v. ūrcu.]

vagiyu III (Dh.M. notes it as the colloq. var. of vagacu) to pretend sorrow.

1121 vaggu (Śab.R.) intr. to become lean, emaciate.
[< *vaṟ-g-; cf. vakku; v.s.v. vaṭṭu.]

1122 vaṅgu intr. to bend, stoop, bow, become crooked; become low or humbled; tr. vancu to bend, to subdue (Bhg.), to serve from a container, empty (Āmu.).

[Ka. baggu, baṅku to bow, become submissive; baḷku intr. to bend; baḷuku, baḷuṅku id.; Ko. vag- to be slightly bowed down, be obedient; To. paḷ- (paḷθ-) to bend down; Ta. vaṇaṅku v. i. to bend; be submissive (Kṟḷ.); vaṇakku to make submissive (Akan.); vaṇar v. i. to bend (Malaip.); vaḷai v. i. to bend, bend low, yield (Cīv.); tr. to bend; Ma. vaṇaṅkuka v. i. to bend, bow, respect; vaṇakkuka tr. to bend; vaḷekka tr. to bend; Kui palga to bend down, stoop; Kuvi (S) waṅg- to be bent; wakh'- tr. to bend; Kuvi (F) vwāng- v. i., vwakh- v. tr.; Klm.(E) vaŋg- v. i.; Nk. Pj. vaŋg- v. i. PDr. *vaṇ-k-, *vă̄ḷ-/*vă̄ṇ-; also v. s. v. vāncu; Kur. beṅk- tr. to bend, curve; beṅkō, baṅkā crooked; Mlt. umgr- to bend, as in respect; prob. forms from *vaṅk- are somehow related to the IA forms: cf. Skt. vaṅkú- going crookedly; Pa. Pk. vakka-, vaṅka-; Skt. vakrá- crooked, bent; Ku. baṅo crooked; B. H. bā̃kā bent; G. vā̃kũ, M. vā̃kā, Sgh. vak bent; Nep. bāṅgo, q. v. Turner, Nep. Dict. Turner suspects contamination with Skt. vyaṅga- crippled, limbless. On the contrary, could the IA set be from Dravidian, where the roots vă̄ṇ- occur?]

1123 vaccu V (before back vowel suffixes, rā-/ra-) intr. to come, arrive; approach; befall; to be possible (with the inf. of a verb in the preceding position) (all classical and Mdn.).

[Ka. bar- (band-); allom. bā; Tu. bar-; Ko. vār- (vad-); To. pōr- (pod-); Ta. vā (va-nt-) to come (Tolk.), happen (Cīv.), be born; varuttu to fetch, get; Ma. vā (vant-); varuka id.; varuttuka to cause to happen; Kui vāva (vāt-); Kuvi (F) vwaiy- (vwat-); Kuvi (S) wa'-; Go. waī- to come, return; wartōl a guest; Klm. var-, va- (vatt-); Nk. var-; Pj. ver- (veñ- [< *veñc-]); KGad. vār- (vadd-), imp. sg. vā; pl. var; Kur. bar- (barc-); Mlt. bar- (barc-); Brah. bann- (bass-). PDr. *vă̄-r-, *vă̄-; see Emeneau, Lg. 21, esp. p. 187 and §17.]

1124 vaṭṭu intr. to be dried up, as a stream (Bhr. I, Kāś.); to grow lean, emaciate (Hara.); n. a dried pickle; adj. barren (of cattle), dried; vaṭṭi empty, useless.

[Ka. battu (a stream) to evaporate wholly; grow lean; baṟe to grow dry, disappear, grow lean; Tu. battuni id.; Ko. vat- (liquid) dries up; varv- (vart-) tissues become dry with fever; To. peł- (peṯ-) (buffalo) goes dry; paṟł- (paṟt-) (tree) dries up; Ta. vaṟṟu to grow, dry (Cīv.), subside, wither; (body) to emaciate (Nāl.); become worthless; vaṟa (vaṟa-nt-) to dry up (Piṅ.); grow lean; vaṟaḷ (vaṟaṇ-ṭ-) v. i. to dry up, become lean; vaṟaṭṭu tr. to dry, parch; Ma. vaṟṟu to grow dry, be reduced; (wound) to heal; vaṟaḷuka to dry up, grow lean; Kui vasa to wither, be thin (-s- < -ṯṯ-); Go. watt- to grow dry, as trees; Klm. vat- to parch; Pj. vett- (NE. veṭṭ-) to dry up; Oll. vaṭ- id.; KGad. vaṭṭ- id.; Kur. batt'- (liquids) to evaporate; batta'- tr. to empty, dry, spend; Mlt. bat- to dry up; Brah. bārr- to become dry, to wither. PDr. *vaṯ-, *vaṯṯ-; also see s.v. vaṇḍu.]

1125 vaḍãku (also vaṇāku Naiṣ.) intr. to tremble, quiver, shake (Bhr. II); n. trembling; tremor; vaḍavaḍa imit. of quivering in cold, etc.

[Ka. baḷku, baḷaku, oṇaku to tremble, shake; Tu. baḷakuni to quake, shake; Ta. vaḷai v.i. to move about, as foetus in the womb; Kui vaṭpa/vaṛpa (vaṭt-) to shake out, flap wings; motion with the hand; Klm. vaḍk- (vaḍak-t-) to tremble, shiver; Nk. vaṛak- to tremble; n. trembling. PSDr. and PCDr. *vaṭ-V- : *vaḷ-/*vaṇ-.]

vaḍacu* IId (Śab.R.; tr. of vaḍiyu, q.v.) to let flow, drip.

1126 vaḍalu (Śab.R.; vaḍulu Brown) (flowers) to wither, to fade.

[< *vāṭ + al; v.s.v. vāḍu; cf. Go. warǝnḍ- to shrivel and shrink (of flowers).]

1127 vaḍiyu[1] III to ooze, drip (Bhr. II); to be filtered; tr. vaḍucu to cause to drip, filter (Śakunt.); vaḍiyāgaṭṭu to filter.

[Ka. oḍi to flow in small stream; oḍi-gaṭṭu to filter through a cloth; Ta. vaṭi to drip, trickle; tr. to cause to flow; to strain, filter, distil; vaṭi filtration; Ma. vaṭiyuka to overflow, trickle; vaṭi n. a strainer, filter; Go. waṛ- to leak, of house; Klm.(E) vaḍp- to pour; Mlt. basar- to flow, as a current. PDr. *vaṭ-/*oṭ-; v.s.v. oḍiyu[1]; ōḍu.]

1128 vaḍiyu[2]* III intr. to dry up; to become lean (late).

[Ma. vaṭiyuka to dry up; GoM. ōḍ- to dry; v.s.v. vāḍu[1].]

1129 vaḍuku intr./tr. to spin, draw thread (late).

[? Tu. (nūl)oḍu a spindle (nūl thread); Ta. oḻukku to draw out as gold thread; ? Go. wadī- to twist or twirl fibre into thread; cf. Kui osa to weave, sew; Kur. ōj- to spin; Mlt. ōj- to twist. PDr. *ōḻ-/*ōc- : *oḻ-V-, *oc-V-.]

vaḍucu* IId tr. of vaḍiyu, q.v.

vaṇāku (var. of vaḍãku, q.v.) to tremble (UH); to fear (late); n. trembling, fear.

1130 vaṇḍu tr. to cook (by boiling, frying, etc.) (Bhr. II); vaṇṭa cooking, vaḍḍ-incu to serve food; vaḍḍ-ana serving food.

[Pj. vend- (NE. venḍ-) to cook; KGad. vanḍ- id. (< *vanṯ-); Kui vaja to cook; vahpa (vah-t-) to fry; Kuvi(S) waj-, Kuvi(F) vwaj-

id.; Ta. var̲u to fry; Ma. var̲ukka to fry, grill; var̲r̲u a grain of boiled rice, etc.; To. par̲f- (par̲t-) to fry; Kur. bār- to bake or fry in oil; Mlt. baṛkar- to be boiled, as fluid; < PDr. *vat̲-; therefore PDr. *van-/*vat̲-; Te. vaṇḍu < *van-t̲-; also cf. Kui vaṇḍa, Kuvi vwand- to taste; manji rice (raw); onda rice (cooked); Kur. maṇḍī rice (cooked); Mlt. maṇḍi rice water; mānḍ- to roast in hot ashes.]

1131 vadaru (also vaduru) intr. to prate, prattle (Bhr. II).
[Ta. vatar̲u to chatter, prate; lisp; tr. abuse; Tu. badaritana defamation. PSDr. *vat-/*ot-; also v. s. v. odaru.]

1132 vadalu (also vadulu) intr. to become slack, loose, as a cloth; be removed, go away; tr. to leave, leave off, abandon, give up, loosen, let loose; vadal(u)cu tr. to remove, untie, loosen (Āmu.).
[V. s. v. udalu, udulu, osulu; Ka. bal̲al to become slack, loose; Kur. od$^{o}$kh̲- tr. to render less tight, detach. PDr. *vac-/*vat- : *oc-/ *ot-, ? *vac-/*val̲-; also cf. vasulu.]

1133 vanaru* intr. to grieve, lament, speak in sorrowful tone (Bhr. I); n. grief.
[Cf. Ka. oṇagu to dry, emaciate; Tu. oṇu̥gelu̥ dry, lean; Ko. oṇg- to become dry in heat; oṇk- to dry in sun or heat; To. wïṇx- to wither; Ta. uṇaṅku to be emaciated (Kr̲ḷ.), be dejected in mind; to pine away; Ma. uṇaṅṅuka id.; Pj. ōl- to dry. PSDr. and PCDr. *ōḷ-/*ōṇ- : *oḷ-V-; alternatively, cf. Ka. oḷar̲u to sound, cry; ūḷ to cry out; Ta. uḷai to sound, howl (Maṇi.); uḷar̲u to shout; uḷampu id. (Akan.); Ma. uḷar̲uka to babble; PSDr. *ūḷ- : *uḷ-V-.]

vancu IId (tr. of vaṅgu, q. v.) to subdue (Bhg.), to bend, to serve food, empty a container (Āmu.).

1134 vandu* to suffer, grieve, sorrow (Bhr. I); to grow pale, emaciated (Bhr. II); to perish (Bhr. II); vanta grief, suffering; cf. vanduru.
[Ka. bardu to die; Ta. varuntu to suffer, be grieved (Kr̲ḷ.); become emaciated (Maṇi.); take pains (Kr̲ḷ.); varuttu affliction (Maturai.); Ma. varuttam trouble, affliction. PSDr. *var-unt-/-utt-.]

1135 vand-uru* to suffer, grieve (Bhr. I, II).
[Same as vandu; prob. metathesis of *var$^{u}$nt- > vantur-, cf. Ta. maruntu, Kur. mandar medicine; altern., -uru may be taken as a different derivative suffix.]

vampu another form of vancu, tr. of vaṅgu, q. v. (Āmu.); n. bend (KS), curve (Āmu.).

vayicu* IIa var. of vaĭcu, q. v. (Paṇḍ., HariV.).

1136 variyu (Dh.M., colloq.) III tr. to test meta, on stone (v. s. v. vrāyu).

1137 varuṭu* intr. to wither, emaciate (Bhīm.).

[Ka. baṟaḍu/baraḍu barrenness; Tu. baranṭuni to grow dry, become lean; To. paṟł- (paṟṯ-) (tree) dries up; Ta. vaṟaḷ (vaṟaṇ-ṭ-) to become dry; Ma. vaṟaḷuka to dry up, grow very lean; Go. warēnḍ- (flower) to shrivel up as seed forms; < PSDr. and PCDr. *vaṯ-aḷ; also v. s. v. vaṭṭu.]

1138 vaṟalu* (SAN; varalu Dh.M.) intr. to be splendid, to shine (Bhr. I); to flourish, spread; to be, to prevail (KS).

[Ta. vaḷar (vaḷar-nt-) v. i. to grow (Kuṟḷ.), to increase, dwell, rest; (vaḷar-tt-) tr. to cherish, foster; vaḷarttu to cause to grow, prolong (Kamp.); vaṇmai bounty (Nāl.); truth (Kamp.); abundance (Kuṟḷ.); Ma. vaḷaruka intr. to grow, increase; aux. to become; tr. vaḷarkka to bring up; Ka. baḷe to increase, prosper (of animals); Mlt. baḍy- (baḍc-) to grow. PDr. *vaḷ-/*vaṇ-.]

1139 valacu[1] V (neg. allom. *oll-, e.g., oll-aka, neg. ppl.) (1) tr. to like, desire, wish, love, be in love with (Bhr. I); intr. to agree, fit, suit, be becoming (Bhr. I); valapu love, liking; olla-ka not agreeing; valadu (Mdn. vaddu) prohibitive, no, not (with inf. of verbs).

[Ka. oli, ole to be pleased; to desire, love, like; ol, val id.; ol likeness; Tu. olapuni tr. to love, fondle; oliyuni to favor, be kind, as superiors; Ta. ol, ollu (oll-iṉ-) to agree (PN); Ma. olluka to consent, love, be fit; neg. ollā/vallā must not.

valacu[1] (2) intr. to be capable, be able (to do) (with inf.) (Bhr. II).

[Ka. oldu, ollade neg. particle; Tu. oli (affixed to verbs) can; e.g., maḷpoli can make or can be made; Ta. ol, ollu to be able, possible (Kuṟḷ.); vallu id. (PN); vallai strength; valavai ability (Cilap.); Ma. olluka to be possible; neg. ollā/vallā must not, ought not. PSDr. *val-/*ol-; v. s. v. valayu.]

1140 valacu[2]* IId (also valcu, q. v. [Bhr. I]) intr. to smell, as fish (Bhr. I).

1141 valayu[1] III and V (allom. val-, e.g., neg. val-adu (indecl.) prohibitive particle, Mdn. vaddu id.); > Mdn. -vāli, -āli indecl. with inf. of verbs, should, ought to, e.g., ceyy(a)-āli should do (all pers., genders, and nos.); intr. to be required, wanted; be liked, agreeable; be proper, be binding (all classical); tr. to wish, desire, want.

[V. s. v. valacu[1] (2).]

1142 valayu[2]* III intr. to turn around (rare, later text).

[V. s. v. balayu.]

1143 valiyu* III intr. to be fatigued (Bhr. I); become thin, be reduced (HariV.).

[Tu. balepuni to be distressed, vexed; Ta. vali trouble, pain; vali v.i. to be painful; olku to grow weak, to pine (PN), become emaciated; be impoverished (Kalit.), be injured (Kalit.); Ma. valayuka to be distressed; valekka tr. to distress; Kui valga be thin, emaciated; Kur. ol$^{o}$kh- to bewail, lament; Mlt. olg- to cry, weep. PDr. *val-/*ol-.]

1144 vasulu intr. to be loosened, become slack; to slip out, to slide.
[V. s. v. udalu, vadalu, osulu.]

1145 vā̃gu to sound, ring; to chatter, babble (late); cf. vāy-incu to play instruments (Mdn.); cf. vā̃cu[1].
[Cf. Ka. bay, bayyu to revile, abuse; Tu. bāṅku, bāṅgu a call (for prayer among Muslims); bayyāṭe abusing; To. pāk- to abuse; Ta. vāṅku tr. id.; vai to abuse, revile (Nāl.); vacavu, vacai bad language; Go. wank- to talk, speak; (peacock) cries; Kur. ba'- (bāc-) to say, command, call; (animals) to cry; Mlt. bāc- (bācy-) to relate, tell; cf. Kui ōga to boast; < *vā̆y-, prob. related to *vāy-/ *vā- mouth.]

1146 vācu IId (Dh.M.; vā̃cu Śab.R.) intr. to swell, tumefy; vāpu swelling on body; tumor.
[Ka. bā, bāyu (bād-, bāt-) to swell; tumefy; Tu. bāpuni to swell; bāpu swelling, tumor; Ko. vāv- (vāt-) (part of body) swells; vāg- (vāyg-) to bulge; To. pōf- (pōt-) (leg) swells; Ta. vāy- (vāy-nt-) to be full (Tēv.); (vāy-tt-) to gather into a mass (Pu. Ve.); Ma. vāykka to swell; vāka to grow; Go. wē- (wēī-sī) (a big blister) to arise; waddī a disease which swells sinews; Klm.(E), Nk. vāy- to swell; Pj. vāp- (vāt-) id.; KGad. vāt- id.; cf. Kur. bayā overflowing, flood; bayār- to overflow (of a river); Brah. bash mann- to be swollen (eyes, etc.); bash-, bē- up, over; paddām inflation. PDr. *vāy-.]

1147 vāḍu[1] intr. (flowers) to wither, fade (NavaN.); to be distressed (Naiṣ.), to droop (Pāri.); tr. vāḍ(u)cu to cause to wither; vāḍpu (Dh.M.) to make leaves wither in fire; cf. vaḍalu.
[Ka. bāḍu to wither, as flowers; become languid; be dispirited; Tu. bāḍuni to fade, wither, shrivel, die; Ko. vāṛ- (flower) withers; (face) becomes haggard; Ta. vāṭu to wither (Nāl.), pine away; n. faded color; vāṭṭu tr. to cause to wither; Ma. vāṭuka v.i., vāṭṭuka tr.; Kui vāra to be wearied, tired; GoM. wārt- to wither; Pj. vāḍ- to shrivel; Brah. bārr- to become dry, wither. PDr. *vāṭ-.]

1148 vāḍu$^{2}$ tr. to use, make use of (articles, clothes, language, etc.) (Bhr. II); vāḍuka usage, using or employing (KS, Bhr. II); a custom, habit.

[Ka. ba<u>l</u>i way, manner; vāḍike usage, custom (l. w. < Te.); Tu. bāḍayi/bāḍige rent (for house used); cf. Te. bāḍuga id.; Ko. vaḷc- to use (domestic utensils); Ta. va<u>l</u>aṅku to be in use, be current; proceed (PN); va<u>l</u>akku n. usage, as of word (Na<u>n</u>.); va<u>l</u>i a way, path (Kṟḷ.), usage; Ma. va<u>l</u>i way, manner, usage, behavior. PSDr. *vā<u>l</u>- : *va<u>l</u>-V-.]

1149 vānu tr. to make, fashion (as pots) (Āmu.); cf. bāna a big pot.

[Ka. bān to make or fashion, as a potter does; make pots; Ta. va<u>n</u>ai to form, shape (Piṅ.); ma<u>n</u>ai to make, create, fashion; vā<u>n</u> beauty, regularity (Kalit.); Ma. manayuka to fashion, make pots; Kuvi (S) wāna-kī- to module; Pj. vāñ- to make (pots); Mlt. bānde the way of doing. PDr. *vān : *van-V-; cf. Pa. vanati, vanāyati aims at; H. bannā to be made; B. banā to do; M. baṇṇẽ be made; G. banvũ; Turner has doubtful etymology from IA, see Nep. Dict. s. v. bannu; ? a borrowing from Dravidian into IA.]

1150 vācu$^{1*}$ IId tr. to blow musical instruments.

[? < Skt. vādyam n. speech, instrumental music, Pk. vajja- n. id.; Pa. vajjaṃ speaking; S. vājo n. musical instrument; G. vājũ n. id.; v. s. v. bājā, Nep. Dict.; alternatively, v. s. v. vāgu.]

1151 vācu$^{2}$ IId (SAN, Śab.R.; vācu Dh.M.) to long for, yearn, desire intensely (Pāṇḍ.); (< *vāy-nc-).

[Ka. bayake, bayke longing; desire; desired object; Tu. bayakuni, bayasuni to long for, desire eagerly; bayke desire, esp. the longing occasioned by pregnancy; Ta. vayāvu to desire (Malaip.); n. great desire, morning sickness (Tolk.); vayavu desire (Parip.); morning sickness (PN); Te. vēviḷḷu (pl. of *vēv-ili) morning sickness (< *veyav-il-); prob. this group is associated with etyma meaning pregnancy, cf. Ka. basi<u>r</u>u, basu<u>r</u>u id. (< *vac-i<u>r</u>-). PSDr. *vāy- < *vac-.]

1152 vāncu* IId (tr. of obsolete *vāṅgu) to bend head, etc., cause to bend (Bhr. I).

[Ka. bāgu to bend, bow; Tu. bāguni, bāṅguni id.; Ko. vāg- to make (pot) bulge on wheel; Ta. vāṅku intr./tr. to bend (Kallā.); vākku n. bend (Nāl.); Ma. vāṅṅuka v. i. to bend; Kuvi (F) vwāng- to be crooked; ? < *vāṇ-k-, v. s. v. vaṅgu, vālu.]

1153 vāmu (ĀVāc.) to scrape together into a heap (as hay) and lift on to the head; cf. vāmi a stack of hay.

[V. s. v. vāru$^{2}$.]

1154 *vāru[1]* (only in neg., vār-aka without interruption, constantly, continually) to be impeded, to refrain from (Bhr. II).

[< Skt. vārayati, Pa. vāreti obstructs; Pkt. vārei; G. vārvũ to forbid; M. vārṇẽ to prevent; see Turner, Nep. Dict. s.v. bārnu; also cf. Kur. bār- (bārc-) to abstain from (food), not to eat.]

1155 vāru[2] (SAN, Śab.R.) (1) tr. to scrape off, chip off the sides of palm leaves.

[Tu. bāruni to cut, comb the hair; chip; Ta. vār tr. to peel off (Akan.); Ma. vāruka to draw lines, cut lengthwise, trim a palm-leaf; Kur. bāg- to scrape, peel or take off the epidermis of the eatable bulbs; bāgr- to comb oneself, be scraped; Mlt. bāg- to pare.]

vāru[2] (2) to make into a bundle (of hay) before lifting on to the head.

[Ka. bācu to scrape together with hand, etc. and gather, as sweepings, etc.; make a heap of and take away; Tu. bāruni to comb the hair; Ta. vār v.i. to be arranged in order (Malaip.); tr. to comb; Ma. vāruka to take in a heap, scoop with both hands; Kur. bāg- to scrape. PDr. *vā-, *vā-r-, vā-ṅk-.]

1156 vāru[3] (Dh.M.) (water) to be drained off from boiled food, to flow or trickle down (prob. formed from the transitive by separating -cu).

[Ka. bār to set a fluid free, to pour out; Ta. vār- (vār-nt-) to flow, overflow (Cīv.); (vār-tt-) to pour; vārppu pouring; Ma. vāruka to flow down; to be strained off; vārkka to pour; cast; Pj. vārp- (vārt-) to strain; KGad. vārk- (vārt-) to strain water from food. PSDr. and PCDr. *vār- < *vā-r-; SDr. and CDr. have forms from *vāṅk- in the same sense, see Emeneau, Kolami, Vocab. No. 1011; ultimately PDr. *vā- with different suffixes.]

vār(u)cu[1] IIa (tr. of vāru[3], q.v.) to strain off water from boiled food; to perform water-offering ceremony (ācamanakriyā-) (Bhr. II, Kāś.).

1157 vār(u)cu[2]* IIa intr. to look for, expect, wait (Bhr. II), wish (Mārk.) (< *to think of, consider).

[Ma. ōrka to think, expect; Ta. ōr, Ka. ōru to think, consider. PSDr. *ōr-/*vār-; also see s.v. rōyu.]

1158 vālu[1] to incline, bend, weigh down, to alight, perch (Bhr. II); tr. vāl(u)cu to bend down (Bhīm.).

[Ka. vālu, mālu, ōlu to bend; mā sloping, slanting; Tu. māluni to lean, incline; ōleguni to recline, lean; Ko. bāḷ- to become exhausted from hunger; Ta. vaḷai to bend, bow (Tiv.); tr. to bend; Ma. vaḷayuka v.i., vaḷekka tr. id.; < *vāḷ-; other forms, v.s.v. vaṅgu.]

1159 vālu[2]* intr. to increase, rise, swell, flourish (Bhr. II, RR), be splendid (BhR), shine.

[Ta. vāḷ splendor (Tolk.); brightness (Kalit.), fame; vāḻ to flourish, prosper; vāy to flourish, be luxuriant; vā to abound, increase. PSDr. *vā-, *vā-ḷ : *vaḷ-ay; for the short grade forms, see s.v. vaṟalu.]

1160 vikku* intr. to swell with pride, to stretch out (later works); to become loose, slack (Naiṣ.).

[< *vir-k-; v.s.v. viriyu, viccu.]

1161 viccu IId tr. to untie, loosen (UH), to spread, expand (KS); to open (BhR), make (flowers) bloom (Bhr. II); to separate, tear apart (Kāś.); intr. (a flower) to bloom (Āmu.), to break, burst (Bhīm.); to be opened; vippu to untie, open a bundle, etc.; viccu adj. unsheathed (of knife).

[Ka. biccu, bircu to loosen, open a bundle; expand eyebrows; intr. to be broken; open, become loose; Tu. biccuni v.i. to burst, fly open; become loosened; bicca unsheathed, as weapon; < *vir-c-; other languages, v.s.v. viriyu, virugu. In Te. Ka. forms, c is the transitive suffix in the tr. set; in the intr. set it is a derivative suffix (originally part of past *-ci). This is therefore a case of morphological merger.]

1162 vijju* intr. to spread, extend (UH; rare).

[< *vir-j-; v.s.v. viccu.]

1163 viḍiyu[1] III intr. to stay, lodge temporarily, as armies in the battlefield (KS, Bhr. I), to set out on conquest (Bhr. I, II); viḍidi a lodging, camp.

[Ka. biḍu (biṭṭ-) to stop, halt, remain; bīḍu a camp, lodging place, house; Tu. būḍu a mansion; Ta. vīṭāram a camp, house (Pu. Ve.); vīṭu a house; Ma. viṭuti lodging; vīṭu a house. PSDr. *vīṭ- : *viṭ-V-.]

1164 viḍiyu[2]* III to become separate from, to leave (UH), to slip off (Bhg.); see s.v. viḍu, vīḍu.

1165 viḍu intr. to leave, part with, become separated; v.s.v. viḍucu, vīḍu.

1166 viḍugu* intr. to blossom, blow, expand.

[Ta. viṭu (viṭṭ-) to blossom (Tēv.); PDr. *viṭ-; v.s.v. viḍucu.]

1167 viḍucu IIa tr. to leave, quit, abandon; release, liberate; intr. to separate, part with; viḍupu liberation, clearance of eclipse (of sun or moon).

[Ka. biḍu to throw, let loose, leave; intr. to be separated; go away;

Tu. buḍupini to leave, forsake; let go, leave alone; shoot (arrows); dismiss, send away; expose; Ko. viṛ- (viṭ-) to release, leave; viṛc- to let go, divorce; To. pïṛ- (pïṭ-) to release; pïḍz- (pïḍǰ-) to get released; pïṛc- (pïṛč-) to drive away; Ta. viṭu (viṭ-ṭ-) tr. to quit (Kṟḷ.); separate; end, discharge (PN); intr. to be separated; (viṭu-tt-) to send away (Tolk.), split, separate; viṭai to become disjointed; Ma. viṭuka v.i. to part, become loose; tr. to abandon; viṭukka to undo, separate; Kui viha to be ended; used up; vihpa (viht-) to separate the corn from the ear by threshing; GoM. biḍs- to abandon; cf. Kur. biṛd- to turn over; give back; Mlt. biḍar- to be dispersed; biḍretr- to disperse; Brah. biṭ- to throw; throw off, shed. PDr. *viṭ-.]

1168 vittu tr. to sow; n. seed; veda sowing (n. and adj.).

[Ka. bittu to put seeds; n. a seed; bede sowing; Tu. bittuni, buttuni to sow seed; Ko. vit-, To. pït- id.; Ta. vittu to sow (Aiṅk.), spread (Cīv.); vitai n. seed (Maturai.); v.tr. to sow seed; Ma. vitekka id.; Kui vīti adj. scattered; Go. wīt- to sow; GoM. wit- (witt-) id.; Klm. vit-, Pj. vit- id.; KGad. vīt- id.; also see Emeneau, Kolami, Vocab. No. 1040, etyma for 'seed.' PDr. *vit-; (> l.w. Skt. bīja seed, Burrow, TPS 1946, p. 10).]

viduru* (ĀVāc.) same as vidulu (rare).

1169 vidulu intr. to be scattered, fall or drop down; vidulcu to scatter, shake off.

[V. s. v. vidur(u)cu.]

1170 vidur(u)cu/vidrucu (Dh.M.) tr. to scatter (Pāṇḍ.); to flap wings.

[Ka. bidir, bidur to be scattered about; to scatter, spread out; toss, unfold, as wings; Tu. biduruni to loosen by itself; Ko. vid- to throw handful of water; Ta. vitir (vitir-tt-) to scatter (PN), sprinkle (Cīv.), throw off; Kui vīti scattered; Kuvi vīd- to flap; Pj. vidrup- (vidrut-) (cock) to flap wings when crowing; Kur. bidig- to lay partly bare; bidṛa'- tr. to scatter about in disorder, spread all over. PDr. *vit-; these forms stem from the same root as the etyma under vittu, q.v.]

1171 vinu IV (allom. vin-/viṇ-, past st. viṇ-ṭ-) tr. to hear, listen to (classical and Mdn.); vin(u)cu (tr.), q.v.

[Ko. vent- to ask; To. pint- id.; Ta. viṉ to question, ask for; viṉavu (also viṉāvu) to question (Kalit.); hear; viṉā vb./n. id.; Ma. vinavuka to ask, pay attention; Kui venba (ves-) to ask; hear; vespa to say, speak; Kuvi(F) venj- (vess-) to tell; veng- to be rumored; Kuvi(S) wen- to hear; Klm.(E), Nk. vin- to hear;

vēṇḍēn he heard (LSI, IV, p. 573); Pj. ven- (vent-, vett-) id.; KGad. ven- (veyy-) id.; Kur. men- (meñj-) to hear, question; mend- to tell; Mlt. men- (menj-) to hear, ask; mendr- to be heard. PDr. *vin-/? *ven-.]

vin(u)cu* IIb intr. to be heard (Bhr. I); tr. to tell (Bhr. I); v. s. v. vinu.

vippu (ĀVāc.; tr. of viccu) to open, untie, loose; (< *vir-p-).

1172 viriyu III intr. to open, blossom, as flower; to break, burst; be loosened, untied; be scattered, be removed.

[Ka. biri to burst open; to blossom; biriku a crack; Tu. biriyuni v. i. to split, crack, burst; birkuni tr. to scatter, disperse, shed; To. pīry- (pīrc-) tr. to open; (pīrs-) to be demolished; Ta. viri v. i. to expand, spread out (Cīv.); be loosened (Kamp.), split; (viri-tt-) tr. to open, spread (PN), untie (Cilap.); n. expanse, crack; virippu, viriyal, virivu n. expansion, breadth (Piṅ.); Ma. viriyuka to blow; virikka tr. to expand; Kui vrīva (vrīt-) to fall to pieces; vriṅga to be loosened, to disperse; vripka (< vrik-p-; vrik-t-) to pull to pieces; untie; briṅgna dispersed by; Kuvi (F) brī- (brī-t-) to topple over; Pj. virŋg- to be loosened; Kur. bird- to pierce, break, throw; Brah. birr- to separate out; cf. pirg̲h- to break, rend. PDr. *vir-.]

1173 virugu (Śab.R.; ĀVāc. vir̲ugu) intr. to break or go to pieces; (milk) curdles (Mdn.); tr. virucu to break; n. breaking.

[V. s. v. viriyu.]

1174 vil(u)cu* IId tr. to sell, purchase (Bhr. II); vela price; viluva value, validity.

[Ka. bil, bili to sell, buy; bele price; Tu. bile price; Ta. vil (vir̲-r̲-) to sell (Kr̲ḷ.); vilai sale, price (Kr̲ḷ.); value (Tēv.); Ma. vilka to sell; vila sale. PSDr. *vil-, *vil-ay.]

1175 visaru/visuru tr. to throw, fling, hurl; to mill flour in a stone-mill; to fan (with a fan); intr. to blow, as wind; n. waving, throwing; fanning.

[Ka. bisuḍu (bisuṭṭ-), bisur to throw, cast, fling; bisu, bīsu to fan, blow, as wind; to mill, grind; Ta. vicir̲u tr. to fan, wave, fling (Tiv.); Ma. visaruka to fan, flutter with wings. PSDr. *vic-V-; also v. s. v. vīcu.]

1176 visuku/visugu (also visuvu) intr. to be vexed, disgusted; be sick of; n. disgust, weariness, vexation.

[Tu. besaru̥ fatigue, vexation, disgust; adj. weary; bēṅku adj. dull; Ta. vicukku n. displeasure; cf. vicai to become angry; Ma. vicakka be angry. PSDr. *vic-V-; cf. Kur. birkha'- tr. to disgust with; make sick of; birkhār- to grow disaffected.]

1177 vīgu[1] intr. to be swollen with pride, be vain; to protrude; to endeavor; vīka valor, endeavor.

[Ka. bīgu to become large, bulky; behave proudly; Ko. vic- to talk impudently to superior; Ta. vīṅku to increase in size; to swell (Kr̲ḷ.); become excessive, tight; vīkkam pride (Tēv.); viyam extensiveness; viyal greatness, width, extension (Tolk.); Ma. vīṅṅuka v.i. to swell; vīkkam n. pride; viṅṅuka to be dense, tight; Kui pīga to be heavy; pigu adj. heavy; Kuvi pikh- to be heavy; Kui bija to be enormously swollen; Kur. bīṇḍ- v.i. to spread out, expand. PDr. *viy- (< *vic-)/*vī-; cf. Ka. bese to be stiff, be haughty.]

1178 vīgu[2] intr. to run away, end, disappear; step aside (Bhr. II).

[Ka. bīgu to go backward, recede; bī to end, cease; to fail, fade, perish; Ta. vī (vī-nt-) to perish, disappear (PN), to leave; deviate (Kr̲ḷ.); Kui viha to be ended, finished; used up. PSDr. and PCDr. *vī-.]

1179 vīcu IIa intr. to blow, as wind; to fling, throw with a sweep; fan.

[Ka. bīsu to swing, wave, fan, throw a net; blow, as wind; mill or grind; Tu. bījuni intr. to swing, blow, as wind; bīsuni tr. to fan, grind, wave, cast; intr. to blow, wave; bīpuni tr. to cast a net, throw; wave hand; Ta. vīcu to throw, fling, fan (PN); swing, as arm; intr. to blow, as wind (Tēv.), be diffused, as smell; Ma. vīcuka to fan, blow; cast nets; vīyuka to fan, brandish; swing; blow, as wind; vīśuka to fan, blow; throw a net; Kui vīka tr. to blow a wind instrument with mouth; vīnja intr./tr. to blow, to fən; Go. mihī- (mih-cī) to throw down violently. PDr. vī-, vī-c-; also v.s.v. visuru.]

1180 vīḍu intr. to be loosened, unfastened; be separated; to leave, quit, forsake; vīḍ(u)konu to leave, see off.

[Ka. bīḍu leaving; Ta. vīṭu v.i. to be destroyed; to die, cease; tr. to let off, leave off; n. leaving, freedom; GoM. viṛs- to loosen; other languages, see s.v. viḍucu. PDr. *vīṭ- : *viṭ-V-.]

1181 vīlu[1]* (ĀVāc.) tr. to make use of (JBh.).

1182 vīlu[2]* (Dh.M.) to be separated; to leave.

[Ta. viḷ, viḷḷu (viṇ-ṭ-) v.i. to open out, unfold; crack, burst; tr. break open, split, leave (Tēv.); Ma. viḷḷu to burst open. PSDr. *viḷ-; also, v.s.v. pigulu.]

1183 vekku intr. to hiccough, sob, be choked in weeping (Nirv.); vekk-ili n. hiccup, sobbing.

[Ka. bikku to take a deep breath, sob in crying; bikkuḷu sobbing; Tu. bikkuni to hold one's breath; to sob; Ta. vikku to be chokeful, to hiccup; tr. bring out with hiccups (Kalit.); vikkuḷ hiccup (Kṟḷ.); Ma. vikkuka, mikkuka to rise in the throat; Kui veka to cough; Kur. bekkh- (bikky-) to be choked; cough; weep through desire; Mlt. beq- to be choked; cf. Kur. hickī hiccough; Brah. hikk- to hiccough; cf. Ma. ekkiḷikka to hiccough; ekkiḷ, ekkiṭṭu n. hiccough.]

1184 vegacu* IId (ĀVāc.) to sob, hiccup (Vikram.).

1185 veccu* IId intr. to be heated (Mārk.); to grieve; n. heat; vecca, veccani adj. hot.

[Ka. beccane warm; bisil (< *vecil) sunshine; bisi adj. hot; Tu. becca heat, warmth; adj. hot; bisi id.; besiyuni to get hot; Ta. vecceṉal hot; veccu n. heat. PDr. *vec-/*vey-; for more etyma, v. s. v. vẽgu, vemmu.]

1186 veḍalu* (> Mdn. veḷḷu) intr. to go or come out; issue forth, set out, start; cf. veḍalabāṭu going out (Bhr. II).

[Ta. viṭal leaving; renunciation; (< *viṭ-al-); for *viṭ-, v. s. v. viḍucu to leave.]

1187 vedaku (also veduku, vetuku, later forms) tr. to search, explore, seek; look for; examine, scrutinize.

[Ka. bedaku to seek, search for; n. search; Kur. bedd- to seek, search, look for; get (wife); procure; find, discover; Mlt. bed- to seek, to marry; < PDr. *vet-; cf. Ta. vita to make a specific mention of, indicate specifically (Naṉ.); GoM. mēhk- to search.]

1188 venaku (ĀVāc.) to seek, search (later text; also occurs in the Viśākha. dial.).

1189 vemmu* (Śab.R.) intr. to be hot, heated (Bhr. II); (< *ve-mp-/*vem-p-).

[Ka. bem heat; adj. hot; Ta. vempu to be very hot (Kalit.); be dried with heat (Kalit.); be distressed (Tēv.); vemmai n. heat, glow (Kalit.); anger, wrath; Ma. vempuka to be very hot; be burnt; vemmu heat (loc.); vempu, vempal id. PSDr. *vem-p-/*ve-mp- : *vepp-; also v. s. v. vẽgu.]

1190 verāju* (Śab.R.) to gather together greedily with hands; to suck liquids with noise (Āmu.).

[Ka. berañju to gather together, to collect, put together; heap up.]

1191 veṟacu* IIa intr. to fear, be afraid (classical); veṟapu n. fear, fright; veṟagu alarm, amazement (classical).

[Ka. beccu, bercu to be scared; to fear; n. fear, dread; beṟagu, alarm, astonishment; Tu. beragu̥ wonder; beraguni to be astonished; Ko. verṇ- (verḍ-) to become extremely afraid; verṭ- to cause (cattle) to have fear; Ta. viṟa (viṟa-nt-) to fear (Tolk.);

vir̲appu n. fear (Tolk.); vir̲ai to be bewildered; ver̲i n. fear (Kalit.); Ma. vir̲ekka to tremble; vir̲a tremor; Kui bree inba to be afraid; brā adj. confused, amazed (< *veṯa-; in Kui *eCa- > Cē- or Cā-); Go. warī- to fear; warūht-, warhutt- caus.; (Dawson) warre n. fear. PSDr. and PCDr. *veṯ-V-.]

1192 velacu* IId tr. to clean, polish (later work).

[Ka. beḷagu to scour, polish; Ko. veḷk- to clean with water; Ta. viḷakku to clean, brighten, polish; sweep, clear up; Ma. viḷakkuka to polish. PSDr. veḷ-aṅk-/*veḷ-akk-; v. s. v. velūgu.]

1193 velayu III (1) intr. to shine, thrive, be splendid (Mārk.); be pleased; to prevail.

[Ka. beḷe to increase, grow; Tu. beḷaguni to shine; Ko. veḷv- (veḷt-) to cause to grow; To. peẓf- (peẓt-) id.; peẓ- (peẓθ-) (food plants) to grow; Ta. viḷai to be produced; to occur (Kamp.); Ma. viḷayuka grow to perfection.]

velayu (2) to be known, come into light (Bhr. II).

[Ta. veḷi to be open or public (Kamp.), come to light. PDr. *veḷ-, v. s. v. velūgu.]

1194 velalu* intr. to come or go out (Bhr. II); cf. vel(u)cu to send out, expel; veli outside.

[Ta. veḷikk-iṭu to set out, start (loc.); vilaku to withdraw, leave, recede; tr. to throw, cast; Kui venḍa to go forward, proceed, start forth; go forth; KGad. veṭṭ- to go out; Pj. valip- (valit-) to expel, drive away; < PSDr. and PCDr. *vel- or ? veḷ-; Ta. and KGad. point to *veḷ-.]

1195 veliyu III intr. (sky) to clear up; (rain) to cease; to fade, as color.

[Tu. boḷkirų clearing of the sky from clouds; Ta. veḷi v. i. to break, as the day; (sky) to clear after cloudiness (Jaffna); become white (Kamp.); < PDr. *veḷ-.]

1196 velūgu intr. to shine, give light, become bright; to burn, blaze; n. light, lamp, brightness, splendor (Mārk.); vella, veli adj. white.

[Ka. beḷagu to shine, become bright; cause to shine; n. lustre; Tu. beḷaguni to shine, glitter; beḷagų brightness, splendor; Ko. veḷg- to dawn; veḷv- (veḷt-) to become pale; To. pȫẓx- to dawn; pȫẓk- to make to dawn; pȫẓf- (pȫẓt-) to be white; Ta. viḷaṅku to shine (PN), become clear (Pu.Ve.); viḷakku to make clear, lustrous (Malaip.); n. lamp, light (Kr̲ḷ.); Ma. viḷaṅṅuka to shine forth; veḷukka to dawn; Kuvi (F) vella white; Klm.(E) veleŋ, velleŋ n. light; Go. (Will.) weṛcī n. light; Go. (Trench) wērcī light, esp. of dawn; Pj. vil white; vilg- (Sth. vili-) to be white; vɪlid light;

Oll. viled white; Kur. bilc- to shine, glitter; sparkle; billī light, flame; Mlt. bilpu moon; bil-bilr- to shine brilliantly; bilpu nīṛu moonlight; cf. biḍy- (biḍc-) to shine; biḍ- to shoot forth, as rays; Brah. (tū)bē moon (bright) light. PDr. *veḷ-/*viḷ-; cf. Ta. viḷḷu (viṇ-ṭ-) to unfold, become clear, etc.]

1197 vel(u)cu* IId (? tr. of velalu) to expel, drive away, as cattle, etc. (Bhr. II); to shed, as tears (UH).

[Pj. valip- (valit-) to expel, drive away; also v. s. v. velalu.]

veḷḷu intr. to go, run, to leave.

[Contraction of veḍalu, q. v.]

1198 vēgu* (also vēvu) intr. to dawn (of day) (Bhr. II); der. n. vēkuva dawn, morning before sunrise.

[Ta. vaiku to dawn, as the day (Perump.); Ma. vaikuka to halt during night; Kui vēga to dawn, to outlast, outlast the night; Pj. vēv- (Sth. vēy-) id.; Nk. vēg- id.; KGad. vēg- id.; Kur. bijj-, Mlt. bij- id. PDr. *vay-/*vey-; PSDr. and PCDr. *vay-k-/*vey-k-.]

1199 vẽgu intr. to be fried; to grieve, suffer; be very anxious, solicitous; tr. vẽcu to fry, grill, oppress, trouble.

[Ka. bē, bēyu (bend-) to be consumed with fire; burn with grief; Tu. bēyuni to boil; be cooked; bēpini tr./intr. to boil, be boiled, cooked; Ko. vey- (vedy-) to be burned; (broth) boils; veyc- tr. to burn up; To. pōy- (pōd-) v. i. to burn; Ta. vē (vent-) v. i. to burn (Nāl.), be hot, sultry; be distressed by grief, be angry (PN); Ma. vēka (vent-) v. i. to burn, boil; Kui vēva (vēt-) to be fried; vehpa (veht-) to be hot, as liquids; Kuvi (F) vey- (vet-) to catch fire; Kuvi (S) wei- to dry up; Go. wē- (wēī-sī) to be cooked; boiled; wahac- come to a boiling point; Klm.(SR) vey- to prepare bread; Pj. vey- (rice) to be cooked; vēp- (vēt-) to be warm; KGad. vey-/vē- to be burnt; Kur. bi'- (bicc-) to be cooked, fried, boiled; biṛ- (biḍḍ-) to be hot; bīta'- tr. to cook, bake, etc.; Mlt. bic- to be cooked, heated; bit- tr. to cook; Brah. bis- to bake. PDr. *vey-/*vē- : *vay- < *vec-); also see Emeneau, Kolami, Vocab. No. 1034; further related etyma, v. s. v. veccu, vemmu.]

1200 vēcu IId (ĀVāc.) tr. to expect, wait, look for.

[Cf. Ko. vēj- to peep; Kui mehpa (meht-) to look at, observe others; Kuvi (F) bec- to peep; Kuvi (S) bēc- to look; see; Go. weht- to explain, show; ? Mlt. bang- to lie in wait. PDr. *vey-/vē-.]

1201 vẽḍu intr./tr. to desire, want (Bhr. I, II); to pray, beg, solicit, request (Mārk.); vẽḍukōlu requesting.

[Ka. bēḍu to wish, desire, solicit, pray; bēḷa, bēṇḍa longing; Tu.

bēḍuni to ask, entreat; bōḍu (with dat.) to be necessary; To. pōḍ- to beg; Ta. vēṇṭu to want (Kalit.), beg, request; intr. to be necessary (Nāl.); vēḷ (vēṭ-ṭ-) to desire (PN), love (Nāl.); vēṇ, vēḷ n. desire; Ma. vēḷka to desire; vēṇa, vēṇṭu n. desire; Klm. Nk. vēl- to ask. PDr. *vēḷ/*vēṇ.]

vĕcu* IIb (tr. of vĕgu) to torment, oppress; to fry, grill.

[V. s. v. vĕgu; also see Kuvi (S) weh'- to oppress; wē'- to maltreat.]

1202 vēyu III tr. to throw, cast, fling; strike, knock; place, put; to thatch a house; as aux., intensifier, e.g., iccu to give, icci vēyu to give away.

[Ka. bese a stroke, whip; Tu. bēpuni to thatch; Ko. vēj- to thatch; To. pēy- (pēs-) id.; Ta. vēy- to cover, as a building; put on, as garland; Kui vēpa (vēt-) to strike, beat, thrash; Kuvi (S) wē- to beat, smite; Kui vega to put a roof; Klm.(E) vēnz- to thatch; Nk. vēnj-; Pj. vēñ-, KGad. vēŋg- id.; Kur. baī- (baññ-) to thatch; Mlt. bes-; Brah. bēn- to put on. PDr. *vey-/vēy- : *vay- (contamination with vaicu (< *vay-) in Te., giving more general range in meanings).]

vēvu* var. of vēgu, q. v. (BhR).

1203 vēl(u)cu* IIa tr. to perform sacrifice with fire, offer to the sacrificial fire (Bhr. II); cf. vēl(u)pu a god.

[Ka. bēḷ, bēḷu to offer into fire, ghee, animals, etc.; bēḷamba an oblation; destruction of human life; Ta. vēḷ (vēṭ-ṭ-) to offer sacrifices (Patiṟ.); to marry (Kamp.); n. marriage; vēḷvi n. sacrifice (Akan.); vēḷvu id.; Ma. vēḷka to marry (as brahmins) before fire; vēḷvi sacrifice; vēḷi, vēḷvi marriage; ? Brah. bēl- to damage, devastate (esp. of crops). PDr. *vēḷ- < *vē-ḷ-.]

1204 vēsăru to be tired, disgusted; vēsaṭa fatigue, disgust.

[Ka. bēsaṟu (bēsatt-) to grow weary, be vexed; n. weariness; Tu. bēsarụ fatigue, weariness, disgust; adj. weary; Ta. vēcăṟu to be weary; be vexed, distressed (Tiruvāc.); vēcaṟal weariness; ? PSDr. vēc-aṯ-.]

1205 vaicu* IIa (also vayicu) tr. to throw, put, place; aux. adv. away, off, etc.

[Ka. bay to deposit, put aside; baycu, baccu depositing; Ko. vay- (vac-) to keep; put; Ta. vai (vai-tt-) to put, place (Kṟḷ.), deposit; guard, set up; Ma. vekka to put, lay, build, plant; aux. to finish an action; veccu placing; Go. bai- to seize, catch; baitt- id.; Klm.(E) vāy- to sow with drill; Nk. vay- to sow. PDr. *vay/*vey-; also v. s. v. vēyu.]

1206 vraccu* IId (inscr. vl̲accu, vraccu, c. 7th century) tr. to ruin, tear to pieces (Bhr. II); (inscr.) to destroy (a grant), to efface or wipe out (the writing in inscriptions); (< *val̲-c-).

[Ka. bal̲i, bol̲i to wipe off with hand; sweep dust; Tu. barjuni to strike; reprove; Ko. varv- (vard-) to hit; To. warf- (wart-) to wipe; Ta. val̲i (val̲i-tt-) to wipe, scrape, rub in with hands (Cīv.); val̲uvu to err (PN); val̲u sin (PN); Kui vrapka (vrakt-) to cut open and disclose contents; bari shattered; vraka vēpa (vēt-) to strike with might.]

1207 vrāyu (> Mdn. rāy-, rās-) III tr. to write, inscribe, transcribe (inscr.; see EI, XXVII, No. 62, p. 241; c. 8th century); to compose, produce, write, draw, paint; cf. rāyasamu a letter, writing (later works).

[Ka. bare to draw, write; bari id.; n. writing; Tu. barepini to write, draw; Ko. varv- (vard-) to write; To. par- (parθ-) id.; Ta. varai tr. to write, to limit (PN); n. line, letter; vari to write, paint (PN); smear, daub (lex.); Ma. varayuka to limit; varekka to make lines; vara a line, streak; variyuka to draw a line; Kui vrīsa tr. to write, scratch; make a mark; write, plow, cut up flesh; n. writing; Kuvi (S) brī'- to draw; rāc- to paint, write, record; GoM. rās- to write. PSDr. and PCDr. *var-ay-; in Te. vr- > r- is quite early; e.g., see rāśi 'having marked (boundaries),' (1310 A.D., NDI, Vol. I, p. 34, Darsi No. 35, line 35); Kui Kuvi < *vrī- < *vari- shows a type of vowel contraction different from the usual one, i.e., the lengthening of the suffix vowel instead of the root vowel.]

1208 vrālu$^{1*}$ intr. to hang loose, to droop; (< *val̲-al).

[Ka. bal̲al to become weary, to droop: be cast down; become loose, to dangle, slip; To. paḍf- (paḍt-) to slip; Ta. val̲ukku to slip, slide; Ma. val̲ukkuka to slip; tr. to let slip; the meaning extension occurs in Te. and Ka. only; also v. s. v. baḍalu.]

1209 vrālu$^{2*}$ (> Mdn. vālu) to perch, alight, as bird; to incline to one side. (A hyper-correction of vālu by changing v- to vr-; only the v- form has etymology, and is also attested in old Te. literature; the meanings of vrālu$^{1}$ might have also helped, through confusion, toward hyper-standardizing the form in question; for similar cases, v. s. v. truḷḷu, vrēyu.)

[V. s. v. vālu$^{1}$.]

1210 vrīlu* intr. to go to pieces; to crack; (< *vir-il-).

[Kui vrīva (vrīt-) to fall to pieces; only Te. has the -il suffix; for related etyma see s. v. viriyu, virugu.]

1211 vrēyu* III tr. to strike, smite; cut off, as with a knife or any heavy weapon (Bhr. I, II); der. n. vrēṭu cut, stroke, smiting; vrēṭu a stroke, chopping.

[This appears to be a hyper-standardization of vēyu; there is contamination of more than one form in this: y-ending bases form the derivative nouns by replacing y by t/p rather than ṭ, e.g., pōyu, pōta; mēyu, mēta, mēpu; in this particular form ṭ presupposes *ṯ as would appear in *vrēṟu (< *ver-, *veṯ-, *veḻ- + -aṯ-), but no evidence is available for this; *ṭ is therefore on account of contamination with ēṭu (< *ēṯṯ-), cf. Ta. eṟi etc.; contamination in meaning is likely with ēyu, q. v.]

1212 vrēlu* (> Mdn. vēlu) intr. to hang, be suspended, to dangle; tr. vrēl(u)cu to hang; (< *veḻ-al-).

[Kui mrēsa (mrēs-it-) to throttle, strangle; n. strangulation; vṛēja tr. to bend back or down; Go. waṛēng- to be hung up; tr. waṛhutt- to hang; cf. Kuvi vīsk- to strangle.]

## S

1213 saḍapu intr. (Śab.R.) to steal; (Brown) to misappropriate.

1214 saggu (Dh.M., Śab.R.) intr. to rot, as liquids; (< *saṟ-g-).

[Brah. saṛ- to rot; Kur. jarār- to decay due to excess of rains; l. w. < IA, cf. Pkt. saḍaï rots; B. saṛā, P. saṛnā, S. saṛaṇu, G. saḍvũ, M. saḍṇẽ; see s. v. saṛnu to rot, Turner, Nep. Dict.]

1215 saḍalu (> Mdn. saḷḷu) intr. to become loose, slack; be loosened; n. looseness; tr. saḍal(u)cu to loosen.

[Ka. saḍil, saḍal, saḍlu to loosen, relax; v. i. become lax; saḍilcu to loosen; saḷḷa adj. loose; Tu. saḍlụ adj. loose, slack; loosened; saḍl-āpini to become loose; l. w. < IA; cf. Skt. śithila-, Pkt. siḍhila-, v. s. v. ḍhilo, Turner, Nep. Dict.; also v. s. v. ḍīlu.]

1216 saṇagu (also saṇ(u)gu; Brown) to mutter.

[? Ma. cinakkuka to mutter, cry ho! ; connection not likely; prob. l. w. < IA, cf. Skt. svaná- n. noise; svánati sounds; Pa. sanati, sanati, saṇati, Pkt. saṇa-, saṇia-; G. saṇkō whizz, M. saṇkā; v. s. v. sankanu, Turner, Nep. Dict.]

1217 samayu III intr. to perish, die, be destroyed, to wear away (Bhr.II).

[Ka. same, save to be destroyed, be diminished; tave to decrease; tavu v. i. to diminish; tr. to destroy; Ko. cam- (camd-) be finished; (camt-) tr. to finish; Ta. camai to be consumed, destroyed

(Kamp.); tr. to finish; to kill; cavu (cavu-tt-) to become weak, be emaciated (Tolk.); tapu to perish; come to an end (Kamp.), die; (tapu-tt-) tr. to destroy; tavu to be reduced; taval diminishing; death (PN); cf. Pj. cam- to go bad, be rotten; < PSDr. *cap-/*tap- : *cav-V-/*tav-V- : *cam-V-/*tam-V-.]

sariyu III (Dh.M.; same as sarusu, q.v.).

1218 sarugu* (Śab.R.) intr. to increase, grow, improve.

1219 sar(u)du (Dh.M.; saradu, sardu Śab.R.) tr. to distribute equally or proportionately; to satisfy each with some part or quantity; to economize; to adjust (Mdn.); sari equality, match; adv. yes, enough (colloq.).

[Ka. sari to adjust; put in proper order; n. equality; propriety; saru id.; Tu. sari adj. equal, like; even; sarikè fit, right, plenty; Ta. cari rightness, suitability; equal measure of quantity (late); Kui sarna straight; upright; Kur. sarya'- to put in its proper place; Mlt. saryar- to be cured, mend, correct; l.w. < IA, cf. Skt. sadṛk > *sadı > sari after the analogy of Pk. tārisa (< Skt. tādṛśa-; Pk. sarisa-; H. saris like, similar; v.s.v. sari, Turner, Nep. Dict.]

sarusu (Dh.M.; sarasu ĀVāc.) to distribute equally.

[l.w. < IA, see s.v. sar(u)du.]

salupu[1]* (var. of calupu, tr. of canu, q.v.).

1220 salupu[2] to ache, pain; n. a shooting pain (of gums, etc.).

[Ka. saḷe, seḷe to draw, pull, to draw up or suffer spasms, as the muscles of a limb; Kui jelba (jes-) to pull, draw. PSDr. and CDr. *caḷ-/*ceḷ-.]

saḷḷu (Mdn. var. of saḍalu, q.v.; Dh.M.).

1221 sā̃ku tr. to rear, bring up, foster (of human beings only); tr. sā̃kuḍu rearing, bringing up.

[Ka. sāku to bring up, foster, nurse; tend, preserve; tāṅgu to support, keep, sustain; Tu. sāṅkuni tr. to foster, nourish, protect; tāṅkuni to take care of, nourish, foster; feed; shelter; tāṅguni to assist; support, sustain; tāṅgu̧ a support; Ko. cāk- (cāyk-) to make to grow, rear, support; To. sōk- to rear (used in songs); tōg- to support burden; Ta. tāṅku tr. to support, protect (Perump., Kalit.); bear (Kṟḷ.); Ma. tāṅṅuka to support; sustain; cf. Kui jōnga to hatch; Brah. sāc- to be to one's liking. PSDr. *cāṅk-/*tāṅk- : *cākk-/*tākk-.]

1222 sā̃gu (var. of cā̃gu, q.v.) intr. to become long, be lengthened; to extend, increase; to spread, as a creeper, etc.; (metal) to be lengthened under a hammer.

[Ka. sāgu id.; Kuvi (S) sāg- id.; Go. sāng- to spread (of a creeper); v. s. v. cā̃gu, cācu.]

1223 suḍiyu[1] III intr. to turn round, (wind) to blow in a whirl.

[Ka. suḻi, tuḻi to turn round, go round, waver; n. round; Tu. sulipuni to whirl, go round; tulipuni id.; suḷipuni to churn, turn in lathe; suḷi whirlpool; To. tuḍy- (tuḍc-) tr. to turn in a circle; Ta. cuḻi to be curved; to whirl, as wind; tr. to curl; n. eddy; cūḻ (cūḻ-tt-) tr. to wind, wrap round (Parip.); surround (Tiruvāc.); (cūḻ-t-) tr. to encompass (Nāl.); cūḻttu tr. to cause to surround; Ma. cuḻiyuka v. i. to curl, whirl; to revolve in mind; cuḻivu whirlpool; cuḻi whirl, circle. PSDr. *cūḻ- : *cuḻ-V-.]

1224 suḍiyu[2]* (Dh.M.) III intr. to burn; (< *cuṭ-i-); v. s. v. cū̃ḍu.

1225 surũgu intr. to disappear, run, flee, in war (Bhr. II).

[Ka. surku to shrink, fade; soragu to wither; Tu. sirku̥ shrivelling; n. weakness; Ta. curuṅku to be reduced; curi v. i. to shrink; Ta. curuṅṅuka to shrivel, decrease; to reduce. PSDr. *cur-unk-; also v. s. v. srukku.]

selãgu* (also selavu; var. of celagu, q. v.) tr. to cut (UH), to plane; sela a hole, a line or streak.

[? Ka. kellayisu to splinter; kelle a shiver; splinter; Tu. ḳellu̥ a splinter; altern., Tu. selȅ a chink, crack; Kui silpa (silt-) to shave; further v. s. v. celagu, celavu.]

selayu[1]* III (var. of celayu, q. v.) intr. to rise, swell, riot (Pāṇḍ.).

[V. s. v. celãgu.]

1226 selayu[2]* III intr. to cut, chop (v. s. v. celagu, selãgu).

1227 sa̮ĩcu* IIc intr./tr. to bear, endure; spare, excuse (classical); to be agreeable, tasty, as food; sa̮ĩpu/sayipu n. toleration, forbearance; sa̮irincu to excuse; tolerate; sa̮iraṇa tolerance; (assimilated loan word).

[< *say-inc- < *sah-inc-; Ka. sayisu, sahisu, sōsu to bear; sayrisu/sairisu to bear patiently, endure; sayraṇe n.; Ta. caki to bear; excuse, forgive; Kur. sah- (sahc-) to suffer from; l. ws. < IA, cf. Skt. sáhate to bear, endure; Pkt. sahaĩ, Pa. sahati, H. sahnā, G. sahvũ, M. sāhṇẽ, v. s. v. sahanu, Turner, Nep. Dict.]

sokku to be intoxicated; v. s. v. cokku.

1228 sogayu* III intr. be beside one's self; to swoon (Bhr. II, Mārk.); sogayika n. intoxication.

[Cf. Kui sōsa (sōs-it-) be intoxicated; < *coy-ay-, or *cov-a-; cf. Ta. toy- intr. to languish, pine; droop; toyyal n. swooning; cōr to swoon, droop; further, v. s. v. sōlu, cokku.]

1229 sorugu (Śab.R., ĀVāc.) to droop, to swoon (later work); to wither, languish.
[Ka. soragu to wither, dry, languish; grow lean; other etyma, v. s. v. cokku.]

1230 solayu III intr. to faint, swoon, languish; (< *col-ay- < *cōl-ay-); v. s. v. sōlu.

sō̃ku (var. of cō̃ku, q. v.) intr./tr. to touch, come in contact with, etc.
[To the etyma given under cō̃ku (q. v.) may be added: Go. sǫk- to apply (ointment to skin, hot water, etc.).]

1231 sōlu intr. to faint, swoon; to reel, stagger; give way, yield.
[Ka. sōlu to fail, fall off in vigor or respect; sōla to defeat; Tu. sōpuni to be defeated, overcome; sōla n. failure; Ko. cōv- (cōt-) to be defeated, become tired; cōl- (cōt-) to be inferior, to fail; To. swi̿l- (swi̿t-) to be defeated; twi̿ł- (twi̿ṯ-) to be defeated; Ta. tōl (tōṟ-ṟ-) to be defeated (Nāl.), toy to languish, pine; to droop; perish; toyyal languishing, fainting (Kamp.); cōr to languish; to faint, swoon; Ma. tōlka to be defeated. PSDr. *cōl-/*cōr- : *col-V-, *cor-V-; *cō-l- < *coy-al-; esp. cf. Ta. toy, cōr; see s. v. cokku, solayu, sogayu.]

1232 sraggu* intr. to decrease, grow less, be diminished, sink, go; (< *sar-g-).
[Cf. saggu, or taggu; ? t- < c-.]

1233 srukku* intr. to fade, become weak; grieve, shrink (Bhr. II), to withdraw (Nirv.); (< *sur-k-).
[Ka. surku, sukku to contract, shrink; fade, curl; Tu. sirku̥ weakness, shrivelling; sirkuni to fade, become weak; Ta. curuṅku to shrink, be reduced; curukku tr. to reduce (Tiruvāc.); Ma. curuṅṅuka intr. to shrivel; decrease; curukkuka to contract, reduce; Go. sūr dry pulled stalks of hemp; Pj. curk- to shrivel, cheeks to sink in; cf. Klm. suk- to fade, wither. PSDr. and PCDr. *cur-uṅk-/*cur-ukk-.]

## H

1234 hattu intr./tr. to hold fast; to hold, stick to; to reach; (l. w. < Ka.).
[Ka. hattu to stick to; to touch; reach; Tu. hattuni id.; for others, v. s. v. paṭṭu.]

1235 heccu IId intr. to increase, in number, etc.; (l. w. < Ka.).
[Ka. heccu id.; Tu. heccuni id.; < *pecc- < *per-c-; v. s. v. perugu.]

## L

1236 laccu* IId (inscriptional) tr. to destroy, ruin (625 A.D., see EI, XXVII, p. 230, No. 420, lines 5-6).

[< *al-c-; v. s. v. aliyu.]